THE AMERICAN ACADEMY OF
CHILD AND ADOLESCENT PSYCHIATRY

YOUR CHILD

THE AMERICAN ACADEMY OF
CHILD AND ADOLESCENT PSYCHIATRY

YOUR CHILD

*What Every Parent Needs to
Know About Childhood Development
from Birth to Preadolescence*

■ ■ ■

David B. Pruitt, M.D., Editor-in-Chief

HarperCollins*Publishers*

YOUR CHILD. Copyright © 1998 by The American Academy of Child and Adolescent Psychiatry. All rights reserved. Printed in the United States of America. No part of this book may be used or reproduced in any manner whatsoever without written permission except in the case of brief quotations embodied in critical articles and reviews. For information address HarperCollins Publishers, Inc., 10 East 53rd Street, New York, NY 10022.

HarperCollins books may be purchased for educational, business, or sales promotional use. For information please write: Special Markets Department, HarperCollins Publishers, Inc., 10 East 53rd Street, New York, NY 10022.

FIRST EDITION

Designed by Helene Wald Berinsky

Library of Congress Cataloging-in-Publication Data

Your child : what every parent needs to know about childhood development from birth to preadolescence / David B. Pruitt, editor-in-chief. — 1st ed.
    p. cm.
  Includes index.
  ISBN 0–06–270158–4
  1. Child development. 2. Child psychology. 3. Child psychopathology.
4. Parent and child—Psychological aspects. I. Pruitt, David B.
HQ767.9.Y67 1998   98–9503
305.231—dc21   CIP

---

98 99 00 01 02 ❖/RRD 10 9 8 7 6 5 4 3 2 1

Contents

Part III ■ SERIOUS PROBLEMS AND ABNORMALITIES

Part IV ■ SEEKING HELP

The Contributors

■ **EDITOR-IN-CHIEF**

David B. Pruitt, M.D.
Professor of Psychiatry
Director of the Division of Child and
    Adolescent Psychiatry
University of Tennessee, Memphis
Medical Director
TLC Family Care Healthplan
Memphis, Tennessee
President 1997–1999
American Academy of Child and
    Adolescent Psychiatry

■ **ASSOCIATE EDITORS**

Claudia Berenson, M.D.
Associate Professor, Psychiatry and
    Pediatrics
University of New Mexico
Albuquerque, New Mexico

William Bernet, M.D.
Associate Professor of Psychiatry
Vanderbilt University School of Medicine
Medical Director

The Psychiatric Hospital at Vanderbilt
Nashville, Tennessee

Jerry Heston, M.D.
Associate Professor of Psychiatry
Division of Child and Adolescent Psychiatry
University of Tennessee, Memphis
Memphis, Tennessee

Paramjit T. Joshi, M.D.
Associate Professor
Director of Clinical Services
Division of Child and Adolescent Psychiatry
Johns Hopkins University School of
    Medicine
Baltimore, Maryland

Penelope Krener Knapp, M.D.
Professor, Psychiatry and Pediatrics
University of California, Davis
Davis, California

James C. MacIntyre II, M.D.
Associate Professor of Psychiatry
Albany Medical College
Albany, New York

■ **DEPUTY EDITORS**
Paul L. Adams, M.D.
Louisville, Kentucky

Virginia Q. Anthony
Washington, D.C.

■ **CONTRIBUTING EDITORS**
Thomas Anders, M.D.
Davis, California

Alan Axelson, M.D.
Pittsburgh, Pennsylvania

Larry Brown, M.D.
Providence, Rhode Island

Ian A. Canino, M.D.
New York, New York

Donald Cohen, M.D.
New Haven, Connecticut

Catherine DeAngelis, M.D.
Baltimore, Maryland

Gerald Golden, M.D.
Philadelphia, Pennsylvania

Allan Josephson, M.D.
Augusta, Georgia

Henrietta Leonard, M.D.
Providence, Rhode Island

Bruce D. Miller, M.D.
Buffalo, New York

Klaus Minde, M.D.
Montreal, Quebec, Canada

Frederick Palmer, M.D.
Memphis, Tennessee

Rachel Z. Ritvo, M.D.
Rockville, Maryland

John Schowalter, M.D.
New Haven, Connecticut

Robert Schreter, M.D.
Luterville, Maryland

Larry Silver, M.D.
Washington, D.C.

Michael Silver, M.D.
Wynnewood, Pennsylvania

Jeanne Spurlock, M.D.
Washington, D.C.

Jean M. Thomas, M.D.
St. Louis, Missouri

Charles H. Zeanah, M.D.
New Orleans, Louisiana

■ **EDITORIAL DIRECTOR**
Hugh G. Howard
Red Rock Publishing, Inc.
East Chatham, New York

■ **CONTRIBUTORS**
Dale Gelfand
Spencertown, New York

Elizabeth Lawrence
East Chatham, New York

Dawn Micklethwaite Peterson
Maplewood, New Jersey

Elizabeth Tinsley
Chatham, New York

Lyn Yonack
Great Barrington, Massachusetts

Acknowledgments

Your Child is the result of a group effort by many of the more than sixty five hundred members of the American Academy of Child and Adolescent Psychiatry and a range of consultants concerned with the needs of children, adolescents, and their families. This book and its companion volume, *Your Adolescent,* focus on the goal of parent education as the primary vehicle to bring about better health and health care for children and adolescents.

The Academy has a long-held belief that parents are a precious resource that must be supported and strengthened for the well-being of children and adolescents. *Your Child* and *Your Adolescent*—which offer the collective wisdom of many child and adolescent psychiatrists dedicated to serving children, adolescents, and their families—represent this philosophy.

The creation of these books was a team effort, much like the collaboration within a functional family or a high-quality child and adolescent mental health–care team. The process included support for the individuals in the group as well as careful coordination of the group. Both are essential for any team project to succeed.

We started with a small group of Academy members working with our wonderful panel of writers led by Hugh Howard. We progressively developed an organization, content chapters, and finally these books, always broadening our circle of consultants and experts, always attempting to reach consensus about what works and what doesn't, what advice to give, and most important, when to say that we don't know.

This project has come to realization with a lot of help. Beyond those listed on previous pages are the following: Alvin Poussaint, M.D., Gloria Powell, M.D., J. Graham Brooks, M.D., Lee Combrick Graham, M.D., Geraldine Fox, M.D., Kevin T. Kalikow, M.D., Jack M. Reiter, M.D., Alvin Rosenfeld, M.D., Dorothy Levine, M.D., Carrie Sylvester, M.D., Martin Drell, M.D., Elizabeth Wright, M.D., Moisy Shopper, M.D.,

Barbara Stilwell, M.D., Shaun C. McDevitt, Ph.D, Bruce Peary, M.D., Andrew Russell, M.D., Joseph J. Jankowski, M.D., Richard Angell, M.D., John O'Brien, M.D., Bennett L. Leventhal, M.D., Owen Lewis, M.D., David Cline, M.D., John Reinhart, M.D., Ms. Abby O'Neil, E. James Anthony, M.D., Harold Koplewitz, M.D., Larry Stone, M.D., Peter Jensen, M.D., David Herzog, M.D., Marilyn Benoit, M.D., Theodore Petty, M.D., and Clarice Kestenbaum, M.D.

Many at my university, the University of Tennessee, Memphis, also supported this effort in the belief that this kind of commitment strengthens and serves the university mission. Among them are Chancellor William Rice, Dean Robert Summitt, and department of psychiatry chairman Neil Edwards; the faculty, past and present, of the Division of Child and Adolescent Psychiatry, including Kris Douglas, Constance Durbin, Laurel Kiser, Marilynn Paavola, Jerry Heston, Ewa Ostoja, Jyothsna Kumar, Mark Sauser, Rita Porter, Robert Pugh, Suzanne Fischer, and Edgar McColgan; and the trainees of the Division both past and present, including recent fellows Anthony Jackson, Kendall Vitulli, Yolanda Gilbert, Yanco Gavrizi, Monica Salgueiro, and Nick Sansait.

I also want to thank Karl Kovacs, executive director of TLC Family Care Healthplan, whose friendship and guidance in our collegial day-to-day work has allowed me a sense of mission in the rapidly changing health-care marketplace, and to Eric Brown, president of Communication Associates, who has helped me over the years to learn the value and effectiveness of clear thinking and talking.

I want to thank several other individuals at the Academy who have supported this work with their insight and assistance through the long writing and editing process, Virginia Q. Anthony, executive director of the American Academy of Child and Adolescent Psychiatry; Patricia Jutz, director of communications; Tamara Hodge-Wells; and Tonya Cook. They have provided immeasurable support.

A special thanks as well to Bettye Fleming, my longtime administrative assistant, who kept the whole project glued together through the many overnight mails, faxes, conference calls, due dates, and deadlines that she, as always, gently and effectively made happen.

Finally, a very special thanks to my wife and colleague, Laurel, who, with our two children, Peter and A.J., has helped me move through the wonderful stages of growth and development as a parent.

David B. Pruitt, M.D.

Foreword

Child and adolescent psychiatry begins with a profound respect for your child, his or her endowments, and a deep regard for the task of parenting.

For more than two decades, I have attended seminars, case conferences, grand rounds, scientific meetings, and committee meetings. Both as a parent and in my professional capacity, I am invariably struck that this respect pervades virtually every presentation about individual children by child and adolescent psychiatrists. Discussions, publications, and stories share an appreciation for the child and the child's strengths and uniqueness. And so, you will find, does *Your Child*.

The Academy was founded in 1953 by eighty-one child psychiatrists who saw a need for a forum to focus on the clinical, educational, and research problems unique to children. The early meetings were informative. The struggles for separation from other medical and mental health groups, for new ties, and for a sense of identity were earnest and absorbing. Differences in values and focus from other professions led to the founding of the Academy as an academic association but, over more than four decades of growth, the agenda here at the Academy has developed to include vigorous advocacy for children and adolescents; an outstanding program of professional education; and an increasing focus on prevention and public health.

In the last fifteen years, the Academy has begun to reach out to you as parents and as members of extended families. We recognize that you are on the front line, whether your role is as a parent, grandparent, or caregiver. You deal daily with childhood disorders and other parenting issues and concerns. Since early identification is one of the most effective forms of prevention, we believe our outreach can help you in preventing or limiting the pain, trauma, and failure experienced by children and perhaps reduce the anguish and heartache felt by parents of children in distress.

Our attempts to inform the public are not

aimed solely at the parents of children who need professional help. Often, in part because of today's very stressful home-work environment, parents need reassurance about the differences between personality and temperament, and education about what constitutes normal childhood phases. The American Academy of Child and Adolescent Psychiatry can provide guidance about when you should be concerned about your child and, ultimately, whether you should seek treatment.

Over a career, a child and adolescent psychiatrist learns a great deal from and about families, about specific resilience and breaking points, about vulnerabilities and elasticities, and about how children with the same parents can be so alike and yet so different. This book is an outgrowth of a vigorous parent-education effort based on that learning. It addresses normal development and normal problems, as well as more serious disorders and concerns. It is a way of sharing child psychiatry's appreciation of childhood, of developmental milestones and childhood achievement with you, the parents, grandparents, and caregivers, who are caring and concerned, anxious, or just inquisitive.

The Academy is very proud of *Your Child* as a key part of our ongoing partnership with parents. We commend David B. Pruitt, M.D., Hugh Howard, the editorial board, and the many authors, readers, and critics who have contributed to this offering.

Virginia Q. Anthony, Executive Director

Introduction

A new father pushes his six-month-old daughter in a shopping cart down the aisles of the neighborhood supermarket. At the checkout line, a grandmotherly woman begins talking sweetly to the baby. After a moment, the woman looks up at the father and asks, "Is she a good baby?"

The father thinks for a minute and then answers. "Well, she's not an *easy* baby, but, yes, she's a very good baby."

Time was, not so very long ago, when the distinction between "good" and "easy" was not often made. By implication, *easy* meant *good*: children spoke only when spoken to, were seen and not heard, never sassed back, ate everything on their plates, respected authority unquestioningly, held still, and never dirtied their dress clothes. Only a generation or two ago, guidance for parents could be equally simplistic: spare the rod and spoil the child; let the baby cry it out, it's good for the lungs; don't hold the child too much, you'll spoil him. Those were the words of wisdom, maxims for successful parenting.

If only parenting—and children, for that matter—were so simple! Today most adults realize almost from the moment they become parents that each child has his own needs or her own way of being in the world. Together with this realization comes an understanding that the child's needs and manner of being evolve and change over time.

You probably knew or will know within a night or two of bringing your baby home from the hospital that your child's needs will not always correspond to or harmonize with yours. More and more, parents and experts alike are coming to recognize by intuition and agonizing trial and error that trying to bend and shape children's needs to suit those of the adults in their lives is difficult at best and painfully pointless at worst.

The journey is traveled by both parent and child. It begins at childbirth, weaves through infancy, toddles on through childhood, and moves in fits and starts though adolescence and on into adulthood. For you and your youngster, the adventure is mutual, the direction shared, and the paths corresponding. Yet the experience is not identical. Just like every other human relationship, the parent-child relationship embraces *two distinct points of view*. As a parent, you have your own perspective, needs, ways, and style, and your own developmental process. Your child has his or her own.

Yet children profoundly need their parents. Your daughter needs you to support and to guide her; your son needs you to supply him with loving limits and to delight in him. For this stage in your own development to be fully enjoyable, rich, and auspicious, it helps if you can cultivate an appreciation of your child's complexity, your own complexity, and the complexity of the parent-child relationship.

Good parenting takes into consideration not only the child's needs, but the parents' needs as well. To be successful, the way you parent must evolve and change over time as the child changes, as you change, and as needs change. However, it is not always easy, even for the most able parents, to recognize and respond to the changes that characterize childhood. What, then, do you rely on to guide you while your child is relying on you?

Surely you have been regaled with the reassuring but rather glib advice, *Trust your own instincts.* You probably heard this from the very first moment you shared the knowledge with a friend or family member that a child would be entering your life. Although you may feel rather unsure, in many instances your instincts will indeed stand you in good stead, pointing you in the right direction to get you through a sticky episode or to unravel a knotty problem with that inscrutable infant that is suddenly yours.

At other times, instinct is simply not enough.

Over time, as his life unfolds, you will get to know your youngster as a unique person. In many ways, he will teach you how to parent, at first through a mutual process of trial and error, and then through direct feedback. However, very young children are naturally incapable of cogently and comprehensibly putting forth their own perspectives, needs, and purposes. Even as your child gets older and more articulate, she will likely have difficulty understanding and clearly expressing her own inner state and behavior. She will count on you to understand her and to help her understand herself and her world; she needs you to guide her as she tries to make herself understood.

This is a tall order. More than occasionally, you will misread or misunderstand your child's communications. From time to time, you will find yourself at a complete loss in terms of what your child is conveying and how you are to respond.

Consequently, parenting leans on more than instinct and familiarity. Usually, it arises from the interplay between your instincts, your intimate knowledge of your particular child, and a practical and discerning understanding of normal child development.

We at the American Academy of Child and Adolescent Psychiatry conceived *Your Child* to provide the kind of information you need to supplement your native instincts and your knowledge of your child. In these pages you will find, in very broad strokes, your child's point of view—what she is likely experiencing at a given age or during a given event or life circumstance—within the context of your relationship. We will look at what to expect from your child, in terms of emotional, cognitive, moral, physical, and behavioral development, at each point along the way. What, for example, does a typical three-year-old feel, think about, and thirst for? What can you anticipate from your six-year-old as he begins school, or if there is a death in the family? How will your ten-year-old respond to the news that his parents are divorcing? What does it mean that your eight-year-old seems to lie regularly?

This information is not presented merely for its own sake. By describing in some detail the developmental milestones and concerns common to all parent-child relationships, by discussing particular questions that may arise during the course of parenthood, and by examining more worrisome problems that all too often present themselves, we hope to provide broad guidance in your day-to-day interactions with your child. Given what you know or are learning about your child's singular temperament, developmental stage, and day-to-day demands, for example, how do you best handle such issues as toilet training, chronic illness, a family move, beginning day care, aggression, sexual behaviors, and the like?

This book offers suggestions for handling practical matters: from choosing your baby's doctor to dealing with sleep problems, from bolstering a child's self-esteem to helping a child manage school difficulties, from selecting age-appropriate toys to finding help for serious emotional problems.

We will also consider when the behavior of the "not easy" child is just right and when it signals trouble; when "good" indicates a problem and when "good" is how it should be. This book is intended to be used as a touchstone—a way of measuring when a certain behavior, though irritating and confusing, is perfectly normal and when it is a signal for professional help. It is a reference intended to offer reassurance, perspective, and guidance.

When all is said and done, successful parenting requires not just instinct, familiarity, and reflexes, but thoughtful reflection as well. Another purpose of this book is to provide the information, and perhaps a dollop of wisdom, to nurture your understanding in such a way that you can facilitate your child's development. Indeed, it is our intention to help you and your child over the inevitable bumps of childhood—even when your instincts are blurred by too little sleep, too much anxiety, too many conflicting responsibilities, and strained patience, flexibility, and creativity.

Parenting is truly one of life's greatest pleasures, as well as one of its greatest challenges. It is the hope of all of us who contributed to this volume that you will find encouragement and help within its pages to guide your child as he or she engages richly and meaningfully in the developmental processes.

How to Use This Book

Your Child is organized to make it easy for you to browse through at your leisure, or to satisfy your curiosity on a given subject, or to direct you quickly and methodically to areas of specific interest when you are pressed to know. The book is divided into four parts plus three appendices.

Part I: The Life of the Child

Part I presents the milestones of a child's development, starting with infancy and working its way through to the preadolescent years. This section presents an approximate chronology of what to expect from your child in terms of physical, emotional, behavioral, cognitive, social, and moral maturation.

The concerns discussed in this section of the book—for example, *My infant doesn't seem to be able to sleep through the night. What if my baby never crawls? My toddler seems to get so clingy whenever he meets new* people. *When will my six-year-old begin to read?*—are typical of those you will routinely discuss with your pediatrician. The issues and information presented here center on what almost every child experiences during the course of childhood.

Within these pages, you may recognize behaviors, feelings, and reactions that have puzzled or troubled you; after reading through the section, you may breathe a sigh of relief—*Oh, that's why she's having trouble sleeping through the night.* or *That's what that tantrum meant!*—knowing that they are not only normal but to be expected.

Chapter 1: Infancy: The First Year of Life describes the initial developmental stage during which you and your child establish a bond. The attachment formed during the first year will serve as the prototype for all other relationships and will enable him to begin to examine the world close at hand. This chapter includes discussions about such topics as eating, sleeping, crying, colic, and well-baby care.

Chapter 2: Toddlerhood: The Child at Ages One and Two looks at the stage during which your child will move further out into the larger world, relying more and more on the capabilities of his own body to explore, investigate, and experiment, all the while remaining deeply and importantly attached to you. Subjects include transitional objects; hitting and biting; socializing; bossiness; negativism; discipline; and the ways in which parents can foster emotional security and self-esteem in their child.

In *Chapter 3: The Preschool Years: Ages Three, Four, and Five,* we follow the growing child as social concerns become more important to her. During the preschool years, she begins to test out the social lessons she learns at home with both adults and children in the larger world. At the same time, the preschooler begins to bring home the lessons she learns in the outside world. This chapter will include discussions of such topics as toilet training; the why question; the world of fantasy; and teaching values.

Chapter 4: The Elementary School Years: Ages Six through Eleven centers on the middle years, in which school increasingly becomes the vital venue for your child's social, emotional, moral, and cognitive development. In this chapter, topics range from helping your child become more responsible; supporting him as he develops greater autonomy; and exploring the meaning of friendship, to such practical matters such as allowance, chores, and television.

Part II: Day-to-Day Problem Behaviors

Part II describes those everyday behaviors, feelings, and reactions that may be bewildering to you but are by no means aberrant. Tantrums, sleep difficulties, and worries about bumps in the night are all perfectly normal parts of growing up. Yet they may be distressing for you and your child. Other behaviors, however natural for the child, may be quite problematic. You may wonder how to deal with your child's lying, stealing, aggressiveness, and bed-wetting, and worried whether there is a need for serious concern. In many cases, even the most puzzling behavior does not signal serious trouble. Yet, it may require your attention and necessitate that you respond in an immediate and measured way. This section places such concerns in the context of the child's development.

In addition, this second part of the book addresses those issues faced from time to time, not by all children, but by many in their singular paths toward adulthood: divorce; death or serious illness in the family: moving; changing schools; going to camp; and other life transitions. By addressing these issues in greater detail, we hope to offer reassurance and direction so that you can interpret and respond to your child's behavior in a helpful manner.

Chapter 5: Challenges at Home concentrates on behaviors that, however normal, are not so easily handled: aggression, attention-seeking, sexual behaviors, tantrums, fighting with siblings, whining, and illness, among others. You may need to be reminded that these behaviors are not a result of anything you have or have not done. You may need a few practical tips on how to handle them. Or you may merely need to be reassured that other parents are dealing with similar doubts or the same disquieting conduct.

Chapter 6: The Family Redefined grapples with the question "What is a family?" Countless children today are being raised by single parents, stepparents, grandparents, gay parents, and foster families. Other factors, including adoption, sibling rivalry, and poverty have a direct impact on a child's development and the relationships he has with those who care for him. They are addressed in this chapter.

Chapter 7: School-Related Concerns includes discussions on such subjects as over- and underachievement, peer pressure, parental involvement, changing schools, cheating, and home schooling.

Chapter 8: The Child and the Community addresses the issues involved in living in the larger community of family, friends, neighbors, and strangers. It touches on such subjects as child abuse, natural and man-made disasters, gangs, and violence in the media.

Chapter 9: The Child with Chronic Illness describes the special challenges that families contend with when a child has a chronic illness such as asthma, diabetes, allergies, headaches, cancer, or AIDS.

Part III: Serious Problems and Abnormalities

In Part III, we move beyond the day-to-day quandaries and concerns to those that in fact represent serious obstacles to a child's development and family life. This section reviews those emotional, behavioral, and developmental problems that usually require professional intervention. The information provided in these chapters will help you understand what is going on with your child so that you can ask a child and adolescent psychiatrist or other mental health clinician the right questions and get the right kind of help for your child and your family.

Today, we understand that when children experience serious problems, it is not only or not simply a product of faulty parenting. Rather it is a result of the elaborate interplay among a child's basic temperament, strengths, vulnerabilities, and biology, the family and community environments. This section presents serious problems within their context and complexity without blame or judgment. It is intended to help parents recognize and understand these serious illnesses and their inevitable repercussions.

Chapter 10: Emotional Disorders elucidates those disturbances, including depressive disorders, anxiety disorders, and post-traumatic stress disorders, in which a child internalizes or feels profound and constant distress to the point that the normal involvements of her life—school, friends, family—are significantly disrupted.

In *Chapter 11: Disruptive Behavior Disorders* focuses on those disturbed behaviors that indicate a considerable degree of internal upset or represent a symptom of a larger, underlying emotional problem. Such conditions include attention-deficit hyperactivity disorder, conduct disorders, and opposition defiant disorder.

Chapter 12: Developmental Disorders deals with mental retardation, pervasive developmental disorder, learning disabilities, and other related problems that impede a child's development.

Chapter 13: Psychotic Disorders examines schizophrenia, brief reactive psychosis, and toxic psychosis, in which a child's thought processes are severely and consistently impaired.

Chapter 14: Sleep Disorders reviews the possible causes and repercussions of a child's sleep difficulties. While sleep difficulties may signal mild, passing problems, they may also represent more persistent, troublesome ones. Among the problems discussed are severe nightmares, night terrors, sleepwalking, and teeth grinding.

Part IV: Seeking Help

Part IV offers practical advice and useful information to guide parents when it seems that professional mental health intervention may be called for. This section presents the who, where, when, and why of getting help. We discuss in detail the many aspects of mental health treatment (individual psychotherapy, medication, cognitive-behavioral techniques, family and group therapies, and psychiatric evaluation and diagnosis), as well as the professions involved (child and adolescent psychiatry, psychology, social work, counselors, and psychotherapists).

As you determine whether your child—and your family—could benefit from professional treatment, *Chapter 15: How and When to Seek Help* offers direction. This chapter helps parents understand just what is involved in seeking help, what mental health intervention can reasonably be expected to accomplish, and how to go about finding the right clinician for your child and your family.

Chapter 16: What Are the Treatment Options? provides a detailed discussion of the fundamentals of choosing and using mental health services—specifically, the various types of therapies available and the issues and problems each typically addresses.

The Appendices include a list of basic identifications and descriptions of commonly used psychiatric drugs (*Appendix A: Psychiatric Medicines*); a list of medical and other tests commonly used by mental health clinicians in assessing or diagnosing children (*Appendix B: Medical, Psychological, Educational, and Developmental Tests*); and a glossary of psychiatric and medical terminology that you may encounter in discussing your youngster's status with his child and adolescent psychiatrist or other clinician. We have also included a complete index to ensure easy access to specific topics throughout *Your Child*.

A Note to the Reader

We used male pronouns (he, him, his, and himself) when referring to the infant in the opening chapter of this book. We used female pronouns (she, her, herself) in the second chapter. Thereafter, pronoun forms alternate from one chapter to the next.

There are a handful of exceptions. These occur in response to conditions or disorders found predominantly in males or females. We chose to use this approach to make the book more readable, evenhanded, and to acknowledge that our readers are the parents of both boys and girls.

The Editors

Part I

THE LIFE OF A CHILD

■   ■   ■

In these four chapters, the milestones of childhood development are described, including those of infancy, toddlerhood, the preschool years, and the elementary school years. In addition to providing a chronology of what to expect from your child, many of the most common physical, emotional, behavioral, cognitive, social and moral issues, and the challenges of parenting that you will confront in raising a child are discussed.

"My family walking through the shoppping center."   *Morgan, age 8*

1

Infancy

THE FIRST YEAR OF LIFE

■ ■ ■

The offspring of some animals walk about by themselves within hours of birth. A newborn fawn, lamb, or duckling, for example, has a high degree of independence. The human child is quite different. Your baby is utterly dependent; without adult care, the baby will die.

A baby needs careful attention—he needs food, warmth, clean diapers, and the rest. Equally important is the baby's need for love and a sense of belonging. There's an element, too, of stimulation, of knowing how to expose the child's senses and perceptions to a world full of play, how to interact and challenge that child as he grows.

The human brain continues to develop after birth, and that development is brought about by stimulation. The stimulation must be of the right intensity and pacing, and must be associated with affect, or feelings. In fact, it is this individual pacing, done by the baby's primary caretakers, that makes up one major task of parenting.

In his first year, a baby triples his birth weight. In roughly twelve months, a newborn incapable of any form of locomotion learns to walk. In a mere six months, he understands that he is an individual, separate from his mother and the world. In the first year, he learns some basic language skills: only a few words are spoken, perhaps, but many more are understood. The baby is also learning the rules of language, grammar, and syntax.

In the pages that follow, you will find an overview of the milestones of the first twelve months, an approximate chronology of what to expect of your baby and when. This chapter also contains detailed discussions of a number of behaviors and issues that concern parents during this time—eating, sleeping, temperament, toys, and others. As you will see, the first year of life is packed with rapid and surprising changes; it is, in short, the single most accomplished of a child's life. It's also the year in which he needs the most help from you.

ON BECOMING A PARENT

There is no such thing, of course, as the perfect parent. No one knows all the answers or has all the skills to manage a new baby. On the other hand, there are sensitivities and qualities to develop that can make you a better parent.

A baby likes hands that hold him comfortably and gently (as well as confidently). A baby likes people who pay close attention to him, whispering and talking. He loves a parent who communicates a sense of love and affection; a parent who cushions the baby's meeting up with his environment; a person who, as the baby ages, helps him learn about limits and separation and delayed gratification. These are some of the qualifications for parenthood.

The parent exposes the child to the world. He or she introduces new experiences and stimuli in a controlled fashion. It's a parent's job to help open the child's eyes, within sensible limits, to the wonders of the world. If you stimulate your child's curiosity at the same time that you give him a confident sense of belonging and a certainty of his own worth, he will experiment and explore.

Don't undervalue your intuition as a parent. There will be times as a mother or father when you sense at gut level that something is wrong. Listen to that little voice. There will be other times when, for a moment, you feel like the only parent in the world, confronted by a situation with no logical solution. You will muddle through. There may be an obvious person to ask, but you may often find that you are the person with the answer. Neither this book nor any other can teach the art of parenting, though much can be learned about babies from reading, talking to other parents, and your own experience. Yet perhaps the single most important gauge in bringing up baby is what your intuition tells you.

As a parent, you also carry baggage. There are perceived social roles—do you think of moms as doing some things and dads others? That's true for breast-feeding, but there really aren't any other biological limits. You need to decide upon mutually satisfactory divisions of labor.

Talk to others, too. Use your extended family to learn about parenting (for example, your baby's grandparents, aunts, and uncles). They have ideas and experiences to offer.

Recognize, as well, that what you bring to parenting is, in part, a product of your own childhood. You may want to re-create the warmth and joy you recall from your upbringing; you may want to give your child something you feel you didn't have. It helps to have your eyes open not only to your baby's needs, but to your own as well.

No one can prepare you for the wave of feeling that will begin the voyage of parenthood. Pregnancy—as exhilarating and as special a time as it is—cannot and does not prepare you for life after the baby is born. The experience is beyond words, and unique to each and every parent and family. You, as a new parent, are specially qualified to invest your best energies, love, and concern in helping your baby to thrive and to launch him on a happy, healthy, successful life.

Milestones of the First Year

The workings of a baby's mind are—and likely will remain—inscrutable. We cannot remember our own experiences of that time, and no newborn can tell us of his as they occur. Yet thanks to a range of imaginative research and careful observation, we have learned a great deal about a baby's first year of life and even of the months before (researchers believe the unborn child to have a capacity to sense the world outside and even to learn in utero). The picture remains unrefined, its details sketchy. Yet even a primitive understanding can help us respond to the newborn as he grows and matures during his first year.

In the pages that follow, we will trace the path your baby will take in those months. Keep in mind that development is much the same from one child to the next, since covering the same developmental ground requires following the same basic path. But the way the child makes his way varies according to his environment and individual variations between children.

Remember, too, that the milestones described below are not a precise mapping of the events to come. The sequence of changes you observe in your child—or each of your children—is likely to follow the pattern described. Yet the pace of individual children differs. One child will walk at nine months, another at fifteen months; both are within the normal range. Some children develop rapidly in the early months, then seem to experience a deceleration in development; the pace changes. A child who walks later may talk earlier.

Development isn't a competition—the fact that your child did (or did not do) something before a friend's child of the same age is unimportant. If, however, you think you detect a pattern that suggests the child's development is significantly delayed or abnormal, discuss your concerns with your baby's physician.

Premature Babies Keep in mind, as well, that if your child was born prematurely then his developmental age may be less than his actual age as calculated from the day of birth. Thus, in considering the developmental milestones that follow, you may wish to calculate your infant's age using the original due date rather than his birth date.

■ THE BABY AT BIRTH

The newborn's eyes focus at a distance of eight to ten inches; the world beyond is a blur. Although they are little more than abstract forms, faces that come within his range are fascinating to the baby. His hearing, though not quite fully developed, is sur-

prisingly close to that of an adult (he may recognize his mother's voice even in utero). By the end of the first month, many infants have the ability to perceive the differing sounds of human speech. In a matter of days, he will also recognize his mother's smell. All of which is a long way of saying your baby likes you to get close to, pay attention to, and talk to him.

The newborn has a number of in-born reflexes, including the *sucking reflex* (put a finger in his mouth, and he will suck on it with surprising strength). There's also a *rooting reflex* (touch his cheek and he will turn his head, open his mouth, and root for the nipple). Other reflexes will include the *grasping reflex* (the baby will close its hand around a finger that touches his palm); the *Babinski reflex* (stroking the sole of the foot will cause the toes to fan out before curling); the *eyeblink,* in which the eyes close quickly when bright lights or rapidly moving objects enter the baby's field of vision; and the *Moro reflex,* a startle response involving outstretched arms followed by an embracing motion. The *neonate*—the medical term for a baby during his first six weeks of life—can be described in many ways, but one of them is as a bundle of reflexes. These reflexes are linked to helping your baby thrive.

The newborn has the wrinkled look of advanced age. His expressions are often peculiar, as he squints, blinks, and crosses his eyes. He will upon occasion catch your eye and look at you, but mostly he'll eat (seven or eight times a day) and sleep (in eight or more naps). A typical newborn will sleep roughly three-quarters of the time, between sixteen and twenty hours at day. His schedule will seem a total jumble, as the parents—themselves alternately exhilarated and exhausted—try to establish a routine.

Initially night and day will seem to converge, but after about two weeks the baby will begin to show signs of adapting to a more recognizable schedule. For some babies, that schedule is reversed with more waking hours at night than during the day. You can help him adjust his clock to yours, giving the baby cues by, for example, extending the time between feedings during the day (see also *Sleeping,* page 24).

Helping the baby adopt a regular schedule that coordinates with yours not only will help the household run more smoothly but will also provide him a secure and predictable basis for further development.

Postpartum Depression   Many women experience a slight depression after childbirth called postpartum blues. Crying spells may occur along with worries about being a good mother. Pregnancy hormones still in the body can produce mood swings, so some degree of sadness after the birth of a child is normal and, in most cases, will pass in a matter of days or a week or two. In about one of ten women, however, the postpartum period brings on or exacerbates a clinical depression. If you feel as if your world is dark; if getting out of bed in the morning is a chore; and, most tellingly, if you find it difficult to relate to your baby and to others around you, talk to your physician.

■ ONE MONTH

As the first month becomes the second, life with baby begins to have a discernable pattern. A routine of eating and sleeping is emerging at about three-hour intervals for breast-fed and four-hour intervals for formula-fed babies.

The child will seem suddenly much more a part of things during the second month when his vocabulary expands to include the charming coos and other sounds of babyhood. He will respond to the sound of your voice and stop feeding momentarily when distracted.

By the age of four weeks, the baby will remain awake for longer periods. The baby sneezes, hiccups, but shouldn't cough (consult the baby's physician if he does). His little reflexive cries have been replaced by real crying; gentle, occasional fussing may have given way to a loud and prolonged period of fussiness in the evening (see *Crying,* page 29).

Food remains at the center of life for the neonate—for the first six months a baby gains almost an ounce a day (some two pounds a month). Yet food isn't everything, as he will now recognize the smell of his mother and respond to caresses. Most one-month-olds welcome agreeable noises around them like music and voices.

■ TWO MONTHS

You can't spoil a baby at two months of age, it's that simple. Throughout the first few months, indulge him—if he cries, pick him up and soothe him. What your baby needs is to develop a degree of trust, of confidence that his needs will be met. No baby of this age cries to manipulate a situation.

This age also features the true smiling, as distinct from the small grins of the contented newborn, drowsy after a feeding (see also *Smiling*, page 17).

Newborns startle: involuntary jerks and uncontrolled spasmodic response are the norm *(Moro reflex).* By two months of age, however, a degree of control becomes evident. He can turn at will, or deliver his hand to his mouth to suck on it. When brought to a sitting position, he can hold his head erect briefly, though it remains wobbly. On his stomach, he'll lift his head up, clearing his airway, looking around; at two months the baby may be able to bear his own weight momentarily when stood up. He will track objects immediately in front of him—their arrival evokes an excited response—and he may bat at a mobile hung above him (see *Play and Toys,* page 32). He can hold a rattle or other object for a few moments before it drops from his grasp. Stimulation (especially if it involves people) will cause him to remain awake longer.

■ THREE MONTHS

During the first months of life, the infant organizes his behavior and stabilizes his physiological processes. To put it another way, the baby becomes coordinated with his environment, establishing regular patterns of eating, sleeping, and wakefulness.

By three months of age, the baby will be sleeping less and the occassional interlude of fussiness in the evening begins to disappear. Colic, too, tends to be resolved by this age (see *Colic,* page 30). His vision is improving, so he can better distinguish shapes and forms. The baby is becoming even more a social being, able to engage the attention of adults. Having reached an equilibrium of sorts with the world outside the womb, the child is ready to begin the process of becoming a separate person.

At birth the child habitually holds his hands clenched; at about eight weeks, he will open them and begin to examine them. He will also explore his own face and features with these newfound tools. On his stomach, he'll lean on his elbows, holding his head and chest up for perhaps ten seconds at a time.

By three months, most (though not all) full-term babies have begun sleeping through the night. If your baby isn't sleeping through, keep in mind that sleeping is in part a function of weight—most babies of eight pounds will sleep four hours at a stretch; at eleven pounds, six- to eight-hour stretches are typical. But your child's temperament is an issue, as well, and a sensitive, difficult baby may have trouble settling down (see also *Temperament*, page 14, and *Sleeping,* page 24.)

There's crying and then there's crying—the *I'm hungry* cry differs from the *It hurts* cry. Gurgles and coos now are to be heard coming from baby, as are vowel sounds like *Ahhhhhhhs,* then with changing intonations *Ahhh-AHHH-Ahhh*; and consonant sounds with *G*'s and *K*'s. He will follow objects or people with his eyes, and will react at the appearance of familiar objects or people.

■ FOUR MONTHS

After your baby's four-month birthday, patterns of life continue to emerge. He is a social being, happy for your company, capable of letting loose with recognizable laughter. His vision has improved, and he can focus normally at most any distance. This means he responds to the sight of food being brought to him. Using what he sees, he can begin to coordinate his hands to reach out to touch objects. With support, he can sit up for a few minutes, holding his head erect and steady.

He can roll from his stomach to his back; some babies of this age can roll back again, too. He can hold his head steady and sit up with some support. At this age, though, the child instinctively uses his mouth to help explore the world: a rule of life for the four-month-old seems to be: *Open mouth, insert anything and everything.* He has begun to try handling objects but hasn't yet become very adept.

In the vicinity of a baby's four-month birthday, the child takes a giant step toward being his own person. Before this age, he has cried out only when he is hungry or uncomfortable; now he makes an important discovery: Upon crying out by choice, he can draw attention to himself. This intellectual leap is of tremendous importance. Even at this age, however, it isn't possible to spoil the baby, so don't ignore his cries thinking he needs some discipline in his life. That comes later.

Another cognitive leap occurs at this time. This has a variety of indications, one of the most apparent being *distractibility.* In mid-feeding, the child will pull away from the breast or let the bottle drop from his lips. The cause isn't a desire to be weaned or even satiation—he's interested, curious about the world around.

At this age, the baby is beginning to understand in an elementary way something of himself and his environment. Some researchers believe that a baby is able to make *Me, Not me* distinctions much earlier, but by four months, the child is also beginning to recognize the difference between *Known* and *Unknown* and between *Normal* and *Strange.* Simple though they are, these distinctions are the building blocks of a worldview.

Consistency is important in enabling the child to develop a context. That doesn't mean a ritualized pattern of eating and sleeping. Rather what the child needs to understand in a warm and fuzzy way is that he can expect to be well fed, warm, and clean; that his little world is full of caring stimulation; and that he has an interactive role to play.

The world responds to baby—parents' faces and voices, simple toys, and mirrors. In fact, the simple exchange of noises and expressions between parent and baby can be the most loving, educational, and welcoming play possible.

■ FIVE MONTHS

A baby of five months is beginning to take in *and* evoke a response from the world around him. The child's eyes will begin to follow a moving object passed before them from one side to the other: he will reach for it, too, and his aim is well coordinated.

By this age, the child likes to be propped up in order to get a better look at the world. He may be able to sit steadily, his hands planted in front of him and arms propping him up. He also will stand with support and be very pleased with himself.

At about this time, baby will squeal and yell, growl and make vowel-based noises, too. He will react to his own name, and will turn his head to try to identify the source of the sound. He will imitate the sounds he hears, as well as facial expressions.

At about five months the coordination will have progressed to the degree that an object can be manipulated, perhaps even handed back and forth from one hand to the other. The grasping reflex the neonate was born with has been replaced by a new ability to control an object. He will examine objects, shaking and turning them, and then mouth them. He'll put his feet in his mouth, too. The first tooth may appear at about six months, though in many babies it arrives later.

■ SIX MONTHS

Your baby sits less awkwardly, his back straighter, but still balanced by hand support. If solid food has been introduced, mealtime will consist of eating—and a lot of playing. He'll want to feed himself and even drink out of a cup but won't be notably skilled as yet (see also *Eating,* page 22). He'll try to tell you what he wants, uttering more consonant sounds than before, including *f, sh,* and *mmmmm* sounds.

He comes to understand at about this time that he is a separate, independent being. It's a monumental event in his development. This cognitive leap evokes mixed feelings in the child, however, because his separateness also represents separation from his parents (for a detailed discussion of this concept and its impact on parent and child, see *Separation Anxiety,* page 18).

A child will also have discovered that he can, at least in some small ways, control his environment—blankets, toys, and objects around him will move when grabbed or pushed or kicked; Mom, Dad, or a caregiver will appear upon being called.

Don't misunderstand the baby's intentions when he throws his rattle on the floor twelve times in succession, and keep in mind there is no disciplining a baby at six months. You will accomplish nothing besides upsetting and possibly confusing him, despite the fact that he seems to be tossing toys about just to annoy you. More likely, he's devising his own method of inquiry: *Did I make the rattle do that banging noise when I dropped it from my high chair? Will someone pick it up?* Be patient with the learning process.

On the other hand, the logic of life should be implicit so the baby can absorb it little by little. His crib is for sleeping and his high chair for eating. The occurrences of the day come in a predictable order, events have a certain logic about them. Habit and ritual are reassuring to a child.

■ SEVEN MONTHS

The seven-month-old can sit on his own for extended periods. He can shift forward onto his hands and back onto his bottom. When drawn to a standing position, he can remain there, holding hands with the attending adult, supporting his own weight. Standing on a parent's stomach, he'll bounce vigorously.

The child's balance is such that both hands are now available for play. His favorite tool for experiencing the world is no longer the eye—looking is fine, but touching is better (though tasting is still pretty good fun, too). He grasps objects and maneuvers them from one hand to the other. He's intrigued by his face in a mirror. He will reach out and pat the reflected image, which he recognizes to be his own.

At this age, the child is increasingly social. He likes people who pay attention, listening and sometimes vocalizing back to them. If there are people at hand, a social baby of this age may seem to be working the crowd, trying to entertain the parent or other adults nearby. Yet the child also can play happily on his own, concentrating intently.

Growth slows during the second six months of life—the average daily weight gain is about half an ounce. The nature of the growth changes, too: the child begins to stretch, his body and limbs lengthening. The added height is enhanced by the gradual disappearance of the folds of flesh and the "Buddha-baby" look. Such changes in proportion will facilitate balance when the child eventually begins to walk.

He will incorporate additional consonant sounds into his babbling, and produce sounds that repeat the same consonant and vowel (e.g., "Ba-ba-baaaaa-BA!"). Most children can roll from back to stomach, as well as stomach to back, by this age. While some perfectly normal children never roll over, others may adopt rolling as their primary means of mobility.

Children have some understanding of *object permanence* at this age. This means the child recognizes that an object he can no longer see still exists; he understands its permanence and will search for objects hidden from him. This suggests that a new, independent world is taking shape *within his mind* that has an existence independent of the sensory stimuli around him (see also *Play and Toys,* page 32).

At about seven months, you will notice your child begins looking to you for guidance when confronted with something new. Before he makes up his mind about it, he wants to get a reading from you. Termed *social referencing,* this advance illustrates the development both of his trust in you and of his ability to manage increasingly complex communications. Upon meeting a stranger, your baby will look to read your face: if your expression is happy and positive, he'll be reassured; if you look worried, he will pause, suddenly cautious. If your baby takes a little tumble and sees a look of panic or grave concern come across your features, he'll probably cry; if you are composed and reassuring, he'll probably maintain a stiff upper lip, too.

▪ EIGHT MONTHS

Language is becoming more than mere sound to the child of eight months. He may say *Bye-bye* in farewell to people he knows. The word *No* is a word he now understands and can obey; upon hearing it, he will stop doing whatever he's doing. Sometimes he himself will shake his head in refusal.

The utterance of a familiar name will cause the baby to look at the person just named. He himself may say *Da-da* in recognition of his father—and, most likely, in reference to a range of other people or things, too. Babbling will now incorporate more sounds, include syllables like *da, pa, wah,* and *ka.* He can clap his hands and wave.

Most children begin to crawl at about seven or eight months of age. To do so, however, your baby needs to master moving individual parts of his body; then he needs to be able to coordinate all of them at once. It doesn't happen overnight, but the pieces come together over a period of months.

Preliminary movements come first—at four or five months, his little arms pushing, the baby powers himself backward (to his surprise and frustration since he is moving away from the object he was seeking). Creeping on the stomach is usually next. At about eight or nine months of age, the movements of the arms, legs, and body come together and the baby crawls.

Some children crawl on their hands and knees, some on their elbows and tummy, still others on hands and feet in a kind of modified squat. Some never crawl at all but move straight to walking. And, no, in case you've heard the rumor, there's no demonstrable link between later reading problems and skipping the crawling stage.

The baby's increasing abilities bring him many opportunities for pleasure but also some for frustration. The child may want to play with something forbidden—mother's china teacup, for example—but you take it out of range. He can't be expected to understand why—his frustrated look will seem to have *And why not?* written all over it. He can't be expected to understand why his fine motor coordination is not adequate to performing a desired maneuver with an object at hand. You can't explain that either.

Helping a child deal with such small frustrations is part of the process of preparing the child for later skills. Allow the child to resolve the frustration himself if possible. If he can't quite perform the maneuver he wants, let him try (he may figure it out), but lend a helping hand before it upsets him. Do it simply, quickly, and let the child go on with his exploring.

If the desired object or activity is dangerous—to the child or your china—distract the child with another activity or substitute another, safer object. Sometimes simply interrupting a child—calling his name—will produce a change in tack. Remove any risky (or at-risk) object immediately. Don't offer a warning first, just do it. In calm, clear fashion explain why (*It's hot* or *It's sharp*).

A crawling or cruising youngster exploring the world doesn't crave ambiguity. He needs clearly defined and calmly stated limits, and the opportunity to begin to understand them.

■ NINE MONTHS

The baby can shift himself from a prone to a sitting position without help. The child is continuing to develop fine motor skills: At nine months, one glance at an object is enough to guide his movement to reach out and grab it.

Hand preference has begun to emerge, too. *Handedness,* as it is called, will be evident when the child demonstrates more dexterity with his left or right hand. Offer a toy and consistently the child will use the preferred hand to grab it. Each of these evolving fine motor skills enables your child to learn about objects in his world and their weight, shape, feel, and other properties.

By nine months of age, the baby will recognize and respond to his own name. By nine months, the baby's "vocabulary" will include consonant sounds as well as vowels, and the baby has begun to master the tones and rhythms of language. The baby has become a great imitator, too, making coughs, tongue clicks, and hisses.

Limits are growing in importance. The last quarter of a baby's first year is a time when establishing limits makes sense.

Limits are not, however, about language. Limits are about actions: A parent who moves quickly, picks up baby, and relocates the child elsewhere delivers the message. Distracting the child is an invaluable strategy when a limit has been reached and the child stubbornly refuses to accept it. Another gambit is substitution. Remember, though, that life can still be frustrating to your child, so be sure your baby's life doesn't begin to be just one limit after another to him.

■ **TEN MONTHS**

The ten-month-old child may be able to master pulling himself to a standing position. True walking seems to be imminent (though it probably isn't); he can walk, though, while holding on to both of your hands.

Your child still needs two naps a day at this age but sleeps less, perhaps fourteen hours a day in a ten-hour stretch at night and two two-hour daytime naps. His ability to make sounds is developing rapidly—individual words and sounds may be repeated endlessly. Imitation of new sounds (as well as expressions and gestures) is a source of pleasure.

The child begins to reveal moods, too. His overall affect may represent such emotions as sadness, happiness, or anger; fear is evident, of strange places in particular.

He has probably chosen one toy as a favorite by this age, but continues to be interested in exploring. He'll open drawers to find out what's inside, and will try to fit objects together.

■ **ELEVEN MONTHS**

At around this age, your child may master the skill of *cruising*, a supported style of walking along, say, the length of a couch. He can squat and stoop, and lower himself back to the floor, settling to his rump with a thump. Climbing up stairs (and perhaps back down) is a new thrill. (The practice must, of course, be closely supervised.)

The eleven-month-old may begin to use objects in his world in imaginative ways to reach some goal—a chair can become a walker, for example. He can pick up small objects and turn pages in a book.

Sounds that are recognizably wordlike will emerge from the baby's mouth at about this time. More than one vowel sound may appear in these *jargon* words, *babee* being a typical one. This is the last step before the infant produces his first real words in the next month or two.

■ **THE ONE-YEAR-OLD CHILD**

The one-year-old is quite mobile. Some children on their first birthday can walk, but most are at least fast on all fours and cruise with ease.

He has likely added a few words to "Mama" and "Dada" in his vocabulary. He knows a dog from a cat in a picture book. He is using his thumb and first finger in a pincer movement to grasp small objects.

He can imitate a dog's bark or cat's meow. He will indicate his desire for certain objects with gestures and sounds; on request, he'll hand over or reach for an object, having come to understand that certain objects are represented by specific words.

Peekaboo continues to be an endlessly fascinating game for the sociable one-year-old who also has become even more of a crowd-pleaser. The one-year-old typically enjoys making his elders laugh—and will often repeat the action to get another, like response.

Feeding time may be complicated by the child's eagerness to use a utensil even though his dexterity falls well short of being able to manage it efficiently. Let him try—and use a second spoon yourself to deliver the bulk of the food.

The one-year-old will cooperate with the dressing process, although at this stage the child is not so much genuinely helpful as he is simply less of a hindrance.

If your twelve-month-old isn't already walking, he will be soon. Eleven to thirteen months is usual; some start earlier (eight months is not uncommon), others later. The normal range includes babies who walk after fifteen months. A useful rule of thumb is: walking comes after crawling by several months. The various muscles must come under more organized control by the brain before the child can begin the even more complicated skill of walking. Early walkers aren't necessarily the natural athletes, by the way; at school age, there will be no distinguishing which children walked early or late.

Your child, on the verge of walking and talking, is ready to take on the life of a one-year-old.

Temperament

Your child has an inborn *temperament.* This assemblage of characteristics predisposes him to respond in certain ways to the world around him. For example, one child will become upset and cry at length upon hearing a loud noise while another will merely startle at an identical sound. Distinctions made on the basis of such differing reactions lead to classifying babies as having one or another basic temperament.

Temperament is largely a matter of style. Long-term studies suggest that a baby's characteristic manner of displaying moods and emotions tends to be a consistent, predictable part of his personality. Thus, identifying an infant's individual style or dominant mood can offer a surprisingly accurate sketch of his temperament for many years to come.

During infancy, your baby's temperament can also prove a reliable aid in helping you to help your child. The shy baby needs to be introduced to new circumstances more gradually than the highly adaptable baby. Knowing your child's temperament can also be useful in recognizing indicators—perhaps illness, maybe a developmental burst, or simply a situation your baby is finding stressful.

■ IDENTIFYING TEMPERAMENT

Consider the way in which your baby handles hunger: Does he express his need for food with demanding screams or a gentler, insistent cry? How about going to sleep: Is it easy or hard for him (and you)?

Your child's overall level of activity is another piece of the puzzle. Still another is your child's adaptability to new or changed circumstances and whether a new situation causes him to withdraw or to join in. Is your child venturesome or apprehensive? Is he inclined to react positively or negatively to a new circumstance? Is there no situation too exciting for him, he loves them all? Or does nothing get him excited? Or is almost anything too much? Is there a tendency for the baby to be self-sufficient (he puts himself to sleep, he entertains himself in the crib)? Some children are enthusiastic eaters and sound sleepers. Others are nervous, and have difficulty settling down to both eating and sleeping. Some babies seek a lot of stimulation, others seek less.

Identifying characteristics can help you locate your child in broader categories. According to pioneering research by Stella Chess, M.D., and Alexander Thomas, M.D., there are three basic "constellations of temperament" among normal children.

The Easy Baby These babies are adaptable, biologically regular in eating and eliminating patterns, and typically respond positively to changes in circumstances. Their intensity level is generally moderate.

The Difficult Baby The difficult baby is the reverse of the easy one and may be best described as strong-willed. His intensity is high and typically strong. He finds change distressing and is biologically irregular.

The Slow-to-Warm-Up Baby The baby with the shy temperament is slow to warm up and to adapt to change. Change is usually met with crying, though typically the intensity of the response is low.

Other Babies Researchers Chess and Thomas found that about 40 percent of the babies they studied were "easy," 10 percent "difficult," and about 15 percent "slow to warm up." The remaining one-third typically exhibited a mix of the characteristics of the easy, difficult, and shy profiles.

■ PUTTING TEMPERAMENT TO WORK

Recognizing that your baby has, for example, a difficult temperament may relieve some anxiety on your part that you've done something wrong or the worry that you're not being a good parent. In the same way, differences between your child's behavior and a playmate's *don't* mean that he is bad or sick.

One of every parent's key tasks is to understand his or her child and to respond to him in ways that enable him to be happy, healthy, and to get the most out of his life. Recognizing his temperament may help you to do that.

With a quiet, sensitive child, let him take the lead. Many babies don't like being looked directly in the eye, it's too much like confrontation. Look away and approach by indirection. Gentle contact—touching the hands or feet, rather than an enveloping hug—may allow the baby to warm at his own pace.

One baby likes being stroked at arm's length, another wants to be virtually enveloped and snuggled close. Most babies don't mind noise, having come from a place where the grindings and grumbling of the intestinal tract are nearby, yet some are awakened from sleep by very little noise. Some thrive on an environment full of life and energy; some seem to prefer quiet.

A difficult baby may challenge you. If nothing you do seems to make your baby happy, you may find yourself feeling inadequate. But don't take it personally: It's your baby's temperament, not your caregiving. There are strategies to try. Some parents find that increasing the amount of physical contact their babies have helps. Try carrying your baby around in a sling or Snugli™. Make extra sure he's warm, comfortable, well fed, and, at sleeping times, well wrapped.

You can't change a child's nature, but you can stage-manage many of his introductory experiences. Recognize, accept, and understand the child's nature, then create an environment that encourages the child to develop confidence, to understand his nature, to make the most of his gifts.

Bonding and Relationship-Building

The just-born baby, placed on his mother's chest, suckles her breast. While still in the delivery room, the father holds the baby. Both parents experience a swelling sense of connection with their brand-new baby and at some instinctive level the baby shares it, too.

This burgeoning attachment is commonly called a "bond."

The bond between parents and child can be established almost instantaneously, but bonding at first sight isn't guaranteed. If you open yourself to the flood of feelings that a tiny person will engender, you will connect with that child.

The bond will, over time, flower into a relationship. This development will result from two-way communication—no, the child can't yet speak, but using an ever broadening array of expressions, movements, and noises he *can* communicate.

The evolving parent-child relationship requires more than filling the baby's needs and helping it feel comfortable and cared for. Enter your child's world and welcome him into yours. Engage the child—during wakeful times, position the baby so he can see you. He looks at you—his eyes will brighten very early at a familiar, welcoming face. You reward him by moving to him. He makes a sound and you respond in kind. You cuddle his diminutive form, and play with him. You tell him about your life, and he'll tell you about his.

Your child's ability to communicate will develop rapidly. By two to three months of age, he will study your face, utterly engrossed, then suddenly smile. A smile in return may be rewarded by more smiling or even a coo. At this age, the infant also has some primitive understanding of the rule *Cry out, and they will come*. The baby cried instinctively at first; but now he has learned to expect a response from a parent or other caregiver. At four or five months, another leap is made when your baby will begin to cry by choice. The child discovers he can draw attention to himself, an intellectual leap of great significance. Soon after this revelation, the baby begins to experiment with coughs and sneezes and even gagging sounds, seeking parental responses.

With the introduction of solid food after four to six months, feeding time will consist of about equal parts eating and social exchanges. The food, the bowl, the spoon, the cup, all are sources of fun. There is research that suggests a child's digestive juices will flow better if there is pleasure in the eating process. If it's fun for you both, communication will be enhanced.

At six months, your baby will be curious at any voice he hears. How much of what is being said does he understand? No one can be sure, though a child of six months can begin to absorb the sound, cadence, inflec-tion, and intonation of speech—so the more he hears, the clearer and more correct it is, the better. Talking also enhances the connection between people of most any age, and this is never more true that between a six-month-old and the people around him. You'll probably never have a more attentive audience.

Your baby needs the special kind of sustenance you are uniquely able to bring him. He needs to be immersed in a loving atmosphere; he needs to sense that this warm little world is provided by his parents. His happiness in his little microcosm of love will be the result in part of an emerging connection with his mother, father, or both. This will help him learn the first lessons of love: The connection he establishes with you is his first try at a relationship, and it will forever be a standard for him as he develops other loving relationships in his life.

SMILING

One day in the second to third month, your baby will scan your face as usual. His eyes will move from the top down, taking in the hairline, the chin and shape of your face, then look into your eyes. The difference on this lucky day will be that, to your delight and his, he will smile back at you.

This expression isn't the drowsy half-smile of satiation a younger baby sometimes offers after feeding. This smile is a specific, social behavior. It is evidence that your child is now capable of sociable exchanges. For a parent, the smiles bestowed upon them by their infants are wonderful little gifts, added incentives to focus more attention on the child.

You will find your baby's smile is a delight; enjoy it as a sign your baby is happy. But don't read a great deal more into it. Babies will examine (and sometimes smile at) crude drawings of faces that have the basic elements in place (eyes, mouth, a recognizably headlike shape). His reaction is probably to *a* face rather than to *your* face, but the smile is a new and important mode of response. By about four months, he will have begun to distinguish parental faces, and to know others closest to him from those who are unfamiliar.

Remember, too, that your baby's smile is a response. He bestows a smile on you because in some rudimentary way he reads the face before him as warm and welcoming. That smile is also a reflection of emotional development, of the child's emerging ability to socialize and to express himself.

Encourage his smile—smile back, greet him with smiles, respond to his with coos or hugs—and the language of the smile will evolve into a method of exchange, too. Sometimes the baby experiences such acute pleasure its body positively quivers with joy, a bodily expression of pure happiness. The child as social being is beginning to emerge.

SEPARATION ANXIETY

A baby at six or seven months of age experiences a basic change in his understanding of the universe. He has become very attached to his mother, father, or caregiver, only to realize he is not at one with him or her, but is a separate being. This recognition can be very upsetting to a child, especially when the parent actually does leave the child's presence. The baby's emotional response is called *separation anxiety.*

Separating from parents is a fundamental part of growing up. As a parent, understand that your child needs to be able to manage separations and the anxiety associated with them. Some children, especially those who interacted with multiple caregivers in the early months of life, appear to have less difficulty making the adjustment to parental absences in the later months. Other children, upon realizing that their parents are leaving their presence, are suddenly seized with the fear that their parents are *abandoning* them.

The separation from his mother/parent/caregiver comes as a revelation that takes some getting used to. Children often respond to separation with crying, agitated behavior, and generalized distress. Ask yourself this: *How would you feel if your baby just disappeared?* The baby's feelings are similar.

After your child reaches six months of age, improvements in eyesight, fine motor coordination, and mobility allow for a great deal more exploration of the world. That also means the child will spend more time separate from parents. This time apart is necessary, contributing to the child's independence. Don't stop cuddling and carrying the child altogether—a sense of security is still essential—but do it less. Don't ignore his calls for attention but, when you know it isn't a matter of safety but a come-entertain-me call, delay your arrival. The child, in a gradual, gentle manner, needs to learn to take on the world himself.

Some children will be used to separation from an early age, but gradual separations may be helpful for the child who has difficulty separating. Arrange to go to a friend's or relative's home for a visit. Let the baby get comfortable and gain some degree of familiarity and comfort with the surroundings. A toy, blanket, or other familiar object may facilitate the process. After a warm but brief farewell, leave the baby for a while with the trusted friend or relative. Even if it's hard for everybody the first time, it'll get easier. Try to practice. The separations should occur at regular intervals and, if possible, with more than one adult at different times.

Again, while practice at separation is essential (complete with gentle partings and warm reunions afterward), time spent with parents continues to be central. Playing with each parent—toy play, peekaboo, reading, feeding, and so on—is still essential.

STRANGER ANXIETY

Another issue for a child of six or seven months is *stranger anxiety.* Many young babies respond happily to most any baby-friendly person. But a previously friendly-to-all baby may suddenly begin responding to strangers with an outburst of crying.

There is a basic technique for minimizing the upsetting effects of a stranger's arrival: An indirect approach is best, in which the new presence enters quietly, avoids looking directly at the baby, and allows the child to take in the new person. It's best done with the child in familiar circumstances, preferably with a parent or primary caregiver in attendance. After a time, a gentle and gradual approach can be made without upsetting the child.

THE BOTTLE OR THE BREAST: WHICH IS BEST?

Some children never know a bottle; some never nurse at the breast. Currents of opinion have shifted over the years, asserting at different times that breast-feeding or bottle-feeding is preferable. Many babies today, however, become acquainted with both.

WHICH IS THE HEALTHY CHOICE?

The clear consensus at the moment among medical professionals is that, where practical, breast-feeding is the preferred choice. Breast milk offers the baby a share of the mother's immunities, while formula lacks such protection. Mother's milk is more easily digested and offers slightly better overall nourishment. Allergies, diarrhea, ear infections, and even obesity are less likely in breast-fed babies. For the parents, there is the convenience factor, as there's no washing of bottles and preparation of formula.

On the other side of the discussion, the bottle does have advantages. The most obvious is that someone other than the mother can feed the child. For mothers returning to work shortly after birth, bottle-feeding may be the most workable option, though a breast pump can be used to express milk for use when the mother is not at hand.

Bottom line? For premature babies and babies born to families in which there is a history of allergies, nursing is strongly advised. Even as few as three or four weeks of nursing can provide your baby with valuable immunities. On the other hand, if circumstances or personal preference lead you to bottle-feed your baby, you need not feel guilty.

EMOTIONAL CONCERNS

Beyond issues of nutrition, physical health, and convenience, there are concerns regarding emotional well-being, both for the baby and the mother. Does breast-feeding have nurturing advantages?

Again, the prevailing wisdom has it that breast-feeding is to be preferred. Nursing helps establish the mother-child bond. For this reason, it has become common practice in many hospitals to encourage the newborn to suckle his mother's breast only moments after birth. Many mothers enjoy breast-feeding not only because they are providing their babies with nourishment but also because the same hormone that stimulates the production of milk also helps make the process of feeding pleasurable for the mother.

Mothers who nurse report feelings of attachment and protectiveness. Breast-feeding may even be a factor in building a mother's confidence in her ability to care for her baby. Yet these are subjective responses and many mothers who bottle-feed report experiencing similar emotional growth and attachment.

The bottle-versus-breast debate must be seen within the context of other issues concerning nurture and bonding. Breast-feeding fosters an exclusive closeness between mother and child; yet the attentive mother, folding the child into her arms and feeding him his bottle, experiences many of the same sensations a nursing mother does, and shares a similar intimacy.

The method of feeding is probably less important to the emotional health of the child than the overall investment of love and attention the mother brings to mothering. A baby whose needs are met promptly and appropriately—the demands for food, the cries for attention, the need for warmth and intimacy of a human kind—will be healthier and happier than one whose mother is less attuned, caring, and attentive.

The development of social relations between parent and child is a key first step in acquainting the child with the world at large, and the food-related mother-and-child interaction plays an important role in shaping the child's early experiences. The process, whether the means of milk delivery is the breast or the bottle, transcends bodily needs for sustenance. The intimacy of feeding offers both human contact and a developing sense of security.

THE OCCASIONAL BOTTLE

As a pragmatic matter, most doctors recommend that even the nursing baby be given a bottle at about two weeks of age and several a week thereafter so the bottle remains familiar. These allow the mother to get occasional breaks. It can make weaning later easier. Too many bottles a week, however, and the baby may begin to prefer the ease of the bottle to the breast. The bottle can be of formula, although, at least for the first few bottles, a mix of expressed breast milk and formula is best.

Eating

A generation or two ago, the generally accepted wisdom was that a newborn should eat every four hours. Many parents insisted upon a regular schedule of feedings: *It's almost four o'clock? Time to feed the baby.*

For some, this strictly regimented routine continues to be the approach of choice, but for most the expectation has changed. Today the rule of thumb for the first few weeks of life is more likely to be, *The baby's crying? He's probably hungry.*

A newborn feeds frequently, perhaps every two or three hours. Keep in mind this is the average; your baby isn't average, so his pattern may differ. Very tall or small babies may eat more frequently. Many babies prove to be day eaters, eating more frequently during the day and less often at night, but for some the pattern is reversed. At eight pounds, a nursing baby will generally feed every three hours, a formula-fed child every four hours.

■ SELF-REGULATION

Most newborns will, if given the opportunity, *self-regulate*. This means the parents' schedule must be flexible, allowing the child to establish a pattern of need (the cries will signal it) and feeding. It isn't for all children: some who *fail to thrive* (don't gain weight) require a more structured pattern consisting of frequent feedings. At the opposite end of the spectrum, some children eat too much. For them, fewer feedings may be appropriate. At your regularly scheduled appointments, your baby's doctor will evaluate your child's physical development and discuss with you the baby's eating habits (see *Well-Baby Care,* page 38).

Don't expect your child to adopt a regular schedule immediately. At birth feeding is little more than a collection of reflex mechanisms; over the first weeks, these are integrated and eating becomes voluntary. The mother, father, or other caregiver needs to coordinate with the baby as this adjustment takes place.

Many new mothers and fathers find that helping their babies master self-regulation is at the fulcrum of learning how to parent. Successful parents establish an equilibrium with their child, one that balances the parents' love and caregiving with the child's emotional and physical needs. That equilibrium is in constant flux—at this age, it can change from one week to the next, not to mention from one month or year to another. Yet working the baby's need-and-feed approach to life into the patterns of your lives can bring confidence, caring, and sensitivity to the parent-child relationship.

Keep in mind, too, that your baby will probably have periods during which his hunger seems almost insatiable. Such growth spurts are perfectly normal. A few days of intense eating doesn't mean that the equilibrium you've reached with your child is gone; the spurts, typically, wax and wane. The breast-feeding mother may feel the added feeding time is burdensome, but it will pass.

■ SPITTING UP AND BURPING

For the first six months or so, your baby's gut is still orienting itself—it isn't quite sure yet which end is up. As a result, regurgitation can occur often. For the soon-to-be parent, this may seem a disagreeable prospect; yet, like changing the diapers of a newborn, it is one of the surprises of parenting: both are really non-events. Wiping away a little spit-up isn't very different from cleaning up a small spill of watery cottage cheese, as long as care is taken to protect your clothing. A strategically positioned cloth diaper on your shoulder is all that is required.

Most babies require burping. The air that collects in a baby's stomach needs to be released, perhaps at the midpoint of the feeding and afterward. To burp him, hold the baby with his head on your shoulder, his body stretched along the length of your chest. Rub or gently pat his back in an up-and-down motion. You'll get results.

■ SOLID FOOD

When should you introduce solid foods? This is another of the many Great Debates of child-rearing. Current wisdom suggests not before four months, often not until six months. Early introduction puts your child at risk of allergy (especially where there is a family history) for no apparent gain (see *Baby Allergies,* page 42).

Your child will have a say in the matter, too. Whether you like it or not, he will play a role in the introduction of solid food. Many children refuse solid food at first, some until seven or eight months of age.

Start with small helpings. When your child is ready, he'll cooperate. Don't try to force him. A week or more will be required for the baby to get into the rhythm of it. Eat-ing sold food involves a new skill—sucking is not the same as swallowing.

Try a new food every five to seven days. By adding them one at a time, you can identify those that the baby doesn't tolerate well (vomiting, rashes, or watery stools indicate intolerance). Start with bland cereals (rice cereal is a good first choice) and then green and yellow vegetables (beans, peas, squash). Follow with fruits (bananas, applesauce, pears).

As the number of foods that has been introduced increases, vary the selection from meal to meal to avoid boredom for both of you. You may want to avoid meats for some months—many babies don't like them at first and they are not nutritionally necessary (breast milk or formula should remain the staple food until about a year of age), so their introduction will accomplish little besides making the stool malodorous. Consistency should be smooth to start with, then lumpy after your child begins to chew things at about eight or nine months, although the child will have no real mastery of chewing for several more months. For that reason, avoid anything more challenging, especially any foods with choke-potential, like hot dogs and grapes.

Are commercial baby foods inferior to homemade? What about table foods versus foods made specially for baby? Again, there are no hard-and-fast rules. One rule of thumb, though: Integrating the baby into the life of the family is an overall goal, so the sooner he eats with you, the better. After all, he smells dinner simmering, too. Over time, you can introduce him to meat, fish, or poultry in moderate amounts, though pureed or minced vegetables from the table are a good place to start.

Fresh foods are preferable, too, at any age. As the variety of foods your child will eat expands to include more foods and flavors, beware of too much reliance on packaged foods. Read the labels: Iron-fortified cereals are advisable, but you want to avoid sugars, salt, artificial coloring, and, where possible, preservatives.

As the baby's coordination develops, let the child use his fingers to eat with. Bread, small pieces of bagel, or banana slices are manageable and satisfy the child's desire for chewing on (that is, gumming) something.

Tool skills and manners can come later. Let him try to feed himself; most children manage with their fingers, if allowed, by their first birthday (spoon skills come later, too, some time in the second year). Ignore the mess until the meal is finished. Keep the activities to eating (*No toys to the table* is a good early lesson). Draw the line between playtime and mealtime.

Yet, at almost any cost, avoid confrontations over food. Making food a battleground may have a variety of consequences later. Give him time to eat. Substitute one food for another if he's not interested at first. Let him play with morsels of bread for a time while you otherwise occupy yourself nearby. Then try again.

Remember, too, that while a child is still nursing or drinking quantities of formula from a bottle, nutrition is not the sole purpose of eating solid food. In fact, it's probably less important that the child eat what a parent regards as a balanced diet at every meal than that the child have the opportunity to use his hands and spoon; to imitate and experiment; and even to try out refusal. For the infant, eating solid food is about learning, about taking on new elements of his world and sharing things with those he cares for.

Sleeping

Sleeping is easy: There are few sights more beautiful in a parent's eyes than one's baby peacefully asleep. On the other hand, the transitions from waking to sleep and back again can be difficult for both parent and child.

Adapting to the changes in the patterns of waking and sleeping during the baby's first year doesn't have to be a source of frustration for all concerned. There is a developmental logic to the changes. Parents who understand how their baby's sleep-wake patterns are evolving can help. This requires that the parents know how to assist the baby and, equally important, when to leave well enough alone.

■ STAGES OF SLEEP

For babies as well as adults, sleep is not a constant state. Patterns of quiet sleeping alternate with more active sleep. *Deep sleep* is just what its name suggests, a time of unconsciousness during which brain activity is slow—it is calm, peaceful, restful sleep, with heavy, regular breathing.

The stage of active or dreaming sleep, also known as *rapid eye movement* or *REM sleep*, is recognizable because the eyes move quickly behind the closed lids. The limbs, too, tend to make occasional, jerky movements, and breathing is shallower. One theory has it that the greater activity in the brain during REM sleep results from the brain trying to organize or process the events of the day.

REM and deep sleep alternate during the night. Periods of deep sleep give way about every fifty to sixty minutes to shorter periods of dream sleep. The baby is likely to move more during REM sleep and, as the child moves from REM back to deep sleep, he may stir and awaken momentarily. For some reason, that passing wakefulness is more pronounced every other cycle, or about every three or four hours. It's at those moments that the child may cry out and wriggle about in the crib.

If the child is allowed to comfort himself, he will usually go back to sleep without parental intervention. That is an ability you want to encourage your child to develop.

■ PUTTING HIMSELF TO SLEEP

Newborns, when sated by a feeding, often drift off as if by fairy dust. By about three months, however, an infant should begin learning to put himself to sleep once he has been settled into his own bed.

Try it: When the baby is open-eyed, relaxed, and due for a nap, put him in his crib (preferably in his crib, not your bed, the couch, or some other spot). He may not fall instantly to sleep but he will quickly learn to do so. Soothing songs, gentle rocking motions, the calm of a parent's presence can be helpful.

If you continue to rely on feeding to induce sleep, your child may find it more difficult later to learn the art of doing it himself. At about six months, babies begin to be much more attuned to their parents' leaving and a sense of separation develops, making bedtime more and more of a challenge (see *Separation Anxiety,* page 18). Having developed some mastery earlier makes going to sleep easier later on.

■ THE BEDTIME RITUAL

Whenever you introduce your child to the process of putting himself to sleep, establish a bedtime ritual. While routines are also important in such other aspects of baby care as eating, sleep routines are especially important because of the body's biological clock that helps regulate sleep. Get the baby ready to sleep, put him into bed, tuck him in, pat him, sing a song, say good night. Do it all more or less the same way each night. The goal is to establish a pattern, complete with expectation on the child's part. It should all seem natural, usual, and the child will become comfortable with it. Such a routine will also reinforce the biological drive for regular sleep patterns.

In the early months, a little gentle playtime with the baby in the crib, perhaps with the rail down and parent alongside, may enhance the sense of the crib as a happy place. A few minutes of play, even a little reading (it's never too soon to begin developing listening skills) may help the process along. The time should be loving, warm, and yet finite with a gentle, firm termination. Many families find it's better to let Dad do it—the mother-child bond can make it harder for both Mom and baby, especially as separation becomes an issue. A security object—blanket, animal, or pacifier—may help, too.

■ AWAKENINGS

That cry you hear in the night may not mean he's awake. He may be thrashing about in the bed, occasionally crying out. But as we discussed earlier, that doesn't mean he's truly awake.

Before going to him, ask yourself *What is the nature of the cry?* If it's pain or real fear, go to the child. If it's *I'm fed up with this crib stuff, come and get me,* then let him cry a little. Often it is nothing but a stirring, a wave that bumps the boat. The child stirs, calls out involuntarily, then drifts back off. The parent who rushes in and makes a fuss creates a problem where there wasn't one; the parent who waits for the waters to settle may be rewarded.

If you do go to him, don't pick him up. Visit, talk, pat, and assure him, even give him a back rub. But try to avoid picking him up. If he won't stop crying should you let him cry? Yes, for a time, perhaps ten minutes—if you can, that is, but don't feel bad if you can't. If his crying persists, return to his side, and go through the ritual of reassurance again.

At these times a pacifier or a thumb may also provide reassurance, or the child may take comfort in a favorite toy or stuffed animal to snuggle with. For future episodes, you may be able to help him find and adjust to such a transitional object (see *The Pacifier and the Thumb,* page 31).

Giving water or bottles to your child in the night may actually make things worse for the baby. The additional fluid makes for wetter diapers, which, in turn, wake the child rather than help him to sleep through the night.

■ THE NEWBORN

The newborn should be positioned on his side or, failing that, his back. Recent research suggests the chances of suffocation in a crib are greatest when a young baby sleeps on his stomach. Wrapping him in a receiving blanket will both assure he doesn't move very much and gives him the cuddled-up sensation he likes.

In order to help your newborn sleep through the night, you should gradually stretch out the periods between eating. Aim for four hours. Encourage the baby to learn to go to sleep by himself (see above). Then adjust the timing of the baby's feedings. If you can wake the child shortly before you go to bed in order to give him a last feeding, you can maximize the number of hours of sleep that follow.

■ AT FOUR MONTHS

Four months of age is a transition time, and your child needs your help more than ever at bedtime or nap time. Establishing the ritual (see above) is essential; yet at times you must also be able to restrain your natural impulse to comfort the child when he awakens.

Again, the child has to master the art of going back to sleep. You can help him master this important skill. That isn't to say the child should be allowed to cry at great length, or that he should be left unconsoled if something is causing him pain. But always pause after you hear a cry in the night. Count to ten slowly—or to thirty if you realize your counting is hurried. Then wait and. . . listen. Any more cries? If not, go back to sleep. Again, you will learn to distinguish the in-the-night startle cry from the other come-and-help me sounds you already recognize.

One technique that can help the parent who has difficulty allowing a baby to learn to put himself back to sleep is, if you haven't done so already, move the baby out of your room; or leave the baby's door open no more than a crack. If you don't hear the baby stirring, the noise won't bother you. And if the baby *really* needs you, he'll let you know.

■ **AT SIX MONTHS**

On average, a six-month-old will sleep about fifteen hours, perhaps nine or ten at night and another six or so divided into two different nap times. Gradually over the next few months, the sleep may diminish slightly (at nine months, the ratio may be ten hours at night to two hours at each of two naps).

The more significant change is likely to be in the pattern of sleep—which is to say, once more, the pattern of awakenings in the night. Your baby may be experiencing *separation anxiety*. Some daytime strategies to encourage independence (see *Separation Anxiety*, page 18) will help the child separate at night, too, but the usual bedtime and nighttime techniques should continue to help the child fall asleep or to return to sleep.

■ **NAPPING**

The ritual for naps should be much the same as that for going to bed at night. Again, the baby should learn how to fall asleep himself, without relying upon a session of nursing or your presence at the crib the entire time. Patterns are important: Try to put your child down for a nap at roughly the same time each day, at the same point in the sequence of the day's events. Adhering to a general pattern helps the child—and the household—maintain some kind of synchrony.

A missed nap isn't a big deal. Putting him to bed early that night is unlikely to compensate for the lost rest, but it will probably mean he'll awaken early the next day. On a day in which the child's normal schedule is interrupted, the best strategy is try to get back to the usual regime the next day.

■ **RECURRING WAKEFULNESS**

You solved the problem of waking in the night at two months when, for the first time, he slept through. At four months, he began waking every four hours, but that passed as, with some effort, you intervened infrequently. But the pattern recurs again, at six months, or eight months, or ten months, or all of them.

Atypical nighttime arousals like these are likely a product of the child's development. The day is packed with happenings, and the child is developing a much greater understanding of the world and his own growing capacities. The excitement spills over into sleep time. The solution? Go back to basics: the bedtime ritual; the non-interventionist approach to nighttime wake-ups.

Remember that the child's evolving cognitive skills excite him but also enable him to contribute to every aspect of his life, including sleeping. He hasn't forgotten what he knew last week about putting himself to sleep—he's just excited about his discoveries and needs you to help him get back to a familiar spot and incorporate his new knowledge. If you remain a constant, a reassuring presence, if you don't interfere but allow the child to do the job, he'll get it.

■ IN HIS OWN CRIB

Where your child sleeps is another decision you have to make as you help regulate your baby's sleep. Most babies are expected to sleep in their own cribs, but recently there has been increased interest in the "family bed," an approach which has long been the standard in some cultures.

There is more anecdotal than scientific evidence about the merits and disadvantages of each approach. Proponents of babies sleeping by themselves say that this arrangement helps the baby develop self-regulation and that the baby learns to soothe himself without direct contact with his parents during the night. Parents who adopt this practice usually have the baby in a bassinet or crib in the parents' room during the days and weeks immediately after birth, or until the baby is able to sleep through the night when the child is moved from the parent's bedroom to the nursery. Using this method, parents avoid the sometimes difficult adjustment of accustoming the child to his own bed when he gets older. Also some parents report they simply sleep better without a baby in

their beds, and certainly being well rested makes for better parenting. Marital intimacy, which is important to young parents, may also be easier without an infant in the bed. A separate sleeping arrangement is the most common approach for American families.

On the other hand, some parents find a great deal of security and closeness when they have their babies and young children sleeping with them. Some parents report their babies sleep through the night much more easily when they use this approach and concerns about smothering the baby are usually overstated.

A major issue with the family-bed practice is *when* to move the child to his own sleeping area. There are no absolute rules here, but most experts suggest there are negative psychological effects for children beyond preschool regularly sleeping with their parents.

When parents practicing the family-bed approach decide the child should move into his own bed, the preschooler who has grown comfortable sleeping with his parents may resist the changes. However, there has not been enough study in this area to draw any useful conclusions about how easy or difficult the transition might be.

As far as marital intimacy is concerned, many parents report that the family bed approach proves no impediment; perhaps the forethought and creativity used by the these couples to ensure a rich sex life away from their children will make for stronger marriages. However, the family bed approach should not be used as a means of avoiding intimacy. Occasionally, after a divorce or separation from a spouse, a parent might reinstitute sharing his bed with the children. Though providing comfort for both adult and child, this practice may not be a good solution in managing the stress of this difficult life transition.

There is no right or wrong answer here. Individual families can consider their options and determine what works for them and their children. The important thing is to make the decision based on the well-being of the child and not as a sociocultural statement or a way to reduce parental anxiety.

Crying

There's crying and then there's crying. There's the little, almost endearing cries of the newborn; about two weeks after birth, your baby will begin to emit ear-piercing shrieks. There's the rhythmic *I'm hungry* cry; the *I'm fussy* cry is quite different, lower in pitch and less insistent. The *I need attention now* cry may follow—typically, long, loud cries, each followed by a breathless pause.

A cry is, in essence, a message from your baby that says *I'm in distress*. Researchers have found that this mode of communication is biologically effective: adults, those with children and without, experience increases in blood pressure and heart rate upon hearing babies crying. Nursing mothers may find their milk begins to flow in response to their baby's cries.

The baby himself isn't able to understand the nature of his distress—that's your job. Your intervention is required. Most parents will be able to distinguish one cry from another within a few weeks, although all crying, no matter what the original provocation, gradually assumes the rhythm of the hunger cry.

Colic could be the cause (see *Colic,* page 30). The nursing mother's diet may be a factor, too—spicy foods consumed by the mother can cross into breast milk and make a baby very fussy. So can caffeine and alcohol, producing stomach upset and irritability. In a bottle-fed baby, the cause may be an allergy to an ingredient in the formula, but typically that's accompanied by other symptoms such as diarrhea.

Perhaps the baby is hungry. In a young infant, there's only one way to find out. If the breast or bottle fails to calm the baby, try the pacifier. Is his diaper soiled? Maybe the child wants company (hold him); or motion (rock, walk about with him in your arms; see also discussion of baby swings in *Play and Toys,* page 32); or attention (entertain the baby with a toy or a song or simply your smiling face). Settle him into your shoulder; researchers have found that this is the most effective hold for comforting a crying baby. Swaddling—tightly wrapping the baby so his arms and legs are held immobile in a receiving blanket—sometimes helps. And maybe he's just got a case of evening fussiness.

■ EVENING FUSSING

In the second or third month of life, this new pattern may emerge. The baby will resist what you have come to regard as a usual afternoon feeding and, instead, experience a period of fussiness. Often this occurs just before the adult dinner hour. The child may feed briefly, he may quiet while being held, but upon being put down, his crying resumes. When the period passes, however, the child will sleep better and longer than before.

The best explanation for this behavior is that the child is adapting. The baby is absorbing more and more of what is happening around him and is overwhelmed by the sheer mass of sights and sounds, interactions, and his own reactions. The baby's usual calm gives way to a little explosion of crying that functions as a release. The evening fusses generally pass by about four months of age.

How should you respond? Perhaps a feeding will resolve the problem. Make sure his diaper is dry. Hold and comfort him, and try entertaining the baby. If none of these strategies works, then let the baby cry for ten minutes, and comfort him again. Repeat the pattern till the fussing ceases. (See also *Colic,* this page.)

■ CRYING PLUS OTHER SYMPTOMS

If the baby's cry is accompanied by other symptoms—breathing difficulty, a blue cast to the skin, rapid breathing (more than sixty breaths a minute), refusal to eat at usual feeding times—then take his temperature. If it's high (using a rectal thermometer, that's more than 100 degrees Fahrenheit in a baby less then two months, 101 or more in a baby up to four months) consult your child's physician.

Some parents find their baby's persistent crying evokes in them seemingly uncontrollable feelings of frustration, helplessness, anger, or annoyance. Such powerful negative emotions can result in parents losing control,

sometimes to the point of physically abusing their babies.

If you feel anger and frustration well up, try to separate yourself from the situation. These feelings don't mean you're a bad parent; on the other hand, you must, first, recognize these feelings and, second, avoid acting on them. If you need help in managing the feelings, call your spouse or a friend or relative and arrange for a respite from caring for the baby. Put the baby safely in his crib and let him cry for a few minutes while you gather yourself in another room. If the feelings persist, however, seek help. Talk to your baby's physician, a child abuse hotline, a neighbor—find someone to talk to and to help care for the baby.

Colic

A baby with colic is an uncomfortable baby. And he has the capacity to make everyone else in the household unhappy, too.

Infantile colic probably starts with an abdominal pain caused by a spasm, usually in the intestines. The three- or four-week-old baby responds the only way he knows how, by crying, alerting his caregivers to his discomfort. Typically, bouts of crying occur in the evening, usually after a feeding, and can last several hours.

During an acute attack of colic, the child may be inconsolable until the pain passes. He may draw his knees to his chest. When you pick him up he may quiet momentarily, but will soon resume crying. Feeding may calm the child but, again, only briefly.

If your child suddenly exhibits symptoms of colic, consult with your baby's physician. The doctor may wish to examine the child to rule out other possible causes of the upset, but more likely he or she will reassure you that it's only colic and it will pass.

Only colic! you may exclaim. A colicky child can bring out every insecurity in a parent. *I don't burp him well enough. . . My milk isn't digestible! . . . Oh, I must not have paid my baby enough attention. . . I'm a failure as a parent.* Set that anxiety aside. What causes colic is unclear, but almost certainly your baby's colic *isn't* your fault.

There are lots of possible explanations, among them allergies, immature intestinal tract or central nervous system, and, perhaps, nervous caregivers. There's also a widely held theory that some children are going to be colicky—it's not a question of cause and effect, they are just prone to develop colic.

There are strategies you can try to calm the colicky baby. Some infants respond to rocking, to movement, to music. A change in formula for the bottle-fed baby may help; the nursing mother might consider a change in her diet. Carrying the baby around a lot, perhaps three hours a day, is said by some writers in the field to help, too.

Perhaps the most reassuring news of all is that by about three or four months of age the colic will usually disappear, as suddenly as it first appeared. There is no link to later digestive, behavioral, or other problems. Colic is simply an irritation of early childhood, which, like childbirth itself, will soften into memory over time.

The Pacifier and the Thumb

Should you discourage your child from sucking his thumb or using a pacifier? As with so many issues in parenting, the experts don't agree upon a single answer.

What they do agree about is that sucking is a natural instinct (remember, the baby will suckle at the breast moments after birth). Sucking is a way the child can soothe himself, drawing upon his own resources.

It is also clear that some children need to suck more than others (ultrasound images have recorded fetuses with their thumbs in their mouths). For children who require such oral gratification, a pacifier or a thumb in the mouth may be soothing. Sucking on a pacifier or thumb stimulates the baby's mouth; the rhythmic sucking will also relax his gut and even the large muscles in his arms and legs.

There is also general agreement that the baby who sucks on a pacifier is less likely to suck on his thumb. Since the pacifier usually drops out of favor by the time a child is three—*and* children who suck their thumbs often do so until age five or six or beyond—the pacifier would seem a preferable choice. Another advantage of the pacifier, to state the obvious, is that it can be made to disappear at any time.

Just as children become attached to pacifiers, however, so do parents come to rely upon the convenience of having one at hand. If you discover that your baby will suddenly stop crying when the pacifier is introduced, the pattern can easily be established—the baby cries in a restaurant, the pacifier is offered; the baby wakes in the night, the pacifier is plugged back in. The pacifier serves a practical purpose, but neither parents nor child should allow it to be perceived as necessary. Regard it as an occasional—and temporary—convenience.

Is there a risk of dental damage? In the early months, a child's reliance on his thumb or pacifier poses no danger to the formation of normal bite. Later, there may be some risk that the thumb, pacifier, or other object will distort the shape of the palate and the arrangement of the teeth as they emerge. There is no consensus, however, as to when or even if dental damage is done. Some experts say that the pacifier and thumb pose no more than a minimal risk; others report malocclusions in children who suck their thumbs after the adult teeth begin to emerge; still others cite cases of much younger children with abnormal dental development.

Is a child at risk of swallowing the device, thus choking on it or aspirating it into his lungs? The risk is negligible, most doctors believe, as long as pacifiers are discarded before they become badly worn or cracked.

If you do opt for a pacifier, a good rule of thumb is to make it disappear between four and six months of age. The child will be mouthing everything within reach at this time, so he can easily substitute rattles and other toys for the pacifier. Gradually the need to suck will diminish.

Play and Toys

Play is learning, an ongoing series of experiments with sounds and textures. It's about the child's own abilities; it concerns the world and its limits and challenges. To a baby, play is never pointless. French psychologist Jean Piaget took this line of thinking a step further: He believed that the essence of knowledge itself is activity.

A baby's environment needs to be safe (see *The Baby's Environment,* page 35), but it also needs to be a fertile source of fun for the child. The child needs to be surrounded by objects that pique his curiosity, that challenge him to explore and learn. That isn't to say that for your child to develop normally he requires a vast array of expensive toys. Your job as a parent is to offer your baby a range of appropriate stimulation. In doing so, you help to entertain, to educate, and to expand your baby's world.

■ BIRTH TO TWO MONTHS

At this age, the best toy of all is a human companion, one that talks, sings, and holds the baby. The primary learning for a newborn baby is about trust. Only a caring, attentive parent or caregiver can teach this lesson.

At about two months, one toy that may have some impact is a black-and-white mobile suspended over the crib. Some babies will watch one with great concentration for many minutes. Patterned sheets, posters, and a shaded lamp that casts shadows will also offer the baby visual stimulation.

The best toys at this stage aren't store-bought but are issued as standard equipment: The baby's hands open at about two months of age from their earlier reflexive clench. In a random choreography even babies don't understand, the hands dance before their eyes, turning and twisting. It's a kind of practice, an early stage in mastering *sensorimotor* skills, as the baby learns how what his senses tell him can be coordinated with his evolving motor skills. In the same way, he may begin to enjoy handheld toys that make noise, rattles being the classic example.

Swings—battery-powered or windup— with molded plastic, cushioned seats and with appropriate seat belts can function as baby minders, providing the child with motion and visual stimulation (and giving the parent or caregiver a break). A baby seat that travels from room to room provides a safe place for the baby that offers a vantage for viewing the goings-on. When purchasing either a swing or stationary seat, be sure to find one that lets your child lie back with his head and spine fully supported.

■ THREE TO FIVE MONTHS

The baby will learn to grab things over this time. Try an inexpensive plastic key chain. It can be washed in the dishwasher, whereas grown-up keys have dirt and grit on them and, when lost, stress the life of the entire household. Try putting the keys *just* out of reach—not to frustrate the child, but to interest him, to get him to reach for them. He will.

■ SIX TO EIGHT MONTHS

Once the baby can sit up by himself, a walker may provide the child with mobility— as well as a method for getting access to other things to put in his mouth, his number one favorite activity at this age.

There is disagreement about whether walkers have any effect on development. There are some researchers who believe that large motor development is delayed in infants who use walkers, perhaps because children in walkers cannot see their feet. On the other hand, new walkers have been designed and are being marketed that, according to the manufacturers, will not interfere with motor development.

Consider two rules: One, if there is any chance the child in the walker will find his way to the top of a stairway, don't introduce him to one; and, two, if your baby does use a walker, make it disappear as soon as the child is capable of initiating locomotion on his own, whether it's by crawling, rolling, or crabbing. By the time the child is about nine months, the walker should be merely a memory.

A six- or seven-month-old child is enchanted by new things. Pleasure is only as far away as a kitchen drawer or cabinet, filled as it is with potential playthings. Although you should judiciously select safe "toys"— not too heavy, no sharp edges, no small parts to swallow—don't hesitate to share them.

At seven or eight months, children begin to understand the concept of *object permanence*. At an earlier age, out of sight was also out of mind, but by this age, the baby is learning that a toy that disappears in a parent's hand may reappear. He'll cover a doll with a pillow, pause, and smile upon uncovering it a moment later. The importance of this advance is immense: It means that the child is now able to retain in his mind a mental image of the object that has disappeared—that is, he understands it is *permanent*. More important, this understanding means that the child's world is no longer ruled solely by what he sees; the recognition of an object's permanence means the child now can maintain mental images. This is evidence that there is a new, independent world taking shape *within his mind* that has an existence independent of the sensory stimuli around him.

The game of peekaboo offers a variation on the theme of object permanence. Called *person permanence*, this emerging concept also means the baby will anticipate a parent's return after an absence. For similar reasons, board books are great fun at this age—it's a continuing wonder that images disappear and reappear as the pages are turned.

What about playpens? They're not taboo. An occasional hour spent in one is fine and reassuring to a parent whose child—just learning to move about—seems about to be into *everything*. However, it is, at best, a short-term solution, as it will be obsolete by the time he walks.

■ NINE MONTHS TO A YEAR

The world is just one big source of playthings for the newly mobile baby. It's your job to make sure the child ends up toying with the right stuff. Among them might be pots and pans, one-piece clothespins, spoons, plastic dishes—household goods that aren't breakable and have no parts that could be separated and swallowed. Good choices at the toy store include toy telephones, large balls, and simple activity toys with switches, handles, knobs, and doors. Wheeled objects that can be pushed around by a baby who is not yet walking independently may give the child the confidence to give it a go on his own.

As usual, firmly and gently enforced limits need to be set. There's little risk of spoiling the child at this age—even though generous friends and relatives may shower the baby with enough toys to equip a day-care center. Reasonable limits may provide a child with the sense that at least a few behaviors are forbidden. This may set the stage for an effective discipline strategy for the years to come.

Too many limits, too many no-nos, will confuse a soon-to-be toddler. But as the first birthday approaches, the child can begin to understand that his world does have some boundaries.

As an understanding of limits evolves, you'll notice your child look back at you as he moves toward a forbidden object or area. He understands where he's going is off-limits, and he's looking for you to confirm it. That's your cue: He wants, and needs, a response from you—perhaps a facial expression, a gesture, or a move toward him.

Play is about more than physical objects like toys, and play concerns more than limits. Another key consideration is playmates. Before reaching their first birthdays, children don't truly play with their peers. That means parents and caregivers assume the roles of playmates, too. Your child may derive endless pleasure from games like peekaboo and "so big." Nursery rhymes, simple songs, and other interactions rich in recognizable sounds and gestures can provide great pleasure—not only for your child but for you, too.

The Baby's Environment

Your baby's world needs to be safe. Unlike the young of some animals, human offspring require adult care for survival, and an essential part of that attention involves protecting children from potential dangers in their environment.

At the same time, your baby's world needs to be full of appropriate challenges. For your baby to learn and develop, he needs the opportunity to interact with his environment; a setting that has been stripped of all stimuli is intellectually barren, too. In short, the richer his world, the greater are the chances for the child to learn. That's where a key element of his environment, appropriate toys, come into play (see *Play and Toys,* page 32, for a discussion of those concerns). But safety is always a key criterion.

■ SAFETY AT HOME

Consider the story of the collector of antique glassware who had floor-to-ceiling shelves to display his collection. When his first child was born, a daughter, he took a gradual approach to baby-proofing.

While the baby was an immobile newborn, the collector didn't move a thing. When she began to crawl, the father emptied the first few shelves. The day before the baby pulled herself to a standing position for the first time, more shelves were emptied of their original contents. He was ahead of her, he said to himself, full of false confidence.

Then one morning the eleven-month-old maneuvered a chair over to the shelves and began emptying the fragile contents within

reach onto the floor with shattering consequences.

The lesson? Baby-proofing clearly isn't a one-time event. It's an evolutionary process that requires as much anticipation as possible—and then constant vigilance. By the time your baby is crawling, you need to have mastered the art.

A comprehensive list of household risks for your baby would cascade beyond the boundaries of this chapter, so consider what follows less as a checklist than a representative miscellany of items to stimulate your thinking.

For a baby not yet capable of locomotion, you need to concern yourself with little more than that his world be warm, clean, and void of objects that could suffocate or strangle a helpless baby. As he develops the ability to reach for and grab objects, his immediate environment should be clear of anything small enough to swallow, heavy enough to hurt, or sharp enough to cut him.

Too many parents have discovered that their child has learned how to roll over when he cries out—after having rolled off the bed. Don't join that club.

As the child begins to be able to move himself around his world, whether he's rolling, crabbing, or crawling, electrical cords should disappear. Chewing on them can cause severe mouth burns; tugging on them can result in injury from lights, irons, or other appliances falling and tumbling babyward. Safety covers on outlets are a necessary precaution.

Necklaces, curtain cords, netting on playpens (especially when it's torn), strings, and light chains all present a strangling risk. Water in virtually any quantity—even a bucketful—is also a danger. Pools must be covered or fenced; bathing is a time for special vigilance.

As your child approaches the crawling stage, you should try it yourself. Get down on all fours and see what you—and eventually your child—can see. Anticipate what can he reach and what will capture his eye. Move risky items out of sight.

By the time a child is pulling himself to a standing position, a coffee table can be the functional equivalent of a jungle gym, a source of fun and physical challenges. Yet an unsuitable coffee table—one made of glass, with sharp edges or a tendency to tip over— is an accident waiting to happen.

Is there old paint that might contain lead in the home? Lead poisoning is a serious health hazard that can result in, among other problems, mental retardation (see *Pica and Lead Poisoning,* page 287). Be sure cleaning and other chemicals as well as medicines are all securely sealed *and* out of reach. Just in case, keep a bottle of the an emetic (ipecac) in the medicine chest. Keep the phone number for the poison control center at hand, too, as induced vomiting is not the appropriate response to all poisoning events.

Before the baby becomes mobile, secure all staircases. Gates or self-closing doors are essential, whether the stairs descend (an early risk for babies with a minimum of mobility) or ascend (accessible to crawlers discovering the pleasures of climbing).

When your child is an adept crawler, let him try out a couple of stairs. Some children seem to have an instinctive mastery of the crawl/climbing motion. This may be a good age to teach the child to climb stairs. Do so, if you wish; but keep in mind that you must insist the child *always* come down backwards (*"Turn around, first, that's right, Davey, turn around"*) and you must *always* go with the child, even after apparent mastery. Protect your child from unsupervised stairway adventures by installing gates at top and bottom.

And don't forget one of the cardinal rules of parenting small children: Adult supervision is essential. No room is truly baby-proof unless a parent is nearby to monitor a child's activities.

■ AWAY FROM HOME

For car travel, the car seat is essential. Both the law and good sense dictate its use. Car seats should always be buckled into the rear seat and, with infant seats, the seat is designed to face the rear of the car for the first year of life or until the child weighs approximately twenty pounds.

When traveling to other homes, to restaurants, or other places that have not been baby-proofed, extra caution is always in order. In an unfamiliar environment, your mobile child should never be out of your sight unless he is sleeping in an appropriate crib, one with slats that are no more than 2⅜ inches apart.

Choosing the Baby's Doctor

Your baby's physician has an important role to play, especially in the first years of life (see

Well-Baby Care, page 38). Selecting a doctor with the right blend of professional qualifications and personal characteristics is important, but to get the best care possible you also need to be able to trust and to confide in the doctor. There are a number of considerations to keep in mind as you identify a pediatrician, family physician, or other practitioner to be your baby's primary care provider.

■ THE INTANGIBLES

Let's start with instinctive judgments— with parenting, they are often important.

As is always the case in dealing with young children, there's a gut-level judgment to be made in selecting a physician. Are you comfortable with the doctor? If you feel condescended to or if you get the I'm-too-busy-to-answer-your-question brush-off, take it up with the doctor. If it's his or her way and you don't like it, find another doctor. Be prepared to cut him a little slack, too. He may have been up the night before answering the phone and trekking to the ER.

You need to trust your baby's physician, but it's important, too, that you feel he trusts you and your instincts. With many practitioners, one look is enough to see why he or she chose pediatrics: the love of babies, the thrill is there anew each time. But the judgment needs to be made on the basis of a range of qualities: accessibility, his (and your) confidence, as well as the physician's qualifications and availability.

■ THE QUALIFICATIONS

Board-eligible pediatricians have graduated from medical school and have a mini-mum of three years of pediatric training; family physicians are also medical school graduates with three years of specialty training. Increasingly, nurse practitioners and physician's assistants are associated with medical group practices. While their training is less extensive, they work closely with fully trained doctors. Satisfy yourself that the practitioner has the training, experience, and commitment to care for your baby.

■ AVAILABILITY

Find out what hours the office is open, too. In the case of two-career families, Saturday or evening office hours may be important, especially for well-baby visits. What arrangements has the physician made for after-hour emergencies? Does the doctor have admitting privileges at nearby hospitals?

■ OTHER CONSIDERATIONS

Inquire of friends whether they have established good working relationships with their children's physicians. Another parent who has made the midnight call to a doctor's answering service knows whether a return call came through promptly. In thinking about a doctor for your baby, remember too that the better time to make your choice is *before* the birth of your baby. You may need or wish to consult with your baby's doctor within days of the baby's birth, and the doctor may visit and examine your newborn within the first twenty-four hours.

Having a physician you trust is an important confidence-builder for any parent.

WELL-BABY CARE

The practice of Western medicine has, all too often, been oriented to illness. For the most part, the emphasis hasn't been on health or even the prevention of illness—the focus was diseases and their treatments.

Well-baby care reverses the orientation. The goal is to monitor the development of the child—physical, emotional, and behavioral—in a way that anticipates normal growth and development and recognizes problems, diseases, or delays as early as possible.

Secondary to the monitoring of your child, the doctor will also be concerned with helping you master some of the basics of parenting. The goal is to forge a partnership with the parent. Ideally, well-baby visits will be occasions for the doctor and parent(s) to discuss concerns the parent has and for the professional provider to offer counsel. Babies don't come with instruction manuals; the ongoing dialogue between parent and doctor helps fill that knowledge gap.

THE PHYSICAL EXAMINATION

If your child leaves the hospital within twenty-four hours of birth, the first well-baby visit will probably be within a few days. More often, the first visit will be at two weeks of age. Thereafter, scheduled visits will typically be at ages one month, two months, four months, six months, nine months, and one year. The doctor may want to see your baby more or less frequently; if the schedule differs significantly from this routine, inquire why it does.

A sequence of inoculations are usually given at well-baby visits. These include: the DPT shots, usually at the two-, four-, and six-month checkups, which are given to prevent the child from contracting diphtheria, pertussis (whooping cough), and tetanus; and a polio vaccine, either in an oral form ("sugar drops") or as an inoculation, usually at two months and four months. Other vaccines that may be recommended are: a hepatitis B vaccine (HBV), usually at birth and the one- or six-months checkup; a flu vaccine (HiB or Hemophilus influenza type B vaccine); and one for bacterial meningitis. Chicken pox vaccines are now available as well.

At each well-baby visit, the doctor will weigh the baby and measure his length and the circumference of the head. These measurements provide a basis for comparison with statistical averages of other children the same age, as well as enabling the doctor to chart the baby's growth from one visit to the next. Your baby will lose weight in the first few days after birth, but within a week will resume his astonishing pattern of growth, tripling his birth weight in his first twelve months.

At each visit, the physician will seek to identify areas for concern. The doctor will perform a physical examination, checking for hip or other skeletal abnormalities and for abdominal masses or enlarged organs. The physician will examine the baby's eyes, ears, and mouth. At intervals blood tests will done, including one at about nine months or a year to check for lead.

CONTINUITY OF CARE

Continuity is fundamental to well-baby care. Following your baby's progress provides the physician with an overall perspective on your child; getting to know you, the parent, is part of the process, too. Observation of the baby and becoming acquainted with the child's family situation provides a valuable context for evaluating changes and illness in your child.

At well-baby appointments, the physician will inquire about the child's overall development: Is he smiling? Can he roll over? What about other movements, motor skills, and vocalizations? The doctor will want to know about the baby's sleeping schedule, eating habits, the nursing mother's diet, and the baby's crying. Does he have colic? What about siblings? How large a part does the baby's father play?

Well-baby appointments should be more than a checkup performed by the doctor; they also become an ongoing dialogue between parent and physician. Do you have any concerns about your child's health or development? As a parent, you are not merely a bystander in attendance to answer the doctor's questions. Your job at home is to take care of the baby, to feed, clothe, teach, eventually to help your child develop discipline and become a responsible, productive citizen of the world. At this early age, your child also needs you to act as his interpreter to his physician.

That means you must take an active role in every aspect of his young life, including asking the doctor questions about what worries you. Tell your baby's physician if you're worried the newborn isn't eating enough. Or that your six-month-old seems never to sleep. Regard your well-baby visits as opportunities to share your worries, suspicions, and questions. Your state of mind—especially if you are anxious or upset—has an effect on your baby. A well-baby visit is the time to talk over your concerns with the physician. He or she may be able to ease your worries.

OTHER CAREGIVERS: BABY-SITTERS AND DAY CARE

Not so many years ago, the societal norm was a working dad and a housewife mom home with the children. In today's world, with two-career families and single parents having become commonplace, many more children—some of them very young indeed—are regularly entrusted to other caregivers.

How soon is too soon? There is no one answer to this question. In the real world, however, economic and other circumstances often don't allow for a parent to remain at home indefinitely. Paid maternity leave in the United States rarely exceeds three months and, frequently, the allowed time is as short as four or six weeks.

If your baby will be going to day care within a few months of birth, you may find making the decision about where the baby goes easier *before* the baby is born.

The younger the baby, the more care is required. Thus, each newborn should ideally have an adult to care for it. In practice, that's often not possible; on the other hand, your baby probably won't get the attention he needs in a situation where the ratio of infant-to-caregivers is four or more to one.

What about the mix? A child of two or three is developing immunities to combat ordinary childhood diseases. In contrast, a baby less than three months old is very vulnerable to such illnesses and at greater risk of more serious complications. If possible, then, select a day-care setting for your infant where there's a narrow range of ages, with children close in age to your baby. This can also help assure that your child will get plenty of cuddling, smiles, and attention.

As the baby gets a bit older, making the move to day care becomes easier. At an age like four months, for example, babies are able to engage adults. This capacity for interaction makes bonding to day-care providers easier.

MAKING THE TRANSITION

Do it gradually. Visit the day care with the child; spend an hour there with him, then go home. Go a second time for two hours.

Make sure the day-care provider edges her way into the picture. After six months of age in particular, this is especially important: New people must be incorporated into the baby's consciousness carefully. The caregiver shouldn't confront the baby—initially, the baby should be given the opportunity to examine the person. Only after the baby has looked his fill should the caregiver approach, look the baby in the eye, smile, and initiate contact.

EVALUATING THE CAREGIVERS

Taking care of babies isn't for everyone. Some people have an innate ability to nurture, a certain personal warmth that babies recognize as welcoming and comforting. Look for it. If that quality is absent, you may want to keep searching for the right setting for your child.

Check references, too: Talk to the parents of at least two other children who go to the day-care facility you are considering. Ask about their child's experiences there and whether the child (and the parents) find it to be a happy, healthy, and nurturing arrangement. You may want to make an unannounced visit, too.

Make sure you and the caregiver share basic notions about setting limits, about how to (and when not to) discipline. Try to determine whether you will feel comfortable with the caregiver, able to communicate. You need to know each day about nap time, tantrums and misbehavior, and, of course, about your child's amazing and clever accomplishments. Look for common sense, experience, a patient nature, good listening skills, and a willingness to do some things *your* way. If there are several caregivers, try to get a sense of each of them individually.

If your choice of child-care provider is a relative, neighbor, or a professional nanny who will devote all of his or her time to your child in your home, the same guidance applies. Where appropriate, check references.

THE SETTING

Look for cleanliness, proper and well-maintained equipment, soft and warm play areas, and an overall cheerful, comfortable environment. Poorly trained pets, cold floors, and open kitchen cupboards are clear signs of an environment that hasn't been properly baby-proofed.

The transition may seem remarkably easy, since some children are simply thrilled to be able to enjoy the companionship of other youngsters. It may be difficult, especially if your child is experiencing separation anxiety. But at its best, going to day care can be invaluable social experience for your child as he learns to meet and enjoy the larger world beyond your family.

BABY ALLERGIES

If your family has a history of allergies, your baby may be predisposed to develop allergies as well. Allergies are a medical concern, but they can also have behavioral effects. The allergy-behavior connection remains controversial, but some researchers believe that allergies in children can produce fatigue, irritability, depression, hyperactivity, sleeping difficulties, and poor concentration. While an infant is unlikely to develop such a range of symptoms, limiting a baby's exposure to allergens now may serve to give that child some protection against allergies later.

In a young baby, the symptoms of an allergic response may not be obvious. It may be months before an allergy to a food reveals itself. Therefore, even in the absence of an apparent allergic reaction, avoid exposing the baby to any allergens to which the genetic mother or father of the new baby had allergic responses as children.

Breast-feeding a potentially allergic child is preferable to bottle-feeding formula. If the child is bottle-fed, consider using soy formula rather than cow's milk. Introduce solid foods no earlier than five months of age, and give them to the child one at a time. If, after a week, no allergic response offers itself to the first food, try another for a week, then a third a week later. And so on. Skin rashes, vomiting, or diarrhea are typical signs of reaction. If a reaction occurs, eliminate that food from the diet for at least six months before reintroducing it again on a trial basis.

Environmental allergens, too, should be avoided. Woolen blankets, feather pillows, kapok-stuffed animals, mattresses stuffed with horsehair, and other sources of animal hair, dust, grasses, molds, or pollens should also be eliminated from the baby's room. Rugs that can harbor quantities of dust should be removed from the home or at least the child's room. House pets, in particular cats, may also produce allergens.

Don't smoke near your baby. The evidence is overwhelming that tobacco, marijuana, and even wood smoke have an impact on babies; some research suggests a correlation between SIDS (Sudden Infant Death Syndrome or crib death) and smokers in the home. (See also *Allergies*, page 279.)

2

Toddlerhood

THE CHILD AT AGES ONE AND TWO

■ ■ ■

Somewhere around your child's first birthday will come the first steps. At that moment, your baby becomes a toddler.

The word "toddler" conjures up perfectly the way she first stretches her legs to gain balance, then waddles from side to side. Yet the very act of walking both corresponds with and brings about a number of events in your baby's life, each of which has important developmental implications.

A child stands up, depending on nothing other than her own two legs to support her. From this new and exciting vantage, the view is different. Objects and people are seen from below, from above, from one side, then another, from far away, and from close up. Then there is new mobility—the toddler can approach what interests her, back away from what disturbs her, and go after what she wants.

At the same time, other new abilities further exploration. The toddler can grasp, hold, and manipulate objects more adroitly. During the second year of life, new control over several muscle systems enables the youngster not only to walk upright, but to run, jump, and execute movements such as eating with a spoon and picking up small objects with a pincer grasp.

Somewhere around the first half of the second year, your child begins to communicate with actual words. Quickly the new talker develops a larger vocabulary and more sophisticated language skills—you'll hear questions as the child understands, discovers, and interacts ever more with the world.

The toddler's body changes, too. The child sleeps fewer hours each day, and her eyes are open to the many wonders of her world. Her reasoning about objects and people becomes more sophisticated. She starts to imitate sequences of actions and to engage in pretend play. She begins to include a recognition of a distinct self—herself—in her thinking and in her play.

Possibly most significant of all is the fact that with those first steps, a child walks alone. The child looks up and, for a moment, understands that others are no longer required for mobility. In essence the baby has severed another tie to the mother's body. Surely this moment brings a sharp sense of the uniqueness and separateness of self.

This chapter will examine the events that complete the period of infancy and produce increasingly complex behavior. We will look at some of the more practical matters—tips on tantrums and negotiating, child care, and

moving into a big bed—that parents of toddlers will likely face. Our subject here, then, is the remarkable passage from infancy.

Milestones

Some time between the second and third birthday, a child completes the period of development called infancy. Like all other transitions from one developmental stage to the next, the end of infancy is marked by changes in biological processes; by the expression of expanding mental and physical abilities; and by the arrival of new social relationships within her world.

■ PHYSICAL MILESTONES

Although a child's body continues to grow rapidly after the first year, the rate of growth is considerably slower than it was earlier. While there is significant variation from one child to another, the average child raised with an adequate diet in recent decades in the United States will be 38 inches in height and weigh 33 pounds by the age of three.

In the early days of toddling about, a baby may appear a bit odd. The child's proportions still suit someone who moves around on all fours. The youngster's head, stuck atop a nonexistent neck, is large in relation to the body. The shoulders and chest are thin, and the belly protrudes. By the time of the second birthday, though, the child's appearance will have slimmed down and lengthened considerably.

Important changes take place on the inside as well, in the structure of the brain and in the level of muscular control. These developments can be witnessed in the control the child has in using arm, hand, bladder, bowel, and leg muscles.

Children also achieve greater capacity to coordinate the information they receive from their five senses with their actions. In order to walk, for example, a child must be able to coordinate leg movements in shifting body weight from one foot to the other while each foot in turn steps forward.

In addition to an increased sophistication in motor capacities, the task of walking requires that the baby evaluate sensory information. The slope of the floor, for example, must be considered as the toddler maneuvers through space. According to what she sees and the way the floor feels to the bottom of her foot, she adjusts her posture and directs her next step. Walking becomes smoothly integrated only when all of its components—upright posture, leg alternation, weight shifting, balance, evaluation of sensory information—are integrated.

Even after babies take their first steps, many months usually pass before they can walk with ease, climb, kick, and jump in a coordinated way. Most are at least twenty months old before they can, with assistance, walk up and down stairs; twenty months before they can kick a ball forward; and twenty-four months before they can jump.

Coordination of fine hand movements increases significantly between twelve and thirty-six months. At one year, a baby can only roll a ball or fling it awkwardly. By age two and a half, the child has developed a level of manual dexterity that enables her to throw a ball at a target with some accuracy.

At two and a half, many children can hold a cup of milk (with sippy top), or a spoon of cereal without spilling. Many can turn the page of a book without tearing it, cut with safety scissors, string large beads with a needle and thread, and build a tower of nine blocks. Some can even dress themselves as long as there are no buttons or shoelaces to contend with.

These are indeed significant accomplishments. Each requires a good deal of practice and developmental maturity to master. With each accomplishment, a child becomes increasingly competent and able to act independently.

Sleeping habits vary, of course, from child to child. At the beginning of the toddler period, most children need two daily naps. Somewhere around fifteen to eighteen months, two naps are too many and one is not enough. A child may resist a nap after breakfast but can barely last through the morning, becoming whiny and impossible. The pre-lunch nap may last an hour or so, but by dinner time, the same thing happens and, by bedtime, the toddler is again completely spent.

By age two, this awkwardness usually resolves into a single nap either at the end of the morning before a late lunch or at the very beginning of the afternoon after an early lunch. Bedtime, too, usually comes quite early.

■ COGNITIVE MILESTONES

As toddlers are perfecting their ability to get around on their own two legs, to eat with

utensils, and to begin to control their bladders and bowels, they also begin to think in a
whole new way. You can see this evolution in
their growing ability to experiment, to solve
simple problems for themselves, to begin
sorting and categorizing objects, and to communicate with words and simple sentences.

During this period of development, children begin to see that there is a relation
between their actions and the world beyond
their own bodies. They engage in deliberate
experiments in order to observe and understand the nature of objects. Watch a child
between the ages of twelve and eighteen
months as she sits on the floor. She acts and
reacts within her present world, attending
only to that which she can directly observe
or experience. She may grab a toy, stretch
her arm out, and let it fall. After watching
what happens as it hits the floor, she then
modifies her experiment: *What will happen
if the toy hits another area of the floor or a
pillow nearby?*

Somewhere between the ages of eighteen
and twenty-four months, the same child
begins to show evidence of symbolic thinking. She no longer needs to directly observe
what will happen. She can conduct her
experiments mentally. She imagines objects
that are not present and considers possible
consequences for certain actions. Images and
words come to stand for familiar objects.
Memory also develops during this period and
she can begin to anticipate and re-create
within her mind.

What this means for the child is that she can
begin to use invention, speculation, and anticipation to solve problems. Try playing this
game with your baby: As the child watches,
hide a ball under a blanket. Then, without the
child observing you, move the ball behind
your back or into your lap. The youngster will
look first under the blanket. Chances are that
the child won't give up after failing to find
something there, as would have happened
only months ago. The toddler will persist in
the search to find the ball. Problem-solving
has become more deliberate.

Around this time, a child begins to engage
in imaginative play. A stick is used as a vacuum cleaner, a toy rake as a doll's comb.
Pretty soon, her stuffed animals are a family
with moms and dads and sisters.

The ability to solve problems, to search
for hidden objects, and to engage in imaginative play all reflect the genesis of symbolic
thinking. The other important indication of
symbolic thinking is the development of language. Language is the symbolic representation through words of people, objects, or
events, present or not.

At eight or nine months, babies begin to
understand certain words and expressions.
Children of this age asked *Where's baby?*
will pat their own chests. They'll point to
their own eyes or ears when prompted.
They'll respond selectively to their own
names and will stop or at least hesitate if
someone says *No.*

Babbling evolves toward the end of a
baby's first year into a string of syllables that
have the tone and stress of actual language
into a word or two in direct imitation of the
other people. The first use of words that is
not direct imitation usually occurs around
the first birthday.

Between the ages of fourteen and eighteen months, toddlers are able to name a few objects if someone points and inquires. They can label pictures of common animals and objects. By twenty-one months, they are able to follow relatively complex verbal instructions. When asked to put their clothes in the dirty clothes hamper, they can, if they are so inclined, do as you ask.

Though children vary in the precise age at which they accumulate language skills, by the age of two, most children will begin to use simple sentences: *Go to store. I want kitty. No go to bed.* They also demonstrate clear comprehension of language directed to them, and can follow relatively complicated instructions. They are able to understand terms that are the opposites of each other. When asked, most can distinguish between a big bear and a small one, for example, or a fat clown and a skinny one.

By this point, the word *No* has crept—or abruptly leapt—into a toddler's vocabulary. Not only is this a word that your child has heard you use and one that is easy to say, but the word itself signals an important shift in your child's sense of self in relation to you. There's a surge of independence between the second and third years; your child will try to separate from you and make independent decisions and judgment calls. *No* has become a message of evolving autonomy. Often *No* will be used merely to exercise veto power. Sometimes you'll hear a loud *No* when the issue seems important only to the child or when the child's behavior suggests she really wants the opposite. This negative behavior announces an important developmental milestone. At the same time, it accounts for the hallmark of the age, *the terrible twos.*

■ EMOTIONAL MILESTONES

As the individual threads of cognitive and physical development come together around the age of two, what begins to emerge is a child with a new and distinctive sense of self as an independent person.

The growing awareness of *self*—and of *other*—enables children to participate more competently in their worlds. The awareness adds to the capacity to tolerate greater independence or *autonomy.* As a new sense of an autonomous self evolves, the child's social relationships, specifically emotional dependency on a primary caregiver (usually mother) begins to shift.

Infants are sensitive to unusual changes in their environment. Even in the first days of life, babies become used to events that occur regularly and pay attention to unexpected changes. Around the age of two, children also become sensitive to events that violate the way things are "supposed to be." They become upset if a doll's arm is missing or if there is mud on the hem of a new dress. At this point, the ability to understand on some level that objects and experiences can be proper or improper according to adult standards has emerged.

Children at this age begin to imitate adults in their play—they use a hammer to bang and a spoon to feed themselves. Somewhere around their second birthday, a boy will begin subtly to fashion himself after his father and a girl after her mother. In addition, children begin to copy behavior.

Increasingly, children this age will strive to accomplish tasks according to the way they observe adults performing them.

Around the same time, toddlers begin to assert more confidently their own individuality. During play, they set goals for themselves. The child may set out to build a tall tower using every block in the room, for example, or to fit every miniature animal into the toy barn. When she accomplishes what she sets out to accomplish, she beams a new kind of smile. This *mastery smile* will likely spread across a child's face as she adds the topmost block to the stack or shuts the door to the barn.

It is also around this time that children begin to let adults know what they want them to do. A child on a swing commands, *Push high.* A child who is having trouble finishing a puzzle turns to her mother with an insistent, *You put.* While it may be perfectly logical—and developmentally appropriate—from the toddler's perspective, to announce her wishes so directly, adults may experience such assertions, unembellished with *please* or *thank you,* as sheer bossiness. Now is probably the time to gently introduce these pleasantries into your child's awareness, as you respond to her request, even though she will not be likely to embrace them right away.

Ultimately, a child's ability to assert her wishes and goals in the larger world—her assertiveness and confident behavior—derives from the feedback and positive reinforcement of parents and adults. Use and support for assertive behavior differs from situation to situation, from family to family,

from culture to culture (see *Bossiness and Negotiation,* page 70).

The emerging sense of self is reflected in the child's language. When the child first begins to speak, one-word utterances will be used to name things. She points to an object or picks it up and says its name. Around the time she begins to join words together, she also begins to describe her own actions and feelings. A child picks up a cat and announces proudly *Me hold kitty,* or takes the last sip of milk and says *All gone.*

For a child to refer to herself in language means that she is beginning to understand that she exists, apart from her world and her caregivers. This developmental accomplishment can also be seen in her growing recognition of herself. At around twenty months, a child who is shown a mirror and asked *Who's that?* will answer without hesitation, *Me.* At this age, boys and girls know their own gender.

By the end of the toddler years, most children have evolved a rudimentary notion of self and other: *This is me and how I do things, and that is you and how you do things.* This amazing developmental leap lays the foundation for both human relationships and self-sufficiency.

By three months of age, babies will be distressed when separated from adults. At about seven months, the distress becomes focused on separation from their primary caregivers. In most instances, the child by about fifteen months has begun to develop ways of self-soothing and tolerating separation.

Having become a toddler, a child is leaving babyhood. A parent is no longer experienced as an extension of the child; nor will your toddler depend solely on you or other caregivers to interpret and navigate the world. But the dependence continues to be strong during the toddler years, and parents can help by being sensitive to their child's shifting needs for both closeness and autonomy.

She asserts herself with a loud *No* or *Me do.* But if you attempt to leave the room, even if she is preoccupied with a toy or book, she will suddenly lose her ability to concentrate and protest loudly or cling adamantly. She wants to control your leave-taking. She will leave you, but you must be there when she returns.

This ambivalent behavior can be confusing to parents. At one moment she is as compliant, responsive, accepting as she ever was; at the next, she rejects willfully your control, help, and involvement. Leaving her with a baby-sitter may engender intense clinging, yet your return may be totally ignored.

Nevertheless, she loves you passionately, and depends on you completely for emotional support, especially as she maneuvers through the perils of growing independence. Your love has created a secure foundation that helps her as she strives for greater independence and your love helps cushion her falls.

While she is wary of strange people and places, she is strongly attached to her parents. It is still difficult for her to adapt to being left for a long period of time with other caregivers. At the same time, she shows curiosity about other nearby people and situations, and will be able to tolerate longer periods of separation if she feels safely attended to by other adults.

However phenomenal these developments are, they do not, of course, enable a child to survive alone. But they do underlie a new form of interdependence within the family. They also set the stage for the way in which the child moves forward to participate in the larger world outside the home.

ESTABLISHING EMOTIONAL SECURITY AND BUILDING SELF-ESTEEM

Once a young child has gained a basic sense of emotional security, she is able to move smoothly out into her world, exploring, learning, and amassing the skills she will need as she grows older.

Emotional security is a product of the attachment, established early in the first year, between a child and an adult caretaker(s)—in most cases, the mother. Out of this attachment evolves a sense of belonging and self-esteem that may influence the quality of all other relationships as well as many later experiences.

During the toddler years, babies awaken to their world. They find novelty and excitement everywhere. Cars and trucks whiz by, strange people come and go. They taste new foods, they accompany their parents to new places, they become aware of other children. There is an infinite number of things to touch and observe. The very same things that attract them, though, may also give them pause. Their world becomes both fascinating and a bit daunting.

As toddlers embark on exploring and learning about their world, both curiosity and fear must be kept in bounds. A child at this age is no longer content to remain at her mother's side or completely under her mother's physical control. Yet she cannot merely wander off on her own. A balance between exploration and safety must be created, maintained, and adjusted as the child becomes more self-assured and competent.

When most children reach their first birthdays, they have solid emotional bonds with their mothers or their closest caretakers (see *Bonding and Relationship-Building*, page 16). Around the seventh month, children begin to show distress when separated from their primary caretakers. Such distress signifies that the babies have become attached to the people who tend to them. As they come to understand that their mothers, for example, will consistently and reliably respond, interact, help, and soothe them, they begin to experience a basic sense of trust.

Once a child has gained faith in her caregivers and feels a secure base of support, having developed the memory capacity to know that mother is there even if not present at that moment, she can venture out in search of greater autonomy. During periods of exploration and autonomous learning, mother and child regulate the distance between them.

Normally, when the distance becomes too great, one or the other is likely to become upset and act to reduce the distance. If the mother leaves for too long, the baby becomes upset and her cries bring the mother back. If the baby wanders off too far at the playground, the mother becomes uneasy and soon goes looking for her.

This kind of mutual, self-adjusting, flexible attachment provides the child with an internal feeling of security. The mother becomes a *secure base* from which the baby makes exploratory excursions and to which she returns every so often to renew contact before venturing out again.

Healthy attachment emerges when a child's need for food and warmth, safety and security is reliably met—and attachment grows from the many nuances that characterize parent-child relationships: touching, holding, eye contact, and verbal exchanges. Early on, parents naturally echo the toddler's new words and intonations.

They mirror emotional expressions: When running back with a skinned knee, the child sees a reflection in the parent's face of her own pouting, tearful expression.

These interactions form the bedrock of a child's emotional security, out of which grows a sense of self, of self-esteem, and an ability to establish and maintain social relationships in the world outside of the family.

What kinds of parent-child interactions foster healthy attachment? This question has intrigued researchers for years, and often weighs heavily on parents. Because no two parent-infant pairings are alike and because the environmental conditions into which babies are born vary enormously, there are different patterns of attachment that meet the basic requirements for development. Security of attachment may also change with changes in parental circumstances. There are, however, a few general patterns of mother-child interactions that seem most conducive to healthy development.

In past generations, parents were warned against being too responsive to their infant for fear that they would spoil the child. The wisdom was, *Just let the baby cry.* Indulging the child fosters unrealistic expectations, the thinking went, and a child learns antisocial behavior. Recent research, however, does not support this belief. In fact, it may be that paying too little attention to infants teaches them that nothing they do has an effect on others. Abusive, neglectful, and even inconsistent care most likely leads to insecure attachment. Secure attachment derives from attentive and sensitive care being given. Mothers who respond quickly to their baby's cries and who are sensitive to their needs during feeding are likely to have babies who are securely attached at twelve months—as long as the responsiveness is not too intrusive or overstimulating.

In general, patterns of parenting that are based on respect, empathy, and responsiveness seem most effective in fostering a healthy sense of self and a strong foundation for other relationships. Parenting in general is optimal when parents are able to remain responsive and sensitive to a child's feelings even when they are inconvenient or in conflict with their own; when parents mirror a child' emotions so that the baby sees and hears her feelings reflected; and when parents are able to tolerate mixed feelings in themselves. Parents who can maintain such responsiveness and sensitivity to their child seem consistently able to provide closeness when a child craves it, to allow greater freedom and responsibility (within the limits of safety and reason) when the child can handle it, and to offer appropriate reassurance when the child feels anxious or frustrated while navigating the world.

Recent studies suggest that the most effective parenting style combines emotional warmth with firmness and, as the child gets older, works to establish an open dialogue with the child. In contrast, a style that is too rigid and authoritarian can make it harder for a child to learn to take initiative, and to develop fully her curiosity and independent thinking. A style that is too indulgent and that worries too much about stifling creativity and individuality can interfere with a child's necessary struggle with frustration, limits, and finally genuine mastery and accomplishment.

Because the child forms the other half of the relationship, she contributes to the quality of the interactions as well. Mothers who have receptive, alert toddlers have an easier time being responsive. Sometimes, a child's temperament hampers an adult's efforts to establish a smooth rhythm (see *Temperament,* page 14). This is often the case with infants and toddlers who are not easily soothed, who get upset if their ongoing activity is interrupted, or who are initially negative to new stimuli. Secure attachments are more challenging in these babies.

In the majority of instances, mothers and their babies develop a comfortable, secure relationship by the third year. It is important to keep in mind that it doesn't take a perfect parent to foster healthy development and relatedness in a child. You only have to be good enough.

LANGUAGE AND SPEECH DEVELOPMENT: WHEN TO BE CONCERNED

Although most children begin to demonstrate a clear understanding and capacity for language starting at eighteen months or so, the actual timetable varies greatly. Even if a child is not speaking by the age of two but gestures as a way of communicating that indicates language comprehension. The child will likely speak soon since this kind of *gestural speech,* using the body to make language, is a good indicator that the child is beginning to develop speech.

DELAYED SPEECH
While parents may naturally worry when their children seem not to be speaking as quickly or fluently as some of their playmates, most worry is proved needless. Yet

there are a number of reasons for speech to be delayed. Deafness and other hearing deficits, for example, can interfere with a child's speech development. If a child's speech seems to be delayed, see your child's doctor and have the child's hearing tested. When language difficulties persist, your pediatrician may recommend consulting a speech or language specialist.

Children who clearly comprehend and use only gestural speech may be refusing to speak. Such refusal sometimes arises when parents are too quick to gratify, making it easy for a child to get what she wants without needing to use words. Often, a third or fourth child does not speak early since older siblings may be talking for the youngster.

STUTTERING

As language development proceeds, some children stutter. Just as children trip over their own feet when learning to walk, some trip over their tongues as they try to keep up with their own thinking. However worrisome early stuttering may be, it is most helpful if parents step back and allow their child to work out her speech. When a child feels pressured because her parents correct her or supply words for her, her stuttering may increase. Her early speech will naturally be a young child's speech, and as such will not always resemble adult speech. It does no good to try to push her along. In most cases, stuttering will disappear with time.

Parents who are worried or troubled about their children's language development should always discuss this with their child's doctor.

Eating

By the beginning of the second year of life, your child will be ready to share mealtimes with you and the rest of the family. Not only will schedules match, but in all likelihood the youngster's tastes and culinary interests will also have become more sophisticated.

Like the rest of us, a toddler's nutritional needs can be easily met by a varied diet of fresh foods—vegetables, grains, fruits, and dairy. Given a toddler's sometimes resolute likes and dislikes, plus your own schedule and the other demands in your life, it may not always be possible to provide a good, varied mix of food on a day-to-day basis. Set your sights on the week's menu and strive to meet your child's, and your own, nutritional needs on a broader scale.

As you prepare family meals, most fresh

foods can be easily adapted for a toddler: simply cooked chicken, meats, and fish cut up into small finger foods; tiny bits of mild cheese; a dollop of yogurt; cooked vegetables pureed or cut into bite-size cubes; steamed or blanched fruit, perhaps mashed or strained (if they have seeds). Be sure, as you give these tidbits to your child, that they are small enough or soft enough not to cause choking.

Avoid giving your toddler fatty foods, nuts, popcorn, or dishes with rich or spicy sauces. Beware taking too much trouble preparing your toddler's food. The more time, money, and emotional investment you put into what your toddler eats, the more maddening it will be when she refuses to eat, or worse, drops the food on the floor.

An ample, varied diet should provide all the vitamins a child needs. However, if your toddler is a picky eater, a daily multivitamin drop or tablet will ensure adequate vitamin intake. Consult your pediatrician.

Sometimes it is not *what* the child eats that concerns parents, but *how* the food is consumed. If you spend considerable money buying fresh vegetables or lean cuts of meat and even more time preparing them, it is understandable that you would feel hurt and possibly angered when your child refuses to eat. When your toddler plays with the food, you have the mess as well as the waste to contend with.

In addition, toddler high-chair behavior often flies against an adult notion of good table manners. A few bites get eaten, a few more get flung about, then the remaining potatoes and bananas become finger art.

Don't take it personally. Remember, you're feeding a toddler who is exercising creativity in exploring the world.

When she's done with her food, she will let you know. No amount of distraction will work for long. It may be that she's ready to be held, or more likely amused, when you've finally sat down to your own dinner.

All this hardly makes for a social and civilized repast. Yet it's important to realize that, while you are trying to feed her so that she can grow and be healthy, you are also trying to teach her to behave in a socially agreeable way. These are two different tasks. Eating her carrots or finishing all the food on her plate is more of a disciplinary issue than a dietary one. She will know when she has had enough, and, in most cases, she will get the nutrition she needs from food that she likes—if you offer her a wide enough variety.

Too often, though, food, eating, and mealtimes can get mixed up with love and discipline. When this happens, a toddler's natural need for control and autonomy will get played out at mealtime. Besides causing considerable disruption and upset during what otherwise should be an enjoyable family occasion, these kinds of power or control struggles can teach a child that eating (or *not* eating) is a way of getting attention. In addition, persistent struggles at mealtime can lead to eating problems later on in development.

If given some say in how and what they eat, toddlers are less likely to have problems later and more likely to become adequate eaters. Growth decelerates in the second year of life; this change of pace is often accompanied by a reduction in eating. With sufficient quantity and variety of food, your child will not starve. If you are concerned that she isn't getting enough calories, have your pediatrician check your toddler's weight and health. If you are told she is thriving, try to relax and back away from the power struggles over food. Enjoy your toddler's wonder as she explores the world's tastes and textures.

By the time a child is two or two and a half, she will be ready to leave her high chair behind. This may be a mixed blessing for parents who are accustomed to the high chair restraining the child at mealtime. With the help of a booster seat, she can scoot right up to the table, ready to join into the social aspects of the meal. Arrange her place setting like everyone else's.

No matter where your toddler sits during meals, it's important to keep in mind that it is not easy for a toddler to sit still and focus for any extended period of time. Before she gets distracted, engage her attention and encourage her independence by providing foods that are easy for her to manipulate. Let her feed herself by any method; spoon or fingers will do the job equally well, depending on your toddler's preference.

This is not the time to insist on proper manners. She will begin to learn table manners by watching and imitating you. In the meantime, don't be overly concerned about the mess and her awkwardness with utensils.

Let her eat in any order and in any combination. While you might not relish the idea of crackers dipped in applesauce or a broccoli and yogurt stew, it may be just the taste your baby will savor. When she has had

enough, accept that she has had enough. Little is gained, even in the area of nutrition, by urging her to eat just a few more bites. When she is ready to get down, let her down. She may return to you for a few more morsels, but once she's away from the table, her meal is likely to be over.

There are some benefits to having your toddler join you for meals. Her eating and manners will become more civilized over time, and she will quickly become a part of your family interactions. There will be times, however, when feeding your toddler earlier will be a welcome and needed change so that you can have a peaceful meal after she's in bed.

Crying

Toddlers' emotions take on new complexity during this period, and their feelings are likely to be powerful and, at many times, overwhelming. A normal part of development is learning how to regulate emotions.

Often, toddlers vacillate between crying and anxiety on one side and frustration and tantrums on the other. It is this profound emotional roller coaster, the likes of which will probably not be seen again until puberty, that can make "the twos" terrible.

Crying in later infancy acts as a call for attention from parents, much as it did during the first year of life. The difference is that as the child gets older, crying can communicate a broader range of feelings, as well as subtler emotional nuances. In addition, the youngster is able to communicate in ways other than crying. The older the child, the better able she will to tell you just what she needs.

A toddler is also developing the capability to tend to many of her own needs and to comfort herself. It continues to be the parents' task to determine what the child's demands mean. Now, though, parents must also judge which demands require their immediate intervention and which the child can learn to address herself. At the same time, parents can begin to help the child understand and identify her own inner states and figure out what to do about them.

Of course, cries of pain, fatigue, and discomfort still very much require a parent's direct and immediate involvement. You want to know and help when your toddler is sick or hurt. Even when the reason for the tears is not immediately apparent, it is important that you approach a crying child with concern and the offer of some kind of comfort.

Teething can cause a toddler to be weepy and irritable. Typically, children teethe throughout their second year. Teething pain can be eased by biting on something cold, such as a special kind of teething ring that is cooled in the refrigerator. Or try rubbing the affected gum with your finger. Sometimes sucking on a bottle will make the pain worse, so you might offer drinks from a cup instead.

Sometimes, periods of tearfulness may signal a *developmental spurt*. As they learn new behavior or approach a new emotional or intellectual milestone, toddlers may naturally feel vaguely disorganized. These kinds of tears may be very hard for parents to interpret. Yet providing extra comfort, perhaps holding her a bit more at these times may be of great help

to your child. Also, you can encourage her to use other sources of comfort—the pacifier, bottle, or a favorite stuffed animal—as she passes through particularly stressful times (see *Transitional Objects and Behaviors,* page 59).

Many tears arise from the *conflict* between what toddlers want, what they're capable of, and what parents are willing to give or consent to. At this age, your child struggles with the desire to be independent, to throw off adult control and dictates on the one hand, and the contradictory desire to stay a baby, to be protected from an increasing appreciation of the danger in the world.

As a result, a toddler may suddenly switch between statements like *Let me* or *I do* or *No* and mournful, panicked weeping if you leave the room for even a minute. You may also notice ambivalence as you try to wean her from the bottle or breast. During the day, she may insist on taking liquid from a cup or may grab greedily at your glass. But, with the same obstinacy, she will cling to her bottle and mother's breast at other times.

■ BEDTIME

Bedtime, the time when a child must say good-bye for now to her parents and her busy world, is frequently the time when *regressive feelings* (a desire to return to an earlier developmental stage) express themselves in tears. A child may cling to her bottle before going to sleep, but allowing your toddler to fall asleep while sucking on a bottle with formula or juice is a habit that can lead to tooth decay and, over time, one that gets harder and harder to leave behind.

Though parents may hope that sleep problems will be resolved in their child's first year, this is hardly ever the case. In fact, after a child's first birthday, when the world holds so many attractive activities, getting to sleep will likely become a greater challenge for both of you.

Nap time dwindles. By the second year, one nap is all that a parent can count on. Your child will be more interested in staying awake, and probably more in need of her sleep at the end of her day.

Rituals, such as reading a bedtime story, become important, as do other transitional activities. A regular routine—perhaps including a *usual* time to take a bath, get in bed, read a story, and so on—allows a child to withdraw from you gradually. Also a special bear or blanket can help ease the transition from wakefulness to sleep (see *Transitional Objects and Behaviors,* page 59).

Another critical ingredient for minimizing tears and struggles at bedtime is a parent's resolve. Be firm about your child staying in her own bed. Expect that she will eventually lull herself to sleep.

If your toddler cries and fusses after all the bedtime routines and rituals are finished, let her know that she is not being deserted, but that the day is over and it's time to go to sleep. Tell her to close her eyes and go to sleep and that you'll see her in the morning.

Crying after you've left the room may be no more than testing. If it persists or begins to build, go back into the room and say *good night* and leave the room. You can repeat these visits a few times, but stay no more than thirty seconds per visit. Reassure her that you are there if she needs you. Don't

take her out of her crib or agree to stay in the room. If you are too interesting, engaging, or stimulating she won't want to go sleep. Try to be low-key, matter-of-fact, even boring.

■ FRUSTRATION

It is important to evaluate a toddler's tears, and their cause, before you act. Crying at this age can be a way of gaining attention from adults. If you rush in before the child can develop any sense of wanting to do for herself, or needing to try again, you may interfere with the toddler's attempts to succeed and to say triumphantly *I did it!* The ability to do things on her own, even to comfort herself, is essential to your toddler's sense of competence and budding self-esteem. As with so many other aspects of child-rearing, parents must walk a fine line between keeping their toddlers safe, being available, or being too quick to get involved in their child's struggles to learn and allowing your child to develop competence.

Shyness and Anxiety

As bold and daring as your toddler seems at times, she is just as likely to be remarkably shy and timid. The world offers myriad fascinating and exciting adventures, but these same adventures may also appear strange, menacing, and downright dangerous. In fact, fearfulness and anxiety are normal emotions at this age (as they are at every age). But they are seldom comfortable emotions.

Adult ways of dealing with anxiety may be to avoid things that make them afraid or to approach them in a measured and thoughtful manner. But toddlers don't have the capacity to understand what is making them afraid and how to deal with it.

Despite the dramatic advances in their development, toddlers are still relatively helpless. They are small, and their control over their bodies is tentative. Their level of mastery, effectiveness, and impact in the world is quite limited. Their power to reason and comprehend is in its formative phase. It's little wonder that toddlers may encounter their world with considerable timidity, and, at times, anxiety.

Your toddler might feel apprehensive when you leave her in bed at night. Slowly, with your help, she will learn to soothe some of her uncomfortable feelings by hugging her teddy bear, or wrapping her special blanket over her head (see *Transitional Objects and Behaviors,* page 59).

Eventually, a child learns to comfort herself with her own thoughts. Late at night, you might even hear her talking to herself as she tries to lull herself back to sleep.

However, if her brother takes her teddy bear away, or if you launder her favorite blanket without her permission, feelings of helplessness, anxiety, or anger may wash over her. When she follows you around only to find that you've locked yourself for a few minutes in the bathroom, feelings of powerless can turn into anger or fear.

When introduced to other children, some toddlers naturally feel shy. A new group of children may be noisy and the situation unknown. When faced with a group of unfamiliar children, such as in a playgroup or day-care situation, your child might cling, suck her thumb, or twist her hair.

Be sensitive and accept your child's shyness and fears. That way you help her understand that all her feelings are okay. Your child will likely cling to you in new situations, but if you respond in a loving and reassuring way (however tempting, it's best not to push or implore), she will let go of you in time.

In situations where your child is truly fearful, you probably won't be able to convince her that she is not scared. It does little good to say *That dog doesn't really frighten you, does it?* or *Don't be silly, it's just a nightmare.* At times, any attempt on your part to talk her out of her anxiety may only increase her fear or upset. However, do offer comfort by telling her when there is nothing to fear. *I understand that you are afraid of the swing. I could watch you so that you won't get hurt. Or if you don't want to swing, we'll find something else to do.*

When a toddler feels anxious or insecure, she will seem less adventurous than usual. She may fret about strange places and people. For a while, she may have extra difficulty going to sleep. She may lose enthusiasm for food and prefer more babyish foods. Anxious toddlers may also revert to earlier behaviors; they might, for example, implore their parents to feed them after months of feeding themselves. This is called regression.

Most times, the anxiety passes as the child gains greater mastery and feels greater control in her world. Some fears, however, may intensify over time. In some instances, the toddler's fear may be very specific—dogs, insects, snakes, the dark, and monsters. Specific, persistent fears are called *phobias* (see *Anxiety and Avoidant Disorders,* page 311).

Children at this age frequently have *nightmares* and *night terrors*, sometimes after a particularly stressful day (and toddlers seem to have many). They can frighten both children and parents. Night terrors usually occur in deep sleep. The child screams or thrashes about, but does not fully awaken. She may seem panicked, sitting upright in the crib, terrified. Or she may seem profoundly sad, lying down, crying as if something dreadful has happened. In most cases, the drama of the night terror disappears in a minute or two. A pat on the back, a few soothing words may be enough to reassure and settle the child back to sleep.

Nightmares are dreams that frighten the child, and from which the child may awaken crying and fearful. You may be able to identify or guess what causes the nightmare—a new baby (or the approaching arrival of one), a new day care arrangement, battles about eating, a recent vacation that changed her routine, or an illness in the family. When the child awakens from a nightmare, you can offer her reassurance, love, and comfort. You cannot, however, expect to prevent nightmares because you cannot eliminate the considerable demands, stress, and anxiety that a normal toddler experiences.

Transitional Objects and Behaviors

Babies and parents call them blankies, loveys, cuddlies, binkies. In the world outside the family, they are called transitional objects. Linus in the *Peanuts* comic strip, though surely beyond his toddler years, still carries his blanket from frame to frame.

These objects—the dirty, torn baby blanket; the ragged, stained teddy bear—are means by which toddlers comfort themselves and learn to tolerate anxiety, specifically in response to separation from their caregivers. By wrapping herself up in the blanket or chewing on the bear's ear, your child holds on to a symbolic piece of you, even when you are not present.

As they get older, children may feel self-conscious about dragging a blanket or old stuffed doll around. You too may find the oatmeal stains and the bedraggled appearance a bit problematic. In the preschool child, a pacifier in the mouth may seem babyish.

Yet as they are expending enormous energy trying to understand and master their world and themselves in it, toddlers are subject to a high degree of anxiety. Chances are, too, that you are out of your child's sights more frequently now—if only in the kitchen while she is playing in the den. Parents leave their toddlers more often in the care of others—to go out at night, to work. Thus, the need for transitional objects does not necessarily diminish at this age and may even increase during stressful times.

Around the age of two, children may begin to insist on wearing a particular item of clothing or a hat. Certain behaviors at this age also serve a transitional purpose. Comfort habits include thumb-sucking, twiddling locks of hairs, ear-twisting, rhythmic sounds, and rocking. When any of these behaviors become excessive, consider what could be stressing your child and offer extra time and comfort.

Other people may make unkind comments when they see a toddler with a pacifier, sucking her thumb, or cuddling her lovey. But most children outgrow their need for these objects or behaviors by the time they reach age four. In most cases, it's neither wise nor necessary to try to wean a child from her transitional objects before that age.

Negativism

From a toddler's point of view, parental care can feel like interference. She finds a delicious-looking morsel in the trash, and someone grabs it from her hand. She begins to scale the bookcase to examine a shiny object at the top, and someone plucks her from behind and places her on the floor.

Many parents insist that their toddler leave the bottle or the breast behind and learn to use a cup. They begin explaining bladder and bowel control and suggest using the potty.

From a parent's point of view, setting limits is necessary to bring culture and safety to a child. A child cannot be allowed to go digging in the garbage or pick up any piece of debris off the street. For safety's sake, she cannot be permitted to climb the bookcase or chase after the dog that wanders into the yard.

A toddler naturally resists any impediments to investigations and creative activities. To your child, it is only natural to register a strong protest to your intervention. To you, such protests may seem contrary and opposi-

tional. In fact, this sudden negative or defiant behavior is the reason that this age has earned the label *terrible twos*.

Before your child began to walk, you could use gentle persuasion and distraction. You could pick up and carry the toddler out of the range of temptation. Because the child was closely bound to you and your body, such movements and rhythms on your part seemed natural.

In a child's second year, she is not as passive a partner. The youngster now has her own independent rhythm and style—and the developmentally driven need to assert them. Now when you gather the child up for a good night's sleep—much needed, after a day of exploring and experimenting—you get protesting squiggles and fussing. No longer is one object as good as another; a small toy offered as appeasement when you take away the piece of garbage your child just picked up off the street just isn't as appealing. Often she acts and reacts as though her independence is based on doing the opposite of what you want.

A toddler lacks the language skills to state her case fully. At this age, she is not able to engage in subtle negotiations but uses the word *No* very effectively. The word suits her purposes perfectly. You ask if she likes bananas, and she will answer *No* as she reaches out for the offered fruit. The *No* becomes a declaration of self—and isn't always meant to be contrary or negative.

While it is easy to view these aspects of toddlerhood as a negative phase, this kind of negative behavior is actually an indication of the child's striving to become her own person. Negativism is just one aspect of a child's development, a declaration of independence, but it does not necessarily signal contrary, rebellious, or willful intent.

If parents react to a toddler's oppositional and autonomous behavior with full power, then fierce defiance, tantrums, and struggle are likely to result. Parents should avoid making every diaper changing, nap time, puddle wading, or garbage excavation into a power struggle.

When parents understand the reasons for their child's protests, they can carry out their parental duties—change the diaper, take the garbage gently out of her hand, lead her away from the stray dog—without a major confrontation or struggle. Some of her ventures into questionable territory can go unchallenged: a child doesn't have to bathe every night; she won't die if she tastes a little bit of dirt; no one will care if she wears the orange sweater with the purple shorts. It's important for parents to pick their battles. Encourage independence where it can be useful and exercise reasonable restraint and prohibition where it is not.

Patience will go a long way. Rather than squashing a child's independence, parents can redirect it. If parents react as though this negativism is a threat to their authority, they may find themselves in a power struggle that can extend beyond the toddler years. When this happens, these kinds of power struggles frequently produce children (not to mention adolescents and adults) who become defensive and who act as though their personal integrity is at risk when submitting to demands of parents, teachers, or other authority figures or, alternatively, become passive and over-accommodating and conforming.

Frustration

Your toddler is developing an awareness of herself as an independent person. She has rights, her own preferences, and a personal style. She no longer sees herself as an extension of you. Nor does she accept your complete control over her and her world. What you may view as willfulness, she experiences as a very natural way of asserting herself. She is growing up and feels secure enough to try to navigate for herself. Try to see things as she does.

Life seldom yields readily to a toddler's will. Her understanding of the world around her is still quite limited. Her physical abilities and competence are not fully realized. She may want to do things that she just can't manage or that are simply impossible. The square puzzle piece won't fit, no matter how hard she tries, into the round space. Her pants won't slip over her head. It is often the case that even the most confidently executed independent action results in frustration.

In the normal course of their interactions, parents unwittingly contribute to a child's frustration. At any given moment, there are a variety of things your child will want to do that you either cannot allow or don't want her to do. You utter a simple *No*. You pull her away from the worm she's following as it inches across the pavement. You grab her hand as she toddles out toward the street. Suddenly, the baby feels hurried, harried, bullied, pressured, interrupted. She responds with fury.

Some frustration is inevitable and necessary. If it were possible to remove all sources of frustration from the child's world, you would also remove a large measure of the motivation for learning. However, too much frustration makes all tasks look overwhelming or impossible, thereby interfering with a toddler's developing sense of mastery and competence.

Whenever possible, parents need to keep on an even keel in dealing with toddlers. At times you may need to hurry your child along, but at others, make time to give yourself up to her pace. Guide her along gently and respectfully. Patiently show her how easily pants can be stepped into or just where the square puzzle piece fits.

Most important, pick your battles. You may have to help her dress so that everyone can get out of the house on time. But perhaps you don't have to leave so many errands until the end of the day that you can't enjoy a slower pace with your child. However patiently you try, though, it is not always possible to strike the right balance between frustration and gratification for your child (see *Bossiness and Negotiation,* page 70).

Tantrums

Just as fears are coupled with anxiety, tantrums can arise from too much frustration. So it's likely that at some point, when your child feels intensely frustrated, she will have a tantrum. Toddlers with emotional temperaments that tend to react strongly will more often have temper tantrums.

Tantrums are the emotional equivalent of a blown fuse. A tantrum is not something a toddler can prevent. Frustration and emotional pressures build; a tantrum releases the pent-up anger and frustration. During a tantrum, the toddler is overwhelmed by internal rage.

In the midst of a tantrum, the child may dash around the room, wild and screaming. Some children fling themselves on the floor, writhing and kicking. Others continue screaming until they make themselves sick. Some turn blue in the face because they cannot catch their breath, or hold their breath until they look gray. In rare instances, children can make themselves pass out by holding their breath.

Tantrums are never pleasant or easy to handle. A child can hurt herself by flinging herself up against heavy furniture or walls. Children often throw tantrums in public so that parents must deal with the child's fury as well as their own embarrassment. Remember that your toddler's tantrums are much worse for the child than for you.

You may not be able to eliminate tantrums completely during these years, but you probably can reduce their number and their intensity. When you must take your child away from something she's happily involved in, force her to do something she doesn't want to do, or restrict her from doing something she likes, do so with tact and sensitivity. Unyielding *dos* or *don'ts* may well result in a power struggle, ending in an explosion of rage.

Be sure to prevent the child from hurting

herself or anyone else during a tantrum. Her overwhelming rage terrifies her. If she sees that she can truly do damage, she will believe that not even you can protect her from her own horrible power.

If possible, hold your child firmly during a tantrum. As she calms down, her rage may melt into tears. Continue to cradle her. If your child cannot bear to be held during a tantrum, don't insist on overpowering her. Remove anything she might break or anything on which she might hurt herself. Wait as patiently as possible for the tide to subside.

Sometimes, when you know the child is safe, the best tack is to walk away. Other times, as the passion subsides, a *time-out* might work (see *Discipline,* page 69).

While the tantrum lasts, it does no good to argue or scold or even try reason. Even though you may feel yourself getting angry, don't scream back. Your own angry outburst will likely only prolong the tantrum. Talk calmly, letting the child know she can regain control.

Don't let your child feel that she is horrible or shameful for having a tantrum. Also, don't unintentionally reward her tantrums. You may be tempted, just to avoid the embarrassment of a public tantrum, to buy that piece of candy or let her ride just one more ride at the amusement park. If she sees that her tantrums have a positive result, however, she could learn to work herself up whenever she wants her way.

AGGRESSION: HITTING AND BITING

Many children hit, bite, and scratch at some point. These unpleasant and negative behaviors may first appear around a child's first birthday as experiments, a way of testing her power. Children may regress to this kind of physical aggression when they are tired or overexcited. These behaviors may also occur during a tantrum (see *Tantrums,* page 62).

When these negative behaviors appear, try not to make too big a deal out of them. Simply hold your child and tell her *No*—biting or hitting or scratching are not okay. Also tell her that you will stop her each time she tries.

Some children act aggressively with other children. They may argue over toys, for example, then hit or push when they don't get their way. If your child does hit, supervise her more closely. Explain that other children do not like being pushed around. Remind her that you cannot let her hurt someone else. Many parents hear the advice *Bite back and let her know how it feels.* This is never a good idea. In fact, biting or hitting only teaches the child that it is acceptable to use physical aggression.

Play

For a toddler, playing is not a simple pas-time: Much more than the pursuit of fun and recreation, it's a complex set of activities. Play is a child's vehicle for investigating her world. Through play, she tests out activities, actions, situations, and herself. In fact, there is little difference between the things she does for fun and the things she does to learn.

Play is fundamental to a child's development. Symbolic play offers children an opportunity to learn about logic, about sequence, about possibilities, and even about self-regulation. The imagination—basic to both the child and the adult—must be developed for the child to become a fully functioning adult. The make-believe of early childhood thus plays an essential role in nothing less than enabling a child to learn how to think.

A child's earliest play typically concentrates on movement and change, grabbing at a rattle as it passes in front of her, swatting at her mobile as it twirls around. As she develops, she gains the equipment to explore, experiment, and learn. She is awake more of the time. She is mobile. She can grasp, hold, and manipulate. She can question and exclaim, with and without words.

For the one-year-old, the world of reality consists of the here and now. Her job is to come to terms with real people and real things as they come before her eyes. For this, she uses her five senses. Her full attention is devoted to what's outside. She busies herself with making sense of what is. She is not ready for what might be in the future. Nor is there a notion of the past.

After a few months, she will begin to experiment. She picks things up and appears to be thinking, *What can I do with this? What does it taste like? What if I drop it on the floor? What if I drop in on a pillow? Can I push it out between the bars of my crib?* A child at this age will use trial and error to figure out how pieces in a large puzzle fit together. Eventually she begins to develop a rudimentary understanding of the rules that govern her world.

Between the ages of twelve and eighteen months, children develop the capacity to engage in symbolic or imaginative play. They use themselves as agents to pretend doing things. At first, your child mimics your actions, following you around the kitchen, chasing unseen crumbs on the floor with her broom. She moves her empty spoon into her mouth and eats make-believe applesauce.

By the time she is two, she can carry out a sequence of pretend actions. Instead of feeding herself, she pretends to feed the baby—shoveling the make-believe dinner into her doll's mouth, wiping the doll's mouth, and burping her.

Another significant development in the way a child plays appears around the middle of a child's second year. Her experiments have revealed to her how different objects respond. Now she begins to notice similarities and differences in how they appear, taste, or feel to the touch. She begins to recognize colors, shapes, textures. She begins to solve some puzzles in her mind. Once she is able to organize objects into groups in her mind, her play begins to involve organizing, sorting, comparing, contrasting, grouping, and labeling. Around the same time, they begin to respond to notions such as time (soon, next week, morning) and number (lots, many).

With the ability to think symbolically, children are able to invent. In their play they begin to treat one thing as if it were another. Your child talks on a banana as if it were a telephone, aims and postures with a stick as if it were a gun (no matter how much of a pacifist you are), scoots her cars along the edge of a sandbox as if it were a road, or wears a saucepan for a hat.

Toddlers still have little real understanding of their world and little control over it.

They easily fall prey to fears of monsters, the dark, dogs, and other real or imagined threats (see *Shyness and Anxieties*, page 57). As they develop cognitively and their play expands, they often combat their feelings of being small and powerless through their imaginative play, which includes wishful, magical thinking. So a little child afraid of the dark turns into a fairy princess with magical powers or a superhero with superhuman strength.

An older toddler may base her play on adult behavior, so that her play is essentially imitative. But, because she is now able to hold mental images of objects and actions, she imitates other people's actions long after she has seen them doing it.

TOY SELECTION: CREATIVE, LANGUAGE, AND EDUCATIONAL TOYS

Unlike their parents, toddlers do not distinguish between educational experiences and play. As they move out into an expanding world, they engage in a process of exploring and discovery. Toys and other objects become instruments for learning and devices by which toddlers gradually acquire and perfect the skills they need to master along the way to adulthood.

Though parents today can select from thousands of toys on the market for their toddlers, a little imagination can work just as well in providing playthings to capture a young child's curiosity.

Toddlers also use their entire bodies to learn. Physical play teaches them about their abilities and limits. It helps them to develop control and competence. As they run, climb, jump, swing, push, pull, roll, and leap about, they become more agile and well coordinated. Physical play channels their energy and relieves much of the stress that comes from new thinking and new activities.

For physical play, children use climbing toys (both indoor and outdoor), stairs (with adult supervision), swings, and push-pull toys. They enjoy scooting around on large trucks and fire engines, pushing baby walkers, pulling plastic and wooden animals. Until her walk is absolutely steady, though, avoid giving her doll carriages or other lightweight, freewheeling toys that are likely to tip or run away.

Besides engaging in large motor activities, toddlers delight in exploring the natural world. Set up a pan of water or help them reach the sink, and they become little scientists, making objects float, sink, and dissolve. Let her add watercolors, bubbles, and ice. Set a wading pool in the backyard (remember, however, that supervision is required every moment there is water in the pool).

Many toddlers also love to make messes and get their hands dirty. Many children enjoy playing with mud, clay, play dough, or finger paints at this age. Other children may not like the feel and look of mess on their hands or clothes. These children may prefer play with sand. (Look for washed sand, and avoid cement or chemically manufactured sand.)

When outdoors, children will spend extended periods of time gathering stones, shells, leaves, and twigs. They sort, categorize, pile up, dig with, break, smell, snap, and examine.

As a child begins to observe how things work, she will be drawn to toys she can manipulate. With blocks she can create structures and topple them over. She will be fascinated by toys with pieces that fit together, including nesting dolls, simple puzzles with large pieces, play people that fit into holes of vehicles or dwellings, variously shaped plastic blocks that fit into appropriate holes, and toys that hook or thread together. As she begins to classify, she will enjoy little cars and miniature farm animals.

In addition, toys act as conduits for many of a child's uncomfortable feelings. As she is learning not to inflict aggression on real people, your child might bite and pinch some of her less favored stuffed animals. When there is a new baby in the house, you may notice that the older toddler attends to her stuffed animals with greater zeal. While she has to control her strong ambivalent feelings about her new sibling, she is at liberty to bathe, nurse, drown, or hate her teddy bear.

Children also need quiet time. Physical tiredness, excitement, and tension can build up to the point that a child no longer knows that she is tired. Quiet occupations give children the opportunity to relax without actually going to bed, and, as such, will serve them for years.

Picture books with big, detailed illustrations and cardboard books that can be chewed on are best at this age. Go through the pages slowly with your child, pointing to the pictures, and describe what is going on. If the words are too difficult, adapt them for your child. Leave books in her crib so that she can amuse herself before she falls asleep and after she awakens.

Scribbling is the first step toward drawing and ultimately writing. Your toddler may enjoy crayons and watercolors. She may like the feel of finger painting, the colors and textures she discovers by painting at an easel.

PLAYGROUPS AND SOCIALIZING

What a child needs most almost until her third birthday is the ability to explore her world at her own pace. It doesn't advance her development to have her join formal classes or activities. In fact, activities which are too structured can sometimes dampen a child's natural creativity and enthusiasm for new experiences.

However, certain group activities can be quite enjoyable for your toddler. At this age, playgroups offer a valuable opportunity for children to play alongside one another. The fact that playgroups also offer parents the opportunity to spend time with other adults, to share common concerns, and trade parenting tips, is an added bonus.

Until a child is three, she usually does not engage directly with other children. As a toddler, she may enjoy playing near other children. When children play side by side, but do not actually engage with one another, it is called *parallel play*. From time to time, a child may glance over at another child and observe how she plays. She may even pick up a few tips of her own.

Sometimes it's hard to remember when you watch toddlers play that they are not really selfish. It's just that, at this age, they don't recognize that other children are all that interesting. After all, your child is still dealing with the notion that she must negotiate with you. No matter how many times you urge your child to play fair, to take turns, or to share, chances are she cannot.

Early on, you may be able to prevent one child from destroying the other's tower or from snatching that tempting pull-dog away from another. However, by the time your child is two, introduce the notion of sharing. Your child may agree to select certain toys that she is willing to share. Other toys may be too special and should be protected as such. And don't expect too much cooperation at this age. If you let her set her own pace, even with her peers, she will develop her own way of socializing that will serve her well as she gets older.

Curiosity

As any parent can affirm, there is no such thing as a quick walk to the corner drugstore when a toddler comes along. Each step offers a new adventure to engage in a new and astonishing sights to stop and observe. There's a pigeon to chase and watch fly away. There's a bottle top or coin lying on the edge of the sidewalk to inspect. There's a flower to smell. With so many wonders to scrutinize, it's truly amazing that you actually ever get to the drugstore.

The fact that toddlers stay awake for longer periods and are interested in what goes on around them gives parents the option to include them in their excursions into the wider world. Your child will be happy to come along with you wherever you want whenever you want—whether it's running errands, dinner with your friends, a long day trip, or weekend getaway.

However, once accustomed to your schedule, your child may not be so willing to nap on the days you do stay at home. Nor will your toddler want to go to sleep at a conventional time. This may lead to irregular sleeping patterns.

On the other hand, routines are important. So naps and bedtimes should be kept to a schedule most of the time. This means arranging your evenings out so that you can put the baby to sleep, and following that routine as closely as possible, even on vacation.

■ MASTURBATION AND GENITAL CURIOSITY

As children begin toilet training, they naturally become curious about their bodies. An interest in genitals, both male and female, is perfectly normal. Little boys play with their penises. Little girls discover the feel and smell of their vaginas and clitorises. Just as they fiddled with their toes and fingers a few months earlier, this exploration is mostly curiosity. It's interesting, plus, it feels good.

Sometimes, a girl will try to insert things into her vagina. It's unlikely that she will hurt herself or rupture her hymen during her explorations. Only if she is overly zealous in her attempts or seems preoccupied with masturbation is there any cause to look beyond natural curiosity for a reason. (See also *Sexual Abuse,* page 259.) If your child begins to play with herself in public, explain that it's okay, but because it is a private thing, touching oneself must be done in private places, like at home in the child's own room.

Sometimes, when children feel stressed or tense, they withdraw to masturbate. Sometimes they will masturbate while watching television, which suggests boredom. When this is the case, offer more engaging activities. Like thumb-sucking or rocking, masturbation can be a way of discharging tension at the end of the day, but if it becomes excessive, it may be a sign that the child feels too much pressure.

Discipline: Establishing Limits and Permissiveness

Discipline is commonly confused with punishment. In the true sense of the word, discipline is the set of methods by which parents guide and teach their children. You use discipline to teach right and wrong, to help a child incorporate a sense of limits and appropriate behavior, and to tolerate delayed gratification. Discipline is not punishment.

Teaching discipline does not happen over night. It is a long-term project. Children are forever testing the limits of adults' patience and the consistency of their discipline. It is likely that you will have to address the same issues repeatedly as well as new issues as they arise.

At its best, discipline means providing calm, consistent limits. That's no easy task. The payoff, though, is that your child will develop self-control, consideration of others' needs and rights, the ability to delay gratification, and to tolerate frustration.

Discipline and the way in which parents implement it must change as the child grows. Parents who see discipline as a matter of showing who's in charge are taking the wrong tack. If a toddler believes that discipline is merely an issue of control, she will likely respond with resistance and obstinacy.

However, there will always be times when, no matter how hard you try to be reasonable and measured, you simply cannot divert a fight. At times, it can seem to the tired parent that children have an uncanny way of finding just the right time to become particularly aggravating: at the end of the day when you are both tired, when you're on the phone, in the middle of important business, during a visit with another adult, or when you're out in public. Nevertheless, it is important to pick your battles and save discipline for important issues.

Hitting and spanking a child when you are angry teaches the child to use physical force to control others. These expressions of parental anger may also undermine your efforts to teach your children to control their own anger.

Time-outs often work to drain some of the passion out of a heated situation. This technique works by having a child sit for a short period of time (perhaps a minute for each year of her age but the time also depends on her temperament) in a designated place, such as a chair, a stair, her room, or crib. The place should not be too stimulating or hold too much fun for the child. This gives her time to get her temper under control. For time-out to work, it must not be seen as a punishment, but rather a special time to regroup and calm down. Sit with your child afterward and talk about why you interfered. Don't lecture, but give the child a clear idea of your expectations for her behavior.

Discipline won't work if you talk to your toddler as though she were an older child. As she becomes more agile with her use of language, she may appear to understand more than she does. Sometimes what looks like defiance may actually be a lack of comprehension.

Don't look for absolute control or compliance. Your toddler will do as you wish if she happens to feel like doing it, if curiosity does not overwhelm her wish to please you, and if she does not feel, at that moment, the need to assert her independence. Frequently, teaching discipline can be a matter of delicate negotiations, rather than putting your foot down (see *Bossiness and Negotiation,* page 70).

Other problems can be addressed by avoiding them in the first place. Move things out of her reach that you don't want her touching. If you don't want her snacking on sweets or drinking sodas, don't have them in the house.

Distraction and substitution will often work to circumvent confrontations. Your child wants your china cup; offer her instead the plastic cup with the friendly bear on it. Your child wants to play with your makeup; suggest that the two of you sit down and color together.

Mealtime is probably not the best time to discipline a child or to assert your authority. By fighting over the amount of food a child eats, or the way she behaves at the table, you may lose much of the joy of eating as a family or in a restaurant. Fights about eating teach a child that food offers a sure way of getting attention. This may contribute to eating problems (or even disorders) later. It is never a good idea to use food as a reward, punishment, bribe, or threat. Food should be first about nourishment, then about being with other people, but not, if you can help it, about control and discipline.

Finally, parents teach proper behavior through example. Your child will learn self-discipline and respect for others by experiencing how you treat her and how you interact with others.

Bossiness and Negotiation

By the very nature of their task—to gain continually greater mastery over their actions and their world—toddlers have to be tenacious. Watch a child during the early days of walking when balance is precarious. No matter how many times she falls, she simply gets up and rushes ahead to the next tumble. Nothing stops her.

You may notice that your child increasingly remembers things, but a toddler's memory is short. As the child tries to do more grown-up things, such as walking, the same step may prove an obstacle time and again, tripping her up. She reacts with the same wild frustration each time. There will be days when it looks as though she will never learn. But she will—with time.

When she was a baby, you simply steered

her away from dangers. When she becomes a preschooler, you will be able to point out the dangers to her. For now, though, you help cushion the fall by child-proofing the house, removing objects that she could swallow from her grasp, placing child gates across stairways, and locking toxic cleaning agents and cosmetics away.

A toddler's persistence is admirable to observe in her physical ventures into independence. It is not always so easy to take when it arises in her social interactions. As she negotiates greater independence, she will naturally seem bossier. After all, she is striving to become the boss over herself.

As you help her navigate greater independence in her relationships, it is your job to keep an eye on that balance between autonomy and belonging (see *Establishing Emotional Security and Building Self-Esteem,* page 49). This is often easier said than done. You are likely her most important social relationship. She will therefore play out much of her ambivalence with you. It is truly difficult to be both a player and an objective referee. Yet, as with her walking, it is your job to steer her away from dangers, cushion her falls, and, increasingly, use words to guide her.

Parents need to strive to keep to a middle course. If you attend too closely or protect too much, the toddler's need for independence will erupt in anger or grief. If there is too much distance, too little attention and responsiveness, your child's need for closeness and safekeeping may break out in anxious clinging.

Often the middle course means learning to negotiate. In negotiations, both people's needs are taken into consideration. Therefore, your need to protect and guide your child will be balanced with her need to be self-directed and self-sufficient.

In most circumstances, your toddler will do as you wish if she happens to feel like doing it. Knowing this, you can arrange things so that you both get what you want.

You can tell your toddler to pick up her blocks. Chances are she will refuse, fight, or throw a tantrum—sometimes all three. Even punishing will not get those blocks picked up, and you will end up feeling like a not very effective bully. Or you can turn the request into a game. *Why don't you pick up the blue blocks while I pick up the red? Who can pick up the most? Let's count as we pick up.*

Now you've made it so she wants to do what you want her to do. Afterward, as you praise her marvelous efforts, your cleverness will be rewarded with a proud child beaming a smile of mastery.

Getting a child dressed and out of the house can pose a challenge to the most patient parent. By offering her a choice—the red overalls or the purple dress—you give her some control and involve her in the process, and your child will likely be dressed before you know it. The more you encourage her to participate, the more pleasurable these necessary activities become.

Sometimes the only way to get a child to do what you want is with rewards. However, bargaining with a toddler is a tricky business. In general, she cannot yet anticipate the consequences of her behavior. Nor can she wait for anything. She wants what she wants *now.*

In addition, her language may suggest that

she understands more than she does. She uses the word "promise," but she is truly confused when you express disappointment that she failed to finish her carrots as she had promised. Sometimes, she uses words to express what she wishes to be true—*It was her doll who made the mess in her room*, or *Yes, her milk is all gone.*

Between the ages of two and three, children can be rewarded with promises of later treats. More often, though, they try to negotiate for a treat now as well as later—they want and probably need immediate gratification.

There will be times, however, when it is important to be firm. You may negotiate about trying a new vegetable at dinner but not about taking medicine. There should be no negotiation about holding a hand to cross the street. The art of negotiation includes knowing when to be firm.

Learning how and when to negotiate will result in less discord between you and your child. As she gets older, your child will be able to remember instructions, to choose between right and wrong, to anticipate the consequences of her actions, and to consider other people's feelings, including yours. At that point, she will base many of her decisions on feelings she developed during this time when her need for greater independence was honored in a loving, approving, and supportive way.

SLEEPING IN A BIG BED

Parents often consider moving their child out of the crib when it's time to make room for a new baby. However, the best time to make the move from crib to bed is when your child is either about 36 inches tall or agile enough to scale the crib walls.

Adventurous toddlers may be able to climb out late in the second year or even sooner—you fail to respond to the child's calls quickly enough, and here she comes. Besides being inconvenient for you, climbing out could be dangerous for your child. Falling out or getting caught in the bars of the crib are both risks; walking around unsupervised is another danger.

By anticipating this step, you avoid the power struggle that can arise when she's intent on getting out of the crib and you want her to stay put.

Your child may agree that with a new baby in the house, the time has come to move up to big-kid status. If you need to clear the crib for the new baby, don't ask your toddler's permission. That risks the child saying *No*—and then you will have another issue to struggle over.

Even if there is no such compelling reason to move to a big bed, as the third birthday approaches, a child begins to feel a sense of ownership and an early desire for privacy. You can use that evolving need for a personal place to introduce the big bed.

Have your child help you pick out the bed (a full-sized single bed with a removable safety rail) or the bed linens. A careful arrangement of possessions around the bed, pictures on the wall, mobiles, a reading lamp that she can turn on and off herself, special toys, a musical box or radio will make the big-kid bed a special place. After all, with all the enormous effort it takes to understand and manage the world, your child needs just the right resting place.

WORKING AND DAY CARE

In today's economic environment, when men and women become parents their career goals or economic situation often require that they both work outside the home. In many homes, both parents must balance the joys of raising a family with the fulfillment of careers and the financial necessity of working. In many families, neither the mother nor the father has the option to stay home after their babies are born. They must contend with the guilt, confusion, and anxiety that go with longing for the balance that is right for their household.

Parents (women or men) who do stay at home, no matter how satisfied they feel with their choice, will give up some income as well as the intellectual and social stimulation work can offer. Whatever your choice, there will be compromise and sacrifice.

Making the decision whether or when to return to work is seldom easy. More often than not, the full weight falls on the parents. Current research in child and family development does not provide clear-cut conclusions on long-term risks or benefits of day care for children with working parents. It does reveal that more parenting by two or more parents is good for very young children. If you have the choice, most experts agree that it is best to wait to return to work at least until you have attached with your baby and feel competent as a parent—somewhere between three and six months.

For most parents, going off to work and leaving their baby behind is difficult. Knowing that you are leaving your child in the best possible hands will relieve much of the anxiety and guilt—if not the actual sense of missing your child.

Some families are fortunate enough to have members of their extended family in the vicinity who may be willing to devote time to caring for the baby. More recently, some parents have been offered access to day care at their workplaces so they can have their children nearby throughout the day. However, for most, day care, like other aspects of parenting, requires a great deal of initial thought, research, and preparation, as well as occasional rethinking as the baby's, family's, or day-care provider's needs change.

The main types of child care are as follows.

IN-HOME CARE

This type of child care involves a parent substitute (au pair, nanny, sitter) staying with the child in the child's home. It may be the best option in the early years since the child remains in familiar surroundings, is not exposed to lots of other children and their illnesses, and doesn't have to travel back and forth. In addition, your youngster will have the complete attention of one person and the two of them may establish a strong relationship, unlike in day-care situations where staff turnover and high caregiver-to-child ratios make such bonding more difficult. It usually happens with in-home care that the caregiver and baby are able to develop a smooth and predictable routine.

However, in-home caregivers are often expensive. Also, by relying on one person without a backup, parents may find themselves in a jam should the sitter get sick or leave abruptly. Many au pairs have no formal training in child care; nor are they required to have training. The point of the au pair program is to travel and experience another culture. They aren't expected to take care of children on a full-time basis, as a nanny, who is formally trained, would. Their role in the host home is to be a mother's helper, not a sole caregiver. Some au pairs may be motivated more by the opportunity to travel and experience another culture than by a genuine desire to care for children. Be selective in choosing your in-home caregiver.

GROUP DAY CARE

Although this is generally not considered ideal for infants, good day-care programs can offer considerable advantages. In the best situations, trained personnel provide a well-organized program specifically geared to toddlers' development and growth. Toddlers have the opportunity to play with and learn from other children.

The disadvantages include less individualized care, more children per caregiver, and the possibility for high teacher turnover and problems when your child is sick. Typically, there is less scheduling flexibility; because many day-care centers follow the school calendar, there may be days when you're working and they are not. In many cases, the cost is fairly high.

HOME DAY CARE

Day care in a family setting in a private home other than the parents' can provide a warm, homey environment at a lower cost than institutional day care. Home day care often caters to fewer children so that there is less exposure to infection and greater opportunity for individualized care. Most home day care offers the possibility of early drop-off and late pickup.

Perhaps the greatest advantage to family day care is that your child will have other children around to play with. By the second year, a child is able to learn from other children, either by imitation or in parallel play (see *Playgroups and Socializing,* page 67). It is less likely that a child will become bored in family day care.

Disadvantages vary according to the individual provider. Home day care is often unlicensed; therefore there may be little health and safety protection. The caregiver may have an approach to child-rearing that differs from yours. Also there may be no backup for care of your child if she or one of her own children is sick.

SELECTING DAY CARE FOR YOUR CHILD

Selecting the best kind of care and the right setting for your child is often an arduous and anxious process. If you are interested in *in-home care,* look for someone who is capable of nurturing and of using mature, intelligent judgment. Always, *always* check references. As you interview possible sitters, try to discover why each applicant chooses to take care of other people's children. This may help you anticipate the way that the day-care applicant will respond to you and your child.

Often, though, it is not possible to get an accurate picture of a person's style and competence until after she has begun caring for your child. It is usually best to have her begin before you have to be away from home. Leave the caregiver with the child for longer periods of time over several days, occasionally returning unexpectedly so you can check up on what's going on.

Throughout your relationship with a secondary caregiver, consider whether she respects your child's personality and developmental stage. Does she push the child, or wait until she is ready to make an advance on her own? Does she understand your child's needs and her communications? How does she speak to the child? How does she comfort her? Does she acknowledge the child's bid for attention?

Also, take into account how the caregiver relates to you. Is she sensitive to and respectful of your feelings as you separate from your child? Does she listen attentively when you describe events that happen when she is not around? Does she encourage the child's attachment to you, making sure, for example, that the child is rested and receptive when you come home? Does she take the time with you to describe the events of the day?

Competitive feelings with the caregiver are unavoidable. Loving parents are bound to feel jealous of the child's attachment to her caregiver and resentful about sharing the child's affections. However, if you lack confidence in the caregiver's ability to be sensitive and responsive to your child and you, you may become more competitive and hovering than you would be otherwise.

You will no doubt notice that the caregiver does things differently than you do. And because the relationship is complicated by competitive feelings, you may feel that everything she does for the baby or gives to the baby is slightly wrong. Your caregiver may feel competitive toward you, as well. Given this context, it is important, as you observe and consider her relationship with your child, not to be critical unless you have genuine concerns about the baby's safety.

It is not necessary that you do things exactly the same way. Children can adjust to, and often benefit from, different caring styles. But there needs to be enough agreement about basic values and approach. Otherwise, there is a risk that you will undermine each other with the child.

When considering *group day care,* look for cleanliness and safety. Are electrical outlets covered, medicine and cleaning agents kept out of reach? Day-care centers should be staffed with well-trained caregivers who like babies and are willing to treat each child as an individual. The staff should be flexible, work well as a team, and accommodate themselves to the sleep and waking rhythm of each baby. The center should offer stimulating experiences and opportunities for learning. However, it is not necessary, or even beneficial, to push too much structured learning at an early age.

The ratio of adults to small children is critical: four babies or toddlers to one adult, maximum. When you are looking for the right center for your child, find out what the turnover rate is and, if possible, if the caregivers are relatively well paid. What is the training required at the center? And, most telling, talk to parents who have children at the center, and perhaps to parents whose children have passed through the center. Ask how responsive the center is, not only to the child's emotional, social, and cognitive needs, but also to the parents' needs. Is the staff available to discuss the child's experiences and reactions during the day? Are they sensitive to feelings of loneliness and abandonment that parents may have when they give up their child?

Many of these same issues and questions arise as parents investigate *family day care*. Look for someone who can tolerate several children and still be sensitive to each child's needs and style. Call other families who leave their children with the family–day care person. Observe closely during transitional times, such as when parents leave in the morning and during reunions at the end of the day. That way you can judge how sensitive the caregiver is to children and parents. Does she hurry the parents out before their children are ready to separate? Does she respond to a child's distress when she is left? Also, at mealtime you may be able to judge how sensitive a caregiver is to a child's developmental level. Are the children allowed to feed themselves? Is the caregiver overly concerned about the children making messes?

PREPARING YOUR CHILD FOR DAY CARE

If it's possible, give yourself plenty of time before you start work to acclimate both you and your baby to day care. Gradually introduce your baby to the person or people who will be caring for her. Make her first few visits short while you stay around.

As it becomes possible for you to withdraw, do so progressively, first by standing off in a corner, then by leaving the room for a few minutes. As your child becomes engaged by the day-care provider or by the setting (the toys or other children), extend your absence. Tell her when you plan to leave the setting, and allow yourself a short absence at first.

When your child notices your return, greet her warmly but casually. It was not, after all, such a big deal for you to leave. Pretty soon, you should be able to leave her for longer periods of time, then for the entire workday.

Finally, trust your own impressions and observations. Watch for signs of discontent in your baby. Sudden changes in her mood or attitude, clinginess, and worry after the initial adaptation may be ways she's alerting you to the fact that this particular situation is stressful and needs adjustment.

PARENT'S DAY OUT

Sometimes a new mother (or father) can get so wrapped up in attending to the toddler's needs that the parent's needs get slighted. Taking a long, steamy shower, sitting down to a meal while it is still hot, or reading a couple of chapters in a novel may begin to seem like luxuries rather than the peace-of-mind necessities that they are.

No matter how demanding your toddler is, how many other responsibilities you have to juggle, and how exhausted you feel at the end of the day, it is crucial that you make time for yourself. Continue to involve yourself in old interests or find new ones. These may include a course at a local college, a study or reading group, an exercise class or sports activity, volunteer work, a dinner and movie with a friend, or just shopping at your own pace.

Though you can take your toddler with you on many of these outings, it's not really a mother's or father's day out if you do. Leave the youngster instead with a friend or relative, a sitter, or her other parent. After all, having an active toddler running about with you is quite different from carrying a sleeping infant in a front pack. And all mothers and fathers, however devoted they are to their children, need time they can call their own—to recharge their "parenting" batteries.

THE NEW SIBLING

There is never an ideal time, at least for your toddler, to welcome a new baby into the family. At least initially, a baby brother or sister can seem more like an unwanted interloper than a playmate and companion.

Look at it from a child's perspective. When the sibling is a newborn, it simply sleeps, nurses, and monopolizes all the attention. When it's a bit older, a younger sibling begins to scoot after your toys. She interferes with your play, knocking down the block tower, crawling off with the doll's bottle. It's little wonder that many parents observe resentment and jealousy in their older child; it is a wonder that so many parents are surprised by their toddler's negative reaction to the new baby. Just because you are delighted, don't expect your older child to be, as a toddler does not automatically understand that parents can love more than one child.

Many parents try to mitigate their child's resentment by having another baby at the most opportune time. However, no one seems to agree at what age a child can best handle a sibling. She will have strong feelings regardless of timing—it's a big change. Therefore, decide to have another child when you feel you can handle it.

Though it's best not to tell your child that a baby is coming in the early weeks of the pregnancy, try to tell her before she hears it from someone else. Also, she may overhear you talking and begin to worry that something bad is about to happen to you. If you see that happening, sit down and talk to her. Explain to her that the baby is growing inside of you and let her feel it move. This may be a good time to talk briefly about where babies come from.

Some hospitals have sibling programs to help demystify the event. A couple of weeks before your due date, discuss with your child your plans for delivery, who will stay with her, and when she will be able to visit you in the hospital.

Having another baby inevitably changes the strong attachment between the parents and the older child. Parents should be careful to remain sensitive to the first child and not to turn too abruptly or too sharply away.

As a mother subtly shifts her focus toward the needs of the younger child, more room may open up for the toddler to experiment with greater independence. Since a toddler naturally strives to act more grown up and begins to identify with the adults in the family, she may be willing, even eager to help with the baby.

Siblings learn much sociable behavior from interacting with each other. They learn what behavior is okay and not okay in the context of a safe, permanent relationship. Within this relationship, they learn to share and compromise. These are not always easy lessons, but in the long run, they are essential to healthy development.

VISITING THE DOCTOR

Beginning with a toddler's one-year checkup, visits to the doctor take on a whole new quality. There is a good chance that a child will be able to walk into the examining room on her own two feet, if not at this visit then at the next.

Starting with the one-year visit, your child will no longer be as passive and compliant at checkups. In most cases, the doctor will actively engage the child, rather than rely exclusively on you to report progress. The doctor may take advantage of the child's curiosity to override her wariness by showing her the stethoscope and otoscope. Perhaps together, they will examine her doll before turning the attention to her. As a result, visits to the doctor after a baby's first year tend to take longer.

During the toddler years, most pediatricians schedule well-child care visits for twelve months, eighteen months, two years, and three years. At her one-year checkup she will get an MMR shot (measles, mumps, rubella). She may also be given an oral polio immunization, HiB (Hepatitis B), and DPT (diphtheria, tetanus, and pertussis) shots at this visit, though some practitioners wait until the eighteen-month examination for these. Many pediatricians have also begun administering a chicken pox vaccine.

Each exam will include measuring and weighing the child, a general physical exam, and a developmental assessment. At one year, for example, the doctor will evaluate the child's ability to sit independently, to pull up and cruise, to walk, to reach for and grab objects, to look for dropped or hidden objects, to respond to her name, to use a cup, to feed herself a bit, to use basic words, and to enjoy social games like peekaboo. If there are any questions or doubts about your child's vision and hearing, ask your child's doctor to examine the child (see *Language and Speech Development*, page 5).

In the eighteen-month visit, the child will probably be interested in participating, but when asked, may refuse adamantly. This surge of negativism and autonomy will exist side by side with her enormous curiosity and appear in her interactions with the doctor.

As the child marches in at her two-year visit, the developmental strides will be dramatic, especially in terms of self-confidence, competence, speech, gender identification, and handedness.

The next visit will be at three years, and in many cases, is in preparation for preschool. Your child is growing up, faster than you can fathom.

3

The Preschool Years

AGES THREE, FOUR, AND FIVE

■　■　■

From infancy through toddlerhood, children develop at an extraordinarily rapid pace. As they near their third birthdays, the rate of growth slows down, and the changes they undergo become less apparent.

Yet the transition from toddler to preschooler seems particularly sudden and a bit magical. One moment a child is a perplexing, changeable, and often volatile creature, unfolding and forming before your very eyes. The next moment, it seems, he has become a relatively sophisticated, sociable, reasonable human being—at least most of the time.

Past the age of three, a child is clearly no longer an infant. He has lost his baby fat, his legs have grown longer and thinner, and he moves around with much more confidence and competence. Chances are he can control his bowels and bladder, ride a tricycle, and dress himself. Listen to him talk: He is developing theories about everything, and testing those theories against the realities around him.

During these years, some decision-making and caregiving subtly shifts from the parents to the child. Part of this shift is due to the fact that, increasingly, a child can manage a larger share of safety and security concerns. He can brush his teeth, put on his coat, get his breakfast cereal out of the pantry. As competence increases, your hands-on, routine care lessens. You can devote more time and energy to ushering him into a wider world of people, things, and ideas, and spend less time actually doing things for him.

Part of the shift is due to the magic of language. Between the ages of three and six, most children are able to use language in more thoughtful and sophisticated ways. More and more, they use words instead of only actions. They describe their troubles rather than cry. Once they relied on hitting and biting when they were angry or wanted something. Now they listen to the voices of their inner development and try a little negotiating instead.

Part of the shift is due to a preschooler's entry into a larger world. This is the age of socialization. By the time a child is three, he enters into the world of other children. Many children at this age engage for the first time in more formal social and intellectual experiences, in playgroups and nursery school.

At the same time, a preschool child is not so accomplished in all areas. At three, he cannot hold a pencil correctly, tie a shoe, or button a button. He cannot concentrate too long on any one thing. His logic relies upon magic; his reasoning is inconsistent and not very rational. In his increasingly elaborate conversations and play, he abruptly follows tangents that make sense only to him. On his way to put clothes in the hamper, he will likely get distracted by a book on the floor or a toy on the desk.

Despite developing independence and competence, he still requires help. But now he is more willing to turn not only to his parents but to others, such as other family members, baby sitters, teachers, an older sibling, peers at preschool. With a sense of emotional security established during the infant and toddler years, the preschooler is eager to look beyond the immediate world and reach out to a larger, more complex social world.

Milestones

This period of childhood appears to be a distinctive stage, with its own special modes of thinking, feeling, and action. In other respects, it appears to be the beginning of a long period of gradual change that extends into adolescence and adulthood. In many ways, this is the time when your child, primed with his unique style and temperament, his sense of belonging and attachment, steps out to make his solo debut into the world.

■ PHYSICAL DEVELOPMENT

A child's physical growth rate continues to slow during the preschool period. Within these three years, a child typically evolves from a round, plump three-year-old, to a slimmer, elongated five-year-old. Until children develop a more muscular tone later on, most go from the plumpness of a toddler to a rather frail looking, reedy preschooler.

Few developmental feats receive more attention around ages three and four than a child's acquisition of voluntary control over the muscles that govern elimination—that is, toilet training.

In the early months of life, elimination is involuntary. When the baby's bladder or bowels are full, his body acts automatically to empty them. Although some children can be taught to eliminate when placed on a potty at five or six months of age, they are not capable of postponing elimination before fifteen months. While some children are able to remain dry during the day by the time they are two and a half years old, most do not achieve such control until after their third birthday. They usually do not learn to stay dry while they are asleep until they are even older. However, by the time they reach preschool age, most are struggling with, and many are succeeding at trading in their diapers for underwear.

■ INTELLECTUAL AND COGNITIVE DEVELOPMENT

In toddlerhood, thinking was based on trial and error. By the elementary school years, a complete shift is made, and thinking will be based on internal processes. The preschool era is the time of this transition.

During this period of growth, a child's abilities to understand, to process and express information, to solve problems, to

remember, and to concentrate are uneven. A preschooler vacillates between logic and magic, understanding and quandary, the reasoned and the unreasonable.

For example, a child effortlessly recalls details of trips to the park, names of dinosaurs, or the location of his favorite toy. But he forgets where he put his coat when he came home, or to brush his teeth before climbing into bed.

Yet, despite the inconsistent quality, the gains preschoolers make in all areas of cognition are significant. As memory becomes stronger and more sophisticated, they can remember from one day to the next, and apply what they learned yesterday to what they are doing today. They begin to anticipate and plan for tomorrow.

Because they can look forward, children can wait a bit. Now, when you mention that grandmother will visit in the afternoon, or that your child can have a special treat after dinner, he can exercise some patience. He remembers that you offered to bake brownies tomorrow and no longer insists frantically on helping you today.

As children's capacities to hold on to thought and emotion expand, they begin making simple choices. Because they remember what they enjoyed last time, they can state what they prefer now.

In addition to memory, a child's attention span and problem-solving capacities grow in sophistication. Children become increasingly creative in the ways they approach tasks. They can sit attentively for longer periods of time, working on a puzzle, for example. With a startling abruptness, though, they may become frustrated, unable to move forward or complete the task, or simply lose interest.

By the age of three, children have the basic ability to allow one thing to represent another. This kind of symbolic thinking is reflected in their ability to use words to stand for objects, people, and actions, and to engage in pretend play. They begin to solve problems through thinking (anticipating and guessing at solutions) rather than depending completely on trial and error. They can imitate actions that they have observed some time in the past in entirely different circumstances.

Even as a preschooler's thinking becomes more sophisticated and rational, the child holds on to old ideas and ways of thinking and this creates confusion. While preschool children have an increasing ability to tolerate and use symbolic thinking, they may continue to have difficulty distinguishing between appearance and reality. For example, a child will become frightened by someone wearing a Halloween mask because he thinks the mask has really changed the person into a witch or a monster.

At four, a child worries that having bad thoughts will actually cause bad results. When children are very angry, they may think about killing people, being robbers, or setting fires. At this age, the child can believe that his thoughts are transformed magically into terrible actions, and that he will be punished.

Around the age of five, a child begins to recognize the difference between thinking and doing. He begins to see that thoughts and actions are not the same, and that his thoughts do not magically produce effects.

Children become more logical in their thinking, and better able to soothe their anxious feelings and control their own behavior.

By a child's sixth birthday, his knowledge of the objective world and grasp of cause and effect have become more sophisticated. Now children demand proof for the information they receive. Adult assertions of fact are often met with the question *How do you know? Why?*

At this age there are also limitations. The child's knowledge is limited, in many areas, uncertain and distorted. After learning about the earth's orbit around the sun, a child riding in a car might announce with great confidence: *I feel the earth going around the sun.* Children at this age still have difficulty in reconciling what they are told with what their own logic and senses tell them.

Thinking may become distorted or confused when information is colored by strong emotion. A mother may have a basic conversation about sex, birth, and babies, for example, only to be asked by her child later, *Didn't you tell me that babies come out of belly buttons?*

By and large, a preschooler's ability to understand and accomplish a task depends on the nature and presentation of the task. Preschoolers do best when they are interested in a task, when information is presented slowly in a supportive way, and when the context is familiar or they have adequate background knowledge.

■ LANGUAGE DEVELOPMENT

When your child was an infant, it was necessary for you to read and interpret the communications he expressed with his body, cries, and early utterances. Although you talked to your child, he responded mostly to your tone; your words meant little. Rather than explain, you showed him that he was safe, loved, and important by picking him up and talking to him when he cried, feeding him, holding him, and returning his smile.

When he was a toddler, you began to use language as a way of establishing a symbolic bond. When your child wandered away from you and found himself frightened by his aloneness, you were able to call out to him and he reconnected with your voice and your words. Still, your relationship relied primarily on nonverbal and bodily communications. When he had a tantrum, you held him. When he reached for the hot stove, you grabbed his hand and said, *No, that's hot!*

Preschoolers react to their world primarily through behavior. They express a great deal through tears and tantrums. Yet now they also possess enough language and their thinking has become adequately complex to be able to join adults in their world of words.

The pace at which individual children acquire and use speech varies enormously. One child may use few words until he is almost three, then start chattering with age-appropriate speech. Another may have several words before he turns one then add very few in the next year. Others start talking at eighteen months and progress steadily.

As long as children participate in human activity and are exposed to language as part of that activity, they acquire language. Learning to speak and understand language does not require any special tutoring. This sug-

gests that all children are born with the capability to acquire language. Note, however, that children who have not developed basic language by thirty-six months of age should be evaluated by their family physicians (see *Developmental Disorders*, page 354).

Language enables children to experience the world in entirely new ways. It is the medium through which parents instruct their children about their roles in the world, about acceptable behavior, and how the world works. Language provides the means by which children ask questions, explain their thoughts and desires, and make more effective demands on people around them.

Language also permits children to forge symbolic connections with the people who care for them. They can thus move away from you physically while maintaining an internal mental connection. You ask, *What did you do in school today?* and suddenly you are included in your child's world. Your child asks: *Where'd you go, Mommy?* and, as you recount the details, the child is able to recall being with you the last time you went to the store.

Using language becomes more complex and diverse once children have passed the toddler stage. Toddlers use their first words to label or comment on what they see. As they develop, they begin to use language for its uniquely human purpose, for talking about things that are not in the room but in their heads, and for expressing ideas that are theirs alone.

Children learn how things work and what they themselves can do through language. Through play and pretend, they put themselves, imaginatively, into other people's places. For example, when a child pretends that he is a librarian, he mimics or creates speech for the character.

Development of language, thought, and intelligence are interwoven. Although a child's ability to talk early is not always a sign of intelligence, in general, the more language a child has, the faster thinking will progress. The more thinking he does, the more language he will use.

As their speech and awareness of the separateness of the listener become more sophisticated, children move from indirect requests *(Bunny's in my crib)* to direct requests *(Give me bunny).* They begin to modify their speech in order to include the listener. When a four-year-old is speaking to a two-year-old, he will shorten his sentences, speak more slowly, and simplify both vocabulary and grammar to make it easier for the younger child to understand.

Young children commonly confuse pronouns when they speak. The use of *you, me,* or *he* depends upon who is talking. To avoid confusion, they will often use proper names and avoid using pronouns altogether: *Baby get dolly* or *Mommy help Joey.*

Typically, a preschool child's ideas are bigger than his vocabulary. Many find it difficult to express thoughts smoothly. There may be a flood of ideas that overwhelms them while they search for the right words. A child may hesitate, repeat syllables, and pause frequently. This may resemble stuttering.

Just listen to what your child has to say. Don't hurry him or finish his sentences or direct him to speak more clearly or slowly. If he is made to think about producing words perfectly, he will likely stumble.

Most three- and four-year-olds are chatterboxes. No matter how familiar or tiring it may be to hear your child go on and on, it is important for him to talk. He's practicing a marvelous new skill. As you spend time listening and having conversations with him, he will continually improve his language skills.

■ SOCIAL AND EMOTIONAL DEVELOPMENT

Some facets of individual personality are visible at birth. Newborns display differences in style that are labeled *temperament* in their levels of activity, responses to frustration, and readiness to engage in new experiences (see *Temperament,* page 14). These traits remain relatively stable over time. Children who draw back from new experiences in infancy are likely to show shyness later when they go to nursery school.

By the time they reach preschool age, a child's personality has begun to evolve. Through interacting with the world, children acquire other traits and characteristics, such as honesty, compulsiveness, loyalty, frugality, compliance, directness, a desire to please. It is usually at this point that you can see the beginning of a child's unique *personality.*

At this age, it becomes essentially impossible to tease out distinct threads in a child's development since emotional development becomes intertwined with social development. Language acquisition and cognitive gains interlace, and in turn, connect with social and emotional threads. This complex development is the basis of the child's growing awareness of his own distinct self as separate from an objective world. This emerging sense of self provides the basis of human relationships.

Crucial to the development of a child's personality is the feedback he receives from others. A five-year-old boy, for example, who carries his chewed-up teddy to school may be discouraged by his parents and teased by his peers. At some point, because of feedback he will make a choice, perhaps opting to wear a favorite cap to school instead of bringing his teddy. A child has to learn not to pinch his baby sister. Instead, he must find some socially acceptable way of dealing with his jealousy and anger.

A child's earliest emotions (like pleasure, anger, disgust, surprise, and fear) are often self-referential. By preschool years, children can experience emotions in relation to others. They feel embarrassment when they attract unwelcome attention. They feel guilty when they fail to live up to the standards they have internalized. They feel envy when someone else receives praise, attention, or an object they want for themselves. They feel pride when they have excelled and others praise their successes and accomplishments.

When children view their actions and thoughts as the cause of all things, they are not able to learn about cause and effect in the real world outside. When a toddler believes that he causes the car to go and the traffic light to change, he can't develop even an elementary concept of how these things work.

When a child does not know that he is separate from others, he confuses his motives with those of others and attributes his thoughts to others. Until he comes to understand his separateness, his knowledge of the world of people and objects is limited and distorted.

On the other hand, when a child cannot grasp that he is similar to others, he has not developed social intelligence. Until he develops this capability, he will not be able to empathize and identify with others. This empathic capacity is needed in order to live as a member of society and forms the basis of conscience.

At three, a child asserts his belief in his own omnipotence and magical powers: *I have superhuman powers. No one tells me what to do. I can destroy you if you don't play with me on the playground.* None of his peers will contradict him, even if they don't quite believe him.

By his sixth birthday, a child's plans and ideas may still be grand, but they are modified by a sense of limits and consideration for others. The child has moved beyond an egocentric view of the world to understand that he is not the cause and center of the universe. Others have rights, motives, sensibilities, and feelings which must be understood and taken into account. At this age, children are also beginning to incorporate basic values and a standard of good and bad. Increasingly they are able to live up to those standards and to create plans of their own that they then can measure against adult standards.

Once children can set goals for themselves and realize that there are standards of performance that they must meet, they begin to interact with adults in a new way. They actively seek their parents' help in reaching goals and meeting standards. This marks the beginning of cooperation and self-initiated, interactive learning.

By the time they reach their sixth birthday, children have more humility about the larger social context where there are rules and standards with penalties for violating them. A child must now weigh his own ambition and self-interest against the ambitions, interests, and standards of others. At this age, a good portion of a child's self-love has been transformed to include others. The child has learned to give to others what he desires for himself.

You can see this transformation in the way your child relates to you. As an infant, you were an appendage whose sole purpose was to respond and cater to him. The realization that you had desires to do anything other than look after him was an affront. By preschool, however, he can acknowledge without being overcome by rage that you have rights and feelings. As he internalizes you as a real, whole person, his love for you changes to include unselfish sympathy and concern. He is now capable of giving as well as taking—and giving what you want, not what he would like himself.

A child's development results from the interaction between socialization and personality formation. Through socialization children acquire standards, values, and knowledge of their society. Through individual personality formation every child comes to have his own unique ways of feeling and behaving.

By the time children are six years old, just as most enter into a full school program, they have learned a great deal about the roles they are expected to play and how to behave in accordance with them; how to control aggressive feelings; and how to respect the rights of others. At the same time, they have developed a clearer sense of themselves, their abilities, and the ways they react in different situations.

Eating

A three-year-old has probably joined the rest of the family at the table. Family meals offer rich opportunities to learn and practice budding social skills. He will learn manners by example, and imitate the behavior of others around the table.

He should have his own place at the table, set just like all the other places. Let him feed himself with a spoon and a fork, drink from a cup, spoon servings onto his own plate, and perhaps even pour his own drink from a small pitcher. He is proud of his developing agility and skill.

Because they spend enormous energy in their daily lives, preschoolers are often big eaters. When offered healthy and varied foods, they will take in enough calories and adequate nutrition. There is no reason to push any particular food. Nor is there reason to restrict foods unless your child has food allergies (see *Food Intolerance and Food Allergy,* page 282). Usually, whatever you prepare for the rest of the family, in most any form, is good enough to offer to your youngster. Help him acquire new tastes, and get him used to foods that your family likes.

Remember, mealtimes should be pleasant family times.

At the same time as you encourage social behavior around the table, allow for his individual style. As children acquire and assert personal taste, they may seem like picky eaters. Some children pass through phases where they refuse to eat anything that is not green. Others insist on noodles at every meal. Even when a child's tastes differ from yours, it is best to be patient and not overly critical. Mealtimes are more enjoyable and food will be less of an issue or problem in the future if power struggles are avoided.

Toilet Training

A baby learns that if he sits in a high chair, he will be fed when he's hungry. He learns to feed himself so he can control what goes into his mouth and when. He learns to walk so that he can move toward things that attract him and away from things that frighten him. He can quickly find you at your desk or follow you into the kitchen. The benefits to these kinds of learning are obvious.

But as far as your child is concerned, the benefits of learning to use the toilet are not so obvious. Performing on the potty may please you and make your child feel a bit more grown up, but that may not convince him. For you, though, the benefits are clear and compelling. This kind of scenario has all the makings of a power struggle.

Don't begin toilet training your child before he is physically capable; you will be asking him to do something he is not mature enough to do. The result may be stress, frustration, tantrums, and defiance. It may even mean that he will delay mastering this milestone or, after finally reaching it, he may feel defeated rather than accomplished. You cannot make him use the potty before he is ready and willing.

Most girls are unlikely to learn to stay dry—even during the day—before their third year and boys may be somewhat later. Starting too early may mean a longer process. Beginning later when children are ready may allow them to learn faster.

Until about fifteen months, your child takes care of his body functions automatically, without any thought. He doesn't realize that he needs to urinate or move his bowels. Nor does he realize that he has done so.

Somewhere between his first and second year, though, he begins to make the connection between the feelings inside his body and the bowel movement or urine he produces. He clutches himself in anticipation and watches what passes out of him. But, at this age, he still doesn't know what to do about it.

If he has a comfortable and secure place to sit and practice—a potty-chair, for example, that can't tip over (one with a removable bowl makes cleaning easier for you)—he will likely experiment and mimic what he sees adults doing.

Introduce the potty only when your child knows what it is used for. Tell him that the potty is where he will put his pee or poop when he is ready. Explain that when he can do that regularly, he can stop wearing diapers. (You might also promise to take him shopping for "big boy" underwear as added incentive.)

Place the potty in the corner of his playroom where he can become friendly with it. Perhaps he'll put his dolls on it. Perhaps he'll take the bowl out and put water in it. Eventually, he will want to sit there himself, probably fully clothed. Do not rush him along by insisting on taking his diaper off. When he is ready to actually use the potty, he will let you know.

Watch for cues that he is about to urinate or have a bowel movement: he may clutch himself, go red in the face, crawl under the table. Then ask if he wants to sit on the potty.

Most children move their bowels once or twice a day. Some are more naturally regular so that you can anticipate their need. Also, a child will usually signal a bowel movement by the look on his face, or by moving to a more private place. The interval between the child's first feeling and the actual event is often quite long. If the child is emotionally ready to cooperate in using the potty, you can use that stretch of time to get him settled.

If the child says no, don't push. If he says yes, stay with him while he's on the potty. Congratulate him when he does produce. Faced with a low-key or casual introduction and the right timing, many children will bowel train themselves fairly quickly.

If your child does not, proceed with respect and patience. Don't force him to sit on the potty, even if you see that he is about to soil his diaper. Try to stay as neutral as possible. If he succeeds on the potty, praise him lightly, and if he does not, don't register disappointment, frustration, or criticism. Also, try not to show disgust if your child

shows an interest in playing with his feces.

For most children, it is a long, slow process before they can stay dry. Early on, the feelings that signal urination usually come around the same time as the flood. *I'm going to. . .* happens simultaneously with *I peed.* Children urinate many times in the day and, when they are absorbed in play, they may not notice their need to go. There are bound to be accidents in the day.

At night, they cannot wake themselves to urinate. Months after your child has stopped wearing diapers during the day, he may still need one at night and during naps.

It is most important for successful toilet training, and for his budding self-esteem, that a child experience a sense of success and achievement. Perhaps after a nap, you notice that his diaper is still dry. Leaving his bottom bare, ask him if he'd like to sit on the potty. If he says no, or sits for only a minute without doing anything, don't comment. If he urinates on the way or as he gets sidetracked by play, clean up the puddle without comment and dress him as usual.

Once he's able to urinate in the potty, offer gentle congratulations, then put a diaper on as usual. After a few successes, without making a big deal of it and without communicating expectations, take the child out of diapers when he's at home and awake. Mop up any accidents casually. Then move up to plastic-coated terry-towel training pants. These will not absorb the whole urination but will reduce flood damage. They are comfortable, and a child can pull them up and down. Continue to use diapers for naps, nights, and trips.

Around this time, a child may show interest in the adult toilet. He will need a firm stool or bench to help him climb on and off, and a small seat clipped over the large one so that he doesn't have to worry about falling in. He may be frightened by the sucking sound that flushing produces—he may fear that he too will be sucked away. If he appears scared about flushing the toilet himself, it may help to wait until he's left the room to flush.

Even when it seems that a child is fully trained, there will be accidents. But once he's accomplished enough to give up diapers, he should not go back. Nor should you threaten, argue, or constantly remind him to go. He needs to develop an awareness of his body and not rely on others to remind him.

Even though there will be times when you need him to go—right before you dress him in a snowsuit for a long car ride into town, for example—he will not be able to urinate unless he feels the need. Nor will he be able to wait until it is convenient for you. Instead, develop your toilet-finding skills, and be sure in the early months to carry a change of clothes.

One last note: Parents may be tempted to toilet train one child just as a new baby arrives. But for many older children, this won't seem like the best time to give up his babyish ways, especially when the new baby is getting all the attention.

Sleeping

By the time children are three, most take only a short afternoon nap or have given up napping altogether. However, after a day of negotiating an increasingly complex social world, a preschooler, whether he naps or not, may welcome the opportunity for a quiet time alone to regroup.

By this age, children naturally feel both a need for privacy and a sense of ownership. Quiet time spent in a special space that is exclusively theirs is particularly valuable. His space, whether it's his room or a corner of a room, should be bright, cheerful, and attractive.

Because this is a space for relaxing, playing, and sleeping, it is probably best not to use your child's room as a site for punishment (which might also inadvertently reward the child with the toys, games, and other amusements the room may contain). Occasionally restricting a child to his room may be called for, but if the youngster's room is used for punishment rather than a refuge, he may come to dread being there.

While toddlers typically fuss about going to bed, by the time a child reaches his third birthday he might not fuss at all. Some children, though, continue to struggle before letting go at night.

As when he was younger, a preschooler will respond to special rituals that announce when bedtime is coming. Bedtime can be much more than mere preparation for sleep. It's a time to wind down as a family, to talk casually about the events of the day and about concerns children have as they anticipate another day.

Don't expect your child to break off in the middle of play or watching television and go immediately to bed. Instead, give him warning that bedtime is coming. Then use the remaining time to wash up, brush his teeth, and perhaps read together. If you suddenly feel pressed to get him into bed, his last experience of the day will be of your nagging and rushing. Read to him in bed rather than in a family room, thereby underscoring the coziness and security of his own room.

When you say good night and leave his room, you may want to promise to return and check on him at some point in the evening. If you make this promise, though, be sure to keep it.

Once a child is in bed, make it clear that you expect him to stay there. That may mean that you sit with him a bit longer; he also must be able to trust that someone will come when he calls.

Because a child this age is only recently toilet trained, he may need to get out of bed to go to the bathroom. Many children use the bathroom as an excuse to get up. A plastic undersheet and a relaxed attitude about accidents will ease a child's anxiety and make bedtime a more peaceful time.

There will be nights when your child has problems falling or staying asleep. As they are dozing off, some children experience vivid images which may be scary or alarming. As a child's mind relaxes into sleep, the imagination takes over and embroiders daytime images. Long after you thought he had fallen asleep, your child may cry or call for you. He might complain that he can't sleep or describe monsters or robbers. Reassure him that he is safe, that there are no monsters or robbers and that you're nearby.

His thoughts and anxiety may come directly from stories he has heard, television shows he's watched, fragments of conversations or news stories he's overheard. Family quarrels or upsets can also lead to trouble sleeping. It might be a good idea to monitor and censor his television viewing or his bedtime stories. If he has heard or witnessed something that upsets him, explain it as truthfully and clearly as is suitable for a child this age.

Every child has reasons to be anxious and, from time to time, anxiety will surface in nightmares. If your child cries out, see if he can calm himself before you respond. If he is unable to and comes to you for support, offer reassurance, tuck him back into bed, and encourage him to return to sleep despite this brief, scary interruption.

Recurring nightmares or night terrors may also occur in children of this age (see *Nightmares,* page 380, and *Night Terrors,* page 381).

Play

During preschool years, the quality of a child's play is characterized by an increasingly sophisticated ability to think, to imagine, pretend, and to create within his head.

A child this age begins to appreciate differences and similarities. His play shows a growing interest in and ability to sort, group, and categorize. He gathers and arranges blocks according to color, shape, or size. He groups all the farm animals in one corner of his play space and the jungle animals in another.

His play progresses from simple attempts to copy or imitate play adults to more sophisticated symbolic play. By the third year, a child can hold some abstract ideas, and concepts that describe things which are not visible, present, or real, so that his play goes beyond mere imitation. A child this age begins to create actively in his play.

Increasingly, pretend play becomes more complex. When he plays pirate, he knows which pieces of clothing to wear, what props to use, what tone of voice to take. He acts out an elaborate drama, complete with dialogue, in the toy parking garage, concluding with a fire truck driving up to put out the fire on the top floor.

As preschoolers begin to show curiosity about (and want to identify with or incorporate) adult standards and behavior, they will be drawn to toys that resemble adult domestic equipment—stoves, tools, and garden sets.

Dolls and stuffed toys function on several levels at once. They guard a child's bed at night after Mom and Dad say good night. They people his imaginary world, eating at his restaurant, learning to read in his classroom.

Not only is a child's ability to think evolving, but his body and his manual dexterity are gaining greater refinement and agility. He can think about how something works and then make it work. He can think about color, then apply it to paper. A child can pretend to be someone else—a bus driver, a doctor, or a playgroup leader, and manipulate the props for his make-believe.

Preschoolers still need suitable play spaces, varied equipment, unscheduled time, companionship, and, from time to time, assistance. Because home has become familiar, they may crave new experiences, new people, and new objects to feed the imagination. Perhaps you can meet your preschooler's imaginative hunger by involving him more fully in daily activities like gardening, cooking, and shopping.

His world may expand within the social world of the neighborhood. He will want to join other children, perhaps going from yard to yard, house to house. You might take him for frequent visits to a nearby playground. Or you may choose to enroll him in regular, structured preschool activities. In all instances converse with him, share your ideas, impressions, observations, and provide information.

■ ARTS AND CRAFTS

Making and creating are important aspects of play and learning at this age. A child has discovered how felt-tipped markers and scissors work. He uses them, not so much to explore as for the fun of creating. If you ask him if he's just drawn a lion, he will probably shrug his shoulders. It hardly matters that his painting doesn't look like anyone or anything—it's a *painting*.

A child's drawing goes through a series of identifiable stages. At three he draws circles and vertical lines. Soon, he makes horizontal lines. Then he combines circular marks with linear marks to make something that resembles a figure.

A very young child draws first and labels afterward. By the time he is four, he might be able to draw a person purposely. By his fifth year, a child's drawings will seem more life-like. When he's five, he may produce a figure with a distinct head and body, legs with feet, arms with hands, and perhaps clothes indicated by buttons and belts. Preschoolers also love playing with sand and water, play dough or soft modeling clay.

■ GENDER DIFFERENCES IN PLAY

Even the most casual observer will note that boys and girls play differently from an early age. Children as young as fourteen months may play with toys traditional to their gender. Boys are more likely to play with trucks and cars while girls choose dolls and soft toys; often they have been given and encouraged to play with gender-specific toys.

Although some boys play with dolls or in the house corner at preschool, by the age of four most become less comfortable with such playthings. While girls sometimes adopt roles of Wonderwoman or Supergirl, they tend to prefer domestic play. By five, the girls will defend their domestic calm against aggressive raids by boys pretending to be superheroes and pirates.

Just what accounts for children's developing ideas and preferences concerning sex-role identities is a subject of much debate. It appears that children become explicitly aware that males and females belong to different social categories around their third birthday; thereafter, and almost always at age five, they tend to prefer to play with children of the same gender and with gender-specific toys. It is not clear how much of this is due to innate gender differences, and how much is determined by parental and social expectations and stereotypes.

THE "WHY" QUESTION

Why is the sky blue? Why do clouds move? Nothing is more characteristic of preschoolers than their love of asking *Why?*

It may be surprising to any parent who has been besieged with such questions that, unlike older children, preschoolers are not yet capable of engaging in cause-and-effect reasoning. They do not reason from the general to the particular (deduction) or from the particular to the general (induction). But rather they think *transductively,* from one particular to another. As a result, they often confuse cause and effect. Because hospitals are full of sick people, they cause sickness; therefore, if you stay away from hospitals, you will not get sick.

A three-year-old who needs more words will reach out for them by asking *What's that?* Naturally, you provide the names for him. Soon, he will progress to *why* questions. *Why is it cold?* As a toddler, had he thought of the question in the first place, he would have tried to find out by trial and error. A preschooler can imagine a broader range of possibilities. The fact that he asks *why* is a sign that he is growing up.

The endless whys can be trying. Asking why can be a way of capturing your attention or asking you to continue talking. Often you don't know the answer. Some whys are simply unanswerable. If you can, answer briefly. If not, you can answer: *That's a good question. I'd like to think about it.* Or *Why don't we go to the library and see if we can find the answer.* Or *What do you think?*

Sometimes, when his questions seem particularly perplexing, you can ask him to talk about what he would like to understand better. Sometimes, the best way to attend to a question is to turn the spotlight back on the inquisitor.

The World of Fantasy

In the third and fourth years, a child's imagination begins to take off. For him, the boundary between reality and fantasy is shifting. He lives in a world where grandmothers live in woods, are eaten by big bad wolves, then resurrected by passing woodsmen. Gradually, though, with age, he understands that such stories are not real.

Children at this age watch everyone around them in new ways. They learn about people mainly by observation and occasionally by imagining elaborate dramas about them. By three, they can use what they imagine to create imaginary characters of their own.

Children often endeavor to become someone else. They notice activities among adults and, instead of merely mimicking, as they did as toddlers, they now try to put themselves imaginatively into the place of another. When a child becomes a baker, he thinks beyond the apron, cap, and flour; he will include the smells of the bread, the tastes of the pies, and the language of the baker. When preschoolers play dress-up, they don't rely on elaborate costumes. They are able to change characters mentally. Props become important. They cook play-dough chicken in a play kitchen. With swords, they become knights; an eye patch makes one of them into a pirate.

Sometimes, children use dramatic play to relive experiences that were emotionally important to them. They become doctors and nurses to reenact a night in the hospital or a visit to the doctor. A child who witnesses a fire may rush home to play a firefighter rescuing a family from a burning building.

At this age, a child's imagination is vivid, complicated, and exciting. Fantasy plays a large role in thinking, in the acquisition of language, in play and social interactions. Through imagination, children are able to assimilate new learning, develop empathy and a sense of humor, and begin to develop conscience. In general, fantasy helps children understand the complexity of the world.

IMAGINARY FRIENDS

Many children between the age of three and five—particularly first or only children—acquire imaginary friends. Imaginary friends are born out of a child's increasing ability to engage in imaginative play and growing separation from the adults who live with them.

Imaginary friends serve many purposes. They provide companionship and ease feelings of loneliness and isolation. They enable a child to have control over some aspects of his life at a time when he can feel particularly vulnerable or uncertain. For children who feel that adults are forever bossing them around, an imaginary friend gives a young child someone to boss around.

A pretend playmate can act out a child's imaginary experiences. Imaginary friends perform miracles, doing all the bad things and experiencing all the good things that a child can only dream of. They can personify all a child's vices while allowing him to hold on to all of the virtues for himself. His imaginary companion can ride horses or fly. He can leave home and live on his own when parents yell. A child would never bite, but his pretend friend does. His friend can be blamed for spilling the cup of milk.

A child will talk about his imaginary friend as if he were real. The friend becomes a beloved and cherished companion. Parents accustomed to being everything to their child may feel a bit jealous. They may also worry about their child's lapse from reality.

In most cases, there is nothing to worry about. Children who create imaginary companions tend to be more imaginative and creative in other areas of play as well. In addition, when imaginary companions become the depository of a child's vices, they mark the beginning of self-criticism. As a child increasingly distinguishes between good and bad, the act of casting off the bad on to his pretend playmate indicates that he is setting up opposition to his own unacceptable tendencies. In that way, imaginary friends represent a step in the child's developing conscience and value system.

Imaginary play should be encouraged and respected as revealing growth of his inner world. If parents ask too many questions or talk too much about their child's fantasies, they trespass on the private and precious nature of such fantasies.

Rather than being angry the child blames his imaginary playmate for his own mistakes, parents can gently explain that it isn't possible for the pretend friend to have done the deed. If a child is older and strongly denies that the imaginary friend is pretend, or if he prefers this friend to the exclusion of developing actual friendships, discuss your concerns with your child's doctor. In the majority of cases, however, imaginary friends help a child make the transition from his own fantasy to a more masterful relationship with the world of real people. As children develop more social skills, most imaginary friends fade away.

Lying

Everyone tells an occasional lie because there is a discrepancy between what is true and what they wish were true. But for preschoolers, there is no distinction between reality and their wishes.

A child accidentally breaks his sister's doll, wishes he hadn't, and wants to avoid getting into trouble. So he claims that the doll fell apart by itself. This is not necessarily lying because the child doesn't know what telling the truth is.

Preschoolers live in a lively world of imagination, surrounded by Santa Claus and the Easter Bunny, by talking animals and stalking cartoon dinosaurs. For children, the line between reality and fantasy is constantly blurring and shifting. It is hard to hold a young child responsible for a realistic and accurate rendition of his impressions and experiences when his life is edged in fairy stories and animal tales. What parents consider to be lying, then, may actually be wishful thinking.

For many parents, the fact that their child lies compounds any act the child may have committed. It's bad enough that the doll is broken, but to see your child speak an untruth can be even more maddening. However, if you confront your preschooler with lying, he may be puzzled. He is probably not capable of connecting the word *lying* and its meaning with his act.

It is important to make it easy for your child to be honest. Approach the child with *What happened to the doll?* instead of *Whoever broke this toy is in big trouble.* Once your child tells the truth, don't overwhelm him with anger or punishment. If you react to his confession with fury, he won't be so likely to admit to his guilt and tell the truth in the future.

Children learn more from what parents do than what they say. Children often hear their parents lie to be tactful or kind or for other reasons. Therefore, it is confusing if you punish the child for lying—but then ask them to tell someone on the phone that you aren't home because you don't want to talk.

Most often, the best approach is to accept the preschooler's lively imagination and broader sense of the truth. Through their vivid or distorted stores, children are often communicating that they need more attention or that they are worried about something.

Preschoolers, however, can begin to understand why truth matters and begin to learn the distinction between what is true and what is not. Rather than viewing lying as an absolute wrong as well as a reason for scolding, you can use it as opportunity to talk with your child and help him develop a sense of truthfulness and honesty.

Shyness

It is perfectly natural for children two and up to become shy when separated from their parents or when they come into contact with unfamiliar people. The majority of children overcome feelings of shyness as they learn and practice social skills.

Most children need some time to warm up and get used to their surroundings. They might cling to their parents when they meet someone they hardly know. When they enter a large group, even with some familiar faces, children may feel shy. They may hold back from joining in, even when the activities seem like fun.

Parents help most by not forcing the issue or criticizing the child. Even when a child's shyness stirs feelings of frustration and discomfort (which is especially common with parents who suffered from shyness themselves), you do best by being patient. Before a social event, prepare your child by telling him who will be there. Help him talk about his fears.

Once in a new or social situation, stay awhile with your child. Don't force him to talk or play with others until he is ready. Offer him a puzzle or toy. If he is able to play next to another child, or focus on something other than the people in the room, he may be able to warm up.

If you notice another child who seems shy, you can gently suggest a way your child can play with him: *That child looks like he's enjoying the puzzle. Maybe you'd like to see if he would like you to help.* However, if he resists, don't push. Be free with praise when he talks or plays with others.

Some children this age are simply not ready to engage in large group activities without a parent nearby. Again, it's best not to force a child into a social situation before he's ready. Take your cue from your child.

Smaller groups can be less threatening. Join a small playgroup made up of the same children and parents. Invite one or two children to your home for playtime.

Some children are born with more of a predisposition (temperament) toward shyness. You will be successful with a shy child if you encourage and don't force. By respecting his characteristic way of dealing in the world, you can build his confidence and avoid future struggles. However, consult your child's doctor if your child seems totally unable to relate to others.

Fears

If a child is by nature shy or nervous, his temperament will not change as he gets older. However, as he moves out of his toddler years, his ability to cope with the stress of everyday life and the feelings it evokes will likely improve.

During the preschool period, there is a marked improvement in a child's ability to separate from caregiving adults, most specifically his mother. Although his devotion and dependence remain strong, he can hold himself calm through minor separations. Words help. You leave the room, saying, *I'm just going out to the car to get something*, and he can hold you and an image of the car in his mind.

The child's growing sense of his own competence is reassuring. He can manage a great many things on his own, and no longer relies on you for every little thing he might need at any moment of the day.

He has discovered other adults beyond his parents: grandmother, a baby-sitter, a teacher, older children. He is beginning to value playmates his own age. When he plays with them, you become a background figure.

His experience has included being left by his parents for short periods—a minute, an hour, an evening—but each time they have returned. Based on this experience, his security in your dependable presence and affection now allows him to take some concentrated attention off you and focus instead on the outside world.

By making your child feel that it is okay for him to take tiny excursions out from your safe harbor, you have made it possible for your child to venture out into the world—and eventually to engage in a school experience. Because he trusts you, he is beginning to trust himself and others in his immediate world.

Yet the ability to cope without you is only tentative. If he is made to feel that you expect more independence than he can comfortably manage, or if something happens to make him feel less secure, he may revert to anxious clinging behavior. There needs to be a sensitivity to allowing enough independence while not forcing too much on him. It is helpful to try to anticipate things that are likely to worry him without being overprotective.

Every child has his own special fears and worries. However, certain anxieties are more prevalent during the preschool years. A preschooler's highly active imagination may make him worry about disasters, especially after a radio or television report. As he catches fragments of adult conversation, words out of context, and stories relayed in dramatic and shorthand fashion, he begins to worry: *What if I got lost in the park? What if my parents were killed in a plane crash?*

Because children are gaining an awareness of a separate self inside a body that belongs to them, they tend to hold their bodies particularly dear. Often they feel anxious about getting hurt. They may express a terror of blood. A staggering number of Band-Aids are used during the preschool years to cover the slightest scratch or hint of blood.

Children also focus on potential pain. A toddler may respond to an injection with a brief cry. A preschooler dreads his next visit to the doctor, shrieks while he's getting the shot, and remembers the incident with fear.

At this age, boys have become aware of their penises. They likely consider them both precious and vulnerable. Despite your explanations, your son may not accept that girls are made a different way. Some boys worry that their penises could be removed as they assume girls' were. A little girl may also be puzzled that she is not like a boy. She may believe that her own body is lacking in some notable way. For both sexes, fear of injury may start with terrible images of being broken or damaged, or having lost a part of themselves.

Help your child navigate such anxiety and fears by letting him set his own pace toward independence, even when this pace is halting or unsteady. Maintain firm and even control over him and his life. Let him know that his safety is still your responsibility and that you do not expect him to take on more than is comfortable for him.

When he is afraid, be reassuring. Because words now have greater power, often a low-key explanation given with reassurance at the time will defuse a child's anxiety. Teasing or mocking about fears is hurtful and cruel, and only encourages a child to hide his fears under a veneer of bravado. Masked, his fears will continue to bother him inside. *And he won't feel that he can tell you about them.*

Fearfulness diminishes as children find that they can cope with many things that happen as a usual part of daily life. Gradually they discover that skinned knees heal, that falling off skates does not break them into pieces, and that mother never loses them or goes off without telling them. Once they see that they are safe and capable, their fears and apprehension diminish.

SCHOOL READINESS

For children who have been cared for at home, this may be the time to consider some kind of organized daily group. A child this age may truly enjoy a preschool or nursery school experience, and, depending on your own situation, you may enjoy or need free time for yourself.

One of the most significant signs that your child is ready to enter into a formal, regular social group is his willingness to be away from you and away from home for short periods of time. If he clearly prefers being with you, you may choose to wait a bit. In a few months, managing without you may be less of a hardship for him.

You can usually tell if your child can manage without you by the ease with which he talks with other familiar grown-ups. The fact that, given a reasonable time to warm up, he is able to interact comfortably with another adult means that he no longer needs you to be his constant interpreter.

Your child may also show increasing interest in other young children. You may have noticed that he enjoys watching or playing with other children he meets around the neighborhood. Or he may be able to join in, after a short time observing, with a group of children at a museum or playground.

Other indications of school readiness become more important as a child approaches kindergarten and first grade.

- his physical health and well-being,
- his motor development—drawing, using scissors, running, jumping, climbing,
- his social competence and emotional well-being—self-esteem, confidence,
- his approach to learning—curiosity, ability to work independently, persistence, listening skills, pride in a job well done,
- his language development,
- and his general knowledge of the world around him.

Aggression

During preschool years, children begin to spend significant amounts of time interacting with children their own age. In order to be accepted as members of their social group, children must learn to control their anger and tolerate frustration when they are not allowed to do what they want. They must also learn to consider the desires and feelings of others, to subordinate their personal interest to the good of the group. Learning to control aggression and to help others are two necessary tasks of young children's social development.

Rudiments of aggression and empathy are both apparent shortly after birth. Aggression can be seen in an infant's angry cries and thrashing about when nursing is interrupted.

A primitive form of empathy may be at play when newborns start crying in response to the cries of other babies.

As children approach the age of two, a new and distinctive sense of self emerges. A child snatches a shovel at the sandbox with the proclamation *Mine!* For a toddler, this is serious business. The child has begun to worry about ownership.

Between the ages of three and six, the expression of aggression changes. Children are less likely to fight physically over possessions. They are more likely to use threats, teasing, and insults. Also at this age, one child might try to hurt another even though there's no apparent trophy at stake.

Some children take out on other children the stresses they experience at home. They bite, hit, or kick younger children. A child might hit a stranger because he longs to hit the new baby at home. Perhaps he hears his parents yelling at each other, so he yells at his playmates. He grabs another child's toy because he doesn't feel loved enough. Some children become disruptive when they feel bossed around too much.

Many studies suggest that boys are more aggressive than girls in a wide variety of circumstances. How much of the difference is due to societal and parental expectations and how much is grounded in inherent differences remain uncertain.

Other studies show that open expressions of aggression—yelling, hitting, pushing—do not reduce anger. Clearly, venting is not an effective way of reducing hostility.

When parents respond to aggression with fierce anger or punishment, they may suppress the child's aggressive behavior. Punishing does not curb aggression; in fact, attempts to control behavior through physical punishment or threats of punishment may increase a child's aggressive tendencies (see *Discipline,* page 107).

Some children use aggression to gain attention. As long as there is no actual threat of harm to the child or someone else, it is best to set firm limits. Yet pay special attention to the child and use positive reinforcement and praise when he engages in cooperative behavior.

Good behavior is crucial to success in the larger world of people. A preschooler needs help curbing aggressive impulses. He will need to learn why it is not okay to bite and that hitting is wrong.

If your child hits you, simply take his hands and say, *I know you are angry, but do not hit me. Hitting hurts, and it is not okay.* Use the same approach when you see your child hit another child.

Most parents try to teach their children to use words instead of physical action. Yet many children are not comfortable with angry words either. A child worries about his parent's anger if he says *I want to kill you.* Though you might find his words upsetting, you will confuse him if you respond by getting angry. At times like these, a child wants to be stopped from doing harm; he needs someone to control him when he feels out of control. Remember, angry words are preferable to physical aggression. Calmly reassure him that he cannot kill you, but that you realize he is angry. You can also suggest alternative words he can use to let you know how angry he is.

Children would rather have good attention than bad attention, but bad attention is better than no attention. If a child notices that whenever he acts in a certain way, he can get you to turn away from what you are doing (including tending to a younger sibling) and focus on him, he may think that the attention he gets from being naughty is worth the trouble.

Because their social controls are not strong enough, preschool children need supervision as they play. Their tempers still flair, and cooperation can be lost in the heat of the moment. It is up to adults to keep everyone safe.

Supervision needs to be subtle and discreet. Don't hover, but be ready to step in before things get out of hand. You may need to sound the warning or redirect play. Children this age do not have the judgment to anticipate danger.

When it is necessary to intervene to protect one child, comfort the injured child. Suggest nonaggressive ways in which a child might handle further attacks such as *No hitting,* or *I'm playing with this now.* By helping children deal with attacks without becoming an attacker, you can keep things from escalating. Other children who observe this can learn that it is appropriate to be sympathetic to a victim of aggression, and that nonviolent assertion in the face of aggression can be effective.

If your child has a tendency to be aggressive, discuss calmly the consequences of such behavior. If he grabs someone's ball and gets clobbered for it, kiss the bump then explain that no one likes having something grabbed out of his hands. Suggest that he ask for the toy he wants, and accept the answer, even when it's *No.* Praise him for trying out your suggestions.

Show your child that other people's feelings are generally the same as his. Reinforce the fact that the most effective way of resolving conflicts comes from sharing, taking turns, and playing together cooperatively.

The Developing Conscience

At three, a child has little ability to feel empathy. If he's asked, *What would you feel if someone did that to you?* he may shrug. He doesn't see what the big deal is, as his imagination does not carry him into the internal world of another person. Nothing matters but his own feelings, and he cannot easily step outside of himself.

At three and four, some children may take pleasure in a cruel act—stepping on a caterpillar, pulling a cat's tail. By five, the same child will cry at the sight of a dead animal in the road. At that point, he is able to put himself imaginatively in the place of the animal and recognize the loss through *identification.*

When a child can understand how another feels, he begins to understand why it's important to inhibit impulses and to restrict aggressive and destructive acts and words. This empathic capacity is implicit in our concept of a civilized person.

The pleasure children take in destructive acts does not disappear, but it becomes repressed. A child shuts such primitive feelings away behind expressions of disgust and revulsion.

The process of repressing and controlling aggressive feelings is not innate, but rather a product of family education. Children give up destructive behavior, not because they simply pass through the phase, but because parents set limits and censure certain aggressive behavior.

Children learn early on what behaviors are good or bad. At the end of infancy, they become sensitive to standards of good and bad. They begin to be able to anticipate adults' reactions and plan their own actions accordingly. Children discover that by assuming parental attitudes toward unacceptable behavior they will please important adults in their lives. Over time, they become more like their parents through the process of identification.

Parents expect children to learn the rules of proper behavior *and* to follow these rules without constant supervision. This happens gradually as a child assumes (internalizes) his parents' judgments, standards, and values, making them part of his own personality. But it can happen only when he has the capacity to think beyond himself and imagine how someone else thinks and feels.

Once children both want to conform to adult wishes and are able to anticipate adults' reactions, they are said to have *internalized* adult standards. Conscience, the inner voice that guides behavior, emerges from these internalized standards. But conscience will not mature until early adolescence.

As children develop a capacity for self-observation and self-guidance, they also develop the capacity for guilt. Children experience guilt when they know what's right but also know they haven't conformed to it and have done something wrong.

With time, children come to understand better what kinds of behaviors are expected of them and to make these standards their own. Nevertheless, the ability to put this understanding into practice is often difficult. It is one thing for a child to control his behavior in the presence of his parents, it is another to exercise self-control when parents are not around. Younger children frequently fall back on more impulsive behavior. The ability to inhibit initial impulses so that more socially acceptable and appropriate behavior can follow is crucial for later development.

Gender Identity

A child's first discoveries of his distinct self are rooted in his experience of his body. An infant stares at his hands, tastes his fingers. Later, in his second and third year, a child becomes preoccupied with how the body works: how well the child can walk, run, climb, hold crayons, throw a ball. Plus, he becomes interested in the products of his body, the urine and feces.

Somewhere around this time, a child discovers his genitals. A boy notices what his penis looks like, how good it feels when he touches it. A girl explores her clitoris and vagina—not so much visually, but by touching, perhaps even trying to insert things into her vagina.

At this point in a child's development, the notion of *maleness* or *femaleness* is introduced. This discovery of sexual differences constitutes a fundamental building block in a child's gender identity.

Gender identity further solidifies a child's concept of self: *I am a boy and I am like my father* or *I am a girl and I am like my mother.* But being *like* entails more than just modeling or mimicking.

The process of gender identity involves observation and imitation as well. Not only do children see what kind of behavior is traditionally and culturally considered male or female, but they learn that boys and girls are rewarded differently for different kinds of behavior.

Beliefs and expectations concerning a child's gender get communicated early and in many different ways. A mother holds her infant daughter and fantasizes about the lacy dresses she'll buy. A father holds his newborn son and imagines playing ball with him. The way children are dressed, the qualities upon which they are complimented, the tasks that are offered to them, the toys that they are given—children receive countless messages about what girls and boys should want and how they should act according to their gender. Gender identity is ultimately based on a combination of all these factors and seems to be firmly established by two and a half or three years of age. After that, it is very hard to change gender identity.

Different cultures also have different roles (gender stereotypes) for boys and girls. Some instruct girls to be docile and passive and boys to hide their emotions. Others allow girls greater involvement in the world and boys greater access to their feelings. Many encourage self-sufficiency in boys and family-centered concerns in girls.

Identification with Parents

As children enter their third year, the clinging and panic at separation diminishes. They no longer need so desperately to be near the adults who hold primary caregiving responsibilities—increasingly they can stay connected by being like them.

At this stage important changes and patterns begin to emerge in the relationships between parents and their child. Freud referred to this stage as the Oedipal period. Increasingly, children begin to identify with the same-sex parent. For a boy, becoming like his father requires that he move away from the person with whom he likely has had the closest relationship, his mother. A girl, on the other hand, will seek to identify with her mother while maintaining a close attachment. Around the age of four, boys begin to wish they had all the wonderful things that belong to their fathers; they even have fantasies of replacing him. Because boys also love their fathers deeply, these rivalrous feelings and wishes cause a period of confusion.

A boy this age is old enough to know that wishing for father to disappear or fantasizing about his death are considered bad. Yet he is young enough still to believe that parents are all-powerful and all-knowing. Therefore, because father knows what he is thinking, the boy fears being punished and feels guilty about his bad thoughts.

Mothers assist in this process by setting limits on their sons' fantasies and by defining them as masculine. The process ends when a boy successfully differentiates from his mother and solidly identifies with his father or other males.

For girls, this passage is different. Around the age of four, a girl begins to have strong wishes to have what her mother has, including father. These feelings cause conflict in the girl. Fathers assist in this process by setting limits on these fantasies and by defining their daughters as feminine. The process ends when the girl resolves the conflict and solidly identifies with her mother.

The process of developing gender identity is a normal part of development. It includes the child's physical exploration of the genitals and is reinforced by the family, community, and societal rules for what to expect from little boys and girls.

Discipline

One of the most problematic aspects of raising children centers around the issue of *discipline.* How do parents respond when children throw tantrums, break rules, refuse to cooperate, or fight with siblings? How can parents use discipline to address troubling or disruptive behavior without spilling over into issues of power, obedience, and anger?

Sometimes parents just want their children to stop when behavior is annoying or harmful. So parents yell, threaten, or punish. However, these responses do not teach children self-control and seldom curtail the behavior they address.

It is part of a preschooler's task to learn behavior that enables him to enter into the world beyond his family. During these years, children begin to come to terms with the countless expectations that society has for their behavior. At its best, discipline helps the child with these tasks.

Children naturally want to learn from the adults around them. But they also want greater freedom and control over their behavior and experiences. Effective discipline helps children balance and negotiate between what they want and what they need in order to function successfully in a social world. It helps a child to learn the difference between right and wrong (which may be culturally defined), develop self-control that is neither rigid nor lax, and respect inner and outer limits. True discipline aims at making sure your child is safe, honest, and good when you are not there to tell him what to do or to provide guidance.

Starting around age three, children begin to use words to control and manage their behavior. After years of having their behavior controlled and managed by adults, they want to take over for themselves. As children develop more self-discipline, they use words to reinforce it.

During play, you might hear your child use controlling phrases that he's picked up from you: *Be careful. Don't touch. Stop it.* The fact that a child talks to himself as if someone else is speaking to him indicates that he is taking in (internalizing and identifying) adult instructions, rules, and sanctions.

Yet, learning self-discipline takes time. Now that your child is of preschool age, he is ready to begin to assume some responsibility for his own safety, security, and social acceptability. You will show him how to behave in countless different situations and circumstances. Except when you need to stop your child immediately—running out into the street, for example—telling him what he must or must not do is seldom an end itself. Instructions add up to a few basic and vitally important principles. Bit by bit, you will withdraw your management, leaving him to apply the principles himself.

First, children learn from your example. If you want a polite, considerate, cooperative and honest child, then you must model that for him. If, in your household, good behavior gets rewarded and bad behavior does not, he will naturally strive toward good.

Explain why you expect him to act in specific ways. That way he can apply the same principle to other situations. He learns nothing he can use if you say, *Because I say so.* Your family will be happier if you do not impose a master-slave hierarchy on it.

If you are always standing over him, ready to correct or criticize, he won't learn to think on his own about what he should or should not do. Plus he will begin to feel that he is bad and can't do anything right and his self-esteem will suffer. A child responds best (and feels better) when he is guided towards correct behavior rather than criticized for his efforts.

Be as consistent as possible. However, there will always be times when consistency won't work. If you tell your child not to interrupt when you're on the phone, what's he to do when the pot boils over, there's someone at the door, or the baby begins to cry?

It is important to apologize if you make a mistake. To say you're sorry, to admit when you're wrong makes you truly human. In this small act, you show consideration for his feelings and respect for the truth. It is also the kind of behavior you want him to emulate.

When parents expect instant and unquestioning obedience, discipline takes on a grim, punitive connotation: We will make this child behave. What a child learns from this is to obey and to fear, but not to think for himself. In many cases, he only learns to appear to be obedient.

There are many reasons that children do not do as you tell them. They may simply want to do something different; sometimes they do not understand what you want or do not remember. Occasionally they want to show their independence, feel contrary, or they want to annoy you. If you detect a deliberate attempt to provoke, your best tactic is to ignore, defuse, deflect, or distract. Whenever possible, look for a means of compromise.

Consequences and punishment are also part of discipline. Punishment shows your child what you will not accept. But it centers on a specific moment and says very little in terms of the kind of behavior you want or expect.

SPANKING AND PHYSICAL PUNISHMENT

There is never any reason or advantage in using physical punishment. Rather than curbing problematic behavior, spanking, hitting, grabbing, or shaking tend to escalate the problem. For children this young, most wrongdoing is due to forgetfulness or impulse. After a child is whacked, all he remembers is pain and indignity, not what he did wrong. His anger may push aside any feelings of remorse he might otherwise have experienced. Nor is he likely to be cooperative afterward—maybe just a bit meeker and more subservient to power.

Most parents would agree that their children should never hurt anybody else to express anger or aggression. No amount of frustration or rage entitles a child to hit or kick. If a parent hits a child—even to show what a good smack feels like—the child learns that when you're big, you can do what you cannot do when you're little. Physical punishment can inadvertently teach children to use physical force to solve problems.

Children learn to operate in the social world largely by the way others operate in relation to them. When parents use physical punishment, there is a greater chance that children will use violence to get their way. These children are the ones most likely to hurt other children. A child who is handled roughly may grab a toy away from another child and add a push for good measure. Or he may attack smaller children when he feels bad inside.

Confining a child to his room can make him avoid his room at other times. Punishments aimed at making a child feel foolish or undignified will only cause him shame. By asserting your own power and his powerlessness, you make a child feel helpless and incapable of being good. If you are truly trying to show him how to behave, don't hurt or shame him.

The best way to discipline a child is by gradually and gently exposing him to the consequences of his actions. When he sees that throwing his toy car in a fit of anger results in breaking, or when he understands that yelling or whining keeps other children from playing with him, he will learn to control those behaviors.

Talk to your child kindly about his behavior. Help him understand the importance of self-control and taking responsibility for his own behavior. Later, when he must face problems without you, he will do best if the inner voice that guides him is a kind, helpful, and supportive voice.

SPOILING

It's very likely that very soon after you brought your baby home from the hospital, you were met with dreaded advice: *Don't pick him up too much. You'll spoil him.* Or *Let him cry it out. Otherwise you'll spoil him.* The specter of spoiling a child hovers each time you feed your baby on demand, give him treats, or praise him.

In fact, spoiling has nothing to do with giving love and attention to a child. Nor does it result from how much the child has. The problem is not what he gets but how he gets it. Spoiling is actually about power and who in the family has it.

A preschool child naturally tests the limits of his influence within his world, just as he tests the power of his body and brain. He wants to know to what degree he can manage himself as well as other people around him. He is concerned with mastery, competence, impact, control, and power.

In order to develop a strong sense of his own competence and worth, a child must discover that he has some influence within his social realm. If he consistently finds that he has too little, he may have trouble taking risks and venturing out in the world later. If he consistently finds that he has too much, he might resist accommodating himself to the countless frustrations and limits in his day-to-day dealings.

However well intentioned, parents can interfere with this discovery by doing too much for their child. A child wants to brush his own hair. He wants to button his own coat. His parents are in a hurry to get out of the house, and they want him to look his best. A child finds that his clothes are picked out for him every day before he can consider what he feels like wearing. He watches an adult finish his block tower before he feels any degree of frustration. He doesn't have to brush his teeth for himself—his parents worry that he won't do a thorough enough job. His toys are always picked up for him—his parents hate a mess and hate even more fighting with him to clean up.

These children are constantly prevented from doing things for themselves. Because their skills are clumsy, inexact, or slow, some children are not allowed to reach a point of frustration. These children rarely have the opportunity to succeed on their own.

On the other hand, if a child discovers that he can consistently override adult power, he will come to understand that he can get his way by bullying. He learns that a well-timed tantrum, prolonged pleading, or pitiable wailing can turn opinion in his favor. Victory may feel sweet at the moment, but a child who feels too powerful can also feel anxious that the grown-ups who are supposed to take care of him are actually afraid of him.

As with most aspects of child-rearing, there is a balance to strike. On the one hand, it is the joy of parenthood to provide children with love and attention. On the other hand, it is also the duty of parenthood to provide firm limits for a child to identify with and incorporate.

Once you decide upon fair and sensible limits, explain them clearly and honestly to your child. He will not always agree with you or like what you decide. If your child can change your mind by reasoned argument or charming persuasion, then he is using real and reasonable influence to good effect. It is not helpful, however, to give in to his tears and tantrums.

A child learns a great deal about give-and-take, negotiating, and cooperating when he has a voice in the decision-making process. As he gets older and ventures out in the world more, issues of what he can have and do become more complicated. There will be times when he will understand, at least as well as you do, what is at stake and what other children his age are permitted. You will be called on to make adjustments in your limits and expectations as he proves himself more responsible.

At all times, your child's rights must be balanced against yours and against those of other family members. If you need to get some work done on the computer and he wants to play a game, discuss the conflict of interest and try to find a reasonable compromise.

Also, help your child understand other people's feelings. The more interested you can make him in how other people feel, the more sensitive to them he will be. Empathy is at the root of unselfishness, which, after all, is the opposite of being spoiled.

Siblings

Very often, when we talk about child development, we assume a context of one child and two parents. Yet many families have only one parent and most in the United States include at least two children. Siblings play an important role in the development of social behavior, sex-role identity, and in the handling of aggression.

Depending on his temperament and the family circumstances, an older child may greet the arrival of a new baby with amiability and cooperation, or he may be openly unhappy and unruly. In many instances, an older sibling takes an early role in the baby's care. He will notice and alert parents when the baby is upset or engaged in a dangerous or forbidden act.

A new baby is also someone to play with. In the first year, you may notice your first-born imitating the baby. Soon, though, it is the baby who imitates his older siblings. As the younger child gets older, he increasingly takes an active role in the relationship. He becomes a more interesting conversation partner for older siblings, and may be able to join in many of their games. Even so, older siblings continue to dominate the relationship. They are more likely to initiate play, and set the tone for the interaction by playing aggressively or cooperatively.

The birth of the second child is often upsetting to the first, especially if it occurs before he is four years old. Prior to the birth of a sibling, most firstborn children haven't had much competition. With the arrival of a new baby, greater demands on the parents' attention reduce the amount of time they interact with their older child.

A firstborn may respond by becoming more demanding. His behavior may become more disruptive. On the other hand, he may become more independent, taking a larger role in initiating conversations and play, or becoming more detached from mother.

Parents who love their first child and look forward to a second may find unbearable the thought that the older child will greet the second with resentment and jealousy. Things will go more smoothly if you accept that you are asking your older child to share your love and attention. However you dress up the facts, the arrival of the younger sibling will affect your older child and will likely cause the older child to compete for your love and want special attention all the more.

An older child will have jealous feelings. These are natural, so it's important that you don't make him feel guilty. Don't ask him if he loves the baby. But don't let him hurt the baby.

The baby will come to look up to his older sibling. Even in the first few weeks, one of his first smiles will surely be directed at him. Help the older child enjoy his new role.

It may also be helpful for him to understand that it is not necessary for him to be grown up to be loved. Allow your first child to be babyish if he seems interested. Offer him a turn in the baby bath and the crib. Sprinkle him with baby powder. Cuddle, swing him, sing to him.

A child who has developed a rather sophisticated command of language may suddenly begin to talk baby talk. While he may be perfectly capable of say *I want juice, please,* he may insist on saying *Ju-Ju?* He has seen the gleam in your eye when you use baby talk with the new baby.

When a child regresses like this, don't fuss at him. It will only be confusing or hurtful if you suddenly scold him for doing something that you do with the baby. However, don't answer him in baby talk. It is important that an older child not feel that independence is being forced on him. He should feel that moving forward in development is his choice.

This is a great time to introduce some practical advantages to being the oldest to balance the disadvantages. Introduce privileges: a later bedtime or special times with one parent.

Fathers can often take the edge off a baby's arrival. Two parents for two children make the pull between differing needs less obvious and painful. Perhaps Father is willing to tend to baby while Mother does something with the older child. Perhaps he is willing to do exciting things with the older child while Mother is busy with baby. Some fathers find that this is an important time to cement their relationship with their older child. For this reason, a single parent may feel more stress with the arrival of siblings.

Some children begin preschool at this time. With a new baby at home, taking up all the space and attention that once belonged exclusively to him, your child may have mixed feelings about letting go of you and forming attachments at school. Be sure that you find time to spend alone with him when he's home from school.

Sibling relationships are seldom consistently friendly or hostile, and most often are ambivalent. Siblings compete for parents' attention and love. Individual temperaments and the match between their temperaments also contribute to the quality of a relationship.

It appears that the sex of each child has minimal effect on the nature of the sibling relationship. What does affect it is the emotional climate of the family. If parents do not get along well or if the family reorganizes through divorce or remarriage, siblings will have more conflicts. On the other hand, brothers and sisters can also offer considerable support and comfort to each other in such circumstances.

When parents show favoritism, hostility increases between siblings. Parents need to monitor their feelings and expressions of favoritism. Even so, it is seldom possible to be consistently fair to each child. There will always be some problems in matching treats,

activities, and vacations to each child's age and stage. Balancing each child's needs and tending to one without neglecting the other always require sensitivity and skill. As long as each of your children depends on you emotionally, there will be jealousy.

At all times, strive to respect each child's dignity. Love them as individuals. Do not compare them or make them feel small to each other or to outsiders. As tempting as it might be, avoid holding one up as an example to the other. There will be enough natural rivalry.

All parents are drawn from time to time into their children's disputes. Intervening seldom settles, and may intensify, their conflict. Children quarrel in part to win attention. When parents intervene, children receive greater attention, and, as all children seem to know, even negative attention is better than no attention. In addition, parental intervention interferes with children's learning how to resolve their own conflicts.

Let your children know that you expect them to respect each other and behave appropriately even when they are not getting along. This is part of becoming socialized.

At the same time, don't force them into each other's company. A five-year-old may have little use for a one-year-old, and these differences in social needs seldom diminish with time. However, if you let your children work out their relationship, they may surprise you with the mutual affection and loyalty which develops over time.

TOY SELECTION: CREATIVE, LANGUAGE, AND EDUCATIONAL TOYS

By the time children reach preschool age, their personal preferences and individual styles are becoming evident. Parents can, therefore, begin to select toys based on knowledge of their children's likes and dislikes. In addition, preschoolers are able to ask for the kinds of toys they want. Their requests may be based on toys they have at preschool, playgroups, at the playground, or advertised on television.

Parents can spend lots of money on toys and games for their children. However, in many cases, children are able to engage in creative and educational play on their own, without the benefit of expensive building sets, puzzles, and counting toys.

Because they are interested in adult standards and behavior, preschoolers are drawn to things that allow them to engage in imitative play: a set of your measuring spoons or cups, boxes, cups, bowls to fill and empty. These can come straight out of your kitchen. As he begins to explore what it's like to be other people, you can provide things for dress-up: simple costumes, hats, plastic helmets, handbags or shopping bags, your shoes, an old nightgown, a tie.

Most children own a set of blocks. They may stack up books from the bookshelf or cans from the cupboards. With your help, they can count spoons for supper, cans of cat food at the supermarket, or blue cars as you sit on the front porch. Ask them to pair socks from the laundry. Help them cut out pictures from magazines and catalogs and make a collage.

Most children enjoy using water, clay, mud, play dough, and sand in their imaginative play. At the sandbox, a child might pretend to mix cement, make cakes or pies, dig tunnels for toy soldiers, make roads for cars, or scoop out a pool for a mermaid.

Physical play becomes more sophisticated. Preschoolers often enjoy riding tricycles or two-wheelers with training wheels. They begin learning to swim. Children this age can use a climbing frame, a wading pool, an art table, easels and art supplies, a swing, a gym set, balancing planks, a playhouse, a toy stove, kitchen set, trucks, puzzles, simple games, and tape players with stories and songs. One day a child might build a house or fort out of large cardboard boxes or imagine one of the boxes is a television. The next day he might dress up in old clothes.

Children of all ages enjoy music. At this age, they are able to use their voices and simple instruments—a xylophone, drums, a recorder—to make music. They delight in dancing, coordinating their body's movement with the music.

Storybooks with attractive illustrations provide both pleasure and the opportunity to refine a child's cognitive and language skills. Plus, the time you spend reading to your child may well be the most special time of the day for both of you.

Every child should have a few toys just because he wants them—even those he chooses because of television advertising.

For some children, there is joy in collecting, accumulating, sorting, categorizing, and grouping things. This is the reason why parents may be asked to buy more books, more dolls, more sports cards, more toy cars, more miniature animals, and the like. However, it is important to limit the acquisitions, too.

Toys that are too noisy, too violent, too expensive, too delicate, or too shoddy can ultimately bring more trouble than pleasure. You will be tempted to limit their use. If you are going to tell your child to be quiet or warn him to be careful every time he plays with the drum or the fragile antique dollhouse, their purchase will hardly be worth the trouble.

Toys with many pieces can become a headache if you have to pick them all up or a heartache for your child if they get lost.

Responsibility and Independence

For many parents, the easy part of raising a child is laying a firm foundation of love, trust, and belonging. The hard part comes as they help their children develop the wings they need to take flight.

Gradually, children let their parents know that they can assume greater responsibility for their bodies, their safety, and their social needs. Although a preschooler still needs you to maintain overall responsibility for his general well-being, he can gradually assume more responsibility for some of his daily routines.

The more you jump in to do what he can do for himself, the more you risk offending his budding sense of autonomy and discourage his move toward greater independence.

Parents can safely help their preschoolers develop a greater sense of responsibility and independence in many ways. First, consider the safety with which a child can navigate his world. If the water in the faucets is too hot, turn down the temperature. Make sure dresser drawers are not too heavy to open. Be sure your child can reach his toothbrush and hairbrush without fingering a razor or becoming curious about the pills in the medicine cabinet.

Give your child simple choices. After all, making decisions is part of growing up. A child must learn to think for himself, not just to do as you tell him. There will always be certain decisions you should still make—about meals or how often he brushes his teeth, for example, or where in the house to eat his snack. But there are plenty of other areas where you can offer him a limited set of options or choices. For example, you can let him choose to brush his teeth before or after a story, to wear overalls or sweatpants, order potatoes or rice in a restaurant.

By the time a child is three, he may be able to assume responsibility for simple chores in the house. He can put his own clothes in the hamper. He can put the napkins around the table. Although he may find chores fun initially, they quickly become boring and repetitive. After the novelty wears off, a young child may find it difficult to remember to follow through on his "job." Positive reinforcements such as a star chart with predictable immediate rewards may maintain interest.

Children whose clothes are easy to manage may gladly dress themselves, especially if parents are not too particular about their fashion choices. Pick clothes that are comfortable and allow for easy movement. Most children can manipulate large buttons and toggles on clothes and Velcro on shoes. Also, pants, shorts, and skirts with elastic waists are easiest to pull on and off.

A child's sense of independence includes not only what he does but how he is treated, especially the respect that he's accorded. For example, if his body is treated as though it belongs to you, like a pet to be brushed and coifed, he will not feel very autonomous.

It may feel natural to urge your child to be affectionate to other adults, to kiss or hug relatives or family friends. However, to the child, being encouraged to make gestures of physical affection he doesn't feel can seem forced or even like punishment.

Of course, being affectionate with other adults may not seem like such a big deal at the time. However, if this pattern of forced physical affection continues, it may be harder for him later to respect his body. For example, in adolescence, the teenager may not feel entitled to say *No* to using drugs or alcohol or to having unwanted sex. The reason parents should help young children develop a greater sense of responsibility and independence—even when it's easier to take over and do something ourselves—is to foster responsible and independent thinking and decision-making. The youngsters will need these as they begin to venture out into the world on their own.

Making Friends

A two-year-old is usually content to watch and play alongside other children (called *parallel play*), and probably will not be ready for cooperative play for another year. Somewhere close to the fourth birthday, if a child has experience playing around other children, he may slip into active participation with little effort. But if he is not used to other children, he will have to learn the lessons of socializing: to take turns, share, and yield. As he learns how to socialize, he will discover the benefits when he modifies his personal ambitions and style. Two can often accomplish much more than one and many more games are possible with a group.

Learning social behavior that is both gentle and cooperative takes a tremendous effort for most children. It is a major developmental milestone. Watch a child enter into a group that has just discovered cooperative play. If the newcomer does not know the rules and is physically intrusive, the other children will not be receptive.

As children become more comfortable with language, they often use words to control the behavior of others. A four-year-old may sound particularly bossy when he commands his playmates: *Stop it! Don't touch my things. Come here this minute.* A child this young has been at the bottom of the hierarchy for some time now. It is natural that he will seek out others to boss around. As he navigates the social waters, you may want to point out to him that friends prefer being spoken to with kindness and to remind him to use *thank you* and *please.*

Preschoolers typically boast. *I'm bigger. I have better toys than you.* This is their way of boosting self-esteem. They also use words to ask for approval or reassurance: *Johnny is a good boy.* While a child's boasting might make you uncomfortable, very few of his peers will notice.

Sometimes a preschooler will become interested in older children. Older siblings represent a vision of what the young child will become some day. And while older children may tolerate a younger child for a while, they will eventually reject him. Your preschooler may be hurt by this rebuff from an older hero. Be sure that you help him find suitable playmates by scheduling play dates, taking him to birthday parties, visiting playgrounds, and involving him in age-specific activities and groups. You may also be able to find a teenage baby-sitter or mother's helper to act as an older presence in your young child's life.

TRANSMITTING VALUES

In recent years, the debate about values has filtered into parents' concern about child-rearing. While most parents would agree that teaching values is an important part of raising children, few would be able to identify just which values to transmit and just how to do so.

Do we want individuals with a greater sense of discipline and control? More caring and responsibility? A sense of fairness and equality? What exactly does building character mean? In short, the issue of transmitting values is not so easily translated into practice.

Some of the concern about values comes from specific social problems: teen pregnancy, drug and alcohol abuse, youth and gang violence, cheating, damaging property, and disrespectful behavior. Some schools address these by offering classes in ethics, emphasizing basic values in classes, conducting special assemblies and informal student discussions, and even by introducing school uniforms.

Public institutions can shape and reinforce values. However, families provide the basics for good and responsible social behavior. Within the family, the child learns such values as control, consideration, cooperation, loyalty, and respect.

Studies suggest that a parenting style, referred to as *authoritative parenting,* works best for teaching a range of values. Authoritative parenting combines emotional warmth with firmness while maintaining an open dialogue with the child. This style contrasts with the old-fashioned *authoritarian parenting (Do as I say because I say so)* and with *indulgent parenting,* a permissive style rooted in the 1960s that is primarily concerned not to stifle a child's creativity and individuality.

The difference in styles can be seen in the following example: A child picks up an apple in the store and starts to eat it. An authoritarian parent yells, *Put that down at once.* An indulgent parent overlooks the deed, hoping to avoid a tantrum. An authoritative parent uses the opportunity to teach the child: He explains that because they hadn't paid for the apple, it would be wrong to eat it. Then the parent involves the child in buying the apple and then encourages consumption.

Children learn about moral behavior from the values and standards their parents communicate and embody. In most cases, parents are more effective if they start out stricter, then loosen the reins as a child gets older. It's a myth that children are fragile, unable to deal with frustration, responsibility, and challenges. Nor is it true that discipline will hurt their self-esteem. Children develop a sense of purpose, positive values, aspiration, and hope when parents handle them with steadfastness, moderation, reason, and empathy.

Some parents are hesitant to impose morals because they are eager to show tolerance for others' values. This can produce demoralized and cynical children. When there is no clear outside authority, people naturally drift to satisfying their own immediate needs.

Recently some parents have returned to religion to help convey a moral message. While this provides a context and place in which to struggle with moral issues, children who attend weekly religious instruction do not have instant morals and values. Morality is conveyed primarily in the small, day-to-day interactions that a child has with parents and within the family.

Learning morality is not simply a matter of learning a list of virtues. A few basic principles, however, form the bedrock of moral behavior. Children must learn to control their impulses. When a child takes another's toy, the natural reaction is to protest and react, perhaps by hitting, but maybe by yelling, or by grabbing the toy back. However, children must learn to think, to listen to that voice that says: *No, it's not right to hit.* They must stop hitting and consider another way to behave.

Yet moral behavior goes beyond suppression of aggressive impulses. Children must develop *prosocial behaviors:* altruism, cooperation, helping, empathy.

Empathy, the sharing of another's emotions and feelings, provides the foundation of prosocial behavior. It includes the ability to interpret and respond appropriately to the distress of others. A toddler might hit a crying playmate, not out of anger or malevolence, but as a way of expressing a strong emotion. This behavior may demonstrate the child's developing sense of empathy and identification. During preschool years, a child's increasing command of language allows him to empathize with a range of feelings. He may express empathy by offering his teddy bear to another child who is crying, or by sharing his lunch with friends.

Another quality that promotes moral behavior is the ability to delay gratification. The capacity of children to wait, to postpone or subordinate their own interest, is connected to their ability to resist temptation when they are older.

Parents transmit values each time they tell and show children how to behave, register pleasure or displeasure, reward, ignore, or punish them. In addition, adults select the social contexts—schools, religious institutions, playgroups, activities—in which children become socialized and learn about values. Most importantly, parents model behavior through behaving in ways they want their children to behave.

4

The Elementary School Years

AGES SIX THROUGH ELEVEN

■ ■ ■

It is opening day of the first grade. As you wait with your child to meet the new teacher, you can't help wondering if this will be a replay of the previous year when your kindergartner clung tightly to your hand, eyes brimming with tears. Perhaps you gently pried the fingers loose and, with a few tears of your own, reluctantly turned your back and walked away.

This year, though, the experience is different. As you offer your hand for support, your first grader looks uncomfortable and inches away, trying to ignore your faux pas and hoping that nobody saw. Then she hears her name in the distance and is off like a shot to greet a friend she hasn't seen all summer. In a matter of moments, she has run off, with barely a wave in your direction, and you are left to marvel at how far she has come in only six years.

Those six years have been a time of discovery. From the moment of birth, we all are explorers, assigned the task of learning about the world and, as we mature, carving a niche in which we can flourish. During infancy, your child's explorations centered on her body: she discovered that she is separate from her mother, that when she cries, she gets food or is cuddled, that she likes her parents' faces but not those of strangers, that her hands can be used to touch, and countless other things.

In her first six years, your child has busily explored and mastered her body skills. She has responded to and communicated with you thousands of times, discovering that she is separate from but lovingly attached to you. Now she says what she wants and thinks. She runs and climbs, she can use a fork, a crayon, and do many more practical things.

During the preschool years, your child, like many others, may have attended nursery school. It is here that she experienced her first group socialization: On one hand, she delighted in playing with other children her age, on the other, she learned that she would not always get her own way, that she had to take turns and think of others if everyone was to get along.

Over the course of the first few years of life, children gradually learn to be more independent, as parents begin to acknowledge the child's emerging physical competence and emotional self-regulation. In our society, first grade is the milestone: Your baby is now ready for school.

In another time or in some remote parts of today's world, this move to a new level of independence would be much more radical. If you were a parent in the Middle Ages, for instance, your child at the age of seven would have been expected to do without parental guidance and enter the world of adulthood with its responsibilities. In the Ngoni tribe of Malawi in central Africa, when the milk teeth begin to make way for the permanent teeth, Ngoni children must stop playing childish games and begin to learn the skills that are essential to survival as an adult.

In our world, of course, we do not expect nor desire our six-year-olds to behave as miniature men and women. But by the time they are ready to start school, we do expect them to know how to behave themselves.

During the elementary school years, your child will cover much cognitive, emotional, and social ground. She acquires knowledge very rapidly—the first grader who haltingly sounds out the word "dog" becomes the fifth grader who announces at the dinner table that her favorite author is Mark Twain.

She acquires social awareness and skill, too. As a preschooler, she had to learn to share and play with other children, but by the end of elementary school, she can play on a team, figure out another person's reasons for doing something, and think about how she looks and acts. In these years, the boundaries of her world expand from the backyard to the neighborhood, from the family to the community of school, church, and acquaintances.

In this chapter, we will explore the fascinating years of middle childhood. We will look at the mental, moral, emotional, cognitive, social, and physical development of these years. Issues such as discipline, lying, and manners will be discussed. We also will address ways to help your child develop a greater sense of competence, responsibility, independence, and self-esteem.

During these years your child will develop an independent identity. As the child moves away from parents, a separate sense of self will emerge. That self evolves as the child masters basic learning skills and functions independently with peers. After the elementary school years, there is puberty and middle school to anticipate.

As you watch your elementary school child become more independent, resist the urge to sit back and let your child occupy herself. She still needs her parents as active teachers, comforters, and participants in her life on her ascent into adolescence.

Milestones of the Elementary School Years

If development were measured solely by the physical changes parents see in their child during these years of middle childhood, one might compare this stage of life with the turtle who ran the slow and steady race. When compared to the explosive growth that took place during the first few years of life and that will occur again in adolescence, this appears to be an apt description.

But there is much more going on in the child than a slow lengthening of limb or a subtle loss of baby fat. The elementary school years are, in fact, a time when a child's psychological, cognitive, and social development is proceeding more like the hare racing at high speed.

As the parent of a child in elementary school, ask yourself how your expectations have changed over the years. Undoubtedly, you expect more of your first grader than you did of your preschooler. You ask that she follow instructions, be able to sit still for a designated period of time, be able to join the family appropriately in rituals or celebrations, and perhaps even do a few chores. These skills are part of her rapidly increasing repertoire, which enable her to function at this higher level.

■ PHYSICAL DEVELOPMENT

The average six-year-old in the United States weighs almost fifty pounds and is about forty-two inches tall. By the time that child enters adolescence, she will double her weight and measure about five feet in height.

Most children during these middle years gain an average of seven pounds a year and grow 2.5 inches annually. Boys double their muscular strength; girls increase muscle strength almost as much as boys.

In first grade, the average height for boys and girls is about the same. Typically, between the ages of nine and ten, girls have a growth spurt and add weight. That's why it is not uncommon to see sixth-grade girls towering over the boys in the class. If your daughter is sensitive about being the tallest in her class, reassure her that others will catch up in the coming months and years. The average boy is as tall as the average girl by age thirteen or fourteen.

While the child is adding length and bulk to her frame, her brain is also maturing and expanding. Between the ages of six and twelve, a child's head circumference increases only one inch to about twenty-one inches, almost adult size. There are many complex, internal changes in the circuitry of the child's brain during this time that allow for learning the many skills and behaviors of this age.

If you look at a class picture of a group of smiling first graders, you can't help but notice wide gaps in mouths where once there were teeth. Between the ages of six and seven, children begin to lose baby teeth to make way for permanent teeth. They loose about four teeth a year over the next five years. Interestingly, in some cultures the first loss of a baby tooth is seen as a sign that the child is leaving childhood behind and is beginning the transition to adulthood. However, we see lost baby teeth as a sign of physical growth and do not link it to behavioral expectations.

In addition to the physical changes that occur in children during these years, there is a refinement in complex motor skills. Running, jumping, and throwing—movements that were awkward and stiff during preschool—become smoother as the child develops more strength and coordination. The preschooler who rode a tricycle and had problems printing her name legibly becomes the first grader who proudly pedals off on her two-wheeler and writes her letters with a precision that leaves little need for guesswork.

■ SOCIAL DEVELOPMENT

Before she is old enough for school, your child spends most of her time with a parent or caregiver. In the first grade, though, over half of the child's waking hours will be spent in the company of peers, more than double the amount of time preschoolers typically spend with friends.

Up until now, your child has had an image of herself as it relates to her family. She sees herself as your daughter, perhaps as a sibling. Now that she is spending more time away from her family, this definition of self isn't sufficient. New identities are formed as a result of new interactions. *The class clown. The best reader in her group. The kid always quick to lend a hand. The girl who stands up to the boys on the playground.* All this from the girl who still seeks her comfort on your lap and cries if someone won't play with her. Your child's evolving identity is all of this and much more.

The elementary school child is spending more time away from parents but usually under the supervision of an adult, usually a teacher. In this environment, the adult instructs the children, maintaining structure and keeping order when necessary. But when children play away from the watchful eyes of an adult they quickly learn in their games to negotiate, compromise, and discuss options.

How do children learn to do this? They learn some skills and rules in school—but even more of these complicated skills are mastered on the playground and in the neighborhood. And they are learned through play.

As they play games and on teams, children learn that they must operate within the perimeters of defined rules and cooperate with others. As they become more skillful at doing this, children develop a respect for rules and the value of the group.

Friendship Although preschool children tend to have playmates of both sexes, as children grow, most begin playing with children of their own sex. In the early years of elementary school, there is still a mixing of the sexes, although not as much as before. Your son, for example, may have attended several birthday parties for girls as a first grader or even played with some girls. But by the time most children are in third grade, they tend to stick closer to children of the same sex.

While a boy may not balk at having to play a board game at home with the daughter of a friend of his parents, he would rather run with his own pack when it comes to playground time. In adolescence this will change, as both sexes develop more interest and awareness in one another.

School-age children probably play with those of the same sex because the way in which girls and boys relate to peers is markedly different. Picture your neighborhood elementary school just after lunch on a crisp autumn day. Dotting the playground, you see small groups of girls, some playing hopscotch, a few jumping rope, some just chatting. The mood is friendly, the noise level not too loud. Then suddenly a group of boys runs and chases each other across the field. The boys are noisy, energetic, and competitive. They show off their physical skills. The decibels are high, one group of girls is shrieking because the boys are now pelting them with spitballs. Some other boys are tossing a hat clipped off an unsuspecting classmate's head. Just a normal day on the playground.

During elementary school, children place more and more importance on being accepted by their peers. The girl who as a preschooler may have been oblivious to being the only kid in the class not invited to a birthday party, now has social antennae strong enough to pick up even the smallest playground slight. By sixth grade everyone will soon hear if a child breaks a social rule. A gossip grapevine emerges, a means by which children exchange information, practice thinking about social reactions, and reinforce their belief that certain behavior is not acceptable. So you shouldn't be surprised when the child who has never said an unkind word about anyone suddenly fills your ear with a daily diatribe on how bossy, sneaky, or show-offish various other children in her class are. This is the time to listen and help shape some of your child's values.

Changing Role of Parents Now that your child is older, you are treating her differently than when she was in preschool. A parent's expectations grow along with the child. You will spend more time reasoning with your elementary school youngster because the child is capable of understanding. You may begin appealing to her self-esteem (*I know you're too smart to do dangerous things*), or using the child's expanding sense of humor to teach a lesson.

As the child matures, the parent is more likely to use consequences, to take away privileges or to arouse the child's sense of responsibility or guilt (*Do you have any idea how worried I was when you weren't home at six o'clock!).* The exclusive use or overuse of guilt, however, can result in a child who is ashamed and lacks confidence.

Interactions go both ways. Children, too, behave differently toward their parents as they grow through childhood. A preschooler who is angry at her parents may whine, yell, or tell her parents she hates them. This same preschooler can then smother you with kisses in a matter of moments. Not so with the older child.

A fight with her parents usually won't result in a fit of kicking and screaming. The school-age child will marshal her mental forces and try to match wits verbally, going to great lengths to argue her point and find the flaws in your argument. Should this prove unsuccessful, she is likely to stalk off and mope. The eight- to ten-year-old may also assume negative or hostile positions on every issue presented to her *(oppositionality)* as a way of coping with disagreement.

The parents of an elementary school student must still provide secure control and limits in some ways; in others, parents must share control and offer choices to the child. Peers are becoming increasingly important and the perimeters of her life are expanding outside your influence, yet your job is far from over. Your independent child still needs you to reinforce understandings of right and wrong, safe and unsafe, fair and unjust. Your child needs to know that you are consistent and dependable.

■ MORAL DEVELOPMENT

All rules are not created equal. Even a very young child knows that it is much worse to hurt someone than it is to forget to brush your teeth. But the distinctions between offenses become more complex as the child moves through middle childhood.

Moral development goes through principal stages. Preschoolers understand physical value—the broken object, for example—but not the importance of motivation (did the child break the vase accidentally or intentionally?).

During the elementary school years the child comes to believe—based on experience and what she has been taught—that there is right and wrong, that law and order should prevail and that the difference between good and bad is clear. A kindergartner or first grader thinks that rules are made by adults and that it is bad to break them.

If you have a child this age, notice that your child often makes choices regarding behavior based on physical consequences and upon her own needs. Thus, the child might reason *No, I won't hit my sister even though I want to because then I won't get to watch TV and I'll miss my favorite program.* The child is primarily worried about being punished.

The child of seven or eight is beginning to understand that hers is not the only opinion, that others view situations differently. For children this age, it is perfectly acceptable to use someone to further their own interests. You may be appalled—not to mention embarrassed—when your child doesn't even try to conceal the fact that she only plays with a particular boy so she can swim in his backyard pool. But don't worry. This self-serving behavior is normal, a common transition from exclusively selfish behavior, through social expediency, to consideration for others. This behavior is also a reflection of the child's growing ability to understand cause and effect. This capacity is part of the changes associated with the *concrete operations* stage described by theorist Jean Piaget.

Moral development continues to evolve—during elementary school, the child depends less upon the parent to define right and wrong. Instead, behavior is influenced by internalized rules and by relationships with peers. During adolescence and young adulthood, a more sophisticated moral code emerges. Moral development is based on an individual's experiences and includes questioning rules, searching for reasons behind rules, and more advanced thinking based on universal principles.

A bright moment in the elementary school years occurs when your child begins to show empathy for others. Toward the late years of middle childhood, your child should become aware that the feelings of others—especially friends and family—are as important as her own. She will adopt a "Golden Rule" outlook on life, believing that she must be kind to others if she wants them to be kind to her. The child at this stage feels pressure to live up to people's expectations. She shows concern for others, demonstrates a willingness to put someone else's interests above her own, and realizes that qualities such as trust, loyalty, and respect are important in her relationships.

As a parent, you have been teaching your young child the difference between right and wrong. During middle childhood, you serve as a moral gauge. *Did I do the right thing?* her eyes question after she refuses to join in another child's defiant stand. Or your son may tell you about a fight or favoritism or foolishness at school. Your expressions and actions may carry more weight than your actual words.

Faith Practices Children want to be like their parents, so those who live by their own rules are more likely to see similar behavior in their children. Some parents firmly believe that one way of creating a foundation of morals and values is with religious faith.

Not all parents are believers or active participants in a church, mosque, temple, or another place of worship. As a result, they do not feel comfortable advocating religious participation for their child. For some parents, however, religion is one way in which children can not only have morals and values reinforced but also see people practicing their beliefs through good works in the larger community.

Participation in a faith community can expose children to worldwide concerns like hunger and famine. Through the expressions of generosity—for example, donations of money, goods, and volunteer services—a child can share the experience of relieving suffering near or far from home.

Faith practices also offer the experience of fellowship. Through common rituals and activities, children, their families, and the society of others in the faith create a sense of community. This sense of a common concern fosters a feeling of both belonging and responsibility for each other.

However, just as religion can be a powerful socializing force, it can also be a tool of intolerance and prejudice. Parents must strive to offer a wider perspective if individuals within the faith community or tenets of the sect preach exclusion (see *Sensitivity to Diversity*, page 142).

■ INTELLECTUAL DEVELOPMENT

When your child was a preschooler, you no doubt learned to keep your instructions short and to the point. You might ask your daughter to bring you her baby brother's diaper; there was a good chance that the task would be accomplished. But if you ask her to bring the wipes AND the baby oil AND a clean blanket, she will likely return with only one or two of them.

School-age children have an increased ability to follow even relatively complex instructions. This is because they have longer attention spans, more ability to use words, and therefore a better capacity to remember. This is an example of one of several important changes that occur in your child's ability to think and learn during middle childhood.

Memory A kindergartner can remember four numbers in a row; most nine- or ten-year-olds have the capacity to recall a six-digit number. School-age children learn and develop strategies to help them remember information. One such strategy is to repeat the information over and over again. Five-year-olds shown pictures of objects and asked to recall are not as likely to repeat the name to themselves, whereas ten-year-olds will use that technique to help them remember. Not surprisingly, the children who use this method remember far more than those who do not.

During middle childhood, children remember by grouping similar objects together. A third grader asked to remember a long list of words may be able to do so by forming clusters of word groups. Thus, a bat, dolphin, bird, and deer are remembered as one cluster because they are all animals; and ice cream, carrots, bananas, and cereal as foods.

School-age children also have a more realistic picture of the limits of their memories. A five-year-old, for example, when shown a set of ten pictures and asked how many she will remember, is likely to predict she can remember them all. Not so for the more pragmatic eight-year-old, who understands that this is not as easy as it looks.

As the child leaves the preschool years and has more and different experiences, and as language abilities develop, the youngster can learn more and associate more with her own personal knowledge. The child can tell you more about what she sees, hears, and experiences. We call this an increase in memory capacity.

More Advanced Thinking As your child enters her elementary school years, her thought processes become capable of more complex tasks. For example, a kindergartner can physically manipulate a pile of blocks. She'll count them and organize them into various piles. Yet when asked to perform the manipulation in her head (without physically moving the objects), the kindergartner probably can't do this. An average eight-year-old, on the other hand, is capable of mentally moving the blocks, imagining how they will look in different configurations and how they can be changed back to the original grouping.

School-age children learn that problems often have more than one solution and that some elements of an object remain the same even when that object's appearance is changed.

Bits of knowledge, once scattered like toys around a child's room, now come together to form logical patterns, enabling the child to think more systematically and effectively. During their early school years children have the ability to think simultaneously about two aspects of a problem, a skill not typical of preschoolers, who focus on one piece of a problem.

The child's ability to communicate improves significantly during these years. When a first grader is asked to describe a set of figures to a child sitting across from her but invisible because of a barrier, she is likely to use descriptions that are specific to her own personal experience. She might say, for instance, that one figure is wearing a hat like Mommy's or the man's hair is like Daddy's. As children mature, however, they understand that they must use more general descriptions that have meaning to the listener as well. The hat can be identified in detail—it's red, with a veil over the face, and a brown feather on top.

Although it may sometimes seem that your child is oblivious to anyone else's point of view, the child during these middle years does make real strides in becoming less self-referential. The child is becoming aware that others may have different opinions. Along with this awareness comes the ability to think about how one's actions will be viewed by others.

Ranges and Patterns of Intelligence

Developing minds are wonderfully varied.

Since early childhood your daughter has been a musical virtuoso, proficient on several instruments. But ask her to perform a simple multiplication problem and she runs to the nearest calculator.

The boy across the street, on the other hand, has no particular skill that stands out. Yet, he consistently gets good grades and, on a recent test for admission to a program for gifted children, did well enough to be accepted while your daughter did not.

At present there is some controversy about measuring and defining intelligence as well as understanding its origin and acquisition—that is, the different contributions and effects of genetic endowment and environmental factors. Traditional IQ tests have limitations. Thus, the gifts of a child who can take a motor apart and put it back together yet has difficulty reading a three-syllable word will not be accurately reflected in such a test—and may go unappreciated in a world where academic accomplishments receive the loudest applause. Such a child may have a special or different intelligence that is not tested on standardized intelligence tests.

The standard way of measuring intelligence—the IQ test—measures only certain kinds of intelligence. Also such tests have cultural biases because of the way the questions are worded or structured. Thus, there is concern that current tests do not accurately measure the intelligence of members of many communities of color.

Even though the issue of measuring human intelligence is a source of continuing debate, there is general agreement about its nature. First, human intelligence is not solely the product of genetics nor of environment, but rather a combination of the two. Second, although experts disagree about what they are measuring when they give an intelligence test, studies show that to some degree these tests do predict school performance. With minority groups, however, the correlation between test results and school performance is less clear.

Your practical, competent, mechanically skilled, or socially astute child may feel "dumb" in school. This child especially needs his parents and family to recognize and appreciate the ways that he is "smart." We know that different kinds of intelligence allow different people to compose symphonies, paint masterpieces, write great books, or execute reverse slam dunks under pressure.

Parents cannot alter their child's genetic (hereditary) endowment to help her do well in school, but they can influence their child's environment. The following environmental influences bolster school success:

- As a parent, you have the potential to profoundly affect your child's school experience. Children are more likely to do well if their parents encourage their curiosity, listen to them, support their educational institutions and teachers, take the time to explain their own actions, and tailor the home environment to reflect their child's abilities and interests.

  Have books in your home and encourage your children to read rather than watching television. Set a regular time for homework and encourage and help the child to always finish it. Expressions of *your* pleasure in the child's increasing academic achievement will promote the child's motivation and energy in the work of school.

- Properly organized interactions with peers will benefit your child, especially in developing social skills and the capacity to solve problems. Although some parents worry about their child's choice of friends and whether they will be a bad influence, remember that peers more often are a positive, constructive influence.

- Some schools are more conducive to student academic success. Studies have shown that "success" schools are not necessarily more modern nor do they have better trained teachers. Rather, they have high expectations for all students. These schools have teachers who expect all their students to do well, who use praise more frequently than punishment, and who give students more responsibility in the school.

Play

Across the animal kingdom, young mammals spend a part of their day engaged in play. Middle childhood has its share of games, too, and, to the casual observer they may seem to be little more than simple fun. Yet, like the play of animal species, children's play teaches them skills that they will need as they grow into adulthood.

When, for instance, the eager Little Leaguer learns that she must wait for her turn at bat, she is given a lesson, albeit subtle, in the adult art of balancing her needs as an individual with the rules of the society in which she lives. Another major difference between the games a child plays before she starts school and those that come during the elementary years is that the latter require practice over a long period of time (competitive sports) and the ability to plan ahead and to delay gratification (as with hobbies and collections).

Later games also depend upon rules to a much greater extent. Consider a game favored by elementary children like hide and seek. Before a group of children begins this game, they typically establish elaborate rules—who will hide and who will seek, how high the seeker counts before she can open her eyes, and so on. Once the rules are established, children who try to change them are considered to be cheating.

Games of older children tend to be competitive and distinguish winners from losers. Moreover, school-age children play in larger groups and for hours at a time if given the opportunity, unlike the preschooler, who prefers two or three playmates and then only for brief episodes.

The French psychologist Jean Piaget and his colleagues studied children of various ages in the act of playing marbles and found that preschoolers played with little regard to competition. They made colorful piles or rolled the marbles around at whim, whereas elementary school children played by the rules and played to win.

When these researchers asked who made the rules, the answers varied: Some offered older children as the source of the rules, while others cited God. When Piaget asked one ten-year-old boy if he might be able to invent a new game of marbles, the boy acknowledged that it was possible but people couldn't play that way because it would be cheating.

The boy explained that if he invented it, it couldn't be a rule. A fair rule is one that is already in the game, he added. Research suggests that most children between the ages of nine and eleven begin to be more flexible about rules. For example, rules can be broken or changed if the majority of players agree.

This reasoning shows a benefit of play: Play allows children to understand human interaction and the roles and responsibilities of the individual and group in society.

Swearing

When your daughter was in preschool, she reveled in bathroom talk and the ultimate insult was to call a foe a poo-poo head.

Now that she's in elementary school, she's developed a strong sense of privacy about the bathroom. Instead, she's taken up swearing.

If you avoid using such language in your home, it's safe to assume that the source was most likely her peers in school.

These are the years when your children will pick up words you'd rather they didn't know. Even before they really understand the full meanings of some words, they sense they are somehow unacceptable by the way other children say them and by the way adults react when they hear the words. Children want to seem worldly and sophisticated. Sometimes they repeat these words—to prove they're cool, to be accepted, and for shock value.

When you hear your child swear, the best approach initially is probably a low-key one. Tell the child firmly that this is not acceptable language and you don't want to hear such words. Parents who get upset and overreact can inadvertently make the child feel powerful—their strong response may actually encourage swearing rather than discourage it.

Lying

Like adults, children lie for a variety of reasons. For example, a child receives poor grades on a report card and is afraid to show it to her parents and hear their reaction. So instead of having to deal with those consequences, she might lie—claiming that the report cards haven't been issued yet.

Or a youngster may lie after a misdirected pitch shatters the kitchen window, afraid of the consequences and punishment. Children may also lie to protect their privacy, avoid embarrassment, cover up for low self-esteem, and to gain the respect of peers.

Even a very young child will lie to avoid blame. In the black-and-white world of the preschooler, one is either good or bad and good people don't do bad things. Since the youngster wants to be thought of as good, the child may deny responsibility for a "bad" act. By the time a child is seven or eight, she has the intellectual capability to understand that a lie is an intentional act of deception.

Your elementary school child understands the principles of cause and effect and can map out a logical route in her mind of the steps she must go through to get what she wants. A lie, in a sense, is a shortcut. However, as the child gets older, she becomes more capable of understanding the negative consequences of lying. She may see that she can deceive her parents sometimes but the result is that they don't trust her, and this causes her more problems than facing the short-term consequences of not getting what she wants.

How concerned should a parent be about lying? In most cases, lying is not a major problem unless it becomes a habit and you see your child lying in many contexts (school, home, with friends). Habitual lying in a child who understands what it means to lie may later be associated with more serious antisocial behavior such as stealing, drug or alcohol abuse, and other forms of delinquent behavior.

This is not to imply that you should ignore lying. Remember, though, that you want your child to feel that she can always come to you, no matter what she's done. Your goal should be to help her learn from her mistake.

Here are some guidelines that you may find useful in dealing with lying:

- Remain calm. If you yell or berate your child, it will be more difficult for her to tell the truth and admit her mistake next time.
- Convey the message that it is the behavior not the child that is bad.
- Try to help the child understand why she lied, and what she could have done instead in the situation.
- Always praise your child for telling you and admitting her mistake. Children who grow up in homes where they feel safe in admitting their mistakes are more likely to become honest, moral adults.
- Be mindful of your own behavior. A child who hears her parent refuse an invitation to a party with the lie that she will be out of town can only be confused when the parent admonishes her for lying. Discuss the dilemma that can occur in social situations: to tell the truth and risk hurting someone's feelings or lie. Help the child develop her ethical thinking by discussing the pros and cons of such complex situations.
- Don't lie yourself—you must set an example.
- When in doubt, believe that your child is telling the truth.
- If your child is caught telling a lie, help her learn that there are consequences by

asking what she thinks you should do about this issue. If the child is harder on herself than the parent would be and suggests a worse punishment than you would have given, then the child is revealing that she is developing a conscience and has feelings of guilt. Talk over those feelings with your child and the importance of telling the truth.

Discipline and Consequences

Every parent knows from experience that children do not always do what you want them to do. When a child misbehaves, the parent must decide how to handle the situation.

Over the years, experts have changed their views on methods for disciplining a child. *Spare the rod, spoil the child*—a philosophy that once enjoyed a widespread following—is not recommended. On the other hand, to do nothing when a child breaks a rule teaches the child that rules don't matter.

Parents must face these questions: How does one best teach a child the rules and, when those rules are broken, what should be the consequences?

In a home where more than one adult is parenting the child, communication and agreement on discipline is the first step. Next is deciding to view discipline not as punishment but as teaching. As a parent, your job is to protect your child from danger and to teach her right from wrong. Thus, she must learn the boundaries of what is acceptable in your household, community, and culture.

Once you have established the rules of acceptable behavior, you must communicate to your child that broken rules carry consequences and decide what those consequences will be. At that point, you have laid out your expectations: *Here are the rules that must be followed and if you break a rule, this is what will happen.* You must then follow through when your child breaks a rule. Parents should also frequently acknowledge and offer positive reinforcement and support when their child complies with and follows the rules. Consistency is a cornerstone of discipline and praise a powerful reinforcer of learning.

Of course, there are numerous ways a parent can teach or discipline a child, some of which work better than others. The three most common parenting styles are what researchers call *authoritarian, authoritative,* and *permissive.*

An *authoritarian* parent attempts to control a child's behavior and attitudes, stressing the importance of obedience to authority and discouraging discussion. Parents who use this method tend to rely upon punishment, which is often spanking or other physical measures.

The *authoritative* parent operates on the belief that both the child and the parent have certain rights and that the needs of both are important. The parent is sure that she is in control and doesn't need to assert physical force to keep the child on the right track. Rather, a authoritative parent is more likely to control her child by setting rules and explaining why these rules are important and why they must be followed.

Authoritative parents will reason with their children and consider the youngsters' points of view even though they may not agree with them. These parents tend to set high standards for their children and encourage them to be independent.

Unlike either the authoritarian or authoritative parent, the permissive parent exercises minimal control. Children of permissive parents are allowed to set their own schedules and activities. Permissive parents generally do not demand the same high levels of behavior as authoritarian and authoritative parents.

What impact do these different parenting styles have on children? One large study found that the children raised by authoritarian parents tended to lack social competence, rarely took the initiative in activities, and were often withdrawn in social situations. Moreover, these children showed less intellectual curiosity, were not as spontaneous, and during moral conflicts usually relied on the voice of authority to decide what was right. Children raised by permissive parents, on the other hand, had difficulty controlling their impulses, were immature, and were reluctant to accept responsibility or to show independence.

The best-adjusted children were those whose parents were authoritative. These children were more self-reliant, self-controlled, and intellectually curious than their peers.

No matter what type of parenting style you use, there will be times—probably lots of them—when your child does something that is completely unacceptable to you and you have no choice but to punish her for the behavior. What, you wonder, is the best way to limit improper behavior?

While many parents spank their children, few experts on child development endorse this approach. Not only is it easy for a parent to lose control and cause serious injury, but this form of discipline provides the child with a model in which physical force is used to obtain compliance. It also sidesteps the issue of helping the child increase self-control and self-monitoring, which is a major of goal of disciplining a child. Physical punishment can also inadvertently teach the child to be aggressive or to be a victim.

Screaming at or humiliating the child are also not constructive punishments. Children learn to disregard screaming and frequent belittling can do serious damage to your child's self-esteem.

What punishments are recommended for inappropriate behavior during middle childhood? Children learn from experience. You can devise logical consequences for their misbehavior to help them learn not to do it again.

If your children fight over the television, the television is turned off. Goofing off at the dinner table, your daughter spills her milk so she has to clean it up. Or your daughter, always rough with her toys, decapitates yet another doll, which is not replaced.

Logical consequences such as these teach children that they are accountable for their actions, without damaging self-esteem.

Another punishment that often works well with this age group is the suspension or delay of a privilege. If, for example, you find out that your daughter broke your rule and biked across town to see a friend, you might want to take her bike privileges away for a few days. Or, if you've been after her all day to clean her room and she still hasn't done it, you may make a clean room mandatory before she is allowed to leave to sleep over at a friend's house. You can also establish a policy where breaking a basic rule results in the child being required to complete a specific five-minute task. In children in the early elementary-school grades, using a time-out may still be effective (see *Discipline,* page 69).

Here are a few basic rules to remember when punishing an unacceptable behavior:

- Be clear about what you mean. If your child senses that you are ambivalent, the instruction may seem less important. Be firm and specific.

- Speak to your child as you would want to be spoken to if someone were reprimanding you. Don't resort to name-calling, yelling, or disrespect.

- Whenever possible, the consequence should be delivered immediately after the infraction, should relate to the rule broken, and be of short enough duration that you can move on again to emphasize the positives.

- Fairness is particularly important at this age so punishments, whether in school or at home, must seem appropriate to the infraction.

CHORES

Your child wants to show you how useful she can be. You can help her do this by letting her help you.

Ideally, chores are introduced when the child is a toddler. Naturally, the early chores are simple ones such as picking up toys after play. During these early years, don't expect these chores to save you much work. What they will accomplish, however, is to teach your child to feel proud of herself and to value competence. You have given her a task and she has risen to the challenge. (See also *Allowance*, page 140.)

As your child grows, so does her capacity to take on more responsibility that not only helps her prove to herself her competence but is actually useful to you. A first or second grader is old enough to make her bed, straighten up her room, set the table, empty the garbage, help put groceries away, and contribute to the work of the household.

In the past, it was common for a family with both a boy and girl in the home to assign them different chores. The girl, for instance, was more likely to be given a job such as washing dishes or setting the table, whereas the boy was expected to mow the lawn or wash the car. Today, however, the emphasis is on creating well-rounded individuals who can go out into the world and pursue their talents, whatever they may be, regardless of gender. Thus, if you have children of both sexes, send them the message that both men and women are capable of doing all kinds of things, chores included. Let your son be responsible for dish washing sometimes and your daughter for washing the car or mowing the lawn. As you've probably discovered, these are skills that, no matter what your sex, come in handy and as parents you can reinforce this message by both performing a wide variety of chores.

Even though most children take pride in showing their parents how much help they can be, there will be times when your child balks when asked to do a chore. Perhaps you've asked her to pick up her room just at the part in her book when the mystery is about to be solved. Most children need to be reminded at times to do a chore. Sometimes you may feel it's acceptable to renegotiate. "You can finish the book before you straighten up your room as long as you do it before lunch."

When speaking to your child about her chores, try to avoid nagging or being too critical. Nor should you assign a chore when you are irritable. If her room doesn't pass inspection, patiently show her how to correct the defect. Don't give her the sense that no matter what she does, it won't be good enough. This will dampen her enthusiasm to please you and make every chore drudgery instead of an opportunity to prove herself.

Self-Control and Self-Doubt

Upon entering elementary school, your child is expected by our society to have the self-control to rein in the impulse to race around the room in the middle of a reading lesson. Instead, your youngster must sit still, listen to the teacher, and bolt only when the recess bell rings.

Self-control is crucial if a child is to succeed in school, both academically and socially. Children who do not learn to regulate their own behavior can have difficulty. Instead of learning their multiplication tables, they fool around and are disruptive; instead of learning how to cooperate and compromise, they're hitting other children who refuse to play the game their way.

In order for a child to develop the self-control that she needs for school and eventually to function in society, she must learn how to control her impulses. Having done this, the child then is able to use the proper response. An example might be the child's impulse to blurt out an answer to a question the teacher is asking. She knows the answer and she's bursting at the seams to just shout it out. But she's been taught to wait her turn so instead she waits and raises her hand.

It takes a long time to learn impulse control, which involves mastering many steps to self-control. Children must learn to inhibit movements, to control their emotions, and to contain desired actions.

Studies have shown that it is much easier for a child to start an action than to stop one. Tell a class of preschoolers to jump and you'll have a roomful of aspiring bunnies. But when you issue the stop order, chances are many will continue jumping and you'll have to repeat your command several times. These children haven't developed the capacity to inhibit their movements.

The same holds true for verbal commands. Even children in the first grade have difficulty consistently following the directions for the game "Simon Says." The children know they are supposed to perform an action only when they hear the words "Simon says," yet most can't help but respond to the command anyway. They fail to inhibit their emotions and conclusions.

During the preschool years, children gradually gain some control over the intensity of their emotions and their motor behavior. They learn that the solution to a problem isn't always as simple as it seems. The ability to more carefully reflect on a problem appears around first grade.

A more complex step in self-control—*inhibition of choice*—is understanding and being able to act upon the knowledge that it is often better to pass up a short-term reward for an ultimately better prize. This skill develops gradually. A six-year-old given the choice between a small toy today or a bigger and more expensive toy next week will opt for instant gratification; an older child will weigh each gift in her mind and be able to decide it is worth waiting for the bigger prize.

Most school-age children have attained some degree of self-control that allows them to attend to learning and develop fulfilling social relationships with their peers. Children who cannot seem to do this may have problems with attention or emotions and may need evaluation by a educational or health professional.

Children as they mature are also developing an increased capacity to make more accurate comparisons between themselves and others. Even as your child is developing the self-control skills that enable her to function more productively, she is becoming aware that she is not the best reader in the class, the fastest runner, or the most popular child.

Children during middle childhood can begin to have doubts about themselves. The girl who thought she could do nothing wrong in first grade may feel as though she can do nothing right as a third grader. Children decide that they are worthwhile human beings on the basis of their competence and on whether they are accepted by others. A child just starting out in school can better rate another child's competence than her own. She may tell you that the girl who sits next to her in class is really smart but the one in the seat behind her has trouble with her letters, an opinion shared by the teacher. Yet no matter what the teacher and the rest of the class think about her ability, she may overestimate or underestimate herself. By third grade, however, the child begins to recognize how others see her. Thus, if the class thinks she is intelligent, she sees herself as "smart"; if she is having self-control and concentration problems, she may be falsely perceived by others as "dumb"—and see herself in the same light.

While there is not much you can do to directly influence the way others relate to your child, you can help your child develop the strong sense of self-worth that will help her overcome her doubts about herself. It has been said that the greatest gift you can give your child is the gift of self-esteem. Indeed, it is true that children who like themselves are more likely to grow up to be happy, well-adjusted adults, whereas those who don't value themselves are more apt to be depressed, anxious, and have a hard time adjusting to academic and social situations.

While there is no foolproof formula for raising a child with high self-esteem, numerous studies have shown that certain parenting characteristics are more apt to correlate with high self-esteem in children. Children who have high self-esteem are more likely to have close, affectionate relationships with their parents than those who do not. Parents of high–self-esteem children are loving and offer their support, attention, and time. Parents need to acknowledge and positively reinforce and support the child who complies with or follows their rules. These parents have set clearly defined and consistent boundaries of acceptable behavior. The child knows the family rules and the consequences for not following them.

Another pattern found in the parents of children with high self-esteem is that they create a home environment conducive to self-expression. The members of the family show respect for one another. Children are encouraged to express their opinions and listen to the opinions of others.

The child who is fortunate enough to live in such a household has the support to develop a healthy view of her competence and value.

Latchkey Kids

When the bell signals the end of a school day, an estimated 2.5 million American children under the age of 15 go home to an empty house. The number of latchkey kids—so-called because some of them carry house keys with them—is growing as a result of more working mothers, an increase in the number of single-parent households, and the difficulty in finding convenient and affordable after-school day care.

What is the effect? According to one large study, maternal employment by itself does not have a direct impact, positive or negative, on the emotional development of children. Other studies suggest that the children of two working parents tend to be more self-reliant, independent, and successful in school. When single mothers are employed, their families may benefit not only from the increased income but from the improvement in the mothers' self-esteem and morale, but the research is not definitive, and some studies suggest that a single mother's employment does not necessarily improve the family's finances. There also appears to be a difference between how well boys and girls adjust.

For most parents, the decision to let a child stay by herself after school is filled with anxiety. Children, too, may have problems with this arrangement. While some relish the chance to be "self-care kids" and on their own for a few hours, others complain of loneliness and boredom. Some children are afraid of being left alone, the most common fear being that someone will break into their home and hurt them. Sometimes children resent that their parents can't be with them after school.

In some states it is against the law to leave children under ten home alone. For some children, that age seems a reasonable standard, but only you can accurately judge your own child's capabilities and maturity. It is dangerous to ask a child this age to baby-sit younger siblings or to load the preadolescent with household tasks or any other responsibilities that may be unduly burdensome. You may have an option as a number of schools are providing after-school day care. But if you are in the position where you see no other viable alternative, there are some things you can do to prepare your child for the responsibility of taking care of herself.

- A graduated approach may work best. For example, leave her alone for an hour on the weekend at first and then gradually increase the time. If she is used to staying by herself, it won't be such a shock the first time she comes home to a quiet house. A ten-year-old may be home alone for up to an hour; by the time the child turns eleven, an hour or even two may be reasonable. At age twelve, the period may be two to three hours.

- Teach your child safety precautions. The child should be taught to lock the door after she lets herself in. Make sure your child knows how to handle unexpected knocks on the door and how to answer the phone without revealing that she is alone ("Mom can't come to the phone right now. May I take a message?"). A list of emergency numbers (911, fire, police, neighbors) should be posted, and escape routes in case of an emergency should be rehearsed. The youngster should also know your work number. You might have the child call you every afternoon upon arriving home after school; most children feel more secure after touching base with Mom or Dad. If you are not easily reached at your workplace, consider investing in a cellular phone or beeper so that both you and your child know that she can always reach you.

- Structure your child's time. The self-care children who get into trouble are the ones who just "hang out," with nothing to do and no parental expectations. Children do much better when they know they are coming home to a house where there are rules and responsibilities. Discuss your expectations about homework and setting the table for dinner, for instance. Your restrictions should also be clear—perhaps an hour of TV or one video. Will the child be allowed to use the stove to heat up some soup, or is the microwave as far as you're willing to go? How about having friends over or going to visit a friend's house? The rules should be clearly understood.

- Be sure your home is safe before you leave children alone for any length of time. If you have guns, they should be locked away, unloaded, separate from ammunition (also locked away), and only you should have access to the keys. Better yet, get them out of the house, as research indicates that the risks of self-injury and suicide are clearly reduced when firearms are removed rather than merely locked away. Alcohol and drugs of any kind should also be stored in locked cabinets that the children cannot open.

- A common problem is fighting between unsupervised siblings. To help minimize conflicts, be clear about each child's responsibilities.

- If your child is leery of being a self-care kid or tries it and doesn't like it, respect the youngster's feelings and find another way to deal with after-school hours. Hiring a baby-sitter is one answer, but you might consider other arrangements, such as play dates with friends, extracurricular activities, community programs, or a combination. Some schools, particularly in large urban areas, offer inexpensive after-school programs that include recreational, rest, and homework time.

Building Responsibility and Growing Independence

There was a time when your child smothered you with kisses when you dropped her off at the day-care center. Then came the start of school and, though less ardent in her affection, she still managed to make you believe every day that she would miss you.

Now that she's moving up the grades, she is more independent and more critical. "No," she insists, "you don't need to walk me to school; that's for babies." "And, please could you not sing along with the radio when you're driving the car pool to soccer practice; it's embarrassing."

The moment we are born we begin the process of emotionally moving away and separating ourselves from our parents. The infant who peacefully lies in your arms becomes the toddler who playfully hides from you and eventually becomes the high schooler who pesters you for the car keys.

Prior to the start of elementary school, your child's burgeoning independence is a source of pride to you. She is doing more things for herself, learning by leaps and bounds, and actually beginning to take on some responsibilities. Even so, the preschool child is still affectionate toward family and has a strong desire to be like the parent of the same sex.

Things change, however, usually around the first grade. The opinions of peers become increasingly important. The child wants, indeed needs, to do more things for herself. She may seem impatient with you. Gone are the days when she unabashedly ran into your arms as the whole class looked on; now she is aware of the other children looking on. This is not a sign that your child loves you less than before. Affection simply makes her uncomfortable, as anyone who has ever witnessed young children watching a kissing scene on television knows.

As children put more emotional distance between themselves and their parents, they often become attached to other adults whom they admire. The adult may be the child's teacher, a coach, or simply a friend of the family. Regardless of who the adult is, his or her opinion is received as wisdom; no argument you make, no matter how lucid, can punch a hole in it. As any parent who has been through this knows, if the teacher says Hawaii is in the Caribbean it must be so. Parents have the right to acquaint themselves with the child's new heroes and should do so as part of their parenting responsibility.

Allowance: Teaching the Value of Money

By the time a child reaches elementary school, she is aware of some of life's financial realities. She probably understands that she can't buy something every time she walks into a store if she has no money. She is aware that the purchase price of your house was more than the cost of a pair of jeans; but if you give her a dollar to spend, she's just as apt to pick out a fifty-dollar stuffed animal as a packet of stickers.

As children grow older, they better understand money and what it will buy. The ten-year-old with a five-dollar bill in hand will scan the aisles of the toy store looking for things that can be purchased with that amount. The child of this age also is more likely to save her money if she sees something that costs more money than she has.

Elementary school students should have a small amount of spending money. This makes them feel more independent and helps them understand that they are responsible for buying some of their own treats.

If your child receives or earns an allowance, let her know the rules you have regarding how the money is to be spent and any chores that you wish to make contingent on receiving payment (see also *Chores,* page 135). Some parents, for example, may object to money being spent on candy. Many children have a tendency to spend every cent, so some parents intent on teaching fiscal responsibility insist that part of the allowance be saved every week. If you pay, establish a weekly payday and stick to it, even when your free-spending child begs for an advance.

GOOD DEEDS, COMMUNITY SERVICE

Elementary school is a good time to instill in your children a desire to help others.

Not only do children in this age group love to do things for other people, in doing so they feel competent and more grown-up. The child also has a feeling of accomplishment. "I collected two big boxes of books and now children in South America have books in their school!" your third grader announces at dinner. She bursts with pride and so do you.

The older a child is, the more volunteer opportunities are available. But even a first grader should be encouraged to put something back into the community. School or church collections of food or clothing for needy families are both easy for young children and rewarding, particularly when you make the point that because she devoted her Saturday morning to cleaning out closets instead of watching cartoons, some needy children will have warm clothes to wear. Brownie or Cub Scout troops can visit nursing homes, collect toys for holiday gifts, bake and serve cookies at a senior center, plant trees in the park, and do lots of other visible, considerate things. Making things for grandparents or sick friends is another appropriate way for a child to become a part of a larger community.

Helping the child to care about others teaches her that each person, even small people, can make a difference. Another benefit of learning to volunteer time and energy in childhood is that the pattern of commitment may continue. Many studies have found that adolescents who help in their communities are less likely to have serious problems such as drug and alcohol abuse as they move toward adulthood.

Manners

You thought you were bringing up a child Miss Manners would be proud to call her own. You heard words like "please" and "thank you" without having to ask *What do you say?* Your youngster used a fork—not her fingers—and usually managed to wait her turn to speak.

Lately, though, you don't recognize her behavior. She wolfs down her food, comes to the table with bits of the backyard under her nails, throws her clothes on the floor, and seems to have forgotten the words "please" and "thank you." Has she forgotten everything you taught her?

Rest assured that this has not happened. Children who grow up in households where family members are kind to each other and who are gently taught politeness and consideration do not forget what they have learned, but they don't always apply it either.

What is happening is that your child is once again trying to be more like her peers. This is another way of declaring independence.

Not every child drops good manners but it is a relatively common problem and one that many parents find exasperating. In deciding your course of action, the question you have to ask is whether this is a serious problem for you and your child.

Remember, the elementary school child has learned that some rules are more important than others. Forgetting table manners, for example, is not as serious as stealing.

Thus, children know that when they let their manners slide it is not a serious infraction. As a parent, you may decide the limits. If your child is being downright rude, you may be more inclined to step in than if she's simply slurping her soup. When you do tell her to behave, be matter-of-fact and firm. Avoid nagging, it usually doesn't work.

Sensitivity to Diversity

"Why are Joe's eyes different from mine?" your first grader asks one morning as you're waiting for the school bus. "Mine are round and his are kind of narrow and funny-looking."

The question is innocent, curiosity the only motive. Yet, you can't help feeling a little uncomfortable, especially since Joe and his father are standing within earshot. So perhaps you try to change the subject, muttering something about telling her later.

Well-meaning parents determined to raise their children to live in our multicultural and diverse society often make the mistake of sweeping differences under the rug. "Don't stare at the girl in the wheelchair," a mother whispers as she hustles her child away from a handicapped youngster. "She's just like we are."

Yet even a young child knows that that isn't quite true. Children, are, in fact, amazingly perceptive to differences. By the age of four, studies have shown that children have a racial identity. Naturally, when a child sees someone with skin of a different hue, she can't help but wonder about the difference. In the child's eyes, the person whose skin is a different color or who can't walk or see is *not* just like her. There *is* a difference. How you as her parent explain this difference will, to a large degree, affect her future perceptions about racial, religious, and other physical differences.

Your child's views about other people are influenced by a wide variety of factors including television, peers, neighbors, teachers, and what they hear you say in the privacy of your home. Thus, if a child is exposed to hearing negative talk about a particular ethnic group, she is more likely to form negative stereotypes about people in that group—and think that talking negatively is acceptable behavior and follow your lead. On the other hand, if she sees that you treat all people with sensitivity and respect, she is more likely to behave similarly toward others.

Children need simple, concrete answers to their questions. When your daughter asks you why a boy's eyes are shaped differently, simply explain that different people have different eye shapes. Joe's parents are Chinese-American, so he has eyes shaped like theirs. You could add that it isn't all right to say that Joe's eyes are funny-looking because that will make him feel sad. Remember, even a small child can understand that certain things make people feel bad inside.

One day your child may come home from school and declare that she hates all black/white/Asian/Catholic/Jewish/Protestant people. Translated, this probably means that she had some kind of an altercation with one child who is of a different race or religion. Simply explain to her that it is only possible to like or dislike people we know and she doesn't know everyone in the world who falls into that group. It's okay to have reservations about a classmate who plays rough or swears or bosses other kids. But it is not all right to dislike him or anyone else because of the color of his skin or the place he worships.

Don't ignore bias incidents. If someone makes a remark to your child that shows prejudice against a particular group of people, you should make a point of telling your child that you do not share this belief. When you or your child are the targets of prejudice, it is important to teach your child how to respond to a derogatory remark as children can easily personalize prejudice. Whereas an adult can shrug off the incident by telling herself that this person is a bigot, the child often thinks that the problem lies within herself. The message she's hearing is that there is something wrong with her, whether it be her skin color, religion, or culture.

Discussing the incident openly is the best approach. Explain that the bigoted person has a problem. If the incident happened at school you may want to talk to the teacher or principal. By being assertive, you empower your child to do the same thing the next time something similar occurs.

Finally, involve your children in activities with children from other cultures and backgrounds. This enriches them and helps them to understand that people's differences and diversity make the world a more interesting place.

Making Friends

It was so simple when your child was a toddler playing in the sandbox. All it took to be her friend was a willingness to play side by side without infringing on space or toys.

The days of such simple relationships go the way of diapers and afternoon naps. The friendships forged during middle childhood are complicated and become increasingly so as children grow older. A first grader, for instance, when asked what makes a person a friend, is likely to say that a friend is someone to play with. Children of nine or ten will stipulate that a friend is a person you like and who likes you, who would never betray you, one with whom you can share feelings and activities, a person who is there when you need her. Indeed, some experts believe that a child's emerging ability to share a special intimacy with friends prepares them for

love and healthy relationships in later life.

Boys during middle childhood are quicker to make friends and are apt to have more companions than girls. Girls, on the other hand, develop more intense relationships and appear more able to distinguish between an acquaintance and a close friend.

Girls tend to discuss feelings and attitudes about people and situations. They compliment each other and exchange presents. A boy's interactions with friends are likely to be in a larger group, typically engaged in a game from which one or more winners or winning teams will emerge.

An elementary school child with no friends is probably unhappy about it. Children are discriminating judges of each other, and if a child cannot make friends there may be a serious problem. You may be able to help your child, however, as studies have shown that the way a parent treats his or her child at home does influence the child's interactions with peers at school.

Children with harsh and punitive parents tend to be aggressive with their classmates and disruptive in class, two qualities that won't win any popularity contests. Shy children often have difficulties in making friends and feel lonely. On the other hand, well-liked children are more likely to have parents whose dealings with them are positive and constructive, rather than negative and controlling.

Here are some things you can do to help your child make friends:

• Set high standards for behavior at home. Children who know how to behave are more likely to make friends than those who don't.

- Allow your child to take on increasing independence when she shows that she is capable of accepting this responsibility. This is a real confidence-builder.

- Be friendly and hospitable to your child's friends. Encourage her to invite a friend to dinner or on an outing.

- If your child tells you she has no friends, talk to her teacher. She may be able to get others to notice your child by giving her special jobs in class or calling attention to her abilities. Sometimes even a simple seat change works wonders.

- Parental modeling of appropriate social behavior can be helpful for children who are having difficulty making friends.

Privacy, Modesty, and Sharing

By the time most children are six or seven, they begin to want a little privacy. Children may suddenly object to sleeping in the same room as a younger brother or sister. The child may start spending more time alone, reading or playing. The idea of having private thoughts and possessions that no one else can see or touch appeals to children especially during middle childhood. Locked diaries and mini safes with combination locks are popular among this set, reinforcing the child's desire to keep things to herself.

Exercising a right to privacy is a natural part of growing up. Unless you believe that something detrimental is happening behind her closed door, respect her privacy. Knock before entering the room and, however curious you may be, resist the temptation to read her diary, go through her drawers, or read her mail.

■ MODESTY

You diapered her more times than you could ever count but these days she won't even let you into the fitting room when she's trying on clothes. The child that as a preschooler used to invite friends in to watch her use the bathroom has suddenly realized that the bathroom door has a lock—and she's using it.

This newfound modesty you're seeing occurs as children become more aware of their bodies and of the differences between boys and girls. The girl who as a preschooler had no qualms about taking a bath with her brother, as a first grader balks at the idea. She wants her privacy.

As children become more aware and concerned about their own bodies, they also are more sensitive to their parents' bodies. Some parents have a relaxed attitude toward nudity. As children get older, they may become embarrassed if they see a parent naked— especially the opposite sex parent. The parent too may feel uncomfortable. As your child gets older and more sensitive about her body, it is helpful to respect her modesty and be discreet.

■ SHARING

By the time most children enter elementary school, they have learned many lessons about sharing. They have learned that when they share, something good often happens. Perhaps the teacher nods her approval or other children want to play with them. Conversely, they learn that when they don't share, there is usually a negative result, whether it's a frown from the teacher or being shunned by the other children.

Although the typical child who enters school knows the rudiments of sharing, sharing skills develop during these years. Children learn to like sharing by seeing their parents, teachers, and peers demonstrate (*model*) this behavior.

In one study, fourth and fifth graders bowled for certificates that could be exchanged for merchandise at a toy store. After the game, the children passed a box labeled "Orphans's Fund" with a picture of a poorly dressed child on the front. Some of the children then saw an adult putting some of her certificates in that box; others did not. Almost half of the boys and girls who saw the adult make a contribution made similar contributions, too. Of the children in the other group, none contributed to the fund for orphans.

Role Modeling

Children are great imitators. They learn to speak by listening to the language they hear around them. They learn to hit when they are hit. They learn to share by seeing others share.

As a parent, encourage development of your child's positive social behavior. One of the ways to do this is to behave in a way you want your child to behave. This is positive role modeling.

Another powerful use of modeling is the strategy of a *coping model*, in which children observe the parent articulate and use strategies to solve problems. The child who sees the parent respond sensibly to such day-to-day events as a missed school bus, a power outage, or a last-minute cancellation by a baby-sitter in a measured fashion has a positive pattern to copy.

One effective method in eliciting positive behavior from school children is called *explicit modeling*. In one study, some teachers held periodic sessions in which they demonstrated sharing and helping behaviors, whereas the other group's teachers provided no extra help. The children in the first group were much more likely to help and share with their classmates than those in the latter group.

Children are more likely to imitate the behavior of a person who appears similar to themselves and who has control over reinforcements; that is, someone who sets limits, makes demands, communicates values, and gives rewards. Aside from parents, teachers are often a child's earliest role models. It is very common to see elementary students—particularly girls—try to imitate the skills and voice the opinions of their teachers because most elementary teachers are women.

In homes where single parents are raising children of the opposite sex, an approach of seeking same-sex role models for the child outside the home and identifying common interests between the child and the opposite-sex parent may prove helpful. Finally, good role models are not selected solely by sex. Other considerations are factors, too, as studies have shown that children are more likely to adopt the teacher as a role model if the teacher has a positive approach and uses positive reinforcement and social praise.

Growing Up Too Fast

Where did her childhood go, you lament as you watch your strapping preadolescent packing for camp. One of the cruelest ironies of parenthood is that there are days when you feel so tied down by the demands of diapers and runny noses that the end seems as remote as a distant planet. Then, in what seems like a blink of the eye, those years have come and gone and your child is forging full speed ahead into an adolescent and adult world that you hope she can handle.

Although childhood to the parents who have watched the process has always seemed much shorter than it has to the children who are living it, this generation of children appears to be growing up faster than its predecessors. Today many children as young as elementary school have a degree of worldliness that many adults find disturbing.

The magazines and television shows that kids watch often portray preteens who dress, look, and act as though they're a decade older. In many elementary schools girls dress seductively, wearing makeup and hairstyles beyond their years, or boys attempt to touch or grab girls inappropriately and use street language to act cool or older than they are.

Children have always been in a hurry to leave childhood behind, especially when there is an older sibling in the house. The younger child sees her older brother or sister getting to do things that are off-limits to her. *Why can't I go to PG–13 rated movies. . . have my ears pierced. . . go to the mall with a friend. . . wear lipstick? You let **her** do it.* These are words that every parent with more than one child is destined to hear.

Whether your child is acting too grown up or not, you need to help prepare your preadolescent to handle the sexual and other pressures that will come with adolescence. The following strategies may help:

- Remind your child that you have rules and that broken rules have consequences. If, for example, your fifth-grade daughter is wearing makeup to school without your permission, make it clear that this is unacceptable, why it is unacceptable, and if she breaks the rule, take away a privilege.

- Discuss sex in a manner that is appropriate to the child's age and deals with the specific question she is asking. A six-year-old who asks where she came from probably does not require a step-by-step account of human reproduction, whereas an eleven-year-old might be ready for (and need) a more detailed description. Discussing the emotional aspects of sexuality and intimacy is as important as understanding the physiology.

- Don't scare your child about sex. A parent should not issue threats about sexual behavior because these may later cause the child to rebel against the parents by acting out sexually. Threats may also create abnormal attitudes toward sexuality that make a sexually healthy lifestyle more difficult later in life.

- Try to relate sexual matters to everyday life. The message should be that sex is not dirty but simply a part of life. For example, in discussing the love and respect that people who are involved in a sexual relationship should have, you might allude to a recent wedding you and your child attended or to the birth of a baby in your neighborhood.

- When your child develops a crush, don't tease.

- If your child uses sexual terms as swear words, calmly let her know that this is inappropriate and that it shows disrespect and demeans people.

- Monitor the television, movies, and videos your child sees and discuss unacceptable behavior of the characters. In many cases, the urge to grow up stems from seeing the worldly characters on television. All too often, the message received is, *I can be cool like her if I talk to girls like that and do the things she does.*

- Avoid giving in to your child so that she has the same privileges of an older sibling. Your older child had to wait until a certain age to attain these "grown-up" privileges. Let the younger one have some goals, too.

TOY SELECTION

A child's work is play, and toys are the tools of her trade.

But what toys? One has only to turn on the television on a Saturday morning to be bombarded with commercials singing the praises of dolls who give birth and space invaders ready to do battle.

Ideally, the toys you buy or make for your child should be age-appropriate. However useful and stimulating a microscope may be to an eleven-year-old, it will probably remain unused on your first grader's toy shelf. On the other hand, buy her a doll with a historical costume and her imagination may take her back in time.

Many companies these days indicate age ranges on their packaging, so as to guide you toward picking a toy that will give your child the pleasure of discovery, not the frustration of being unable to master it.

In choosing toys for your child, keep in mind the different skills that certain toys help develop. For example, fine motor skill is essential if a child is to write her name. Toys that improve fine motor coordination include jacks, marbles, a yo-yo, magnets, a harmonica, pick-up sticks, video games, and a computer mouse and keyboard.

To help a first-grade child develop her overall coordination and strengthen large muscles, a jump rope, roller/ice skates, bat and ball, mitt, kites, ring toss, or a small bike would be good toys. An older elementary schooler can handle a larger bike, basketball hoop and ball, sled, skies, skateboard, in-line skates, and swim fins.

Toys can nourish the child's imagination. Children in the early school years love to pretend they are the postal carrier delivering mail or the teacher teaching the ABCs. Give a child a doctor's kit and she'll operate on her stuffed animals. Six-year-olds of both sexes love dolls and stuffed animals. Boys should never be teased about playing with dolls, and girls should not be teased or discouraged if they play with trucks or other toys traditionally regarded as being for the pleasure of boys. Aside from dolls and stuffed animals, puppets are great toys for giving voice to a child's imagination. In the imagination of a child the box that your new refrigerator came in can be transformed into a space station or a puppet theater.

Children love to make things. Encourage your child's creativity by making sure she has a supply of paper, pencils, markers, paints, clay or play dough, and crayons. Tinkertoys, Lincoln logs, and Lego blocks are great for budding architects and contractors, and jewelry-making kits, lanyard lace, ceramics, a weaving loom, and musical instruments and tapes also are toys that help children develop their creative side.

Other toys that encourage children to think are board games (young children need simple games), puzzles, books, and science kits. Board games can provide positive play for the whole family.

An ever larger range of computer software is available to help children learn their letters, to master reading and writing, and to learn about the world. Select carefully when shopping for computer programs; be sure the software is age-appropriate and that it offers both educational value and entertainment. As the child's reading skills improve, access to the Internet can also offer your youngster the chance to exercise curiosity and explore new areas of knowledge. As with the television, but even more so because of its interactive capability, use of the Internet requires supervision and safeguards.

As you peruse the aisles of your local toy store, think active play rather than passive. So many toys these days involve little more than a finger pushing a button or two. There's more fun and benefit to be had in activities that allow the child to become actively involved.

Motivation

Humans behave the way they do for a reason. This great instigator of behavior is called *motivation.*

Human behavior is motivated: To accomplish the simplest task, people must perceive a benefit or payoff. That benefit may be internal, a private pleasure appreciated only by the individual or the payoff may be external. A child who wants to please her parents, for example, may clean her room. The parent then lavishes praise and the child basks in the glow of parental approval.

Most parents want their children to do their best, whether it be in school, sports, or other activities. Motivation is, in fact, of central importance to a child's ability to learn. The question usually asked is, *How best to motivate a child?* A corollary to that, however, is *How best to help a child develop self-motivation?*

Children are usually motivated in school by the use of incentives. Sometimes the incentive is external like the prize of a pencil for the best speller or a packet of stickers to the child who reads the most books. Other times, especially as children get older, the incentive is more self-directed. The child wants to read more books than anyone in the class to prove something to herself, her parents, or her teacher.

A major dilemma for many parents is whether they should offer incentives to motivate a child toward good behavior or better grades. Your child may first bring it up, mentioning that her friend gets one dollar for every *A* and wondering why she doesn't get such a good deal. The goal you should be working toward is to have your child want to do well in school or be well behaved because in doing so she feels better about herself (an internal motivation). There are, however, times and situations where it doesn't hurt to offer some incentive. Here are some things to think about in offering rewards or incentives to your child:

- *Don't overdo it.* Make incentives the exception, not the rule. Don't apply them to regular chores but to one-time tasks. Moreover, allow a couple of weeks before you offer another incentive.

- Consider using nonmonetary rewards. Instead of money, offer a privilege, outing, book, or toy.

- Make sure the child understands the connection between the task and the incentive. If you study your math every night this week, I will take you ice-skating on Saturday. If she holds up her end of the bargain, you must fulfill yours.

- Whenever possible, provide the incentive as soon as possible after it is earned. A promise of a summer camping trip for a straight-A report card sounds good, but if it comes months after the fact its value as an incentive is lost. A better incentive would be a trip to a toy or bookstore the day after report cards come out.

EXTRACURRICULAR ACTIVITIES

During middle childhood the physical boundaries of your child's world expand, and with that expansion comes an awareness that there are many interesting things that people do.

This is a time when children clamor to try new things. Your child comes home from school asking to take art lessons. Your daughter announces over dinner that a Brownie troop is forming and wants you to sign on the dotted line. *Can I play on the soccer team. . . take ballet. . . have clarinet lessons. . . be in the drama club. . .* The list of activities goes on and on.

These years are for exploration. *Do I have the talent to be an artist when I grow up? Could I ever be a good enough gymnast to compete in the Olympics?* Children can discover whether their interests and talents match by trying new things. Perhaps you think your eight-year-old has no special artistic talent, yet she wants very much to take an art class. Why not let her? It probably won't take her long to realize that she will never be a professional artist but this exposure may teach an appreciation of art that gives her pleasure throughout her life. And many talents come as a surprise to parents.

Extracurricular interests keep children busy and away from television or spending too much time playing computer games. A child who spends afternoons at the baseball field practicing her pitch isn't watching cartoons, and she's getting the exercise her body needs. There are questions to ponder, however, such as once an activity is started should it be continued? How will you handle issues regarding practice?

Many of the activities kids enjoy after school and on the weekends also offer an opportunity to make new friends. Children in elementary school love to feel as though they are a part of something. Hence, the popularity of clubs and activities such as scouting.

Although extracurricular activities should be encouraged, be careful not to let your child get overscheduled. Some children are put on a treadmill of activity from the moment school ends until bedtime. This is too much for even an energetic child to handle. Make sure your child gets plenty of time to read a book or simply relax. Make it clear that school is your child's first priority and these other activities should not interfere with homework.

Popularity

One day your child may come home from school, chin quivering, eyes darting everywhere but your face. You wonder what's wrong. Has something happened? The youngster grudgingly admits not having been invited to a birthday party or some other event. *Why don't kids like me? Why can't I be popular?* asks your child, still young enough to expect an answer that will magically resolve the issue.

Most adults can still recall a time when they felt like an outsider, when everyone in the world was liked but them, when all it took to make their day was a kind word from the class leader. It is natural for children to want to be liked and to have friends. Friendship is as necessary to childhood as immunizations or learning the ABCs. But not every child is destined to be voted homecoming queen or student body president.

Elementary school children crave approval from their peers but soon realize that it is more important for some peers to like them than for others. At dinner every night you may hear about the girl in the class that everyone wants to sit next to or the boy who no one will play with. Within every classroom a hierarchy evolves, with those at the bottom being ignored or rejected and with an exulted few at the top.

A child's social development in later years may be related to her place in the group during these early school years. Just what does make a boy or girl of nine or ten especially popular? Physical attractiveness is probably an important factor, especially among girls.

But unusual beauty may lead to a child's neglecting more enduring aspects of personality development. Other attributes include the willingness to help others, being able to remind others of rules, the ability to offer suggestions in difficult situations, being oriented toward the group, and nonaggressive behavior. Conversely, children who are most often rejected by their peers are more likely to be excessively talkative, active, and aggressive.

Most people do not draw large numbers of admirers. Thus, it is important to teach your child that having many, many friends is not necessary; having a small circle of friends, though, is crucial to the child's emotional well-being.

As a parent you cannot make other children like your daughter, but you can teach your child attitudes that will enable her to be more comfortable with herself.

- Many parents in their desire to make the child feel good send the message that whatever she does is special. This sense of importance has value in establishing the toddler's self-worth, but needs to be tempered with reality as the child reaches school age. If not moderated by reality, it will be translated in the young mind as, *Hey, I'm pretty great, better than anyone else, in fact.* The child who believes she is better than her peers is seen as arrogant, especially if she expects preferential treatment. In contrast, a child who is more apt to demonstrate humility may be well liked by others because she is sensitive to other people's feelings and doesn't feel that she is above the rules.

- In an attempt to become popular, a child may decide that acting a certain way or developing a persona is essential. You can counteract your child's urge to develop a false front by explaining that it is normal and acceptable to act differently in different situations. It's all right to be shy in one setting and rambunctious in another. Emphasize that it isn't possible for everyone to be her friend. What is more realistic, however, is that she feel good about herself and her friends.

- Children can be close buddies one moment and enemies the next. Sometimes small incidents have a way of snowballing. If your child has a fight with a close friend and it appears that neither party has the skills to resolve the mess, offer to help. You might also enlist the help of the other child's parents.

- Let your child know that her friends are welcome in your home. When her friends come over, make them feel their presence is appreciated.

SUMMERTIME

In most households children wait for summer the entire school year. When summer does arrive, the novelty can wear thin in less time then it takes to unpack a backpack.

Within days the mantra *I can't wait till it's summer* is exchanged for *I'm bored.* And as any parent knows, one bored child equals one miserable adult.

The key to making summer a time that your whole family looks forward to is scheduling activities to keep the children active. Summer is a great time to plan family vacations. Sign your children up for local activities such as tennis, swimming lessons, arts and crafts, or playground programs. These are enjoyable for most children and give parents a much needed break for a few hours.

When parents work full time, summer poses a problem beyond boredom: child care. Some parents hire baby-sitters to work during the summer, others rely on day-care centers, all-day camps, many of which provide busing, and even sleep-away camps for part or all of the summer. However, many parents are forced because of finances to leave their older children unattended while they work (see *Latchkey Kids,* page 138).

Despite all the options available to help your child enjoy summer, try to avoid overscheduling her so that she's running from one activity to the next. Children also need a little unstructured time as much as they need activity. So give her some time to lie on the lawn, watch the clouds drift by, and wonder what it would be like to be up there looking down.

Television

American children today watch too much television.

There are two basic problems with television: The programming itself and the fact that children who sit hours on end glued to the tube are *not* doing the things kids should be doing, like playing with friends, daydreaming, shooting hoops, perfecting a pirouette, collecting bugs, and all the other things that make childhood a magical time.

The average American child from birth to age eighteen spends more time in front of the television than in the classroom. In the average American home the set is on six or more hours a day. In television-oriented homes, there are few books or records and family trips to museums or parks are rare.

When a young child watches television, she has difficulty differentiating fact from fiction. A seven-year-old who sees the villain shot by the sheriff isn't entirely sure whether the actor is really dead or just pretending. An eight-year-old who watches a television couple with their arms around each other wonders if they are really married or whether they are very good friends in real life.

Another basic failing of television is that it is so fast-paced that there is no discernible continuity of action from one sequence to another. This makes it difficult for even a nine- or ten-year-old child to follow what's going on since there is no time to stop and think for a moment between scenes. How does this effect a child when he's not watching television? One study found that children who watch a lot of television had lower than normal expectations about how long it takes to learn from a textbook. These children tend to read less than their peers and do not do as well in school.

Any parent who allows a child to watch television should be concerned about the content of shows. Television has an enormous power to shape opinion. A negative use of that power is portraying sexual, racial, religious, and age-related stereotypes. Studies have shown that when children watch culturally sensitive educational shows such as *Sesame Street*, which portrays children from many ethnic backgrounds as friends, they are more willing to get to know children of other races or religions.

In addition to stereotypes, television serves up a daily diet of violence. An estimated 80 percent of the programs that children watch contain violence. There is widespread agreement that children who are allowed to see violence on television show more aggressive behavior than those who don't. Even preschoolers who watch a show such as *Superman* are more likely to be more aggressive toward their playmates than a child whose television is restricted to *Mister Rogers' Neighborhood* or other nonviolent children's programs.

The child who is allowed unsupervised access to television is getting a head start on sexuality and attitudes toward other issues before parents themselves can frame the discussions. Characters in prime-time shows act out sexual relationships in scenes that only a few years ago wouldn't have been allowed on the air. Smoking, drinking, and even drug use is often portrayed as normal and acceptable.

Even TV commercials teach children to want toys they can't have and food that isn't healthy for them.

What then is the solution? Most experts agree that less television is a step in the right direction. This is not to say that all television is bad. There are high-quality shows for children and adults, but you have to look for them.

Children should not be allowed indiscriminate use of the television set. It shouldn't be in the child's bedroom. Parents should not only control the programs their children watch but should limit the time they're allowed to watch TV. Some experts suggest that during the week a parent should limit television to no more than one hour a day. The television should never be on during mealtimes or other family times.

When your children watch television, try to watch it with them. When parents watch a show with their child, the child gains a better understanding of what she is seeing because the parent is able to help put things into context and discuss values with their child. Parents can also turn off shows that are not appropriate for their child.

Finally, children learn by example. It's not enough to tell your child not to watch television, if you too are a television addict. Teach her to be selective and discriminating by limiting your own television viewing.

WORKING WITH SCHOOLS

One of the most beneficial things you can do for your child during these elementary school years is to be involved with the school.

One way of doing this is by volunteering to help out whenever possible. Elementary school children love to see their parents at school. If you have any doubt about the truth of this statement, make a point of running into your child the next time you're at the school shelving books in the library or distributing the school newsletter. Her face will brighten when she sees you.

When you are involved in your child's school, you are sending the message that you care about her day and what happens in it. Moreover, you are more likely to get to know teachers and other school personnel and to get a feel for what is going on both in and out of the classroom. Parental involvement is critical to school success. It is also important that the parent support, within reason, the authority and order of the teachers.

There are dozens of ways a parent can help make their child's school a better place. The needs of every school vary but most are dependent upon a Parent-

Teacher Association (PTA) for various extracurricular activities and fund-raising. As a PTA volunteer, you may want to volunteer to arrange class parties or accompany your child's class on a field trip, help children select books in the library, or tutor those who are behind in their reading skills, or act as a parent liaison between your school and the school board.

Some working parents assume that because they are away from the home all day, they cannot be involved in their child's school, but this isn't true. Even though you may be unable to commit yourself to being at the school on a regular basis, you can still actively participate in the evenings or on weekends, whether it be making costumes or painting sets for the class play, calling parents to inform them about school activities, or helping out at your child's class booth at the school fair.

Even if you decide that you simply do not have the time for any volunteer work, you should still make a point of establishing an open line between yourself and your child's teacher. During the early weeks of school, send in a note introducing yourself to the teacher or place a phone call. Be sure to attend back-to-school or open-school night if your school has one. It's an opportunity to hear the teacher talk about the curriculum. Most schools also offer an individual conference between parents and teacher, which is your chance to address any questions or concerns you may have about your child's progress.

As you prepare for your conference, write down your concerns, questions, and any points you want to make. Even if your child has been having problems with the teacher, be friendly and cooperative, not combative, which will only put the teacher on the defensive. The message that should come through loud and clear is that you consider the teacher and the school part of your team, a team whose goal is to help your child do her best. *What can we all do to make things better for the child?* should be the issue on everyone's mind.

Remember when dealing with the teacher or school principal: You are your child's advocate and it is up to you to speak up if you suspect a problem. Without a strong parental voice in the student-teacher-school equation, many students can fall through the cracks.

School Problems

Before a child starts school, parents often wonder whether their child's behavior is normal. Even when a child seems particularly difficult or fussy, most parents assume (or hope) that such exasperating behaviors fall within the realm of normality. In most cases, it is only after a child enters school that serious behavioral problems come to light. There a child's behavior can be observed and measured against that of other children of the same age. Whether the child has learning disabilities, emotional disorders, behavioral disturbances, or a combination of problems, there may be negative consequences. The youngster's social interactions, academic accomplishments, and school attendance may suffer, producing difficulty with learning, achieving, making and maintaining friends.

Second only to the family, school is probably the most important socializing influence on children. In many cultures, success and failure at school is virtually the equivalent of success or failure as a person. School is the child's primary occupation. It's where the child spends the greater part of each day. Therefore, success at school is important for both social and emotional development. When children are unsuccessful at school, tremendous difficulties for both the child and parents are common outcomes. Often parents personalize their child's successes and failures at school. Parents tend to hold themselves responsible for their child's difficulty at school and can become frustrated and exasperated. This in turn has a similar effect on the child.

When children start school, they are stepping into an unfamiliar world. At home, they are still dependent and usually feel cherished and secure. Yet at school they are relatively independent, trying to learn to make some decisions for themselves in a more impersonal group. The rules for belonging, for being valued, are unfamiliar, often shifting from year to year and from class to class. In school, children must work to earn approval from their peers and teachers, whereas at home they may feel accepted and secure merely by being part of their family.

Young children tend to miss school because they do not feel well enough to attend, usually due to stomachaches or headaches. With older children, truancy becomes an expression of underlying problems. At any age, problems with school attendance have academic and social implications.

Most children receive sufficient emotional support and understanding at home. From this base, they are able to negotiate both the social and academic demands of school life. For some children, however, home life and school life are not in harmony. Troubles at school can easily create difficulty at home, and troubles at home can plague a child's school experience. The child who has to go back and forth from one troubled life to another is doubly vulnerable to anxiety, depression, frustration, anger, fear, and despair.

A child upset by tensions at home will likely be distracted from his schoolwork. When this results in poor academic performance, tensions at home may increase. Frustrations and worries that stem from home life may be acted out with teachers and peers, causing behavioral problems. Eventually, parents will be called into the school to address their child's problems.

Children who have learning or social problems at school might conceal them at home. As time passes, a chasm of silence, deception, and anxiety can widen, causing tensions. Sometimes when a child has problems at school, the youngster may become withdrawn and be sullen or rebellious and irritable at home.

Parents can contribute to or distract from a child's success at school in the attitudes they express toward school, academics, and teachers. Often when parents themselves have been competent or successful in school, they are more supportive of their child's achievements. Parents can reinforce appropriate school-related behaviors, such as regular attendance, completing homework, reading, and studying. In general, homes that provide appropriate educational stimulation are less likely to have children with school problems, yet they can also establish overly high expectations.

Parents also influence how children relate to their peers. Those who are relatively successful in their own social relationships tend to have an easier time helping their children work out their peer relationships. When a child has poor peer relations, is regularly teased or rejected by his peers, serious school problems, as well as emotional problems, may develop.

There are a number of ways in which parents can ensure that their child's home and school life are in productive harmony:

- Encourage your child to talk about school. Go beyond the routine, open-ended question *"How was school today?"* Initiate more meaningful, deeper conversations about school.

- Find time regularly to review—together—what your child brings home from school.

- Help your child with homework without actually doing it. Show interest. Make sure the youngster has adequate space and material to work.

- Help engender interest in school lessons by making connections with other things in the child's life. Apply, for example, mathematical skills to cooking, sports scores and statistics, shopping, or drawing. Go to the library or bookstore to look for additional reading material. Play board or computer games that elaborate on the subjects being studied in school.

- Volunteer for school activities such as chaperoning a field trip; solicit an invitation to address your child's class about your work.

- Don't link poor grades to a system of punishments or, on the other hand, academic accomplishments to a system of bribes of money or material things. A child should learn to regard success or a good grade as its own reward.

- Talk with the child's teachers frequently. Discuss behavioral and social matters as well as academic issues.

- Keep informed about your child's curriculum, school, and school system.

- Being calm at home can help a child handle difficulties at school. Therefore, make a special effort to maintain a stable, supportive home environment. This is especially important at times that are naturally more stressful at school such as the first few weeks of school life, the beginning and end of the school year, and transitions from elementary school to middle school or on to high school.

- Encourage and enable your child to get involved in extracurricular activities. These will enhance natural interests and talents and the youngster will be able to cultivate friendships with other children who share the same interests. In doing so, it is helpful to the child to have some input into the kind of activities he might like and not overwhelm or burden the child with an overly demanding or busy schedule.

- At the same time, children also need unstructured time. After school, it may be perfectly fine to have some down time simply thinking, daydreaming, creating games, engaging in imaginative play, or playing spontaneously with friends and siblings. If a child feels too much pressure to be productive all the time, he may start to resent these activities and rebel in his behavior.

Even when parents do all they can to help their children strike a productive balance between school and home, they may find themselves frustrated by the school itself. As most students, teachers, and parents know, there are certain behaviors that are unaccept-

able in school. Yet there are a number of ways in which schools may unwittingly foster the very behavior they find objectionable. When children are having school problems, parents should be alert for certain problematic areas in the school setting.

Some schools are less sensitive to students' individuality than others. When schools squelch individuality by demanding rigid uniformity, students who differ more than slightly from the norm may be given the impression that being themselves is bad, inadequate, or unacceptable. This negative self-perception can lead to distorted perceptions of social situations as well as diminished intellectual efficiency and motivation.

Some schools seem to communicate inappropriate expectations for troubled students. Sometimes, by labeling students as emotionally disturbed or behaviorally disordered, they set up the expectation of failure.

In other cases, schools set classroom standards that are either too low or too high. Schoolwork that is too demanding leads to frustration, which can cause aggression, regression, or resignation. Schoolwork that is too easy can provoke a sense of boredom and lack of focus, which can result in disruptive behavior. When schoolwork does not reflect a child's intellectual ability, the child may avoid school altogether.

Some schools or classrooms fail to manage behavior with consistency. When a child cannot predict a teacher's responses, the youngster may feel anxious and powerless to figure out appropriate behavioral alternatives. It is confusing for a child when a specific misconduct is punished at one time and overlooked at another. The lesson learned may be that favorable consequences following good behavior cannot be relied upon. This lowers the incentive to behave properly.

At the same time, it is crucial that schools provide reinforcement for desirable behavior and avoid reinforcing inappropriate behavior. If a child who is always acting up in class gets all the attention, however negative that attention may be, other children may rightly feel passed over and ignored. The lesson could be that good behavior and high achievement are hardly worth the effort.

When children spend a lot of time learning irrelevant skills, or when they cannot understand the relevance of the material, they may begin to misbehave or become truant. Ultimately, they will fail to engage in the material and feel that they are wasting their time. This becomes more of an issue as the child gets older.

Finally, schools should provide models for desirable conduct. Teachers whose attitude toward academic work is cavalier, who treat others cruelly or disrespectfully, and who are disorganized, tend to foster similar attitudes and conduct in their students.

Given that a child spends almost twelve years in school, it is crucial that parents take an active part in their children's academic pursuits and maintain regular contact with the teachers. In this way potential school problems can be identified early enough to devise strategies and appropriate interventions.

Part II

DAY-TO-DAY PROBLEM BEHAVIORS

■   ■   ■

In these five chapters, you will find discussions of issues faced from time to time, not by all children, but by many, in their singular paths toward adulthood. Some are everyday behaviors, feelings, and reactions that are perfectly normal but are distressing for you and your child; others are more problematic. We offer guidance for dealing with a range of such day-to-day problem behaviors as your child's lying, stealing, aggressiveness, or bed-wetting; for dealing with a death in the family, moving, changing schools, and other life transitions. As always, our goal is to offer reassurance and direction so that you can interpret and respond to your child's behavior in a helpful manner.

"Football is my favorite sport."   *Ahmed, age 7*

5

Challenges At Home

■ ■ ■

The day-to-day challenges of parenthood can be daunting even when your child is perfectly healthy. One day your two-year-old is banging his head against the wall in a fit of temper, your kindergartner thinks a snake is hiding under her covers at night, and your older child is waking up in a wet bed. What, you wonder, do these things mean?

The answer is probably nothing. While parents often doubt themselves and their parenting skills, many children's behaviors are not the result of anything the parent has done (or not done). More likely the child is going through a normal developmental phase. The purpose of this chapter is to address some of the common issues and concerns of childhood. Some, such as simple tantrums and conflict between siblings, occur in all families, while others—bed-wetting, breath-holding, hyperactivity, and aggression, to name a few—may or may not be problems in your home.

Aggression

Each one of us has some aggression inside of us. As adults, we learn how to control such urges; as a parent, you will more than likely be challenged at some time by your child's aggressive and/or destructive behaviors.

Perhaps the first sign occurs in playgroup when your two-year-old nips the arm of a playmate who dared reach for the toy that your child wanted. With a slightly older child, the aggression may take the form of verbal threats or insults against a classmate. Some children are model citizens around their friends and peers, preferring instead to demonstrate their aggressive behavior at home toward parents or siblings. You might find your child breaking toys, coloring on the walls, or even kicking and hitting.

Learning to control aggression is an important part of social development in early childhood. Feelings of anger that may lead to aggression *are* a perfectly normal part of a child's range of emotions, although individual children vary greatly in how intensely they express anger. As a parent, a big part of your job is to teach your child to control hurtful or angry behavior. In order to help your child do this, it is helpful first to understand what constitutes aggressive behavior.

An aggressive act is by definition one that is intended to hurt someone. Therefore, if your preschooler, in the excitement to show off a drawing made in school, knocks down baby brother, the explanation is probably normal impulsiveness not aggression.

A behavior cannot be considered aggressive until the child understands that physical acts of aggression are painful to the other person, and that by causing this pain, the youngster can have an impact on the other person. For most children, this realization comes during the toddler years.

There are two basic ways of understanding aggression: *instrumental aggression*, which is aggressive behavior directed toward obtaining something one wants; and *hostile aggression*, specifically aimed at hurting another person, whether the motive be revenge or a means of establishing dominance and superiority.

Studies have shown an increase in aggressive behavior especially toward siblings during a child's second year of life. Up until eighteen months of age, children are likely to smack, kick, or bite a sibling. As a child approaches two years of age, however, the youngster seems to discover other nonphysical ways to hurt others. He demonstrates the capacity to walk away from a physical fight and might instead rip up another's prized picture.

Most parents notice an increase in aggressive behavior around the age of two. At this age, the toddler develops a clearer picture of himself as an individual with ownership rights. Most two-year-old children are not good at sharing their toys and there will probably be an occasional tug-of-war over a toy. The point is not the toy itself—neither child shows any interest until the other wants it—but the ability to emerge the winner.

Children between the ages of three and six are less likely to have a physical altercation over who gets to play with a certain toy. However, verbal insults, threats, and teasing increase during these years. Although most children learn to manage aggressive feelings as they grow older, some get even more hostile over time.

Parents who have aggressive children may wonder what has caused their child to behave in this manner. There are thought to be three major factors at play in the development of aggressive behavior. First, aggressive behavior is a necessary component of evolution. Basically, Charles Darwin's theory of the survival of the fittest states that to be successful, any animal or human being must compete with others for the things they need to survive and reproduce. This favors individuals who are competitive and geared toward meeting their own needs even at the expense of others. According to Darwin, over time a species develops the characteristics of its most successful members, who have had to be aggressive in order to survive. While such aggression may have served a role in our collective evolution, it does not have this benefit for individuals today.

As a parent, however, you have some control over the other two factors thought to contribute to aggressive behavior: *rewarding aggressive behavior* and *modeling behavior*.

Some children behave aggressively because they are inadvertently rewarded for those behaviors. Studies of preschool children have found that generally after a child takes a toy away from a classmate, he is actually rewarded in that the victim either hands over the toy or goes on to something else. Thus, the aggressive child learns that this is a way to get what he wants and subsequently he doesn't hesitate to repeat this behavior. Over time this becomes a pattern of interaction for the child, especially when he wants something right then and there.

Think about the way you react when your child displays aggression. Parents sometimes unintentionally give signals of approval to aggressive behaviors, such as paying more attention to the child, laughing at the incident, or giving a nonverbal message of being proud of the child's aggressive act.

The third factor in aggressive behavior is that children model their actions after those of an adult. When a child breaks a rule and is spanked or beaten, that youngster is more apt to behave aggressively in social situations. In a series of experiments, researchers had groups of preschool children watch an adult with an inflatable doll. In some cases, children were in the same room while an adult yelled at, punched, and hit the doll's head with a mallet. Others watched the attack on television, while still others saw an adult dressed as a cartoon cat perform the violent acts. Children in a control group watched the adult in nonaggressive play with the doll.

Later, each group was given a chance to be with the doll. Those children who had seen the violent adult—whether in person or on television—behaved in a violent manner toward the doll. The researchers concluded that the children learned that aggression was acceptable from watching the violent adult.

■ **HOW TO RESPOND**

- Examine your methods of discipline. If there is physical violence in your household or if family members consistently use coercion, a child is more likely to mimic the model seen at home and use similar tactics at school and on the playground. Instead of spanking your child when the youngster hits a playmate, try sending the aggressor out of the room for a time-out. In this way, you minimize the negative attention-giving, thereby reducing the chance of giving any nonverbal signal of acceptance.

- Children crave attention and sometimes will use aggressive behavior to get the attention they need. If you suspect the inappropriate behavior is an attention-getting ploy, try lavishing your attention on the victim, while ignoring the aggressor. Pay attention to the aggressive child only when the youngster is playing cooperatively and then be generous with praise.

- Don't expect your young child to share his toys. Most children until the ages of three or four are not happy about giving up a toy to a visiting friend. Encourage sharing, praise it when you see it, but don't punish the youngster for not sharing. Let the child see you sharing with others. When your child does have a friend over, try to prevent problems by putting away special toys.

- If your young child is destructive around the house, it is probably a function of natural curiosity and clumsiness, not malice. Put breakable items out of reach, give your child safe areas to explore like a special kitchen drawer. If an item cannot be moved, tell your child not to touch it and if the youngster disobeys, use verbal disapproval or a time-out.

Usually a child takes something apart out of curiosity but sometimes things are broken intentionally or in anger. If toys are deliberately broken and the item belongs to the child who has ruined it, explain that you will not replace it. If the item belongs to someone else and your child gets an allowance, have him pay for part of it. The realization that the child is *responsible* for replacing the item should teach the youngster a valuable lesson about respecting others' property.

Attention-Seeking

The attention you give your children nourishes his emotional well-being much the same way food nourishes and keeps his body healthy. Love and attention are vital to a youngster's well-being.

Children crave acceptance, praise, and those moments of undivided attention that tell them they are special. Unfortunately, they don't always understand that there are appropriate times to seek their parents' attention and times when parents are focused on other things and unable to give them the attention they seek immediately. Very young children understand only their own needs, and when children want attention, they often resort to annoying behaviors such as whining, clinging, complaining, and interrupting. If they still don't get the attention they are seeking, temper tantrums may ensue. Such behaviors are intended to get parents to attend to the youngsters' needs *immediately.* Most of these attention-seeking tactics are used by toddlers and preschoolers because children this age have not yet learned to delay gratification. As the child develops, he will learn to be more patient, to be able to be considerate of the needs of others, and to delay the need for instant gratification.

A young child's limited vocabulary can also make it difficult to explain exactly what is desired. This leads to frustration and impatience, which can easily escalate into a bout of whining or even a temper tantrum. Moreover, during these early years your child is in the awkward position of trying to separate from parents and become more independent, yet feeling uncomfortable in these new situations. This continuous emotional push and pull makes the child more volatile. Some attention-seeking also turns into a power-play. *I can too make Mommy put down the baby! All I have to do is scream and kick the floor.*

If you have a young child who is continuously seeking your attention at inopportune times and in inappropriate ways, remain calm while he whines, complains, interrupts, or even has a tantrum. Don't respond to a demand until the child has calmed down, otherwise the message will be sent that whining works. When the request is made appropriately, praise the child and try to respond.

Try to be proactive and anticipate bad behavior: Before you start a lengthy phone conversation, explain to your child, "I'm going to be on the phone for a while. Please don't interrupt me while I'm talking." Find the child an activity for your phone time. The idea is to deal with the bad behavior before it happens rather than coping with it *after* it happens. On the other hand, if you find yourself in the middle of an unexpected telephone conversation but it can't be interrupted when your child is demanding your attention, try to get the child to count to five slowly while you finish what you're doing. When it happens next, ask the youngster to count to ten.

For most children, time will allow the maturation process to do its job as long as you set consistent limits. By the time most children are seven, they are capable of thinking through cause and effect. Consider the first grader who has seen the negative effects of interrupting and who wants permission to go for a bike ride. The youngster sees the supervising parent on the phone and is more likely to wait until the conversation is over to ask, recognizing that the odds are better for getting permission if he waits.

Most school-age children have learned to control their anger when they don't get what they want. If your child is still having tantrums or fits of anger, ask yourself whether you have set enough and appropriate limits. Do you spend lots of time with your child? Is the youngster under too much pressure?

During the elementary school years, children's emotions and behaviors are relatively tranquil. However, as your child becomes a preadolescent, expect some behaviors designed to grab your attention. Some of this attention-seeking may be reminiscent of the preschool years, with your son appearing to test your patience. Some of this is developmentally appropriate as he gradually moves away from you toward greater independence.

Expect arguments. Your older child's mental resources are more advanced and you will be amazed at the youngster's ability to argue a point. View arguments as discussions and a chance to teach the child about debate. Refuse to lose your cool and don't respond to the child unless he stays calm, too.

Above all, make a point of spending time with your child. Although the child may pretend otherwise, now *is* a time when you are needed.

Whining

Whining is a method of seeking attention, and one that can be extremely grating. One reason parents hate to hear it is that whining expresses negative feelings so effectively.

Like the child who suddenly throws himself on the floor in a temper tantrum, the whiner wants something from you and wants it *now*. The difference is in his approach.

Whining is actually a subthreshold tantrum. Although the whiner may be easier to take to the grocery store than the child who collapses in a sobbing heap at the checkout counter, the whiner can test the most patient parent's endurance. Whining, in fact, often works for a child because adults reward the whining to make the whining stop.

All children whine at times. But if you have a child who uses this tactic often, you should handle it as you would a temper tantrum. First, make sure that you don't routinely give in to demands or the youngster will learn that whining produces desired results. Sometimes *parents* whine, too. Consider whether the child has learned to whine from an adult or an older sibling. Is it a learned behavior?

When the child is whining, explain that you can't understand him and that you will talk to him when he can use a normal voice. When you get to the point where you can't stand it any longer, send the child for a time-out or ask him to sit in a "whining chair" until he can state his request in a normal tone of voice. When the child demonstrates some mastery over whining, reinforce and encourage the child and listen and consider his request.

Immature Behavior

As your son plays with the girl next door, you can't help noticing how much younger he seems, even though he is, in fact, three months older.

Her vocabulary is more extensive, her speech clearer. She skips when your child can barely hop and, while it doesn't take much disappointment to push your son's tantrum button, this girl seems to have a firm handle on her emotions even in the face of upset.

Is something wrong with your child? *Rest assured*—in most circumstances like these, there is nothing at all wrong with the less mature child. The normal rate of development is variable and he is simply developing at his own pace.

It would be so easy, both for parents and for the doctors who treat children, if all human development followed a set clock. If we could predict that all babies would walk by their first birthdays or that every child would start having temper tantrums by age two, it would take some of the guesswork out of parenting. But children are individuals, each with a unique temperament and genetic makeup. There is no communal clock.

Thus, what we have is a range of skill development and those who fall within this range are considered developmentally on target. Your infant may walk at nine months, while your brother's child takes his first step at fifteen months. Yet both fall within the normal range of development.

Immature behavior manifests itself in many ways. Whining, clinging to a parent while the rest of the kindergarten marches through the classroom door, tantrums, and hitting or playing aggressively are all examples of immature behavior. Most children have learned to control these behaviors by the time they are in kindergarten or first grade. Some simply take longer to attain the sophistication level of their peers. Others may regress due to the birth of a new baby or a radical change in the family such as divorce or the death of a loved one.

Immaturity itself is less important than whether it is causing the child trouble. Is your child having difficulty making friends? Does your youngster get into trouble with the teacher? If things are going well at school, maybe your child behaves in an immature fashion only around you. This suggests self-control skills that the youngster can exercise at will. Maybe this is a time to examine family dynamics to see if you are inadvertently rewarding the child for not acting his age.

How should a parent handle immature behavior? The best course is not to ridicule the child for immature behavior but to offer praise for appropriate behavior. Don't assume that the youngster always knows what is acceptable and what isn't, so offer reminders: *No, I will not listen when you whine. Use your big-kid voice so I can understand what you want.*

Temper Tantrums

Everything was going fine. You and your two-year-old had a pleasant time at the park and on the way home you stopped at the grocery store. Then it happened. Standing in the checkout line, you shook your head at a request for a lollipop. The next minute, your child was on the floor, kicking and screaming. And every pair of eyes in the store is on your child and on you, the parent of *that kid!*

Every parent whose child has moved beyond infancy has been through it. Tantrums are one reason that the term *the terrible twos* was coined. In fact, two-year-olds do not have a monopoly on this emotional meltdown. Children barely past their first birthday have been known to voice their displeasure so that the entire neighborhood wakes up and listens; most three-year-olds can kick and scream with the best of them. Even school-age children have their own form of temper tantrums. While the average third grader doesn't roll on the floor and try to kick the wall in, you may hear professions of hatred from the child's mouth, along with slamming of doors and accompanying sobs.

If your child is going through a period of temper tantrums, do not despair. One day this stage will pass and your child will be more cooperative. No matter how good a parent you are, most children will have at least some tantrums during their childhood.

The ages of eighteen months to three years are a time when stubbornness, opposition, and even outright defiance are normal. Expect *No!* to be your child's favorite word. The youngster's negativism is simply a normal step in the process of becoming more independent. Sometimes parents become weary with their children's temper tantrums, but don't be discouraged.

This is not to say that every child is effected equally. Perhaps life with your first child was relatively tranquil, the tantrums few and far between. Then your second child may seem to have one tantrum after another. A child's temperament is thought to be a factor, as some children simply have a more difficult time than others getting through this developmental phase. Typically, even during infancy these children were unpredictable, resisted change, and were emotionally intense.

There are parenting techniques you can use that may avoid some tantrums.

- Don't punish the child simply for saying "No." Try to ignore negativism if you can.

- Give the child two acceptable choices. For example, don't pick out one outfit and expect the youngster to agree with your choice. Instead, find two acceptable outfits and give the child a choice.

- Give a warning before a transition. If the child is happily playing with a friend and you suddenly announce the end of playtime, a fit of temper may erupt. However, if you say that in a few minutes it will be time to say good-bye, this gives the youngster time to get used to the idea. Transitions from one activity to the next are sometimes hard for young children, so parents need to be sensitive to some of these developmental issues.

- Try to limit your own use of "No." Use positives.

When the inevitable tantrum occurs, how should you handle it? To a large degree that depends upon the type of tantrum. A temper tantrum expresses anger but that anger may be fueled by different causes. Some tantrums, for instance, are the result of a child's frustration—the youngster can't button his shirt so he explodes. Or he wants something that he can't have, perhaps a cookie just before dinner. Some tantrums simply are the result of the child being tired at the end of a busy day.

How you handle the tantrum depends upon what provoked it and the needs of the individual child. Some children, for example, calm down quickly when picked up and held by an understanding parent; others scream louder, kick harder, seeming to need physical release before they are ready for the comfort of Mom's or Dad's arms.

When your child has a tantrum out of frustration over an inability to do something, try comforting while encouraging the youngster to keep trying. Explain that you are proud of the child for trying to tie his shoes and that soon he will be able to do it.

When a tantrum is initiated by a child's desire for something that is unallowable, the approach is different. First, don't give in to the demands—if you do, the child will learn that a tantrum is effective. If possible, ignore the tantrum, even if you have to move to another room. Most tantrums run their course within a few minutes, especially if the child doesn't have an audience.

After the screaming stops, be friendly and try to act as though everything is back to normal. With an older toddler, try to get the child to verbalize feelings: *I felt angry because. . . .* If the tantrum occurs over your child's refusal to have a bath, let the screams go on for a few minutes and then carry the child to the tub and give a no-frills bath. Again, the youngster mustn't get the idea that a tantrum can be used to control a situation.

Some children during a tantrum seem to be capable of injuring themselves, banging their heads, holding their breath. Children, like adults, avoid pain, so it is unlikely that your child will physically hurt himself (see *Breath-Holding*, page 171).

Naturally there will be times when you can't ignore the tantrum. If your child is damaging property, kicking and breaking things, you must intervene. When anger turns against a parent or another person, move the child to his room. Send the message that aggressive behavior is not acceptable.

Breath-Holding

There are few behaviors as frightening to a parent as a child who, usually in a fit of anger or frustration, holds his breath until he turns blue or even loses consciousness.

Breath-holding is a problem that typically begins between the ages of six months and two years. Most children outgrow the problem by the time they are four or five. Usually a breath-holding attack is precipitated by another event. Angry over not being able to select groceries on a shopping trip, a child may fall down and begin crying and then hold his breath until turning blue around the lips. In many cases, breath-holding occurs when a child is in the midst of an escalating temper tantrum. Young children often become frustrated, and hold their breath.

Whatever the cause, it is important for the parent to understand that these attacks are generally harmless and brief. An estimated 5 percent of children have an abnormal reflex that allows them to hold their breath long enough for them to actually pass out, which is frightening to the parent.

During a breath-holding episode, have your child lie flat to increase blood flow to the brain. Time the attack; usually they last under a minute. Don't put anything in the youngster's mouth because this could cause the child to choke. *Never* shake a youngster in an attempt to restart breathing, as this can cause blood vessel damage around and inside the brain. Do not try to resuscitate your child unless he doesn't resume breathing quickly.

If your child is a breath-holder, you can expect the attacks to occur anywhere from once a day to once a month until the child outgrows the behavior.

Although a typical breath-holding episode is harmless—if terrifying to parents—there are situations in which you should call your child's physician. If they occur more than once a week and are increasing in frequency, seek an evaluation by your pediatrician. You also should call the doctor if your child holds his breath for more than a minute or has muscle jerking during the attacks. If your infant is under six months of age and/or turns pale instead of blue, notify your doctor immediately or call 911.

In dealing with breath-holding attacks, try to have a relaxed attitude and not show anxiety or concern. Go about your business once the attack passes and, above all, if the attack was prompted by your refusal to give the youngster something he desired, don't be tempted to give in now. You don't want your child to learn that such behavior results in his wishes or demands being fulfilled. That might result in perpetuating rather than diminishing the breath-holding episodes.

Impatience and Impulsiveness

When a young child wants something, he wants it *NOW*. Patience—the ability to wait for something—is a behavior that you as a parent must teach your child.

Young children can be quite impatient.

The infant screams when hungry and stops only when fed. The baby is many months away from learning that a few minutes' wait will produce satisfaction.

Fortunately, as children's reasoning abilities expand, they realize that waiting for what one wants is sometimes necessary. Even though waiting a half hour to turn on the television may seem an eternity, most six- or seven-year-olds have realized that indeed that time will pass and before long they will be watching their favorite program.

Of course, some children are slower to learn patience than others. Children who are perfectionists tend to be very impatient, especially with themselves if they fail to accomplish something on the first try.

Help your child learn to tolerate frustration. Doing things *for* them doesn't develop a tolerance for frustration but *avoids* the issue. If he is drawing a picture, for example, and having difficulty, help him do the hard part so that he can get on with the rest and avoid the frustration that could erupt into a tantrum. New challenges should be introduced when the child is in a good mood, not when a nap is overdue or a meal running late.

Praise is also an important component of teaching patience. Next time your child waits patiently for something, be sure to let the youngster know how impressed you are. Finally, make sure your own behavior sets a good example. Many adults, too, exhibit too little patience.

As with patience, the ability to control one's impulses is learned. During the early months and years of life, children tend to be impulsive, driven by curiosity and the need to explore. Even though you tell your toddler to stay away from the stairs, the staircase may still attract the child the moment your back is turned. When your child wants a toy that a playmate is holding, the impulse is to grab for the toy. This is not a thought-out or calculated move, but an impulsive way of achieving a desired end.

By the time most children have entered school, they have learned to control their impulses. They've learned that they can't grab toys away from others if they expect others to play with them. At this point, most children have the ability to consider an action before they act it out.

There are some children, however, who display impulsive behaviors at an age when they should be able to exercise control. These children may consistently show poor judgment. The impulsive child can't seem to wait to be called upon to speak out in class or for a turn to bat during a baseball game. The youngster may be caught stealing from the local supermarket or behave aggressively toward other children. This child may seem unable to consider the consequences of an action *before* acting.

Some children with these characteristics are simply spontaneous individuals and risk-takers. If you suspect your child falls into this category, try to help the youngster learn to think through a situation.

Don't lecture or place blame. Instead, help the child think through his actions and consider what will happen if he behaves a certain way. Talk about specifics: If, in a given situation, he behaves one way, how will his peers respond? Offer alternative behaviors and get the child to consider what playmates will say and do. Talk about his friend's feelings—will a given action cause emotional hurt or pain? Over time, help your child learn to *think* before he *acts*.

Some children who are unusually impulsive may have attention-deficit/hyperactivity disorder (see *Attention-Deficit/Hyperactivity Disorder,* page 337). If your child's impulsiveness causes school problems, if he is having difficulty concentrating on tasks and is overactive, then consult your child's physician.

The Active Child

A great deal of physical activity is normal during childhood—kids, to varying degrees, love to run and play. Sometimes, however, a child seems to be literally bouncing off the walls and no matter how hard you try, you can't seem to interest the youngster in settling down for a story or for some quiet activity. If you have an active child, he may be in constant motion or you may notice erratic bursts of energy.

Some children are very active and are a challenge to the caregivers trying to keep up with them. But overactivity itself is not a diagnosis or disorder. Overactivity is simply a behavior that may be a part of attention-deficit/hyperactivity disorder (see *Attention-Deficit/Hyperactivity-Disorder,* page 337), a condition that occurs in 3 to 5 percent of children. ADHD interferes with learning because these children have difficulty paying attention, following directions, and remembering information.

Children who are overactive may also be impulsive, and act without considering the consequences. They may also have difficulty directing activity. Children who are overactive and who are having problems in school should have a comprehensive evaluation.

In overactive as well as hyperactive children, there are behavioral techniques you can use at home to help control activity:

- Keep your household well organized. Routines help the active child to develop a sense of orderliness. Make wake-up, bedtime, mealtimes, snacks, and chores as consistent as possible.

- Provide an outlet for his energy. Make sure he gets time outside to play. A fenced yard or, in the winter, even a garage, is a good place to play. Limit the number of toys he has because too many toys can increase his distractibility.

- Make sure your child gets adequate rest. When an active child is tired, impulsiveness increases.

- Avoid places where your child is at risk of becoming overstimulated: a crowded mall or a fast-food restaurant at lunchtime on Saturday, for example. Limit time in places where the expected level of quiet, good behavior is impossible for the child, such as a long religious service, a lengthy visit to the library, or a movie he finds boring.

- Develop and implement limits. Overactive children can tolerate fewer rules than the average child. But make sure the rules you do have are consistently enforced.

- Accept your child's limitations. Don't criticize his overactivity and don't expect to turn him into a quiet child who can sit still for long periods of time.

Habits

Like adults, children sometimes perform an action so often that it becomes automatic; it's hard for the child *not* to do it. When this happens, the child is said to have a habit.

A child may develop a habit because of anxiety or pressure. Children who bite their nails, for example, tend to be high-strung. When a nail-biter is anxious about a school project, the child's fingers automatically find their way into the mouth.

Many childhood habits are the result of the child's need to comfort himself. The child who sucks his thumb remembers and finds the pure comfort and well-being of infancy when life consisted of lying in a parent's arms and sucking on a bottle or breast. Thus, when your son is tired or after an argument, you may find him with his thumb in his mouth. Another so-called "comfort" habit is rocking or head-banging, a behavior found in older infants. Again, this behavior is more likely to occur when the child is tired or frustrated.

How is a habit best handled? In the past, nail-biters were subjected to everything from splints on the fingertips to bitter medicine, neither of which was usually successful. If your daughter bites her nails, try giving her a manicure. It can be a nurturing and comfortable grooming activity and it also communicates to her that her hands and fingers are attractive. Perhaps she will want to keep them pretty by not biting them so much.

If your child is self-comforting with a habit such as thumb-sucking, then scolding, punishment, or bad-tasting medicine will not cure the habit. Nor does nagging and punishment solve the problem. In fact, such parental responses can make the problem worse since the child feels even more stress. Most children give up thumb-sucking on their own over time, but if your child's habit is severe enough to be causing dental problems, your dentist may suggest a mouth appliance to curtail thumb-sucking.

Despite our best efforts, however, some children do grow up with habits. They may address it later when they themselves become cognizant of the habit; in some cases, this occurs when peers notice the habit and the child becomes self-conscious and tries to modify or stop the habit. For the parent, one productive approach may be to examine the stresses in your child's life and to try to reduce the need for a comforting habit like nail-biting.

Sexual Behaviors

Children by nature are inquisitive, exploring everything around them. At the same time, they are also discovering things about themselves and their bodies. The day you come across your child with his pants down playing doctor with a friend, you may find yourself at a loss for words. Is this normal behavior and, if so, what is the best way for you as his parent to react?

Sexual feelings are, in fact, perfectly normal during childhood and even infancy, and an essential part of healthy psychological development. Most sexual play during early and middle childhood involves exploration of their bodies and masturbation, in which the child touches his own genitals. Many children, especially young ones, also play sexual games with a friend of the same or opposite sex. They may pull their pants down and examine each other, with or without touching, watch each other go to the bathroom, and practice kissing and hugging just like grown-ups.

Although you may have just learned of your preschooler's sexual behavior, the child probably discovered pleasurable genital feelings in infancy. As the child matures, it is natural for the youngster to become more curious and to touch the genitals because it feels good.

However, some children also touch their genitals when they are tense or nervous. These children tend to touch themselves more frequently than those who are doing it simply for the pleasurable sensation. Sometimes they need professional help because the behavior may be a symptom of anxiety, and the child may be indiscriminate about where he indulges in such behavior. If your child repeatedly masturbates in public or exhibits other unusual sexual behaviors (imitating intercourse, for example), consult your child's physician, who may recommend consulting a professional with expertise with children (see also *The Traumatic Effects of Child Abuse,* page 323).

Preschool children also have strong feelings about the people they love. Your son may announce one day that he's "in love" with a girl in his class and wants to kiss and hug her just like parents do. You may notice how physical he's become with you, kissing you, wrapping himself around you. This is an age when children love to touch and be touched. They're curious about their own bodies and also the bodies of others.

Preschool children are more likely to be found masturbating and engaging in sex play with friends than are older children. Yes, school-age children do masturbate, but they are more apt to do it in the privacy of their bedrooms. Recognizing this to be normal is important for parents as a step in helping their children learn culturally appropriate expressions of sexuality.

Most experts recommend a casual approach. You don't want to overreact. Parents who slap their children's hands or tell them what they're doing is "dirty" may make the child more determined then ever to masturbate, or it can make the youngster ashamed of his body and contribute to sexual problems later. Moreover, young children may fear that something bad will happen to their genitals because of excessive masturbation.

On the other hand, you don't want to ignore masturbation or other sexual play. If you do, your son will think it is all right to masturbate in front of others. Explain that this is something that should be done when alone, in the bedroom or bathroom. When there is more than one child involved, make them aware that you know what they're up to. You can indicate your disapproval without punishing or making them feel ashamed. Oftentimes distracting the children and keeping a closer watch on their play is all that is necessary to discourage this activity.

A NEW BABY IN THE FAMILY

Understanding the frustration of a first child is easy: Until the moment Mother and Father bring home a new baby, the firstborn has been the focus, adored and fussed over and catered to by parents and extended family. After having had Mom's and Dad's full devotion, a little usurper arrives, a helpless bundle of neediness that requires constant care and attention. It's a situation even the most well-adjusted child has trouble coping with graciously.

Yet steps can be taken to ease that transition. Make the child feel a part of the process well before the baby arrives. The older sibling will find the adjustment easier if she knows well before birth that a baby is growing inside Mommy. There's a thrill of recognition for her, too, if she's allowed to feel the baby kicking.

When a baby joins the family, you can defuse the anxiety and resentment of the older child by inviting the youngster to participate in the baby's care. Tasks should be age-appropriate but even a young child will feel useful in a "grown-up" way if she's pushing the carriage or putting on baby's socks or patting his back to burp him. An older child can help with feeding and may enjoy reading favorite stories out loud to the sibling. Any exercise of the skills she has developed serves to reinforce not only her sense of mastery but also her place as the older, more accomplished child in the family.

Make sure to schedule time with your older child by herself to do things you've always enjoyed doing together. Make her feel as special as her younger sibling is. (See also *The New Sibling*, page 79.)

Conflicts with Siblings

Rivalry between children who live in the same house is common and can take many forms.

The arrival of a baby triggers jealousy in even the most secure child. When a cute, cuddly stranger is suddenly competing for— and usually winning—their parents' affection and attention, and even that of extended family members like grandparents, a young child may feel ignored and less important.

Then there are the physical conflicts that occur when your toddler dares encroach upon a favorite toy belonging to your preschooler. You may find your younger child screaming, pinned to the floor by the older sibling.

As children get older, most learn to hold their physical aggression in check, but that does not stop them from squabbling and having feelings of jealousy *(You love him more than me!)*. Hurtful remarks can become commonplace as even young children are adept at knowing the right buttons to push to get a reaction from their siblings.

So expect that sibling conflict will be a part of family life. There are ways, however, to create an environment in which jealousy between siblings does not hamper your relationships with your children and theirs with each other.

■ THE NEW BABY

The arrival of a new baby, especially when your child is between the ages of one and three, can be a traumatic event, particularly to the firstborn child who is used to exclusive rights to his parents. Children often regress when the baby comes home. A toilet-trained child, for example, may start having accidents. Or the child's speech, once so clear, becomes difficult to understand and baby talk reappears. The older child sees the baby getting the attention that was once hers. Visitors stream in bearing gifts. Mom and Dad are tired and preoccupied. It shouldn't come as a surprise then when your two-year-old suddenly forgets how to walk and wants to be carried everywhere. Another symptom of sibling rivalry is anger toward the baby, manifested sometimes in rough handling.

While these are normal symptoms and typically resolve within a few months, there are some steps to make the transition easier for everyone.

- Prepare your child for the arrival of the baby. Let the older child feel a part of the process. Solicit the youngster's help in decorating the baby's room, picking out toys, and feeling the baby kick.

- If you will be moving your older child out of a crib and into a bed in preparation for the new arrival, make the switch at least a couple of months before the birth. If the move is made without preparation, your child may feel displaced and unloved.

- Praise your child's mature behavior. Communicate the message that he is your big boy, your helper, and soon will be a big brother, too! Make him feel that the arrival of the baby makes him special, too.

- Don't attempt to get your child to master a new skill such as toilet training immediately prior to the birth of the baby, even if he seems ready. Wait until after the birth when he has had a chance to adjust to the change in your household.

- When you are in the hospital, call your child frequently. Most hospitals today also allow young children to visit their mother and new sibling.

- Upon arrival home, hand the baby to someone else and spend a few moments alone with your older child.

- Allow the older sibling to help you take care of "our baby." Although a young child should never be allowed to carry an infant, you can supervise the youngster as he sits in a chair (with side arms) and holds the baby.

- If your child regresses after the baby's arrival, don't be critical. Give the youngster extra attention, especially for being a "big kid."

- A child who becomes aggressive with a baby should not be spanked; this only teaches that hitting is acceptable. However, you should intervene immediately and send the older child to his room for a time-out. Moreover, be careful of not having the baby and older child alone in the same room for the first few weeks, until you are sure the older child's anger will no longer be directed toward the baby.

■ CONFLICTS BETWEEN OLDER CHILDREN

Some days it may seem as though your children walk around with rulers measuring everything you do for one against what you did for the other. It is natural for children to have some jealousy at times. Generally, the better you get along with each child, the less that child will begrudge the attention that you give to brothers or sisters.

To help foster a more cooperative attitude between siblings, try not to make comparisons. Your child has to know that you love him for himself. If, either verbally or in more subtle ways, when he brings home an average report card, you compare his to his straight-A older sister, he is bound to be resentful, toward both his sister and you. Instead, treat each child as an individual. Teach them that it isn't necessary to compare everything and that things can't always be equal. Perhaps one day one child gets to do something special with you and the next time it will be the other's turn.

When your children argue, unless the altercation turns physical, try to stay out of it. When you do intervene on behalf of one or the other, it only reinforces the jealousy of the one who is blamed because that child, too, wants to be favored by you. If a parent jumps into the fray at the first sign of trouble, that actually encourages disputes because each child is eager to see the other get into trouble.

When it isn't possible to allow your children to resolve their differences, demand that they stop fighting, refuse to listen to arguments, and try not to place blame (unless one is blatantly at fault). Try to get them to focus on a solution, whether it be compromise or going their separate ways for a while. Emphasize the importance of making up and moving on so that they don't dwell on their animosity toward each other.

Fairness

It's not fair! These are three words that parents hear frequently.

Whether the issue of the day is how many cookies each gets or a teacher who lavishes large shares of praise on one or two individuals or punishes another harshly, children are amazingly adept at ferreting out even subtle hints of unfairness.

Although even young children may accuse you of being unfair, a child's perception of fairness becomes more sophisticated as his reasoning skills and sense of morality develops.

Under the age of four, your child wants a cookie simply because he wants it. He won't try to justify his urge for a cookie. In his mind, he should have it because he wants it.

Between the ages of four and five, a subtle change occurs as the child learns to justify his request based on a physical characteristic. For example, if you have three cookies and he and his sister both want one, he may justify getting two cookies because he's a boy.

In the early school years, children are great egalitarians. In their thinking, if everyone gets the same, conflict is prevented and everyone is happy. If you see children of this age arguing, you can bet that no allowances are made for extenuating circumstances. The doctrine seems to be: *Fair is equal.*

When most children are around eight, however, their increased ability to problem-solve enables them to logically take into account factors that may influence fairness. For example, if a group of kids are asked to clean up a playground and a handful of the group does most of the work, most children between eight and ten would agree that the hard workers should get more of the reward than the slackers. During these years, children also tend to take into consideration mitigating factors such as poverty or physical handicaps when deciding how rewards should be divided.

After the age of ten children, like adults, are more apt to consider specific circumstances when asked about fairness issues. Older children would be likely to say that it would be fair to help a classmate sound out a word during reading class but not to whisper the correct spelling of a word during a spelling test. At this age, children are able to take into account more than one person's claims and the demands of a specific situation. They have learned that while all members of the group should be given their due, this does not always mean that everyone is treated equally.

In resolving disagreements between children, keep in mind that the expectations each child has for himself and others change as they develop. Know that fairness is a goal to be met over time. Trust your good judgment and your children's rivalry will decrease.

Twins

One out of every ninety pregnancies in the United States today results in the birth of twins. Although with advanced prenatal diagnostic techniques, the vast majority of expectant parents have ample time to plan for the arrival of two newborns, there are bigger issues than the simple logistics of feeding and diapering.

The world has always been fascinated by twins, especially when they are identical twins. People have a tendency to compare their attributes, trying to discern which is smarter, who is the leader, whether they walked at the same time, and so on.

If you are the parent of twins, it is important to encourage each child's individuality, especially if they are identical twins. Each child needs to know that he is special, not because of the coincidence of his birth, but because of the person he is. Therefore there is controversy whether the twins should be dressed in identical outfits. Don't allow yourself or others to describe them in a comparative way—one twin should not be the reference point for the other.

Twins are usually closer emotionally than the average siblings and that's an advantage in that they each have a live-in playmate. But early on, you should start introducing them to other children, so that they rely less on one another. Encourage them to have their own friends and interests. One may want to take ballet, the other play soccer. Avoid referring to them as "the twins" but use their names. Make it known to friends and neighbors that they are not a package deal and that it is perfectly acceptable to invite one over without the other. Insist that they be in different classrooms at school. Once they have moved beyond the toddler years, avoid dressing them in the same outfits unless they insist.

As a parent of twins, it is extra challenging

to be fair. *I read one's story first tonight, so I must read the other his story first tomorrow night.* This shouldn't be an issue as long as each child feels that he is loved and has his own special place in your heart and in your home. Even if you as parents follow these guidelines, often extended family members, especially grandparents, do not. It may prove helpful in the long run to share your ideas about raising your twins with them, too, asking them to practice the same approaches.

Tattling, Teasing, and Bullying

Most parents at some point witness these behaviors, whether their child is the instigator or on the receiving end of the teasing and bullying.

■ TATTLING

If you've ever spent time at a playground, you know that young children seem to delight in tattling on a playmate. *Mary stole my ball! Peter's hogging the slide! Elise kicked Sarah!* Sometimes it may seem that the children do more tattling than actual playing. Yet, after one child tattles on the other, all hard feelings seem to vanish—until the next episode.

Some tattling is to be expected from your toddler and preschooler as part of the normal socialization process. Once your child enters school, however, the tattling takes on moral undertones. Children between the ages of five and seven are extremely concerned about right and wrong and merciless in their fervor to expose wrongdoing. After that age,

however, children learn that everything is not black or white, and that sometimes a person does something that is technically not right— lie, for instance—to spare a friend's feelings. By the time most children are around nine, tattling at school occurs less often because they have learned that it does not win points with their peers. Older children who repeatedly tattle on classmates will find themselves alienated from peers.

The rules that apply at school may seem mysteriously absent at home. While your twelve-year-old wouldn't think of tattling on a friend, he seems to relish making you aware every time his younger sister's behavior crosses the line. The best rule when it comes to sibling tattling is that unless you are witness to the crime, either ignore it or discipline everyone involved. If you take the word of one child over the other, you may be dispensing flawed justice. Encourage them to work out their differences themselves.

Try to discourage tattling but don't create a blanket rule against it. Teach your children that there is such a thing as "good reporting" when a child should report on circumstances in order to help keep a sibling safe. If, for example, your younger child knows that your older one is skipping school or involved with dangerous activities, he should feel comfortable telling you without being accused of tattling.

■ TEASING

Teasing is typically used by children ages three and up. In most households, the teaser is usually the older child. He knows just what buttons to push to upset his younger sibling.

Although he loves to tease others, he usually doesn't react well when he is teased.

If you have a child who is constantly being teased by another, try to encourage the youngster to ignore it. Explain that often one child teases another out of jealousy. Teasing is a way of trying to diminish the other child and make the teaser feel better. Depending upon the age and temperament of your child, this may or may not work.

If the teaser is your child's sibling, you have more control. Let him know that what he is doing is causing his sister pain. Ask why he teases, what he hopes to gain, and how he would feel if someone did that to him. If the situation doesn't improve, you can try leveling consequences for teasing. Tell him that the next time he teases his sister, he will give up his favorite television show or whatever you deem an appropriate consequence.

■ BULLYING

Many children get into occasional scraps at school or in the neighborhood. By the time most children are in first or second grade, they have moved beyond the stage where arguments are resolved with fists.

The bully, though, shows a recurrent pattern of aggressive behavior. He is the child who purposely trips the girl in front of him in the class line and then laughs when his victim falls or starts to cry. On the playground at recess, he barges into a game of jump rope, snatches the rope away from its owner, and uses it as a weapon when the other children try to retrieve it. Unlike the others, he has not learned self-control.

A bully often is selective, picking out one or more children who he senses are most vulnerable, and then heaping on the physical and verbal abuse. Bullies tend not to be well liked, even by those who are not among his victims. A bully often has low self-esteem and does not do well in school. Children who are bullies are at a higher risk of developing a conduct disorder (see *Conduct Disorders,* page 349) during adolescence, which may later lead to delinquent and antisocial behavior.

Most parents are not aware that their child is bullying others until someone—usually a teacher or the parents of a victim—calls. Bullying is a behavior that often merits evaluation and treatment, so you should consult your child's physician. You may also want to consider family therapy to make sure that you are not inadvertently rewarding this problematic behavior.

Fears

While childhood is a magical time when anything seems possible, it is also a fearful period. Children can have real fears of anything, from the neighbor's poodle to the water in the bathtub. In examining a child's fears, understand that they are a normal part of development and often appear as a child is attempting to adjust to a particular stress in school or at home. Fears also surface when a child is trying to deal with aggressive or competitive feelings.

The first fear that most parents encounter is the fear of separating or *separation anxiety* that typically surfaces during the first year of life. At about six or seven months of age, most babies begin to be fearful of strange places and people. As long as the infant can cling to a parent, he's fine; but if you leave the room, he'll let out a wail that will certainly get your attention. (See also *Separation Anxiety,* page 18.)

The baby at this age is just learning to crawl and getting a first taste of independence. The infant is learning that when people or objects are out of sight, it doesn't mean that they don't exist anymore; you can disappear into the next room and the child can follow. The older infant is now learning that he has some control over his environment and he wants to exercise that control in familiar surroundings and with familiar people. Hence, the *stranger anxiety.*

Studies have shown that most babies will adapt to a stranger if they are given time and allowed to approach the stranger. However, often when the stranger makes the first contact, the baby becomes fearful and begins to cry. A similar fearfulness occurs once the child begins to walk. Again, the child's life is changing and anxiety results. Babies this age often wake up several times a night, screaming as though they have had a terrifying nightmare. The frustration and excitement of the day may account for the nighttime awakenings.

If you have a two-year-old, you may notice that the child is suddenly afraid of the vacuum cleaner or loud, sudden noises. The two-year-old is continually exploring the environment around him, which at times is unfamiliar. Abrupt change or unexpected sounds in his environment can make a young child fearful. Some children at this age experience emotional and behavioral "meltdowns," a sign that stimulation and excitement are overwhelming.

For the preschooler, fears often begin when the child starts having feelings of aggression. Perhaps you have a new baby in your house. You may have what seems like a fearless child who, at the age of three or four is suddenly afraid of everything. The youngster doesn't want to stay with a baby-sitter, can't sleep in a dark room, makes you check every night for monsters under the bed, and cringes when the neighbor's friendly dog approaches. Most likely, the new arrival in your house has stirred up anxiety, anger, and competitive feelings. The older child is trying to hold in these negative feelings, so instead they surface as fears.

Parents often make the mistake of reading more into a fear than is actually there. A child suddenly afraid to flush the toilet probably doesn't have a deep emotional disturbance. Chances are the youngster's psychological development is progressing just fine. But if you take the fear too seriously, you may end up reinforcing it.

Offer reassurance, recognizing that the fear will not go away overnight. If you think the child is dealing with angry feelings, offer acceptable ways for the child to express aggression. Talk about how you feel when you get angry and what you do to feel better.

Don't force a child to confront a fear. If the fear is of dogs, don't drag the youngster toward the next friendly dog you see; that will only make the child pull farther away. This fear is something to be resolved in time and in the child's own way and at his own pace.

Don't let up on discipline and limits. Some parents bend over backward to please a fearful child. This can make the situation worse. The child needs the security of knowing that you have set certain limits and those limits exist no matter how he feels. Ultimately, these limits may help the child resolve the fears because they help to provide boundaries within which the child can function.

THE DEATH OF A PET

For many children, their first real experience with loss occurs when a pet dies.

By the age of three, most children begin to worry about losing something that they love, whether it be a parent or a beloved dog or cat. When it happens, the reaction can vary. Some children can express their grief, while others appear almost oblivious—but weeks later, they're walking around with sad faces, wetting the bed, having nightmares, or becoming aggressive.

You may be tempted as a parent to shield your child from the pain of loss. However, if the family dog dies, the solution to your child's grief is not to ignore what has happened and immediately replace the pet with another. Your child needs to know that it's all right to feel sad and that you feel it too. Let your child know it is normal to miss pets after they die and encourage the youngster to come to you with questions or for extra hugs. Some families even plan simple burials when pets die as a way of saying good-bye and showing respect for the child's loss.

Invariably, the death of a pet will spark fears about a child's own mortality and about yours too, so be prepared for some conversations about death in general. You may want to explain that everyone dies eventually but that most people are old when that happens.

One point to make clear is that death is not simply going to sleep. Children who hear mention of the sick family pet being "put to sleep" may be afraid to close their eyes at night for fear that they too will die. Explain the process: With a dying dog, tell the child that the dog is very sick, in pain, and won't get better.

THE PERFECTIONIST CHILD

Just about everyone knows a child so anxious to be perfect that he refuses to read aloud because he's afraid to make a mistake. Or a girl who gets headaches in the days before delivering an oral English report or a piano recital.

Perfectionism can be crippling to the child and frustrating to a parent. Common among exceptionally bright children, signs of perfectionism can appear in children as young as three or four. As the perfectionist gets older, he may have a limited social life, as his unrealistically high expectations get in the way of making and maintaining friendships.

Perfectionist children typically view themselves and their activities in absolute terms. There are no gray areas: Something or someone is either perfect or useless. These children usually project their own unyielding judgment onto others, and assume that everyone else judges them and their accomplishments as harshly as they do.

Often holding such high standards results not in success but failure. Children who feel intense performance anxiety may freeze up during an exam or an oral presentation. Stomachaches and headaches can lead to school absenteeism, causing the student to fall behind.

Feeling overwhelmed by their own expectations, perfectionistic children procrastinate. As long as a project is never good enough or complete enough, a child may feel safe in knowing that he will never be judged and his true value and ability never truly measured. An unfinished or inadequately prepared project always holds the promise of perfection.

Not all children who are concerned with details are perfectionists. Perfectionism is a problem only when a child is chronically worried; when attention to detail is attached to significant anxiety; or when the child wants to stop the behavior or feelings. For some, experience and a little reassurance will ease their unrealistic expectations.

You can help, too. Show your child that you are not perfect. Think about the messages you send your child: It is one thing to want success, it is another to push the youngster to value achievement above all else.

When anxiety in the face of a project threatens to overwhelm a child, help organize the task and break the project into manageable pieces in order to diminish the anxiety and make procrastination unnecessary.

Finally, if reassurance does little to loosen anxiety's grip on your child, seek professional help.

Dealing with a Sick Child

Children, especially preschoolers, seem to get sick often. One week it's an ear infection; the next vomiting and diarrhea; and at times it's a runny nose and fever.

Luckily, most childhood illnesses are short-lived and usually not serious. It is more likely that the child will bounce back more quickly than the parent who comes down with the same ailment.

Accept the fact that, no matter what you do, your child will get sick occasionally. Prior to adolescence, the typical healthy child comes down with an average of three or four colds per year.

Childhood illness is difficult both for the parent and the child. Even a three-day stomach virus can turn a parent's world upside down. The working parent usually has no choice but to take time off from work. Then there is dealing with an ailing child and perhaps with vomiting and diarrhea. There is the added stress and helplessness of watching someone you love dearly struggle with an illness.

For the child, an illness, in addition to causing pain or discomfort, is frightening. *Grandpa got sick and then he died,* the child may be thinking. *Is that going to happen to me?* It also can be embarrassing and humiliating, especially for an older child at school, who suddenly can't control his bowels. Moreover, a younger child may think the illness is punishment for something he has done or thought about doing.

Although an illness is not easy for either the parent or the child, here are some suggestions that may help you both to get through these times.

- *Be honest.* If you know that something will hurt, let your child know ahead of time. *Yes, the shot will hurt for a moment and it's okay to cry,* you might say. Let the youngster know that you understand how it hurts but that the shot is necessary to get better. Sometimes it helps to give the child a choice. *Do you want it in this arm or that arm, standing or sitting?*

- *Try not to let your child see how worried you are.* Adopt a matter-of-fact, pleasant look on your face when you enter your sick child's room. If you look worried, you will only cause the youngster to worry, too.

- *Don't force a child to eat.* Most sick children don't have much of an appetite. As long as your child is drinking fluids to avoid dehydration, don't insist upon solid food. Most children's appetites return within a few days.

- *Avoid spoiling your child.* A little pampering is fine during an illness. You may find yourself fixing special foods to tempt your child's finicky appetite, reading more stories than usual, and loosening your rules regarding fun things like television. However, illness can bring out the bossiness in some children. Care and nurture are appropriate but remember there may be limits to what you should do for your child. Make it clear that you are there to provide company and to help your child feel better, but also know when to back away.

- *During the time of recuperation, keep the child busy.* Once a child starts feeling better—but not well enough to return to normal activities—you should make sure that there are playthings at hand to keep the youngster occupied. Some suggestions include books, puzzles, craft projects to be done in bed, and a cassette recorder. Doing light schoolwork may make the transition back to class easier, and with less homework to catch up on.

Offer reassurance. Remember, it is frightening to be sick when you're young. As an adult, you know that your child's strep throat will feel much better after a few doses of medication. All the child knows, however, is that it feels as though someone's delivering a sharp stab to the throat with every swallow. The child needs to be reassured the pain will go away soon. As for going back to school, your youngster shouldn't return to day care or school until the fever passes but should be encouraged to return as soon as he is physically able. If you have concerns about whether your child is ready to return to normal activities, discuss them with your child's physician.

Feeding and Eating Problems

When he was a baby, his stomach seemed to be a bottomless pit that you spent a good part of your day trying to fill. Now, though, your preschooler could care less about food. Some days it seems as though he doesn't eat even one decent meal, despite coaxing, bribing, and begging.

Getting a child to eat is a major source of frustration for many parents. You worry about your child not eating enough to promote growth. When parents decide to take things into their own hands, it becomes a battle of wills and a power struggle at the table may result. *You will sit in this chair until you finish your dinner,* a frustrated parent dictates to the child who has no interest in eating the food on his plate. An hour later the child is still sitting there, the food cold and barely touched.

Before you become concerned about a child's change in eating habits, it is important to understand that you cannot compare the infant appetite with that of the toddler and older child. During your child's first year of life, the youngster's birth weight probably tripled, a phenomenal rate of growth that will never occur again. Naturally, to sustain such growth, the child was ravenous, at the breast or bottle numerous times a day and, in the later months of that first year, attacking solid food with relish.

Between the ages of one and five, however, most children only gain about four or five pounds per year. Thus, it stands to reason that the body does not need as much food as it did when it was growing more quickly. As a result, a decrease in appetite is fairly normal.

Children will eat when they are hungry. Forcing a child to eat large portions at every meal when he is not very hungry may make the youngster shun the food altogether, especially if the child is going through an oppositional phase in development. It may send the unhealthy message that the clean plate rule applies regardless of hunger and can turn into an unpleasant power struggle, making mealtimes difficult for the whole family.

When it comes to eating, the rules should be simple. You don't want to make food more important than it is, so don't use it as a reward. Don't offer bribes for eating everything on the plate or specific foods like green vegetables. That doesn't apply to dessert, as eating dessert after the rest of the meal is a healthy principle, not a bribe (*If you finish your meal, you can have dessert*). Don't make the youngster feel guilty if your casserole doesn't appeal to him. A child should not learn to substitute food for love.

Mealtime should be a pleasurable experience for everyone. This means no criticism over your child's lack of appetite or unwill-ingness to eat dinner. Nor should the child be kept at the table for not eating after the family has finished eating their portion. This will only make the youngster associate mealtime with unpleasantness.

The following are additional tips to help eating become less of an issue in your home:

■ PREVENTION

As you begin to introduce your baby to solid food, there are things you can do to make eating more pleasurable and less a battle of wills. When you are feeding the baby cereal, do not trick the child in order to slip the spoon in. Let the child initiate and pace the feeding. If he turns his head or refuses to open his mouth, for example, it probably means he doesn't want any more. Initiate finger feeding between six and eight months of age and give your child a spoon so that he can try to feed himself by his first birthday. Babies should be self-feeding by the time they're fifteen months old. Once the baby is feeding himself, he will stop eating when his hunger is satisfied.

■ IMPROVING A POOR APPETITE

Many children develop poor eating habits despite well-meaning adults. For instance: When your child picks at breakfast, you offer a snack at 10:00, making the youngster too full for lunch. Sometimes a child's appetite returns with gusto after skipping a meal or two.

Although snacks are fine, limit them to twice a day. Choose nutritious foods (not sweets) and keep the snack small. If you find that your child neglects dinner, try eliminating the afternoon snack and see if the appetite for dinner improves.

Many babies and young children neglect their food because they are allowed to drink milk all day long. As a result, their stomachs are too full for food. If your one-year-old is a milk-drinker, limit milk intake to sixteen ounces a day.

Finally, respect food preferences. If your child doesn't like eating carrots and gags every time you insist a carrot be consumed, substitute another vegetable. If the food dislike is not quite so strong, you can make a rule that at least a few bites of peas or whatever the food happens to be must be eaten. Many parents institute a one-bite-per-year rule when it comes to disliked foods. Thus, if he is six years old, he has to eat six peas if he wants to have dessert.

■ WHEN TO BECOME CONCERNED

The vast majority of poor eaters are perfectly healthy kids, most of whom will develop normal appetites as they enter adolescence. However, there are times when poor eating can be a symptom of illness or can by itself be of concern. Consult your family physician if your child is losing weight, has not gained any weight in the past six months, gags on or vomits some foods, or has physical symptoms such as chronic stomachaches or diarrhea.

EATING TOO MUCH, EATING TOO LITTLE?

All parents wonder about the eating habits of their children. Yet few areas of child-rearing are such a source of concern.

One parent wonders, *"Is he eating too little?"* and another worries, *"Is he eating too much?"* A father worries, *"He's loud and obnoxious at the table, especially in public."* A doting mother obsesses, *"My child won't talk when eating and really only eats when alone."*

There's the worry, *"Is there enough variety in a diet of bread and milk and apples?"* and, much the same, the concern that *"He won't eat anything green!"* The complaints go on: *"He eats so fast"* and *"My son eats so slowly!"* and *"None of them will ever try anything new!"*

Does any of this sound familiar?

Eating preferences are a part of childhood. Most are passing challenges to a parent's good sense and patience. However, some eating behaviors persist over a sustained period of time and can lead to dietary deficiencies. Eating difficulties can also become a battleground between parent and child.

Eating habits in children are quite variable. Some children eat a great deal, some are picky, sparse eaters. Some eat quickly, others eat as if they had all day to finish a meal. Yet the single most common factor in eating difficulties in children is, in short, independence. The toddler who insists upon feeding himself; the young child who refuses to eat what his parents insist he must eat; the older child who resists the discipline of parents with regard to food selection and mealtimes—all three are displaying completely natural behaviors that are searching for independence.

Bed-wetting and Soiling

Bed-wetting or *enuresis* is a relatively common problem, occurring in 40 percent of three-year-olds, 30 percent of four-year-olds, and 20 percent of five-year-olds. Most doctors do not consider occasional bed-wetting to be a problem until a child is at least six. Ten percent of first graders wet the bed at least once a month. Remaining dry at night requires neurological maturation, which occurs on a variable timetable.

Contrary to what was once believed, most children who wet the bed do not have emotional problems. Nor do most have physical abnormalities, beyond a bladder that may be slightly smaller than average. Many bed-wetters have a parent who may have wet the bed, so heredity is thought to be a factor.

The majority of children who wet the bed outgrow the problem between the ages of six and ten regardless of treatment. However, because bed-wetting is a nuisance for the parent and can be humiliating for the child, there are steps you can take that may help reduce the problem or at least make it easier for everyone when an accident does occur.

- **Limit fluids.**
  Since your child's bladder cannot hold its contents all night, don't challenge it with extra fluid. Limit your child's last substantial drink to two hours before bedtime.

- **Urination.**
  During the day, encourage your child to hold urine for long periods to increase the size of the bladder. Prior to going to bed, make sure the youngster urinates in order to start the night with an empty bladder.

- **Praise.**
  On mornings when your child wakes up dry, be sure to offer praise. Some parents like to award gold stars or stickers for dry nights.

- **Protecting the bed.**
  You may want to have your child wear thick underwear under the pajamas to help keep the bed dry, though some older children may find such steps embarrassing. To protect the bed, invest in a wash-

able vinyl mattress pad. You can keep the blankets dry by placing a sheet of plastic between the top sheet and the rest of the bedding.

- **Responding to a wet bed.**
  No one likes waking up in a wet bed, so it is unreasonable for a parent to think that any child would choose to be a bed-wetter. Punishment, teasing, and criticism will not help this problem go away, but can prolong the course and cause subsequent emotional harm. Your child needs sympathy, support, and encouragement.

- **Self-awakening at night.**
  If your child is found to have an unusually small bladder, he probably will have to learn to get up once or twice a night to empty it in order to stay dry. Some parents wake their child up for trips to the bathroom before the parents themselves retire. If you are considering this approach, remember that the youngster must eventually learn to wake up independently.

- **Taking responsibility.**
  You should teach your child that when bed-wetting does occur, the youngster should get up and change his nightclothes. Keep extra pajamas near the bed to make it easier. Unless the bed is soaked, teach the child to put a towel over the wet spot and get back into bed without waking you up. This helps teach the child to take responsibility for solving the problem.

If none of these strategies helps control the problem, you may wish to consult your child's physician.

■ ENCOPRESIS

Soiling or *encopresis* is the repeated passage of feces into inappropriate places such as the underwear. Young children who have recently been toilet trained often have accidents in their pants but this is not considered encopresis until the child is at least four years of age. Both enuresis and encopresis can be either *primary,* in cases where the child has never mastered bladder or bowel control, or *secondary,* in which a child, after a period of attaining control, begins to bed-wet or soil again.

Encopresis is five times more common in boys than in girls and 25 percent of children with this problem are also bed-wetters. Usually the child who has encopresis holds his stool in, often because he is constipated and therefore it hurts when he has a bowel movement. This, in turn, makes the stool harder and more painful to pass. In severe cases, the child has a large amount of dry impacted stool in the rectum and watery feces will leak out and soil the child's underpants.

Most children who have encopresis do not have a physical abnormality that prevents them from attaining bowel control. In many cases encopresis is associated with a stressful family situation such as divorce, the birth of a sibling, or starting school. Sometimes a child will actually smear feces, an indication that there may be a problem in the emotional relationships at home. Rather than openly expressing anger, the child shows resentment by soiling. If this continues, consult your child's physician.

If your child has encopresis, it is helpful to retrain the bowel in order to establish a regular time each day when he sits on the toilet. See that he eats a diet high in fiber (fruits, vegetables, grains), which should improve the constipation. You may want to try rewarding him every time he has a bowel movement in the toilet.

Above all, never shame or punish the child. If you detect an overall pattern of oppositional behavior, you may wish to consult a child and adolescent psychiatrist or other professional for an evaluation. A treatment plan might be devised, which may include family or individual therapy. Emotional problems can lead to both bed-wetting and soiling, particularly in a child who has had a traumatic or frightening experience. For example, a child who has been sexually molested may have either of these or other symptoms of post-traumatic stress (see *Childhood Trauma and Its Effects*, page 319).

Dressing

As simple as the act of dressing oneself may seem, it can provoke frustration in some households, especially when everyone is rushed. The frenzied parent, painfully aware of every tick of the clock, agonizes as the child spends three minutes in the act of getting one button through the hole, only to see that it's the wrong hole. From the child's viewpoint, your offers to help speed the process along are seen as interference and create a stress.

Thus, the parent must be both extremely patient and tactful, which isn't always easy when you're pressed for time.

Children usually begin undressing themselves between the ages of twelve and eighteen months. By the time they reach their second birthdays, they are adept at getting *out* of their clothes. Around this time, many children begin to try putting *on* their clothes, too. This can be extremely frustrating as the child struggles to master tasks that are still beyond his fine motor capabilities.

You can ease the transition by buying clothes that don't require buttoning or zipping. Pull-on shirts, pants, and dresses are good, as are sneakers with Velcro closures rather than shoelaces. Even with the easiest clothes, your child will need some help initially. This is where tact comes in. You don't want the youngster to feel a failure, yet you don't have two hours to invest in letting the child complete the process. You may want to try sharing the job. For instance, if the child has difficulty getting socks over the toes, you do that part and then let the youngster pull them up. That way the child feels a sense of accomplishment.

Another potential area of conflict is what to wear. When your child's closet is full of all sorts of clothes, he may emerge with unsuitable color combinations or be under- or overdressed for the weather. It is helpful to sort clothes at least twice a year and put away out-of-season clothing. In this way, you have exercised some control over what the child may choose to wear.

Try offering a choice between two or three acceptable outfits. To facilitate dressing in the morning, you may also want to go through the process of choosing the next day's clothing the night before and have it laid out and ready to put on.

Most children by the age of five are capable of dressing themselves, although they still may need help with zippers and shoelaces. Some children, although perfectly capable, suddenly refuse to dress themselves or procrastinate so that they are not ready when the rest of the family is leaving.

If persistent stalling means missing the school bus, take the child to school—but make sure that you arrive a little late, so your youngster realizes there are consequences when dressing isn't completed on time. Try setting a timer and make a game out of beating the clock. Remember to reward success.

TRAVELING WITH YOUR CHILDREN

Under the best of circumstances, traveling can be stressful. Add children to the equation and it can make you resolve never to leave home again.

That would be a shame. Family vacations are a wonderful time to put the pressures of everyday life behind and really focus on being together. Moreover, it exposes children to things they don't see in their daily lives and to appreciate diversity.

The key to enjoying *and* surviving a vacation with children—especially young children—is careful planning. The spur-of-the-moment weekend jaunt where you hurriedly stuff a few things into an overnight bag usually won't suffice when youngsters are involved. Invariably you'll end up leaving some necessity behind.

- In planning your vacation, consider the ages and interests of your children. While a week of touring big city museums may be your idea of a dream vacation, a trip to the beach or an amusement park will probably make for happier children.

- Once you decide on a destination, research your options. Some hotels are child-friendly; others may be too formal for families. A good travel book devoted to your destination may recommend child-friendly restaurants and activities to interest the whole family.

- Make a list of the things you will need before you begin packing. Pack toys and books and that special blanket or stuffed animal that your child won't go to bed without. Even if your child doesn't use a night-light at home, take one with you, especially if the youngster is to sleep in a separate room.

- Bring a car seat if your child requires one.

- Pack a first aid kit, too. In addition to any prescription medicine your child may be taking, include bandages, an antibacterial ointment, a thermometer, a pain reliever such as children's Tylenol, a diarrhea medication recommended by your doctor, insect repellent (not necessary in cities but invaluable if you are planning a beach or camping vacation), and a medication for motion sickness.

- Pack a separate bag to keep with you in the car or plane. Pack diapers, wipes, extra bottles, baby food, and a change of clothes if you are traveling with an infant. For older children, pack sandwiches, water bottles or juice boxes, fruit, and plenty of snacks. If you are traveling by plane, don't make the mistake of assuming that your children will eat during the flight. Your children may not eat the food, even if you order a special child's meal.

- Prior to the trip, have each child pack a backpack with things to keep them amused on the plane or in the car. Books, paper and crayons, a Walkman and tapes, travel games, a deck of cards, and activity books are some ideas.

- Don't try to cram too much into your vacation days. While a small child may tolerate a trip through one museum, don't expect your youngster to be a model citizen as you go from one museum to the next. Instead, find a park or playground. Make the child feel that this is a vacation for kids, too, and that everyone has some say in how the time is spent.

GOING TO CAMP, SLEEP OVERS, AND PARTIES

As a natural part of growing up, a child begins to move away from the safety net of home and to venture outside, seeking new experiences. As the youngster becomes more comfortable, new relationships with others begin to develop, too.

Even during the preschool years, your child discovers that it's more fun to play with a friend than with Mom or Dad. At this point, the youngster probably will be invited to a birthday party. Depending upon age and personality, the party may be cause for some anxiety. Your child may be torn between wanting to go but being afraid.

Don't be surprised if your child insists you stay at the party. At many preschool parties, in fact, the host parent actually prefers to have the parents stay. Once most children feel comfortable, they usually let go of the parent's hand and join the activities, returning periodically to make sure that Mom or Dad hasn't deserted them. Sometimes, however, a shy and intimidated child will cling to a parent—and refuse to have anything to do with the games unless you too agree to join in. At these times a sense of humor helps. It is best to just go along with the child and not push too hard. Eventually—perhaps not at this party but at a later one—the youngster will have enough confidence to let go of your hand and go it alone.

During the early school years (sometimes even before), most children have a strong desire to sleep over at a friend's house. Peers have become more important and children have a natural curiosity about their friends: what does his room look like, what kind of food does he like to eat, what television is he allowed to watch? Even before you think he is ready, your child may start asking for a sleep over. If you really think he's not ready to stay at someone else's house, you may suggest that he have his friend sleep over at your house. If that isn't acceptable, you may want to start preparing him for this experience by explaining that it will be different from at your house.

However anxious they may be for the experience, many children have a problem with change. Perhaps the food isn't cooked just the way they like it, the beds are too soft, or the television's too loud. For some young children, minor details such as these are enough to sabotage the entire sleep over. Going into the experience prepared for differences, your child will have a better chance of having a good time.

Some children, however, just aren't ready to be away from home even though they may try hard to be. This revelation typically comes late at night when they can't sleep at the friend's house and you're asked to come and take the child home. If this happens, be patient. Despite high hopes and good intentions, your child just wasn't ready to be away from you all night long. Praise the youngster for trying; and wait a few months before trying again.

As children grow older, the need to test their wings intensifies and suddenly the occasional night away from home just isn't enough. In many parts of the country, a ritual that has become almost a rite of passage is leaving home for summer camp, which may be as short as a week or as long as the summer school vacation. In some families, children are sent to sleep-away camp from the time they enter elementary school, but most children adjust more easily to being away from home if they are older. A common age for the first camp experience is in middle school.

Like the preschooler who has ambivalent feelings about attending a birthday party, many older children feel similarly about the first camp experience. On one hand, the prospect of being away from one's parents for an extended period is exciting and reinforces their feelings of independence. On the other hand, it can be downright frightening.

Although most children are apt to have some mixed feelings about camp, it helps when children truly want to go and camp is not something that's being thrust upon them. Moreover, children should have a say in selecting camps. If, for example, your child expresses great interest in going to tennis camp but you insist on an arts camp, the youngster probably will be more reluctant to go than if the destination were tennis camp.

Whenever possible, visit the camp prior to making a decision. Even when children have only visited a camp, their level of comfort will be greater come the first day than if they had never been there before.

When the child's away at camp, write often. Let the youngster know that you miss him and are looking forward to seeing him. If the camp has a parents' visitation day, make a point of attending. And no matter how much fun the youngster is having, don't be surprised if your child misses you. After a few weeks apart, many parents and their children develop a newfound appreciation for one another.

6

The Family Redefined

■　■　■

One dictionary definition of the word family is "a group of persons of common ancestry"; another is "a group of individuals living under one roof; a household." While both these definitions may be sufficient for the Census Bureau, a great many intangibles are certainly missing.

Family means different things to different people. Each of us has our own associations with the word that are colored by our childhood experiences.

Our family teaches us how to be human. From our earliest bond as a newborn with Mother and Father through the day we leave home, the family is where we learn how to communicate our needs and form reciprocal attachments. Through language, spoken and unspoken, we learn to understand others—to establish rapport, to listen for multiple meanings, to both express and contain powerful emotions, to develop a sense of irony and humor. We learn empathy and compassion. These skills and others are essential to getting along with others and building meaningful relationships. The family is a social microcosm, or small society, in which the rights and the needs of others are first learned. The limits of individualism are first taught within the family, too, and the child learns and experiences values and learns what is right and wrong.

Ideally, a child's family life is sufficiently secure and nurturing to allow the child to discover who she is and what she can do. If the child is accepted and appreciated, idiosyncrasies and all, she will more easily accept herself and other people. If she is not judged harshly and is forgiven mistakes, she will learn from them. A child allowed to go (within the limits of safety) where curiosity leads and who is given opportunities to develop individual talents will become a self-confident member of society.

All of us have a powerful need to belong. The first unit to which a child really belongs is the family. Later there might be a group of friends, a basketball team, and the high school orchestra, but the family will always be the center of the most basic kind of belonging. A family defines a child's origins and *sameness*—the brown eyes, perhaps, the red hair, Dad's love of music, Mom's uncanny mathematical ability—but also the *differentness*, the child's individuality. With the family, the child is an integral, irreplaceable part of a group of loving people on whom she can depend and who will always care about what she does and how she's feeling.

This feeling of belonging, so critical to a child's emotional well-being, is reinforced by a sense of family history and the youngster's place in it. Stories from the past as well as the present, told by parents, grandparents, and other extended family, confirm the child's role as an important "character" in the continuing family saga. The family acts also as a vehicle for transmitting cultural traditions, which expands the child's sense of belonging outward to the greater community.

It is the parents' role to provide the optimal environment for the child's healthy development. Parents are the leaders for the family; they make the decisions and are the source of protection, provision, and discipline. When their relationship is one of mutual support, trust, and esteem, they are better equipped to fulfill the various tasks that make up effective parenting, such as nurturing, listening and communicating, building trust, setting boundaries, and establishing goals and tasks.

In simplest terms, parenting is an unconditional commitment to one's children. It means protecting them from stress and poverty, giving them freely of one's time, translating the world's mysteries, and serving as a buffer against its hardships until they are mature enough to meet them on their own. And when children falter and fall, it means offering sympathy and support.

The nature of the family in America has changed radically over the last few decades. What was once traditional is now the exception. Instead of a father in the workplace and a mother at home raising the children, many families are now characterized by single parents, stepparents, stepsiblings, gay parents, adopted children, foster children, or relatives other than parents raising the children. In these instances, a family *is* a collection of relatives living under one roof, as the dictionary suggests, but held together by an emotional glue that defies easy definition.

Family Rituals

The routines and rituals that mark a family's day, week, and year serve not only to organize family life but also to reinforce the emotional bonds that tie family members together. They range from the mechanical weekday morning schedule, when children have to be prepared for day care or school and Mom and Dad are getting ready for work, to the more complex rituals of important holidays and religious worship.

In many families, taking leave and coming together are accompanied by habits that might be seen as small rituals—the good-bye kiss, the welcome-home hug, the chat over an afternoon snack about the child's day. Evening mealtime is an important ritual, however simple it might be, because often it is the only time of the day when your family can sit down together to share not only a meal but their abiding interest and concern in each other.

A relaxed and convivial dinner is an important daily affirmation of parents' love, although once children start school you'll be lucky to collect everyone together for dinner every night. Yet several nights a week is fine. *Don't* invite television to be a guest at the table, no matter how loudly your children protest. If you actively engage them in dinnertime conversation, they will learn to prefer that to any TV sitcom.

"Dinnertime conversation" does not mean simply that the grown-ups ask the children what happened in school that day. It also means that the parents actively share information about their own daily experiences with each other and with the children.

Involve the children in before- and after-dinner chores, too. Helping with preparation and clean-up emphasizes the importance of family mealtime and their contribution in making it a pleasant experience. Children who come to the table at the last minute, wolf down their food, and jump up to go back outside or to their rooms seldom have much interest in exchanging information and ideas with the rest of the family.

After-dinner activities can include cleaning up, games, playing musical instruments, singing, projects, and homework. Even if television is the activity of choice, that, too, can be a family ritual: The family learns one another's favorite shows; the members negotiate what each gets to watch; they laugh together, and, in general, share the time rather than going off in solitary fashion to watch their own televisions.

Bedtime rituals are among the favorites of both children and parents. Most children love being read to or told stories; a parent who's a good storyteller is an asset indeed, and will be called upon to spin a nightly yarn long after the children have learned to read on their own. After the story you might spend a few minutes chatting about anything on the child's mind, particularly a worry or anxiety. This quiet time together prepares your child for sleep, deepens your relationship in part through the exchange of hugs, and strengthens the child's feeling of safety, trust, and being loved.

Religious beliefs and rituals are central to many families' lives. Include your children as early as is practical for you. Communal worship and other spiritual practices can enhance the moral guidance you yourself provide every day. They also affirm the children's sense of belonging to a historical tradition as well as to a living community of fellow worshipers.

Holidays provide another opportunity for rituals. These celebrations are by their nature inclusive, and children look forward to them every year. Even at a fairly young age children can take part in the preparation for Thanksgiving and Christmas or Hanukkah—seasonal table decorations, ornaments, cookies, handmade cards. If we can let go of having everything exactly right and hold on to a sense of humor, holidays can be a source of joy, fun, and relaxation for everyone. In families that cherish the warmth and togetherness of holidays, grown children return year after year to relive that magical season.

Research is finding how important family rituals are. They are a factor in building both relationships within the family and in mastering some of the basics of relationship-building in general. Some family rituals just happen, the natural result of cooperation and affection. Yet rituals also need to be worked at and developed. They don't just happen; they can only occur when unstructured time is available as they don't lend themselves to being squeezed into a rushed schedule. Rituals should be nurtured, consciously maintained, and modified over time as the children grow and develop. As the life of the family evolves, rituals can be both a source of pleasure and a great help as the family makes its way through periods of stress and transition.

Separation and Divorce

Divorce has become common in American life. The rate of divorce in the U.S.—about 50 percent of all marriages—is one of the highest in the world. Some divorcing couples take a certain comfort in that statistic, reasoning that because stigma of divorce has diminished, their children do not suffer as much as children of previous decades.

Yet the breakup of the family cannot be regarded as a *normal* event for any child. It is one thing to know other kids who've experienced divorce and quite another to have it happen in one's own home. The child wants Mom and Dad to stay together. Divorce means loss and abandonment, pain and grief, changes, and the unknown. Someone leaves the child.

In a few cases divorce is the only tolerable alternative to a home environment that is violent, abusive, and harmful to the child. In other cases, where the parents' relationship is strained but not violent, where daily discourse is marked by argument, distrust, and tension, professional counseling may help both parties learn how to communicate better, express needs and feelings, and resolve conflicts. Especially when there are children involved, parents should make every effort to save their marriage. Working through a crisis strengthens the marital bond, renews commitment to the family, and restores the children's sense of safety and security. The children, too, learn that conflicts can be resolved.

If, with or without professional help or other attempts to shore up a failing marriage, a couple decides to separate, they must keep in mind that their children need them more than ever. The period leading up to the decision to divorce has doubtless been hard on the youngsters, no matter how hard the parents have tried to keep them out of the middle. The actual, physical separation is the concrete culmination of the children's fears. But if both parents try to keep disruption to a minimum and their own dealings amicable and respectful, the children will suffer less.

If divorcing parents are unable to rise above their own anger and bitterness and see to their children's needs, the long-term consequences can be wrenching. Divorce usually brings with it a host of upheavals: the loss of the everyday relationship with one parent, generally the father; a sharp decline in family income, which may translate into moving to a new neighborhood, going to a new school, or losing a full-time mother to the workforce. More important, there may also be an accompanying and pervasive sense of unease, insecurity, and fear of abandonment.

Some young children react to this breach in their familiar world by acting out—becoming more aggressive and uncooperative, getting into fights—or by turning their anxiety inward, regressing, withdrawing into depression. Preschoolers and school-age children may blame themselves for the parent's leaving, perhaps imagining their bad behavior drove Mommy or Daddy away.

Older children feel deep sadness and loss. Their schoolwork suffers, and behavior problems are common. In junior high, when the opinion of their peers is so important, they may feel ashamed and isolated, even if some of their friends have gone through the same experience. Their self-esteem may plummet. As teenagers and adults, children of divorce often have trouble with their own relationships and may continue to experience problems with self-esteem.

Whatever the child's age at the time of the divorce, the effects of divorce can be felt at subsequent stages of development as well. A child whose parents divorced when she was three, for example, will work through the divorce again as a school-age child, a young teen, an older teen, and as a young adult. Divorce is not a one-time, single-episode trauma. The predivorce, separation, divorce, postdivorce, and stepfamily stages all produce stress.

The family structure is inevitably altered after divorce and during the transition to a single-parent home. While mothers and fathers once performed different roles and functions in the two-parent family—one parent may have been more effective as a disciplinarian, the other may have been the nurturer—the sudden absence of some of these functions is one consequence of the change. When the household suddenly has but one parent, it is difficult for that parent suddenly to fill all the roles and functions, although the child's developmental need for them remains.

■ HOW TO RESPOND

If you and your spouse have decided to separate—and there is absolutely no chance of reconciliation—don't wait until the last minute to tell your children. You're turning their world upside down as it is; why compound it by, for instance, announcing to them when they come home from school one day that their father has moved out and isn't coming back? Instead, give them time to absorb the news, to ask questions, and to express their feelings while they have both parents there.

If possible, you and your spouse should talk to the children together and present an explanation you've both agreed on beforehand. Keep it simple, straightforward, and honest. Honesty doesn't mean openness, and it isn't an invitation to go over your spouse's various faults—his affairs, her alcoholism, whatever. A more useful approach would be to say, for instance, that your fighting has been making everyone unhappy and that you've decided your home would be calmer and not so tense if Mom and Dad lived apart. Assure them that the decision is between the two of you and has nothing to do with anything they've done.

Acknowledge that the divorce will be painful and sad for everyone but affirm that you both love the children and will always be their parents. Be specific about the logistics of the new arrangement—where Mommy and Daddy will be living now, where the kids will be living, how often they will get to see the other parent, what else will change, and, most important, what will not. Some parents are upset by their children's responses: for example, the child who seems to care more about the whereabouts of favored toys than the separation. Try to accept the child's responses and to see them from the child's point of view. Children often focus only on what they can handle.

In other words, present the news honestly and then assure the children that although Mom and Dad are splitting up, neither one will ever leave the kids or stop loving them.

No matter how well you've handled breaking the news to your children, you will be asked to explain it again and again. It's a huge, overwhelming thing to deal with, and the subtleties and ramifications may not emerge for all of you for some time. Be open to discussing it over the coming weeks and months, particularly if you notice that your children seem angry or withdrawn or are complaining of more headaches and stomachaches than usual. Encourage them to express their feelings, however inarticulate and perhaps hurtful to you. Respect their own hurt and anger, but gently correct any misconceptions about you or your spouse, especially those that have to do with abandonment and losing the other parent's love.

Perhaps the single most important and most difficult thing each parent can do to ease the devastation of divorce is to encourage an ongoing relationship between the child and the other parent. Try to complete the legal procedures as quickly as possible—a prolonged custody battle is demoralizing for a child—and do it amicably. Agree to work together through the coming years as two parents who are both concerned about the well-being of their child. If you can, schedule regular conversations, either in person or by telephone, to keep each other apprised of problems, important events, and milestones.

As divorcing parents, you will have to decide upon custody and visitation arrangements. Many issues need to be considered in reviewing the options. With younger children, for example, you will need to balance their need for more parental contact and supervision with practical considerations— every-day visitation might seem best for the child but not as workable a solution. There are advantages to each of the arrangements and all can be made to work given the working support of both parents. But keep in mind that the driving principle must *always* be the question *What is BEST for our child and what does OUR child need?*

Whether you choose joint custody or sole custody with visitation for the other parent, once that issue is settled, honor it fully. Don't turn visitation into a bargaining chip. Don't fight in front of the child or use the child to keep a fight going. Resist the temptation to pry information out of your child about your former spouse's new life. Do not complain to your child about late support payments or the other parent's absence at a piano recital. Your child will notice and doesn't need you to rub it in. Don't test the youngster's loyalty. Respect and support your child's need to maintain a unique, loving relationship with the other parent, free of your negative input.

If you're the noncustodial parent, stick religiously to your visitation schedule. Your child needs to see you regularly and share her life with you, to be able to count on you and your visits, and it is your obligation to make those visits a priority in your new life. Don't plan something grand or special for every visit; your time together should feel natural and normal. If the youngster is with you over a weekend, include normal activities like homework and school activities. For older children, include friends of your child's in some activities. All of these are parts of everyday life, after all, and the more closely you can approximate that, the more secure and stable your child will feel.

In general, resist the urge to turn your child into a confidant, a replacement for your spouse. It is unfair and inappropriate to burden the youngster with your concerns and anxieties. They belong to you, the grown-up, not to a child. Even given difficult circumstances, childhood should be as innocent and safe and unfettered as it can be.

In that vein, try to keep family life normal, predictable, and routine. That includes maintaining the same household rules and expectations that applied before the divorce. Sometimes parents feel so guilty they let rules slide a little, but children need the security of structure and boundaries now more than ever. Don't let chaos set in. (See also *Family Rituals*, page 199.)

Finally, it's important to recognize that taking care of yourself and your children after divorce is a very tough job. The emotional, psychological, and economic toll on both parents can be enormous. If you feel overwhelmed or close to burnout, ask for help— from extended family, close friends, minister or rabbi, or a mental health professional. Often kids and parents both benefit from support groups aimed specifically at addressing the effects of divorce; many civic and religious organizations offer such workshops at low or no cost. Seeking help is not a sign of weakness or failure. If anything, it signals your strength and dedication to your family.

With the commitment and goodwill of both parents, children of divorce can come through the experience having gained resilience, independence, and perhaps compassion.

Single-Parent Families

The economic and social changes that have affected the U.S. over the past few decades have transformed the American family. What was once considered the norm—two parents, father employed, mother at home, stable financial picture—is now the exception. Half of all marriages end in divorce. Roughly half of all children spend several years in a single-parent household. Some mothers have never married, some parents experience the death of a spouse, and some single individuals adopt children.

According to the statistics, a single-parent family is at greater risk for such negative outcomes as a decline in income, poverty, social isolation, child abuse, and behavioral problems. While it cannot be denied that the stresses on the family are great, these outcomes are not in any way inevitable. If a single mother—single mothers far outnumber single fathers—can juggle the multiple tasks of caring for her children and taking care of herself, her family stands an excellent chance not only of surviving but of thriving.

Even with child support, most single parents are hard pressed to meet all their financial obligations. The decline in family income may necessitate moving to a less expensive home or into an apartment in a different neighborhood, transferring the children from one school to another, giving up vacations, cutting back on purchases, and often other, more radical measures to provide for basic needs.

The great majority of single mothers work. Their absence from the home carries both benefits and disadvantages. As a working mother, you may feel guilty about not being home with your children, particularly if they're young. You may be plagued by child-care problems.

In contrast, you may also feel a sense of competence and accomplishment because you're paying the bills and keeping your children fed and clothed. This is no small achievement. (You might also take comfort in the fact that, according to several studies, daughters of working women tend to be stronger and more independent and have a more positive view of women in the workplace.)

Yet keeping both work and family life functioning smoothly is not easy and at times impossible. Child care is a perennial concern, but finding a satisfactory answer to that problem is only one of the tasks facing the single parent. After a full day at work you return home to what may feel like a second shift—buying groceries, cooking dinner, cleaning up, doing laundry, and finally giving time to your children. It's a rare parent indeed who can routinely manage a schedule like this without feeling exhausted. When lack of time and money keep you from pursuing any personal interests, meeting friends occasionally, or going to the movies, burnout is a real danger. Small children tend to fall apart at the end of the day, and their demands may be more than you can handle. You may find yourself snapping, even yelling at them.

If you have gone through a divorce or your spouse has died, your children are experiencing their own grief. Behavioral problems can surface, such as increased aggressiveness or emotional withdrawal. Your children's needs only compound your struggle to come to terms with your circumstances. You may respond with guilt and resentment or even rage that they are making it all so much more difficult for you. You may also bitterly resent what your ex-spouse has done to you, making parenting discussions very difficult.

■ HOW TO RESPOND

To adequately meet the demands of the family, it is crucial that you attend to your own needs, too. Don't be afraid to ask for and accept help with housework and children. Enlist the aid of grandparents, aunts and uncles, neighbors, good friends, and baby-sitters, and empower them to perform parental functions. Give yourself time off to do some of the things that give you pleasure.

As your children get older, give them more responsibility for household jobs appropriate for their age—feeding pets, setting the table, starting dinner, washing dishes, doing laundry, sweeping, or vacuuming. Children benefit from the ability to contribute through routine chores in any household, not just a single-parent one.

School-age children are rarely eager to take on belt-tightening measures and may resent you for making it necessary. Explain the realities to your child—without giving in

to the temptation to blame your ex-partner or paint a more frightening picture than actually exists—while assuring the child of your continuing love and caring. As much as possible try to keep the child's routine the same as before, with social and extracurricular activities intact.

Keeping to routines established before single-parenthood will also help with any difficult behavior that arises afterward. Be understanding: Your children need time to adjust to a painful transition. Do not, in your guilt, allow behavior in your child that would have been unacceptable before. Boys in particular may challenge a mother's authority. If you are in this position, you will need to reestablish again and again how the rules are made and what the consequences are when they are not obeyed. Do it lovingly, compassionately, but firmly. Ask your former spouse to support you. Family therapy may be beneficial if your children are having a particularly difficult time adjusting.

Under the best of circumstances, being a good parent is one of the toughest and most rewarding challenges in life. Doing it as a surviving or divorced parent is even harder, but parents everywhere are proving it can be done.

Stepfamilies

With the current high rate of divorce and remarriage in the U.S., the number of children living in stepfamilies, now about 10 percent, is growing. For the adults, remarriage is something they have looked forward to; the custodial parent in particular can now better share the emotional and financial responsibility for the family, and when both partners' emotional needs are being better met, they can be more available for their children.

Children experience remarriage differently. Many young children, even after years of living without a second biological parent, continue to harbor the hope that their parents will reconcile and remarry. A stepparent dashes that hope. There is no guarantee that just because a parent loves someone that the child will even like this new spouse.

In addition, over the years of single parenthood children grow very close to their mother or father, and they may perceive a threat to that relationship, especially when stepsiblings join the family circle as well. These new siblings often seem like complete strangers. No matter what, stepfamilies significantly change the previous relationship among family members.

Then there's the matter of split loyalty. Some children worry that they are being disloyal to the absent parent if they allow themselves to like or show affection to the stepparent. It is important to recognize that what may be another chance for happiness for you may, for your children, be more closely associated with loss, conflict, anger, and overwhelming change.

Consider your own expectations for your new partner. Do you expect that, over time, your new spouse will be treated as a parent? Are you prepared to empower that new co-parent? You cannot, for example, allow your child to refuse to recognize authority simply by asserting *You're not my real parent!* You

must be prepared to lend your authority. On the other hand, it should be clear to you as the biologic parent that your future spouse is devoted to your children.

This is usually a slow and gradual process and cannot be rushed. Children have to learn to trust the stepparent before they feel comfortable with new relationship and family structure.

■ **HOW TO RESPOND**

When your relationship with a new person becomes serious, tell your children about him or her before you introduce them to each other. Answer any questions, allow them to express negative feelings, and assure your children that your relationship with them will not be altered by this new attachment.

When you decide to marry, encourage your children to take a role in the wedding. It is an important ritual for *all* of you, for it signals the beginning of your new life together, and if your children feel a part of the process, the family will be off to a better start.

Then comes the hard part: moving in together. Allow a period of time for transition and adjustment as family members get accustomed to each other and learn their roles in the new configuration. Stepsiblings will complicate the process, especially if, as is usually the case, space is at a premium and bedrooms must be shared. The loss of a private haven may be offset somewhat if boundaries of some kind are maintained—for instance, separate toy boxes and bookshelves and desks.

Do not expect miracles of your blended family. Younger children may adjust reasonably quickly, but older children have stronger opinions, more established routines and roles, and, at least in their own eyes, more to lose of their old life. They may aggressively challenge the stepparent or withdraw emotionally. Keep the lines of communication open with your children. Help them articulate and work out their negative feelings before they become habitual. But openly, actively, and firmly deal with disrespect or blatant disobedience.

If you are the stepparent, you face a somewhat different challenge. You're entering a family with its own style, a structure with set routines, rules, rituals, and expectations. If you respect your stepchildren's privacy and particularly their relationships with both their parents; if you do not force a relationship before it's had time to develop naturally; if you do not assert your authority but rather leave the role of primary disciplinarian initially to your spouse, then you stand a good chance of being accepted by the children. Over time, a balance should grow between you and your new spouse regarding parenting roles and responsibilities.

There will probably be behavioral acting out of some kind initially. Don't take it personally. With time, patience, and good humor on your part, these conflicts should ease as the children grow more comfortable and learn to trust you. Supporting and sharing in their interests—be it Little League or cello recitals—goes a long way, too.

If tension and conflict do not recede over time, or are exacerbated, consider professional help, perhaps for the whole family. Remember that the best foundation for a reasonably harmonious blended family is a warm, solid, and mutually supportive marriage. Over time, the same trust and commitment will usually grow with your stepchildren.

Adoption

The last quarter century has seen a rising interest in adoption in the U.S. Many couples put off starting their families until their late thirties and forties when it is more difficult to conceive. Other couples want to bring children of other races and from other countries into their homes. The ranks of prospective parents are changing, as single men and women, as well as gay and lesbian couples, claim the right to be loving and nurturing parents.

Couples and individuals who make the decision to adopt—and who persevere through the months and sometimes years of the adoption process—are by definition committed to their children and are often more knowledgeable about child development than nonadoptive parents. Usually they have also been prepared by the adoption agency for the special challenges their child will present to them over the years and into adulthood. This emotional (and usually financial) commitment helps ensure that most adopted children have good chances of having parents who are well adjusted and happy. But, just like biological parents, adoptive parents don't always realize the demands placed on them by the child.

Children adopted at a later age have a greater potential for behavior problems. On the other hand, whatever the problems you encounter, you are rescuing a child from an uncertain, unstable, and insecure existence, with the promise of permanence, continuity, and love. Learn as much as possible about the adoptive child's background so potential problems can be anticipated. The more years a child has experienced an uncertain, neglecting environment, the more commitment the adoption requires.

Once the adoption is completed, perhaps the most critical task facing adoptive parents is telling their children that they're adopted. Theories about the best time to introduce the subject have changed over the decades. Fifty years ago every effort was made to match the child to adoptive parents so that it would be easier to *conceal* the fact of adoption. These days most experts agree that the child's emotional health is better served if knowledge of the adoption is imparted early. That initial conversation must be repeated again and again through childhood and adolescence, with new questions and concerns arising at different ages and stages but the same basic issues recurring: *Who am I? Where did I come from? What were my birth parents like? Why did my birth mother give me up?* And, sometimes, they ask, *What was wrong with me that they gave me up?*

Children are amazingly intuitive and can often sense when something—such as the truth about their origins—is being kept secret from them. Young children may be unable to verbalize their unease and, in their egocentric way, may construct horrifying fan-tasies or wonder if they have done something wrong.

■ HOW TO RESPOND

Adoption should not be a secret. If you yourself are still struggling with any aspect of the adoption—your inability to conceive, concern that your child's feelings might be hurt upon learning of the adoption, fear that your youngster will reject you in response to the news—do everything you can to work through these feelings so that you can talk to your child honestly and reassuringly.

By being open right from the start you spare your child needless worry and fear. The word *adoption* is not so loaded when a child has heard it used in a loving context since toddlerhood. The adoption story will be one the youngster will want to hear repeatedly, and although the greater implications may not be clear to the child, the reassurance that she was deeply wanted and loved strengthens the feeling of security that underlies healthy self-esteem. Some parents are so positive and open about the adoptive process that from the beginning they celebrate the day the baby came to them in addition to the child's actual birthday.

Be prepared for conversations in the years ahead as your child grapples with the biological and emotional aspects of adoption. Answer the questions completely no matter how many times the youngster has asked them before, and try not to feel threatened by a seeming obsession with birth parents, particularly as the child gets older. Share whatever information you have about the birth parents. To the question "Why didn't they want me?" you might answer that you don't know exactly what the reason was for giving your child up, but maybe they were very young and too poor to take good care of their baby, so they did the best thing they could—give up the child to a family they knew would provide a loving home. Assure the child of your love and of a permanent place for the youngster in your family and home.

As children enter school, peer relationships become increasingly important. Being part of the group requires a certain amount of conformity, of looking and dressing and talking like the others. For some adopted children this presents a problem because they *do* look different, not only from their friends but from their own families. If your adoptive child came from another country, describe that country, point it out on a map, relate the unique things you know about its people, and celebrate the differences. Think of creative ways and times to help the child learn about her origins. Don't go overboard, however. While it's important to bolster pride in where the youngster came from, remember that a great concern of the child is to fit into *your* family and community.

Gay Parenting

The number of families in the U.S. in which either one or both parents are homosexual is rising. Gay men and women are adopting children, and members of lesbian couples are having babies through artificial insemination. Gay celebrities with children who have come out of the closet in recent years have helped propel the issue into the public forum.

But in a society in which many people are still uncomfortable with the idea of homosexuality—and much more so with homosexual parents—gay couples face many challenges in their quest to redefine the nature of the family.

For many people, the main objection to gay families is the notion that such a setting cannot possibly be "healthy" for the children involved. One unspoken assumption is that the children of gay people themselves grow up to be gay. What research has been done on this particular question indicates that the children are no more likely than children of heterosexual couples to be homosexual; they perform as well in school and appear to be no more vulnerable to emotional and behavioral problems.

No matter what the makeup of the family, what ultimately counts most in child-rearing is not the sexual orientation of the parents but how well they bond with and nurture the child, as well as facilitate each aspect of a child's development. That doesn't mean, however, that kids don't have a difficult time coming to terms with having two moms or two dads, with being different in a way that may be harshly judged by their peers and some in society. A better understanding with more abundant studies and accurate information will hopefully counter misperceptions.

■ **HOW TO RESPOND**

Fitting into the community and assuming a comfortable place in the life of a neighborhood is a valuable component of the family experience. With this in mind, many gay couples choose to live in communities that are more open to differences, thereby allowing their children to feel more at home among ethnic and sexual variations from the mainstream model of the family. Support is more readily found in such communities, and groups offer support and assistance to gay couples who must continually battle the perceptions of the outside world.

Most gay parents encourage openness and honesty with children from the beginning. Attempts to keep the parents' relationship a secret only suggests that it is something to be ashamed of, an attitude that may be hard to correct later. As with a heterosexual marriage, it is not necessary to explain the exact sexual nature of *your* relationship, particularly to a young child, but be prepared for questions that are sure to arise if the youngster's friends tease her. Assure the child that both parents love her and are just as dedicated as other parents are to their children. Love is an essential element in what makes a family, and if you can take joy in your own individuality, you can convey that acceptance and joy to your child.

Foster Families

Foster parents provide an essential service in the child protective system, that of caring for children who require a safe, temporary home away from their biological parents. Most foster parents are motivated by love and compassion, and all are faced with the daunting task of caring for children who may have a history of neglect or abuse, or who may have been through several foster homes already.

Foster parents also face the dilemma that they are warned not to become attached to a child, and yet it is the consistent, uninterrupted emotional commitment that gives a child a sense of security and stability and the capacity to form other emotional bonds later in life. That makes it all the more important that you consider carefully the simple, introspective questions, *Why am I doing this?* and *What do I expect to gain from this?* In many cases, simple altruism, the desire to help, to do good is the answer and it's an admirable one. But confused motivations can complicate what is already a challenging task.

■ HOW TO RESPOND

If you are new to the foster care system, certain guidelines may be helpful. Keep in mind that while returning the child to the biological parents is the ultimate goal, that will not happen as long as the original home environment is unsafe. Because it is in the child's best interests to keep foster placements to a minimum, try to make your home the last stop—before the child's return to biological parents or an adoption, either by you or another family.

After you've gone through foster care training and are offered a placement, be sure first to ask questions about the child to ascertain whether or not you can manage the youngster. Don't feel guilty about being selective beforehand; rejecting a child *after* placement in a home is very damaging to an already fragile sense of self. Ask the social worker why the youngster is being placed and about the child's background. Has the child any special problems or needs? Is this the first foster home? Does the youngster have siblings? Do the birth parents or extended family have visitation rights? If the child is an infant or toddler, ask about the special needs created by fetal alcohol syndrome or exposure to drugs in utero. Ask as many questions as you need to feel comfortable about your decision.

Some couples are hesitant about taking in a foster child if they have children of their own. It may be difficult and disruptive for biological children, but one common strategy is to take in only foster children younger than your own children. Your decision to become a foster parent should depend on how strong and stable your family is and how much time you can realistically devote to a needy extra child.

Once the child is in your home, keep written records of such things as calls and visits to and from social workers, visits with the child's parents, observations about the child, and anything else that may be useful to social services, the courts, and adoptive parents. Maintain contact not only with your foster child's social workers but with the lawyer assigned to the case.

Social workers are often overwhelmed and harassed, so try to remember that they're doing the best they can within a system that is slow, flawed, and overburdened. When you discuss the child with the social service worker, be as specific as possible—this is where your notes will come in handy—and try not to get into an adversarial position. If you can't get a satisfactory response to your questions, ask to talk to the supervisor and perhaps have a problem-solving meeting to clarify issues and solutions.

Many foster parents can provide children much more than room and board—attention, nurturing, structure and predictability, and a sense, however temporary, of belonging. Understand at the outset that this is no easy task, that your patience and commitment will be tested, but that the rewards to the child are immeasurable. Learn all you can about child development and the special problems of children from dysfunctional homes, some of whom are born with physical and developmental problems. You will get training when you enter the foster parent program, but any other knowledge you bring and develop will enhance your ability to be an effective and caring foster parent.

Cultural Differences

The U.S. has always held out to immigrants the promise of political freedom and economic opportunity, but it also presents a multitude of social and cultural challenges, particularly to those who come from very different traditions.

Immigrants are caught between two worlds. They face enormous pressures to conform to American culture, yet for the most part feel more comfortable surrounded by the familiar trappings of home—language, religious rituals, food, music, clothing. For many adults assimilation occurs in work and professional arenas but home and social life may still revolve around the traditions of their country of origin. For their children, however, the story is usually quite different.

Immigrants face the same problems in raising children that all parents face, compounded by the fact that the long-held values they brought with them are often discordant with those of the dominant culture. American movies and television highlight a very different kind of family life from that many immigrants consider proper, let alone acceptable. In families transplanted from patriarchal societies, for instance, fathers may feel threatened as their wives and children gain more mobility and clamor for greater say in their own lives.

Culture clashes are more dramatic with adolescents, for whom peer approval is so important, but younger children too can struggle for social acceptance. Conformity in dress—the right sneakers or hairstyle—is one obvious way to overcome looking different. Learning the language, including the latest slang, is another. In fact, immigrant children generally learn English more quickly than their parents and then serve as translators. This may give them a level of power that, while it can be discomforting to their elders, also gives the child respect and a contributing role in the family.

Yet another path to assimilation that some children unwittingly follow is school performance. A good education is one of the strongest components of the American dream. Foreign-born children generally do better academically than native-born children, spending less time watching TV and more doing homework. But the longer they live in the U.S. and the more time they spend among their U.S.-born peers, the more they, too, develop other competing interests and hobbies which may result in a decline in their academic achievement. Their long-term goals may also become less ambitious.

A question to ponder is how and to what extent to assimilate into a society that offers unlimited educational, economic, and professional opportunities but whose popular values are counter to yours? Guiding your family through the acculturation may require tempering the beliefs of your native culture with the spirit of American opportunity and flexibility. Your children will quickly embrace American ways and values, but they are still children and must be guided by you.

■ HOW TO RESPOND

Maintain those aspects of your life that make it meaningful for you. Religious beliefs, celebrations, and practices are probably prominent among these; as in any family, they offer solace, support, joy, continuity, and stability, as well as a sense of connection to the community. If you worship outside the home, continue to do so with your family; if daily rituals are part of your worship, make sure the children have the opportunity to participate in them.

Although it may be difficult in the beginning, gradually become more involved in the life of your new community. Your children's school activities and other interests are an excellent opportunity to do so. Volunteer in school or chaperone field trips. If you are not fluent in English, look into ESL (English as a

Second Language) courses at local schools, churches, or service agencies such as the Literacy Volunteers of America. But don't give up your native tongue or insist that your children speak English all the time. Being fluent in more than one language is a skill that both you and they can use to advantage in school and many professions.

Make your children study. Don't let television usurp time better spent doing homework, reading, or practicing language lessons. On the other hand, be careful not to deprive them of playtime or the chance to socialize with friends. Children do not function well under the constant pressure to achieve and excel; their emotional development often suffers. Emphasize—by example, especially—the value of hard work and goal-directed behavior, but also remember that they are children.

If you or other family members are having difficulties adjusting, take advantage of special programs offered by churches and social agencies that address the problems unique to immigrants. In larger urban areas you may find counselors of similar ethnic background who can guide you through the various legal, educational, medical, and social complexities of life in your adopted country.

A Chronic Illness in the Family

All parents are familiar with the minor illnesses of childhood—colds, ear infections, strep throat, fevers that can knock a child out for a few days—and, fortunately, can expect their child to recover and get back to normal activities. About 2 percent of children, however, are afflicted with chronic illnesses serious enough to hamper physical activity and regular school attendance. For their parents the challenges are several: managing the special care that children with these illnesses often require; dealing with the parents' own feelings of anger, guilt, grief, and powerlessness; and helping their children cope emotionally and live as normal a life as possible. (See also *The Child with Chronic Illness,* page 274.)

If chronic disease has struck you or your spouse, you may be faced with similar challenges. Certainly some of the emotions are the same, although they are probably more manageable than if you have to watch your child struggle. In addition to the financial and physical strain, chronic illness often means constraints on some of the activities you enjoy with your family. It may mean limits on athletic exertion. If it's more severe, even picking up a child or going out for ice cream may be impossible. You may not have the energy to help with homework.

Whatever the severity and duration of your illness, it's important to help your child understand your condition and not be frightened by it. Explain it in terms and concepts they can readily grasp (one father of a six-year-old calls bacteria-fighting blood cells "soldier cells"). Be as positive as is realistic, emphasizing your strength and all the good things you're doing to get healthy again. But also point out whatever limitations apply and must be respected.

As they begin to get a fuller picture, your children will have questions, usually of a practical rather than scientific nature. Encourage them to also express any fears or concerns. Validate their feelings, correct any misconceptions, and reassure them that Mom or Dad is still the same person who loves them very much.

There are practical considerations for a family with a chronically ill parent. Child care may be required for preschoolers and for younger children after school. The children themselves can be enlisted to help around the house, and most children are happy to do the little things that make a difference for an ailing parent. A child who reads fairly well can read a story aloud—a wonderful switch of roles that will make the youngster feel needed and important. The important thing is to keep family life as normal as possible so that the child isn't robbed of childhood.

If you must be hospitalized, prepare the child by explaining the reason, and offering assurances that the doctors can take better care of you than the family can right now. Even surgery can be described in a matter-of-fact, benign way, without gory detail. The child should be allowed to visit you in the hospital—unless you and the doctor have a compelling reason to believe the experience would be more frightening than reassuring. Remember that children can conjure up visions far more terrifying than reality if something is kept from them.

Again, try to keep home life routine and predictable, with as little interruption as possible in the schedule, except for the visits to the hospital. The healthy parent should spend time with the children each day to reinforce the feeling of safety and normalcy, but should also seek ways of renewing her own energy, of dealing with her own sadness, added burdens, and grief.

RAISING GRANDCHILDREN

The extended family—grandparents, aunts and uncles, cousins, in-laws—is an important resource for both parents and children. Grandparents routinely provide child care, financial assistance, and emotional support. Occasionally they are called upon to provide much more: the temporary or full-time care and responsibility for their grandchildren.

Different kinds of events precipitate this need for a change in family structure, and they nearly always are traumatic, if not devastating, for the grandchildren. Parents may die prematurely because of accident or illness. In communities where AIDS has taken a heavy toll on the adult population, families made up of a grandmother and grandchildren are not unusual. Parents may be unable or unwilling to care for their children because of chronic drug or alcohol abuse or other dangerous lifestyles. Some of these parents are abusive to the point of harming their children and grandparents step in to become full-time parents.

Grandparents are generally ready to simplify their lives, relax, and enjoy the golden years. A grandmother suddenly forced to give up that vision and take over the role of parent must deal with many emotions—grief, anger, loss, resentment, and perhaps guilt—in addition to coping with some of those same emotions in her grandchildren. There can also be a sort of culture shock as the grandparent confronts the inevitable changes from one generation to the next in music, recreational pursuits, and even in basic notions of family, authority, and parental roles. The transition is never an easy time for anyone, and yet because of the blood bond, the reassuring familiarity, the feeling the children have of still belonging to *someone*, a family remains. For children in this situation, that is the best possible scenario.

If you are raising grandchildren, don't forget your own needs while you are ministering to theirs. The advice that applies for any parent under stress is relevant to you. Ask for help when you need it, from other family members, your pastor or rabbi, a professional counselor, or support groups. If the children are having trouble in school, make sure their teachers and counselors understand your home situation. Ask for their advice. Give yourself a break whenever you can; chasing a toddler or a seven-year-old around can be exhausting.

Aging Grandparents

The American population is aging. Baby boomers, when they reach the age of sixty-five after 2010, will constitute nearly a quarter of the population. What will make this generation of seniors different from their predecessors is their relative good health, thanks to advances in medicine and increased public awareness of the importance of staying fit.

Children often have their own anxieties about old age, which can be compounded by their parents' ambivalence. Witches in story books have white hair and hunched backs and gnarled hands; the sight of an old woman with those features may be frightening to a young child. A beloved grandfather's growing inability to maintain certain physical activities might understandably be upsetting as well. It is the parents' job to help a child not only to understand that aging is part of the natural process of change that occurs in each person's life but also to appreciate the gifts that come with age: wisdom, patience, a connection to the past, and more time to share with grandchildren.

■ **How to Respond**

Encourage your child to talk about these feelings. The youngster may not find it easy to articulate fears or may feel uncomfortable discussing such a sensitive topic—so if you sense anxiety or uncertainty, try gently to draw the child out. Explain that while Grandpa may seem not himself sometimes, there is a simple, logical reason for his cane, tremors, or forgetfulness. Assure your child that there's nothing to be afraid of.

Be aware of your own feelings about aging. Kids pick up on their parents' fears and biases. Just as it's unwise to obsess about being thin around your adolescent daughter, so is it unwise to greet each new gray hair with panic and each new wrinkle with loathing. Avoid saying "Oh, she looks so *old!*" when an actress who's been around a while comes on screen. Don't yell "Hurry up, old man!" at the slowpoke driver in front of you. Such careless comments only reinforce the stereotype that old is bad, slow, useless, or should be retired or discarded.

Maintain a strong relationship with grandparents. Children lucky enough to have a solid connection to extended family, including grandparents, have a decided advantage in their social and emotional development. Most grandparents are eager to be part of their grandchildren's lives—to tell family stories, create memories together,

and pass on traditions. If they are open to it, perhaps your child could spend part of summer vacation with them. If they live nearby, they might work together on hobbies and projects—bird feeders, model trains, nature studies—that you and your spouse may not have time to help with. A photo and memorabilia album of the family is a wonderful ongoing project that can give a child a personal sense of history, continuity, and belonging. If you live far from your parents, encourage your child to maintain contact through letters, E-mail, regular phone calls, and video and cassette tapes.

Expose your child to older people. Most are alert, healthy, and active; look into community programs that bring together children and the elderly. By helping your child build a positive attitude toward and respect for older people, you are not only strengthening the bond between generations that is so important to both, you're also striking a blow against ageism.

Death and Dying

Just as many grown-ups are uncomfortable with the notion of growing old, many more are apprehensive about the final stage of the life cycle. For some, the easiest way to deal with death is not to discuss it at all, especially with children. But by skirting the issue parents do a disservice to everyone and, on a more philosophical level, may be denying themselves the chance to enhance their own appreciation of the richness and preciousness of life.

◾ How to Respond

The subject of death need not be a ponderous one when discussed with young children, who are as curious about it as they are about any other event or experience. The sight of a dead bird might trigger a preschooler's first questions and offers an excellent opportunity for a calm, factual, age-appropriate discussion. You might explain that everything that lives eventually dies—flowers, bugs, animals, people—and that living things have different life spans. A particular moth might live only a few days, but the family dog will live for a good many years and people for much longer, until they have children and grandchildren like Grandma and Grandpa.

Whatever your religious beliefs, your child needs to understand that physical death is irreversible. The dead bird will not take wing again, nor do dogs or people ever come back to life. A very young child may have trouble grasping the concept, but may take comfort in the idea that after death all things return to the earth, to give back the elements that make up new life—flowers and earthworms and cows and people. You might further explain that as living things get older they wear out and don't function quite so well, and hence must make way for newer, younger, fresher beings. A school-age child readily accepts the idea that the earth would be much too crowded if older creatures did not die to make room for newcomers. The association of old age and natural death also makes it easier for the child to be comfortable with both.

Avoid using the word "sleep" when talking about death; the association, which is made in genuine kindness and concern, can make a child extremely nervous and fearful about going to sleep at night. In the same way describing a dead person as having "gone away" may be understood as implying an eventual return. When "unnatural" death does strike, explain that we do the best we can to protect ourselves and our loved ones but that we cannot always keep death at bay.

If a pet dies, spend some time with your child talking about it and perhaps making a ritual out of the burial. A child feels the loss of a beloved pet keenly, and it helps if you can share the youngster's sadness. Don't run out and get another pet right away. Let the child decide when the time has come to do that.

If a close relative dies—a parent, grandparent, uncle or aunt, sibling—the child's feelings must be acknowledged and given room for expression. Too often grown-ups either are so caught up in their own grieving or in trying to protect a child from their own emotional devastation that the child may feel abandoned and even more fearful. Grieving is a healthy, natural response to loss, but a child must be helped in the process.

Make sure the youngster does not think that her own thoughts or deeds caused the death. The child needs to hear that the death was not her responsibility—it is common for children to think thoughts like *If only I hadn't made her get so mad!* Children also commonly attribute power to their fantasies (*I wish she would die!*). Make sure the youngster understands that the death was unrelated to the child's thoughts or actions.

A child who loses a parent is at psychological risk. It is the difficult task of the surviving parent to help the child at the same time that he or she is coping with the loss. The child's reactions can take the form of anger, regressive behavior, eating and sleeping problems, or withdrawal. However your child expresses grief, understand that it may not be in the way adults express theirs, and simply accept it. Give the youngster as much of your time as you can, and offer reassurances that you're not going away, too. Sometimes it can take a long time for a child to recover from this loss enough to return to normal activities, so keep other disruptions to a minimum.

If a sibling dies, the trauma is sometimes greater even than when a parent dies. The surviving child may have lost her best friend. The child may feel guilty because they fought sometimes and said and thought mean things about each other. As difficult as it will be for you, do not neglect the surviving child, who will need a great deal of consoling, support, and understanding. Call on your extended family to help. Grieve together for the lost child, but do not idealize him or her, or your other child may feel unable to make up for the loss.

Moving

A child of any age will usually balk at the idea of leaving a familiar home, an old neighborhood, good friends, and a school in which teachers, fellow students, and routines are reassuringly familiar. Most children do adjust once they have settled in the new home and the new school, but for others the process results in emotional setbacks.

This is particularly true when the move is part of a larger crisis such as divorce or the death of a spouse, or if the family moves repeatedly. Statistics suggest that for each relocation, the children are 3 percent less likely to graduate from high school.

If you can, try to plan a major move around one of your child's academic transitions, when the youngster would have to change school buildings anyway—between elementary and middle school, or elementary and junior high, or junior high and high school, however the school system divides the grades. In this way your child may not feel quite so new and conspicuous; the other children will be new to the building and to the different schedules and requirements too.

Unfortunately, few people have that much control over when they move. Jobs are no longer as secure as they once were, and, however reluctantly, parents must go when and where the jobs are. A newly widowed parent might need to move to be closer to family. But the upset of moving can be alleviated by preparing children beforehand.

■ How to Respond

Because the time period between leaving old friends and making new ones can be painful and scary for children, try to make the transition less abrupt. Get all the information you can on the new neighborhood or part of the country you're moving to and share it with your youngster, using pictures, maps, and brochures (available from the local Chamber of Commerce). Point out recreational areas, famous landmarks, football stadiums, proximity to theme parks—things that will make the new town sound more appealing.

Plan the actual move together. Make it an adventure. After you've arrived and settled in, try to revisit the old neighborhood and old friends, even if it means traveling a bit, and perhaps invite your child's best friend to come visit. Keep in touch with telephone calls and letters, too.

In the new neighborhood scout around for a family with a child the same age as yours and arrange play dates so that your child has a buddy in school. This is particularly effective if you arrive before the school year begins, but it's a good midyear strategy, too. Social cliques are more easily penetrated if the new child already has a friend within the group. Sign your youngster up for activities with the Scouts, at the YMCA, or at a church, temple, or synagogue.

If you yourself are positive and excited by the prospect of moving and meeting new people—and if you can keep the internal life of the family consistent and stable—your child will have an easier time adjusting. The experience may even help build social skills and self-confidence.

Unemployment

Job loss has become a distressingly common event. While it might be of some comfort to the newly unemployed person to know that he is not alone, there is no doubt that his family will feel the impact, both emotionally and financially.

Unemployment tests the strength and health of a family in a way few other crises do. The loss of income and the resulting belt-tightening are certainly painful, but the blow to a parent's identity and ego can be even more devastating. But family bonds can be both preserved and strengthened if job loss can be perceived less as a crisis than as an opportunity.

Many children react very little to the news of job loss. Others respond with stomachaches, sleep disturbances, behavioral problems, or a drop in school performance. If the unemployed parent becomes depressed or abusive, children may display more severe symptoms.

▪ HOW TO RESPOND

Even young children should be told what's happened to Mom or Dad, but in language they can understand. A preschooler will generally accept a calm, positive explanation quite readily, but you should encourage the child to ask questions and voice any fears. The concerns will probably be simple to address: *Will Daddy be home during the day now? Will there still be money to get that new toy?*

An older child very likely has some knowledge of the concept of unemployment—any exposure to the media assures that—and may therefore understand the larger ramifications for the family. The youngster may express concern about suddenly being poor, or having to move, maybe to another neighborhood or a smaller house, or having to change schools. For most children the thought of this kind of upheaval is traumatic. To the extent that you can, assure the child that you will keep changes to a minimum, and that, although everyone in the family will have to make some adjustments in spending and expectations, you will attempt to prevent major disruptions of family life.

Anyone in a stressful situation benefits from feeling useful, and children are no exception. They are usually eager to pitch in. If your child is old enough and volunteers to deliver newspapers or mow neighbors' lawns, permit such jobs so long as they do not take up too much homework or play time.

The best way to protect your children from undue anxiety is to remain upbeat yourself. This may not be easy, because job loss can shatter an adult's self-image as a competent individual who can provide for the family's needs, now and in the future. Keep in mind that you are not alone in this situation; nor do you have to go through it alone. You may feel a sense of loss, betrayal, worthlessness, or powerlessness; it helps to voice these common and understandable feelings with your spouse or friends, a pastor, or a support group.

If your spouse is unemployed, be prepared to listen and support and point out his or her strengths. Avoid giving too much advice or checking up regularly on the status of the job search. Marriages are often strained by the job loss of one partner, so it is vitally important that both partners maintain mutual support and communication in order to spare the children as much tension as possible.

Above all, keep a sense of perspective. Unemployment is not the end of the world. With humor, flexibility, and a commitment to maintaining the children's safety and security, you can pull through.

POVERTY AND THE FAMILY

In 1996, 22 percent of American children under eighteen lived in poverty. The poverty rate of young families has almost doubled in the past twenty years. In a study comparing eighteen industrialized nations, poor children in the U.S. were worse off than their counterparts in all but one country. (Interestingly, high-income American children were better off than their peers in all the countries studied.) These statistics reflect the inequality in income distribution, low state and federal expenditures on social programs for children, and the low priority given to the problem of child poverty.

Families have fallen into poverty over the last two or three decades as the result of several factors. The rate of divorce has risen to half of all marriages. The average income of single-parent families, usually headed by women, falls by 37 percent within four months of a divorce, and fewer than half the children living with their mothers get child support from their fathers. Out-of-wedlock births are rising as well. The real value of family income, even among dual-worker families, is declining at the same time that public assistance funds are being cut.

The effects of child poverty are compelling: hunger and malnutrition, inadequate housing, greater vulnerability to such health problems as HIV infection and other infectious diseases, and child abuse. Poor prenatal care, low birth weight, and malnutrition combine to make children even more susceptible to environmental stresses, with the result that their cognitive, emotional, behavioral, and social development can be at risk of serious impairment.

Child poverty isn't an unsolvable problem, but it takes political will to acknowledge the social costs and address the root causes. There is much less public support in the U.S. than in Europe and Canada for approaches such as child-care subsidies for working parents. Every other nation in the study mentioned above has some kind of child or family allowance, including minimum child support for single parents who are not receiving any support from the other parent.

On the other hand, poverty does not necessarily condemn its victims to a lifetime of lowered expectations. Many children have triumphed over poverty and gone on to become productive and fulfilled adults. There are also many successful community programs that focus on strengthening families—and extended families—and providing them with opportunities for education and training in meaningful work.

7

School-Related Concerns

■ ■ ■

As their children enter school, parents are faced with the task of finding—or creating—a learning environment that "fits" their particular child. Most parents send their kids to public school. Parents who can afford private schools have a wide range from which to choose; a few parents elect to home-school for at least part of their children's school years. In all cases it's important to know what your choices are, to investigate and evaluate them, and after you make your decision, to stay involved in your child's schooling through the years.

■ PRIVATE SCHOOL VS. PUBLIC SCHOOL

Many parents assume that private schools are always better than public schools. They cite a number of reasons: smaller classes, a larger and more varied curriculum, better teachers, greater discipline in the classroom, more opportunities for advanced and independent study, or that they like a school's religious affiliation. The student body is often more homogeneous academically (and economically). In the coming years, graduates of prestigious private schools can reasonably expect a greater chance at being accepted by prestigious universities.

These points certainly do not apply in all cases, as private schools vary greatly in their educational philosophy, methods, resources, and quality. And high tuition is not necessarily a guarantee of high standards or high merit.

The more relevant point is that your public school may offer an excellent learning environment for your child—without the expense—as well as services and facilities to support special needs and interests. In urban areas, some schools track children of different abilities in different programs. Others have "gifted-and-talented" programs. Then there's your child's social life to consider. It probably revolves around neighborhood friends who go to the local public school and reflect a diversity of backgrounds and philosophies that will serve your child for a lifetime. Your own involvement in the school can become an integral part of your involvement in the life of the community.

Whatever the merits of private and public education, investigate your options before deciding on a school, keeping your child's temperament, talents, and interests in mind. Sit in on classes and observe the interaction between children and teachers. Is the atmosphere one in which your child would be comfortable? Talk to other parents, and to the principal and staff—do they seem receptive to your questions and ideas? Note facilities that would be of interest to your child, as well as clubs and other extracurricular programs.

■ SINGLE-SEX SCHOOLS

Numerous studies conducted in recent years have challenged the long-standing premise that coeducational schools are the best learning environment for both boys and girls. Some educators have observed differences in teachers' behavior toward boys and girls: they tend to call on boys more often, are more tolerant of boys' disruptive behavior, give less attention and encouragement to girls, and use male pronouns and male examples in their lessons. Girls in coed schools generally do not do as well in math and science. In girls' schools, on the other hand, girls may be able to focus on and excel in academic and other pursuits without the distracting competition for boyfriends and popularity that may begin as early as seventh and eighth grade. For these reasons single-sex schools for girls—as well as single-sex math and science classes in coed schools—are gaining popularity.

The evidence is less compelling that boys perform better in single-sex schools. Some educators argue that boys and girls need to learn to work together, that boys need female role models, and that boys may become more intolerant in a single-sex school of the kind of diversity coeducational schools afford. Others point to the fact that while boys may do better in math and science, girls are generally superior in English and other classes and the presence of both sexes makes for a more balanced academic environment.

The decision of whether to send your child to a single-sex school depends on your educational goals as well as on your child's personality and preferences. A shy girl, for instance, who is intimidated by boys in the classroom may flourish in the more equal and nurturing atmosphere of a girls' school. A boy who needs more structure and a rigorous learning environment may be better served in a boys' school. In any case, it is important that you and your child visit the school first, sit in on a class or two, and talk to students and their parents. A day or a half-day spent in school is highly recommended for parents.

SCHOOL UNIFORMS

For more than a generation, school clothes have been synonymous with play clothes to the great majority of children. School dressing styles (like parental style) evolved from neat and tucked-in to decidedly more casual. Except in some parochial and prep schools, uniforms became largely a thing of the past.

In recent years, however, educators and politicians as well as parents have reexamined the possible role of school uniforms as an instrument for order, discipline, middle-class tradition, and reducing violence in and out of the schoolyard.

Advocates argue that uniforms erase economic distinctions, and the values that allow for students to judge each other by designer labels. While parents may be incredulous that baggy pants and oversize T-shirts comprise a fashion statement, wearing the right clothes can be a preoccupation with kids, particularly in middle and high school, and it can mean conflict with parents, who must bear the expense. Other claims in defense of uniforms are that they bolster attendance rates, improve academic performance, and promote discipline and respect for teachers. Not least of all, in some urban areas where gang members identify themselves by their clothes, or where children have been assaulted for their expensive sneakers and other clothing, uniforms are said to contribute to school safety.

Not everyone is convinced that school uniforms are a panacea. Detractors point out that a clear connection between uniforms and improved learning has yet to be made, and that the focus on uniforms will contribute little to genuine school reform. Others are concerned that uniforms conflict with the goal of teaching children greater tolerance for diversity. The principle of freedom of expression may also be compromised by such regimentation.

School districts that have introduced uniforms generally do so on a voluntary rather than mandatory basis, usually with a high compliance rate. They often implement the policy among elementary and middle-school students, for whom the issue of clothing is less inflammatory than for high schoolers. In most cases the school has wide community support—from parents, teachers, students, and businesses, which sometimes donate uniforms to children who cannot afford them. This broad-based support is a major reason uniforms have been so successful in the communities in which they have been introduced.

Separation

A child readying for school who has attended some form of day care as an infant or toddler is accustomed to the daily ritual of separation. That may ease the anxiety of the first few days of nursery school or kindergarten, but your youngster will probably be only a little better off than children for whom preschool is a new experience.

Understanding what a momentous step this transition is for your child will better equip both of you to prepare him beforehand. Before the first day of school, talk to your child about what to expect—the activities (nap, snacks, storytime), the schedule, the toys, the other children. If possible, arrange a play date or two with another child in the group so that he has a friend on the big day. Take him to the school to familiarize him with the layout (where the bathrooms are, which cubbyhole or coat hook is his) and to introduce him to the teacher. Not feeling alone will go a long way toward making his first day less strange and puzzling.

If your child demonstrates difficulty with separation, consider staying for a portion of the first day or two, and possibly longer. As he becomes more comfortable, make your stays shorter, until eventually you stay only long enough to help him off with his coat and boots, greet the teacher, and see him engaged in an activity. Don't prolong your good-bye—lingering may only reinforce his worries—but do remind him that you'll pick him up at the end of the school day. (For a child with little concept of time you might name a more concrete event, such as "after your teacher reads you a story.") Make every effort to return when he expects you to; don't make him wait and worry that you've forgotten him. Especially during the first days, your youngster may hold in tension and anxiety while you're gone and then express it quite vocally when you return or even burst into tears. Allow him to do so, with assurances that you missed him too, but that you'll get to spend the rest of the day together. (If he's to be picked up by a baby-sitter or another family member, make sure they understand the importance of picking him up on time.)

Until your child is completely adjusted to separation, be prepared for a possible regression in some behaviors, such as clinginess, sleep difficulties, thumb-sucking, perhaps a reluctance to go back to school. Taking a beloved teddy bear or blanket may help him feel more secure. Consult the teacher about the best way to handle this.

If your child seems really unhappy, he may simply not be ready for preschool; if it's possible for your schedule, allow him to stay at home for a few months more before trying again. Alternatively, a preschool with a different style might help.

The demands of even nursery school—as mild as they might seem to you—may be draining for a young child who is not ready to sit still for long periods, follow directions, take turns, or eat and rest at appointed times. As reading and writing become part of the program, even a child who is bright enough may not be sufficiently mature to handle them. Children do not benefit from being pushed into formal academic programs before they're ready; it's important to allow them to learn from play and free exploration and to respect the pace of the individual child.

Perhaps the single most important factor in facilitating separation for your child is your own attitude. If you are feeling ambivalence, guilt, or anxiety about sending him off by himself, he is likely to sense these emotions, which will only add to his own natural reluctance. It's important that you acknowledge and work through your feelings. If you're sat-isfied that he's going into a safe, pleasant, caring environment, help him by being positive and cheerful and by showing him that you like and trust his teacher. Understand your emotions and then, if needed, be firm and confident helping your child through this important transition.

Be prepared to repeat the process of separating when your child enters first grade—"real school"—and perhaps again during the change to middle school. For some children the beginning of *every* school year may be a little bumpy. Change is exciting, but it can be scary, too. With your understanding, patience, and sometimes a needed but gentle nudge, your child should weather each passage and do a little growing up in the process.

Over- and Underachievement

Over- and underachievers have one thing in common: They are children of at least average but often higher intelligence. Overachievers push themselves to perform at a high level, either academically to the exclusion of other pursuits, or both academically and athletically, for instance. They may work obsessively, berate themselves for grades lower than an A, and have no social life or time to enjoy activities or hobbies.

Underachievers perform below their potential, as measured by certain assessment procedures or by the observations of parents and teachers. They may flunk tests, hand in sloppy homework, or not turn in homework at all. In class they may be quiet and withdrawn, or aggressive and disruptive.

■ CAUSES AND CONSEQUENCES

The motivation to do well is present from an early age in many people, but sometimes pressure is exerted by parents whose dreams and expectations bear little resemblance to their child's own interests and abilities. A compliant child may choose to please his parents by getting straight A's, regardless of his own interests and the pressure this performance places on him. Some overachievers, however, are perfectionists who, even without pressure from parents, are critical of themselves, intolerant of mistakes, and afraid to try new things for fear of failure.

On the other hand, a child may follow his own inclinations even if these take him in the opposite direction from his parents' plans, thus leading to family conflict when his report card is covered with C's and D's. Or he may rebel against unrealistic expectations by not trying at all, or by doing the minimum. Many gifted children are underachievers.

The compulsion to over- or underachieve can ultimately be damaging not only to the child's school experience but also to his sense of self-worth. Both behaviors should be of concern to parents.

■ HOW TO RESPOND

Each child comes with his own talents and interests, and it's your job to honor those and encourage—not force—him to achieve his potential. Teachers, guidance counselors, or school psychologists can assess an underachieving child's abilities and determine what program would best help him achieve. He may be more gifted at music than geography; he may find science class frustrating and yet be able to find the energy and aptitude to dismantle and reassemble a toy. An ideal curriculum must be personally meaningful as well as challenging, and should foster self-directed learning in a low-pressure environment.

At home, you can help build self-confidence by easing up on criticism, comparisons to siblings or friends, or expressions of disappointment that he can't do any better. Reward diligence, good study habits, careful and thoughtful schoolwork, and any effort to do the best he can with warm praise, even if his effort produces a C average.

If your child is gifted, he may have difficulty fitting in with his peers. In middle school he may compensate by focusing exclusively on schoolwork or by performing at a lower level so as not to stand out. Discuss the situation with teachers and the school psychologist, who may devise an individual education plan (IEP) for him, and ask for updates. (See *The Gifted Child,* page 234.) Because social development is a critical part of your child's emotional health, encourage him to pursue activities that bring him into contact with peers of similar ability and interests, such as the chess club or the orchestra. A truly exceptional child may be happier in a single-sex school or any school in which high academic achievement is valued and rewarded.

Self-acceptance is a valuable trait to cultivate in yourself and to model for your child. Understanding that we all make mistakes and can, in fact, learn from them is an important lesson for both the under- and overachiever. As a parent, step back and let your child struggle to accomplish tasks on his own.

Explain that like everyone else he is better at some things than others, and encourage him to try new activities and hone new skills for the sheer pleasure of it. Set an example by not berating yourself for mistakes or setbacks but instead working steadily at a given task, enjoying the process as much as you anticipate the results, until it is done.

PEER INFLUENCES IN SCHOOL

As children move into middle school, the focus of their social relationships begins to shift from parents and family to peers. The ability to form close, satisfying friendships is a critical element of psychological growth and maturity. Friends offer one another understanding and acceptance and the chance to be themselves. Friendships bolster self-esteem, social skills, and a sense of connectedness and belonging. Children with solid friendships tend to do better academically.

The transition to middle school often means a change in the friendships of earlier years. Social pressures intensify as kids begin the process of defining who they are—and are not—in relation to their peers. Cliques form, often around shared interests like sports and music but also around appearance and the kinds of clothes members wear. Kids who are not naturally good at making friends but who want to belong sometimes suppress aspects of themselves—their love of reading, for instance, or the fact that they like their teachers—in order to fit into a group with a more negative view of school and school-related pursuits. Or they may be drawn to children who swear or smoke or steal, for instance, because they carry the allure of greater freedom from parental rules and expectations.

If your child's academic performance is suffering and he suddenly voices a dislike of school, such friendships may be the reason. If so, it is probably not a good idea to declare an outright ban on spending time with those friends—that tactic usually backfires. A better approach is to supply an alternative. Encourage relationships with children whose behavior you *do* feel more comfortable about; open your home to them and arrange special trips and activities that are of mutual interest. Befriend their parents as well—they may be just as eager to find acceptable companions for their kids. Explain gently what specific behavior worries you about your child's friends and the likely consequences of continuing that behavior. As you do with your own child, focus on the behavior rather than making blanket statements about the child as a whole. Don't say *You can't play with Aaron because he's a bad boy, period.*

If your child has grown up with love and respect, if his family environment is caring and supportive, he is likely to make healthy choices of friends. The troublemakers—the kids with an attitude—may hold a passing appeal, but you can generally trust your youngster to end up with buddies who share his values, interests, and outlook.

Parental Participation At School

All schools, both public and private, should welcome and encourage parents' involvement in their children's schooling. And your participation as a parent should be a given. One reason, in this era of budgetary constraints, is that parents often make programs and activities possible that might otherwise be out of the question—after-school enrichment courses, field trips, plays, scholarships, career presentations. Another more important reason is that researchers have found that children whose parents are actively involved in the school are more likely to be successful academically. That alone is a powerful motivation for parents to volunteer whatever time and resources they can to their child's school.

For parents who work, of course, it's hard to find that kind of time in a busy schedule. At the very least, make every effort to meet your child's teachers on the first day of school or during open house in the early fall. Most schools schedule at least one meeting a year between you and your child's teachers to discuss progress. Invite teachers to visit your home; dessert and coffee will suffice. Teachers are often eager to foster parental involvement. If this is not a policy, try to make it one. Go to the parent-teacher meeting even if your child is doing well, because you may gather information and insights that are new to you. Sometimes children's behavior or work in school reflects problems you may be unaware of; or you may discover that your child has a special talent that's never been displayed at home. You are likely to have questions yourself (it helps to write them down beforehand), such as what grades are based on or if your child seems happy in the classroom. You'll also get a sense for how the teachers feel about your youngster and what you might do to clarify any misunderstandings.

The teachers benefit from learning of any problems at home or recent traumas (such as divorce or the death of a grandparent) that might shed light on possible changes in your child's behavior, absences, or missed homework. Follow up your conference with a note to the teachers, thanking them for anything that they do particularly well or is of special benefit to your child. Like everyone else, teachers are motivated to do a better job when they feel supported and appreciated.

If your child is having problems, particularly with a teacher, ask for a special conference. Go with an open mind, prepared to listen to the teacher's viewpoint rather than being defensive or accusatory. Share with the teacher your child's concerns as well as your own ideas, expectations, and an assessment of your child's strengths and weaknesses. Remember that while you are your child's advocate, it is best to think of the teacher as your ally, not your adversary. But if the teacher seems unwilling to accept your input and work out a strategy for helping your child, talk to the school guidance counselor and the principal.

Parent-teacher conferences are only one way, albeit an important one, to learn about and support your child's school. More active involvement includes helping out with class activities—chaperoning on field trips, assisting with special projects like nature walks and collecting food for the homeless, making costumes for a class play, or helping the school librarian. Some parents share their professional expertise by talking about their chosen field or doing hands-on work such as teaching a science class or helping to put together a class newspaper.

Joining the Parent Teacher Association or Organization (PTA or PTO) is a good way to assist larger efforts to support the school. PTAs help support after-school programs, science fairs, and a variety of other activities; they sponsor speakers and conferences on topics relevant to parents and educators; they are the liaison between parents, teachers, and school administrators; they serve as a bridge to the surrounding community; they may work on curriculum issues and in resolving conflicts. If you have a great idea for a new program, are unhappy about a school policy, would like to offer your services writing grant proposals, or wish there was a way the middle-school kids could be made more tolerant of ethnic differences—join the PTA.

Or go one step further and run for the school board. As a board member you will have the chance to help shape and change policies and raise academic standards. Serving on a board requires a commitment of time and effort, however, as well as an abundance of patience and perseverance. But it can also be extremely rewarding to work for the good of all the children, not just your own, in your community.

Children with Special Needs

All children have differences in learning styles or differences in physical and emotional capabilities. The challenge of meeting the educational needs of all children is a primary concern in the school community, and adequately informed and involved parents can have a considerable impact on the success of the school program. While it's important for parents of all children to be in contact with their children's teachers and school administrators, it's absolutely essential for the parents of children with special needs.

More than 4.5 million children in the United States are classified as exceptional, with physical, mental, and emotional disabilities. Since 1975, with the Education for All Handicapped Children Act and subsequently with the Individuals with Disabilities Education Act, all children have been guaranteed an appropriate education regardless of their abilities or physical and mental conditions. Other laws require school districts to search actively for and to provide services for children with disabilities between the ages of three and five to better prepare them for school. While gifted children do not qualify for special help under federal laws, about half the states mandate some kind of special educational support for them.

Which children qualify? Loosely defined, children who have physical or mental handicaps, behavior disorders, learning disabilities, or speech and language disabilities are considered exceptional. The law requires school districts to evaluate every child whose teachers and parents request it. If a problem is detected, the school must provide appropriate services; if it cannot, it must cover all expenses associated with private instruction. Not only are schools required to develop an individualized education program (IEP) for students with special needs, but they must also include parents in the decision-making.

Until the 1970s, schools usually grouped children with physical disabilities in special classes apart from other children. Experts no longer agree that segregating kids with disabilities provides the ideal context for learning. On the other hand, whether they should be integrated, or *mainstreamed*, into regular classrooms is the subject of continuing debate. Do these children benefit from small classes taught by teachers with specialized training, or are they better served by exposure to the same education and culture as other children? Would a special teacher's help in a mainstream class be better? Today mainstreaming part or all of the school day is generally considered the most desirable educational setting, not only for special needs students but for all children. By helping children to accept and respect individual differences, the quality of education for all students is enhanced. For students with severe disabilities, however, high-quality special classes or community-based residential schools may be an option for consideration.

Often schools offer specialized instruction for children with disabilities outside of the mainstream classroom for part of the day. Frequently called "resource rooms," these classes provide the individual attention these children need without isolating them from their peers. It's important to make sure that your child is being removed from the general classroom for the right reasons. Special education classes are not designed to address the needs that the main classroom fails to meet; they are intended to provide enrichment and support. In addition to the resource-room option, there may also be self-contained classrooms for children who are unable to benefit from the mainstream class or, because of disabilities, are unable to participate in that class.

One of the best ways to make sure your child gets the best education is by maintaining frequent communication with his teachers. Frequent notes, calls, and conferences will keep you and the teachers and administrators more aware of your child and his needs and progress. You are your child's best advocate and are best able to get the school's full support.

■ Learning Disabilities

The educator's term *learning disability* and the psychiatrist's term *specific developmental disorder* cover a wide spectrum of problems, ranging from fairly mild reading or arithmetic problems to social and emotional problems that interfere with the child's ability to function in the classroom. Most children with learning disorders exhibit at least average intelligence; in fact, one of the criteria for diagnosing learning disabilities is a large discrepancy between IQ and achievement test scores. It is estimated that between 10 and 30 percent of schoolchildren have learning difficulties of some kind and the numbers may be increasing.

Remember that what may casually be labeled a learning disability may be something else: a mismatch between child and teacher or between child and curriculum (which can lead to daydreaming, boredom, or acting out); a reflection of conflict at home or in school; or perhaps a *learning difference*, which describes a child with an unusual learning style.

On the other hand, a teacher who is not trained to recognize learning disabilities may label a child as lazy, uncooperative, or unmotivated instead. Some teachers and parents have trouble understanding that learning disabilities may afflict bright or gifted children. It's not always easy to identify some learning problems, and some may not be recognized

until after months or even years of school.

What are some of the symptoms that may signal a learning disability? Your child may not be doing as well as his teachers expect, based on their assessment of his capabilities. Try to ascertain the nature of his difficulty: Is he reading well below grade level? Does he have trouble understanding what he reads, following instructions, paying attention, or focusing on one task at a time? Is he easily excited or distracted, and does he have trouble sitting still? If so, request that he be assessed by a professional trained to evaluate children with learning problems (See also *Learning Disorders*, page 360.)

One common condition that causes learning problems is attention-deficit/hyperactivity disorder. ADHD is diagnosed in a child who from an early age exhibits symptoms of inattention, hyperactivity, and impulsivity. These symptoms usually result in the child having difficulty with schoolwork. Many children with ADHD also have associated learning disabilities that require assessment and treatment for optimal outcome. (See also *Attention-Deficit/Hyperactivity Disorder,* page 337, and *Learning Disorders*, page 360.)

■ Other Children with Special Needs

Many children with special needs have conditions other than learning disabilities.

Physical Disabilities Children who are blind or visually disabled, deaf or with hearing disabilities, or have orthopedic disabilities comprise about 1 percent of American children aged three to twenty-one. Children with physical disabilities have the same needs as other kids, and their education is best done by mainstreaming into regular classes, if the child is physically able to attend school. Mainstreamed children usually receive support services by special teachers, who take them from their classrooms for short time periods during the day. Alternatives to mainstreaming include separate classes, schools, or, in selected and limited situations, community-based residential schools.

Some schools try to resist the total mainstreaming of children with physical disabilities because of the added expense and responsibility. Your child may need an aide to help him move about the school or interpret his teacher's words, for instance, or the physical structure of the school may need to be altered to accommodate a wheelchair. Don't let these considerations deter you from pursuing the best situation for your child.

Emotional and Behavioral Disorders Children who have emotional and behavioral difficulties are often either withdrawn or overly aggressive. School professionals should provide an evaluation of the child's condition and develop a plan recommending either keeping him in the regular classroom or enrolling him in a special class. Supportive services and therapies should be provided by professionals trained to treat children with emotional and behavioral disorders.

The American Academy of Child and Adolescent Psychiatry and the Council for Exceptional Children have called for schools to stop using expulsion as a way to discipline children whose behavior isn't appropriate, even those who are dangerous or violent. The law requires that schools use alternative settings to "provide positive opportunities for all to work and learn," thereby eliminating certain future failure for these children.

Speech and Language Disabilities Problems that prevent children from communicating with others include difficulty with articulation, language, fluency, or voice. The severity of the problem dictates the method of treatment, which may involve special education teachers as well as speech or language specialists. (See *Language and Speech Disorders*, page 364.)

Specialized Health Care Needs An estimated 100,000 children are dependent on some form of medical technology for their survival because of accidents or disabilities. Other children are considered medically fragile and may have special health problems that prevent them from normal classroom participation. These children need effective educational opportunities and mainstreaming into regular classrooms with out-of-classroom activities whenever necessary. The special-needs child learns from this regular classroom exposure, as do the children without any special needs.

The Gifted Child

The definition of giftedness has changed somewhat over the years, particularly as the complexity of raising and educating gifted children has become better understood.

According to the new definition, giftedness is *asynchronous development*, which means that gifted children develop cognitively at a much faster rate than they do physically and emotionally. The brighter the child, the greater the asynchrony. Raising a child of exceptional abilities can be an exhilarating experience, but parents and teachers must be prepared both to nurture those gifts and at the same time remember that the child is a child, not a small adult.

How can you tell if your child is gifted? Some early signs are unusual alertness and curiosity, empathy, a long attention span, high energy level, early and extensive language acquisition, a sharp sense of humor, and a vivid imagination. A child may also be gifted musically or artistically. If your child exhibits several of these characteristics, you might consider having a professional evaluation. Early identification affords you the chance to learn as much as you can about the special needs of a gifted child and how best to help him develop his gifts.

Perhaps the most important thing to keep in mind is that you need to treat your gifted child like a child, with a child's social and emotional needs, in spite of his intellectual precocity. It may be easy to forget that your articulate six-year-old who tells sophisticated lightbulb jokes might also be afraid of the dark. Teachers, too, sometimes expect overly mature classroom behavior from a gifted seven-year-old who's breezing through *Little Women* or can multiply thirty-two by eighteen in her head.

If your financial resources are limited, explore ways in which you can take maximum advantage of public programs, museums, and other opportunities in your area. Talk to your child's teachers and ask for suggestions as to how you can, within the limitations of your budget, encourage his exploration of the gifts he has. Public libraries, children's theater groups, school bands and choruses, and local universities are all possible sources of enriching activities.

Keep in mind, however, that one temptation many parents of gifted children cannot resist is to cram as many activities and enrichment programs as possible into their children's schedules. This strategy runs the risk of child burnout. Like all kids, gifted children need time to play, to hang out with their friends, or to do nothing at all. Also like other children, they should be allowed the room to discover and explore their own interests and talents. If you expose your child to a wide variety of experiences, he's likely to be particularly attracted to one or more. Follow his lead: Not every child will benefit from piano lessons; yours might decide he's more interested in the guitar; or he might have no interest in music at all and would rather build rockets or take a photography class. Support his interests at home, in museums and concert halls, in a special summer camp, or with travel.

The state of being out of sync, both within themselves and in relation to their peers, makes gifted children potentially more vulnerable to frustration and emotional turmoil. Living with a gifted child can be exhausting for parents and other family members: he has to know the *why* and *how* of everything, he may occasionally challenge your authority, and he may be easily bored if he's not sufficiently challenged. He may throw a tantrum because his six-year-old hands cannot produce what his ten-year-old mind wants them to. His peer relationships may be stressful, particularly in pre- and lower school, where he may be seen as bossy and domineering. In middle and high school he may be faced with the conflict of wanting to fit in and yet feeling different. Many gifted children seek the companionship of older kids or adults or become loners, preferring their own company.

It is therefore critical that parents not only provide a supportive home environment—in which the gifted child is appreciated for who he is and respected for his uniqueness—but also become strong advocates for their child in school. Meet early and often with teachers and work together to develop a plan to meet your child's special needs. If possible, offer support in the form of supplementary resources, enrichment classes, or assistance in the classroom. Let teachers know how much you appreciate any efforts they make to keep your child engaged and challenged.

If you can handle it financially, you might want to consider all possible opportunities; a daughter, in particular, may well thrive in an all-girl school. Some cities have magnet public schools that specialize in such areas as performing arts or math and science. These schools are usually tuition-free but may require an entrance exam. Many public schools have Gifted and Talented programs in which high-ability students are tracked and given special out-of-the-classroom activities and challenges. If your school does not, there

are several other options within the system: early entrance, grade-skipping, advanced courses, compacted courses, credit for outside courses, and others. However, with grade-skipping in particular, assess your child's emotional and social readiness before you agree to it, as this option may further the desynchronization between cognitive and social development. Discuss it with him beforehand—he may not like the idea of being the youngest or smallest kid in the class; he may balk at the idea of leaving old friends. Academics aren't everything; flexibility and creativity—your own and the school's—are crucial.

Boasting

At some time or another most children engage in boasting about accomplishments, possessions, or acquaintances, often with adults as their role models. This behavior occurs most commonly in the seventh and eighth grades, as peer relationships assume greater importance. In and of itself, boasting is not unusual. When it becomes habitual, however, you might want to consider why.

▪ CAUSES AND CONSEQUENCES

Boasting is an attention-getting behavior, and a child who relies on boasting may be signaling that he needs more of your support and involvement than usual. Often a child who is stretching himself into new areas of achievement or development will temporarily want his parents to become more involved in his life, as if to provide reassurance that despite the growth into independence, his parents are still there. It's easy for parents to step back from their child at such times, assuming that with increased self-reliance he won't need or want their involvement to the same degree as in the past. Ultimately this will be true, but times of transition often leave children needing more, not less, parental support, at least for the short run.

Boasting can also be a clue to a child's feelings of inadequacy and his need for the approval of his peers. Like adults, children want to be liked, and they may fear that without some special reason their peers won't find them acceptable. Habitual boasters may be suffering from low self-esteem, even though what they are claiming is true.

The validity of a child's boasts may make little difference to his peers. An older child may be rejected by friends who don't believe his claims. But sometimes a child has good reason to brag; he may in fact be the smartest at math or the best artist. In some cases, the acclaim his parents heap on him may backfire, by making him feel that his talent is the only reason others would want to befriend him. Some children simply become so fixated on their accomplishments they can think of little else, which can make them rather tedious company for their peers.

■ HOW TO RESPOND

What's the best course of action if your child has started to boast more than you think is healthy? If he's bragging about fact rather than fiction, coach him in the value of humility, especially when he's in the company of those less endowed or able. Suggest that he try to put himself in the other child's position to understand how a less fortunate friend might perceive his boasting. Teach him to take turns when talking to other kids and to show interest in what they say. Developing empathy and a sensitivity to the feelings of others will in time help temper inappropriate or habitual boasting.

Should your child's boasting be unfounded, take the time to listen between the lines and figure out why. Is he having trouble making friends in general? Does he boast about things he's done (but actually hasn't) or toys he owns (but actually doesn't) in order to buy friendship? If he seems to feel he has nothing else to offer, his self-esteem could probably use a boost. Think about ways you might help him, perhaps by spending more quality time with him, apart from his siblings, or by engaging him in activities in which you know he excels. Let him know that you enjoy his company, that he's fun to hang out with, that you're interested in what he has to say. By listening well and teaching him the give-and-take of normal interaction you'll be giving him some tools with which to approach new friends. Quietly encourage his special strengths and abilities and thereby bolster his confidence as he ventures out into the sometimes cruel world of peers.

Bullying or Dealing with a Bully

Another way that children grab the attention of others is through bullying, whether physical or verbal. Bullying is exceedingly common; almost 10 percent of schoolchildren in grades one through nine are the victims of bullying by peers on a regular basis. Because it has always been a problem of childhood, adults too often shrug it off as something victims just have to learn to live with, saying that boys—the most common offenders—will be boys.

Children who are bullied experience real suffering, however, that interferes with their social and academic development. Studies show that the aggressive behavior of a bully will interfere with the victim's ability to think clearly. Imagine how well you would perform your job after enduring terrifying threats or taunts just before work or during lunch. Some young victims of bullying have even committed suicide rather than continue to endure such punishment. In fact, the suicides of three youths prompted Norway to implement a campaign against bullying in 1983. So effective was the campaign that in 1994 neighboring Sweden declared bullying illegal.

Bullying can be physical or verbal. Boys rely on physical threats, regardless of the gender of their victims. Girls' bullying is usually verbal, usually with another girl the victim, and their threats are more psychologically manipulative than boys' threats. Girls, who generally place greater value on relationships, are apt to threaten to spread false rumors or to withdraw friendship if their victims don't comply with their demands. While physical threats may seem more terrifying than verbal threats, victims are just as devastated by ostracism or other social injury, and their complaints should be taken just as seriously.

Many parents wonder where to draw the line between typical childhood meanness and bullying. Occasional name-calling and pushing don't qualify; as unpleasant as they may be, all children encounter this kind of behavior and learn through trial and error how to respond to it. When pushing and shoving become hitting and throwing someone against the wall, or a child starts extorting money or possessions from another child, or vicious rumors cause social isolation—and when these confrontations become regular occurrences—meanness has turned into bullying.

Contrary to popular opinion, bullies are not necessarily all bluster. Children who bully thrive on controlling and dominating others. They have often been physically abused and bullied themselves, and have gone from being bullied to bullying others. They will go so far as to inflict injury on those who don't give them what they want, and they seem to derive great satisfaction from seeing their victims give in to their requests. Their aggressive nature causes them to see accidents as intentional, and they often strike back impulsively. If your child happens to be the unlucky perpetrator of such an accident, the bully is unlikely to listen to reason, no matter how convincing your child's explanation.

■ CAUSES AND CONSEQUENCES

What causes a child to become a bully? Experts say it happens when parents repeatedly fail to follow through with threatened sanctions against a strong-willed child, who continues the unwanted behavior until the parents' anger finally escalates to aggression, even to the point of striking the child. This pattern, coupled with the parents' failure to provide positive interaction such as hugging and praising, teaches the child to be even more aggressive. Some experts claim that a lifestyle of aggression is already in place by the time a child is two. Studies have also shown that children prone to bullying behavior are often left unsupervised and watch more violent television. They lack empathy for others and are unaware of how others see them. In some cases, bullying children are also imitating adult behavior.

Victims of Bullying Children who are targeted by bullies also fit a particular profile. A victim is often smaller or younger than his tormentor and has a hard time defending himself. More sensitive or cautious than other children, he usually blames himself for the attack. He may feel worthless, anxious, depressed, and insecure. Since other children are uncomfortable when a peer doesn't stick up for himself, they stay away from him, reinforcing his self-loathing and sense of worthlessness. Those who are victims at one age are most often victims later, and since even one year of being the target of a bully can hamper a child's future success at school, repeated victimization can spell disaster for developing social skills as well as for academic achievement. Victims often come from overprotective families in which the children have little practice handling conflict in appropriate ways.

Is your child a victim? Rarely do children targeted by bullies bring their problem to their parents' attention. They are more likely to offer excuses for their lost lunch money or missing hat. If you suspect your child may be the victim of bullying, provide lots of opportunities for him to open up to you, and when he does, listen intently, without interrupting. *Active listening*, in which you restate what your child has said or revealed about his feelings, is a useful tool for encouraging further discussion.

■ **HOW TO RESPOND**

First, listen to what your child describes to you. Ask him what he thinks should be done. What has he tried, what works and what hasn't worked?

If you've ascertained that your child is being bullied, seek help from the teacher and school. Most bullying occurs on playgrounds or in unsupervised halls or corners, and teachers need to be made aware of this. While schools have seldom acknowledged the seriousness of bullying or taken action to curb it, research has alerted some school authorities that it's happening at their schools and that they need to take measures to prevent it. Ask that your school administrators find out about programs other communities have used and implement them.

You can also help your child deal with bullies. First, don't suggest that he fight back. Perhaps the easiest and most effective method is to walk away and avoid the bully. When that's not possible, however, humor can be a powerful deterrent. Help your child practice funny responses with you at home, so that he'll have several clever comebacks at hand the next time the bully confronts him.

Learning how to be assertive will also help; the simple act of insisting that the bully leave him alone often has a surprising effect. Explain to your child that the bully's true goal is to get a response, and that by crying or cowering your child is setting himself up for further abuse.

Feeling supported by friends can help a bullied child feel less isolated and may even discourage the bully from pursuing him. Arrange times for your child to be with friends and encourage him to include friends during shopping trips or other outings. Having friends to stand by him when a bully threatens is enormously comforting and empowering.

What to Do If Your Child Is a Bully
While some people may consider bullying a sign of masculinity or strength, it is actually a signal for parents to do something. The importance of curbing bullying behavior as early as possible cannot be stressed too much. There is incontestable evidence that bullies travel a path of escalating patterns of abuse that can culminate in court convictions

and even spousal abuse; ultimately the person a bully hurts most is himself.

Understanding that your child's need to dominate others stems from his own feeling of inadequacy is a good place to start. Learning compassion is an important lesson that may need constant reinforcing. Model good relationships at home, both between spouses and between parents and children, and provide your youngster with lots of love and affection. Limit or at least monitor his television viewing and provide him with plenty of opportunities for more active outdoor play. Talk with his teachers, who may be eager to coordinate a plan with you to curtail his bullying behavior. Professional help, either from the school counselor or a private clinician, can be invaluable.

Be clear about what constitutes acceptable behavior and what does not, and spell out the consequences of not following the rules. Impose nonhostile, nonthreatening, nonphysical sanctions when your child breaks the rules, every time your child breaks the rules. Consistency coupled with love can reverse even deeply ingrained bullying.

CORPORAL PUNISHMENT

Corporal punishment is the practice of disciplining a child by inflicting physical pain, usually by means of an open hand, ruler, or paddle. Few experts recommend the use of hitting or spanking in the school or at home, and most organizations concerned with the welfare and education of children, including the American Academy of Child and Adolescent Psychiatry, have published policy statements against corporal punishment.

Instead of correcting errant behavior, this form of punishment tends to humiliate the child, destroy the trust most children place in adults, and ruin the nurturing atmosphere of both home and school. Hitting can erode a child's self-esteem and train him early on that striking out with the goal of hurting another is the proper response to conflict. Children whose parents use corporal punishment may become more aggressive and hostile toward others. Another objection is that it's simply not effective.

Once considered a standard method for modifying children's behavior, corporal punishment in schools is now expressly outlawed in many states and cities. Legislation to prohibit corporal punishment is pending in several other states. Nevertheless, studies show that one to two million incidents involving corporal punishment in school occur each year in the United States, which is one of only two Western countries in which it is not banned altogether. (The United Kingdom is the other.)

If your school sanctions corporal punishment and you do not, protest to the school board or the PTA. Make clear you will not tolerate the use of corporal punishment with your child. You will likely find plenty of support among other parents, particularly if you arm yourself with the abundance of research documenting the adverse effects of corporal and other degrading forms of punishment.

Cheating

If your child has been caught cheating in school, you should be concerned. But if it's the only time, don't assume that you have a reprobate on your hands. Cheating is a common occurrence, especially as children progress to the middle grades. But school isn't necessarily the first place they learn how to break the rules.

■ CAUSES AND CONSEQUENCES

The first experience most children have with cheating occurs while playing games.

Since winning often seems to be the point of a game, young children may not understand why they shouldn't do everything they can to win. By six or seven, most children are able to reason and understand the need for rules, and consequently most rule-breaking subsides. Cheating during the elementary years is fairly unusual, since grades are less of an issue than are learning to read and becoming proficient at basic math skills. But with the middle-school years may come increased pressure to bring home good grades, and it is often during this period that kids learn to cheat, usually by using crib notes, copying from others' papers or tests, or outright plagiarism.

Distinguishing between cheating and cooperative learning is important, however. Helping each other with homework or working through math problems together is an educationally sound method of learning and should not be discouraged. Often children learn best by teaching others.

■ HOW TO RESPOND

Parents can do several things to maximize the likelihood that their child will not cheat. Early in your child's school career, demonstrate by words and actions that learning is more important than grades. Firsthand involvement in his learning is a much more meaningful way to assess his progress than asking what grade he earned on a science test. Exploring the natural habitat of a frog after reading about it in a science magazine shows genuine interest and excitement about learning as an end in itself. Making too much of a high or low grade sends the message that the grade is more important than what it represents, and your child will pick up on that and do whatever he can—including cheating—to meet your demands.

One of the most effective ways to teach children is by example, and nowhere does that hold more true than with cheating. How do you respond when you are undercharged at a store? What if you're given too much change? Do you gloat aloud over how you've persuaded a friend on the police force to bend the rules and tear up your speeding ticket? Or passed your child off as younger than he is to get a reduced-price ticket?

Remember that your values are apparent in everyday situations. As tempting as it may be to cut into line at the bank, it's not worth the sacrifice of a good, albeit small, moral lesson.

Because cheating is unusual in the early school years, your child's cheating at this age could signal a problem. It may be his response to a loss, whether the death of a grandparent or a neighborhood friend's moving away. Spend a little extra time with your youngster to ease him through the transition period. Inform his teacher of the change in his life, too, so that the teacher, too, can be aware of any special needs he might have.

If your middle schooler is caught cheating, let him know that you are disappointed, but don't overreact. A harsh response can cause kids to continue this behavior out of anger and spite. Instead, find out what motivated him to cheat. Was he unprepared for a test? If he was so afraid of bringing home a poor grade that he decided to cheat, you might ease up on the pressure to get all A's and help him with his study skills. A crib note, however, is a sign the cheating was planned. Be sure to let him know that you and he cannot tolerate cheating and that you value his integrity above all else.

Most children who are caught cheating are extremely embarrassed and concerned, rightfully, about their parents' reaction. By using this experience as an opportunity for your child to learn more about himself, you gain greater trust and teach him that you are there to help him get back on track regardless of what he's done. Establishing that rapport will go a long way during the challenges of the teenage years.

Competitiveness

Whether parents should encourage competitiveness has been the focus of much debate. At one extreme are parents who deny the validity of any form of competition among children, choosing to do away with games, grades, and events that pit children against one another. At the other end of the spectrum are those who believe that unless a child learns to be competitive at a young age, he will never succeed as an adult in our highly competitive society. As with many such controversies, the practical needs of your child probably lie somewhere in the middle.

Regardless of what their parents do to temper it, children learn competitiveness early in life, especially when there are other children in the family. Sibling rivalry can spur heated and persistent competition, and when the children involved are the same gender, two years or less apart, and one has an outstanding talent or ability, rivalry is at its fiercest. But even without siblings, kids spontaneously encounter competition with neighborhood or playgroup friends—*Who can run fastest and get to the corner first?*—or during games, or when one child is singled out for special attention. The urge to compete probably is part of a survival and adaptive mechanism. Still, teaching kids about cooperation rather than competition may prove to be healthier and more useful in the long term.

But your child needs to learn that winning or being the best isn't the most important thing to you. Too much emphasis on being number one can harm his self-esteem if he falls short of the goal. Having love and approval based on winning or getting the best grade can undercut your child's certainty that he is valued by you just the way he is.

■ How to Respond

Some children are more inclined to be competitive than others, and you need to determine your child's level to find the best classroom environment for him. If your first grader has less of a drive to compete and is placed in a highly competitive classroom, he may feel out of place, withdraw, and not feel confident enough to risk making mistakes by trying. A class in which his personal best is valued most and the joy of learning is emphasized more than grades would be a more benevolent, nurturing environment. For an older child, a school that fosters competitiveness in and out of the classroom can push him to cheat. Again, stressing personal best instead of top honors reduces the pressure and allows for a more natural, enjoyable learning experience.

While you want to encourage your child to do his best, and give him the tools with which to do that, showing him that you will love and value him regardless of honors and achievements will go a long way toward easing an unrelenting drive to compete.

School Avoidance, Refusal, and Truancy

Mom, I don't want to go to school.

For most parents, hearing their child say

this occasionally is no cause for concern. Not wanting to do something one is obliged to do is not uncommon for a child—or, for that matter, for an adult. But if your child complains often about school or refuses to go, there's usually something more to it than the need for some downtime.

About 5 percent of children avoid school or refuse to go altogether at some point during their school career. School avoidance is most common between the ages of five and seven, and again between eleven and fourteen, both periods of a child's life when major changes are occurring, the first being entry to elementary school, the second entrance to middle school.

■ CAUSES AND CONSEQUENCES

During the first years of school, children are setting out on unfamiliar territory, and fear of the unknown can cause any child to be a bit more clingy (see *Separation Anxiety*, page 18). Most children seem to get over this after the first few days or so, but for some it may recur after a few weeks, and morning battles over going to school can become the norm. Separation anxiety—the fear of being away from you—can be upsetting, not to mention disruptive of everyday life. Even if your child has gone through separation anxiety earlier in his life—when you began working away from home, for instance—the challenges of kindergarten and first grade can renew his distress.

Few young children know how to identify and express their fears straightforwardly. For some children, headaches, stomachaches, and other ailments are their means of expressing their anxiety. The first step with a frequently ill child is to consult your pediatrician to rule out physical causes. Once you're assured of his physical health, you can work on other possible reasons for his objection to school.

Fear of someone or something at school or on the way to school might be the reason he doesn't want to go. Talk to your child about what happens at recess or when walking to or from school. Sometimes children are ashamed of feeling worried or scared and therefore reluctant to discuss their fears. The problem might be something easy to resolve, like taking another route to school to avoid a barking dog; it might be concern over schoolwork or an upcoming test. Sometimes separation anxiety produces physical symptoms like headaches and stomachaches. The anxiety may appear after a physical illness like the flu or a cold. The child may have stayed at home from school for a few days and then seemed ready to go back, only to have head- and stomachaches appear.

While older children don't usually experience anxiety in the same way as when they were younger, changes in their lives or losses they experience can trigger a desire to stay at home. If a preadolescent refuses to go to school for more than a few days, though, the problem can become more serious as the child's fears and anxieties are reinforced by avoiding school and staying at home.

■ HOW TO RESPOND

As difficult as it may be, you need to insist that your child go to school. Allowing him to stay at home will cause his fears or problems to grow, and you won't be doing him any favors. It doesn't hurt to tell even young children that school is required by law.

If you discover that he doesn't want to go to school because he's being taunted by a bully, get the school involved right away and do what you need to make him feel safer (see *Bullying or Dealing with a Bully,* page 236). Suggest that he walk to school with a friend or stay within view of the teacher at recess.

Maintaining daily routines at home can be an enormous source of comfort for kids during difficult times. You might add a special morning ritual, carving out ten minutes, if you can, for quality time to read or just talk before you each leave for your workday.

Find out about class work from his teacher. If an upcoming test is causing anxiety, help your child study and even practice taking a mock test at home. Often all that's needed to turn the problem around is to give your child some control of the situation and a sense of mastery.

Taking steps to evaluate and deal with it is essential. Seeing your pediatrician may be a wise step, especially if there have been physical complaints, because a child who isn't in school is considered truant if he's not receiving medical attention. If you cannot resolve the problem fairly quickly, it's important to involve the school, too, for academic, emotional, and behavioral help and in deciding the best course of action to take. If teachers have noticed academic problems, your child may have a learning disability he's been able to deal with until now.

School Failure or Repeating a Grade

Traditionally, when a child failed to meet the academic standards for his age group, the solution was to hold him back a grade to help him get a more solid grasp of the subject matter and improve his chances of succeeding in future grades. Today, however, the research overwhelmingly proves that repeating a grade does little academically to help a child but much to diminish his self-esteem. Students who are having difficulty tend to make the same academic progress whether they repeat a grade or are promoted to the next. Inevitably, though, their self-esteem and social growth suffer if they are held back.

Many schools have a pre-first grade or a readiness first grade for children who have finished kindergarten but don't seem mature enough for a regular first-grade class. These classes, which usually have fewer students, serve as a bridge between kindergarten and first grade and offer the extra support and coaching some children need. Often more structured than first-grade classes, they help kids grow accustomed to school routines and provide a more nurturing environment. Another alternative for younger children is a multi-age group, which combines two grades in one class. For older students, moving from one grade to another might occur in the middle of a year, allowing the child to repeat a semester rather than a whole year.

■ How to Respond

If your child's teacher recommends that he be held back, schedule a conference with the teacher, principal, and other school staff who interact with your child. Ask their opinions of your child's level of maturity and ability to grasp concepts. Explain that retention is seldom recommended by most experts and suggest that the school develop an alternative arrangement that will address your child's academic deficits and yet be sensitive to his emotional and social needs. Be willing to participate in any plan that's decided upon, since a parent's help and involvement in a child's schooling almost always improves his chances for success. If he repeats a semester, helping him to maintain social contacts during the transition will improve his chances of weathering the change. Monitoring his homework on a daily basis, and offering assistance when he needs it, will provide structure and routine. In some schools, peer tutors can provide additional help.

Since students who don't pass a grade are twice as likely to have a learning disability, insist that your child be tested. Your district's public school is required to provide testing, even if your child is enrolled in a private school. (See *Children with Special Needs*, page 230.)

Going to a New School

Entering a new school can be a daunting prospect for most children. Whether your child is entering middle school in the same system or entering a new school because you've moved, the experience can set him back in terms of behavior and confidence.

Beginning middle school or junior high can trigger insecurities and fears in a child. Not only will he go from being among the oldest in his school to being among the youngest, he will also face more teachers than he had in elementary school, and more complex schedules, lockers, different classrooms, and other adjustments. Worrying about changing classes and having the right materials for each one can cause anxiety, and his self-confidence can be further undermined by unsympathetic older students. To compound the problem, middle schoolers are approaching adolescence and tremendous physical change.

The child whose family moves in midyear faces an even more difficult adjustment. Starting in a new school that's already in session means entering a social environment where friendships and ways of interacting are already established, and that can cause a newcomer to feel like an outsider. Couple that with a feeling of loss for the school and friends he left behind, and it's easy to see how your child might feel lonely and intimidated. (For suggestions on how to deal with this transition, see *Moving*, page 218.)

■ HOW TO RESPOND

The preparation you do to help your child enter a new school can make an important difference. Whether he is enrolling at the beginning of or midway through a school year, visit the school in advance and meet with teachers and staff. Get a feel for the physical layout of the building and his classroom, pointing out important places like the lunchroom and bathroom. If your child will be changing classrooms, ask the teacher for a schedule and the room numbers, and walk the routes with him. Find out what the first tasks or routines of a typical school day will be. Be sure to take care of any paperwork, including immunization forms and records, before the first day. Get a list of school supplies he'll need and make a special shopping trip to allow him to choose them himself.

Ask the teacher to suggest one or two students in the class who might be friendly to your child, so he will have some faces to recognize. If possible, call the parents of those children and arrange a get-together ahead of time. Having a friend or two on the first day can dispel many fears.

Finally, expect and accept as perfectly normal a certain amount of regression on your child's part during the transition. Separation anxiety may flare up again, evident in disrupted sleep patterns and a reluctance to leave home. He may cling to you more than usual and need extra hugs. Offer him plenty of extra support, but don't abandon the usual family routines, which can provide much-needed comfort and reassurance. (Also see *Separation Anxiety,* page 18.)

8

The Child and the Community

■ ■ ■

When an infant enters the world, she comes equipped with her own unique style and a cluster of temperamental traits. She is received by a family which, likewise, has its characteristic style, in addition to its personal history and set of values and beliefs. The larger social context in which her family lives advances its own collection of manners, values, and convictions, as well as a rather broad sense of purpose and worth. All of these individual, family, and social conditions are constantly colliding and interacting, fashioning the child in her community.

As long as parents remain at home with their young children, they retain a high degree of direct control over outside influences. However, as others come into the home—grandparents, friends, baby-sitters—they bring in ideas, values, and voices from the outside. The older a child gets, the more directly she will interact with her community.

There is no doubt that children learn their primary social lessons in the family. They absorb an understanding of how to deal with people from the way they are treated and from the way their parents treat others. Children model their own style of negotiating, differing, arguing, fighting, loving, sharing, caring, and expressing their feelings and desires on their relationships with parents, siblings, and extended family members. They then take what they learn into the larger world.

In a sense, development happens within the center of a social vortex. Through the messages they receive about socializing and the input they get in their social interactions, children develop a social identity. When they are able to steer their way through their community with relative ease and when their own individual styles and values are in reasonable harmony with those of their community, their growing sense of self and competence is enriched.

Through their dealings in the community, children necessarily move away, not only from their nuclear family, but also from an exclusively egocentric perspective. As time goes by, because they operate within a context larger than self and family, most children acquire a greater sense of belonging, purpose, and responsibility.

What exactly do we mean when we talk about *community*? Usually, the term refers to the social context in which each individual belongs. It is a place where people are linked, not just by proximity, but often by common concerns, involvements, and values. In many cases, the term implies reciprocity, care, and compassion.

For many, "community" conjures up images of homogeneous, cohesive villages or neighborhoods from days gone by. Today, a child's community probably extends beyond a few square blocks. Most children these days operate within a number of interrelated, or intersecting communities, including their extended family, their neighborhood or town, their religious group, and their ethnic or racial group.

Day care and schools define another kind of community. When parents leave their children in the care of others, whether day care, nursery school, or elementary school, for several hours a day, the nature of the children's experiences changes in a decisive way. The type of day care, nursery school, and school that children attend directly influences their development.

In addition, as children get older, they become involved in communities based on shared interests such as arts, academic, or sports activities. The community outside enters the home daily through letters, magazines, newspapers, television, radio, books and the computer. Today many children travel more extensively and at a younger age than ever before. They are, therefore, able to witness and experience aspects of diverse communities around the world. Consequently, we can talk today of our children belonging to a global as well as an immediate community.

For all the advantages that today's more complex and sophisticated community brings, there is a cost. Often we look back on the past, and the idea of community appears in a rosy light. Our nostalgic image usually encompasses a tight-knit, ever-concerned fellowship of neighbors and friends that offers a sense of kinship and belonging, of homogeneity and safety. Mirrored in this image is the belief that years ago, everyone cared for everyone else, and that neighbors knew and kept an eye on the children as if they were their own. In this picture, a child on her way to school had to worry only about remembering her lunch or if she would be invited to a classmate's birthday party.

Whether this image is historically accurate or not, it is clear that the very idea of community has changed in recent years, just as our notion of family has. Sadly, for some children, community is just the place they come from, an indifferent location where few people know their neighbors and even fewer feel concern for their neighbors' welfare.

In most instances, helping children explore their community is no longer a matter of merely teaching them the way to the corner drugstore. These days, a child on her way to the drugstore might come across a homeless man begging for money, or other children, little older than she, hanging out on the corner, smoking cigarettes or marijuana. It is a tragic reality of our times that some children fear daily for their own safety on the streets of their neighborhoods and in their classrooms.

Within their homes, children hear news on the radio of wars raging on the other side of the world and of murders committed in their home city. On television, they see images of homes submerged in flood waters or whole towns devastated by hurricanes. On the Internet, they play games with beer-drinking frogs or carry on conversations with strangers thousands of miles away.

Consequently, raising a child to be a citizen in this larger, more complicated and demanding community is both exciting and daunting. Just how do parents promote a safe, rich, supportive relationship between their children and the community?

As most parents know, it has become virtually impossible to monitor and control all of a child's interactions. In addition, as a child gets older, too much parental control becomes counterproductive because it does not allow a youngster to develop independent, internal controls. Besides, children tend to react willfully against rigid parental limits. Thus the task requires that parents exercise appropriate control and measured judgment. Mostly, rather than engendering fear, it is a matter of encouraging good sense and internal controls in their children. Yet these are fine lines to walk.

For many parents, teaching their children merely to manage in the community is not sufficient. Many want their children to cultivate a clear sense of personal responsibility in regard to their community, to consider the greater good as they make personal decisions, and to find meaningful ways to contribute. In order to encourage a sense of social responsibility, parents must nourish their children's natural empathy. In addition, as they get older, children should learn to take personal responsibility for their own actions in the world. In that way, they come to care about what goes on around them and about people and places that do not touch them directly or tangibly.

In this chapter we will look at the behaviors and events that can arise from the complex interrelationships between the individual child, her family, and her community.

Rules and Boundaries

As children mature, most come to respect rules and boundaries. They also evolve their own standards and boundaries. These aspects of development play a critical role in a child's interactions in her community.

Very young children are, by nature, egocentric. Concerned primarily with their own wants and needs, they find it difficult to understand that the interests of others are distinct from their own. Adults can usually enforce limits and rules with relative ease for young children; they can pick up and move a very young child or remove the object of temptation from view or reach.

The older children get, the more they are able to use reason to understand rules and limits. By the time a child begins school, for example, she can understand that others have their own wishes and needs. She will notice that sometimes other perspectives differ from hers and that the interest of others conflicts with her own. Because her egocentric viewpoint is leavened with an increasing awareness of the other, reciprocity—*I'll do this for you if you do that for me*—enters into her interactions.

By the age of eight, most children are able to weigh the needs and feelings of others as they make decisions and judgments. The process of balancing their own needs with the needs of others forms the heart of their sense of morality. For most children, the notion of fairness becomes pivotal around this time.

A child's perception of fairness and justice is key to the willingness to follow rules and respect boundaries. In addition, a child this age will expect others to treat her, her standards, and limits, with equal fairness and justice.

At this age, children are able to cooperate.

As a rule, the ability and willingness to cooperate serve children well in their dealings in the world. But cooperation is something they learn at home. Families that emphasize *cooperation* over *obedience* provide children with an important social lesson. Rather than insisting that "these are the rules and you must follow them regardless of circumstances," parents who shape rules and limits within the context of day-to-day living, with all its contingencies, offer children the opportunity to become thoughtful about what they do and the choices they make.

In addition, when families teach that, as participants in a social unit, all members must consider each other's feelings and needs, and find ways to compromise in their daily living, the inevitable clashes of values, needs, and styles will offer valuable examples of negotiating and cooperating. A child will then be prepared to apply these lessons in a larger circle of peers and adults.

All children—and homes—need rules and limits. Without structure and rules to guide their behavior, children feel abandoned, lost at sea without a map to guide them, an oar to propel them. A household would be nothing less than chaotic (and messy) if no one put anything away, if everyone insisted on dinner at a different time, and everyone operated on separate timetables. Discipline, rules, and limits bring order to a child's life. Even as rules and limits shift, as they must as a child grows up and circumstances change, rules teach the skills the youngster needs to manage and control her impulses. Simply put, rules and limits, as they are imposed externally or as they become internalized, become key to their social functioning.

Where health and safety are concerned, rules need to be more strictly followed. Examples of non-negotiable rules should include never riding in a car without a child-safety seat or a seat belt, and not taking somebody else's medicine. However, flexibility with other rules offers your child the opportunity to understand how things work and why judgments are made. If rules are too rigid, your child will likely question automatically whether they're fair. As she gets older, she might refuse to comply simply because you insist on compliance. In most cases, children accept rules more readily when they understand the logic of them.

Here are some other rules about rules:

- **"Do as I say, not as I do" seldom works.**
  Although all parents at some time or other wish they could correct their child's behavior without addressing their own, double standards only invite confusion. If you want your child to act in certain ways, model those behaviors for her—whether it's about eating sweets, speaking in a respectful way, or hitting. As far as your child is concerned, you are her model, and whatever you do must be okay for her to do. This is not to say that adults and children are expected to have identical rules. It *does* mean that adults who don't follow their rules set an example to children who may then conclude that they don't have to follow the rules set out for them.

  There is another problem with the "do as I say, not as I do" philosophy. It is important that children recognize a clear and accurate connection between words and actions. When there is a disconnection between what a child sees and what she hears, words lose their power. In addition, she may begin to doubt the truth of her perceptions. Out in the world, a child may then not be able to trust the information that she receives. At the same time, she may put out confusing messages of her own because her words and behaviors are out of sync.

- **Make sure that what you ask for is reasonable.**
  Children evolve their own standards. Many times, your child's standards will differ from yours. You may, for example, be frustrated by your child's need to finish one project in an exacting way before moving on to another task. Yet, if you insist that she acquiesce to your sense of the way it should be, you can create a dilemma for your child as she struggles to please or appease you. In addition, you may provoke an otherwise unnecessary power struggle, and perhaps an avoidable tantrum.

  When your child is out in the world, she needs to be able to respect others' standards. In order to do so, she must be permitted to value her own standards, and to consider what she wants even as she strives to accommodate the wishes of others.

- **Trust your child to do the right thing.**
  Within the limits of your child's age and stage of development, allow her to have

responsibility for her behavior. Let her feel that you trust her to take charge of herself. If you give her permission to play at a friend's house, for example, keep in check the urge to rattle off a list of dos and don'ts. This will only undermine her belief that she *can* be in charge of herself.

- **Allow for negotiation and flexibility.**
  Children who have a voice in the home have less difficulty speaking up in the community. This is important because it not only allows them to say *No* to dangerous situations and behavior, but also it engenders a sense of impact and consequence. By allowing your children the opportunity to question and challenge authority at home, to renegotiate rules that might be unfair, and to have a say in how they are treated and disciplined, you help them learn about compromise, respect, and making responsible decisions—valuable lessons at any stage of life. They also learn which rules are negotiable and which are not.

- **Let your child experience the consequences of her behavior.**
  When danger and damage are not concerns, allow your child to see the logical outcome of her behavior and choices. Many children, for example, become distracted or recalcitrant when it's time to get ready for school in the morning. If, after you have worked out a reasonable morning routine, your child is still unresponsive, and you find yourself nagging, take a less controlling role. After your

child misses the bus and gets to school late once or twice she will begin to understand how her morning behavior gets her off to a bad start.

Many parents lament, "I don't understand it, no matter how often I tell her not to, she still does it." We have all been around adults who nag their children to little apparent effect; all their correcting and scolding does little to diminish their children's bossy, boastful, or whiny behavior. The more an instruction is repeated, the less likely it is to be heard.

A child will discover out in the world that such behavior is just not acceptable. Most children will curb unacceptable behavior so that they can be part of the group at school or play. In this way, a positive peer or community group can provide the best corrective for minor problems in a child's behavior.

Fears and Anxieties

Most children experience anxiety for the first time when, around the age of eight months, they look into someone's face and realize that person is not Mother. Although a baby would not be able to conceptualize the experience as such, *stranger anxiety* signals a child's first awareness of community.

Not surprisingly, most children (and many adults) feel nervous as they make their way into a greater social world. In most cases, such anxiety in the face of a larger, often unfamiliar world is healthy and protective. Normal anxiety arises in the face of actual danger *(Will I fall off this swing and hurt myself? Will that barking dog bite me?)* or in response to a situation that could cause embarrassment or loss of self-esteem *(Will I look stupid in these clothes? Will I fail this test?)*. As she continues to grow and explore her world, every child will experience anxiety from time to time.

With age, experience, and understanding, many fears diminish. For an eight-year-old, hearing a sudden loud noise or being left alone in a room does not hold the same menace that it may for a three-year-old. On the other hand, with age comes increased awareness, and often greater anxiety. When children hear or read news reports about kidnappings, murders, wars, or threats to the environment, they may well feel anxious. Such fears usually fade as events fade from the headlines, yet sometimes a child will need a little extra help processing what she hears or sees in order to resolve her fear.

When the anxieties don't fade or diminish, and when they begin to interfere with a child's ability to make her way in her social and academic worlds, more serious problems may be starting. In cases like these, professional intervention may be required (see *Emotional Disorders,* page 307).

■ How to Respond

When fears and anxiety appear to be a normal and passing response, offer your child reassurance and understanding. Ask her to talk about what's troubling her. Generally speaking, if you know the cause, you may be able to ease your child's discomfort, if not dispel it altogether.

Some important tools to helping your child deal with her fears are:

- **Acknowledge what she's feeling and be sympathetic.**
  Although you may know that there is, in fact, nothing to be afraid of, her fears are real feelings. Ask her to describe her fears. What does she think would help her overcome them? By eliciting her involvement, you help her bring her reason and intelligence into play, thus strengthening her coping skills and fostering her sense of mastery.

- **Don't discount her fear.**
  Comments like "Oh, you're being silly" or "You're a big girl; don't act like a baby" do little to alleviate a child's anxiety. In fact, such responses negate her worth and may compel her to hide her feelings and perhaps develop other symptoms.

- **Don't force your child to confront a fear.**
  If she seems willing, gently encourage, even coax her to face the source of her anxiety. However, if she does not respond to gentle urging, forcing the issue may make her even more afraid. Remember that as a parent you are a protector as well as a teacher.

- **Be careful not to overreact or cater to a fear.**
  Children will pick up on their parents' fears, so be careful that you don't telegraph a fearful message. If you're afraid, chances are she'll learn to be afraid, too.

If you are overly protective, you may unwittingly reinforce a fear. When children get a lot of attention through anxiety, they may begin to use it to get their way. If your child seems to respond to the additional attention, find other ways of indulging her needs so that she doesn't use her fearfulness to get her emotional needs met.

- **Take seriously your child's response to her experiences out in the world.**
  If a very young child develops excessive anxiety in relation to her day-care situation or her preschool, for example, consider whether the timing or placement is best. When possible, delay or decrease her time away from you and home, or make more acceptable arrangements. Should an older child develop strong anxieties around social situations, you may want to cut back on her extracurricular activities in order to allow for more time at home.

- **Prepare your child for new experiences.**
  Talk to your child about what she can anticipate in a new setting or with a new group of children. Ask her to imagine what it will be like.

- **Use reading material to help her understand her concerns.**
  Books that deal with similar situations or feelings illustrate to a child that she's not alone. They also allow her to examine the source of a fear from a distance. Reading a book together may help your child feel more comforted.

Disasters: Natural and Man-Made

The ozone layer is thinning. There are threats of nuclear war, industrial pollutants, and acid rain. We face the possibility of earthquakes, hurricanes, floods, forest fires, mud slides, and tornadoes. Even if today's world is not actually a more perilous place than ever before, it can certainly seem that way, perhaps even more so to a child who lacks the benefit of experience, history, and mature judgment to put today's news into perspective.

Between television, newspapers, magazines, school, and home computers, children are confronted daily with information about disasters, wars, and tragedies. Such frightening information can provoke a torrent of distressing feelings that even the most well-adjusted child may be hard pressed to handle.

Many times, children at certain developmental stages are particularly sensitive to distressing news. Around the age of two and three, for example, just as a child is launching herself into a larger social realm such as day care or nursery school, she may be more likely to worry and become anxious. Because she is in the throes of separation with all its attendant uncertainties, news of danger or disaster may impress her with special poignancy.

In fact, during any transitional time—the beginning of elementary school—or during any time of change at home—the birth of a sibling, a divorce, a remarriage—a child is likely to experience more anxiety. In general, the more unsettled a child feels at home, the more intimidating the world is likely to seem. At these moments, the potential for disaster seems to loom large in a child's imagination.

▪ HOW TO RESPOND

As parents, we try to protect our children from harm and allay their fears. Yet, with so much information and so many sensational images, a fearful child is not always placated by a few calming words.

Studies show that many children react strongly to news about such natural and man-made catastrophes as earthquakes, war, and environmental disasters. The nightly news presents dramatic reminders of how much suffering there is in the world. Hearing parents and other adults discuss their own distress about such disasters, children may feel helpless and anxious.

However haunting the news and images are, adults are able to distance themselves from the impact. Yet children lack the intellectual sophistication and perspective to process much of the information they receive. Television especially brings an immediacy that is disquieting to children. They cannot easily place events in the context of history and geography. They don't always understand that what they see in their living room is happening far away. Because television blurs the boundaries between here and there, then and now, children can assume that the events pose an immediate threat to them.

When they hear about other children caught up in the event, they may directly identify. All this can be frightening and overwhelming to a child.

A Parent's Role Children need a sense of hope to understand and cope with the more fearful aspects of their world. Children who feel optimistic about their world and future tend to feel safer even in the midst of disaster. Your child needs to know that even when terrible things happen, there is always hope for the future.

In general, children who are secure in their emotional attachments and confident in their ability to face and master their immediate environment tend to feel more hopeful. The resulting self-confidence translates into a greater ability to consider and cope with distressing information in a measured and appropriate manner. Thus children who have been able to negotiate their world with relative success can often handle feelings of helplessness stirred up by news of tragic events.

Other ways to help your child handle the unavoidable or uncontrollable are:

- **Don't take it for granted that you understand the nature of your child's anxiety.**
  Even though your child expresses worry about specific disasters, listen closely as she describes her fears. What your child finds scary may be very different from what you think are the frightening elements. Consider your family situation. Perhaps there are other issues—at home or at school—that prompt her worries.

- **Communicate honestly.**
  Acknowledge that disasters happen, often unexpectedly. But emphasize that they happen rarely. With natural disasters, there is generally sufficient warning to

give everyone time to get to safety or take precautions. If you live in an area that is vulnerable to such disasters as tornadoes or floods, be reassuring. Develop and rehearse an emergency plan with your family.

Knowledge counteracts uncertainty, thereby raising a sense of control. Therefore, make easing your child's anxiety an academic affair. Find and read together material about the subject—weather, for example. By helping her use cognitive skills to overcome anxiety, you teach her an effective coping method that will serve her in all areas of her later life.

- **Avoid exposure.**

Try to shield a younger child from visual images of the consequences of natural disasters. Children often do not have sufficient ability to put events in perspective or to understand the concept of geographic distance. There is no reason to expose her to images that may only cause distress and worry.

- **Explain that disaster is nobody's fault.**

Because disasters stir up feelings of helplessness, children often look around for a comprehensible explanation. And because young children usually feel that everything relates directly to them, they may believe that when something bad happens, it's their fault. Perhaps, a child may reason, a catastrophe has happened as punishment for some wrong she has done—real or imagined.

Explain that, more often than not, bad things happen for no reason. It may be helpful to introduce the notion of mystery and randomness. Though these concepts may be difficult for a young child to grasp, it may help her to understand that there are things that no one can control completely.

- **Address your child's ambivalence as well as her fears.**

Many disasters, such as war, fascinate as well as frighten children. As she experiences and experiments with her own aggressive impulses, for example, your child may enjoy playing war or reading about it. Unlike a child's fantasies, though, the realities of war are disturbing.

Talk to your child honestly. While respecting her natural fascination with the idea, explain gently that most dramatic events are complex. For instance, unlike a sporting event in which one side wins and another loses, and all team members go home, war is complicated and tragic for all involved.

Although many people work hard to prevent it, war is a reality of the past and the present. Reassure her that most wars today happen far away. If she hears about a war in a far-off place, locate the area on a map for her.

- **Explore manageable solutions to problems.**

Environmental issues seem to have particular resonance for young children. The fact that animals and their habitats are threatened seems to stir up feelings of identification, concern, and worry. At the same time, there are ways in which even young children can have direct and obvious impact on the environment, thereby exercising active control of their anxiety.

Talk with your child about the things she can do to be environmentally responsible, like turning off lights and shutting off faucets. Discourage littering and encourage recycling. Perhaps older children would enjoy writing to government officials or corporate officers with their protests and suggestions. Show your children how to become environmentally conscious consumers by reading product labels with them. If your child has an interest in animals, show her ways to become involved in the responsible treatment of animals.

Finally, talk about your own choices. If you car pool or use mass transit, explain how that conserves resources. Plant trees and wildflowers in your yard; recycle and buy products made from recycled materials. Discuss the relationship between such seemingly mundane items as household products and the depletion of the ozone layer. When your children see you measure the effects of your actions, they will likely bring the same thoughtfulness to their behavior.

The Community's Role Chances are that if you live in an area that is particularly vulnerable to natural disasters, local schools will have programs to address potential crises with the students. If this is not the case, ask your school board to invite a mental health professional into the school to discuss with teachers and parents ways of coping with disaster and any related fears children may harbor. This may help the school to develop a policy about how to help their students after a disaster.

Many schools have environmental programs as part of the curriculum or after-school activities. Such programs usually look at the current environmental problems while offering concrete suggestions for taking better care of the earth. In so doing, they enable children to understand the delicate balance of life on our planet and encourage them to become active participants in their own futures.

Safety in the Community

Almost daily the news presents another terrifying story—a child is abducted or raped, shot or run over, sometimes right in front of her house or in another seemingly safe place. Given such sensational examples of dangers in our society, just how do parents make their children mindful of the need to be safe without making them afraid to leave the house?

Whether the world is as menacing as the news would have us believe, as parents we must be responsive to the dangers that the world holds. We use sunscreen on our children and ourselves to guard against skin cancer. We lock our houses and cars. We stay alert in parking lots and malls. We avoid dark, deserted places. We tell our children to watch out for cars as they play outside and instruct them never to take candy from strangers or get into their cars.

While parents may view these actions as exercising common sense, a child can see them as confirmation of her worst fears: why prepare for disaster if it's not going to happen? Parents have to balance the need to make their child aware of the very real dangers in the world with her need to trust and delight in the world. Children bring an innocence and sense of wonder to their experiences in the world; teaching wisdom without betraying that wonder is no easy task. In most cases, it is a matter of teaching judgment, not fear. Although you don't want your children to see the world as a dangerous, menacing place, you want them to approach new situations and people with full awareness and a degree of caution.

■ How to Respond

A Parent's Role Parenting in today's world requires addressing today's concerns. Early on, find a way to talk to your child about difficult subjects, even though you may think she is too young to be concerned with such things. Children generally hear only what they can handle. And most children handle a lot more than we give them credit for.

Follow the cues your child provides. If she becomes fidgety or distracted during your discussion, she may be telling you that she has heard all she is able to hear for the moment. No doubt, the subject will come up again.

Usually if a parent doesn't bring up the subject, a child will. Sometimes children ask about sex, war, kidnapping, sexual abuse, AIDS, abortion, and drugs before you've had time to gather your thoughts. If you have established easy and open communications, the stage is set for the most difficult subjects.

How you talk to your child is more important than *what* you tell her. Your tone and your words will help her make the distinction between what she does and does not need to fear.

STRANGERS. Make explicit the distinction between the way she is expected to behave with adults she knows and with adults she doesn't know. It is perfectly okay to ignore strangers' questions. However enticing, she should refuse all offers of candy, kittens, money, or toys.

Let her know that most adults would never ask a child, especially a very young child, for help to find a lost dog, for directions, or for the time. When a stranger persists with such requests, tell her to run away, without worrying about being rude. Even when someone appears to be nice, he might not be, so emphasize that no one can tell right away whether a stranger is trustworthy or intends harm.

Role play with your child. Give her examples of specific situations and responses. For example: What do you do if a stranger shows up at school and says I sent him to pick you up? What do you do if someone asks you to help him find his lost cat?

HOME ALONE. Today, many children ten and older come home after school to an empty house (see also *Latchkey Kids*, page 138). If your child must take care of herself for the afternoon while you are at work, work out specific rules and routines for her. Have her call you at work as soon as she gets home. Prepare a plan for emergencies. Make arrangements with neighbors and friends in case your child needs something special.

Your child should know to lock the door when she's home by herself. In most cases, if your child is home alone, she should not answer the door if someone knocks unexpectedly. If she does open the door to someone she doesn't know, she should indicate that an adult is home but unable to come to the door.

If she comes home to find the door open when no one is supposed to be there, she should not go into the house until a neighbor or another adult can check into the situation.

SEXUAL ABUSE. Many parents are unsure or squeamish about bringing up sexual matters, especially with their children. Yet, there are ways of laying the groundwork so that you can talk to your child without scaring her. Establish an open dialogue about sexual issues early on. If you introduce the subject of sex in a discussion of abuse, there is the danger that the idea of sex may become automatically linked in your child's mind with danger and anxiety.

If you have fostered in your child a sense of ownership regarding her body, she will likely have an instinct about what is okay for her body and what is not. You build on her natural sense of ownership of her body by letting her pick out her own clothes or wash herself in her own way. Also, avoid pushing her to kiss or hug other adults when she

clearly does not want to.

Finally, when parents treat their children's bodies with respect, children tend to demand that others treat their bodies in a similar manner. Children who are consistently hit, grabbed, or physically punished at home may feel that adults are entitled to misuse their bodies simply because they are bigger.

It is important that children learn, through how they are treated and what is said to them, that their bodies are their own. No one, under any circumstance, has the right to touch their bodies in any way that makes them uncomfortable. Children as young as three or four can listen to a candid discussion about sexual matters. By understanding when and how sex is acceptable, they can begin to understand the distinction between appropriate and inappropriate touching. Unfortunately, however, most sexual abuse is committed by someone the child knows and trusts.

In general, a child should know that no one should touch her in any area that would normally be covered by her bathing suit—with the possible exception of doctors and nurses during medical exams. Nor should she agree to touch anyone else's private areas. If someone urges her to do so, she should tell her parents or teachers. Instruct your child that she can say—very loudly—*No! Stop!* and, most effectively, *I'm going to tell!*

Often sexual abuse—especially incest—can continue only if a child keeps the secret. Children may agree to keep the secret out of fear that the abuser will harm her, a pet, or other family members if she tells. Some children are paralyzed by shame because they feel some pleasure in the abuse. In addition, it takes little to convince a child that the abuse is her fault. Frequently, children are abused by people they love and feel loyal to. Teach your child that *no matter what, no matter who,* she can talk to you when something bothers or upsets her.

Should your child tell you about a sexual incident, remain calm. Reacting with horror or disgust, however understandable, can increase your child's sense of guilt and shame. This could keep her from sharing future confidences with you.

If your child has been sexually abused, seek the advice of a mental health professional who has experience working with children. Also, many communities have agencies that offer services specifically to victims of sexual assault (see *The Family Redefined,* page 197, and *Childhood Trauma and Its Effects,* page 319).

AIDS AND OTHER SEXUALLY TRANSMITTED DISEASES. Many schools offer programs to discuss AIDS in an age-appropriate manner. Even if your local school has such a program, you should also address the issue with your child long before sex becomes an actual concern for her. Today, news of these diseases is dramatic and scary, and in most cases, parents are able to deal with their children's confusion and fears most effectively.

Emphasize, even before your child has to worry about sexual responsibility, that she should always try to act responsibly in all social interactions. Help her understand, in a developmentally appropriate way, what AIDS and other sexually transmitted diseases

(STDs) are. Explain how people get such diseases and what can be done to prevent them. If your child learns about them at school, be sure to ask about what she learned, what she understands, and what other questions or concerns she has.

Child Abuse and Neglect in Other Families

A generation ago child abuse and neglect hardly seemed an issue. Today it is clear just what a grave problem it is in our society. The sensational stories in the newspaper alert us to it daily. How, though, should you respond if your child says that her friend is being beaten by her parents? What if you suspect that a neighborhood child is being sexually assaulted? How can you be sure that what you suspect is truly abuse and not just differing parenting styles, a family in crisis? At what point do you offer help and at what point do you report abuse to local officials?

■ HOW TO RESPOND

Different families and different cultures define discipline in different ways. What seems like abuse to one parent may be "sparing the rod, spoiling the child" to another. Some parents truly believe, with the best of all intentions, that a good whack or a serious spanking is the best way to discipline a child.

In addition, sometimes when parents are particularly stressed or going through a particularly difficult time—during a divorce, after being laid-off from a job, or following the birth of another child—their patience may be thinner, their reactions to their child harsher. Also, parents who suffer from such emotional problems as severe depression, manic-depressive disorder, psychosis, or addictive disorders, may find it difficult to be tolerant and consistently loving with their children.

In certain cases, harsh, punitive parenting may be effectively addressed through counseling. As a friend or neighbor, you may be able to offer help and support. Indicate that you notice how stressed the parent seems. Suggest that during times of stress, it is helpful to talk to someone. There may be support groups or parenting classes available in your community. Also, if possible, offer to help out by watching the children for a while.

However, if a child truly is being abused, either sexually or physically, or neglected, counseling by itself is not an adequate response. It is crucial that the child's safety be secured directly and immediately before any of the other issues are considered.

How do you, an outsider, judge whether a child is being subjected to extreme corporal punishment or abuse? Bruises, black eyes, bloody noses, and lacerations are all indications of abuse. When an area on a child's skin remains red for several hours after she has been slapped or whipped, the injury merits further evaluation; this probably indicates abuse as well.

Abused children may have a variety of psychological and behavioral symptoms. Some behave aggressively or are sexually provocative; others are passive and withdrawn; still others show no obvious signs at all. If they are subject to continuous abuse, they may lag behind in academic achieve-ment. Often, they appear extremely angry, impulsive, fearful, or depressed. With young children, you may see such regressive behavior as bed-wetting or excessive clinging. Nevertheless, it is hard to determine that a child has been abused merely by her behavior. In fact, some abused children seem to appear outwardly normal (see also *Childhood Trauma and Its Effects,* page 319).

A Parent's Role If you have good cause to suspect that a child you know is being abused, you must contact your local child protective services agency. This is especially true if there appears to be a pattern of abuse. If you are unsure whom to call, contact one of the hot lines found in your telephone book. Most reports are handled confidentially.

There is no question that, in issues of abuse, there is a lot of uncertainty. In addition, getting the social welfare agency involved creates its own set of problems. Nevertheless, if you think a child is being seriously mistreated, it is better to err on the side of the child's physical safety. While you may hesitate to call for fear of angering or embarrassing the parents, or getting them into trouble, a child's physical and emotional health takes precedence. And truly, few parents want to hurt their children. Sometimes, the only way to help them control themselves is by involving child protective services.

Antisocial Behaviors

Early on, children learn what sorts of conduct are expected of them. Babies notice what brings smiles to their parents' faces and what evokes that dreaded word, *No.* Children begin to understand what behaviors get them what they want—attention, affection, praise, and that second cookie. And they begin to perceive what behaviors arouse undesirable responses—anger, yelling, withdrawal, and punishment. In addition, because children seem to have a natural empathic sense, often they act out of true concern for other people's feelings and rights.

This is not to say that once a child has a fairly solid grasp on right and wrong, on fair and unfair, she will always follow the path toward good behavior and avoid bad. All children misbehave at times. There are many complicated reasons that children sometimes get in trouble.

Usually when a child misbehaves it is because she misunderstands what is expected of her. Gradually children comprehend and internalize their family's standards of behavior. However, this process is neither wholesale nor progressive, and children will accept family standards in uneven ways.

Also, a child's ability to understand and accept family standards depends on the constancy of the cues at home. If a parent says one thing and does another or if a parent is inconsistent with praise or punishment, a child may well feel confused about what is required of her. And usually, children are answerable to more than one adult. One parent may promote one kind of behavior while the other parent encourages another.

Even when a child understands quite well what is expected of her at home, the world offers her other, often attractive options. At times, she will find the rules strange and the expectations confusing. She may notice when she starts day care, nursery school, or elementary school, for example, that other children act in ways that she never thought of or that are unacceptable in her home. She may observe a child hit when she knows that hitting is not allowed. On television, she may see other children using words that are not permitted in her home. She will probably experiment with these new behaviors, and occasionally, her confusion will come out in her behavior.

In addition to the natural desire to try out new behaviors, children sometimes misbehave because they want to assert themselves and their own autonomy. Around the age of two, children begin to behave in ways that may be exasperating to parents but are perfectly normal expressions of their new abilities and curiosity. After going out into the world, a child will come home, all full of herself, brimming with new experiences and impressions. On those days, she might express her pleasure in her independence through her conduct.

As children become more involved in a social world outside the family, they experience a wider range of behaviors and styles. In a child's attempt to figure out who she is and experiment with herself in her world, she may mimic her peers. Occasionally, parents may look upon this as problematic. Parents may insist that their child eat only healthy snacks, for example, so that when she pleads relentlessly for soda and cookies, they may believe she is rebelling against family values.

It is a simple fact that when parents leave

their children in the care of others, they relinquish much of their control. Thus, they may view behavior that differs from that which they wish to engender as bad. In addition, parents may be surprised how easily children forget the rules. Swept up in play with their friends, they may disregard what is expected of them and move, in the moment, with the rhythm of the group.

Sometimes children misbehave because there is chaos and distress in their lives, perhaps internal, perhaps external, and they know of no other way to express it. Some behavioral difficulties can be traced back to neurobiological problems that took root during pregnancy, delivery, or the postnatal period. Some difficulties arise out of other problems, such as learning disabilities or hyperactivity (see *Attention-Deficit/Hyperactivity Disorder,* page 337). This suggests that there are biochemical or neurological underpinnings that find expression in behavior.

Frequently, children whose home life is disrupted by the birth of a sibling, a death, a divorce, a move, or a remarriage communicate their upset in their behavior. As a rule, though, when the upset is addressed or allayed and the condition managed, a child's behavior will become more reasonable.

■ HOW TO RESPOND

In most instances, parental understanding, gentle guidance, and a bit of flexibility will help a child find a moderate course in terms of her behavior. Chances are that support and understanding from a parent will bring a child's behavior back to a reasonable center.

Even an isolated act that seems serious,

throwing a rock through a neighbor's window or spray-painting graffiti on a wall, for instance, is probably mischief rather than delinquency. However, there are times when internal and external checks and balances fail to take hold, and a child behaves repeatedly in purely self-destructive or objectionable ways. Some homes are so consistently chaotic, bleak, and troubling that a child's misbehavior becomes chronic. In such cases, children may engage in actions that break serious home, school, or community rules and laws. Occasionally, such behavior indicates or foreshadows a pattern of delinquency.

The family serves as the primary socializing force in a child's life. When parenting is relatively consistent, supportive, loving, and flexible, children learn to control their impulses and behavior, delay personal gratification, and respect other people and their rights. Parents who encourage their children to be responsible for their actions limit the risk of antisocial behavior. Often this means not letting your child get away with small infractions. Parents who, for example, make sure that their child apologizes for hitting another child in the playground, returns the gum she shoplifted, or is responsible for the window she broke, minimize the chance that such small violations will escalate to seriously defiant behavior.

Some families are so stressed, however, that they are ill-equipped on their own to provide an aggressive, impulsive child with sufficient nurturing and guidance. Children in such families are at risk for developing major behavioral problems (see *Disruptive Behavior Disorders,* page 335). Frequently, communities can provide some support for such families and their children.

Early identification and intervention can prevent behavioral problems from becoming entrenched in children. When children enter day care, preschool, and elementary school, other adults can observe their behavior in the context of their peers. In addition, certain emotional problems may find their first expression in a child's social behavior. At the point at which high-risk behaviors are identified, these social institutions usually have the resources to address problems. If they do not have the resources, a child and family may be referred to outside help.

In many cases, children are able to overcome home environments which are chaotic, bleak, and deeply troubled because someone in the community took an active interest in them. An adult in their community—a teacher, a grandmother, a minister or rabbi, a coach, a youth worker, a volunteer Big Brother or Big Sister—reached out a nurturing hand and established a bond of affection and guidance.

Stealing   Many childhood acts make parents uncomfortable, of course, but high on the list is stealing. Perhaps you learn that your youngster has stolen something from a friend or a store. How do you judge the situation and how do you respond?

Within a preschool child's egocentric world, the concept is: *The candy bar is there, so it's there for me; therefore, I can take the candy bar.* She may simply not understand that taking something that doesn't belong to her is wrong.

Most older children know better. Stealing for a school-age child is usually an isolated act, the result of a whim or impulse. However, the child who steals repeatedly may be stealing because she feels deprived, either of material possessions or loving support. Children take things even when parents insist they provide both creature and emotional comforts. Repeated stealing can speak of anger, resentment, or hostility.

When your child comes home with something that doesn't belong to her, stay calm. Listen to her explanation, then offer firm yet sensitive guidance.

Asking your child directly if she stole the doll may result in her lying to cover her shame. Be sensitive to her dignity, but be clear that, however tempting, taking something that doesn't belong to her is wrong. When she takes something from a friend's house, go with her as she returns it. When she takes something from a store, go with her as she pays for it.

Be aware, too, that you are your child's moral compass. If you come home with stationery or pens from your office for your family's personal use or if you brag about a mistake in your favor by the bank teller, your lessons about honesty will be a lot harder for your child to understand.

Fire Setting   All children are fascinated by fire. A child of three to five years old may express her *fire interest* by pretending to be a fire fighter, cooking on a toy stove, and asking questions about fire. The older child may engage in *fire play*: lighting matches or candles. Sometimes, when children play together, they may become distracted from the rules and involve themselves in dangerous play with fire.

In rare occasions, external stress or emotional upset will display itself in a behavioral disorder known as *fire setting*. This repeated, malicious, impulsive setting of fires (also known as *pyromania*) is frequently just one rebellious behavior in a pattern of antisocial actions, including stealing, vandalism, and truancy (see *Disruptive Behavior Disorders,* page 335).

Be clear with your child about the dangers of fire and firm about her behavior. Keep matches and lighters out of the reach of young children. If your child's interest in fire seems excessive or if she is unable to curb her behavior so that her interest seems likely to result in destructive acts, you and your child may need professional help. This is especially true if your family is experiencing extraordinary stress; your child's behavior may be a cry for help and attention. Contact your pediatrician or local mental health agency for a referral to a mental health professional.

Delinquency Delinquency is usually not a concern until early adolescence. There are, however, certain environmental factors and patterns of childhood behavior that point to a future risk for delinquency.

The risk of delinquency is greater in families where there is inadequate supervision, care, and involvement. Not surprisingly, parenting that is neglectful, intolerant, and unloving causes problems that may surface in delinquency.

Excessive conflict among family members or intense marital discord can cause profound distress in children which may then be expressed through their behavior. In families where aggression and violence are used to discipline or disagree or where drugs or alcohol are used to deal with depression or mental illness, children tend to imitate such behavior. In addition, parents with such personal difficulties often use inconsistent or unduly harsh punishment and send mixed signals about their expectations. This kind of parenting tends to confuse and anger children, and may contribute to the development of delinquency.

Children who come from homes in which there are a number of these problems seem to be at highest risk for delinquent behavior later on. On the other hand, even in troubled environments, supportive, consistent parenting during the early years acts as a buffer, diminishing the likelihood of delinquent behavior during adolescence.

Behavioral problems may signal that a child is having trouble managing her emotions. She may use delinquent behavior to get attention. This is often the case if parents are preoccupied with marital problems or emotional or work problems. As parents fail to monitor the child's activities, delinquent behavior may serve to pull them back in. Delinquent behavior may also divert attention away from, or call attention to other problems, such as abuse or parental alcoholism.

Outside influences, too, play a part. Exposure to violence on television and movies has been shown to desensitize children to violence (see *Violence in the Media,* page 269).

In some cases peer pressure is a factor. Children become particularly vulnerable to peer pressure when they are also at risk due to family problems.

Almost all young children engage in acts that could be viewed as "antisocial," such as hitting, cheating, lying, and stealing. Yet very few go on to become delinquents, much less criminals. However, when such acts consistently go unnoticed or when adults fail to impose consequences on such acts, there is a greater chance that the behavior will escalate and develop into real problems.

As children grow up and need less direct supervision, any problem with behavior that has not been addressed already will likely get worse. If such problems as learning or reading difficulties are not picked up and dealt with in first, second, or third grade, a child might have significant problems later in school which could manifest in disordered conduct (see *Conduct Disorders,* page 349). Luckily, many schools are equipped to recognize and remedy learning problems.

If your child exhibits certain behavioral problems, it is important that you respond in a measured way. Ask your child why she thinks she's acting the way she is. Consider if there are other factors that may be bothering her and ask her about them. Avoid reacting harshly or with rigid punishment.

Being loving and supportive can be difficult when you're angry and worried about your child's misdeeds. In many cases, when you look beyond the conduct itself, you may see that your child is struggling with feelings and issues that are getting the best of her. Try not to lay blame on your child, yourself, or

her school, but look for the meaning behind the conduct. If the behavior continues after you've addressed it with her or if it interferes with your child's academic, family, or social life, consult a mental health professional (see *Disruptive Behavior Disorders,* page 335).

Substance Use and Abuse

While substance abuse seems like a subject that concerns parents only as their children near adolescence, it's not unheard of for children to experiment and use alcohol or drugs as early as age eight.

By fourth grade, many children feel pressured by their peers to try alcohol and drugs. By sixth grade many children have tried beer or wine; some have even tried hard liquor.

Nearly half of fourth to sixth graders have tried smoking cigarettes. Tobacco is frequently the first forbidden substance a child tries, often as a result of peer pressure. Though not strictly a psychoactive substance, tobacco is considered a "gateway drug," that is, the most common doorway through which children enter into the world of substance abuse.

Substance use almost always begins as experimentation in the company of friends, usually as a result of strong peer pressure. It can easily escalate into dependency. Children have difficulty seeing the link between actions today and consequences in the future. Moreover, children naturally believe they're immune to the problems that besiege others.

If you find a teenager smoking or sipping

a beer, you may be concerned, but chances are you won't be entirely surprised. Though you want to pay attention to the adolescent who is drinking and/or smoking, many try these once or twice without advancing to more problematic behavior. Yet it is essential that if you catch a preadolescent child smoking or drinking you take it seriously. Such behavior in a young child may well be an indication that she is at risk for addiction as well as other troubled conduct later on. It may also indicate serious problems simmering under the surface. The younger a child is when she experiments with these substances, the greater is the long-term potential for abuse.

As a growing child becomes more independent, parental supervision and influence lessen and the influence of friends increases. Children who are struggling to deal with feelings of depression, hyperactivity, intense performance pressure, anxiety, loneliness, or anger, or with chaotic or abusive family lives are more vulnerable to the negative pull of some of their peers. In addition, they may welcome tobacco, drugs, and alcohol as ways of dealing with their problems.

■ **HOW TO RESPOND**

Experts agree that prevention must begin well before adolescence. Talk with your child about tobacco, alcohol, and other drugs before they become an issue. Casual discussions in which you solicit her thoughts and share your opinions will likely be more effective than a heavy lecture about the evils of weed and demon rum.

As you talk to your child, remember to consider her age. Younger children may not be able to understand the notion of addiction. With them, describe concrete consequences such as the harm these substances cause to the body. Since smoking is something that even a young child can observe, that may be the place to start. Talk about how bad smoking makes people smell, how the effects can manifest in poor complexion. Smoking makes breathing difficult. Many people who smoke have bad coughs and get sick easily.

When you get to alcohol, describe how drinking can make people act in embarrassing ways and do stupid things. Be sure your child understands the difference between illicit drugs and medicinal drugs.

Ten- to twelve-year-olds should be given information about what drugs are out there and the consequences of substance use and abuse. Explain the effects that habitual substance use can have on a person's health, finances, and relationships. Introduce the notion of addiction. Also let your child know that substance use is an ineffectual means of dealing with problems and difficult feelings. Although they may numb or cover over feelings in the moment, they actually dull a person's ability to solve problems. When the effects of alcohol or drugs wear off, the problems remain.

Provide the necessary support for your child to refuse drugs. Role play, allowing your child to practice her refusal responses. Despite all the ads and programs to the contrary, just telling her to say "no" isn't enough. If repeated "no's" don't work, instruct your child to walk away from her friends. And she should always leave if illicit substances are being used.

Children are increasingly targeted by tobacco and alcohol advertisers. Talk about TV, billboards, and magazine ads. Counter the myths purported in these ads that life is enhanced by using alcohol and tobacco and that these substances make a person richer, smarter, sexier, and more popular. Teach your child to be critical about what she's being told (and sold) by advertisers. Explain that advertising is done by people who want people to buy their products.

If you're watching a TV show or movie in which a character gets into his car and drives home—and arrives safely—after having a few drinks, take advantage of the opportunity to talk about the dangers of drinking and driving.

Probably the most important factor in determining whether your child will use drugs, alcohol, and tobacco is whether you use them. Don't assume that she will be able to recognize and understand the distinction between what you're telling her and what you're doing. Children whose parents smoke and drink are far more likely to follow in their footsteps because of the increased exposure and availability.

Many parents are reluctant to broach the subject with their children, since they smoked or experimented with drugs and alcohol in their youth. However, your own history should not deter you from being straightforward, clear, and sure about your expectations for your children. Address drug and alcohol use with the same certainty that you explain your other values.

If asked, state simply that you have smoked or tried drugs and alcohol. If it's true, tell your child that your experience taught you how misguided those behaviors were and how glad you are to have stopped. However, this should not be an opportunity to confide in your child. The important message is that just because you experimented with drugs and alcohol in your youth does not mean it is okay for your children. Be clear about it without apologizing.

Because peer pressure is so influential when it comes to substance use or restraint, get to know your youngster's friends. Whenever possible, get to know their families as well.

Children who have developed a sense of self-worth and competence feel less need to be followers in order to be accepted by others. Conversely, a strong need for peer acceptance can render a child less tolerant of being different and create a greater pull to conform to such group behaviors as smoking or drinking.

If you catch your child smoking or drinking, address it immediately. Talk to your child to discern what is behind such behavior. Because smoking or drinking in children is indeed a serious issue, make sure there is a significant consequence: have your child do a report on lung cancer or alcoholism; go with her to the park to pick up cigarette butts; ground her. Although the consequences do not have to be harsh, a child should feel that engaging in such serious behaviors has repercussions. Problematic behavior that is consistently overlooked or discounted tends to escalate.

If your child repeats the behavior, she may

have gone beyond experimentation. Professional help either with a mental health clinician or through a drug-treatment program may be advisable (see *When and Where to Seek Help,* page 387).

■ COMMUNITY RESOURCES

Many schools offer prevention programs. These tend to help students resist peer pressure and to question their assumptions about substance use.

Community antidrug groups such as Mothers Against Drunk Driving (MADD) are an important resource. If you need information or support, look to such grassroots organizations.

Violence in the Media

In a single day, television offers thousands of images of violent acts—simulated beatings, shootings, stabbings, rapes, and other forms of cruelty. While television broadcasters and filmmakers insist, despite considerable proof to the contrary, that there's no link between TV and movie violence and aggressive behavior in children, graphic demonstrations of how adults handle anger make powerful impressions on children.

Few people doubt that television and movies influence our buying habits, affect our values, and shape our behavior. Because enacted violence appears not only in adult shows but in children's programming as well, the effect can be profound, especially on those children who are already inclined to aggressive behavior.

The impact of visual images of violence may be immediately evident, or it may surface years later. In some instances, after repeated exposure to violence, children become immune to the pain and suffering of others and to the horror of violence. A child can identify with victims, and/or victimizers. She might imitate victimizing and violent behavior. Or she may become more fearful of the world around her.

Sometimes watching a single violent program can cause a child to act more aggressively. In fact, children, especially those who are already aggressive, tend to engage in increased aggression for a number of days following a violent show.

■ HOW TO RESPOND

The average child in this country watches five hours of television every day. Parents need to supervise and limit their children's viewing.

Consider the effect television has on your child. School-age children who are allowed to watch television during the week may rush through homework, piano practice, and other responsibilities so that they can sit passively in front of the television. Some parents do not permit any television during the week. Others monitor television watching on a day-by-day basis, allowing certain shows during the week.

Consider restricting the total number of hours of television a week. If a child knows that she can watch only five or six hours, she will save the time for select shows. When children have unlimited access to television, they tend to sit on the couch and channel surf. Chances are they will come across intensely violent images in passing.

When your child has a friend over, do not give in to the temptation to let them sit in front of the television. Television will preempt their opportunity to socialize and engage together in imaginative play.

Talk, negotiate, and set limits about movie or television show selection. In order to know what types of shows your child enjoys, watch at least one episode of each program she regularly watches. If you're concerned about her choice, talking to her about the program may help sharpen her judgment.

Discuss aggressive and unacceptable behavior that you see on television. Talk about real-life consequences of such behavior. Ask your child how she thinks the characters could have better solved their problems.

Help your child understand that television and movies are imitations of life, but not real life. Point out how the media simplify complex life problems. Few problems are solved in the span of an hour or half hour. Discuss the difference between violence, suffering, and danger in life and on the screen.

Encourage your child to watch those movies and programs that demonstrate such positive values as helping, caring, and cooperation. Just as viewing violence can foster aggression, watching shows that put forth humane conduct fosters kind and considerate behavior.

Restrict shows and movies that you deem too violent or otherwise inappropriate. To ensure that your child doesn't watch such shows at the homes of friends, discuss your views with other parents.

Remember: Your child should learn about life from you, not from your television set.

Violence: Guns, Gangs, and Children

Violence has become an unavoidable element of American life. For some children, it represents merely an aspect of the video games they play or the movies they watch. For others, violence touches their lives in very real and frightening ways. Many children witness violent acts. Some are victimized by violence. And a few commit violent crimes.

Juvenile violence is escalating at a shocking rate. While most juvenile crime involves older adolescents, children as young as ten years old are being arrested for murder, aggravated assault, rape, robbery, burglary, larceny, theft, and arson.

■ Guns

A generation ago, gun violence involving children was so rare as to be shocking. Nowadays it is no less shocking but, sadly, it is far less rare. Gun violence knows no geographic, social, or age boundaries. It affects children in urban areas and small towns, children from affluent families and those living in poverty.

Many children worry, with justification, that they might be shot on the way to school or stabbed in the school hallway. Some children pass through metal detectors before they reach the classroom.

The United States has one of the highest rates of criminal violence in the world, largely due to the availability of firearms. Given the increased likelihood of conflict escalating into homicide when guns are present, a child who has access to a firearm is at increased risk of violence.

Today, more young people die from gun violence than any other cause.

Gangs As soon as children start school, they begin to group themselves according to shared interests and styles. Children may socialize together because they all enjoy sports, excel in academics, or like the same music. In preadolescence and the teenage years, children form groups that they refer to in labels, such as "preppies," "jocks," and "grunge." These groups offer children a sense of belonging and social confirmation.

However, some groups organize around expressions of power, aggression, and violence. Ironically, many children who are drawn into such gangs experience deep feelings of powerlessness, alienation, and confusion. Offering a sense of belonging and confirmation, these gangs are menacing to children on the outside and often dangerous and misguided for those who belong.

Despite the fact that gangs first appeared in economically depressed urban areas, they are not endemic only to the inner city. Gang members, male and female alike, come from poverty and affluence. They come from broken or chaotic homes or intact, seemingly loving families. They live in urban tenements, suburban, or rural homes. In short, gangs are a cross-gender, cross-country, cross-class, and cross-cultural problem.

When children join gangs, they tend to make public expressions of violence and to commit crimes at a younger age. Gang members are more likely to use guns and to bring weapons into school. Although children are most likely to join gangs between the ages of eleven and fourteen, children as young as eight become members.

Children who join gangs are looking for a variety of experience otherwise missing from their lives: unconditional acceptance and support; a sense of belonging and participation; respect, recognition, and status; safety, security, and control; a sense of excitement.

■ HOW TO RESPOND

As discussed earlier in this chapter, when children come from homes that are bleak, chaotic, and neglectful, they are at higher risk for acting out their confusion and distress in their community. What is more, when violence is used in the home to discipline and express a range of feelings—including helplessness, frustration, and depression—children tend to mimic such expression. Children need to feel safe and secure, to know that there are adults who care for and watch over them. They need expectations and standards to be clearly communicated and discipline to be fair and consistent. When these needs are met, it is less likely that a child will engage in violent behavior or attach herself to negative peer groups.

Families that provide nurture, support, and comprehensible, flexible discipline provide a dose of prevention against the pull of negative peer groups and violent culture—even when children are particularly vulnerable because they have difficulty in school or other problems.

Often, members of the community play an important role in offsetting community violence. Whenever teachers, clergy, or volunteer mentors get involved with a child in the community, they offer inoculation against destructive pulls and help her navigate a difficult family or community life.

Many communities act as buffers against violence through neighborhood watch programs, community center outreach, church programs, and after-school activities. Groups of parents, teachers, school boards, PTAs, churches, youth agencies, and local law enforcement agencies have come together to devise cohesive strategies either to prevent gangs from emerging and/or to combat existing gangs. Probation and youth service agencies often work in the schools or in the community to develop gang prevention programs and outreach programs for both students and parents. The Office of Juvenile Justice and Delinquency Prevention (OJJDP) of the U.S. Department of Justice can supply individuals and organizations with ideas for programs to deter gangs.

Children who feel a connection at school, whether through academics, sports, clubs, the arts, or other aspects of the school community are more likely to resist the draw of a youth gang. Several city school systems have developed task forces to address gangs. Even though gang violence has been known to erupt in schools, schools that offer a sense of belonging and concern, that provide adequate security, remedial education, and social resources can be one of the best solutions to the gang problem.

Whether safety is engendered in their families, in their schools, or in their communities, children who feel a basic sense of trust and consequence will be able to keep the idea of violence in a saner perspective. These children will turn to grown-ups when another child has a gun or weapon at school or in the community, or when other children are urging that they join in on gang activities. Many times, they will feel empowered enough to say no.

GUN SAFETY

Many parents keep a gun in the home for protection. However, more often than not, having a gun in your house puts you or a family member—including your child—at much greater risk of being killed than someone breaking into your home. A stranger breaks into a house and shoots family members with the gun they bought to defend themselves. Children accidentally shoot themselves, their sibling, their playmate, as they play with a gun they've found. Children commit suicide with the family gun. Family members settle arguments with guns.

The best insurance against your child dying from a gunshot wound is getting rid of your gun. However, if you choose to own a firearm, then you must enforce strict rules about safety.

- Make certain that all guns are locked in cabinets at all times. Most children find their way to most anything, however well hidden. There really is no such thing as a child-proof gun. A padlock key offers little protection. Police recommend that you use a combination lock. Avoid using an obvious number for the combination, such as birthdays or anniversary dates. Keep ammunition locked in a separate location.
- Never allow your child access to your firearms—no matter how much safety training you may give.
- Never keep a weapon loaded.
- Equip your firearms with trigger locks.
- Make sure your child understands that a gun is not a toy. Regardless of what she may see on TV or in the movies, using a gun in real life can kill or severely disable someone.
- Tell your child to walk away whenever there is so much as talk of looking at, playing with, examining, or otherwise being in any sort of contact with a gun.

9

The Child with Chronic Illness

■ ■ ■

Every parent wants good health for his or her child. We realize colds, stomach bugs, and ear infections are inevitable. Even so, as parents, we want our children to be healthy and to be able to enjoy the innocence of childhood.

Unfortunately, many children and their families are confronted by chronic diseases. Some diseases are passing challenges that resolve themselves after a few months or years. Others have symptoms or require treatment for life. For some young children, the experience of a chronic disease may eventually be completely forgotten, though for others the disease becomes part of their lives.

A *chronic disease* is an illness of long duration, lasting by definition three months or more (as distinct from an acute ailment like the flu or a minor infection that comes and goes in a matter of days or, at most, weeks). The chronic disease becomes a day-to-day factor in the child's life, and in the life of the family. The disease and its emotional and behavioral consequences may affect the child's school performance, as well as his relationships with friends and family. The time required for medical treatments and the financial impact of the disease may produce additional stress for the family.

The child with a chronic disease—and his family—must adapt to the life changes required by the diagnosis of a chronic disease. The love and support of both parents and siblings is a fundamental part of treatment. Parents play a critical role in keeping life for the ailing child and the rest of the household as normal as possible.

This chapter focuses on specific ailments.

Each is different and presents unique challenges; such common, chronic ailments as asthma, diabetes, and epilepsy are discussed in detail. Despite their differences, however, the experiences of dealing with these and other illnesses have much in common. In addition to consulting the entry devoted to the disease with which you are concerned, see also *Coping with Chronic Disease: A Parent's Role* (page 275) for strategies in dealing with the challenges you face, and *Coping with Chronic Disease: Challenges for the Child* (page 277) for a better understanding of what your child may be experiencing.

COPING WITH CHRONIC DISEASE, PART I
A PARENT'S ROLE

Chronic diseases in children vary widely in symptoms, severity, treatment regimens, and prognosis. Yet for children and families confronting any chronic disease the goal is the same: to help the child grow and mature as normally as possible with a minimum of disruption to the life of the child and the family.

ACKNOWLEDGE YOUR RESPONSE

Before you can help your child deal with his ailment, you must first recognize and deal with your own feelings.

Anger, disappointment, fear, and guilt are predictable parental responses to the news a child is chronically ill. A cloud of concerns may seem to envelop you: financial worries; confusion at dealing with the specialists and the complexities of the medical system; and the emotional turmoil every parent experiences. It is perfectly normal and understandable for a parent to rail at the Fates, "*Why does it have to be my child!*"

Keep Your Cool

Stay calm or, at least, let your child know and see that, even though you are upset, you are still in control. A parent's attitudes can have a significant impact on the child. Your anxieties can translate in your son or daughter to increased worry or even panic (*"If Mom's that upset, it must be hopeless or worse than I thought!"*). However, it is unreasonable to try to appear as if nothing is wrong. Let your child know you are concerned but that you will be there to support him.

Don't take your child's illness personally. You don't have the disease, your child does. You play a supporting role, but the principal performer is your child.

Guilt, anger, anxiety, fear, and self-doubt are common emotional responses to a diagnosis of a chronic illness. Be aware of your emotions and their impact on your behavior and relationships. Anger may be misdirected to your medical team, family, or child. Placing blame on the other parent for the child's illness, mistrust of the medical team, and overprotectiveness of your ill child are common responses, too.

Identify Your Responsibilities

You will need to establish relationships with the medical professionals who will provide the help your child requires. Meet with the members of your child's health-care team, and ask questions. You will need to educate yourself about the disease, reading about it, perhaps seeking sources of new information on the Internet, finding other parents who have experienced some of the challenges you now face.

You will have to accept responsibility for making treatment decisions. You will have to be a participant in your child's care, assisting in therapies prescribed and providing the physical, emotional, and financial support required.

Establish a committee of command. In most cases, the best approach involves both parents meeting with physicians and helping to make decisions. Your child should have a voice, too, if he is old enough and well enough to understand. Take advantage of the guidance offered by your child's primary physician or pediatrician. A physician with a specialty in treating your child's disorder may also be a key counselor. Prominent roles can be played by therapists, nurse practitioners, family members, and trusted friends. Consider the advice of the professionals you encounter at special schools, camps, and counseling facilities, too.

Remember the Rest of the Family

Caring for an ailing child may require sacrifices on the part of other family members. Prolonged hospital stays, continuing therapies, and other demands and changes produced by the disease and its treatment can throw the routine of a family out of balance.

Initially, the illness may take center stage in the life of your family. Beware of allowing your life to be consumed by your child's illness to the exclusion of other family members, activities, and established patterns. No one—not you, the sick child, nor anyone else—will benefit. Your goal should be to reestablish day-to-day patterns that incorporate the treatment regimens and necessary lifestyle adjustments into the mainstream of the household. Consider the impact of the disease on the child's brothers and sisters who may feel anger or guilt.

In the case of a diabetic child, for example, the best approach is to focus on the child while controlling his diabetes. Gradually the spotlight should fade and the lights come up on the larger drama of the family as a whole, in which the diabetic child is but one player, the diabetes one factor in his life. For the child with epilepsy, a seizure lasts only a few minutes—at most other times, the epilepsy is secondary in the child's life. Try to maintain a larger perspective: the disease does not define the child.

Live a life of your own, too. Seek respite care. Maintain a social life, individually and collectively as a family. Call upon friends and family members to help you. Normal life must go on. It's better for you *and* your child.

COPING WITH CHRONIC DISEASE, PART II
CHALLENGES FOR THE CHILD

Childhood involves learning about how to live in the world. It's hard enough for healthy children, but for the child living with a chronic illness, a whole new set of challenges complicates the process.

For a young child, his chronic disease is likely to be bewildering; an older child, whose maturity allows him to understand the ambiguities and challenges of his circumstances, may experience intense anxiety and even panic.

The healthy child struggles for independence. For the child confronted with lifestyle restrictions—dietary or exercise limitations, the need to recuperate from surgical procedures, or the side effects of medications—his illness may tend to foster passivity and dependence. For example, a chronically ill child whose mobility is limited can begin to feel anxious about any sort of movement and, simultaneously, has little opportunity to discharge tension as an active child would do. Some children become self-centered.

Honesty and Acceptance

To help your child deal with his disease, you need to be honest with him—and with yourself. Children have a remarkable capacity for sensing when they are being told less than the truth. Leaving the child ignorant of his condition will foster fear and risk isolating the child. The clearer an understanding a child has of his diabetes, for example, the better able he will be to assume age-appropriate responsibility for its treatment. You must understand and then help your child to learn and understand. Talk, cry, get angry—not *at* your child, but go through the process *with* the child.

Tailor your explanations to your child's level of development. Discuss with your physician how to broach the subject and how much to explain. As your child develops an understanding of his disorder, the more he will be to able to feel in control. Illness can actually offer a child a chance to experience a sense of mastery as he learns to manage aspects of his disorder or its treatment.

Avoid Being Overprotective

The child who spends too much time shielded by a parent learns less about taking care of himself. Understand the child's limitations and help the child work within them. Challenge the child to extend himself, to excel in areas where he can. Don't overindulge; in general, the family rules should apply equally to the child with a chronic illness. There's no parallel universe for the sick and they must live in the world, too. The child with allergies, epilepsy, or another chronic condition must still learn the dos and don'ts at home and school.

The Child's Self-Image

Attaching a label to a child is often necessary. If he has cancer or cystic fibrosis, his teachers, caregivers, and a range of others in the family and out in the world will need to know. Yet labeling has its risks. A child can be reduced from a unique individual to merely symptoms of a disease.

Don't think of the child with a chronic disorder as a patient; and don't confuse your child's identity with his illness. To put it another way, don't let the illness stand between you and your child. Your child mustn't sense you see him as the weak link who is letting the rest of the family down.

Being sick isn't a character weakness. On the other hand, it isn't a badge of honor to be rewarded like an act of bravery. Try to keep a balanced view of your child. Don't let the disease take precedence over the child, as the focus shouldn't be on the sickness but on the child's normal development.

DON'T ISOLATE THE CHILD

A chronically ill child has different experiences than do well children. He may feel unique in a lonely way because he may not share all of their experiences, because his illness may limit his ability to do things other kids are doing. This is even more painful for him if he knows that you, his parent, are worrying about him.

To the greatest degree possible, treat your child as if he had no chronic disease—and help your child to feel the same way. Don't establish limits in your mind *or* in the child's. Your child, like any other, needs his parents' expectations and hopes, their dreams and their discipline to help shape his future.

Allergies

In an adult, allergies can be uncomfortable and inconvenient. In a child, they are often only a minor irritation—but, in some cases, they interfere with behavior, learning, and normal development.

■ IDENTIFYING THE SIGNS

Allergies are an overreaction by the body to the presence of substances like mold, pollen, or smoke to which the allergic person is sensitive. Symptoms of an allergic reaction may include a congested or runny nose; watery, itching eyes; itching skin, sometimes with hives or other skin rashes; sneezing, wheezing, or persistent coughing; headaches or earaches; vomiting, constipation, diarrhea; and even bed-wetting and soiling. The skin discomforts may escalate to eczema, in which itchy skin provokes scratching that, in turn, produces inflamed scaly skin. Sneezing and wheezing may become asthma (see *Asthma,* page 283).

A child with allergy sensitivities may also have skin that displays a tendency to welt after being scratched and circles under the eyes (sometimes called "allergic shiners"). Itchy eyes may cause a child to rub his eyes persistently; a constant runny nose may make the child habitually wipe his nose.

In children, the effects of allergies may

also be more generalized. These behavioral effects may include fatigue, irritability, depression, hyperactivity, and poor concentration. Sleeping difficulties are also common among allergic children.

■ CAUSES AND CONSEQUENCES

While not yet proven to the satisfaction of many researchers, there may be an association between allergies and behavior or mood problems. As a result, some professionals evaluating a child's behavioral or mood problem may attempt to rule out allergies as a possible cause.

By definition, allergies are acquired sensitivities to specific substances. That means the first time a child encounters ragweed, for example, he may have no allergic reaction. With additional exposures, however, the child's immune system may begin to react—and to overreact.

The presence of an *allergen* produces an immune system reaction. The allergen—often an innocent environmental substance like animal dander, dust mites, or mold—deceives the body into thinking it is a dangerous invader. One response is that blood plasma cells produce a protein called immunoglobulin IgE. Each time the allergen is identified, more IgE antibodies are released and they accumulate in the body. In the mucous membranes, the IgE cells produce such allergic symptoms as weepy eyes and runny nose.

■ HOW TO RESPOND

The cause of your child's symptoms may be unavoidable environmental allergens like dust, molds, or pollens. On the other hand, if your child's eyes are puffy after sleeping, the cause may be the contents of that stuffed animal he treasures, his pillow, or pets in the bedroom. Detergents, soaps, cleaning agents, and a wide variety of chemicals and materials that we encounter everyday are allergens to those sensitive to them.

Identify the Allergens The logical first step is to find which allergens produce symptoms. There is a cause-and-effect relationship, so track down the causes.

They can be environmental factors—grandpa's pipe smoke, dust in the house, the dander from the cat—but foods, too, may produce symptoms. The degree to which food allergies are to be blamed for such symptoms is unclear and the subject of continuing controversy. Many physicians remain unconvinced of the connection. However, if you suspect your child may have an undiagnosed food allergy or sensitivity, as a parent you are uniquely positioned to test for it, particularly in a preschool child. The process involves monitoring the child's intake of food and the subsequent appearance of any symptoms. Keep in mind, however, that too much focus on controlling food can lead to behavior problems in some children, so approach the process with care.

Keep a Journal Record what foods your child consumes and when. Watch the child's behavior and any allergy symptoms, and enter those observations, too. This may be difficult in school-age children when you have less control over their diets. Try involving the child as an investigator into his symptoms.

Be as objective as possible. Many parents believe sugar makes their children hyper; and children often behave according to parental expectations. If your observations lead you to consider a restrictive diet for your child, make sure your observations are accurate. Depending on the symptoms, the child may wish to endure them rather than be singled out as different from his peers.

Although not related to allergies, be aware of foods with caffeine. A small child receives a higher amount of caffeine per body weight than an adult does upon consuming a caffeine-containing beverage.

Milk is the single most common food allergen. Wheat is probably second on the list, but not far behind are peanuts, almonds, corn, tomatoes, eggs, pork, yeast, chocolate, and citrus. In cases where simpler means have not isolated one or another causative food, you may want to try the elimination diet. This involves avoiding all those foods mentioned above, as well as beef and other meat products for five days. In order to determine whether an eliminated food is a cause of your child's allergic responses, reintroduce one of the banished foods each day after the five days of abstinence.

If an immediate or delayed reaction is observed, eliminate the food for a period of six months, then introduce it again. The child's system, given a rest from defending itself against the offending food, may be able to tolerate it. Your child's physician should be able to provide additional guidance on an elimination diet.

■ ALLERGY TESTS

If you are unable to find and eliminate the allergens, blood tests may be conducted by an allergist to measure allergic reactions in the blood to various animals, chemicals, dust, fibers, foods, and pollens. Called RAST (for *radioallergosorbent*) tests or *cytotoxic* testing, they are done on blood samples in test tubes. The results require interpretation. A positive test doesn't provide an absolute answer, but may indicate that further tests are appropriate.

A test called a *rhino probe* may be done, in which a smear from the inside of the nose is examined for allergic cells. Another option is to test the skin itself, introducing allergens in tiny amounts to the skin. Also called *intradermal provocative testing*, dilute solutions of allergens like dust or dander are scratched into the surface of the skin and then observed for allergic reactions—if redness or hives appear, the child is sensitive to the injected allergen. All of these tests are conducted by health-care professionals.

■ ALLERGY TREATMENTS

Avoidance is the preferred treatment. Again, if the offending substance can be avoided, as with certain foods, this is often a successful approach.

Some allergens are unavoidable, however, like dust, pollens, and molds. If the hypersensitivity is to common agents, then a child's sensitivity may be altered by introducing minute amounts of the offender into the child's system. This may be done by sublingual treatment (placing a drop beneath tongue, where the substance enters the bloodstream without passing through the stomach and intestines) or by injecting it into the skin.

Allergy medications—taken orally, by injection, or applied directly as eye drops, creams, inhalers, or nose sprays—relieve allergy symptoms. They may, however, have behavioral side effects of their own. Sleepiness and crankiness are common with certain medications such as antihistamines, as is hyperactivity with some asthma medications.

■ ALLERGY PREVENTION

If either parent is an allergy sufferer, a wise course is to avoid exposing your child to any allergen to which either parent is sensitive. If your child is sensitive to animal dander, for example, limit exposure to animals.

Perhaps the best news of all is that allergy symptoms may lessen or disappear with adolescence.

FOOD INTOLERANCE AND FOOD ALLERGY

In some children, there is a direct relationship between the food they eat and their ability to function at home and in school. A poorly balanced diet—in particular, the failure to consume an adequate breakfast—or the presence of foods or food substances to which the child is intolerant or allergic can have effects on the brain's function. These may, in turn, manifest themselves in behavioral, concentration, and learning problems.

Too often, however, such relationships are exaggerated or even imagined. Concerned parents observe a behavior in their child, read in the popular press that one food or another might be responsible, and conveniently conclude there's a cause-and-effect relationship. Then they eliminate the suspect food from the child's diet.

Don't simply attribute a behavior problem like hyperactivity to chocolate or monosodium glutamate (MSG) and then banish the food or additive forever. It's probably not that simple.

Food allergies involve an immune system response, in which the body attacks a common and usually harmless food (such as peanuts) as if it were an unwanted invader, producing an allergic reaction. This reaction may be limited to skin hives, lip swelling, and drooling; it may progress from wheezing and raspy breathing to severe breathing difficulties (see *Asthma,* page 283).

In contrast, a common food sensitivity is lactose intolerance, in which a child is unable to absorb milk or other dairy products. A shortage of lactase, the enzyme that helps digest lactose, the sugar found in milk, may produce gas or diarrhea when lactose-containing foods are consumed. Food intolerances are uncomfortable but not a major heath risk.

True food allergies and food intolerance don't go away and the food that produces the symptoms must be avoided. If you suspect that your child is allergic or intolerant of a food or foods, consult with your child's physician about appropriate steps to diagnose and minimize the effects.

Asthma

Asthma—a disorder in which breathing difficulties occur—is the most common chronic disease of childhood. It usually involves wheezing and daily coughing, often at night. Asthma may be triggered by allergens or may be a response to viruses or exercise. It is a condition that, in many cases, has emotional and behavioral as well as medical components.

■ IDENTIFYING THE SIGNS

If your child has been diagnosed as having asthma, you know the symptoms all too well. During an *asthma attack,* as the episodes are called, breathing becomes labored, resulting in a wheezing or whistling noise on breathing out. The asthma sufferer finds exhaling more difficult, experiencing a tightness in the chest and may cough.

Any discussion of asthma necessarily concerns allergies (see *Allergies,* page 279) because asthma attacks are most often triggered by allergens, ranging from a bee sting to simple house dust. Other potential causes include a viral respiratory infection like a cold, a sinus infection, a medication, or emotional stress. Sudden exposure to cold or dry air or physical exertion can also bring on an asthma attack.

About one in every fourteen American children has asthma and in most cases asthma symptoms appear before the sixth birthday. The tendency to asthma can also be inherited, so the children of asthmatic parents are much more likely to develop asthma.

■ CAUSES AND CONSEQUENCES

During an asthma attack, the tiny airways in the lungs called *bronchial tubes* are narrowed because the smooth muscle that surrounds them constricts. The membrane that lines them also swells, the mucus there becomes thick and sticky, and air has more difficulty passing through the tubes. The result is wheezing.

Asthma is an organic disease—its symptoms are very real and can even be life-threatening. Yet there is a element of *somatization,* too, meaning that the mind has an effect on individual attacks and influences the overall course of the disease. Asthma can also have a significant impact on a child's self-esteem and self-confidence.

The sensation of not being able to get enough air is very frightening. Breathing difficulty first produces fear and, when the problem is not resolved, panic inevitably follows. Even after an asthma attack passes, the fear remains: *Will it happen again?* and *When?* A sense of helplessness often accompanies the asthma attacks and their aftermath. This cycle of fear, anxiety, and helplessness adds to the emotional aspect of asthma.

Asthmatic children may learn that, while scary, the symptoms and fear of attacks may serve other purposes—for example, to get attention or to express rebellion or simply to get a reaction. Occasionally children who have symptoms of asthma—typically, attacks of wheezing—are not responding to allergens in their environment but to events in their lives like the birth of a sibling. The child's wheezing may refocus attention on himself, and may represent an expression of his jealousy and anger at the shifting of attention in the family. Such cases are unusual, but require that the child be provided means of expressing feelings in other ways than through his asthma.

In some children, chronic anxiety or stress over time is a factor in the development of asthma. Violent arguments or physical abuse in a home, for example, may produce asthma attacks that reflect the seriousness of parental conflict. Clinical studies have demonstrated more difficulty in controlling the symptoms of chronic illness in families in conflict and in those that communicate poorly. Changing such patterns will help not only the asthmatic child but the entire family.

While every asthma attack must be taken for what it is—a potential medical emergency—the asthmatic child must also be taken for what he is, a young person struggling to adapt to the world. The disorder in the vast majority of cases is very real indeed, but individual attacks can be produced by myriad allergic *and* emotional factors.

■ How to Respond

Asthma attacks can be life-threatening, involving rapid respiration, cough, increased heart rate, and vomiting. In emergency cases, constant coughing is accompanied by *hypoxia* (oxygen deficiency in the blood), which causes the lips and nails to turn blue. This is a medical emergency, requiring immediate medical assistance.

Medical Intervention Inhalers can be used to dispense several types of medication and should be used to *prevent* attacks. The same medications are used during attacks, but are best administered with a *nebulizer*, a device that introduces the drugs into the lungs as a fine spray.

Some medications (called *bronchodilators*, including albuteral and metaproternol) release the muscular tension around the bronchial tubes. These medications are usually used along with drugs that reduce the swelling and inflammation of the tubes (Cromolyn sodium, Intal, or corticosteroids). In emergency cases, adrenaline may be administered by injection.

Eliminating the Allergens Asthma medications are important, but a second, equally important component of any treatment regime for an asthma sufferer involves identifying and eliminating possible allergens that may trigger asthma attacks.

Secondhand smoke in the home from cigarettes, pipes, or cigars must be eliminated. If you or anyone in your family smokes, a child with asthma is a good reason to quit. At the very least, take your habit outside. The following are common allergens: woolen blankets, feather pillows, kapok-stuffed animals, mattresses stuffed with horsehair, and other sources of animal hair, dust, grasses, molds, or pollens. Avoid exposing the child to other allergens if possible. Vacuuming frequently, removing rugs from the child's room, and installing filters on the heating and air-conditioning systems may also help reduce allergens. If house pets are found to be a cause, you may face the difficult decision of finding them other homes. Initially you can try banning the pet from bedrooms. (For further strategies, see *Identify the Allergens*, page 280.)

A Parent's Role Include the child in the treatment process. Explain what is happening to his body and the workings of any medications. A sense of helplessness may be counterbalanced by the child's ability to act, to self-medicate with inhalers when wheezing begins. The drugs can provide the child with a sense of control.

As his ability to understand increases, continue to educate your child about his asthma. This will enable him to develop an emotional acceptance that will also help him deal with fears and concerns. A support group or even an electronic "conversation" at a Web site may further foster his understanding by learning from others meeting the same challenges.

As a parent, you must keep your cool, too. Your child will sense your anxiety, and it may fuel growing worries and a sense of panic. Calmly reassure your child. Clinical evidence shows that emotional problems are more likely when parents have difficulty dealing with their children's asthma; a cycle of increasing anxiety can result. Separation anxiety disorder can also develop in cases of asthma (see *Separation Anxiety Disorder,* page 308).

Don't allow the condition to limit your child's sense of curiosity or adventure. Just because he is sensitive to animal dander doesn't mean he can't go to the zoo. Don't foster a sense of fear of physical activity; encourage participation in a range of activities.

If management of the disorder proves difficult, consider talking to your child's pediatrician about consulting an allergist. Again, key to overcoming asthma is a sense of mastery on the part of the child. Everyone in the household needs to know what can be done, that attacks aren't inevitable. They don't have to be. Understanding that—and working to develop a treatment approach—are key parts of getting the child well. (See also *Coping with Chronic Disease,* page 275 and 277).

Diabetes

A few generations ago, diabetes was virtually untreatable and inevitably fatal. In 1921, insulin was discovered and its administration has rendered diabetes eminently manageable. Today, diabetes remains a lifelong challenge, but the child with diabetes can expect to live a fulfilling and productive life.

■ IDENTIFYING THE SIGNS

Diabetes is uncommon before the age of four. Typically, the child becomes ill, loses weight, urinates frequently, and is constantly thirsty. An accompanying symptom may be an overall sense of lethargy. Consult your physician if you observe these symptoms, or other signs like failure to gain weight or unexplained and frequent vomiting.

■ CAUSES AND CONSEQUENCES

Diabetes mellitus, as the disorder is formally known, occurs when the pancreas fails to produce an adequate supply of the hormone insulin. One possible explanation for the failure of a previously healthy pancreas is a viral infection that, in children who are genetically susceptible, gradually destroys the cells in the pancreas that make insulin.

Insulin controls the amount of sugar (glucose) in the bloodstream. Insulin is necessary for the energy-producing glucose to enter the cells of the body. Too little insulin results in an excess of glucose in the blood but not enough in the cells. If left untreated, this surplus of blood glucose produces the symptoms of diabetes and its potentially life-threatening complications, in particular diabetic ketoacidosis, in which the changes resulting from elevated blood glucose levels lead to unconsciousness or coma. Some adults have diabetes which can be managed with diet, but juvenile-onset diabetes (or insulin-dependent diabetes mellitus, IDDM, or Type 1 diabetes, as it is also known) must be treated with both diet and insulin.

■ HOW TO RESPOND

On the one hand, managing diabetes is an almost mechanical process involving the replacement of the absent insulin in the blood in a manner that closely resembles the balance of the normal body. The insulin, administered as shots, must be delivered in the right quantities and at the proper times. Monitoring the glucose, the dietary discipline, and other approaches will also help maintain the body's blood sugar at proper levels.

Insulin Shots If the diagnosis of diabetes is confirmed by blood tests and urine tests, a lifelong regimen of insulin shots will likely be required. Parents typically give the shots until the child is able to give them himself, usually at about the age of eight. The shots are usually given twice daily, before breakfast and dinner. Parents also should regularly do tests of blood sugar levels to be sure the diabetes is well controlled.

In some children diabetes proves more difficult to control than in others. "Brittle" or "unstable" diabetes may require three or four daily insulin shots, the installation of a diabetic insulin pump, and even periodic hospitalization to bring blood sugar levels well under control.

Dietary Approaches The administration of insulin to the diabetic child is a matter of life and death. A less dramatic component of any treatment regimen, yet one of increasing significance as the child ages, is the management of your child's diet. The goal is to maintain levels of glucose (sugar) in the blood within a normal range. The child with well-controlled blood sugars will feel better and grow better, and will be less likely to have other medical complications from his diabetes. These long-term complications can include atherosclerosis, high blood pressure, and circulation problems. It is also important to understand that while compliance does decrease the risks, it does not guarantee there will be no complications. Be honest; then, if complications do occur, your child will have been prepared and will be less likely to blame himself.

This means there are forbidden foods, namely those rich in simple sugars like those found in regular candy, cookies, and other sweet treats. The availability of sugar substitutes has made it much easier for diabetics to tolerate these necessary restrictions. Meals should be balanced, consisting of a range of healthy foods, with an emphasis on foods high in fiber like fruits, vegetables, and whole grains.

The child's diet must also be regimented according to a strict schedule. The three meals should be consumed at regular intervals, and supplemented by three regularly scheduled snacks at midmorning, midafternoon, and bedtime. An exercise program may also be prescribed, because physical activity can help control diabetes.

Emotional Intervention Controlling diabetes—especially in children—presents challenges in helping the child accustom himself to its regimens and social challenges. Emotional support, guidance, and reassurance from parents and others are almost as crucial as the life-saving insulin.

The diabetic child has a chronic disease that will remain with him as long as he lives—and how long and how well he lives may be a direct consequence of how well he manages his diabetes. Understanding the implications of this is too difficult for a small child, yet the importance of establishing healthy habits should be a major orientation. Your child should play an active role in the process, whatever his age. As the child matures, the process will become less a parent-child partnership and more the child's sole responsibility as he assumes control over the shots and the glucose monitoring.

Coping with diabetes is a unique challenge; but it has similarities to the process of living with other chronic diseases or disorders. For some general guidance, see *Coping with Chronic Disease*, page 275.

Pica and Lead Poisoning

Infants and toddlers are eager for experience, exploring the world around them. Instinctively, they examine, touch, and smell just about everything they can get their little hands on.

Then they open their mouths and, if the object in hand will fit, they pop it in and give it a taste test, too.

This oral phase of exploration is perfectly normal, but it is a potentially risky behavior requiring both anticipation and vigilance by parents. Poisons and medicines should be stored in secure cabinets. All objects available to the toddler must be scrutinized, with issues of cleanliness, sharpness, and size in mind. Anything that could get caught in a child's throat and cause choking should be out of sight and out of reach.

Even after such precautions are taken, remaining elements in a child's environment can pose potential health risks. The paint on the walls or the soil in the garden or in potted plants simply doesn't belong in a child's mouth, even for a moment. Pica and lead poisoning, two disorders of young children, can result from such ingestion.

■ PICA

The term "pica" comes from the Latin word for magpie, a member of the crow family and a scavenger with a taste for just about anything. Like magpies, infants and young children with pica tend to consume non-nutritive substances.

They do so not once but persistently and recurrently. In toddlers, the substance may be ashes, clay, chalk, cloth, dirt, hair, peeling paint, bits of paper or cardboard, plaster, or string. In older children, the substances may be animal droppings, bugs, leaves, small rocks, or sand.

Boys and girls are about equally affected by this disorder. Pica is more likely to occur in children under two and living in poor families, and those children with mineral deficiencies (in particular, shortages of iron or zinc). Mentally retarded children are also more prone to pica. Associated poisoning can also occur, as can intestinal blockage and obstruction, resulting in dangerous emergency medical complications.

■ LEAD POISONING

At about the time a child is learning to walk, the risk is greatest for lead poisoning. The child's activities increase with his mobility; standing tall on two legs, the toddler can reach twice as much lead-filled wall space or other potential trouble. Innate curiosity—coupled with the desire to taste everything—almost guarantees that a house with lead will soon have a toddler with lead in his system, too.

■ IDENTIFYING THE SIGNS

Unlike problems that offer the parent fair warning, lead poisoning can surprise the parent. Before its symptoms are apparent, damage has already begun. The symptoms may include listlessness, abdominal pain and constipation, anemia, delayed growth, headaches, convulsions, and mental retardation.

In some states, lead testing of infants is mandatory. In fact, many doctors recommend that every child with a behavior problem or living in specific impoverished neighborhoods be checked for lead. However, lead poisoning often goes undetected until a child enrolls in school. Hyperactivity, difficulty in learning, or other physical or emotional indications may lead to lead testing.

■ CAUSES AND CONSEQUENCES

In the developing child, lead is dangerous poison. Lead cannot be eliminated by the body. Therefore, it accumulates and can have significant and permanent effects on many organs, including the brain. Small amounts of ingested lead can cause learning disabilities in children; larger amounts can produce mental retardation. Hearing loss, stomach and intestinal problems, anemia, and short stature can result from chronic lead poisoning. The effects on intelligence and development are only partially reversible.

Until 1977 the mineral lead was an ingredient of many paints. That means that countless homes have lead paint on the walls, ceilings, and trim work. Many young children are tempted to eat paint chips. The paint dust raised by remodeling or paint-stripping or even general activity in the house, too, poses a risk because it can contaminate clothing, then a child's hands, and in that way be ingested.

■ How to Respond

Consult with your physician if you suspect either pica or lead poisoning. The consumption of any nonfood substance that is potentially a poison is a medical concern and may require treatment.

Pica is preventable, largely through close parental supervision of playtime. If nutritional deficiencies in your child are identified, vitamin or mineral supplements may be prescribed or dietary changes suggested. Most children outgrow pica after age three.

In the case of lead poisoning, a combination of increased supervision and the elimination of lead sources such as lead-based wall paint may be required to eliminate further danger (see *Potential Sources of Lead*, page 289). But more important is the prompt treatment of the child to immediately reduce lead levels.

When the levels of lead are slight, a low-fat, well-balanced diet and an iron supplement may be all the treatment required. Iron binds to the lead and both are eliminated. Follow-up lead tests will determine the effectiveness of the treatment.

In more serious cases of lead poisoning, a chelating drug will be administered, either by injection or as oral medications. These drugs attach to the lead in the bloodstream and are excreted by the body.

In cases of severe, long-term lead poisoning, hospitalization and special education may be necessary.

Lead Testing If you live in an older home or apartment building, have your child tested annually. Typically, a screening test is done with a drop of blood from a finger prick and, if test results prove positive, a second test is done on a larger volume of blood drawn from a vein in the arm. This second, venous sampling will provide a more precise reading of the level of lead contamination. Teeth, hair, nail clippings, and urine can also be tested, and a bone X ray can confirm long-term lead exposure.

Potential Sources of Lead If tests reveal that your child has elevated levels of lead, you must identify the source of the poisoning in the home, play areas, or other locations. The contamination must then be eliminated.

Innocent-appearing paint chips can contain lead. Older cribs may have lead paint on them. Other sources include lead in plumbing pipes, fittings, or solder; engine exhaust fumes; or occupational exposures to lead from anyone in the family who wears contaminated clothes home from work. The exposure of nursing mothers to lead also puts their infants at risk through lead-containing breast milk.

Again, if you have any reason to suspect lead contamination, have your child tested.

Precocious Puberty

Puberty is a normal part of growing up. There is, however, no "normal" schedule for the physical and emotional changes associated with puberty. When a child enters puberty earlier than usual, the term *precocious puberty* is applied.

■ IDENTIFYING THE SIGNS

It is possible for some girls to develop breast buds and a small amount of pubic hair as early as seven or eight years of age, and for menstruation to begin as early as age ten. Some boys may experience testicular enlargement and growth of pubic hair at ten. On average the changes begin somewhat later but, again, normal children may experience growth spurts as early as nine-and-a-half (in girls) and, in boys, prior to the eleventh birthday.

In rare instances, a glandular abnormality may produce the changes of puberty prematurely.

■ HOW TO RESPOND

If your daughter enters puberty before eight-and-a-half years of age or your son prior to age nine-and-a-half, consult your physician. The doctor may wish to determine whether a glandular abnormality or other medical problem is causing this early puberty.

Emotional Intervention When puberty occurs early, the challenge to a child experiencing the changes prior to his peers is more than a matter of hormonal and bodily changes. At a time when fitting in seems so important, the child begins to stand out. This can prove to be a temporary asset, as the taller, more physically mature child may automatically have the respect of smaller peers and may even assume leadership roles in school or play. However, chances are the child with a head start on maturity won't maintain that lead; relinquishing that status may also require a difficult emotional adjustment during adolescence.

In general, boys find early maturation an advantage. Their larger size often results in superior athletic performance and added social prestige. In girls, the positive and negative effects are more ambiguous but may tend to lower self-esteem.

The physical and emotional changes may occur very quickly and the child, male or female, doesn't feel like he knows himself (or she herself) from one week to the next. The changes create stress if the child suddenly feels uncomfortable with his or her body. Again, boys tend to revel in growth and added strength, but girls may be uncomfortable with the weight gain that normally accompanies puberty. If your daughter thinks she is overweight during this period, she may resort to fasting or a restrictive diet to slow the changes. Understanding, education, and communicating with your child are important.

Mood changes may also accompany puberty. That previously docile child you knew so well may, with surprising speed, be transformed into a preteen quite willing to take issue with your opinions and demands. Studies suggest that children who mature early physically are perceived by adults and peers alike as more socially mature than they actually are. This can have a confusing impact on the child's experience and behavior.

The Parents' Role For a child with no medical condition causing early puberty, make sure he understands that nothing is wrong; some people mature earlier, some later. The range of normal is very wide and includes the nervous and gawky nine-year-old girl and the sixteen-year-old boy embarrassed by his short stature. Your child doesn't want to feel different; assure him that it's just a matter of timing, that the other children will reach this stage soon enough.

You will need to strike a balance between noticing the changes and *not* overreacting. Drawing attention to changes in an already self-conscious child will not help. The weight she is gaining, for example, shouldn't become a focus of family discussion; that will only add to her self-consciousness. Yet at an appropriate time, you should calmly talk with your child about the changes he is experiencing.

Don't confuse physical development with emotional maturity. Girls with breasts and boys with burgeoning muscles don't neces-sarily know how to behave in ways that are as mature as their bodies might suggest. Conversely, the child who is less mature physically isn't necessarily slower to mature emotionally. Physical and emotional maturity tend to parallel one another, but do not proceed in lockstep.

Premature Sexuality Be aware, too, that a child who physically matures earlier than her peers may suddenly find herself the object of attention of older teenagers. This may mean your child will learn about—and be exposed to—language, behaviors, and experiences for which her same-age peers and earlier experience have not prepared her.

The risk of sexual advances and resulting abuse by older individuals is very real in the girl who finds herself an adolescent so quickly. There's a certain thrill to her new maturity, to being treated as if she were much older. This flattering attention can, however, turn into sexual advances. An emotionally immature child, suddenly living in a rapidly maturing body, may not be equipped with the emotional perspective and coping strategies necessary to fend off inappropriate attentions and to reject seductive advances.

Pregnancy is a very real risk to such girl-women, and some studies have shown that girls who mature early are statistically more likely to become pregnant and have children earlier. In the same way, boys who mature early are statistically more likely to consume alcohol, use drugs, smoke cigarettes, become sexually active, and find themselves in conflict with the law than their slower maturing peers.

If your child has continuing difficulty in making the adjustment to his or her physical changes or if you find yourself unable to communicate and are concerned about how you and your child are adjusting, consult your child's physician.

Recurring Headaches, Stomachaches, and Other Pain Disorders

Every child complains of an occasional headache or stomachache. These are often due to common childhood infections, a sudden change in diet, stress, or fatigue. These familiar symptoms are usually mild and temporary. Typically, they disappear almost as quickly as they appear.

■ IDENTIFYING THE SIGNS

In occasional cases, children repeatedly complain of such discomforts—for which neither parent nor physician, upon examination and evaluation, can identify a cause. In some instances, a physical disease may be present, but the accompanying symptoms seem out of proportion or unrelated to the illness.

Stomachaches If your child develops a pattern of unexplained stomachaches, try to identify potential causes in the context of the child's life. Psychological or emotional reactions may be accompanied by physical changes in the stomach and gut which produce the symptoms. At age four, for example, a stomachache may be an indicator not of gastrointestinal disease (although there is gastrointestinal distress) but of nervousness in the face of a social situation. At five or six, a stomachache and vomiting may occur if you insist your child consume a food he strongly dislikes. A stressful school situation can produce similar symptoms.

Headaches In the same way, your child may complain of an occasional headache at age five; by age seven more frequent headaches may be accompanied by fatigue or excitability. Exhaustion, too, can be a factor in triggering headaches. At age eight, both headaches and stomachaches may occur when you require your child to complete certain tasks he regards as disagreeable. Separation anxiety (when a child is separated from home, parents, or other people to whom he is attached) is sometimes accompanied by such pain complaints.

■ CAUSES AND CONSEQUENCES

If your child complains repeatedly of headaches or stomachaches but no identifiable cause has been found, your child may have what is called a *somatoform disorder*. The discomfort is very real to him, just as the stresses that produce them are real and troubling. Such unexplained physical complaints may require medical intervention and justify changes in lifestyle.

Be sure there is not another cause for your child's pain before you conclude that the pain is triggered by emotional and psychological causes. Constipation may often be accompanied by stomach pains. Some viral infections produce abdominal cramping. Respiratory infections can cause swollen glands which, in turn, can produce abdominal pain. Food intolerance, too, causes stomachaches, as do a range of more serious illnesses like appendicitis, infections like streptococcus, bowel obstructions, and pneumonia.

If the stomachache is accompanied by diarrhea, constipation, persistent loss of appetite, or other symptoms of illness, consult your child's physician. Localized, sharp pain and muscular tightness in the abdomen are danger signs. If there is a chance the child has ingested poison or if he has difficulty breathing, has a high fever, falls asleep between periods of pain, or has had a fall or sustained an injury that might explain the complaints, seek medical help immediately.

Headaches are rare in children under four. They may occur, especially at the end of a long afternoon's play, for example, but small children may not be able to describe how they feel to an adult.

Between ages four and seven, children are more likely to begin to complain of headaches. Most headaches are occasional events and some may be triggered by a child's desire to mimic adults—they want to be like their elders, one or more of whom may periodically experience headache.

If your child has a severe headache which occurs suddenly, lasts for several hours, and does not abate when treated with acetaminophen (Tylenol), consult your child's physician because another condition may be the cause. Other worrisome accompanying symptoms are nausea, vomiting, and visual disturbances (the child complains of blurred or otherwise distorted vision).

Recurring somatoform headaches and stomachaches typically are temporary and do not interfere with a child's life. Children tend to outgrow recurring headaches and stomachaches by adolescence. The peak age for headaches is age twelve, for stomachaches, age nine.

In families with an ill or dying family member, headaches, stomach upset, and loss of appetite are common responses in otherwise healthy children who are anxious about the health of a loved one (see *Coping with Chronic Disease,* page 275).

If the headaches or stomachaches arrive like the ring of an alarm clock on school days, they are likely related to other issues (see *School Avoidance, Refusal, and Truancy,* page 242, and *Separation Anxiety Disorder,* page 308).

In some children, continuing or recurring pains may interfere with the child's school, family, and social life. In preschool children, there may also be such accompanying symptoms as acting immaturely, irritability, excessive clinginess, and a tendency to be accident-prone. In school-age children, academic problems, social withdrawal, or emotional distress may accompany the child's increasing complaints of pain and, in occasional instances, indicate a more serious disorder (see *Anxiety and Avoidant Disorders,* page 311). Excessive worry about upcoming events, schoolwork, or the child's worry about his own competence may, in certain cases, indicate the presence of depression (see page 329).

■ HOW TO RESPOND

Pain is subjective regardless of the cause of the pain. A toothache that one person finds debilitating is nothing more than a nagging distraction to someone else. How much it hurts depends on a variety of factors, including an individual's experience, physiology, and psychological state.

A child's own report is the best indication of pain. The ability of the child to describe the sensation he is experiencing depends on a variety of factors, including the source of the pain and the child's age, experience, and psychological state.

Infants and toddlers may be unable to express their pain verbally. Their outward reactions to pain may be physical expressions and crying, but increases in heart rate and blood pressure are also usual. As a child grows older, he has more experience with pain and greater capacity to cope with discomfort.

The parent's job is to allow the child to express his pain and to listen. Together, they can work to respond appropriately. That may require developing appropriate coping strategies to gain control over aches and pains, which may involve consulting the child's physician.

Emotional Intervention If your child has stomachaches or headaches of unidentifiable cause, take the child aside and calmly talk through the situation. Explain that the family physician has not found an illness that is causing the pain. Be gentle in explaining that taking medicine won't help the pain to get better. Reassure the child that the two of you may be able to find other ways to make the discomfort go away.

If you've identified stressful situations that appear linked to the complaints, discuss how life's challenges can sometimes seem very hard. Describe what you've observed, and explain that the buildup of some of these pressures and worries can be avoided. Use a metaphor: *"It's like a soda can. If you shake it, the pressure builds up inside. It needs to be released, gradually, or it'll explode all over the place. The same kind of thing is happening inside you—and we need to figure out a way to help you to release that pressure."*

GIVE YOUR CHILD A SENSE OF CONTROL. By recognizing situations which are stressful for your child, by thinking about and accepting his anxieties, the stresses can be managed before headaches or stomachaches develop. Helping your child to understand and to employ this strategy will help reduce his anxiety.

Explain to your child that his complaints are not punishment; headaches are not his fault. If your child believes headaches are the consequence of bad behavior, for example, a pattern of headaches can be accompanied by a sense of helplessness and, with certain children, depression may develop. Reassure the child that stress causes everyone's body to react. Some children develop headaches, while in others stomachaches may occur.

If you and your child can identify the cause, he may be better able to anticipate the headaches. Appropriate rest periods, reorganization of activity schedules, or, in some cases, the use of selected medication, may allow your child to eliminate or minimize the pain.

DON'T REINFORCE THE BEHAVIOR. A child's discomfort can seem worse to him if he senses concern on the part of a parent. Try not to reinforce the child's fear by becoming visibly alarmed. Passing discomforts can become habitual or chronic if the child becomes caught in an ascending spiral of anxiety. Again, explain to the child how the problem occurs; that it isn't serious; and what steps can be taken to address it.

TRY KEEPING A LOG. If your child frequently complains of head or stomach pains and you can't identify the stresses in his life that could be triggering the pains, try keeping a simple log of the symptoms. Older children can be encouraged to help and become investigators into what may make the pain better or worse. Record when the child reports his pain in relation to day-to-day activities. Is there a pattern—school-day mornings, play-date afternoons? How long do the pains last? Are there events that seem magically to make the problem appear or go away, like the arrival and departure of a particular person? Are there other, associated complaints?

Have there been changes recently in the child's life? A new school or a friend who moved away? A troubling event like the death of a pet? Something especially fearsome on television? Are there problems in the home between the parents or with a sibling?

Does the child have trouble sleeping? If the stomachaches are accompanied by sleeping problems, a recent change in eating habits, and a sudden disinterest in familiar friends or activities, your child may be depressed and you should discuss with your pediatrician whether to consult with a child and adolescent psychiatrist. If you suspect sexual or physical abuse, see *Physical and Sexual Abuse,* page 259, and *Child Abuse,* page 260.

■ **MIGRAINE HEADACHES**

When a child regularly complains of headaches that are clearly uncomfortable and there is a family history of migraines, you may wish to consult your child's physician. Migraine headaches typically begin with flashes of light or other visual perceptions; often, nausea is an accompanying symptom, or your child may avoid bright light. The headache may last up to twenty-four hours, during which time the child will have little appetite or energy. No one medication treats all migraines, but a number of products are available that have proven effective.

In learning to deal with pain syndromes, you are dealing with a potentially chronic problem that, while different in many particulars, resembles other chronic ailments. See *Coping with Chronic Disease,* page 275.

Seizure Disorders

Seizures have often been described as lightning storms in the brain, and the description fits. Epileptic seizures result from abnormal electrical activity in the brain which may produce unexpected, intense physical movements or loss of consciousness.

■ IDENTIFYING THE SIGNS

Seizures vary considerably. *Focal seizures* (also referred to as *partial seizures*) involve part of the brain and may or may not be associated with visible movements; similarly, the child may or may not lose consciousness, and may look as if he is in a dreamlike state.

Generalized seizures involve a sudden and unexpected loss of consciousness, followed by a physical collapse and rhythmic contractions of the arms and legs. After a few minutes, the child will return to consciousness, though usually he will be disoriented.

Because your child is unlikely to have a seizure when in the presence of the doctor, the physician will depend upon you to observe exactly what happens before, during, and after your child's seizures. This will enable the physician to identify which kind of seizure activity occurred.

If seizures only occur when your child has a high fever, they are classified as *febrile seizures*. Symptoms may include loss of consciousness, rolling of the eyes, and stiffening or even convulsing of the arms and legs. Febrile seizures are usually generalized and brief.

If seizures are recurrent, the child is said to have *epilepsy*.

■ CAUSES AND CONSEQUENCES

Most febrile seizures are not harmful to the child and occur in children who are otherwise quite normal. Febrile seizures rarely occur after age five.

Seizures may result from injury or infection in the brain, lead poisoning, or chemical imbalances in the blood. In many cases, there is no identifiable cause.

Some focal seizures ("staring spells") may be mistaken for daydreaming. However, a child is not simply a dreamer when his attention cannot be attracted by calling his name or gesturing within his line of vision. If the child does not recall the events of the preceding moment when he does respond, the episode may well have been a seizure.

■ HOW TO RESPOND

If your child experiences a seizure, it will likely pass without immediate medical intervention. During the seizure, however, you should protect the child from injuring himself. Position the child on his side to allow saliva to drain and to prevent choking if vomiting occurs. If the child is eating when the seizures occur, remove any food in the mouth with your finger if possible. Remain with your child for the duration of the seizure, and offer comfort when the child is responsive. Consult your child's physician immediately afterward.

If a seizure lasts more than two or three minutes or if a second seizure follows immediately, call for emergency medical assistance.

In some children who experience focal seizures, the disorder is hard to recognize. Often the seizures go undiagnosed, and the child is categorized by parents or teachers as a daydreamer or as uncooperative. Such children may have academic difficulties in school that are attributed to disinterest, lack of motivation, or to other emotional or behavioral causes.

The search for the cause is the first approach. There should always be a careful medical evaluation of seizures in a child. You and your child's physician may seek consultation with a pediatric neurologist. Blood tests, X rays, brain-wave examination (electroencephalogram), or other tests may be ordered to determine the cause. If a cause is identified, such as fever, infection, or injury, it will be given appropriate treatment.

If seizures recur, an anticonvulsant medication may be prescribed. When taken in appropriate doses, these drugs prevent further seizures in the majority of cases.

Seizures usually occur less often with age. Adults are about one-fifth as likely to have a convulsive episode as is a child.

Emotional Intervention Reassure your child first. He isn't abnormal, handicapped, or disabled just because he's had a seizure or seizures. Although it may be embarrassing for the child to lose control in a seizure, his seizures should not be regarded as a shameful secret. In fact, educating your child's teachers and playmates to the nature of the condition is the best way to get past outmoded notions about epilepsy.

Your child may be hesitant or apprehensive after having a seizure. He may want to avoid taking part in physical activities for fear of losing consciousness. He may tend to isolate himself to avoid the negative reactions of his peers.

Your job—as a parent, as a family—is to bolster your child's self-image. His self-esteem may be shaken by worries about future seizures. Tell the child that he is perfectly normal prior to a seizure, and returns to normal afterward. It's just for a few moments that the child is not himself—and you, the child, and the doctor will work to eliminate those moments.

Your child does, however, need to be given the opportunity to express his anxiety and concerns about the disorder. His seizures may alarm you, but you can help him adjust to them if you keep your anxiety about the seizures under control and if you emphasize his successes in other aspects of his life.

The child with epilepsy who takes anticonvulsant medication daily shouldn't be made to feel it's a sign of a problem in his life. The medication helps him to stay healthy and he can feel he is taking control by taking the drug and assuming responsibility for adhering to his medication regime. A Medic Alert bracelet is a good idea for a child subject to seizures.

Beware of being overprotective. Don't let fears of another seizure prevent your child from taking on new challenges. On the other hand, don't overindulge the child either. Help your child understand that his primary goal is to strive to enjoy, grow, learn about, and expand his universe just as his peers are doing.

Epilepsy is a disorder that presents unique challenges to the epileptic child and his parents; however, as with any chronic disease, there are common challenges to parent and child alike. For a discussion of some of those challenges, see *Coping with a Chronic Disease,* page 275.

Cancer and Life-Threatening Diseases

When a child has an illness—whether it's minor or major—he needs special treatment. Any child with a serious or potentially fatal disease suffers a wide variety of emotional as well as physical pains. This presents parents, siblings, and friends with opportunities as well as burdens. Cancer, cystic fibrosis, and sickle-cell anemia are three life-threatening disorders that are a great challenge to any family. (Much of the same guidance applies to the child and family facing life-threatening diseases as to those confronting chronic diseases; see *Coping with Chronic Disease,* page 275.)

■ CANCER

Cancer isn't a single disease; there are more than two hundred kinds of cancer. Each type of cancer, however, results from uncontrolled growth of certain cells that, over time, will destroy healthy tissues if the cancer is not treated.

Many childhood cancers are highly curable, including some leukemias and lymphomas. But the very word "cancer" still evokes fear—and a sense of fatality.

■ CYSTIC FIBROSIS

This inherited disease affects certain glands in the body and their secretions. Cells in the lungs, pancreas, and sweat glands are most often affected, though the sinuses, reproductive organs, liver, and intestines may also be involved.

Cystic fibrosis is often confirmed by a "sweat test," in which the quantity of salt lost in perspiration is measured. Children with cystic fibrosis secrete excessive amounts of salt in their perspiration; their skin may have a salty taste and salt crystals may be visible on the surface of skin. The child with cystic fibrosis tends to be underweight and to grow slowly.

Insufficient amounts of certain enzymes needed to digest fats and protein properly result in stools that are foul-smelling and bulky. The lungs, too, are often seriously affected, and the child with cystic fibrosis may have a persistent cough. The goals of treatment are to manage lung secretions so as to improve lung functioning; to replace or supplement inadequate digestive enzymes; and to replace salt lost through perspiration or excretion.

■ SICKLE-CELL ANEMIA

This blood disease is found primarily among persons with African-American or Mediterranean ancestry. In some states, a blood test is conducted at birth to determine whether a newborn has the disorder. A genetically inherited abnormality, sickle-cell anemia is passed on to a child only if both parents carry the defective sickle-cell gene.

Sickle-cell anemia results from abnormally structured hemoglobin molecules in the red cells. The abnormal red cells are vulnerable to changing shape, becoming sickle-shaped instead of round. When this happens, the sickled cells may block small blood vessels. This can cause intense pain and precipitate a pain crisis in which medical intervention may be required. The blood cells are destroyed and anemia results, with a range of potential complications. Over time, repeated severe episodes can result in irreversible damage to one or more internal organs, including the kidneys, lungs, or liver.

■ HOW TO RESPOND

Parents may blame themselves for a child's disease, especially if the disease has a genetic component. Some parents may also experience a kind of mourning, a *grief reaction*, when the diagnosis of one of these life-threatening disorders is made. It will be hard to deal with the frequent hospitalizations, surgery, or with chemotherapy or other medications and their powerful side effects.

For children with cystic fibrosis, there are the added challenges presented by the need for such special treatment approaches as a mist tent, and the need to master postural lung drainage, in which the child is positioned such that gravity will drain fluids from the lungs.

Anxiety is the single most common emotional reaction in children with cancer, cystic fibrosis, sickle-cell anemia, or other life-threatening diseases. In young children who require hospitalization, this anxiety often accompanies the separation—resulting in bouts of crying and panicky behavior, as well as feeding and gastrointestinal problems (including diarrhea, vomiting, and loss of bladder control). Slightly older children under similar circumstances may revert to less mature behavior. As a result of repeated hospitalizations and painful procedures, a child may develop specific fears (phobias) or

more generalized post-traumatic stress responses (see *Anxiety and Avoidant Disorders*, page 311).

Easing the anxiety is an important part of the process in living with the seriously ill child. In the hospital, familiar toys, clothes, and other favorite belongings can help make the hospital stay more like normal life at home. Kind acts are somehow more memorable when a child is sick—small gifts, remembrances of happy moments, surprise visits—any and all can lift the child's spirits.

Children vary in their understanding of and reaction to a serious illness and the issues surrounding death and dying. Although developmental research and guidelines suggest specific age ranges at which children master certain concepts of death, the individual child often defies these averages. One six-year-old may have an amazing understanding of the ambiguities of life and death, while a particular twelve-year-old may have more rigid—and less subtle—understanding.

The key is *listening* to the child. Take your cues from him, understanding what he says. *Then* try to share with him your understanding. Correct his misunderstandings as best you can. Support groups for children and parents may be helpful in improving coping with a child's chronic illness.

This is very difficult for adults and particularly parents. You are caught up in the cruelest struggle a parent can face—wrestling with the fact that your child may die. You need to talk to others about your thoughts, fears, and feelings. You may need a support network of family, friends, and professionals. You also need the time and as much energy as you can muster to listen to and hear your child's understanding of the journey he must travel. If you allow the discussions to happen, your child may tell you his real concerns, some of which you can help address, others of which you can help him endure.

Be cautious, too, not to overreact every time you get word of some new disease breakthrough or treatment. It may not be a lifeline at all, but a cruel false promise.

To the greatest degree possible, look to your child's strengths and health. Don't establish limits in your mind—or the child's. The sick child, just like any other, needs his parents' expectations and hopes, their dreams and their discipline to help shape their futures.

TALKING TO A CHILD FACING DISEASE OR DEATH

Even after years of experience, most doctors feel anxious in dealing with a dying child. It's no wonder that most parents find the prospect of discussing a child's impending death with him hard to imagine. The child with a curable but difficult disease isn't a great deal easier to confront.

UNDERSTANDING DEATH

In truth, a child under six will not be able to understand that death is permanent. The child may instead focus on a single facet of the death as an event: *"Will I still like chocolate, Mommy?"* Still the young child will sense his parents' emotions, and these will be hard for him to understand.

Between ages six and eight, the child develops a better sense of the consequences of death, but usually only at about age nine does death begin to be understood and accepted as irreversible and final.

TO TELL OR NOT TO TELL THE CHILD

A child will deal with the knowledge of his own death differently than his parents will. For some parents, denial of their child's illness offers a kind of emotional protection. In dealing with young children in particular, parents may decide not to tell the child his disease is a fatal one.

Consider your child's willingness to confront the truth about his death. Some children cannot or will refuse to understand; there is no need to insist. Others will come to accept the knowledge slowly; there's nothing to be gained by insisting upon instantaneous understanding and acceptance.

Before telling a child, think through how the discussion is to unfold. Talk the issue over with your physician or clergyman. Determine who is the best person to open the discussion, whether the child will be most comfortable hearing first from a parent, the doctor, or another person close to the child. If a person other than a parent is there to discuss the issue, a parent should be nearby to be with the child when and after he is told.

When talking about a child's impending death, do not offer the information as a pronouncement. Rather, the prognosis should come in the course of a conversation. The child may need to talk at length about death's meaning; the subject may come up again and again. An understanding may emerge in the child's mind only after repeated conversations.

DEFINING DEATH

It isn't easy, but you'll need to devise an explanation that works for you and for your child. When a person dies, he no longer breathes, speaks, or eats. It isn't temporary and, no, he isn't coming back. Death is a natural part of the life cycle.

Don't resort to talking about death as a kind of sleep. That's a distortion you'll have to correct later and only means you'll have to have still another hard conversation. And in the meantime your child may be afraid to go to bed at night for fear of dying. In fact, fear of being alone when dying is a common anxiety for the child who faces death.

No One Is to Blame

A young child understands the world in reference to himself. By this logic, he may think that a bad thing, like an illness, is a consequence of his own actions. It may seem preposterous to you, but to him such thinking is real and troubling. Make sure your child isn't inadvertently left feeling the fault lies with him.

Be Prepared for Denial

The child may refuse to accept what you tell him. An emotional eruption may result. That response is understandable.

Put Them in the Picture

The child needs to be able to trust his caregivers, parents, and medical professionals alike. One way to foster a trusting relationship is to give honest explanations of treatments, medications, and the likely outcomes. Be truthful: A lie, as innocent as it may seem, will probably have to be unlearned later. If a procedure is going be uncomfortable, don't pretend it's painless. Be honest with yourself, too.

Keep the child informed about the treatment. He should know what is being done, why, and told what to expect. Answer his questions. If you don't know the answer, say so.

A dying child may be able to express fear, loneliness, and other emotions through drawing or playing. The creation of pictures may help the child express things for which he does not have words and thus exercise some degree of control over his illness and feelings about death. The child may also be able to communicate his pain or fear through drawing, and even show you his misunderstandings about the causes of the illness.

The child must be given hope. Even when death is inevitable, the child should be assured that his parents and physicians will do everything possible in fighting the illness. Dignity, too, is important. The child's wishes and his desire for privacy during the different phases of his illness, including his death, should be respected.

Every child is different; there is no standard reaction to facing death. However, the manner in which the news is given and the support offered the child by parents and others around him will have an effect on the child's reception of the news. Children can be brave in the face of death; some are overcome with fear or anger. But all children require the support and affection of their families to help them accept the truth.

CHILDREN WITH AIDS

In a few short years, this previously unrecognized disease has become a terrifying presence on the social and medical landscape. For a while, the disease appeared to be a danger almost exclusively for homosexuals and intravenous drug users; it was easy and convenient to regard it as somebody else's problem. That narrow view was transformed by the appearance of the disease in children.

AIDS—acquired immune deficiency syndrome—is the result of an infection with HIV (human immunodeficiency virus). Once infected, the body's immune defenses are gradually weakened over a period of years by the virus. The impaired immune system is then subject to infections and cancers. Until some future medical breakthrough, full-blown AIDS is a fatal illness.

AIDS AND HIV

These two acronyms are linked to one another but they're *not* synonymous. A person infected with HIV is termed *HIV-positive* but doesn't necessarily have AIDS. In an adult, years are likely to pass before HIV infection erodes the immune system to the degree that the symptoms of AIDS appear. In a baby infected before or at birth, however, the infection generally progresses to AIDS more quickly than adults. In some babies, the disease progresses rapidly and they die before reaching their third birthdays. Other babies have a disease course that may last many years.

Most children with HIV received the infection prior to birth. The virus can cross the placenta in utero, be passed via blood or other bodily fluids during birth, or passed to the nursing infant in infected breast milk. Mothers-to-be with HIV must get special treatment to try to prevent transmission of the virus to their fetuses. It is estimated that a quarter of children born to HIV-positive mothers will develop HIV infection, but new treatments for pregnant women may reduce the transmission rate to fewer than one in ten babies of HIV-positive mothers.

LIVING WITH THE HIV-POSITIVE CHILD

Deadly diseases inevitably produce fear; those such as AIDS that are also communicable breed suspicion and other strong individual and public reactions. AIDS is no exception.

The facts are these: HIV is transmitted from one child to another only by blood and certain bodily fluids. Since normal childhood activities pose little risk of bloody injury, the risk of transmitting the disease is similarly small. AIDS is not going to be passed on to another child, parent, or caregiver by holding hands, using the same toilet seat, or feeding the child.

Going Public

Most children infected with HIV can safely attend preschool and school. Unless your child has open lesions or aggressive behaviors like biting, he should be able to attend school without restrictions.

There are still conservative communities where the public reaction to a child with AIDS is more likely to be rejection than compassion. Yet being honest with your child is still the preferred course. The information provided the child should be age-appropriate. At six, for example, a child can understand he is sick but not comprehend the nuances of AIDS.

Children who are asked to keep a secret from the world may feel caught between two camps, isolated and helpless. The burden of coming to grips with the notion of death is hard enough without complicating the difficult issues with secrecy. See also *Coping with a Chronic Disease,* page 275, and *Talking to a Child Facing Disease or Death,* page 300.

When a parent has AIDS, a child who has not been infected with HIV will likely encounter the hospitalization and eventual death of that parent. For a discussion of those issues, see *A Chronic Illness in the Family*, page 213, and *Death and Dying,* page 216.

Part III

SERIOUS PROBLEMS AND ABNORMALITIES

■   ■   ■

In each of these five chapters are a number of disorders that can represent serious obstacles to a child's development and family life. While these emotional, behavioral, and developmental problems are uncommon, they usually require professional intervention. The information provided in these chapters will help you understand what is going on with your child so that you can ask a child and adolescent psychiatrist or other mental health clinician the right questions and get the right kind of help for your child and your family.

"A boy resting outside on a summer day."

Eric, age 9

10

Emotional Disorders

■ ■ ■

There will be countless times in your child's life when she feels anxious, fearful, sad, angry, and frustrated. Occasionally, these or other powerful emotions will seem overwhelming to her and unsettling to you. Despite their intensity, in most circumstances these emotions are normal responses. In a short while, the upset will pass.

Most children's normal, healthy emotional development proceeds without being sidetracked by strong, unrelenting feelings. As young children, they attach first to caregiving adults. In the school years, they connect with peers in rich and productive ways. They learn through interactions within their environment, and their central nervous systems mature. They develop control over their emotions and, along the way, they evolve a competent, independent sense of self.

In some children, however, worries, frustration, or unhappiness are not merely passing, healthy responses to life's day-to-day events. The feelings are too strong and out of proportion, and interfere with their ability to function at home, in school, or at play. We expect the child to experience emotions when confronted with a specific environmental stress—a move, the birth of a sibling, or an illness in the family. Once the stress is relieved, we also expect that the feelings will dissipate. If the distressed feelings persist, we must wonder if there is another problem.

There are several things to consider when trying to determine whether your child's reactions are out of the ordinary. Younger children have a more difficult time putting thoughts and feelings into words and have less control of their strong emotions. Is your child expressing emotion by acting out her difficulties through play or artwork, or through behavior that reflects anger or frustration? Are your child's strong feelings interfering with her ability to function at home, in school, or with friends?

Try to be objective about your own emotional reaction. Parents who sense their child's emotional pain will often themselves become very upset. Furthermore, parents often feel responsible or guilty about their child's pain. Sometimes parents have been blamed by others for the emotional difficulties their child may be experiencing.

This chapter will look at some of the major emotional problems that children can experience, including such disorders as separation anxiety, depression, and obsessive-compulsive disorder, and will consider ways to assess the seriousness of the problems and the need for professional help.

Separation Anxiety Disorder

At about eight months of age, the baby usually has attached to the adults who provide warmth, nurturing, and care. The baby has a profound devotion to her parents and other caregivers. As your baby develops an aware-ness of your importance, she will protest your disappearances when she sees you leave. She feels bereft, cries, and protests fearfully.

This reaction is called *separation anxiety*. It signals a normal and significant cognitive accomplishment: Your child has developed an attachment to you and the ability to distinguish you from all others. As circumstances and development demand that she separate from you, she must learn to trust that you will return and that she will survive the strong feelings stirred up by separation. Developing a basic trust in those who love and care for her is at the core of healthy emotional development (see *Separation Anxiety,* page 18). By the time your child is two or three, she should be able to separate from you, enter a new situation, and manage her anxiety with relative ease. Throughout childhood, periods of clingy behavior and mild separation distress naturally occur in the face of unsettling events or significant changes.

Some children have severe and persistent difficulty in mastering the internal challenges of separation. These children get flooded by intense anxiety when facing separation. Their symptoms range from considerable discomfort to a full-blown panic attack.

■ IDENTIFYING THE SIGNS

For separation anxiety to be termed a disorder, it must be greater or more persistent than would be expected based on a child's age, and the anxiety must interfere with her daily functioning. A child who suffers from separation anxiety disorder is haunted by terrible worries about her parents' health and safety. She may fret about getting lost or being kidnapped. She may report seeing people peering into her room. She may fuss about going to school or anywhere else that would take her away from one or the other parent. Being alone or going to sleep without an adult nearby can bring about tantrums, panic, stomachaches, nausea, or even vomiting.

When apart from caregiving adults, some children with separation anxiety disorder withdraw from or avoid social involvement. Some seem apathetic or have difficulty concentrating on schoolwork or play. Other children are preoccupied with concerns about death and dying while others harbor phobic dread of animals, monsters, the dark, muggers, kidnappers, and car accidents (see *Anxiety and Avoidant Disorders,* page 311).

Children with separation anxiety disorder demand their parents' constant attention, without regard to how busy the parents are talking on the phone, working, or dealing with other children. Because the child's behavior and complaints interfere with a parent's daily routines, many parents become frustrated and even angry about their children's separation difficulties.

■ CAUSES AND CONSEQUENCES

When a child experiences excessive separation anxiety, parents should first examine their own feelings about separation, since anxiety can be communicated even nonverbally from parent to child (*and* from child to parent).

Practically all young children experience mild distress in response to a significant life event or change; often that distress is appar-

ent in clingy behavior and a reluctance to separate. Seeing their child's emotional pain, some parents become distressed themselves. They then find it hard to soothe the child. The parents' anxiety further upsets the child which, in turn, causes the parents more anxiety. This cycle often intensifies until the child refuses to go to school or sleep alone, or begins to complain of stomachaches or headaches. At this point, separation anxiety problems are often brought to a physician's attention.

Anxiety about separation may increase in situations where a parent becomes overly involved with or more distant from the child, such as during a divorce. When a child has serious medical problems, parents can unwittingly contribute to separation difficulties through efforts to care for and to protect (or overprotect) their child.

Many youngsters who have early and severe separation anxiety continue to experience chronic anxiety and persistent school attendance problems as they mature (see *School Avoidance, Refusal, and Truancy,* page 243). In some cases, children may develop agoraphobia, in which they are fearful of going out or entering places that don't provide an easy escape. In addition, it appears that there can be a connection between separation anxiety disorder and depression (see *Depressive Disorders,* page 329).

■ HOW TO RESPOND

If your child's fear of separation seriously limits her activities and interferes with your life and her daily routines, seek professional advice. Your child's physician will be able to recommend a child and adolescent psychiatrist or other mental health professional specializing in treating children with anxiety disorders. The evaluating professional will involve parents and may include other family members, as well as the child. The treatment process will likely begin with an evaluation of symptoms, family and social context, and a careful review of the child's development.

Managing separation anxiety—as with all childhood emotional disorders—usually requires a combination of treatments. Just how the problem is approached depends on the child, the family, and the specific treatment setting chosen. While anxiety conditions can cause considerable distress and disability, effective treatment can enable the child's healthy development to continue.

Treatment will center around reducing the symptoms of anxiety; relieving distress; preventing complications associated with the disorder; and minimizing the effects on the child's social, school, and developmental progress. If the problem manifests in school avoidance, the initial goal will be to get the child back to school.

Family Therapy If the child is young, the anxiety is mild, and the symptoms recent, family therapy is often effective in defining the problem and reducing the ways in which family members inadvertently add to the anxiety. Through family therapy, parents learn to respond to the child in a reassuring way while she learns to tolerate the anxiety of separation.

Parents are provided guidance and support in therapy as they encourage separation at appropriate times. Even parents of an anxious child must expect her to go to school and sleep alone. As the child is able to get through the school day or sleep through the night, she is rewarded with praise and appreciation for her courage. At the same time, family therapy helps parents maintain loving, consistent, age-appropriate expectations for the child (see *Family Therapy,* page 409).

Cognitive-Behavioral Therapy In many cases, cognitive-behavioral psychotherapy techniques can be effective in treating separation anxiety disorders. Such approaches help the child examine her separation anxiety, anticipate situations in which it is likely to occur, and to understand its effects (see *Cognitive-Behavioral Therapy,* page 407). This can help a child recognize the exaggerated nature of her fear and develop a corrective approach to the problem. Moreover, cognitive-behavioral therapy tends to be specific to the anxiety problem and to involve the child's active participation, which usually enhances the child's understanding.

Medication When separation anxiety is severe, a combination of therapy and medication may be used. Antidepressants medications such as doxepin (Sinequan), fluoxetine (Prozac), imipramine (Tofranil), nortriptyline (Pamelor), paroxetine (Paxil), or sertraline (Zoloft), or anxiety-reducing agents like clonazepam (Klonopin) or lorazepam (Ativan), may be prescribed.

Anxiety and Avoidant Disorders

Anxiety is an innate and useful emotion. Without fear or worry, a child would never learn to avoid running out into traffic or feel motivated to study for a science test. Reactions to noises, heights, and loss of physical support are present at birth.

Everyone—adult and child alike—experiences anxiety. Anxiety is an important emotion, signaling that danger or a sudden change is at hand, alerting and readying the person to respond.

By eight months of age, babies experience fear of separation from parent figures and fear of strangers; for many, special objects such as blankets and stuffed animals ease this kind of anxiety (see *Separation Anxiety,* page 18, and *The Pacifier and the Thumb*, page 31).

When the baby is able to separate herself physically (having learned to walk) or when her mother is separated from her, as occurs with day care or the birth of a sibling, she may also feel anxiety. It is not uncommon for children to regress at such times, or turn again to thumb-sucking or a cuddly toy for comfort.

By age three, most children can separate temporarily from parents with minimal crying or clinging behavior. However, separation is still a strain for them: After several hours of successfully braving day care, a child may have difficulty falling asleep, or she may awaken frequently in the night. Preschool children express normal anxiety through tantrums, aggressiveness, and excessive napping. They may also fret about getting hurt or about something bad happening to their parents while they are away.

Once they begin school, most children have at least fleeting worries that peers and important adults such as teachers may disapprove of them. There are many ways in which school-age children express their anxiety: their voices tremble; they bite their nails, suck their thumbs, or lick their lips raw; they complain of headaches or stomachaches; they get into arguments with other children. At the same time, many older children bravely sit through scary movies and amusement park rides in an attempt to master anxiety.

It is important to remember that some children experience greater anxiety than others. Others are shy, timid, and slow to warm up to new people and situations by temperament. Still others are characteristically uneasy or nervous.

■ IDENTIFYING THE SIGNS

Some children, however, experience intense anxiety almost constantly. This anxiety interferes with their ability to make and keep friends, to operate and cooperate within the family, and to manage the challenges of school. Children whose lives become dominated by fearfulness and tension may be suffering from anxiety disorders.

Anxiety disorders and their manifestations vary from child to child. Signs generally include excessive worry, agitation, and wariness. The child may worry about the future or the past. Even when there is no actual danger or threat, a child may talk about feeling scared, nervous, upset, restless, or under pressure; she may feel overwhelmed by dread and uneasiness. To try to hold on to control, the child may seem watchful and suspicious or may show certain ritualistic behaviors to protect herself, like carrying a lucky charm. Some children allay tension by ruminating about an event or situation over and over again (see also *Obsessive-Compulsive Disorder,* page 315).

Panic Attack One variety of anxiety disorder is seen in the occurrence of panic attacks. During these discrete, intense episodes of anxiety there is a combination of emotional and physical symptoms. During panic attacks, the child feels intense fear or discomfort, a sense of impending doom, or sensations of unreality. Physical symptoms include shortness of breath, sweating, choking, chest pains, nausea, dizziness, and numbness or tingling in her extremities. Sometimes the child is afraid she is dying or losing her mind.

Children who have panic attacks generally appear high-strung. During a panic attack, they may report that they can't think. Following a panic attack, children may feel apprehensive that they will have other attacks. Panic attacks may or may not accompany agoraphobia (in which the child is fearful of going out or entering places that don't provide an easy escape).

Phobias When a child develops an exaggerated and inexplicable fear that focuses on a specific object or situation it is called a phobia. Phobias may limit activities. A child who suffers from an animal phobia, for example, might refuse to spend the night at a friend's house if the friend has a dog. A child with agoraphobia may feel uncomfortable on a busy street or crowded mall. Children who have intense fears of medical settings might kick and scream before visiting the doctor, even though all previous visits have been relatively uneventful.

It is not unusual for young children to identify blood, darkness, fire, germs, dirt, heights, insects, small or closed spaces, snakes, spiders, strangers, or thunder as objects of their anxiety. In most cases, phobias are short-lived and create minimal interference with the child's day-to-day life.

Social Phobia Many children feel reluctant to enter into new social situations, but given the opportunity to observe and warm up, most are able to join in. Some, however, are gripped by excessive or unreasonable anxiety and disabled by fear or apprehension of other people's judgment or expectations. This is termed social phobia. Children who have social phobia may cry, throw tantrums, cling, or stay close to a familiar person when confronted with new social situations. Although restless, they tend to shrink from contact with others, refuse to participate in group play, and stay on the periphery of social activities. They may also complain of pain, fatigue, and stomachaches and may be preoccupied with worries about their general health or appearance.

For children with these anxiety disorders, anxiety becomes unrelenting and overwhelming, out of proportion to circumstances. A small challenge or change in routine may provoke an exaggerated response. Overly anxious children appear clingy, needy, dependent, withdrawn, uneasy in social situations, and overly vigilant. Anxiety problems which are severe and persistent may result in school avoidance (see page 243) or reluctance to participate in social activities.

■ CAUSES AND CONSEQUENCES

Most researchers believe that a predisposition toward timidity and nervousness is inborn. If one parent is naturally highly anxious, chances are greater that a child will also show anxious tendencies. At the same time, a parent's own uneasiness is often communicated to the child, compounding the child's natural sensitivity. A cycle may then be established whereby child and parent reinforce each other's uneasiness and tendency to worry or be anxious.

Panic attacks or panic symptoms can also occur with other problems (see *Separation Anxiety Disorder,* page 308; *Childhood Trauma and Its Effects*, page 319; and *Fears and Anxieties*, page 252).

Children who suffer from extreme nervousness often fail to achieve their full potential. They may be overly conforming and eager to please, perfectionistic, and unsure of themselves. They tend to redo tasks in order to live up to their own high standards, and often require excessive reassurance that what they are doing is good enough. Excessive and persistent worry frequently filters into all areas of a child's life—school, sports, family, and social interactions.

Most parents have heard their child complain of nightmares, stomachaches, or headaches when facing new or difficult situations. However, children with excessive anxiety experience these physical symptoms regularly. They may also complain about muscle tension and cramps, and need to urinate frequently. Overly anxious children may sweat, blush, and startle easily. These physical symptoms (associated with severe anxiety) often bring these children to their family physician for evaluation.

Accompanying the anxiety may be feelings of depression; over half of all children who have panic disorder also have major depressive disorder (see *Depressive Disorders,* page 329). In older children, persistent anxiety may be accompanied by suicidal feelings or other self-destructive behaviors. Sometimes older children and adolescents experiment with drugs or alcohol in an attempt to soothe or mask anxious feelings.

■ HOW TO RESPOND

Listen carefully and respectfully to what your child tells you about her fears. Point out that worry and fear are natural parts of life, and that all children her age feel afraid at times. After she's had a chance to talk, reassure her that although her feelings are real, they can be handled, and as she gets older, she probably will overcome her fears.

If she's afraid of monsters in her closet, look into the closet with her. If she's afraid of the dark, get a night-light. Introduce her gradually to the source of her apprehension. If she fears dogs, bring her into contact with the friendly dog at a neighbor's. With you by her side, she may be able to reach out and touch the animal. While you cannot make her fears disappear, you can help her gain a more realistic perspective concerning actual risk and danger.

Encourage your child's use of such transitional objects as blankets, favorite hats, stuffed animals, or pictures. Look with her at the cause of her fears. As the child gets older, remind her of other times she was afraid but was able to enter into new situations, like day care, or enjoy an unfamiliar setting, like camp. Be sure to praise her when she acts in spite of her uneasiness—it's an accomplishment of which she should be proud.

Sometimes a child's fear or fearfulness goes beyond normal anxiety and begins to invade her life and limit her activities. If the intense anxiety lasts more than few a months, seek professional advice. Your child's physician will be able to recommend a child and adolescent psychiatrist or other mental health professional specializing in treating children with anxiety disorders.

The evaluating professional will involve parents and may include other family members, as well as the child. The treatment process will likely begin with an evaluation of symptoms, family and social context, and a careful review of the child's development.

A medical and family history will be taken to determine the existence of any medical conditions, like diabetes, that could produce similar symptoms. Any medications that might cause anxiety will be reviewed (like some drugs used to treat asthma). Since large amounts of caffeine, typically consumed through soft drinks, can cause agitation, the child's diet will also be considered. Other biological, psychological, family, and social influences, and conditions that might predispose the child to undue anxiety will be taken into account as well.

Managing anxiety disorders—as with all childhood emotional disorders—usually requires a combination of treatments. Just how the problem is approached depends on the child, the family, and the specific treatment setting chosen. While anxiety conditions can cause considerable distress and disability, effective treatment can enable the child's healthy development to continue.

Treatment will center on reducing the symptoms of anxiety; relieving distress; preventing complications associated with the disorder; and minimizing the effects on the child's social, school, and developmental progress. If the problem manifests itself in school avoidance, the initial goal will be to get the child back to school as soon as possible.

Cognitive-Behavioral Therapy In many cases, cognitive-behavioral psychotherapy techniques are effective in addressing childhood anxiety disorders. Such approaches help the child examine her anxiety, anticipate situations in which it is likely to occur, and to understand its effects (see *Cognitive-Behavioral Therapy*, page 407). This can help a child recognize the exaggerated nature of her fears and develop a corrective approach to the problem. Moreover, cognitive-behavioral therapy tends to be specific to the anxiety problem and the child actively participates, which usually enhances the child's understanding.

In some instances other therapies such as psychotherapy (see *Individual Psychotherapy,* page 404) and family therapy (see *Family Therapy,* page 409) may also be recommended.

Medications When symptoms are severe, a combination of therapy and medication may be used. Antidepressant medications such as doxepin (Sinequan), fluoxetine (Prozac), imipramine (Tofranil), nortriptyline (Pamelor), paroxetine (Paxil), or sertraline (Zoloft), or anxiety-reducing agents like clonazepam (Klonopin), or lorazepam (Ativan), may be prescribed.

Obsessive-Compulsive Disorder

We all use some personal rituals and routines to establish order in our lives. This is especially valuable when we face pressures, challenges, or rapid changes. At such times routines and even personal rituals may calm us.

For some children, however, excessive rituals and rumination emerge from their attempts to order their internal feelings of anxiety and chaos. In the extreme, a person's organizing thoughts may become obsessions and personal rituals may become compulsions. If a child is distracted by obsessions or driven by compulsions to the point that normal functioning and development are dramatically disrupted, she may be suffering from obsessive-compulsive disorder (OCD).

■ IDENTIFYING THE SIGNS

A child with OCD usually experiences both *obsessions* and *compulsions.* Obsessions are unwanted and intrusive thoughts, images, or impulses that a person recognizes as senseless or unnecessary, tries to resist, but feels she must give into. They may take the form of repetitive words, thoughts, fears, memories, numbers, pictures, or elaborate dramatic scenes. Obsessions often concern cleanliness, contamination, safety, aggression, or sexuality.

These thoughts intrude repeatedly and involuntarily on a child's thinking. Despite the fact that the child cannot control these ruminations, she usually realizes that they arise from her mind. With OCD, these ruminations go well beyond natural worries about real-life problems.

Compulsions are repetitious and ritualistic actions, carried out in response to an internal sense of obligation or rules. Examples of common compulsions include hand-washing, hair-pulling, ordering, and checking and rechecking, or such mental acts as counting, praying, and repeating words silently.

Typically a child will understand that her compulsions are unnecessary and senseless but, at the same time, has great difficulty *not* doing them. The child may have elaborate rules for chronology, rate, order, duration, and number of repetitions. Compulsions may be linked to obsessions or represent efforts to lessen certain thoughts, impulses, or fears. Often there is little apparent logic connecting the rituals and the fears they are designed to prevent or mitigate. Rather than reducing anxiety, obsessions and compulsions frequently increase it.

■ CAUSES AND CONSEQUENCES

Obsessive-compulsive disorder has a biochemical component, with similarities to depressive disorders (see *Depressive Disor-*

ders, page 329). OCD is more likely to occur with children whose parents also have (or previously had) the disorder. OCD is also more common in families with a history of Tourette's disorder (see *Tics and Tourette's Disorder,* page 318) or problems with anxiety and mood swings.

Children with OCD may continue to achieve in their academic and extracurricular activities. However, their social and family lives are frequently affected by the child's severe symptoms. For example, washing rituals can consume hours each day, dissolve an entire bar of soap at each session, and leave the child's hands raw and bleeding. Counting and ordering compulsions can interfere with accomplishing the simplest of tasks. Rituals executed repetitively from night to early morning not only prevent sleep for the child, but keep the rest of the family awake as well.

Early on, as the obsessions and compulsions are emerging, parents often try to convince themselves that their child is only involved in peculiar habits or passing through a phase. The child may say that she, too, sees the odd nature of her behavior, leading her parents to believe that the symptoms are within the child's control. However, children who suffer from this disorder have lost some control over their thoughts and actions.

The child may also attempt to include her parents in the rituals. When the child is successful in pleading, extorting, or bargaining, the compulsion can involve the parents as well, and giving in to the compulsive activities or aiding in their performance seldom relieves the child's anxiety.

▪ HOW TO RESPOND

If your child's OCD seriously limits her activities and interferes with your life and her daily routines, seek professional advice. Your child's physician will be able to recommend a child and adolescent psychiatrist or perhaps some other mental health clinician specializing in treating children with OCD. The evaluating professional will involve parents and may include other family members, as well as the child. The treatment process will likely begin with an evaluation of symptoms, family and social context, and a careful review of the child's development.

Managing OCD—as with all childhood emotional disorders—usually requires a combination of treatments. Just how the problem is approached depends on the child, the family, and the specific treatment setting chosen. While OCD can cause considerable distress and disability, effective treatment can enable the child's healthy development to continue.

Treatment will center on reducing the symptoms; relieving distress; preventing complications associated with the disorder; and minimizing the effects on the child's social, school, and developmental progress. If the problem manifests in school avoidance, the initial goal will be to get the child back to school.

Parents may feel embarrassed by, apologize for, or minimize the child's OCD symptoms. However, once parents recognize the symptoms, which is usually early in the development of OCD, professional evaluation and treatment are crucial. OCD symptoms do not usually abate without help. Because children with OCD are likely to be apprehensive, the ability of the evaluating professional to establish a solid relationship is critical to success.

Individual Psychotherapy A good therapeutic relationship can absorb much of the child's anxiety and promote open discussion. Psychotherapy can also address related problems: anxiety about family problems or divorce; loss of self-esteem; unrealistic expectations; perfectionistic striving; regulation of sexual or aggressive impulses; and the general effects of having a chronic psychiatric illness during one's development. Because OCD is often chronic, effective therapy can require months or even years. (See also *Individual Psychotherapy,* page 404.)

Family Therapy This approach addresses the ways in which symptoms reflect and affect family life. It provides an opportunity to identify ways in which family members unwittingly perpetuate symptoms as well as other problems that could be promoting symptoms. It also offers support to family members as they learn about this disorder and ways in which they can help the child. (See *Family Therapy,* page 409.)

Cognitive-Behavioral Therapy Found effective in treating OCD, cognitive therapy focuses on changing the irrational beliefs and distorted thoughts at the root of the disorder. Many children with OCD feel uneasy talking about their thoughts and rituals because they usually involve bathroom or sexual material, but therapy can help a child deal with conflicts and reactions surrounding obsessive-

compulsive behavior. The youngster may even have trouble thinking about positive events and her own good attributes, taking any failure or setback personally and magnifying negative events. Cognitive therapy focuses on identifying and correcting distortions and on helping the child to change her thinking.

Behavioral techniques have also proven useful in treating OCD. Treatment may include, for example, a method by which the child's anxiety is slowly reduced so that obsessive-compulsive behavior is prevented. The child may also be gradually brought into contact with a feared object or event; then the youngster's obsessive-compulsive behaviors in response can be gently thwarted. The goal is to help the child recognize the exaggerated nature of her fears and develop a corrective approach. (See also *Cognitive-Behavioral Therapy,* page 407.)

Medication Certain medications in combination with psychotherapy are helpful in reducing the symptoms of OCD. Among the drugs prescribed are various antidepressant medications such as fluoxetine (Prozac), clomipramine (Anafranil), and fluvoxamine (Luvox).

Hospitalization In most cases, a child with OCD can be effectively evaluated and treated as an outpatient. Admission to a hospital is not necessary unless the family's capacity to support the child is thoroughly depleted or overwhelmed, or the OCD symptoms cause the child to become self-destructive or dangerous.

Tics and Tourette's Disorder

A tic is a rapid, repeated twitch of a muscle that produces a quick, sudden, and uncontrollable movement. The affected muscles will begin to twitch for no apparent reason. Parts of the body most frequently involved include the face, neck, shoulders, body trunk, and hands. Sounds that are made involuntarily are called vocal tics.

Most children who have tics develop them between the ages of six and ten. Tics are three times more common in boys than girls. Tics can be voluntarily suppressed for brief periods, and most are mild and hardly noticeable. However, in some cases they are frequent and severe and can affect many areas of a child's life.

■ IDENTIFYING THE SIGNS

The most common tic disorder is called *transient tic disorder* and it may affect up to 10 percent of children during the early school years.

Tics that last one year or more are called *chronic tics*. Chronic tics affect less than 1 percent of children and may be related to a more unusual tic disorder called *Tourette's disorder*. Children with Tourette's disorder have both body and vocal tics. Some tics may disappear by early adulthood, and some may continue. Children with Tourette's disorder may also have problems with attention and concentration. They may act impulsively, may develop obsessions and compulsions, and may blurt out certain words or phrases including, in rare instances, obsceni-ties. Tourette's disorder sometimes occurs along with obsessive-compulsive disorder (see page 315).

■ CAUSES AND CONSEQUENCES

Transient tics are common, often occurring in bright, highly sensitive youngsters probably in response to stress. Children who are overly shy or self-conscious are more likely to have more frequent tics than those who are more relaxed. Transient tics disappear by themselves over time. The tics associated with Tourette's disorder, however, do not simply disappear.

Although the precise cause of Tourette's disorder is not known, it appears to run in families. There is some evidence that certain stimulants (for example, methylphenidate) used to treat attention-deficit/hyperactivity disorder in children may worsen or exacerbate an existing tic. The course of Tourette's disorder is unpredictable, but the symptoms often become less evident over time.

■ HOW TO RESPOND

Children with tics or Tourette's disorder cannot control these sounds and movements and should not be blamed for them. Punishment by parents, teasing by classmates, and scolding by teachers will not help the child control the tics and may damage the child's self-esteem.

The best approach to transient tics is to ignore them. In the vast majority of cases, they go away on their own. You may help speed their exit along by helping your child become more relaxed. You can help do this by making sure the youngster is not over-scheduled, has plenty of free time for play, and by not being overly critical.

If the tics become frequent (more than ten a day), last for more than a year, interfere with school or friendships, or involve coughing, sounds, words, or profanity, see your child's doctor. Through a comprehensive medical evaluation, often involving such specialists as a pediatric neurologist and a child and adolescent psychiatrist, a determination of whether a youngster has Tourette's disorder or some other tic disorder can be made.

Treatment for the child with a tic disorder may include medication such as clonidine (Catapres), haloperidol (Haldol), or pimozide (Orap) to help control the symptoms. The professional can also advise the family about how to provide emotional support and the appropriate home environment for the youngster.

Childhood Trauma and Its Effects

All children experience some stressful events. The majority, however, grow up in kind, loving, nonabusive families and never experience a life-threatening disaster like a hurricane, earthquake, or bomb explosion. Most children never witness a murder or drive-by shooting. But some do face and are overwhelmed by traumatic events.

Trauma is defined as an event more overwhelming than a person ordinarily would be expected to encounter. For example, while a divorce in the family is stressful, it would not be considered a life-threatening traumatic event. In contrast, one parent knifing the other would. Children who experience horrible external events may experience emotional harm or psychic trauma. Left untreated, all but the mildest of childhood trauma can have an impact on the child.

Researchers have identified two basic types of psychic trauma: *one-episode* or *single-blow psychic trauma*, which results from a single, sudden, and unexpected event such as a rape, a bad car accident, or a devastating tornado; and *repeated trauma,* which arises from long-standing, repeated events, such as sexual or physical abuse. Each type of psychic trauma has characteristic signs.

One-Episode Trauma Also called Type I post-traumatic stress disorder (PTSD), single-blow trauma produces a number of characteristic symptoms. Children who experience one-episode or single-blow trauma usually retain detailed memories of the event for a long time. No matter how much a child may try to forget, these memories remain vivid. Unlike regular memories, these are uncontrollable; they intrude into their day-to-day activities and can interfere with play, school, and family life.

Nightmares are also common among children with post-traumatic stress disorder, as are recollections of the traumatic event that occur during waking hours and intrude into the child's thoughts.

These children may tend to startle easily

and be very vigilant. Children often attempt to gain mastery over the randomness and lack of control experienced in a sudden disaster by asking "Why me?" They become preoccupied with finding reasons and ways in which the traumatic event could have been averted. When this reworking and rethinking is not successful, a child can become pessimistic about the future and feel little purpose in life. Some children also experience visual hallucinations both immediately following and long after the single-event trauma. After witnessing his mother's murder, for example a child may see monsters lurking in corners that are understandably terrifying.

Repeated Trauma Also called Type II post-traumatic stress disorder, repeated trauma occurs in children who have been abused often and for a long time. Chronic trauma is also common in children who have been reared in violent neighborhoods or war zones. Increasingly it is found in children who witness violence in the home or in their communities. Many of the same symptoms that accompany Type I or single-episode trauma occur, as well as additional ones with Type II. Because the trauma is repeated or prolonged, the child develops a sickening anticipation and dread of another episode. After being repeatedly brutalized, children may have a confusing combination of feelings, at times angry and sad, at others fearful. Often these children appear detached and seem to have no feelings. Such emotional numbness is a hallmark of this type of trauma.

■ Identifying the Signs

Immediately following any kind of traumatic event, children commonly experience brief and usually limited denial and emotional numbness. They will often try to stop thinking of the traumatic experience. Children who suffer through repeated traumatic horrors develop and use a variety of psychological mechanisms to cope.

Some children (such as youngsters who are regularly abused physically) may develop a type of self-hypnosis that enables them to deaden, at least in their minds, the pain of the trauma. This is called *dissociation,* and reliance on such emotional distancing as a frequent coping mechanism can have negative effects on a child's development.

Long-standing or repeated abuse also produces rage in children. Anger festers, occasionally exploding as tantrums and violent behavior. A child may turn this rage against herself, engaging in self-mutilating and self-endangering behavior, or by making physically damaging suicidal gestures. She may direct her anger outward through aggressive or delinquent behavior, or identify with the aggressor by turning the rage toward other children, victimizing and humiliating them. On the other hand, the child may also experience aggression as dangerous, so her behavior may become extremely passive, too, resulting in victimization.

Internal changes may occur as the child tries to adapt to both the trauma and the loss caused by the trauma. For example, psychic numbing may minimize the pain. Holding tenaciously to the specific memory of the trauma may be an effort to master the experience. Developing a belief in omens—attaching meanings to unrelated occurrences like associating a teacher's yellow sweater with bad weather, for example—may be an attempt to reduce the child's feelings of helplessness. However, the resulting state of unresolved mourning and continuing grief interferes with the child's ability to move on with her life.

In cases where the event has resulted in disfigurement, disability, or prolonged pain, a child may feel guilt, shame, self-revulsion, or rage if her peers shun or tease her. Suicide attempts or self-mutilating behavior may occur among these children.

Reliving the Traumatic Event Traumatic events may be repressed but are not fully forgotten. The child may reexperience the trauma through any of her senses. She may experience vivid and unwelcome flashbacks, often during quiet, unfocused times, such as when bored in class, falling asleep, listening to the radio, or watching television.

In the child's play or behavior, she will recall and attempt to rework the event. Her drawings and stories may incorporate and reflect the traumatic event(s). Although referred to as "play," repetitive post-traumatic play is more often grim work. Reliving the event represents an attempt to master fears that continue to haunt or overwhelm the child.

Tragically, trauma shatters the natural sense of invincibility and trust basic to normal childhood. This shakes the child's confidence about the future and can lead to limited expectations. Traumatized children often have a pessimistic view of career, marriage, having children, and even life expectancy.

Other signs common to children who suffer post-traumatic stress disorder include sleep problems; nightmares; exaggerated startle response; panic; deliberate avoidance of reminders of the trauma; irritability; immature or regressed behavior; and hypervigilance.

■ CAUSES AND CONSEQUENCES

Childhood psychic trauma (PTSD Type I and PTSD Type II) occurs as a result of overwhelming, horrible external events over which the child has no control. The experience renders the young person temporarily helpless.

Childhood trauma can be closely related to other serious emotional disorders both in childhood and later in adulthood. It is not uncommon to discover that a child who is brought to a mental health professional for other problems—conduct disorder (see page 349), major depression (see page 329), attention-deficit/hyperactivity disorder (see page 337), obsessive-compulsive disorder (see page 315), panic disorder (see page 312), antisocial or violent behavior (see *Anxiety and Avoidant Disorder,* page 311)—has also experienced an intense, terrible trauma or series of traumatic events.

Childhood trauma darkens the child's vision of the future as well as her attitudes about people. Young people who have been traumatized will voice cautious, one-day-at-a-time attitudes. They may say that you can't count on anyone. Sexually traumatized girls may shrink from men (using avoidance to cope with the trauma) or approach them with overly friendly sexual advances (in an attempt to master the trauma by trying to relive it). Traumatized children tend to recognize the profound vulnerability in all people, especially themselves.

Trauma-related fears often persist into adulthood. While some anxious children express apprehension about growing up or getting married, sexually abused children may grow up fearing sexual contact.

Passing fears—of strangers, the dark, being alone—are not uncommon at certain developmental stages of childhood and also appear in other emotional disorders. However, extreme panic and avoidance of these situations may be the result of earlier exposure to severe trauma.

Within the traumatized child, internal changes may occur which can affect her later in life, surfacing in adolescence or early adulthood. Without treatment, some childhood traumas can result in later problems characterized by violent behavior, extremes of passivity and revictimization (people who were raped or incestuously abused as children often fail to protect themselves from rape), self-mutilation, suicidal or self-endangering behavior, and anxiety disturbances.

■ How to Respond

Early intervention in childhood psychic trauma is important. Families that offer support, understanding, and a sense of safety as close to the time of the traumatic event as possible can effectively limit the effects of trauma on a child. Your child's physician may also recommend consulting a child and ado-

lescent psychiatrist or other mental health professional for evaluation and treatment.

Individual Psychotherapy Therapy that allows the child to talk about the trauma or integrate it into her play may help the child move beyond the pain to cope better.

Play therapy—psychotherapy in which the child is encouraged to use actions and play materials to express emotions, thoughts, and fantasies—allows the younger child to reenact the traumatic event in a safe environment, moving gradually to verbal expression. For example, drawing the scene of the event may help the child start talking about the trauma.

Therapy may make it easier for the child to describe feelings. In time, she may be able to understand her symptoms, behavior, and characteristic ways of dealing with the trauma. Moreover, talk and play eventually give a child the opportunity to look at the traumatic event in context and to gain perspective. Gradually, the child is helped to see the event as an encapsulated experience, a personal tragedy that occurred in a moment in time, rather than as a fate that determines and controls the rest of her life.

Medication Occasionally, medication is prescribed to treat symptoms of post-traumatic or acute stress disorder. Among the medications that might be prescribed are antidepressants such as imipramine (Tofranil) and nortriptyline (Pamelor), and anxiety-reducing agents like clonazepam (Klonopin) or lorazepam (Ativan).

Children who experience trauma can be

helped and are responsive to treatment. With the sensitivity and support of their families, such youngsters can accommodate the memories of their trauma as individuals who survived, and go on to lead healthy, productive, satisfying lives.

The Traumatic Effects of Child Abuse

In the view of some experts, child abuse in this country has reached almost epidemic proportions. According to a recent report, more than two million children are subjected to neglect and physical, emotional, or sexual abuse every year.

There is no standard definition of what constitutes child abuse, but each state has statutes that describe the forms of child abuse. Regardless of distinctions in legalistic terminology, however, experts agree that the abuse cases reported represent a small percentage of the actual number of children who are victims of severe abuse.

■ CAUSES AND CONSEQUENCES

Most parents prefer to think of chronic child abuse as something that happens to *other* people's children. While it is evident that certain kinds of stress make abuse statistically more likely—poverty, job loss, marital problems, extremely young and poorly educated mothers—abuse also occurs across all economic lines and in seemingly good homes. Many people blame the prevalence of violence on TV and in the movies, and while that theory has not as yet been fully substantiated, media violence may contribute to our acceptance of physical aggression toward children. It is worth noting that cultures in which corporal punishment is not sanctioned have much lower rates of child abuse.

Without intervention or therapy, abused youngsters grow up into troubled adults, suffering from a variety of symptoms such as low self-esteem, depression, relationship difficulties, extreme aggressiveness or passivity, and substance abuse. Many in turn become abusers of children themselves.

■ IDENTIFYING THE SIGNS

Abuse of any kind leaves an indelible mark on its victims. If you notice your child's behavior changing dramatically, try to find out why. Some sexually abused children display overtly sexual behavior around their peers or adults; in fact, it may be the most specific behavioral symptom of sexual abuse. If your child masturbates openly, inserts objects into her vagina to masturbate, acts out sexual intercourse during play, or tries to touch the genitals of others, these may be signs of sexual abuse.

A young child who has been sexually abused may also be fearful, withdrawn, sad, or angry; the youngster may complain more of stomachaches and other physical ailments, including genital pain or rash; there may be regression to earlier behavior like bedwetting; social skills may suffer, and peer relations become difficult. An older child may exhibit the same symptoms and also be more aggressive and disruptive in school, and grades may drop. Sexually abused children are often depressed.

■ HOW TO RESPOND

Even well-adjusted, even-tempered parents occasionally experience so much stress that they find themselves screaming at the kids or threatening punishments they would never dream of carrying out. But if you find yourself falling into a pattern of snarling and yelling, smacking bottoms or slapping faces, stop and take stock of your own emotional state. You may be at risk of abusing your children. If the demands of your life are simply more than you can handle—particularly if you have to manage them alone—don't be afraid to ask other adults for help.

Call on relatives, friends, or baby-sitters to give you a break now and then. Try to arrange your schedule so that it is less complicated; stick to priorities and drop the frills, at least for a while. If you or your partner feel a constant rage you cannot always control, do *not* take it out on your children. Get professional help as soon as possible. If necessary, send the children to stay with relatives until you have cooled down and learned better ways not only to cope with stress and anger but to handle conflicts with children. Family therapy should be considered.

Sexual abuse all too often occurs within families as well. In fact, in roughly two-thirds of cases the abuser is a parent or other family member (and is most often a man, although women abuse, too). Often the abuser already has the youngster's trust so it is fairly easy to manipulate the child into some kind of sexual act, either as a spectator or a participant. Then the abuser swears the child to secrecy, threatening fearful consequences if the events are reported to others.

Wise parents therefore understand that the best way to protect their child against sexual abuse is to build self-esteem from early childhood and teach the youngster to trust her instincts in matters of physical intimacy. If your toddler doesn't want to hug Grandpa or climb into Uncle John's lap, don't force the child to do it just to please them. *No* is an acceptable response to unwanted physical affection (and Grandpa and Uncle John should understand beforehand the important lesson being taught here so they do not take offense).

An open, relaxed, and respectful attitude toward sexual matters is fundamental. Don't be afraid to use the words *penis, testicles, breasts, clitoris,* and *vagina* when language development and comprehension allow. Explain that certain parts of your child's body are private and should be touched only by the youngster's parents and doctor, and perhaps a known and trusted baby-sitter when bathing or dressing. Explain further that those parts of other people's bodies are private, too.

Help your child understand, in language appropriate to age and development, the meaning of boundaries. Rather than make this an explicitly sexual issue, discuss it in terms of general safety, and perhaps with the help of a little role-playing teach the child some strategies for handling a situation in which the rules of privacy are being violated. Reinforce the basic premise that if an adult's behavior in this area doesn't seem right, the child has the right to say no to it.

Explain further that while some secrets— like the new bicycle you're hiding in the garage to give to her sister for Christmas—are good, fun secrets, others are not. Breaking a piece of your good china and then hiding the pieces is not a good secret. Being forced by an adult or a teenage relative or baby-sitter to do something that makes your child feel confused or bad is not a good secret, especially if there was an explicit warning given never to tell anyone.

Begin these discussions in early childhood, refining and adjusting them as your child gets older. The better prepared and more self-confident the child is, the less is the risk of falling prey to an abuser.

If your child tells you that she has been abused, take the assertion very seriously. Most of the time when children talk about being abused, they are telling the truth. Occasionally, however, a child may make up a story about being abused or even come to believe abuse occurred when actually it did not. No matter what, listen and take seriously what your child is saying and then determine what action and investigation is necessary.

If your child comes home from kindergarten and says the teacher hit her in the face, you should call the teacher and ask what happened. The teacher may provide a perfectly reasonably explanation for why the child has a black eye. If your child returns from visitation and reports that his stepmother hurt his penis, you should call the father and stepmother and compare notes. Perhaps the child had a rash and the stepmother was applying prescribed ointment.

If the child appears injured, consult your pediatrician as soon as possible. The doctor will examine the child and, if he suspects abuse after conducting a preliminary investigation, the doctor will contact child protective services. In addition, the pediatrician may direct you to a child and adolescent psychiatrist or other mental health clinician qualified to work with children. Counseling for both the child and the parents is of immense value in dealing not only with the child's trauma, but with the parents' rage, guilt, and sense of helplessness. If it appears that the child was abused, let her know that she has done the right thing in telling you, and that you will take care of the situation and make sure it does not happen again. Assure the child again and again that she is safe and that it was not her fault: Sexual abuse is *never* the child's fault.

Selective Mutism

It's the first day of kindergarten. Your daughter feels really shy and nervous. For the whole day, she sits silently. When asked a question, she nods her head. But within a couple of days, as she settles into school, she's back to her old chatty self.

The girl down the street has just moved to this country from Venezuela. She knows a few words in English, but feels so self-conscious that she doesn't speak to anyone outside of the family. It's surprising to see how talkative she is in Spanish with her family and how silent she is elsewhere. But in a few weeks, as she gains greater skill in her new language, she begins to engage in tentative conversations with her neighbors and schoolmates.

In such situations, it is understandable

why a timid and uncomfortable child would refuse to talk. But some children refuse continuously to speak in certain situations. This pattern can interfere with social relationships and educational achievements. These children may be suffering from an emotional disorder called *selective mutism.*

■ IDENTIFYING THE SIGNS

Children with this disorder have developed normal speech and language and are capable of normal conversations. However, they typically refuse to speak in school or engage in conversations with adults outside of the family.

Despite the name, it is not clear to what extent selective mutism is truly within the child's conscious control. During the time that a child is mute, she might remain completely silent, or communicate in whispers or small words. It is likely that she will appear alert and interested, making eye-contact and attempting to communicate through gestures, pantomime, sign language, drawings, nods, or shakes of the head. When not mute, she may be quite talkative.

Children who suffer from selective mutism may also exhibit many of the features associated with anxiety: excessive shyness, timidity, social withdrawal, clinging behavior, fears and phobias, compulsive traits, and depression. A child with selective mutism may also be aggressive, hostile, and combative, though these behaviors are more likely to be played out at home.

Selective mutism usually appears between the ages of three (when language normally is established) and eight. Typically, it is identified during the first and second year of elementary school. In most cases, this disorder begins insidiously, though in some cases it begins abruptly, usually following a traumatic event (see *Childhood Trauma and Its Effects,* page 319).

■ CAUSES AND CONSEQUENCES

While the exact cause of selective mutism remains subject to debate, there is a higher incidence among children who develop language difficulties after a traumatic event and among those who must suddenly acquire another language because their families are recent immigrants. Once an immigrant child can speak and understand the new language, a continued refusal to speak at school probably indicates a problem.

It may be that children prone to selective mutism are slower to mature, not only in speech development but in other physical and cognitive areas. These children tend to have greater difficulty controlling their bladders and bowels, for example. In addition, some are clumsy and awkward. This suggests a possible neurobiological component to the disorder.

There are some indications that troubled family interactions or seriously depressed or distant parents may contribute to the appearance of this disorder. In some cases, a trauma or specific stress—the death of a parent, sexual or physical abuse, a prolonged and unavoidable separation between the child and her family—may cause a child to decide not to speak.

Selective mutism, if it persists, can pervade many aspects of a child's life. Her schoolwork and performance may suffer; she may be subjected to cruel teasing by her peers; and she may further withdraw emotionally and socially.

■ HOW TO RESPOND

Left untreated, selective mutism typically lasts from several months to a number of years. While a few cases clear up on their own, your child's physician may recommend consulting a child and adolescent psychiatrist or other mental health professional qualified to work with children.

The evaluating professional will note to whom the child speaks, under what circumstances, and the level of language sophistication that the child has attained. The evaluation will also include a careful history of hearing problems or ear infections and speech and language development. Whether the condition is related to a neurological disorder or mental retardation will also be considered.

Treatment may combine a number of approaches: behavioral modification (see *Cognitive-Behavioral Therapy,* page 407), psychotherapy (see page 404), family therapy (see page 409), speech therapy, and, on occasion, the use of antidepressant medications if there is underlying depression. With early, effective treatment, there is a high rate of success in treating selective mutism.

Disorders of Attachment

For a variety of reasons, the relationship between an infant or very young child and her primary caregiver may be disrupted or disturbed, interfering with the formation of the intimate bond that is an important building block for all healthy relationships. Such problems may cause delays in the child's physical, intellectual, and emotional development. Later, the youngster may become either inhibited or indiscriminate in the ways in which she attaches and relates to others. These features may signal *disorders of attachment.*

■ IDENTIFYING THE SIGNS

A parent or a physician usually notices signs of trouble in attachment in the first year of a child's life. Often, a parent brings an infant or child to the doctor with repeated complaints of severe colic, poor eating, or spitting up. The doctor may also discern that the baby is detached and unresponsive, and that she fails to engage in the type of social interactions expected of a child at her age.

Indiscriminate acceptance of strangers is considered normal up until the age of eight months. Children who suffer from these disorders, however, may attach with inappropriate intensity to any adult figure after this age. Others may continue to shrink from contact. In many cases, these children will continue to show inadequate growth and poor weight gain. This condition is called *reactive attachment disorder* or *failure to thrive.*

■ CAUSES AND CONSEQUENCES

Early failure to thrive and disturbed social relatedness can arise out of a number of circumstances. A mother may experience a debilitating postpartum depression or require a prolonged hospitalization following childbirth; the infant may be sickly or premature and remain in the hospital for an extended period of time.

There also seems to be a link between low birth weight and difficulties in attachment. In addition, there is a higher incidence of attachment disorders among children whose parents are extremely young, come from great poverty or emotionally deprived circumstances, have histories of behavioral or relational difficulties, or have mental illnesses. Attachment problems arise when a child experiences severe emotional and sensory neglect, too little holding, talking, and interacting with her adult caregivers.

Some parents may believe that they are caring adequately for their babies. However, they may not really know what the child requires and may fail to understand her various communications. There may be little eye-contact with the child and a lack of or inconsistent responsiveness to the baby's needs or wants. In these instances, parents frequently misinterpret expressions of distress, assuming the child to be physically ill. This may prompt a visit to the child's physician, at which time the disorder is diagnosed.

These children are at increased risk for growth retardation, frequent illnesses, and possibly death from complications of malnutrition or infection. Even when malnutrition and infection are not immediate concerns, children with this disorder are at risk for continued serious impairment in their social, emotional, and physical development. Children with severe autism or mental retardation (see *Pervasive Development Disorder*,

page 368) may display similar symptoms. A comprehensive medical and psychiatric evaluation will distinguish between these conditions.

■ HOW TO RESPOND

Immediate professional intervention is needed to establish adequate feeding and weight gain, to treat complications of malnutrition, and to provide reasonable stimulation and interaction. In mild cases, this can be undertaken in an outpatient setting or in the family home.

The mother and other caregivers will be offered instruction and encouragement to foster suitable parent-child interactions and caregiving patterns. In addition, time will be spent teaching the parents what to expect the baby to do at different stages, and to offer them support and help in understanding the baby's needs and behavior.

If a mother feels alienated or socially isolated, supportive *group therapy* can help (see page 411). If a mother is experiencing her own clinical depression, she may receive treatment, including therapy and antidepressant medications.

Because attachment disorders can be life-threatening, hospitalization may be necessary when the condition is severe or recognized late. In most instances, babies respond immediately to improved nutrition and nurturing provided in the hospital.

However, taking the child away from the mother and putting the child in the hospital may make things more difficult for the mother. She may feel alienated, detached, depressed, and inept. Therefore, when possible, a treatment plan should be developed to keep the child at home. When the child's physical needs require hospitalization, every effort should be made to involve the baby's caregivers in the treatment process. Once the baby is stable, a plan is devised to help the parents become more skilled at attending to their child's health and safety after hospital discharge.

With timely and effective treatment, children with disorders of attachment can continue their development and make satisfactory social connections as adolescents and adults.

Depressive Disorders

As parents, we want our children to be happy. Yet despite our best efforts to please and protect them, children encounter disappointment, frustration, and, at times, real heartbreak.

All children feel sad or needy sometimes. However, there are some children who seem constantly sorrowful, hopeless, and helpless. Seriously depressed youngsters experience disturbing symptoms that are beyond the range of normal sadness.

■ IDENTIFYING THE SIGNS

There are two basic types of depression: *major depression* which lasts at least two weeks; and the milder but chronic *dysthymic disorder*, in which a long-standing depressed mood seems to be connected to the child's

temperament or personality. Young children often do not talk about feeling depressed or down; therefore, vague, nonspecific physical complaints (headaches, stomachaches, other pains and aches) can be the first indications of severe depression in a school-age child. Other young children with depression may also be irritable; experience anxiety at separation from their parents (see *Separation Anxiety Disorder,* page 307); or have exaggerated fears (see *Anxiety and Avoidant Disorders,* page 311). Not all children who suffer with severe depression appear depressed, but instead may seem irritable or moody, swinging from great sadness to sudden anger.

Usually, there are other clues or signals that a child is depressed. She may lose interest or pleasure in most activities. She may complain about being tired most of the time or lack the energy to engage in her normal activities. She may sleep or eat too little or too much. She may have trouble concentrating or making decisions. Feelings of worthlessness, anger, or guilt may find expression in suicidal thoughts or ruminations about death.

Children with *dysthymic disorder* have milder but still harrowing symptoms of depression—a depressed, irritable, volatile mood; appetite and sleep changes; diminished energy; low self-esteem; feelings of hopelessness; poor concentration and indecisiveness—that last for a year or longer. Though dysthymic disorder is uncommon in childhood, it may begin prior to adolescence. The depressed moods color every experience, impression, and response. These children may go about their activities as though wrapped in a despondent gauze, with only brief periods of improved mood and outlook.

■ CAUSES AND CONSEQUENCES

Depression is a complex and multifaceted condition. Likely rooted in a genetic and/or biochemical predisposition, depression also can be linked to unresolved grief, possibly in response to early real or imagined losses of nurturing figures. Depression may also reflect that the child has learned feelings of helplessness rather than feeling empowered to seek solutions for life's problems. Depressed thinking tends to be negative, hopeless, and self-defeating, reinforcing feelings of depression.

Some seriously depressed children have experienced early life or environmental stresses including childhood trauma (see page 319) or the death of a parent or other significant people. They may live in families where they regularly witness or are victims of parental aggression, rejection, or scapegoating, strict punishment, or parents abusing one another. Such family pressures may contribute to the development of a depressive mood disturbance in a child.

Depression also runs in families. Often one parent of a depressed child has suffered with depression. A depressed parent is also likely to be less responsive to her child. Thus, both genetic risk and life experience can contribute to her depression.

Depression usually interferes with a child's social and academic functioning. When a child is seriously depressed, school performance deteriorates and she loses interest in school and peer activities. She may complain of headaches or stomachaches or develop severe fears or phobias (see *Anxiety and Avoidant Disorders,* page 311).

Sometimes the symptoms of restlessness, agitation, and decreased concentration may mislead parents or teachers into thinking that a child has attention deficit disorder while, in fact, the child is depressed (see *Attention-Deficit/Hyperactivity Disorder*, page 337). It is not uncommon for children who are evaluated for one condition to be diagnosed with the other disorder since the two different disorders can coexist.

■ HOW TO RESPOND

In trying to decide if symptoms are serious enough to seek help, talk to your child. Let her know that you see her sadness. By showing interest and the desire to help her understand her feelings, you bring hope to the child.

Without pressuring her, point to activities she enjoys and handles successfully. Help build self-esteem by recognizing small triumphs and admiring her competence. As you listen to her, she will naturally feel protected and cared for.

At the same time, try to determine whether the child seems capable of handling the feelings on her own or whether she seems overwhelmed. If the symptoms persist, particularly if they are dangerous or seriously interfere with the child's life, ask your child's physician for names of a child and adolescent psychiatrist or other mental health professional experienced in working with children.

Treatment should begin with a full evaluation, which usually includes all members of the family. An assessment will be made to rule out an underlying physical disease or illness that could also produce depressive symptoms.

Parents will be asked to describe symptoms and such behavioral changes as irritability, moodiness, loss of interest, and sleep and appetite changes, and to report the duration of symptoms as well as any possible precipitating event.

Many parents who are also depressed may have trouble accurately describing the child's symptoms. They may either view everything in negative terms, therefore exaggerating problems, or be so preoccupied with their own depressive symptoms that they fail to observe the child accurately. In such families, it is not uncommon for parents to be unaware of their child's sadness, suicidal thoughts, or sleep disturbances.

Individual Psychotherapy Therapy offers support and empathy while encouraging exploration of the depressed feelings and symptoms. Treatment may alternate between play and talk because a treatment goal is to help the child talk about her feelings. If a specific circumstance or event has precipitated the depression—divorce, for example—therapy gives the child a chance to resolve some of her feelings and accept even a difficult reality.

For younger children or children who have trouble expressing themselves in speech, play therapy can provide an opportunity to communicate feelings and perceptions. Through play, the depressed child is able to communicate or enact in play her sense of loss, powerlessness, aggression, or danger—and eventually deal with these painful emotions.

Cognitive-Behavioral Therapy Often effective in treating depression in older children, cognitive therapy focuses on the irrational beliefs and distorted thoughts which are part of depression, such as a negative view of the self, the world, and the future. Usually a depressed child personalizes failure, magnifies negative events, and minimizes positive events and attributes. Cognitive therapy focuses on identifying and correcting negative thought patterns or distortions and on helping the child change her thinking (see also *Cognitive-Behavioral Therapy*, page 407).

Group Therapy This approach in children aims to help them develop social skills that can lead to a greater sense of mastery and self-esteem. Children may find it easier to express feelings in a supportive group environment. Support groups for parents can help them manage specific problem behaviors, use positive reinforcement, communicate with children in an age-appropriate manner, and become better listeners for their child.

Family Therapy Family therapy addresses problems that may worsen depression in children such as a lack of generational boundaries (in which parents or caregivers treat their children as peers), severe marital conflict, rigid or chaotic rules, or neglectful or overly involved parent-child relationships. In addition, family sessions may help identify other depressed family members and assist them in getting their own treatment (see also *Family Therapy*, page 409).

Medication Medications are sometimes used as part of a comprehensive treatment approach with a depressed child. Research is underway to clarify the role of medication and the response in the developing child. Some recent studies have shown improvement with use of antidepressants. The more commonly prescribed antidepressants are fluoxetine (Prozac), imipramine (Tofranil), nortriptyline (Pamelor), paroxetine (Paxil), and sertraline (Zoloft). Other antidepressants include bupropion (Wellbutrin) and venlafaxine (Effexor). Before an older child begins taking a medication, specific target symptoms should be identified in a discussion between the child, the parent, and the physician. Possible side effects and other aspects of the medication should also be fully discussed.

Hospitalization A depressed child should always be assessed for the risk of suicidal or self-endangering behavior. If a child is preoccupied with death by suicide or has a well-thought-out plan, hospitalization may be needed. Otherwise, as long as the child is able to function and her family is relatively supportive, intensive therapy can be done on an outpatient basis.

Bipolar Mood Disorder

Some children are troubled by both depressed and elevated moods. The child's mood may shift suddenly from one extreme to the other; in other children, there is a rapid cycle between high and low moods. Although the disorder is not common in children, youngsters with severe mood changes may have a bipolar mood disorder.

■ Identifying the Signs

In bipolar disorder, manic episodes usually alternate with episodes of depression and with normal moods. The manic element of *bipolar* or *manic-depressive disorder* is signaled by an elevated, expansive, angry, suspicious, or irritable mood lasting at least one week.

During a manic episode, a child irrationally distorts her view of herself and has inflated self-esteem. She may talk constantly and rapidly, and have difficulty sticking to one idea or subject at a time. She is easily distracted, appears agitated and restless, and sleeps very little. Most alarming, she may engage in reckless and dangerous activities. Bipolar disturbance usually interferes with school functioning and/or peer and family relations.

Children with bipolar illness are often extremely hard to tolerate. Hyperactive, silly, giggly, and aggressive in their verbal communications, they may use profanities and sexual comments loosely during a manic episode. Delusions of grandeur (*believing*, for example, not just pretending, to be Superman) can lead to dangerous behaviors, like running in front of cars or jumping off roofs. A manic child is often unable to eat and sleep and she may be insensitive, mocking, or cruel to others.

■ CAUSES AND CONSEQUENCES

Bipolar disorder occurs more commonly in families with mood disorders. As a result of their own intense moods and feelings, some parents with mood disorders have difficulty being consistent and effective in their parenting.

Children with mania may resemble those with severe attention-deficit/hyperactivity disorder (see page 337). However, manic children have greater mood swings, often appearing euphoric, irritable, or suspicious.

■ HOW TO RESPOND

Treatment of bipolar disorders (manic-depressive illness) in children should begin with a full evaluation by a child and adolescent psychiatrist or other mental health professional.

Individual Psychotherapy Since bipolar disorder is a lifelong condition, it is crucial that the child learn about the disorder and how to live with it. When identified, symptoms can be successfully treated and controlled. In addition, stressors that may precipitate symptoms can be avoided or reduced and coped with. When coping skills are learned, these children and their families can lead emotionally rich and productive lives.

Cognitive-Behavioral Therapy Often effective in treating the ups and downs of bipolar disorder in older children, cognitive therapy focuses on the irrational beliefs and distorted thoughts which are part of the mania or depression. In dealing with periods of depression, the therapy may address the youngster's negative view of self, the world, and the future. Such negative thought patterns may have been formed or reinforced by the child's family environment. Cognitive therapy focuses on identifying and correcting negative distortions and on helping the child change her thinking (see also *Cognitive-Behavioral Therapy*, page 407).

Group Therapy Group therapy for children helps them develop social skills that can lead to a greater sense of mastery and self-esteem. Children may find it easier to express feelings in a supportive group environment. Support groups for parents can help them manage specific problem behaviors, use appropriate positive reinforcement, communicate with children in an age-appropriate manner, and become better listeners for their child.

Family Therapy Family therapy addresses family problems that may worsen bipolar disorder in children, like a lack of generational boundaries (in which parents or caregivers treat their children as peers), severe marital conflict, rigid or chaotic rules, or neglectful or overly involved parent-child relationships. In addition, family sessions may help identify other depressed family members and assist them in getting their own treatment (see also *Family Therapy*, page 409).

Medication Once other possible causes for the symptoms such as substance abuse, a medication reaction, another medical condition, or other behavioral disorders have been ruled out, a mood-stabilizing medication like lithium may be prescribed. Other mood stabilizers that have been prescribed are carbamazepine (Tegretol) and valproic acid (Depakene). Before a child begins taking a medication, specific target symptoms should be identified in a discussion between the child, the parent, and the physician. Possible side effects and other aspects of the medication should also be fully discussed. In some children, antidepressants may be needed in addition to the mood stabilizer during the depressed phase, and an antipsychotic medication may be used in combination with the mood stabilizer during the manic phase.

Hospitalization If recognized early, manic-depressive episodes can be treated on an outpatient basis or in partial hospital programs. When there is self-destructive or aggressive behavior toward others, hospitalization may be necessary. Some children with mania may require hospitalization to ensure their safety.

11

Disruptive Behavior Disorders

■ ■ ■

As parents, we often measure our children's well-being by their behavior. In the family, at school, in the community, with their playmates, we notice how they act and interact. Sometimes we are reassured by what we see and, at other times, we wonder if our children's behavior is cause for concern. We also tend to see our children's behavior as a reflection of ourselves as parents, and frequently worry whether we are being good enough parents.

Every child misbehaves from time to time. In the vast majority of instances, misbehavior is short-lived and of no great concern. However, there are some children who communicate by *externalizing distress* through their behavior. This is in contrast to emotional disorders (see page 307), in which a child may feel very depressed or anxious and tends to *internalize* the distress. With a disruptive behavior disorder, the child tends to move away from these internal feelings toward actions.

A child's disruptive behavior upsets others in the youngster's life, and generally is more distressing to other people than to the child. In short, children with externalizing disorders are often as troubling as they are troubled.

Since disruptive behaviors usually have a direct and negative impact on the people in the child's life, it is not uncommon for the child to be viewed as being "bad." Seldom do children with troubled behavior report their own distress. Instead, they get labeled by adults, typically parents and teachers. However, labeling can be misleading because disruptive behaviors are often symptoms of an underlying psychiatric disorder or problem.

Disruptive behavior disorders account for most referrals to child and adolescent psychiatrists and other mental health professionals. Some studies put the number as high as two-thirds of all referrals.

In some instances, a behavior unequivocally signals serious internal problems, such as when an older child pushes a younger child from a rooftop resulting in very serious injury; or a young boy systematically tortures small animals; or a girl repeatedly sets fires. But in many cases, it's not easy to assess and judge whether distressing or disruptive behaviors are signs of deeper, more serious emotional problems. Studies show that parents are troubled by misconduct, whereas children are troubled by fears, loneliness, and inner unrest.

When evaluating a child's behavior, it is also important to consider the child's temperament and characteristic personality and behavioral style. Each child is born with certain temperamental traits that determine how the child will behave, learn, and interact with others.

Temperament is one component of behavior—in a sense, it is the *how* of behavior rather than the *why* (motivation). Consider two children asked to perform the same task. Even when they have the same *motivation* and similar abilities, their performance may differ. Why? *Temperamental differences* are often the explanation. Even children of the same parents who grow up in the same environment may have distinctly different temperaments.

Temperament in children can be classified broadly into three styles: *easy, slow to warm up,* and *difficult.* From the earliest days of life, babies show singular ways of acting and reacting in the world. Even in the youngest infant, parents may note a distinct style in the child's level of activity and in rhythms of sleeping, eating, and eliminating. Babies also vary in the way they approach or withdraw from new situations, in the intensity of their emotional responses, in responsiveness to sensory experiences, in adaptability, mood, distractibility, attention span, and persistence. Whenever parents try to figure out if a child's behavior is problematic, keep in mind there is a broad range of what's considered normal behavior.

Temperament is shaped by a number of circumstances, including a child's neurophysiological makeup and genetic inheritance. Conditions during pregnancy, delivery, and the postnatal period can also have an impact on the developing brain or biological systems, which in turn affects behavioral development. Psychosocial factors, such as parenting styles or family and social strains continually influence behavior and may alter temperament—a child who is naturally cheerful, outgoing, and optimistic will have difficulties remaining upbeat if he is constantly criticized, neglected, or abused.

In addition, behavior is neither simple nor constant. When we talk about children's behavior, we also include their ability to concentrate and attend to tasks and activities; the way they control, manage, and organize their movements, expressions, and thinking; the way they interact with others; the degree to which they respect and comply with limits and rules; and the overall manner in which they function in the family and in the community. Each aspect can change during a child's development or as circumstances change. A child's ability to concentrate, to share with others, to consider another's feelings, to listen to others and follow directions, for example, may vary in response to upsetting events, new circumstances, internal changes, and maturation.

How then do parents judge when their child's behavior signals a larger problem? How do they gauge the feedback they get from others, from their child's teacher or the parents of playmates? When does normal misbehaving cross the line into disordered behavior?

This chapter will look at a group of disruptive disorders in which a child's problems and uneasiness is expressed primarily in the way he acts. The disruptive behavior disorders include *attention-deficit/hyperactivity disorder* (ADHD), *conduct disorder,* and *oppositional defiant disorder* (ODD).

Attention-Deficit/ Hyperactivity Disorder

From time to time, in the normal course of their explorations and interactions in the world, most children bubble over with restlessness. On their feet, they dash from here to there. In a chair, they squirm, twist, churn, wriggle, and jiggle. With so much to do and so much going on around them, there's neither time nor reason to sit still.

While such activity is normal during early childhood, some children continue to operate as though they live within a high-speed kaleidoscopic world. For children who have attention-deficit/hyperactivity disorder, images, sounds, and thoughts churn constantly, distracting them, making it impossible for them to stay fixed on any one task or activity. These children often start running almost as soon as they learn to walk.

Sometimes when people speak, hyperactive children are so distracted or so inattentive that they don't even notice. Such children have great difficulty sitting still, planning ahead, or attending to what's going on around them. They often find it impossible to consider and conform to expectations and requirements of the world around them. As a result, their difficulties often cause disruption, annoyance, and disappointment to others in their environment. In addition, these children are more accident-prone and difficult to manage.

Once called *hyperkinesis* or *minimal brain dysfunction*, attention-deficit/hyperactivity disorder (ADHD) occurs in between 3 and 5 percent of all children, perhaps as many as two million American youngsters. Many more boys than girls are affected, though the disorder is being identified increasingly in girls. On the average, at least one child in every classroom in the United States needs help for the disorder.

Characteristic behaviors are inattention, hyperactivity, impulsiveness, and disorganization. Children who are inattentive have a hard time keeping their mind focused on any one task for long. They become easily bored or distracted. Children who are hyperactive seem to be in continual motion. They are overly impulsive and don't curb their automatic reactions. It appears that they do not think before they act and frequently they appear disorganized, forgetful, and unprepared.

However, because all children at times display occasional hyperactivity, short attention span, and impulsive thinking and behavior, especially during times of stress, unrest, or excitement, it is important not to misidentify them as having ADHD. Children with ADHD exhibit these symptoms much more consistently over time than other children their age or developmental level. In addition, anxiety, depression, and other emotional problems can produce symptoms that resemble ADHD.

■ IDENTIFYING THE SIGNS

Although signs of this disorder are often evident during toddlerhood or even earlier, most children do not come to the attention of their pediatricians or mental health professionals until they start school. Like other behavioral disorders, ADHD is most often identified by adult people, not by the child. Adults have varying tolerances for excessive activity, so that the same behavior may be accepted as exuberant by one teacher but considered a serious problem by another. Some parents do not know what level of activity, concentration, and compliance to expect from their children at different ages and may worry about their child's level of exuberance, energy, and restlessness.

In addition, problems may be present at school but not in the home, or at home but not at school. Some children are bored, discouraged, restless, and unable to follow instructions at school, not because they have ADHD but because they don't find the type of structure or challenge that suits them. Some children who suffer from undiagnosed learning disabilities express their frustration through behavior. They may have difficulty concentrating. They can become restless and fidgety and, ultimately, disruptive in the classroom.

ADHD is a chronic disorder. Its symptoms can be mild, moderate, or more severe, depending on the child. Many times, a child will try harder to focus if he likes his teacher. If he's involved in a subject or task that he's good at or particularly interested in, such as during a favorite TV show or story hour, he may seem better able to contain himself. Children with ADHD usually have more problems in large groups and do better one on one. Some children with severe symptoms have problems constantly and in all settings: at home, at school, and at play.

There are three different types of ADHD. The least common one includes children who are predominantly fidgety and hyperactive, tending to blurt out answers in the classroom, but maintain adequate concentration. A child with the second type of ADHD is characteristically inattentive, easily distracted, and disorganized, but not hyperactive. These children daydream, forget, or lose things, procrastinate, and fail to complete their work. Children with the third type of ADHD have a combination of the symptoms and behaviors of the other two types. This third variety of ADHD is the most common and most severe form.

In general, children with ADHD look normal physically and at times their behavior is normal, too. However, for children with this disorder, fidgety, restless, and distracted behavior is not just a temporary reaction to stress. If ADHD goes unrecognized and untreated, a child can experience a lifetime of emotional pain, frustration, academic underachievement, even failure, and social isolation.

In infancy, early indications of the disturbance may be reflected in temperament. The baby may sleep very little or for very short periods of time. When awake, the baby may be very demanding. Feeding problems such as poor sucking, crying during feedings, needing to be fed often for brief periods, or difficulty settling into a comfortable sucking rhythm can also be early indications of ADHD. Sometimes, these infants become picky eaters. Irritability, fidgeting, crying, and/or colic can make children hard to soothe or cuddle. They may not like being held. Sometimes, they develop self-soothing behaviors such as excessive thumb-sucking, head-rolling, head-banging, or rocking.

Once such children begin to crawl, they may be in constant motion with little regard to their parents' presence or absence. They may seem oblivious to and undeterred by parental warnings of danger. If the child is accident-prone, which is often the case with ADHD, the youngster will require close supervision. Frequently, parents find it nearly impossible to maintain a daily routine with these children because they are so irregular.

As all parents know, toddlers and preschoolers are naturally active. Most have short attention spans, and many are fairly impulsive. For these reasons, identifying the child with ADHD at this developmental stage is often difficult. Children later diagnosed with ADHD tend to be toddlers who ran instead of walked. Always on the go, always changing focus, they seem in perpetual motion, without goal or purpose. They may impulsively bolt from the table before finishing meals, refuse to sit through a story, and fidget while watching television.

A young child with ADHD may be prone to intense temper tantrums. He may have great difficulties in entertaining himself and in playing cooperatively with others. Some ADHD children are very aggressive. Unstructured activities such as independent work are difficult. However, for many ADHD kids, even structured or focused activities—like painting, drawing, or games—are also problematic because of the difficulties in being able to concentrate and remain seated, making completion of the task unlikely.

Although some hyperactive children are precocious in terms of gross motor skills, they may still be clumsy and accident-prone. For many, fine motor coordination and language ability are delayed. Sleeping problems can continue into the school-age years.

While most preschoolers and young school-age children can be impulsive, children with ADHD are impulsive to a degree that is distracting and dangerous. They may grab toys or hit other children without any obvious provocation. They may dash out into the street for no apparent reason. They might steal a candy bar or comic book on a whim without considering the consequences of their actions.

The symptoms of ADHD are usually evident by the time the child is five or six years of age (although, looking back, they usually were apparent earlier). The older child with such symptoms as restlessness, impulsiveness, and short attention span may have another emotional disorder such as depression (see page 329), anxiety (page 311), bipolar disorder (page 332), or substance abuse (page 266). It is also possible they have milder ADHD that was not identified at a younger age.

Children with ADHD seem unable to delay their responses. At school, they often are impatient and unable to wait their turn. An overly impulsive child might blurt out an answer (not always correctly) before a question is completed or while another child is attempting to answer. The child's schoolwork may show lack of thought and focus. School papers and assignments are frequently incomplete or full of errors.

Typically, a hyperactive child in the classroom won't stay seated and is in constant motion, pacing or running about inappropriately during class. Children with ADHD may be so fidgety as to literally fall out of their chairs. Play and leisurely activities cannot be engaged in quietly—the youngster with ADHD seems to be verbally impulsive and to talk incessantly.

Yet, the very same child may be able to concentrate for considerable stretches of time on certain activities that are enjoyed or that come easily, such as drawing cartoons,

watching television, or playing video games. Such selective attention seems related to motivation and pleasure in the task. Children with ADHD have difficulties in social situations and frequently have few friends. Many of these children are less mature when compared to their peers.

It is still not clear whether hyperactive children have difficulty perceiving and understanding social cues or whether they perceive them correctly but fail to respond appropriately. In normal circumstances, most children adjust their behavior through learning so that they can enter into a game, for example, or a group project without interrupting the rhythm that has been established. Children with ADHD cannot easily adjust their behavior to the demands of specific situations. They are more likely to simply barge in and disrupt the process. They often appear very self-centered.

On the playground, they might push into games and conversations without being invited. They might run into other children, pushing, hitting, shoving. While there may be no particular anger, hostility, or malicious intent in this intrusive physical contact, it often results in quarrels and fights with other children. At other times, school-age children with ADHD may be oppositional and argumentative, characteristics that can become habitual as the child's personality develops.

■ CAUSES AND CONSEQUENCES

Despite years of research, the cause of ADHD is still not fully understood. Evidence to date indicates that there are many factors underlying ADHD, among them genetic and neurobiological vulnerabilities. The basic problem is thought to be in the area of the brain that inhibits responses. This leads to the inattention, impulsiveness, and physical overactivity seen in ADHD. A child's environment may also contribute to the development of the disorder or worsen the symptoms.

In some cases, the cause of hyperactive behavior is not ADHD but high levels of lead in the blood; fetal alcohol syndrome (in which excessive alcohol consumed during pregnancy has a range of effects on the unborn child); exposure to other drugs in utero; the result of a serious head injury; or a consequence of an infection of the central nervous system. In the 1970s, attention focused on food additives, although later it was concluded that additives were not a cause of the syndrome. In the 1980s, public attention turned to sugar in its search for an explanation for ADHD. Many parents still limit sugar and foods rich in sugars but controlled studies have discounted the sugar theory as a cause for ADHD.

Pressures in the child's home, coupled with neurological vulnerabilities, seem to increase the likelihood that a child will manifest problems related to ADHD. The prevalence of children with hyperactivity, impulsiveness, and inattention is greater in disadvantaged, large inner-city environments. This may be due to interrelated conditions such as poverty; malnutrition; lead poisoning; poor prenatal and neonatal health care (which can lead to prematurity or low birth weight); maternal drug or alcohol abuse during pregnancy; and family disturbances, including violence and drug and alcohol abuse. Any one or a combination of these elements can play a significant role in developing and perpetuating ADHD symptoms.

While the exact degree to which a chaotic environment contributes to ADHD symptoms is still unclear, it does appear that parents who are able to provide support, stability, educational stimulation, and hope can help children with ADHD compensate over time for their vulnerabilities.

The symptoms of ADHD in these children makes parenting more challenging. Dealing with ADHD symptoms, and the inevitable frustration that results, may cause many parents to doubt their parenting skills. Parents of children with ADHD report greater social isolation, self-blame, and depression than other parents. When these factors translate into a parenting style that is more intrusive, controlling, and disapproving, the child's emotional development, competence, and self-esteem can be adversely affected.

As parents try to establish limits and discipline, for example, many become exasperated by their child's inability or unwillingness to listen. Despite every effort to curtail certain behaviors, parents often complain that the child doesn't learn from mistakes or doesn't seem responsive to praise or punishment.

This vicious cycle of negative interaction, stress, and sense of failure for both child and adult are also seen in the classroom between teacher and child. In addition, a school or classroom setting that is unstructured and disorganized can intensify ADHD symptoms.

Once a child enters elementary school, he

is expected to be able sit still and complete tasks for longer and longer periods of time. The more concentration required, the greater the likelihood that ADHD symptoms will interfere.

In addition to a child's conduct in class, his schoolwork will show the effects of the disorder. Unable to give close attention to details, he is prone to making careless mistakes. It might appear that the child does not listen when spoken to directly or does not follow through on instructions or finish schoolwork. Youngsters with ADHD may have difficulty organizing their thoughts and schoolwork.

Most hyperactive children avoid, dislike, or refuse to engage in tasks that require sustained attention. As a result, homework and schoolwork often go unfinished, especially when it is boring, repetitive, or difficult. In addition, they often don't finish chores at home.

Children with ADHD tend to underachieve at school, failing to reach their potential and functioning below their grade level in reading, spelling, and/or arithmetic. Because they have trouble paying attention and find it hard to organize their work, they actually may have trouble processing and remembering information.

In addition, children with ADHD may have difficulty remembering things in order (*sequential memory*). They may also have trouble controlling their pencils, required for handwriting and drawing, the result of poor fine motor skills. Clumsiness while skipping or running is an example of difficulty with large motor skills. Even when they are clearly intelligent, such children seem unable to discipline their thinking so that they can focus on or follow a particular line of thinking.

The less success ADHD children have with schoolwork, the less motivated they are to pursue academics. With many of these children, even their most concentrated efforts seem to bring little success.

A sense of failure may also permeate the social relationships of children with ADHD. Their impulsive behavior bothers other children. In addition to getting into trouble themselves, these children tend to get others into trouble. Consequently, they often find themselves unpopular with peers, and enduring friendships are rare. Sometimes, the only other children who are willing to play with a child with ADHD are those who are younger or have similar problems.

Since children with ADHD are impulsive they tend not to think about consequences, and this often leads to socially unacceptable or risky behavior. Excessively impulsive children may walk on a roof ledge, or lean way too far out an upper window. Risk-taking behaviors are more common in children with ADHD, who may also be accident-prone.

It is hardly surprising that children with ADHD tend to have low self-esteem. Many find themselves in trouble constantly or receiving lots of criticism. Many feel socially isolated and lack the mastery and competence that other children gain from navigating social and academic challenges. Therefore many children with ADHD enter a cycle of failure and criticism that is perpetuated both at school and in the family. Unless these children have the opportunity to experience adequate pleasure, love, and success, feelings of failure become chronic and can lead to depression.

ADHD commonly exists with other problems, such as specific learning disabilities. Children with ADHD may also have depression or anxiety disorders (see pages 329 and 311). Almost half of children diagnosed with ADHD are also diagnosed with oppositional defiant disorder or conduct disorder (see pages 345 and 349).

■ HOW TO RESPOND

ADHD is a treatable condition that requires a comprehensive approach. More than two hundred studies have shown that stimulant medication can produce striking results. Other treatment approaches, singly or in combination, may include cognitive-behavioral therapy, social skills training, parent education and support, and remedial education.

If your child is diagnosed with ADHD, learn as much as you can about the disorder. Talk with your child's doctor, teachers, and parents of other children with ADHD. Investigate what your child's school can do to provide *remedial education* or special tutoring to compensate for learning difficulties or to address associated reading disorders and other learning disabilities or language delays (see *Learning Disorders*, page 360). Parents of children with ADHD are their youngster's best advocates and need to be involved in monitoring school progress and in getting their children the help they need. Many communities have ADHD parent support groups and parents often find comfort and help in meeting and talking with others in similar situations.

Cognitive-Behavioral Therapy Behavioral therapy can help children control their aggression, modulate their social behavior, and regulate their attention and physical movements. Parents and teachers identify positive behaviors, for which the children are rewarded and encouraged. Cognitive therapy can teach older hyperactive children self-control, self-guidance, and more thoughtful and efficient problem-solving strategies (see *Cognitive-Behavioral Therapy,* page 407).

Social Skills Training When coupled with other therapy, social skills training has been effective in helping children smooth out their difficult social behaviors. Through such training, children can learn to evaluate social situations and adjust their behavior accordingly. The most successful therapies are those that provide training in the child's natural environments—such as the classroom or in social groups—as this may help the child apply the lessons learned directly to his life.

Typically parents participate in their children's social skills groups and provide opportunities outside the group to practice the skills the child has learned. For instance, parents might invite friends over for a variety of simple activities. Over time, they provide the opportunity for their children to progress successfully to more complex social activities.

Despite such programs, however, hyperactive children may continue to have socialization problems when involved in play and activities with the children without the disorder.

Parent Training Programs Some parents are helped through parent training programs. In these sessions, parents learn strategies for managing their children's behavior. These are practical approaches to dealing with a child with ADHD.

For example, you need to be sure you have your child's attention when giving instructions; further, you need to issue instructions one step at a time rather than issuing multistep requests. Parents learn to increase structure in the child's life. They can help the child work toward successful experiences, which can help counteract some of the negative effects of the disorder. The emphasis is on observing the child and communicating clearly. Parents are taught negotiating skills, techniques of positive reinforcement, and other means of managing the behavior of the child with ADHD (see *Parent Management Training*, page 352).

Family Therapy This approach addresses the family stress normally generated by living with ADHD. Using a variety of techniques, families can change patterns of communication or interactions in order to help the child with ADHD. Sometimes, in the course of treatment, it may be discovered that a parent also has the disorder. Treatment of that parent may be helpful since the adult's behavior can affect how the child responds to treatment. (See *Family Therapy*, page 409).

Medication Since the 1930s, *stimulants* have been used to treat what we now call ADHD. Stimulant medications include methylphenidate (Ritalin), dextroamphetamine (Dexedrine), and pemoline (Cylert). Such medications increase the child's attention and reduce excess fidgeting and hyperactivity, allowing the child to focus on his work. It is thought that the stimulant medications improve the brain's ability to inhibit distracting stimuli and decrease impulsiveness. In many cases, children with ADHD who take medication can concentrate for longer periods and are better able to complete tasks and comply with requests.

The most common side effects of stimulant medication are reduced appetite and difficulty falling asleep. Some children report stomachaches and headaches, especially during the first few days of treatment. If these side effects continue, they can often be controlled by reducing the dosage of medication for a few days. It is crucial that the treating physician monitor your child's height and weight to assure that physical growth is progressing normally.

Although the results from the use of such medication can be dramatic, using stimulants to treat a child with ADHD is a serious decision. It has been suggested, too, that in some cases the diagnosis of ADHD has been used to justify medicating children who are perceived as active, expansive, or difficult by adults who lack the patience and willingness to tolerate them. There are a variety of factors to consider, among them the severity and duration of disorder, the short-term and long-term benefits of medication, and the potential side effects. Ask your child's psychiatrist to describe how the decision is made whether, when, and how to prescribe medication as well as the kind of follow-up needed to monitor its use. (See also *Medications*, page 413.)

When stimulants fail to modify the symptoms, or cause problematic side effects, antidepressant medication may be helpful in treating the symptoms of ADHD. Among those prescribed are imipramine (Tofranil), nortriptyline (Pamelor), and bupropion (Wellbutrin).

Children with ADHD are at higher risk for academic failure, social isolation, low self-esteem, depression, and disruptive behavior. For some, it can be a lifelong disorder, but for those children diagnosed and treated early, the condition can be effectively managed and their lives can indeed be productive, successful, and fulfilling. Most of these children develop greater control over their behavior and become less impulsive as they grow and mature.

Oppositional Defiant Disorders

All children are oppositional from time to time. There are also times in normal development when oppositional behavior is expected. This is especially true when the thrust towards separation is most intense, around the ages of two and three, and again in early adolescence.

However, openly uncooperative and hostile behavior becomes a serious concern when it is so incessant and fierce that it stands out when compared with other children's behavior and when it affects the child's social, family, and academic life.

■ **IDENTIFYING THE SIGNS**

It's not easy to distinguish oppositional defiant disorder (ODD) from age-appropriate normal oppositional behavior. Symptoms of the disorder tend to mirror, in exaggerated form, child-rearing problems common in all families. In addition, different families have various levels of tolerance for oppositionality. In some, a minor infraction of the rules produces major consequences, while in more tolerant homes, oppositional behaviors are largely ignored until they cause ongoing difficulties.

In children with ODD, there is a pattern of uncooperative, defiant, and hostile behavior toward authority figures that seriously interferes with the youngster's day-to-day functioning. Regularly, they lose their temper, argue with adults, actively defy adult rules, refuse adult requests, and deliberately annoy others. The symptoms are seen in multiple settings—at home, at school, in the neighborhood—and are not simply the result of a conflict with a particular parent or teacher.

Blaming others for their mistakes, these children often appear touchy, angry, resentful, spiteful, or vindictive. Although overtly aggressive behavior tends to be limited, some children engage in mild physical aggression. However, their language tends to be aggressive and often obscene.

Children with ODD were, in many instances, fussy, colicky, or difficult-to-soothe as infants. During the toddler and preschool years, when a certain degree of oppositional attitude is considered normal, ordinary points of contention in the family become battlegrounds for intractable power struggles with these children. These oppositional episodes typically center around eating, toilet training, and sleeping. Temper tantrums are usually extreme in a child with ODD.

Children with ODD consistently dawdle and procrastinate. They claim to forget or fail to hear and, as a result, are often referred for hearing evaluations, only to be found to have normal hearing. The issue is not obeying what was heard rather than a problem with not hearing.

As the child matures, struggles may center on keeping his room neat, picking up after himself, taking baths, going to bed on time, not interrupting or talking back, and doing homework. In all instances, winning becomes the most important aspect of the struggle. At times a child with ODD will forfeit cherished privileges rather than lose the argument.

Milder forms of ODD are limited to the home environment, while, at school, the child may be more passively resistant and uncooperative. More severe forms involve defiance toward other authority figures such as teachers and coaches.

The child typically has little insight and ability to admit to the difficulties. Rather, he tends to blame his troubles on others and on external circumstances. He is always questioning the rules and challenging those he perceives to be unreasonable.

Before puberty, the rate of ODD is higher in boys than in girls. In adolescence, the disorder is equally shared.

■ Causes and Consequences

It appears that oppositional defiant disorder arises out of a circular family dynamic. A baby who is by nature more difficult, fussy, and colicky, may be harder to soothe. The parents often feel frustrated and unsuccessful as parents. If they perceive their child as unresponsive or "bad," they may begin to anticipate that the child will be unresponsive or noncompliant. They may then become unresponsive or unreliable in return, adding to the child's feelings of helplessness, neediness, and frustration.

As parents attempt to assert control by insisting on compliance in such areas as eating, toilet training, sleeping, or speaking politely, the child may demonstrate resistance by withholding or withdrawing.

As a child matures, increasing negativism, defiance, and noncompliance become misguided ways of dealing with adults. In this way, the disorder may be a tenacious drawing out of the "terrible twos."

The more a child reacts in defiant, provocative ways, the more negative feedback is elicited from the parents. In an attempt to achieve compliance, the parents or authority figures remind, lecture, berate, physically punish, and nag the child. But far from diminishing oppositional behavior, these kinds of responses toward the child tend to increase the rate and intensity of noncompliance. Ultimately, it becomes a tug-of-war and a battle of wills.

When such patterns typify parent-child relationships, discipline is often inconsistent. At times, parents may explode in anger as they attempt to control and discipline their child. At other times, they may withhold appropriate consequences which soon become hollow threats. As the child continues to provoke and defy, parents lose control. Then, feeling regret and guilt, especially if they've become verbally or physically explosive, the parent may become excessively rewarding and gratifying in order to undo what they now perceive to have been excessive discipline or punitive consequences.

When a child starts school, this pattern of passive-aggressive, oppositional behavior tends to provoke teachers and other children as well. At school the child is met with anger, punitive reactions, and criticism. The child then argues back, blames others, and gets angry.

These children tend to have difficulty adapting at school. Their behavior can cause disruption in the classroom and interfere with social and academic functioning. When their behavior and defiance affects their schoolwork and performance, children often experience school failure and social isolation. This, coupled with chronic criticism, can lead to low self-esteem. Usually, ODD children feel unfairly picked on. In fact, they may believe that their behavior is reasonable and the treatment and criticism they receive unfair.

In many cases, oppositional disorders coexist with attention-deficit/hyperactivity disorder. In fact, the impulsivity and hyperactivity of ADHD can greatly amplify the defiance and uncontrolled anger of ODD (see page 337). Symptoms of ODD may also occur as part of major depressive disorder (see page 329), obsessive-compulsive disor-

der (see page 315), or mania (see *Bipolar Mood Disorder,* page 332). Some children with separation anxiety disorder (see page 308) may also have oppositional behaviors. Clingy attachment merges into or possibly reflects oppositional defiance. There also seems to be a correlation between ODD in a child and a history of disruptive disorders, substance abuse, or other emotional disorders in other family members.

■ HOW TO RESPOND

Parents who are concerned that their child may have ODD should seek a professional evaluation. This is important as a first step in breaking the cycle of ineffective parenting of the "bad child." During the evaluation process, parents may come to appreciate the interactive aspect of this disorder and look for ways to improve their management of the child. Books and parenting workshops given under the auspices of churches, schools, and community agencies may also help parents respond better to the needs of their children.

Once ODD has been diagnosed, the child and adolescent psychiatrist or other professional may recommend a combination of therapies for ODD. Among the options your clinician may recommend are following:

Parent Training Programs Some parents are helped through formal parent training programs. In these sessions, parents learn strategies for managing their children's behavior. These are practical approaches to dealing with a child with ODD. The emphasis is on observing the child and communicating clearly. Parents are taught negotiating skills, techniques of positive reinforcement, and other means of managing the behavior of the child with ODD (see *Parent Management Training*, page 352).

Individual Psychotherapy The therapeutic relationship is the foundation of a successful therapy. It can provide the difficult child with a forum to explore his feelings and behaviors. The therapist may be able to help the youngster with more effective anger management, thus decreasing the defiant behavior. The therapist may employ techniques of cognitive-behavioral therapy to assist the child with problem-solving skills and in identifying solutions to interactions that seem impossible to the child (see *Cognitive-Behavioral Therapy*, below). The support gained through therapy can be invaluable in counterbalancing the frequent messages of failure to which the child with ODD is often exposed. (See also *Individual Psychotherapy*, page 404).

Family Therapy Problems with family interactions are addressed in family therapy. Family structure, strategies for handling difficulties, and the ways parents inadvertently reward noncompliance are explored and modified through this therapy. This approach can also address the family stress normally generated by living with ODD. Sometimes in the course of treatment, a parent is also found to have a psychiatric disorder. Treatment of that parent may be helpful since the adult's behavior can affect how the child responds to treatment. (See *Family Therapy*, page 409).

Cognitive-Behavioral Therapy Behavioral therapy can help children control their aggression and modulate their social behavior. Children are rewarded and encouraged for proper behaviors. Cognitive therapy can teach children with ODD self-control, self-guidance, and more thoughtful and efficient problem-solving strategies. (See *Cognitive-Behavioral Therapy*, page 407).

Social Skills Training When coupled with other therapies, social skills training has been effective in helping children smooth out their difficult social behaviors that result from their angry, defiant approach to rules. Social skills training incorporates reinforcement strategies and rewards for appropriate behavior to help a child learn to *generalize* positive behavior, that is, apply one set of social rules to other situations. Thus, following the rules of a game may be generalized to rules of the classroom; working together on a team may generalize to working with adults rather than against them. Through such training, children can learn to evaluate social situations and adjust their behavior accordingly. The most successful therapies are those that provide training in the child's natural environments—such as the classroom or in social groups—as this may help them apply the lessons learned directly to their lives.

Medication Medication is only recommended when the symptoms of ODD occur with other conditions, such as ADHD, obsessive-compulsive disorder (OCD), or anxiety disorder (see pages 337, 315, and 311). When stimulants are used to treat attention-deficit/hyperactivity disorders, they also appear to lessen oppositional symptoms in the child. There is no medication specifically for treating symptoms of ODD where there is no other emotional disorder.

Conduct Disorders

Children misbehave for a variety of different reasons. Perhaps they don't understand the rules, they feel they need to assert their own autonomy, or maybe they wish to test the limits imposed on them. However, some children misbehave because they are experiencing internal distress: anger, frustration, disappointment, anxiety, or sorrow. The younger a child is, the more likely he is to call attention to his distress through his behavior. As a child matures, however, there is an expectation that he will be increasingly able to resolve much of his distress on his own and will express his feelings through words rather than outwardly directed misbehavior.

There are also children, however, whose behavior is consistently troubling to others. In these cases, the children's behaviors are outside of the range of what is considered normal or acceptable for their level of development. Perhaps most alarming is that many of these children show little remorse, guilt, or understanding of the damage and the pain inflicted by their behavior.

Increasingly, we read stories in the newspapers of children who routinely set fires, torture animals, or torment other children. We hear of young children who join gangs and cruise the streets, terrorizing others. In extreme cases, there are those who physically, sexually, or murderously assault others.

When their behavior is extreme and highly disturbed, the temptation is to dismiss these children as scary, lost, or bad to the core. Increasingly, there is a tendency to relegate them to the criminal or juvenile justice system. Yet, by doing so, we may overlook the fact that some of these children have serious underlying emotional disorders.

Conduct disorder is the most frequently diagnosed childhood disorder in outpatient and inpatient mental health facilities. It is estimated that 6 percent of all children have some form of conduct disorder, which is far more common in boys than in girls.

The earlier a child displays extremely disturbed behavior, the worse the likely outcome. Some studies report that high levels of activity and unmanageable behaviors at the age of four anticipate behavioral problems in later school years. This is the best time to intervene. Behavioral problems at eight are reliable predictors of adolescent aggression. Many of the underlying causes of childhood behavioral problems, including family violence and abuse, can be prevented or successfully managed. It's important to look beyond obvious negative behaviors to identify underlying biological, emotional, or social vulnerabilities that might be present and treatable.

■ IDENTIFYING THE SIGNS

Children who are physically and verbally aggressive much of the time should be evaluated to determine whether they have a conduct disorder. Their aggression typically is expressed toward people and animals, in the destruction of property, in lying and theft, and in serious violation of society's rules.

In order to diagnose conduct disorders, a clinician will look for a repetitive and persistent pattern of behavior which violates the basic rights of others. Usually, a child with a serious conduct disorder will engage in a number of unacceptable activities and seems to lack empathy and have little or no remorse, awareness, or concern that what he is doing is wrong.

For example, children with conduct disorders might bully, threaten, and intimidate others. Typically, they initiate physical fights, sometimes using weapons such as bats, bricks, broken bottles, knives, and guns. These are the children and, later, the adolescents and adults who get involved in muggings, purse-snatching, armed robbery, sexual assault, animal torture, and rape. Some children deliberately set fires, vandalize, and destroy others' property.

Children with conduct disorders might shoplift or break into other people's homes, buildings, or cars. They might mislead people or systematically lie to obtain goods or favors or to avoid obligations. Examples of violating rules include repeatedly staying out of the home overnight, breaking curfew, running away from home, and truancy. The severity of these behaviors differs from child to child.

Clinicians distinguish between types of conduct disorder. Children younger than ten years of age, especially those previously diagnosed with oppositional defiant disorder (see page 345), are said to have *childhood-onset conduct disorder*. When the symptoms and behaviors of conduct disorder are not evident until after the child has reached ten years of age, the diagnosis is *adolescent-onset conduct disorder*. Youngsters with childhood-onset CD are typically more aggressive; they are likely to have few or no friendships with their peers. They are also at greater risk of persistent conduct disorder or of developing antisocial personalities as adults. Few girls develop childhood-onset conduct disorder; girls are more likely develop adolescent-onset conduct disorder.

■ Causes and Consequences

The diagnosis of conduct disorder implies a multitude of potential criminal behaviors as well as numerous possible biological, psychological, and social problems. Because of its inclusive nature, the diagnosis of conduct disorder is common.

It is likely that biochemical underpinnings and genetic vulnerabilities interact with environmental forces and individual characteristics to cause conduct disorders. When there are serious problems during pregnancy, delivery, and the postnatal period, for example, youngsters may demonstrate a variety of neurobiological problems as development proceeds. These include slowed development of gross and fine motor coordination (required for throwing a ball, skipping, or writing) and impaired short-term memory. It is not uncommon for children with these kinds of problems to show poor judgment, trouble regulating feelings, and difficulty controlling their actions as well. They have trouble modulating their behaviors, feelings, and even their biological rhythms of sleep and appetite.

Many conduct-disordered children have learning problems, especially in the area of verbal skills. However, since many come from homes in which actions speak louder than words, lack of parental stimulation and modeling may account for these weaker verbal skills. Difficulties in reading and language contribute to academic difficulties, especially in the higher grades when so much depends on understanding and using the written word. Language deficits may also contribute to an inability to articulate feelings and attitudes, so that a child out of frustration might resort to physical expression.

In many instances, unrecognized and untreated learning disabilities and cognitive deficits create deep frustration for a child. Thus the entire school experience gets filtered through defeat and humiliation. A child may then stop attending school or skip challenging classes. Once he leaves the structure of school, which might have been a major opportunity he had for experiencing positive success, he may engage in delinquent behavior. For some children, delinquent behavior, however unlawful or unacceptable, provides them with both the status among their peers and the opportunity for some reinforcement that they are unable to find at school.

Antisocial behavior abounds in poor inner-city areas, together with high rates of family instability, social disorganization, infant morbidity and mortality, and severe mental illness. These factors may well cause and perpetuate severe conduct disturbances in a child.

More and more, child psychiatrists and other mental health professionals are recognizing the role played by prior physical, sexual, and emotional abuse in the genesis of certain kinds of aggressive and inappropriate sexual behaviors. Substance abuse or mental illness in parents—psychosis, severe depression, or manic-depressive disorders—can have a grave impact on the children in the family.

Substance abuse and conduct disorders commonly coexist in a child or teen. It is not unusual for deeply troubled children, some eleven or twelve or younger, to use drugs and alcohol. Children use drugs and alcohol for a number of reasons. They may try to self-medicate for anxiety, depression, thought disorders, and hyperactivity. They may wish to blot out memories of abuse or treat insomnia. Some children think they need drugs or alcohol just to be able to face another day in a violent, abusive household.

The most violent children are likely to be those who have been the most severely abused. Their way of dealing with the abuse is to dissociate their feelings from action (see *Childhood Trauma and Its Effects,* page 319). They thus appear to be cold, detached, and lacking in empathy. Yet, because it is sometimes the most deeply disturbed children who tenaciously maintain their bravado, boast of their offenses, and threaten others with further violence, they are often passed over to the justice system. These are the children whose mental health needs are most often neglected and who are at highest risk for criminal and violent behavior in adolescence and adulthood.

Conduct disorder can also occur along

with other disorders such as attention-deficit/hyperactivity disorder (see page 337). Though depression is more often associated with withdrawal than aggression, it can include irritability and rage (see *Depressive Disorders*, page 329). Furthermore, episodic destructive behaviors or sporadic episodes of robbery and burglary may represent the manic phase of a bipolar disorder (see page 332). Especially violent children may demonstrate psychotic thinking (see *Psychotic Disorders,* page 372). Suicidal behavior is not uncommon with children who have conduct disorders. Rather than dismiss such attempts as manipulative behavior, adults must take them seriously, not only in terms of the immediate danger, but as desperate expressions of frustration, pain, anger, and impulsiveness. Conduct-disordered children are usually not very articulate about their feelings and may demonstrate their pain with self-destructive behaviors.

■ HOW TO RESPOND

No single treatment approach has been shown to be effective for conduct disorder. Because children with conduct disorders may suffer from myriad biological, psychological, and social vulnerabilities, a combination of treatment methods seems most effective. Frequently this combination of therapy will include liaison with community resources including juvenile court staff or probation officers.

When children with severe behavioral problems are brought to a child and adolescent psychiatrist or other mental health professional, treatment usually begins with a comprehensive evaluation. This will likely include a detailed medical history and psychological testing. A neurological examination is often valuable to determine if any central nervous system dysfunction contributes to the child's problems. A psychoeducational evaluation may uncover intellectual and learning problems that could cause academic and behavioral problems that will put a child at risk for truancy and disruptive behaviors.

The clinician will probably try to determine if the child has any control over his aggressive acts and if he can anticipate a violent episode before it happens. An attempt is also made to ascertain whether the child feels any remorse or empathy toward victims after such episodes.

Parent Management Training Many times, treatment for conduct disorders is family-focused. Parent management training has been used with considerable success with aggressive children, particularly when parents themselves can make changes. When parents can participate fully, this method helps parents to encourage appropriate behaviors in their children and to use discipline in more effective ways. In order to interact with their children in new ways, parents learn to use positive reinforcement, to link misbehavior to appropriate consequences (see *Discipline and Consequences,* page 132), and to develop ways of negotiating with their children. Once the parent-child relationship smoothes out, many children are better able to navigate their social and academic worlds in a more productive manner.

Family Therapy This approach can help families learn less defensive ways of communicating with each other. It can foster mutual support, positive reinforcement, direct communication, and more effective problem-solving and conflict resolution within the family. (See *Family Therapy,* page 409.)

Social Skills Training Skills training focuses on children in order to enhance their problem-solving abilities. Through such programs, a child can learn to identify problems, recognize causation, appreciate consequences, and consider alternate ways of handling difficult situations. Efforts are made to diminish mistrust of others, especially adults, and to help the youngster open up more and seek support and encouragement. Most children with conduct disorder feel alone and alienated from the adults in their lives.

School-based treatment programs are in wide use throughout the country, whether in special residential treatment environments, designated community-based schools, or specific programs in mainstream schools. These programs can reintegrate the student back into regular classes as the child's behavior allows.

Individual Psychotherapy A therapeutic relationship with a caring, consistent, older individual, when coupled with other treatments that help structure the child's behavior and with cognitive-behavioral therapies (see page 407), the youngster with conduct disorder symptoms may be helped in figuring out why he does what he does. As the child grows older, the clinician helps the child better understand his emotions and actions and how to deal with both.

Medication Since conduct problems tend to arise from a tangle of biological, emotional, and social stresses, there is no single class of medication that has been found especially useful. Even when another psychiatric disorder has been clearly defined—such as hyperactivity, depression, manic-depressive illness, or schizophrenia—medication is seldom sufficient on its own to alter conduct-disorder symptoms. If the child has underlying ADHD (see page 337), the use of stimulants may help reduce negative behaviors and impulsiveness. Lithium, a mood stabilizer, and anticonvulsants have also been shown to reduce impulsive aggression. Used judiciously to address specific clinical findings in each individual case, appropriate use of medication can enhance the success of other treatments.

Given the rather dramatic and disturbing quality of the conduct-disorder symptoms, it is important to keep in mind that not all behaviorally disturbed children progress to become seriously antisocial or criminal as adults.

On the other hand, more often than not, ongoing, adequate medical, emotional, educational, and social supports are required for many years—sometimes well past the age of eighteen—if children with severely disturbed behavior are to develop into adaptive adults, and go on to live meaningful lives and become productive members of society.

12

Developmental Disorders

■ ■ ■

It is the wish of all expectant parents: *Please let my child be born healthy.* In the moments after her birth, you anxiously count fingers and toes to reassure yourself that everything looks perfect, and that your baby is fine and healthy. Most of the time that's the case.

Sometimes even at birth there are signs that there is a problem that might impede the child's development. Initially these signs are most likely physical. We know that an infant born with certain physical characteristics such as those seen in children with Down's syndrome, for example, will have some degree of mental retardation. More often than not, however, developmental problems are not apparent for many months or even years. A parent takes home a physically healthy baby who may then lag behind her peers in her development of language or motor skills. Or, as is often the case, everything seems normal until the child is well into elementary school and unable to read with proficiency or demonstrate other academic skills.

In this chapter we will discuss some developmental disorders. Some such as autism and mental retardation can be very debilitating, although some individuals with these disorders are capable of functioning at a higher level and learning more than was once thought. We also will explore learning disorders that can be frustrating for both the child and parents, and can threaten academic success. The chapter will also focus on how to recognize these developmental disorders and how best to respond to them.

Mental Retardation

Mental retardation is the currently accepted term for a disability in which intellectual abilities are significantly below average. Such limited intellectual abilities can cause problems with a child's daily functioning—communicating, self-care, home living, social development, relating to other children, play, and success in school. More severe mental retardation can often be identified early in life, but it is not a disease or an illness in itself.

In some children with mental retardation, delays in development are apparent in infancy. With others, the limitations in intellectual ability are not evident until the child enters school and begins having difficulty meeting academic expectations.

Roughly one in a hundred adults is thought to have mental retardation, but as many as 3 percent of school-age children are diagnosed to be mentally retarded. The higher prevalence during the school years may reflect the fact that some children with mental retardation improve their adaptive abilities and functioning so that the diagnosis no longer applies. The disorder is more common in boys than girls, perhaps because congenital anomalies and prematurity is more common in boys.

How is a diagnosis of mental retardation reached? Sometimes it is apparent at or soon after birth. An infant born with Down's syndrome, for example, has certain physical characteristics easily identified by the physician, and one of the consequences of this genetic disorder is mental retardation, which can range from mild to severe. Other children may show physical differences that suggest mental retardation, like an abnormally small head, low-set ears, flattened nose bridge, wide or high-arched palate, short or long limbs, or abnormally shaped fingers or toes. The presence of such physical characteristics does not mean a child is mentally retarded, but suggests the need to further evaluate the child and closely monitor development.

The degree or severity of mental retardation is classified by IQ (intelligence quotient) test scores. The average IQ is 100. Children with an IQ between 51 and 70 are considered to have mild mental retardation; those with an IQ between 36 and 50 have moderate mental retardation; a score between 20 and 35 indicates severe mental retardation. An IQ below 20 would be termed profound mental retardation. IQ scores suggest the types of interventions required and gives clues to the long-term outcomes.

Many schools classify children with mental retardation by levels of academic functioning. A child who masters the skill of a typical third grader is labeled *educable*. If the maximum skills are those of first grade, the child is termed *trainable*.

The diagnosis of mental retardation is made by measuring a child's IQ, but this is not an easy task when a child has limited language or motor skills. Other developmental tests may be used to measure language, motor, thinking, and social skills. While developmental delays are often identified in this process, such delays may or may not be a consequence of mental retardation. Some children will catch up over time while others will later be recognized as having mental retardation.

■ IDENTIFYING THE SIGNS

As most new parents know, it's easy to suspect a problem when the younger baby next door is doing something that your child hasn't mastered yet. No matter how many times you study the developmental charts that assure you that not all typical babies are walking at twelve months, you can't help but wonder if something is wrong when your child isn't toddling around.

Trust your intuition and seek help if you are concerned. Always talk with your child's physician about any significant delay in language, motor, or social development.

Most of the time nothing is amiss. However, some signs are worthy of investigation. A delay in the development of language is the most obvious (see *Language and Speech Disorders*, page 364, for details on the milestones of language development). If your child is not talking by age two or two-and-a-half, that is reason for investigation. In the same way, seek a professional evaluation if, at three, your child has a few words but is still not able to communicate; or, at four, the child has some language but seems frustrated with getting her thoughts out. Seek help, too, if your four-year-old child seems not to understand you, and you find yourself making eye contact, speaking slowly, and limited to no more than one request at a time.

Some children with mental retardation have delayed motor development. Some sit, crawl, and stand later than expected. They may learn to walk but still be awkward when running or climbing. There may be room for concern if your preschool child has difficulty using crayons, pencils, scissors, or eating utensils, or with buttoning, zipping, and tying. Some children show difficulty with learning, as they fail to remember the names of objects or people and struggle to learn colors, numbers, or letters. They may seem to have less ability to use fantasy and imagination when playing and continue to prefer to play by themselves when their peers have begun to play with other children.

Remember: Not all children with delays like those described here will have mental retardation but they all should be evaluated.

■ CAUSES AND CONSEQUENCES

There are many causes of mental retardation. Sometimes the cause is readily apparent while in many instances, especially in individuals with mild retardation, no cause is discernible.

Most cases of mild mental retardation are due to environmental and psychosocial factors, such as lack of stimulation, inadequate nutrition, and exposure to toxins such as lead. About 25 percent of cases of retardation are due to either a chromosomal or metabolic abnormality. The most common chromosomal abnormalities contributing to mental retardation are Down's syndrome and fragile-x syndrome.

Down's Syndrome This is the most common form of mental retardation. Approximately seven thousand infants are born in the United States each year with Down's syndrome, representing roughly one in seven hundred live births. It is due to an extra chromosome.

Fragile-X Syndrome This the most common form of inherited mental retardation and second only to Down's syndrome in frequency as a known chromosomal cause. It is estimated to occur in about one of every 1,250 male births and one of every 2,500 females. Unlike most cases of Down's syndrome, it is carried from one generation to the next.

An example of a metabolic disorder that leads to mental retardation is phenylketonuria (PKU), a congenital deficiency of a particular enzyme (phenylalanine hydroxylase). Infants born with this rare disorder have normal brains that quickly begin to deteriorate because of the absence of the enzyme. Because a special diet can prevent the severe brain damage of untreated PKU, many states require a simple blood test at birth to screen for this disorder.

Certain conditions during pregnancy can increase the risk of mental retardation. These include toxemia; placenta previa; exposure to radiation during the first trimester; the ingestion of certain harmful drugs during pregnancy; alcohol use by an expectant mother; and maternal malnutrition. In addition, intrauterine infections such as German measles, complications of premature birth, and birth trauma can cause mental retardation.

Sometimes infants who are born with average intellectual potential develop diseases like meningitis and encephalitis that damage the brain and nervous system.

The consequences of mental retardation depend upon its severity. It is estimated that 30 to 70 percent of adults with IQs between 60 and 80 live independent lives without special help from outside agencies. On the other hand, people with a more severe level of retardation generally require supervised living arrangements and more support.

■ **HOW TO RESPOND**

If your child shows signs of developmental delay or mental retardation, a thorough evaluation should be done to determine the extent and cause of the problem. Discuss your concerns with your family doctor. All public school systems are required to have services available to evaluate children in need. These evaluations may involve consultations with specialists such as a pediatrician, child psychiatrist, clinical psychologist, neurologist, audiologist, and speech pathologist.

In many cases of mild retardation, the early years pass without anyone realizing that the child is anything but a little slower in learning the basics than her peers. Unfortunately, it is often only when she begins school and falls behind her classmates that suspicions are raised and the child gets the special help she needs.

Getting Help Once a child is diagnosed with mental retardation, the goal is to help her reach her full potential and learn to cope with her disability as effectively as possible. Treatment must address the complex interplay of neurobiological and psychosocial factors. A comprehensive approach involving several disciplines may be appropriate: speech and language therapy, occupational therapy, special education services, environmental changes, skills development, behavioral intervention, psychological services, social skills training, and medications are all possible needs and interventions.

If the diagnosis is made during infancy, your state, county, or municipality may have infant stimulation programs which focus on developing the infant's cognitive, physical, and emotional development. These programs also make the parents aware of the child's strengths and weaknesses. In most cases of mild mental retardation, the delays in development are the result of too little stimulation in the children's environments. Programs such as Head Start for toddlers and preschoolers can help identify mental retardation or other special needs and develop an individualized intervention program before the child begins public school.

Regardless of the severity of your child's disability, federal law gives her the legal right to an education from birth through age twenty-one. The majority of children with mental retardation can be taught in special education classes in public schools. Children with more severe retardation may require schools or even residential programs specifically designed to meet their needs. Most children with less severe levels of mental retardation are "mainstreamed" (included in regular classrooms) for at least part of their school day. This concept of inclusion is likely to expand in the future in public schools.

Most communities have some resources and supports, like recreational and social programs, for people with mental retardation.

Parental Adjustment The diagnosis of mental retardation can be difficult for parents to accept and understand. Most parents have high hopes for their children. Hearing that a child's potential is limited can be painful. Parents often feel angry, sad, betrayed by nature, and may take on a burden of guilt, feeling that it's all their fault and that somehow they failed their child.

Allow yourself the pain of hearing the diagnosis and the confusion when thinking about your child's future. Seek help through your family doctor or the professionals who evaluated your child. Parent support groups are available in most areas. Health-care and school personnel can refer you to resources in your community for appropriate help and guidance. Find a professional team that can both inform you of your child's current needs and help you plan for the near and long-term future. Since planning for more than six months at a time is often frustrating, learn to think in six-month units of time: For example, each spring, plan for the following fall.

Planning for the Future A major concern for the parents of a youngster with mental retardation is the future. *Where will she live? Who will take care of her when we are no longer up to the task?*

Many adults with mild mental retardation grow up to live independent or semi-independent lives. They hold jobs, drive cars, raise families, and are productive members of society. Those with more limited mental abilities often are able to live in supported living or group homes where with some supervision they can care for themselves. These adults can often be trained for jobs that require skills within their abilities. Employment in the community with supports provided to the employer and employee to ensure success is a reasonable goal for many adults with mental retardation.

CEREBRAL PALSY

Cerebral palsy (CP) is a movement disorder thought to be the result of a brain abnormality or brain damage incurred during pregnancy, delivery, or in early life. The prevalence of moderate to severe cerebral palsy is thought to be roughly one or two cases per thousand live births. It can be associated with mental retardation.

There are two main types of cerebral palsy. *Spastic* cerebral palsy involves increased muscle tone in certain muscle groups that produces constant muscle contractions. Over time, this can lead to musculoskeletal deformities. In *nonspastic* cerebral palsy, there are involuntary movements of various muscle groups, which can increase during times of stress or excitement.

A comprehensive treatment approach is appropriate. In addition to the care provided by your child's doctor, other interventions may be required by an orthopedic specialist, neurologist, developmental pediatrician, speech therapist, nutritionist, or physical and occupational therapists, as well as psychological support by a child and adolescent psychiatrist or other mental health professionals.

FETAL ALCOHOL SYNDROME

Although it is entirely preventable, fetal alcohol syndrome is one of the most common causes of mental retardation. Excessive alcohol exposure during pregnancy produces an incidence of approximately two cases of fetal alcohol syndrome in every thousand live births.

Children with fetal alcohol syndrome often have low birth weights, smaller than normal head circumferences, tend to be irritable, and may be mildly to moderately retarded. They may have poor coordination, decreased muscle tone, and a short attention span.

Treating fetal alcohol syndrome should include parental counseling, and the children often require special educational programs and assistance in behavioral management. Family therapy is also recommended to help the family cope with the many aspects of this disorder.

Learning Disorders

In classrooms across the country, there are children struggling to learn. They are of at least average intelligence—some, in fact, are extremely bright—yet for a variety of reasons, they have difficulty learning.

The terms *learning disorders, learning disabilities,* and *learning differences* describe various impairments in academic skills. In order to help the child, however, it is important to distinguish clearly which skill(s) is impaired. The worrisome disorders that we will discuss in this section are not due to physical disorders, such as a hearing loss or visual impairment. Children with learning disorders process information differently from other youngsters as the result of neurological changes in the brain. Learning disorders interfere with the child's ability to learn or to express what she knows.

These disabilities may run in families and are often preceded by delayed development of language during the preschool years. Perhaps one in ten school-age children have such problems. Boys and girls are likely to be equally affected, though boys are more prone to become frustrated and to misbehave, so they are more often referred for testing and thus are more frequently diagnosed than girls. Early identification can prevent or limit frustrations and failure at school, which often leads to other emotional, social, or family problems.

Reading Disorder Proficiency in reading is often considered *the* key to success in other academic areas. Reading achievement is closely linked with mastery of spelling and mathematics, and reading difficulties may make mastering other basic skills more difficult as well. Typically poor readers are poor spellers, although the converse is not necessarily true.

A child with a reading disorder reads significantly below expected level. Recent research has found that difficulty with reading is related to the ability to distinguish subtle differences in sounds. There are forty-four units of sound, or *phonemes,* in the English language and the first step in reading is to connect the proper sound to the symbols of the alphabet on the page. Children who are far behind in reading skills may have problems with associating these sounds with the symbols they see, as well as with interpreting words, tracking words, visually discriminating between similar letters (mistaking d for b, for example), and various other cognitive skills necessary to master reading. These may include difficulties in sounding out words and, eventually, reading comprehension.

Delays in learning to read may be the result of a combination of cognitive, psychological, and social factors. The most frequently associated diagnosis with reading disorder is attention-deficit/hyperactivity disorder (see page 337).

Note that the term *dyslexia* also refers to a learning disability in which a child has difficulty in learning to read. This problem is identified when the child has difficulty in identifying words—*word blindness*—or a tendency to reverse letters and words in reading and writing. The name dyslexia was once common, but since its narrower definition includes only certain signs of reading difficulties, the term dyslexia more recently has been superceded by the broader category of *reading disability.*

Spelling Disorder There is considerable overlap between reading and spelling difficulties. However, the processes involved in learning to read and spell are different. It is sometimes thought that if a child has learned to read, then spelling will naturally follow. But that is not necessarily true.

Children may read words they cannot spell, and may spell other words without being able to read them, further suggesting that reading and spelling skills are independent of one another. Spelling problems tend to last longer than reading problems. Unlike more visual skills, phonics is important in the development of spelling, although visual memory for spelling patterns may play a major role in spelling proficiency.

Disorder of Written Expression The emphasis on expressing one's thoughts or ideas in writing surfaces relatively late, typically in late elementary or early middle school. Children who have difficulty expressing themselves in written compositions may have isolated or multiple problems.

In order to write, the child needs to master two tasks. First, the child must have control over the muscles of the hands. A child who has had difficulty learning to color, use scissors, to button or zip clothing, or learn to tie shoelaces may have difficulty learning to control the pencil and to form letters. Second, the child must master the language of writing, that is, the ability to put thoughts on paper using the correct words in the proper order and to be able to spell and to use correct grammar, punctuation, and capitalization. Children with problems of written expression may have handwriting problems, but they always have problems with the language of writing.

Children with this disorder are particularly at risk because writing problems tend to be given less credence than reading disabilities and children who have both writing and reading problems have severe learning disabilities. It is not uncommon for parents and teachers to blame writing problems on the child, ascribing the difficulty to laziness, noncompliance, or poor motivation. Consequently children with writing disorder are particularly vulnerable to frustration.

Mathematics Disorder Four basic factors are involved in math achievement: language, conceptualization, visual-spatial ability, and memory. Some children with language disabilities cannot relate the symbols of math problems to everyday situations, which may make it impossible for them to calculate word problems. A child who is failing math may have a visual processing problem that makes recognizing numbers difficult. Trouble concentrating and excessive impulsiveness, common traits among children with attention-deficit/hyperactivity disorder (see page 337), may impair a child's ability to organize mathematical details. Some children who fail math have memory problems, forgetting what they are doing or what numbers they are using for computation, a problem that is especially noticeable during mental arithmetic.

Disability in mathematics is not as well understood as problems related to other subjects, and the diagnosis of a math disorder is generally not made until several years after beginning school. Since math is learned, math difficulty can be due to poor teaching or to long periods of absence from school.

Social-Emotional Learning Disability Children with this disability usually have both social and academic problems. Their social disabilities are often attributed initially to persistent school failure, isolation from other children in special classes, and the high prevalence among them of behavioral patterns associated with attention-deficit/hyperactivity disorder that provokes disapproval of peers and teachers. However, it is now recognized that some youngsters also have serious problems with social skills acquisition.

Such learning-disabled children often have chronic difficulties with interpersonal relationships. They fail to interpret appropriately the emotional responses of others and do not make correct inferences about other people's emotional behaviors. Sometimes these learning disorders are referred to as *nonverbal learning disabilities.*

Parents commonly observe their child's inability to make friends. The youngster may not be invited to parties or to join in play. The child is excluded from the group, and finds herself isolated or on the fringes of the group. Although children with social-emotional learning disability may be intelligent and have good general academic knowledge, they may be unaware that others are not interested in their particular preoccupations. In this sense, these children appear to be insensitive to the wishes and desires of others.

Motor Skills The ability to control one's movements is important to school success. A child who cannot jump or run with the same ease as the other children may develop poor self-esteem, which can adversely affect school performance. Those whose fine motor skills (the ability to use their hands) are lacking may not be able to write, draw, or even tie their own shoelaces. Children with poor fine motor skills may have hand-eye coordination deficits. Some children know what they want to do but can't execute the appropriate sequence of motor movements. Many of these children also have problems with speech articulation. Motor memory deficiencies may account for motor skill disabilities. For example, a child will temporarily forget how to make a certain letter.

■ IDENTIFYING THE SIGNS

Most learning disabilities become apparent during elementary school when a child fails to keep pace with classmates, although in some cases the disability is recognized later. Poor school performance is one general symptom of a learning disorder, although not all children who do poorly in school are learning disabled.

Signs of a possible reading disability include excessive use of finger-pointing (an indication that the child may have problems visually tracking words), the inability to instantly recognize familiar words, difficulty in sounding out unfamiliar words, and problems with remembering and retelling a story that the child has just read or that has been read to her. Errors are made because words are remembered by features like their initial letters or length. These children read words by sight recognition and have difficulty with new words. They tend not to spell phonetically.

Children with motor skill deficiencies may have awkward pencil grasps. When writing, they frequently hesitate and cross errors out, often making their work illegible. Those with mathematics disorder may also have difficulty forming numerals and in putting them in proper sequence. They may also have difficulty in applying computational skills to problem-solving. Although younger children learn to count, it is ordinarily not until formal math instruction is begun that the diagnosis is made.

■ CAUSES AND CONSEQUENCES

It is often unclear what causes a learning disability. In some cases a certain disability may be apparent in several family members, indicating a genetic component. In some children, there appears to be a difference in the way the brain functions and processes information, although the brain does not show evidence of damage. For others the cause is never apparent, leading some experts to speculate that these disorders are the result of developmental delays or immaturity.

Although the causes may be unclear, the consequences are not. If not promptly recognized and treated, a learning disorder can lead to chronic academic failure, low self-esteem, and to social and emotional problems for the child.

■ HOW TO RESPOND

If you suspect that your child has a learning disorder, talk to the teacher and the principal. Public schools can assemble a diagnostic team or, as parents, you may elect to have a private evaluation done. The evaluation team may include a developmental pediatrician, child neurologist, child psychiatrist, clinical psychologist, and an educational specialist.

There are three parts to an evaluation for learning disorders. First, an intelligence test helps identify your child's level and ability and specific difficulties. Next, specific achievement tests measure reading, writing, and math abilities. The third part of the evaluation measures specifically how your child processes information, integrates and understands it, stores information, and how the information is retrieved by talking or writing. This psychoeducational evaluation will identify whether there is a learning disorder and if so, the specific nature or type of disorder and the appropriate remedial interventions necessary.

The impact of a learning disorder is often minimal if that disorder is diagnosed and treated early in a child's school career. Treatment will involve working with professionals and developing a plan (called an *Individualized Education Plan* or IEP) to fit the individual needs of your child. In some cases that may involve a change in schools or a special education class for all or part of the day. Some children with slight disabilities may be capable of staying in their regular classroom as long as they have extra tutoring after school.

School success is essential for a child's feelings of self-confidence and self-esteem. Poor school performance can result in secondary emotional or social problems, resulting in misbehavior in school or at home. Children with learning disorders may be anxious or depressed and have difficulty relating to their classmates; family stress may also result. Counseling may be advised to address such emotional, social, or family problems. Children whose learning is hampered because of the signs and symptoms of attention-deficit/hyperactivity disorder (the inability to concentrate and/or hyperactivity) may benefit from the use of medication as well (see page 337).

Language and Speech Disorders

One of the most fascinating things you will do as a parent is to watch your child's ability to communicate develop. The birth cry of the newborn soon evolves into the coos and babbles that will in the ensuing months become simple words.

Like all human development, speech and language does not adhere to a rigid timetable. There is a wide range of so-called normal development. Your first child, for example, at fifteen months may have been speaking in simple sentences, a feat that your second child doesn't accomplish until closer to the age of two, perhaps because of his sibling interpreter.

The acquisition of language is one of the first learning tasks of our young children. It is also one of the most important because failure to master one's native language and speak it correctly often is a harbinger of later academic problems. Difficulties in verbal expression can be the result of speech or language problems or both. Speech is defined as the ability to communicate through sounds; language is the ability to communicate through speech.

In order for a child to have the capacity to develop normal speech and language, four systems must be intact. They are:

- **The child's environment.**
  A youngster must have adequate interaction and stimulation to learn to speak. Quite simply, babies who are spoken to often, learn to speak. Learning to speak includes mastering rhythm, inflections, and sequencing. Those who live in homes where people talk little to each other typically have a more difficult time developing language skills.

- **The child's input system.**
  In order to learn language, a child must be able to clearly hear and not be hearing impaired.

- **The central speech and language system.**
  The acquisition of a language depends upon an intact and functioning central nervous system. Although the neurological basis of language processing in children is not fully understood, it is believed to be principally a function of the left side of the brain.

- **The production system of speech.**
  Clear speech depends upon the ability to correctly shape the sounds of language. A child who has a defect of the larynx, throat, nasal, or oral cavity will have difficulty being understood.

A child must learn two types of language. *Receptive* language is the ability to decode words and sentences. In order to be able to do this, a child must be able to interpret what she hears and assign a meaning to words and sentences. This requires that she be capable of applying selective attention to speech sounds. She then must discriminate between similar sounds she hears. From there, she learns to identify basic units of sound as words with meaning.

The second basic type of language is *expressive* language. Used to express ideas, expressive language involves the ability to call up relevant words from one's repertoire, then to arrange them in phrases or sentences that conform to our standards of grammar, and then be able to incorporate the ideas into sentences in a manner that can be understood by others.

■ IDENTIFYING THE SIGNS

Most children begin to speak between the ages of one and two. By age two, many youngsters have a vocabulary of about fifty words and can combine two or three words in a statement. Subsequently, both vocabulary and the ability to speak in longer and more complex phrases develops rapidly.

Speech problems can include delayed speech, articulation problems, and stuttering. *Language problems* may involve difficulties receiving, processing, or expressing language.

Most children's mastery of language proceeds unevenly. Between the ages of eighteen months and five years, words form in her mind faster than they can roll off her tongue. As a result, about 30 percent of preschoolers have difficulty pronouncing certain words or sounds, although almost all children can be completely understood by the time they are in first grade. Stuttering is also common during these early years. Most young children stutter at one time or another for a few weeks or months. Stuttering is a long-term problem in only about 1 percent of children.

Thus, a few bumps on the road to speech and language development is considered normal. However, studies suggest that as many as 4 to 5 percent of children do have a speech and language impairment. As a parent, how do you know if your child is among this group?

There are certain milestones or signposts that speech development is proceeding on course. If your child's development lags well behind this general timetable, you should discuss your concerns with your child's doctor.

- At about one month of age your infant's activity should stop when she hears a sound; and she should be making sounds herself.

- Generally the three-month-old looks in the direction of a speaker, smiles in response to speech, and coos.

- Usually the normal five-month-old responds to her name and is beginning to mimic sounds.

- A seven-month-old will respond with gestures to words like "up" or "bye-bye."

- At ten months, most infants speak their first words and can accurately imitate pitch variations.

- A twelve-month-old will respond to certain verbal requests and gestures (for example, "Come here" or "Give it to Mommy") and is beginning to attach names to certain objects.

- A twenty-one-month-old should be able to identify pictures of familiar objects and should be using words more than gestures to express what she wants.

- By age two, young children should be able to combine words such as "We go," or "Push me." She should be able to understand fairly complex sentences and refer to herself by name.

- Most three-year-olds are able to sustain a conversation, putting two or three sentences together and moving from topic to topic.

- By the time your child is four, her speech should be clear enough to be understood (for the most part) by a stranger.

Signs that your preschool child has a problem in language and speech development include:

- At six months she does not turn her eyes and head to a sound coming from behind.

- At ten months she does not respond to her name.

- At fifteen months she does not understand and respond to words such as "no-no," "bye-bye," and "bottle."

- At eighteen months she is not saying at least ten words.

- At twenty-one months she does not respond to simple directions.

- At two years the child does not point to body parts when asked to do so.

- At two-and-a-half years she cannot be understood by the family.

- At three years the child uses no simple sentences, does not ask questions, and cannot be understood by strangers.

- At three-and-a-half years she consistently fails to add the final consonant. Thus it is *ca* instead of *cat*.

- At four the child still stutters frequently.

- At any age, she speaks in a monotone, in and inappropriate pitch, consistently speaks too loudly or too softly, or often in a hoarse voice.

■ CAUSES AND CONSEQUENCES

There are many things that can cause a child to have problems developing speech and language skills. Sometimes there is a physical cause for a speech and language problem such as a hearing loss. A child whose hearing is impaired will be slow to develop language and the words she does say may not be spoken clearly. Delayed speech and language acquisition are common in children with mental retardation, brain damage, and pervasive developmental disorder, while cerebral palsy and an abnormality such as a cleft palate can result in speech disorders. In many cases, however, there is no physical cause for a speech or language disorder.

Language dysfunction may be of receptive or expressive language or both. Think of the last time you tried to conduct a telephone conversation over a bad connection. An individual with a receptive language disorder spends every day as though she was trying to do just that. Many find it hard to distinguish the forty-four different units of sound, or *phonemes,* in the English language and have difficulty blending them together into words. Children with impaired language reception often have problems sounding out words phonetically. Not surprisingly, these children typically have problems in school, especially with reading, spelling, and writing. They tend to be restless and inattentive in class and slow to adapt socially.

Expressive language disorders include: problems with resonance and voice; and fluency disorders such as stuttering, articulation disorders, and problems in language formulation. The child who knows what she wants to say but just can't seem to get it out, who can't tell a story, or who commonly can't think of the words she wants may have an expressive language disorder.

Resonance and Voice Difficulties Disorders of resonance and voice include pauses in conversation, repetitions or prolongations of sounds, and lapses in response. These disorders typically require the services of a speech therapist.

Stuttering The most common fluency disorder is stuttering, a problem that usually begins when a child is around three or four, although it can appear even in adolescence. The vast majority of preschoolers who stutter outgrow the problem. The most productive course of action is to ignore the stuttering. Don't make your child repeat her words, don't correct her. About 1 percent of stutterers, however, get worse rather than better and require speech therapy. Over the years there have been many theories as to the cause of stuttering. Currently many speech therapists believe that the vocal cords in a stutterer are prone to spasm as a reaction to stress, which interrupts the air flow required for normal speech. Therapy is geared toward teaching techniques that help minimize this disruption.

Articulation Disorders These are the most common disorders of expressive language. Examples include the substitution of one sound for another, the inability to produce a certain speech sound, and sound distortions. In some children, articulation problems occur infrequently; in others the problem may be so severe that their speech is consistently unintelligible. A child with an articulation disorder may have an abnormality in the oral cavity that interferes with proper speech. Hearing loss sometimes is responsible for an articulation disorder.

Children with expressive language disorders typically are shy in class and may, to avoid talking, rely on gestures or on single words or phrases to get their message across. It is common for these children to be quiet in class so as not to attract the attention of the teacher. Even when they know the answer, they resist raising their hand to avoid having to talk. Some of these children may have a history of delayed language development. Many, although not all, have difficulty learning to read. The problem often becomes more apparent as the child grows older and the writing demands of school intensify.

■ **HOW TO RESPOND**

If you suspect that your child has a speech or language problem, consult your child's doctor. A speech-language evaluation can help clarify the nature of the difficulty and prescribe appropriate therapy to improve the problem.

The first step in an evaluation may be a hearing test. A child with a history of ear infections, for example, may have suffered a slight hearing loss that could be interfering with speech development. The doctor also will ask you questions about the child's early development to determine if there was anything amiss. A psychologist may conduct testing for learning disorders or mental retardation. A speech therapist may well be consulted for further evaluation and to suggest treatment. Early diagnosis and appropriate speech-language therapy is important. Therefore, if you suspect speech and language disorders in your child, seek professional assistance as soon as possible.

Pervasive Developmental Disorder

The term *pervasive developmental disorders* (PDD) includes a group of disorders characterized by qualitative impairments in the development of social interaction, communication skills, and imaginative activity. Two types of PDD are autism and Asperger's disorder (see *Asperger's Disorder*, page 371).

Most infants are social creatures who need contact with others to thrive as much as they need food and water to survive. You need do nothing more than enter the room and your baby smiles, coos in delight, and with every muscle in her body indicates her wish to be picked up.

Occasionally, though, a child does not respond in this expected manner. Instead, the child seems to exist in her own world, a place characterized by repetitive routines, odd and peculiar behaviors, and a total lack of social awareness and interest in others. These are characteristics of the pervasive developmental disorder *autism*.

Autism is one of the most severe developmental disabilities of childhood and has a prevalence of between two and five per ten thousand children and perhaps higher. This disorder occurs three to four times more frequently in boys than girls, and is fifty times more common in the siblings of children with autism than in the general population.

■ IDENTIFYING THE SIGNS

Typically, autism is identified by the time a child is thirty months old. The disorder is often discovered when parents consult the youngster's doctor, having become concerned that the child is not yet talking, resists cuddling, and avoids interactions with others.

Upon questioning, the parents of a child with autism often recall that even as an infant the child did not want to be cuddled. The social smile that we've come to associate with babies was absent or extremely delayed, and the child did not respond with the anticipatory excitement that the normal infant shows prior to being picked up by a trusted loved one.

A child with autism is generally withdrawn, aloof, and fails to respond to other people. Most children with autism will not even make eye contact. When hurt, the child will not seek the comfort of a parent's arms. These children do not play with others but instead spend their time in solitary activities.

Certain behaviors suggest that children with autism may have abnormal responses to sensory stimuli. Children with autism may place their hands over their ears to avoid the stimulation of loud noises. Conversely, at other times they may be unresponsive to sound and thought to be deaf. They may also lick or smell objects or toys they pick up.

Children with autism often engage in odd and ritualistic behaviors that reflects a need to maintain a constant environment. They are likely to have certain routines that must be followed otherwise they will erupt into a rage. A child with autism, for example, may have to touch objects in a certain order or food must be presented to the youngster in a certain way. The child with autism may demonstrate strong taste aversions, eating a very narrow range of foods.

It is common for children with autism to engage in strange body movements such as constant rocking, whirling, teeth-grinding, and head-banging. Sometimes the behaviors are carried out to the point where injuries are sustained, suggesting an insensitivity to pain.

Many children with autism do not speak at all or may only mimic sounds. Those who do speak often will reverse their pronouns, referring to themselves as he or she. Nonsense rhyming and other idiosyncratic language also is common.

The severity of autism varies widely, from

mild to severe. Some children with autism are very bright and do well in school, although they have problems with social adjustment. Others function at a much lower level. Intelligence tests conducted on children with autism reveal the majority to be in the mentally retarded range but, because many children with autism don't communicate verbally, IQ testing should be performed by professionals with expertise in evaluating developmentally delayed children. Occasionally, a child with autism may display an extraordinary talent in art, music, or another specific area.

■ CAUSES AND CONSEQUENCES

The cause of autism remains unknown, although current theories indicate a problem with the function and possible structure of the central nervous system. Although conditions such as maternal rubella, encephalitis, and meningitis appear to predispose a child to autism, these are not considered causes. There is now substantial evidence that autism is a genetic disorder, although the specific mode of inheritance remains unclear. We do know, however, there is no validity to the theory that autism develops because of parents' behavior toward the infant.

■ HOW TO RESPOND

If your young child exhibits some of the characteristic symptoms of autism, see your child's physician for a thorough evaluation. This evaluation usually includes a clinical history, hearing test, neuropsychiatric interview, and observational assessment. A variety of psychometric instruments are available for the assessment of children with autism such as the *Childhood Autism Rating Scale* (CARS), the *Autistic Diagnostic Interview* (ADI), and the *Autism Diagnostic Observation Schedule*. A few children require more extensive testing of the blood, urine, and brain, but such additional studies are usually conducted in order to confirm that the condition is not the result of a brain or metabolic disorder.

While strides in the treatment of autism have been made in recent years, this is still a difficult disorder to treat. The successes are limited and depend upon the severity of the problems. Currently, the most effective treatments involve a combination of special education, behavior modification, and sometimes the use of medications. There is no specific medication for autism so before prescribing medications, your child's doctor will seek to identify behaviors, such as aggression, compulsivity, hyperactivity, social withdrawal, and depression, to monitor while medication is being taken. The treatment program must be carefully tailored to the needs of the individual child.

Autism may worsen as a child moves into adolescence, although a small number of youngsters with autism actually improve during the teen years. About 40 to 50 percent of children with autism develop some degree of speech. Many have some improvement in their ability to interact socially, but it is rare for a person with autism to have a sexual relationship based on intimacy or to marry. Treatment may lead to broad and positive changes in the child's development and produce an overall reduction in autistic symptoms and behaviors.

ASPERGER'S DISORDER

In the past, children with Asperger's disorder were often diagnosed as having autism. While this disorder does share some characteristics with autism, there are some important distinctions.

In general, the child with Asperger's disorder functions at a significantly higher cognitive and intellectual level than the typical child with autism. While about three-quarters of children with autism test in the mentally retarded range, those with Asperger's disorder test in the normal range. Unlike the lack of language or, in milder cases, the severe language delay associated with autism, children with Asperger's usually are using words by the age of two, although as they get older their speech patterns are often odd, their words spoken in a monotone. Similar traits are often found in family members.

Like the child with autism, one with Asperger's disorder does not successfully interact with her peers. These children tend to be loners. They have little empathy for others and are highly egocentric, displaying eccentric behaviors. A child with Asperger's, for example, may spend hours each day preoccupied with counting cars that travel past on the street or watching only the weather channel on television. Coordination difficulties, as well as speech delays, are also common with this disorder. Some research has shown Asperger's disorder clustering in families.

The treatment and intervention for children with Asperger's disorder follow the same general guidelines as those for children with autism. Children with Asperger's disorder also have an increased vulnerability to psychiatric disorders such as mood disorders (see page 332), schizophrenia (page 373), and obsessive-compulsive disorder (page 315).

The outcome for children with Asperger's disorder is generally more promising than for those with autism, probably because of their higher intellectual and communication abilities.

13

Psychotic Disorders

■   ■   ■

Psychotic disorders, which are also referred to as thought disorders, are among the most serious of mental disorders. The symptoms of schizophrenia, brief reactive psychosis, and toxic psychosis are upsetting and often frightening to both the parents and the child. In most cases, a child with one of these disorders requires professional attention as soon as symptoms develop.

Imagine the concern and fear of the parents of a child of nine who suddenly becomes very agitated and apprehensive. The youngster tells his parents about hearing voices that are yelling bad things at him. He may tell them he's afraid that there's poison gas in his bedroom or that the police are watching their home because aliens have landed there. He is unable to answer his parents' questions, yet he continues to ramble, often incoherently, and his parents have trouble following his thinking. Such experiences are terribly frightening for child and parents alike.

Psychotic disorders are characterized by an impairment of the thinking processes that enable the child to perceive thoughts, actions, and even the world as they really are. When so impaired, the child is incapable of thinking logically. The disorganized or unusual behavior and emotional reactions of a child with psychosis follow no particular pattern but rather can be described as illogical; inappropriate to the situation; puzzling to the observer; uncharacteristic for the child; or as making no sense. A child with a thought disorder may speak in a disorganized, incoherent, or incomprehensibly vague manner. The child with a thought disorder may speak rarely or in torrents of words that have little to do with reality. The concept of "conversation" may not be applicable, as there is an absence of the mutual perception, awareness, and understanding basic to a normal conversational exchange.

Believing that one has heard, seen, or otherwise experienced something that is not present, an *hallucination*, is common to some psychotic thinking disorders, as are *delusions,* false and often bizarre beliefs that a person clings to, despite overwhelming evidence to the contrary. Careful diagnosis by an expert is necessary to distinguish between true hallucinations or delusions and imaginary companions or excessive fantasizing, which are not characteristic of thought disorders.

Evidence of unusual, distorted, or impaired thinking can occur in other mental disorders in children. Youngsters under seven years of age often have trouble thinking logically and tend to associate unrelated matters simply because their ability to organize thoughts is immature. Children with mental retardation, especially those with a mental age below seven years of age, also may think illogically. Children with developmental disorders that result in impaired communication skills may appear to think illogically when the difficulty is actually a result of their deficit in language skills. These symptoms may be misdiagnosed as thought disorders.

Hallucinations occur in some children with seizure disorders (see page 295) and in some youngsters with post-traumatic stress disorder (see page 319). The obsessions of children with obsessive-compulsive disorder and the body image distortions characteristic of the teen with anorexia nervosa clearly interfere with logical thinking, but these disorders are not psychotic disorders.

The subject of this chapter is the mental disorders which seriously impair children's abilities to function in reality, including schizophrenia, brief reactive psychosis, and toxic psychosis. Any child with disordered thinking or behavior should be evaluated immediately by a clinician with expertise in these serious mental disorders of childhood.

Schizophrenia

Schizophrenia is a chronic psychotic disorder that typically begins in late adolescence or early adulthood. An estimated 2.5 million Americans have been diagnosed with this severe mental illness. This disease is found in about 1 percent of the world's population but is rare in children under twelve years of age. Schizophrenia is a disorder that affects males and females equally, although in young children it is more common in boys.

Schizophrenia is more likely to emerge during the college years or in adulthood. There are, however, a few children who have the symptoms of this disorder before age twelve. The diagnosis is difficult to make in young children because they often cannot clearly describe such symptoms as delusions and hallucinations. The stage of a child's development also has an impact on diagnosis: a normal preschool child's conversation may move illogically from one topic to another; in an older child, however, that pattern may be symptomatic of the disorganized thinking that occurs in a psychotic disorder.

■ Identifying the Signs

Children with schizophrenia are impaired in their ability to understand reality in a manner consistent with their age, development, intellectual capability, education, and culture. Adults and children alike who develop schizophrenia have difficulties in the *form* of their thinking, which may involve illogical thinking, trouble organizing thoughts, or loose associations; they may also have an impairment in the *content* of their thinking, exemplified by hallucinations and delusions.

Illogical Thinking A child with schizophrenia frequently speaks in a manner that makes it difficult to piece together the elements of what is being said. The word "because" may be used inappropriately. Assertions made in a single sentence may contradict one another. Unnecessary or inappropriate reasons may be given for statements. A child might justify forgetting something because of something else utterly unrelated— *I left my books at school because the teacher wore a blue hat.* Another verbal example of illogical thinking might be, *I didn't like the cake but I like it as a cake.* Keep in mind that children under seven may also talk in a rambling or disorganized manner, yet that is typical for their stage of development.

Loose Associations Loose associations are defined as unconnected shifts from one topic of thought to another. In a child with schizo-

phrenia, the elements in the child's conversation seem unrelated. The listener is often confused, puzzled, and unable to follow the thread of the conversation because the child has offered no verbal connections for changes in topic.

Hallucinations When children experience hallucinations, they usually assert they are hearing or seeing something or someone that doesn't exist in reality. Their brains process "experiences" in a manner similar to dreaming. Thus, the "experiences" are strictly internal events and are not based on information from their environment.

Hearing voices is a type of hallucination in schizophrenia. Children have described these voices as telling them to "kill my sister," "run away from home," or "to do bad things." Some children with schizophrenia report hearing voices that called them derogatory names. Sometimes they recognize the voice as a relative's or friend's; other times it is described as a stranger's voice. Hallucinations in young children with schizophrenia may also be related to such familiar childhood themes as monsters, cartoon characters, or toys. Some children report visual hallucinations in which they see anything from fierce monsters to benign shapes and scenes.

Delusions Young children do not often develop delusions. These fixed, false, and often bizarre beliefs that cannot be changed by logical argument are much more common in adolescents with a psychotic disorder. Delusions are rare in children under seven but when a young child has bizarre delusions, it is often a sign of a serious disorder such as schizophrenia.

Delusions are outside the realm of what is acceptable for a specific community, culture, or religion. A child's conviction that certain foods will poison him is an example. Bizarre delusions are those outside the realm of the possible, such as a child's belief that his actions are controlled by messages from the television. On the other hand, some children have false beliefs which are not delusions, like the preschooler who reports a chair deliberately tripped him or the school-age child who believes his friends are responsible for his losing his temper.

Schizophrenia doesn't always follow a set pattern. Some children with schizophrenia will become withdrawn, others boisterous; some become fearful, others unexplainably aggressive. These children have severe problems relating to their environment and to the people around them. They fail to establish social relationships with other children, communicate poorly, and they misunderstand verbal and nonverbal social cues from others. They behave in bizarre ways, causing further social rejection. Children who develop schizophrenia may also have unusual fears, experience puzzling or fluctuating emotional states, and may have developmental delays.

■ CAUSES AND CONSEQUENCES

No one has as yet been able to identify the cause or causes of schizophrenia. Abnormalities in brain development have a role. Genetic factors are also involved—this is supported by the higher incidence of the disorder within families where one or more members have thought disorders. The malformation or changes in the brain may also be the result of a viral infection during the second or third trimester of pregnancy. A variety of studies provide data to support each of these theories, but most researchers believe that ultimately a constellation of several factors will be identified as the cause of schizophrenia.

Schizophrenia is a lifelong disease which can be controlled but not cured. Over the years great gains have been made in controlling the disease with medication, therapies, and family education. Typically the child has periods with severe symptoms but, with treatment, there is considerable improvement. Unfortunately, each episode may result in some loss of capacity to function at the child's previous ability level.

■ HOW TO RESPOND

If your child is having any of the psychotic symptoms discussed earlier in this section or is severely withdrawn and emotionally unresponsive, you should seek help. You may want to start with your child's doctor, who will then refer you to a child and adolescent psychiatrist or other mental health clinician if schizophrenia or another psychotic disorder is suspected. Both you and your child will need support as you struggle to accept and deal with one of these serious and frightening disorders.

Treatment usually begins with a comprehensive evaluation. The child and adolescent psychiatrist will question you about the child's developmental history and symptoms, and interview both you and your child and spend time observing the child's behavior. A neurological examination is often valuable to determine if any central nervous system dysfunction is contributing to the child's symptoms. A psychoeducational evaluation may uncover intellectual and learning problems as well as problems the child may be having in getting along with other children the same age. As part of this evaluation, a battery of tests may be administered to assess everything from intelligence to the child's ability to think logically. During the comprehensive evaluation, careful consideration will also be given to other possible disorders before reaching a diagnosis of schizophrenia.

Hospital Care During periods of acute illness, hospitalization may be necessary to provide a safe and structured environment. The immediate goal is to control the acute psychotic symptoms. It is important to work closely with your child's psychiatrist, nursing staff, and educational specialists to construct the best plan for your child. Once he leaves the hospital, the plan should help him learn as much as possible in school and reach his highest level of functioning with his communication and thinking disability.

Medication If your child is diagnosed with schizophrenia, medication treatment will be geared to his particular symptoms. Antipsychotic medications may be prescribed to help decrease excitability, to improve the ability to think in a logical manner, and reduce hallucinations. These med-

ications have greatly improved life for many people with schizophrenia. The medications appear to work by blocking certain chemical receptors in the brain. Among the antipsychotic medications that may be prescribed are chlorpromazine (Thorazine), haloperidol (Haldol), and thioridazine (Mellaril).

Antipsychotic medications may cause side effects such as sun sensitization, loss of bladder control, weight gain, blurred vision, dry mouth, the feeling of faintness, severe muscle spasms, and tremors. Several newer antipsychotic medications seem to have fewer side effects.

Other Therapies While antipsychotic medications are effective in controlling or reducing some of the acute symptoms of psychosis, they usually do not help the social withdrawal that is common in people with schizophrenia. Thus, psychotherapy and family counseling usually are key components of treatment in an effort to help the child with schizophrenia live as normal a life as possible and to help the family cope with the child's illness.

Brief Reactive Psychosis

Occasionally children and adolescents suddenly develop psychotic symptoms that last for a few hours or days. This disorder is called brief reactive psychosis. These youngsters have typically been under great stress. They may have experienced a death in the family, witnessed acts of violence, or have themselves been abused sexually or physically. Some children whose emotions tend to fluctuate, who are impulsive, and who have difficulty maintaining stable relationships also experience brief reactive psychosis.

▪ IDENTIFYING THE SIGNS

Sudden disorganization of behavior, speech, and emotional reactions are the key symptoms of brief reactive psychosis. The child may appear agitated, confused, and may adopt bizarre behavior or dress. For no apparent reason, the child may suddenly start screaming; or he may adopt the opposite approach and withdraw into a silent shell. When he does talk, his speech may be nonsensical, full of incomprehensible and repetitive phrases. Hallucinations or delusions sometimes occur in brief reactive psychosis but are usually short-lived.

▪ CAUSES AND CONSEQUENCES

Brief reactive psychosis appears to be linked to extremely stressful events in the child's life. Other causes have not been identified or extensively studied in children. The acute psychotic symptoms often resolve quickly with total recovery in a few days. After the episode, however, some children may feel depressed, have lowered self-esteem, and feel anxious about future attacks.

▪ HOW TO RESPOND

Support and safety are two primary concerns in helping a child experiencing reactive psychosis.

Medication Antipsychotic medications are often effective in treating acute psy-

chotic symptoms; among those that may be prescribed are chlorpromazine (Thorazine), haloperidol (Haldol), and thioridazine (Mellaril).

Other Therapies Medications will not eliminate the problem that caused the psychosis in the first place. Thus, individual psychotherapy (see page 404) is often recommended to help the child learn to cope with the emotional trauma that precipitated the episode. (See also *Childhood Trauma and Its Effects*, page 319.)

Hospital Care During periods of acute illness, hospitalization may be necessary to provide a safe and structured environment. The immediate goal is to control the acute psychotic symptoms.

Toxic Psychosis

Toxic deliriums or toxic psychoses occur when a medication, illicit drug, alcohol, medical condition, or head injury results in a person developing temporary psychotic symptoms.

▪ IDENTIFYING THE SIGNS

Unlike schizophrenia or other psychotic disorders where impaired thinking and communication are major symptoms, toxic psychosis is more likely to cause vivid, disturbing hallucinations or other perceptual problems. These sensory experiences may be extremely frightening and may be accompanied by agitated, uncontrolled, and even aggressive behavior. Children with this condition appear to suddenly "lose their mind" and become disoriented, unable to identify who or where they are or why they are behaving in a certain manner. They may also have signs of fluctuating alertness.

■ CAUSES AND CONSEQUENCES

In childhood, the most common cause of toxic psychosis is medication. The condition can occur as a symptom of too much medicine, such as when too large a dose of the psychostimulant methylphenidate (Ritalin) is given. It may also occur as a side effect to a normal dose of a common medication, including over-the-counter antihistamines or other cold medications. Other causes in children are alcohol, amphetamine-like drugs (for example, "speed" or cocaine), or hallucinogenic drugs (LSD, psilocybin).

Some children hallucinate when they have high fevers. Certain illnesses, such as kidney disease, may also result in the buildup of waste products in the body that have toxic effects, producing disorientation and hallucination.

Most children who develop a drug-induced psychosis recover once the drugs are out of their systems. The gravest danger occurs during the psychotic episode, when a person may accidentally cause serious harm to himself or others.

■ HOW TO RESPOND

Toxic psychosis requires immediate medical intervention to identify the cause and provide appropriate treatment. Consult your child's physician or take your child to the local emergency room immediately.

Hospital Care Persons experiencing toxic deliriums may need to be protected so that they will not harm themselves or others. A quiet place and the presence of a trusted person may be the best environment. Continual verbal support and encouragement can be very helpful. Some children may require a brief stay in the hospital.

Medications In some cases, antipsychotic drugs are administered to control the distorted perception (hallucinations) and decrease the child's agitation.

As part of the diagnosis, your doctor may advise laboratory tests to determine whether a particular medication, illicit drug, or chemical triggered the psychosis. If the cause of the psychotic episode was drug or alcohol abuse, a substance abuse evaluation and treatment program may be necessary.

14

Sleep Disorders

■ ■ ■

As an adult, perhaps you've learned not to take a good night's sleep for granted. While most people come to expect occasional sleep problems as they age, we also tend to think that our children are immune to such difficulties. After all, the expression "to sleep like a baby" was coined to describe the blissful state of oblivion we typically ascribe to childhood sleep.

In actuality, children, like adults, don't always sleep well. Along the developmental path, roadblocks often fall between children and their ability to get a good night's sleep. Studies have shown that many of the so-called problem sleepers during infancy are still having problems as preschoolers. In one study of eight-month-old infants with sleep problems, 41 percent were still problem sleepers at the age of three, and 84 percent were still having sleep difficulties three years later.

Falling into a sound asleep at the end of a busy day spent in exploration should be the most natural thing in the world. Why then do children have sleep problems? The explanations vary, depending upon the developmental stage of the child. A toddler, for instance, grappling with the anxiety of separating from parents, may have problems falling asleep (see *Separation Anxiety*, page 18). When she finally does sink into slumber, it is only to awaken several times during the night. Individual and family variations in infant temperament, nutrition, physical discomfort, milk allergy, family conflict, and bad sleep habits all can contribute to sleep problems in young children.

In this chapter we will explore some of the most common sleep problems that face children. We are indeed fortunate to live in an era when sleep problems are beginning to be taken seriously and there are health-care professionals who specialize in the research and treatment of sleep disorders in both children and adults. For the most part, though, childhood sleep problems do not require the expertise of specialists. The nightmares, night terrors, and sleepwalking—some of the topics we will explore in this chapter—that may be keeping your child and perhaps you, as well, from getting a good night's sleep usually resolve in time.

Nightmares

Few parents have escaped being summoned in the middle of the night by an anxious or crying child who reports dreaming that she was falling off a cliff or had seen monsters.

A child's night, like an adult's, is punctuated by dreams during rapid eye movement (REM) sleep, a sleep stage that occurs four or five times over the course of an average night. Most dreams are relatively uneventful and easily forgotten. Some are wonderful while others classify as nightmares.

Nightmares typically begin at age three or later. Although everyone has a bad dream from time to time, many children have nightmares that frighten them enough to disturb their parents.

■ IDENTIFYING THE SIGNS

Nightmares usually occur late in the night as the periods of REM sleep grow longer. The child awakens from the nightmare, fully aware of what's going on (this level of awareness distinguishes a nightmare from a *night terror,* of which a child has minimal recall; see *Night Terrors,* page 381). Depending upon her nature and how frightened she is, she may summon you with her cries or come into your bedroom to tell you about the nightmare. Or she may calm herself and fall back to sleep. In the morning, she will usually be able to recall and tell you about the dream.

CAUSES AND CONSEQUENCES

Nightmares are often a response to stress or anxiety and may increase in frequency and intensity when a child is under stress. Traumas or events that cause fears in your child's life may be associated with nightmares. For some children, a scary bedtime story or movie may result in nightmares. Certain medications or the withdrawal of certain drugs also can induce bad dreams.

Occasional nightmares are not cause for alarm. They are most common between the ages of three and eight, when the child has an active fantasy life. Times of transition, such as when the child moves into a new home, starts school, or makes another life adjustment may also be a cause of nightmares.

■ HOW TO RESPOND

If your child has an occasional nightmare, your hugs and reassurances are probably the best response. You can also try to decrease some of the stress in her life. Be patient and supportive. A young child who has a night-mare about a monster and is then frightened to turn out the light will not be satisfied with your logical explanation that monsters simply don't exist. Rather, it may be more reassuring if you help her search her room (don't forget under the bed). When your search fails to turn up anything more threatening than a stuffed animal, she may feel less anxious about going to sleep. Another solution may be to let her sleep with the light on or with a night-light.

Avoid exposing your child to violent television programs or movies. In a sensitive child, even frightening bedtime stories can produce nightmares. Rather than telling stories that glorify fear or danger, choose tales in which people conquer their fears in the end or chose bedtime stories in which fear is not a prominent theme.

Some children have recurring nightmares that eventually begin to take a toll on their daytime behavior. Daytime irritability or fearfulness may be an example of this. If this is happening in your house, you may wish to talk to your physician about consulting a child and adolescent psychiatrist or other child expert, especially if there has been a traumatic event in the child's life (see also *Childhood Trauma and Its Effects,* page 319).

Night Terrors

The first time your child has a night terror, you may confuse it with a nightmare, albeit an abnormally severe one. If night terrors occur frequently and you watch your child scream and thrash in bed, her eyes wide with fear, you suspect you're dealing with something other than a bad dream.

Sleep or night terrors are not bad dreams. A child during a night terror, in fact, is not dreaming at all. Once the terror ends, the child soon goes back to sleep and, unlike the person who has had a nightmare, will have no recollection of the event the next morning.

It is most likely not an indication of severe emotional problems. We now know that, for the most part, these sleep disturbances in children are probably the result of a temporary delay in the brain's maturation. As the child begins to shift from one stage of sleep to another, there is interference with the usually smooth transition.

Night terrors typically surface when a child is around eighteen months old. Night terror attacks, like other parasomnias such as sleepwalking, are more common in boys than girls. In some children, night terrors may change to the related disorder of sleepwalking with increasing age.

■ IDENTIFYING THE SIGNS

Unlike a nightmare, a night terror usually occurs shortly after the child has fallen asleep, generally within the first three hours. Suddenly you may hear screams. You go into your child's room to find her kicking and thrashing, perhaps even punching the bed. Her eyes are open, wide with terror, but she doesn't respond to your questions. If you try to hold her to calm her down, she may push you away or even hit you.

Most night terrors last between thirty seconds and five minutes, although some have been known to last as long as twenty minutes. Some children have infrequent attacks, while others may have them every night. Usually once the child calms down, she returns to sleep immediately.

■ CAUSES AND CONSEQUENCES

Night terrors tend to run in families, as does sleepwalking. If both parents had night terrors when they were young, a child has a 60 percent chance of developing the problem; if one parent had night terrors, there is a 45 percent chance the child will also. Three percent of all children between the ages of eighteen months and six years have night terrors.

Aside from heredity, stress and excessive fatigue are thought to be factors in triggering night terrors.

Although it is frightening to see your child in the middle of a night terror, try not to be alarmed. As they mature, children usually outgrow these attacks.

■ HOW TO RESPOND

If your child is having night terrors, try to stay calm. Your main concern during the episode is that she not hurt herself. Stay in the room with her and intervene if you think she's in danger of falling out of bed or injuring herself, but otherwise don't restrain her.

Sleep monitoring in a laboratory is not recommended for night terrors but if you are uncertain about whether your child is really having a night terror or you need reassurance, some doctors recommend that the parents use a video camera to film the episode so that a doctor can verify the condition.

Some parents find that a brief (less than an hour) nap during the day may help reduce the incidence of night terrors. A new therapy to help prevent the attacks involves waking the child up prior to the time when attacks generally occur. A parent who wants to try this method should note the time the attacks occur for five successive nights. Then the parent should wake up the child ten to fifteen minutes prior to the time of the expected night terror. Keep the child up for five minutes or so and then let her return to bed. Since most night terrors in young children occur while the parents are still awake, this is an easy method of treatment and it may be worth your while to try it. In many children treated with this method, the problem disappeared after a week.

Medication For persistent night terrors, your child's physician may prescribe an anti-anxiety medication for a short period to change the sleep profile and eliminate the night terror.

Sleepwalking

Sleepwalking, like the related disorder night terror, is an arousal disorder of sleep that is thought to occur when the brain has difficulty making the transition from non-REM sleep to REM sleep, the sleep stage in which we dream.

Sleepwalking is actually a term that encompasses more than simply the action of walking. Sleepwalkers have been known to dress, pick flowers in the backyard, and rearrange furniture.

Perhaps as many as 40 percent of children have one sleepwalking incident; 1 to 6 percent have anywhere from one to four attacks weekly.

■ IDENTIFYING THE SIGNS

Sleepwalking typically occurs during the first one to three hours of sleep. Some children will get out of bed and walk around the house. A young sleepwalker's body movements are poorly coordinated and she doesn't seem to have a particular destination in mind as she aimlessly wanders through the house. Although her eyes are open during the episode, she will appear to be in a daze. If you wake her, she will be confused and disoriented. In the morning, she will have no recollection of the incident. Most episodes last anywhere from a few seconds up to thirty minutes.

Some young children will not actually walk but will simply sit up in bed, appearing to be awake when they actually are asleep.

■ CAUSES AND CONSEQUENCES

As with night terrors, sleepwalking tends to run in families. Other factors thought to induce an episode of sleepwalking include fatigue and prior sleep loss. In children, the problem typically surfaces during the preschool and early elementary school years, with the highest incidence found in children between the ages of six and twelve. Most

children who sleepwalk outgrow the problem by adolescence.

Sleepwalking in children is not a sign of an emotional illness. The biggest problem posed by childhood sleepwalking is the risk of injury. Children have been known to fall down stairs, hurt themselves bumping into furniture, or endanger themselves by leaving the safe confines of the home.

■ HOW TO RESPOND

Since arousal disorders such as sleepwalking are difficult to predict, it is important that the parent of a child who walks during sleep create a safe environment to minimize the risk of injury when these incidents occur.

Sealed windows, locked doors, and a gate at the top of the staircase will help protect the child who sleepwalks. To make the house safer, you also may want to avoid leaving objects, electrical cords, or small furniture in the middle of the bedroom where it can be tripped over. Some parents purchase an alarm that is triggered when the child leaves her bed.

In some children, sleepwalking incidents can be reduced by giving the child a brief late afternoon nap and by reducing stress in the child's life.

Medication   In severe cases, the anti-anxiety medication diazepam (Valium), which changes the sleep pattern, has been successful in reducing the frequency of sleepwalking episodes, although a tolerance may develop and, when the drug is discontinued, the sleepwalking will resume. If your child continues to sleepwalk into adolescence, a neurological examination to rule out sleep-related seizures may be warranted.

Bruxism

Bruxism is characterized by the grinding or clenching of the teeth during sleep.

About one in every seven people has bruxism. The disorder is most common between the ages of ten and twenty, although 50 percent of normal infants have a short-lived version that occurs during teething, typically at around the age of ten months.

■ Identifying the Signs

If your child has bruxism, the chances are you've heard a loud, grinding sound coming from her room at night, usually shortly after she's gone to sleep. In many cases, the dentist is the first person to recognize bruxism.

■ Causes and Consequences

There are several causes speculated for bruxism. Sometimes it can be caused by a problem with the *occlusion* of the teeth (the way the upper and lower teeth fit together in the mouth). In other cases, bruxism may be attributable to stress. Some individuals who grind their teeth at night are found to be suppressing anger or anxiety. Adults who have bruxism often find the problem increases after they drink alcohol.

The main consequence of bruxism is damage to the teeth.

■ How to Respond

If your child has bruxism that is damaging her teeth, your dentist can create a plastic guard that she can wear during the night to protect them from additional damage. Mouth braces or other orthodontic devices also may help if the child has an irregular bite.

Individual psychotherapy to reduce emotional distress may be necessary to get to the source of the problem, although bruxism may return when treatment stops.

Part IV

SEEKING HELP

■ ■ ■

In these two chapters you will find practical advice and useful information to guide you when you think professional mental health intervention may be called for. This section presents the who, where, when, and why of getting help, and the kinds of mental health treatment available—individual psychotherapy, medication, behavioral and cognitive techniques, family and group therapy, and psychiatric evaluation and diagnosis.

"My family."   *Amy, age 8*

15

When and Where to Seek Help

■ ■   ■

As parents, we want our children to do well, to thrive and mature into healthy, happy, well-adapted individuals. Despite all our intentions and efforts, however, few children pass through childhood without challenges. Many children must deal with illness, neurological problems, learning disabilities, a move, a divorce, an illness or death in the family, or parental remarriage. A child's development can also be impeded by trauma, abuse, or parenting that is not well matched with a child's temperament or special needs or is routinely neglectful or inconsistent.

For most children, such events pose only a temporary challenge. They are resolved over time and the children are able to continue on their developmental journeys. Sometimes, however, children and their families need outside help in coping with these challenges or in dealing with their repercussions. Some children face a series of family and social upsets. Such children and their families may require professional help or treatment to address the difficulties so that youngsters can resume healthy development.

Determining when children need help beyond what their families can provide is not always easy for parents or other adults. Nor is it always clear what kinds of help are best suited to a given child's family and problems.

In this chapter, we will discuss the actual process and procedures involved in seeking help; the signposts indicating that professional intervention is warranted; what exactly treatment means; and what it can accomplish.

When and Where to Seek Help

Parents are often in the best position to recognize when their child is having a problem. Even when parents do recognize that their child is having trouble, it is not always apparent that professional help is necessary.

The first step in assessing the cause of your child's difficulty is to ask him. Sometimes, gently asking your child questions— *Why are you constantly sad? Why did you steal that toy from Annie's house? You seem upset, is something bothering you? Why are you so mad?*—will reveal the issues with which he's struggling. Giving him adequate time to respond is necessary; talking honestly with your child about his feelings may also be helpful.

Consulting your child's physician or teacher, or your minister, priest, or rabbi may help you identify problems—both in the child and within the family—that could be causing the upset. Frequently, a teacher will notice your child's trouble and call you in. Working together, you can often get the child back on track before schoolwork or social interaction is affected.

As a rule, it is the combination of parents' growing concerns and the observation of outsiders such as teachers, physicians, and family members, that lead parents to consult a clinician for their child. There are a few

signs, when present over an extended period of time, that indicate that your child has problems which could benefit from treatment. For children younger than six years of age, these include:

- Behavior problems in day care or preschool program.
- *Excessive* fears, worry, anxiety, or crying.
- Hyperactivity or fidgeting beyond that observed in other children his own age.
- Trouble sleeping or persistent nightmares.
- Constant disobedience, aggression, or provocative opposition to authority.
- Frequent, unexplainable temper tantrums.
- More problems separating from parents than other children.

For older children six to twelve years old, signs include:

- Marked decrease in school performance.
- Poor grades in school despite the fact that the child is trying hard.
- Excessive fears, worry, anxiety, or crying.
- Hyperactivity or fidgeting beyond that observed in other children his own age.
- Persistent risk-tasking..
- Constant disobedience, aggression, or provocative opposition to authority.
- Inability to make or keep friends.
- Inability to cope with problems and daily activities.
- Striking weight loss or weight fluctuation not related to a known medical condition.

- Significant change in sleeping and/or eating habits.
- Excessive complaints of physical ailments.
- Aggressive or non-aggressive violation of other people's rights, opposition to authority, truancy, thefts, fire-setting, or vandalism.
- Threats to run away.
- Self-mutilation or self-destructive or other dangerous behavior.
- Sustained, prolonged sadness and withdrawn mood and attitude, often accompanied by poor appetite, difficulty sleeping, or thoughts of death.
- Frequent outbursts of anger.

Once you decide that help is necessary, making your way through the mental health system might be perplexing. Researching and selecting the right kind of professional help is like other decisions you make for your child. It is a matter of timing, gathering and considering options, and making a commitment to your choice.

However, unlike selecting a school or camp, parents often bring their own conflicted and troubled feelings to the process of seeking help. Children's emotional distress and internal pains cause considerable disruption to the child's and the parents' worlds, as parents get caught up in this turmoil and anguish, too.

In the midst of so much internal and external distress, parents may have difficulty being objective. Parents frequently blame themselves, or fear that others—teachers, family members will blame them.

Keep in mind that many times a child in crisis reflects a family in crisis. Parents who are involved in intense marital conflict, divorce, grief, physical illness, substance abuse, or their own emotional, psychiatric disturbance are not always able to make the best determinations about how to seek help and the best treatment for their child.

If you are concerned about your child's emotional health or behavior but don't know where to start, ask friends, family members, your spiritual counselor, your child's school counselor, or anyone else you know who has had experience with psychiatric treatment. Once you start asking questions, you may be surprised at how many people you know have sought help for their family and child's emotional and behavioral problems.

Your child's pediatrician or family physician can often help you decide on the best path for your child and your family. You can also contact your child's school counselor. If there is an Employee Assistance Program through your work, speak to its representative. Many insurers and managed care plans have 800 telephone numbers to connect you to services that can assist you in finding behavioral health services covered by your health insurance. Consult your local medical society, local mental health association, or county mental health administrator. National organizations like the American Academy of Child and Adolescent Psychiatry and the American Psychiatric Association can be contacted at their national headquarters or at local branches found in many cities and regions for referrals. Often local hospitals, medical centers, or the department of psychiatry at a nearby medical school will offer mental health services. You can also find names in the yellow pages under "Mental Health Services," "Physicians (Psychiatry, Child)," "Psychologists," or "Psychotherapists." However, parents should be cautious about using yellow pages as their sole source of information and referral: Get as much information about this important decision as possible from friends, school personnel, professionals, and other sources.

Profiling the Practitioners

The variety of mental health practitioners can be bewildering. There are psychiatrists, psychologists, counselors, pastoral counselors, psychiatric nurses, psychiatric social workers, and people who call themselves simply therapists. Few states regulate the practice of psychotherapy, so almost anyone can call himself a "psychotherapist."

On the other hand, most states do recognize and license *psychiatrists, psychologists, nurses,* and *social workers.* While having a degree or other credentials does not ensure that someone is a skilled and effective clinician, chances are that those practitioners who hold a state license or certificate will have more skills and training than those who have not met such standards. It may be helpful to understand some of the distinctions between these practitioners as you search for a mental health clinician to treat your child.

Psychiatrist A psychiatrist is a physician, a medical doctor whose training and education includes a medical school degree (M.D. or D.O. degree) and at least four additional years of study, research, and clinical training in psychiatry. Based on their training, psychiatrists have a thorough understanding of mental and medical issues. They also have an in-depth knowledge of medications and are licensed to issue prescriptions. Those who have completed their training may take a national examination.

Child and Adolescent Psychiatrist These medical specialists are fully trained psychiatrists who have had two additional years of advanced training with children, adolescents, and families. Those who have completed their training may take a national examination administered by the American Board of Psychiatry and Neurology. If they pass this examination, they are then board certified in child and adolescent psychiatry.

Psychologist Although some psychologists possess only a master's degree in psychology, many have earned a doctoral degree in clinical, educational, or research psychology. During their course of study, most psychologists are trained in the evaluation and nonmedical treatment of emotional problems and become knowledgeable about research techniques and psychological testing procedures.

Social Worker Usually a social worker has earned a master's degree at a college or university. In most states, social workers can take an examination to be licensed as clinical social workers. Some social workers are employed by general medical hospitals and government agencies to help families cope with a variety of issues, including child abuse, spouse abuse, delinquency, and poverty. Other social workers who are in private practice, or are employed by mental health centers or psychiatric hospitals, may provide counseling or psychotherapy for individuals, couples, or families.

Psychotherapist The term "psychotherapist" does not denote a particular degree or training. It refers only to that fact that one is engaged in the professional practice of psychotherapy (see *Individual Psychotherapy,* page 404). However, many who practice psychotherapy are not self-designated as psychotherapists but have earned professional degrees and completed postgraduate training in one or more methods of therapy during the process of becoming psychiatrists, child and adolescent psychiatrists, psychiatric nurses, psychologists, or social workers.

Often various mental health clinicians perform different functions in the treatment process. In this book we often use the general term *clinician* to describe professionals who are concerned with diagnosing and treating mental disorders and illnesses. Yet, as we've just discussed, not all such professionals are equally well trained to provide for the needs of your child. For example, certain kinds of psychological testing are typically the province of psychologists, while social workers usually have training in family therapy. On the other hand, the training of a child and adolescent psychiatrist prepares that clinician to integrate medical understanding when performing a psychiatric evaluation (see page 394). In the same way, when medications are required, the only mental health clinician licensed to issue prescriptions is the psychiatrist.

It is advisable for parents to attempt to find a clinician who has advanced training in child, adolescent, adult, and/or family therapy. Yet it is also important to find a comfortable and productive match between your child, your family, and the mental health clinician.

FINDING THE RIGHT CLINICIAN

Although clear thinking can be difficult during times of upset, consider carefully what you and your child want and need.

Try to think through these questions:

■ What are the problems or concerns you want help with?

■ What style of interaction will you find most helpful? Will you and your child work better with someone who offers advice and direction? Who listens and solicits your thoughts and solutions? Or a combination?

- ■ Are you looking for individual or family therapy?
- ■ Would you and your child be more comfortable with a male or female clinician?

Be honest and voice your concerns and questions directly to the mental health clinician from the beginning. During the first interview, observe how your child and other family members respond after meeting with the child and adolescent psychiatrist or clinician. Did each of you feel as if you had been listened to? That you, your child, and your feelings were respected? Was there a sense of safety or support or understanding? Listen to your instincts and find a second candidate if the first clinician doesn't seem to connect solidly with you and your child, although this may require more than one session.

Once treatment has begun, a good child and adolescent psychiatrist or clinician will help you find ways of coping or solving problems and will build on existing individual and family strengths. Even when families have reached an impasse or are in crisis, they still have some healthy ways of behaving, reacting, and coping.

Before you make the decision to have your child enter treatment, you should clarify some basic issues. Ask these questions:

- ■ What clinical areas does your clinician identify as crucial for you and your child?
- ■ How often will you meet and for how long?
- ■ How will the proposed intervention address the problems?
- ■ How much does the clinician charge? Is there a sliding scale? Does your insurance or health plan cover some or all of the charges?
- ■ Is there a charge for missed appointments? How much notice is required to cancel without being assessed a charge?
- ■ Does the clinician work collaboratively with other professionals in case other needs arise, like testing or medication?

When you find the right fit for you and your child, remember that the clinician is only part of the solution. It is essential for you and your family to establish a partnership with a skillful, supportive, and effective professional.

What Professional Help Really Means

In consulting with a child and adolescent psychiatrist or other mental health clinician many parents worry about being judged. They are anxious and have many questions: *Is my child normal? Am I normal? Am I to blame? Am I silly to worry?*

As you start the process, remember that the mental health clinician is there to support and help the family find a solution to the problem, not to place blame. The clinician will listen to your concerns, help you and your child define the problem, and identify some short- and long-term treatment goals.

Parents frequently have other questions about treatment. *Can you help us? Can you help our child? Does my child really need treatment? Do I? What is the diagnosis? How can the family help? What's next?*

Remember: No brief treatment, however effective, is capable of "fixing" you or your child. Treatment will not transform a headstrong and highly active child into an obedient, malleable individual. Nor will therapy transform a youngster who is shy and thoughtful into an assertive, boisterous go-getter. Treatment *can* help individuals and families find solutions and ways to cope better with some very complex problems.

Practitioners vary enormously in style and method. Traditional psychotherapies focus on identifying emotional conflicts and bringing them into clearer awareness. The clinician encourages direct expression of feelings as a way to lessen the tendency to act out or express feelings through behavior. Within families, the professional will work to foster direct and open communication rather than communications which are covert or subversive.

Psychotherapy means change but is not about the clinician changing your child. People enter therapy because *they* want change, to alter in some way their thinking, feelings, or behavior. Therapy allows or *facilitates* changes in individuals, couples, and families. In children, the treatment focuses on the child's emotional conflicts or on parenting or family problems that may be interfering with development and normal functioning (i.e., school, learning, and socialization).

While the child and adolescent psychiatrist or clinician guides this process, your child and family must do the actual work to institute change. Change is never easy, yet great anxiety or distress often provides the opportunity for change. Once the initial problem has been resolved (or becomes less disruptive to the child and family), the treatment may end. Nonetheless, other problems (for example, marital problems, stress, or depression in other family members) may also need attention. When family members are willing, treatment may continue, moving other problems into the center of the process for work and resolution.

The length of treatment is determined by many different factors, including severity and the complexity of the problem(s) that need to be addressed; the amount of time, effort, and emotional tension a family can tolerate; the responsiveness of the child and family to particular treatment methods or techniques; and the cost of treatment. In the best of all circumstances, therapy ends when all who are involved agree that the work is done.

The Psychiatric Evaluation

Professional help frequently begins with a comprehensive psychiatric evaluation. Whether the family comes to a child and adolescent psychiatrist or other clinician in private practice, a mental health clinic, child guidance center, or hospital emergency room, the problem must be carefully defined and understood before the work can begin. Typically performed by a child and adolescent psychiatrist or a team of mental health clinicians, the psychiatric evaluation will establish the plan and goals for treatment.

Usually the evaluation consists of a series of interviews, requiring several hours during one or more sessions. During these interviews, the child, family, and clinician work together to formulate different hypotheses concerning the nature of the problem(s). They will also examine possible causes, exacerbating circumstances, and other related problems.

A psychiatric evaluation will involve all areas of the child's and family's lives. At first, the clinician will identify the child's strengths and assets. At times, the inquiry may strike you as irrelevant or embarrassing. However, the more information a clinician has, the more accurate will be the understanding of the problems and issues.

The clinician will want to know when you believe the problem started, whether anything in particular seems to make it worse, what has been done to address it, and what worked and what didn't. He will ask about the child's overall health (including immunizations) and developmental progress. *When did your child begin to sleep through the night? And talk, walk, feed himself, and complete toilet training?* Questions will also be asked about the pregnancy and delivery; about siblings and their individual histories; and about relationships.

Parents' health is also relevant, in particular if there is a history of mental and physical illnesses, health problems, attention-deficit/hyperactivity disorder, or substance abuse. *Has treatment been sought before? What helped and what didn't?*

To answer questions about the child's physical health and psychological or cognitive functioning, the clinician may arrange for specific tests (for example, blood tests, X rays, and special psychological, educational, and speech and language assessments). With your permission, your family physician, school personnel, relatives, and other mental health clinicians involved with the family may be contacted (preferably by you, the parents) as part of the comprehensive evaluation.

By combining biological, psychological, and social information with developmental history and the strengths of the family and the child, the clinician lays the foundation for formulating a diagnosis and developing a treatment plan.

■ THE INTERVIEWING PROCESS

Questions early in the evaluation tend to be open-ended to allow for broad descriptions of experiences and impressions. As a diagnostic picture takes shape, the clinician may focus questions to test hypotheses. As a clearer understanding emerges, the clinician should share his observations with the parents and child.

The evaluation process is more than simply gathering information and developing hypotheses. There is also a relationship developing between the child, family, and the child and adolescent psychiatrist or professional clinician. Within this relationship, the actual work of treatment will take place.

Interviewing the Child Children are often initially interviewed in the company of their parents. But during the evaluation many clinicians may also want an opportunity to interview the child alone. Some children require several brief contacts before they begin to trust the clinician and are able to speak honestly about feelings or behaviors. In general, children are the best reporters of their feelings while parents are the best historians and are better able to describe observable behavior.

During the evaluation, the clinician will note the child's attention span and mood, and look for signs of persistent or intense anxiety or depression. A reluctant child will not be pressed for answers. Shy or fearful children may respond better to a number of shorter interviews or to less threatening topics, often in play therapy. The clinician may speculate about what the child may be feeling; seemingly irrelevant questions may be intended to make the child feel safer.

Interviewing the Family The clinician will want to talk about how you and your family operate. The family is, after all, the context within which children develop emotionally, physically, socially, and cognitively. The behavior of one family member inevitably influences the others and is, in turn, influenced by them. A child and adolescent psychiatrist cannot assess a child's problem without assessing the family, too.

The clinician will want to get a reading on life in your household. He may ask about the time you spend together, whether the child meets family expectations, and if you feel you are responsive to your child's needs. The clinician may ask about your worries. *What made you seek help now? Has the problem become worse or less tolerable? What do you think caused the problem? What have you done about it?*

You will be asked personal questions that may seem beside the point, such as how happy your marriage is and how well you and your spouse negotiate disagreements. Parental conflict is often an important circumstance, so the clinician will try to get a sense of other serious problems in the home or in the family. Depression, unresolved grief, illness, financial difficulties, or a family move can each have a profound effect on your child. Sometimes the effect is different from one child to another in the same family.

The clinician will ask about the intensity and quality of your child's peer relationships. *How many children does your youngster routinely play with? What kind of play do they engage in? What are your youngster's favorite hobbies, recreation, or activities?*

In both family and child interviews, a psychiatrist will want to learn how well your child behaves and achieves at school. The clinician may add to the information you provide by directly asking day-care, preschool, or elementary school personnel about the child's relationship with teachers and other students, ability to attain academic potential and achievement, and the existence of any disciplinary concerns.

Understanding the Clinician The evaluation process is interactive. It provides an opportunity for the clinician to get to know your child and your family *and* for you to get to know the clinician. During the evaluation sessions, you and each member of your family should feel supported and listened to.

Watch how the clinician interacts with your child and your family. Tone, posture, and choice of words are indicators of how well the clinician understands the family's worries, fears, and hopes. Over time, you will need to discuss information such as test results and treatment planning; you will need explanations of complex medical or psychiatric information in a way that each of you can understand. Your child—and you—need to feel comfortable with the clinician.

As much as families want to be told that everything will be all right, not even the best psychiatrist can predict how things will turn out in the long run. But effective clinicians know that things can get better, knowing that other children have gotten better. When that vision is communicated, it eases suffering and builds relationships.

Many families feel apprehension and anxiety when they seek help. When a child and adolescent psychiatrist or other clinician communicates professional competence and concern, the child and parent are reassured.

PREPARING YOUR CHILD FOR THERAPY: WHAT PARENTS CAN DO

Since children are strongly influenced by their parents and families, the appearance of an emotional or behavioral problem in a child is often linked to the family. Many times parental troubles—marital conflicts, preoccupation, neglect, depression, stress, or general chaos—are expressed through a child. Sometimes family problems can inadvertently reinforce a child's natural vulnerabilities or problems.

The solution to a child's emotional or behavioral difficulty often lies *within* the family. When parents seek therapy out of concern for their child's health or behavior, this act alone often sends an important message to the child, that the parents recognize a problem and are prepared to try to fix it.

You should be involved in your child's treatment from beginning to end. You have roles as an historian during the evaluation and as a consultant during the treatment. You yourself may also seek treatment, whether it's individual therapy, family therapy, or in a family support group.

If your child is in individual therapy, parallel work with parents and siblings can lead to important shifts in the dynamic equilibrium of influences within the family. Such work within the family can improve the long-term outcome for the child's future development.

Preparing your child for treatment involves being receptive to and curious about the therapy process yourself. Since you are a partner in the process, ask questions. You need to be willing to look at things honestly and directly, to change and grow along with your youngster.

From the very beginning of the evaluation, be straightforward with your child. Explain in clear language why you are taking him to a professional. For example, tell him that you and his teachers are concerned about how he is feeling and behaving. Explain that it often helps to talk to someone who understands children and that together you will try to understand exactly what is bothering him. Explain why you think he needs treatment. Acknowledge that you may need help to be a more effective parent.

At each step in the process, describe to your child the person with whom you will be meeting, the setting, the people who will be there, the length of the session, and the other arrangements. Your child should know the clinician's name. Having this information can help your child feel more in control. Encourage your youngster to be open and honest when answering questions. Encourage him to ask his own questions. Sometimes it is helpful to reassure you child that it may take some time to feel relaxed enough to talk freely. Explain that therapy is a special and private time set aside to allow him to talk and think about anything he wants. Tell him that eventually he and the clinician will begin to understand why he feels troubled.

To engage in a therapeutic relationship, your child needs your support and encouragement. This is not always easy. Sometimes your child may leave a session with an idealized image of the clinician. You may feel competitive, sensing that someone else is helping your child in a way you could not. At other times your child may storm out of a therapy session very angry and complaining about the clinician or about having to undergo therapy. You may worry that your child will talk critically or reveal embarrassing secrets about you.

Deal honestly with the clinician *and* with your feelings and concerns. You, too, need to have trust in the clinician and believe in the process to effect change for your child and family.

DEALING WITH MANAGED CARE SYSTEMS

Managed care is a review and approval process that monitors the need, type, and use of medical services in an effort to save on costs and increase profits. In recent years, this approach has become a widespread means of controlling health-care costs and of trying to certify the quality of treatment.

Managed care can indeed control costs, but it also influences and even dictates treatments. Managed care tends to emphasize short-term treatment, and focuses on dealing with a current crisis or on changing very specific, concrete behaviors.

Care is authorized by a *utilization review*. This review is usually done by social workers, nurses, or others (often referred to as *case managers*) either by phone or by reviewing a written report prepared by your clinician. Many managed care companies direct their enrollees to obtain treatment from clinicians in a specific network (see *Preferred Providers,* below).

Frequently the clinician evaluating or treating your child will be required to present the evaluation or treatment to a case manager *before* your insurer authorizes payment for additional treatment. If this is not done, you could be responsible for paying all the charges yourself. To avoid delays and disruptions in treatment, contact the insurer when you are considering seeking treatment. The appropriate phone number is usually to be found on the back of your health-care card.

Case managers use guidelines developed by the managed care company hired by your health-care plan. Written treatment plans prepared by the child and adolescent psychiatrist or mental health clinician may be required. Sometimes an entire medical record may need to be submitted for review. In the case of psychiatric disorders, managed care reviewers typically authorize payment for a limited number of outpatient sessions or days of inpatient care. To obtain approval for additional treatment, the clinician must discuss the child's progress and needs with a case manager in the managed care organization.

Problems about confidentiality may arise, too, during the utilization review. There may be issues or "family secrets" that you regard as private and are reluctant to have revealed and discussed by your clinician with the case manager. Formerly, these were kept between you and your doctor. These may be important matters your child has shared with the clinician during treatment but that infringe on your private relation with the psychiatrist.

Discuss such concerns with your clinician. Often, he will respect your desire for privacy, but be aware, too, that some of the facts that you regard as private may also be vital to getting your child's treatment approved by managed care. That means they may also be fundamental to justifying to the insurer the need for continued treatment.

If treatment is denied but you and the clinician think that additional treatment is necessary and covered by your health plan description of benefits, follow the appeals process outlined in your health plan. Your children and family may also benefit from treatment that does not qualify as "medically necessary" and is not covered by your plan. If that is the case, you may wish to consider contracting with your clinician to pay for treatment the way you purchase other valuable services.

Some managed care plans limit your choice of child and adolescent psychiatrist or other mental health clinician to their *preferred providers,* a group of doctors, social workers, or psychologists enlisted by your insurer at contracted rates. Typically, these preferred providers have agreed to accept a reduced fee. If you choose to consult with someone else, your insurer may not pay for these services. In the same way, care given at *out-of-network* hospitals may not be covered by your insurance.

Traditionally insurers paid only for inpatient and outpatient care. Today, depending upon your plan, a fuller array of services such as day hospital, day treatment, home-based care, respite care, and family-support services may be covered at least in part. These lower-cost and less restrictive services may offer a number of advantages over inpatient hospitalization (see also *What Are the Treatment Options,* page 402).

Some mental health plans set maximums on annual or lifetime costs for mental health care. Prudent parents and employers study these limits closely before signing up for health insurance. Once this amount is used up, coverage ends and a child's subsequent mental health bills will be the responsibility of the parent. If this happens and your child needs continued care you cannot afford, you may need to seek help from your state-supported public mental health system. Unfortunately, this may mean changing clinicians and disrupting your child's care.

As you purchase health-care insurance for your family you should carefully evaluate the mental health coverage. Consider the following questions in evaluating the plans:

■ Is the mental health coverage managed by an outside company?

■ Is there a list of preferred providers? Are child specialists included? Are there child and adolescent psychiatrists? What happens if you want to see someone not on the list?

■ Are you responsible for a *deductible*? (Many insurance programs do not cover treatment from the first dollar but require you pay for an initial annual increment or deductible of $100 to $500 or more.)

■ What are the co-pays, if any? (*Co-pays* are the portion of the cost of each service for which you are responsible out-of-pocket.)

■ What are the limits on the number of visits covered? Who decides how many visits are allowed?

■ What hospitals are covered under the plan? Does the plan cover other services like day treatment or respite care?

■ Are there lifetime or annual dollar limits for mental health coverage?

■ Is there any recourse (such as appeals or grievance procedures) if you are not satisfied with the provider or the recommendations of the utilization review?

■ What, if any, diagnoses or preexisting conditions and treatments are excluded from coverage?

There may be times when you will have to act as your child's advocate to get services that are not covered by your plan. Mental health and family advocacy groups and professional associations such as the American Academy of Child and Adolescent Psychiatry may provide you with assistance and important information about local services. The support of other parents may also be helpful when you are trying to obtain needed services for your child.

Emergencies

Children in crisis turn to their parents or other adults for help. The parents themselves may be anxious, angry, or distracted. School counselors or teachers may be overwhelmed or unaware. When adults are at a loss as to how to help the child, they are likely to declare the situation beyond control and seek immediate outside help.

Clear-cut psychiatric emergencies include suicidal or homicidal threats or behavior. Other possible emergency situations include: severe anxiety or panic attacks; psychosis;

drug overdoses; drug use by young children; and violent, assaultive, or destructive threats or behavior.

In all emergencies, the first order of business is to ensure the safety of the child. Call your health plan's emergency number or consult your family physician. If there is any delay, go to a hospital emergency room. Psychiatric hospitalization is often useful in helping a suicidal, impulsive, or psychotic child regain control, or with a child who is very depressed and has not responded to intensive outpatient therapy. Inpatient stays are usually brief. In some communities, less restrictive but safe environments like a crisis residence or group home may be available.

Older children may ask for help independently. Or they may feel that there is a barrier in communicating with their parents, and a crisis can be an indication of homes that are chaotic, negligent, or abusive. Psychiatric emergencies are often linked to troubled relationships within the family and a stressful situation at home. For example, family crises which threaten family stability include divorce, abandonment, illness, or death.

Many children are brought for emergency treatment by their parents or relatives. Others are sent for emergency treatment on the recommendation of school, juvenile court, police, health and mental health organizations, and other community agencies, the family physician or pediatrician, and neighbors.

During the evaluation of a psychiatric emergency, the clinician will assess your child's physical, emotional, intellectual, educational, and social functioning. Recent events will be carefully reviewed, in particular any that indicate trauma, drug use, and other emotional stressors. During the evaluation, the clinician will also review family structure and relationships and will explore whether relatives or friends can give support.

Emergency assessment seeks to clarify what precipitated the crisis. Was it physical abuse or loss? Other underlying conditions may also emerge, such as a severe depression (see page 329), conduct disorder (page 349), a psychotic disorder (page 372), an anxiety disorder (page 311), separation anxiety disorder (page 308), or a medical problem with psychiatric symptoms.

Once the child and family can feel safer and less stressed—when the panic, anxiety, and chaos of the emergency has subsided—the clinician can begin to investigate underlying issues and consider how to prevent future crises. It is important that everyone understands that the emergency problem is often not just a temporary crisis, but rather a reflection of complex personal and family difficulties that need a fundamental solution.

16

What Are the
Treatment Options?

■   ■   ■

Once you and your family have seen a child and adolescent psychiatrist or other qualified mental health clinician and the evaluation process has been completed, you should have some idea of the complexity of the problem and a proposed plan of action. This should include one or more treatment therapies: individual, couples, family, or group. Individual treatment may include medication therapy.

A proposed course of treatment is based on the child's diagnosis and the course of her problems over time. There are other important conditions, including the family's emo-

tional resources, their comfort with different types of therapy, the availability of services, and insurance or financial resources.

Clinicians develop treatment plans according to their training. Whether the clinician is a child and adolescent psychiatrist, psychologist, clinical social worker, pastoral counselor, or psychiatric nurse will influence the shape of the plan. If you are being treated in a hospital or mental health clinic, the recommended course of treatment will be affected by institutional policies, attitudes, and styles. Your managed care company may also favor certain treatment approaches.

This chapter will explain and discuss some of the words, concepts, and therapeutic services that are part of psychiatric treatment for children, adolescents, and their families.

The Continuum of Mental Health Care

Different communities have different types of treatment available for children with emotional and behavioral difficulties. The complete range of programs and services is called the *continuum of care*. Not every community has all services, but some of the more common services are described briefly below.

- **Private office or outpatient clinic.**
  In such settings, clinicians will meet with patients (individuals, children, couples, families, and groups) for scheduled sessions (typically, thirty to sixty minutes). The frequency of visits depends on the needs of the child.

- **Intensive case management.**
  Case managers will coordinate different services from a spectrum of help (psychiatric, financial, legal, and medical) to ensure that the child can live successfully at home and in the community.

- **Home-based treatment services.**
  These services involve a team of trained individuals who visit at home and develop a treatment program to help the child and family by working with the youngster and other family members.

- **Family support services.**
  Such community agencies offer a range of services, which may include parenting training, parent support groups, nutritional counseling, and playgroups to help families care for their children.

- **Day treatment programs.**
  These intensive programs will provide psychiatric treatment and school or special education services. Children usually attend five days a week.

- **Partial hospitalization or day hospitals.**
  Here children will receive all the intensive treatment services of a psychiatric hospital during the day but return home at night to enable them to maintain continuity with their families.

- **Emergency/crisis services.**
  These are twenty-four-hour-per-day services for psychiatric emergencies that will be provided in hospital emergency rooms or by mobile crisis teams.

- **Respite care services.**
  While receiving respite care, a patient will stay with trained individuals outside of the home for brief periods of time to provide parents with a respite from the burdens of caring for their child.

- **Therapeutic group home or community residences.**
  These special residences will accommodate small groups of children whose home life does not provide sufficient sup-

port, structure, and nurture. Children in these settings often also attend a day treatment or special educational program.

- **Crisis residences.**
  These settings will offer short-term (usually fewer than fifteen days) crisis intervention and treatment for small numbers of children or teens. Patients are supervised twenty-four hours per day and may still attend their own schools.

- **Residential treatment facility.**
  Seriously troubled children will receive intensive and comprehensive biopsychosocial treatment in a campuslike setting over a longer period of time, typically twelve to eighteen months.

- **Hospital treatment.**
  Children will receive comprehensive psychiatric treatment in a hospital. The length of treatment varies. Some communities have specialized psychiatric hospitals. Others have special units for psychiatric services within a general or community hospital.

Individual Psychotherapy

Psychotherapy is based on the development of a therapeutic relationship between a patient and the psychotherapist. One important feature of this relationship is the development of sufficient trust on the part of the child to allow the youngster to reveal to the therapist her thoughts, feelings, and inner experiences. The clinician, by using her knowledge of psychological processes, human development, and psychiatric disorders, is able to work to relieve the child's discomfort and suffering and to promote the development of new skills and ways of coping.

The goals of psychotherapy are to relieve suffering; to restore emotional stability; to increase tolerance of a full range of emotions, including anger and frustration; to promote age-appropriate independence in thought and action; to maximize the child's use of her innate abilities; and to resume healthy development. Psychotherapy is a method of treating psychiatric disorders, emotional and behavioral problems, and developmental crises and delays. To the extent that these goals are accomplished, a child will find more pleasure and meaning in her life and will build greater resilience.

The practice of psychotherapy includes different approaches, styles, techniques, and interventions. Most psychotherapies foster self-exploration while offering some support and direction. Most clinicians, regardless of their training, draw from various schools of psychotherapy theory, and modify their approach according to each child's needs and capacities.

In the privacy of the clinician's office and within the safety of a therapeutic relationship, the child will begin to talk or play as a means of expressing herself (thus, the terms *talk therapy* and *play therapy*). The clinician observes the child and listens very carefully, noting patterns and themes. During psychotherapy sessions, which are often scheduled once a week and last from thirty to fifty minutes, the youngster is encouraged to explore thoughts, experiences, and feelings. Without moral judgment or criticism, the clinician listens to the child and encourages self-exploration in the child during these times. The clinician may ask for clarification, offer interpretations of internal emotional conflicts, make connections between current problems and past experiences, and help the child develop different ways of coping.

The power of any psychotherapy lies within the relationship between clinician and child. Within the safety of that relationship, the youngster is encouraged to become curious about and to discuss feelings, behavior, and inner struggles. By exhibiting a caring, understanding attitude toward the child, the clinician allows greater expression and minimizes embarrassment. Even with very nervous or apprehensive children, good therapeutic relationships can absorb much of the anxiety and promote open discussion. Therapy instills hope for the child to overcome her problem. The clinician uses this hope to help the child get better.

Parents play several essential roles when their child is in psychotherapy. Because children are dependent, they rely on their parents' judgement about the recommendation for treatment. This requires that the parent understand the problem and feel confidence in the clinician. The child relies on the parent to bring the child regularly and to provide payment for treatment.

Another key component of individual psychotherapy with children is the *parent work.* The parents will meet with the child's therapist or with an alternative clinician, with the purpose of understanding the child's difficulties and how these difficulties impact on the child's life, development, and the rest of the family. Parents are offered guidance in developing new approaches to parenting and family management. A goal of the parent work is to help the parents tailor their parenting to the needs of the child.

■ **PLAY THERAPY**

Clinicians use play therapy to help the child express and communicate feelings and emotions. Clinicians also listen and observe for themes in the child's play and how the child uses play materials which may clarify the child's problems.

Play therapy can be used to help children reenact traumatic events in a safe environment. For depressed children, play may provide a vehicle whereby they can act out their feelings of loss, powerlessness, anger, and frustration. Drawing can serve as a bridge between play and talk. As children become more comfortable in therapy, they may use more verbal expression, and the clinician can help children to describe their feelings, and to begin to understand their problems, defenses, and methods of coping.

In therapy, both talk and play eventually give children the opportunity to put their experiences and feelings in perspective. When children are having difficulty dealing with painful life circumstances, therapy gives them the chance to understand their feelings and move on to adapt to reality.

The exact length of any course of psychotherapy varies. When symptoms disappear, children or their parents may understandably wish to end treatment. However, the time of ending is best determined in conjunction with the clinician, who is able to assess whether the underlying problems are sufficiently resolved that the gains can be maintained. Sometimes in treatment things may appear to worsen, or the child may protest the treatment. At such times, it is essential that parents meet with the clinician to understand what is occurring so they can agree whether to continue and to support the psychotherapy.

There are different forms of individual psychotherapy, which include supportive, psychodynamic, and cognitive-behavioral. For each, the length and frequency of sessions and the duration of the treatment varies.

Psychotherapy is not a quick or easy fix. Rather it is a complex, intense, and rich process that can provide insight and can reorient a child toward a future of self-realization.

PSYCHODYNAMIC PSYCHOTHERAPY

Psychodynamic psychotherapy is also called *psychoanalytically oriented psychotherapy*, and includes child psychoanalysis. It is about understanding the psychological forces that motivate a child's actions and that color the youngster's thoughts and feelings.

Psychodynamic psychotherapy can help identify a child's characteristic patterns of response to inner struggles. Such patterns are also called *defenses*. This type of therapy operates on the assumption that once the underlying issues and patterns are brought to light, the child can develop better mastery of her emotions and choose more wisely what she wants to say and do. Psychodynamic psychotherapy is part of the foundation for many other forms of psychotherapy.

Psychodynamic psychotherapy is often the preferred treatment for complicated conditions, including those in which more than one problem affects the child. Such children have more than one diagnosis or may have experienced medical or social trauma. Often these illnesses are resistant to other treatments. Psychodynamic treatment is useful when the child's problems have led to delays in social and emotional development. It is an important treatment option in many psychiatric conditions, including childhood depression, anxiety disorders, eating disorders, and gender identity disorders. For children who are experiencing significant life stresses (for example, from divorce, illness, or death of a family member), psychodynamic psychotherapies are also frequently an important treatment option.

Psychoanalytically oriented psychotherapy consists of thirty- to fifty-minute sessions where privacy and protection from interruption are assured. The frequency of the sessions and the duration of treatment vary in accordance with how much inner change is to be accomplished and how strongly entrenched the child's defenses are. In stressful life situations where the goal is to help the child to understand and adapt to new circumstances, the treatment may be less frequent and of brief duration. In contrast, with more complex and longstanding problems, the treatment will more likely be twice a week and of longer duration. The lengthiest and most intense form of psychodynamic psychotherapy is child psychoanalysis in which the child is seen four times per week for several years. Evidence shows that child psychoanalysis is an effective treatment for young children with severe and complicated problems.

In psychodynamic psychotherapy, the clinician aids the child in gaining an understanding of her inner world in order that she may create her own effective response to her environment. Rather than giving advice, the clinician assists the child in developing her own coping strategies. The child improves because she has gained insight into her feelings and inner struggles within the context of a compassionate, respectful, and reliable therapeutic relationship in which she has felt deeply understood.

Cognitive-Behavioral Therapy

In the past few years, cognitive-behavioral approaches have proved especially useful in the treatment of children with emotional and behavioral problems. As the name implies, *behavioral therapies* focus on external behavioral symptoms rather than internal feelings and motivations. Behavioral therapy addresses the symptomatic behavior directly. By improving behavior, feelings will also change.

A cognitive approach improves a child's moods and behavior by addressing faulty patterns of thinking. How a person interprets events shapes how she feels and acts. Cognitive therapy guides a child toward more realistic and positive thinking. The focus is on how the child's distorted thinking leads to emotional and behavioral problems.

In cognitive therapy, children learn to identify, test, and correct specific distortions in their thinking. They learn to recognize negative thoughts, and see the relationship between thinking, feelings, and behavior. Common errors in thought include exaggerating fears; anticipating disastrous outcomes; overgeneralizing from negative experiences; and ignoring times when things go well. Once a child recognizes that she had been automatically reacting negatively, she can examine how realistic those reactions are, consider alternative explanations, and imagine other outcomes.

Cognitive-behavioral therapy offers children tools for thinking about their world. Cognitive-behavioral therapies work especially well with children because the techniques are active and specific to a given problem. The therapy may be shorter than in psychodynamic therapy (perhaps one or two twenty-minute sessions per week), which suits many children. Cognitive-behavioral therapy also tends to be short term and solution oriented.

As with psychodynamic psychotherapy, the initial goal is to develop a rapport between the child and clinician and to gather information. Through a collaborative relationship, the clinician attempts to engender interest in the child, and together they examine, experiment with, and assess the child's belief system and perceptions.

Children with excessive *anxiety, phobias,* or *separation anxiety disorder* may be encouraged to chart automatic thoughts and disturbed feelings, to explore worst-case scenarios, and to use self-soothing mental images and fantasies in overcoming their anxiety.

Highly anxious or phobic children might be encouraged to use relaxation techniques or to talk themselves into a more soothing or reasonable emotional position. Through *systematic desensitization* (gentle, repeated exposure to a situation or object that frightens or upsets the child), the youngster may learn to conquer the phobia or avoid an anxiety state. A child with obsessive-compulsive disorder, for example, may be brought into contact, through either gradual confrontation or imaginary exposure, with the feared object or event; attempts to engage in obsessive-compulsive behavior are then gently thwarted (see *Obsessive-Compulsive Disorder,* page 315). This helps a child recognize the exaggerated nature of her fears and develop a corrective approach.

In cognitive theory, *depression* stems from irrational beliefs and distorted thoughts. Usually a depressed child personalizes failure, magnifies negative events, and minimizes positive occurrences and attributes. These negative thought patterns may be the result of the loss of a parent at an early age or of adopting the thought patterns of a depressed parent. Often these negative thoughts are not based on a realistic perception by the child of her abilities and circumstances. In cognitive therapy, the clinician and child identify unpleasant thoughts, explore their origins, and devise more realistic and more positive ways of dealing with day-to-day problems.

Behavioral therapy targets specific symptoms, such as social withdrawal, low activity level, self-deprecating behavior, and aggressive behavior. A child then learns to monitor negative thoughts she has about herself, evaluate their validity, and reinforce positive alternatives. The youngster is taught to set more realistic goals and standards of performance, to refrain from punitive self-statements, and to think of herself in kinder, more encouraging terms.

The cognitive-behavioral clinician working with a child with *conduct disorder* or *anti-social behavior* will start by determining to what degree the youngster can anticipate and control her aggressive acts and whether the child feels remorse or concern after such episodes. Clinicians frequently use *problem-solving training* to help aggressive children deal with difficult social and interpersonal situations. The clinician helps the child learn to identify and express her feelings of upset more appropriately and to devise alternative behaviors. The child learns about the consequences of her behavior. The focus is on the child being accountable for her choices, decisions, and behavior. The youngster then begins to see the advantages in changing her behavior. Gradually she may be able to interact more successfully in social situations. After a few successes, she starts to consolidate what she has learned, her behavior improves, her thinking becomes more positive, and she feels better. Her family and friends respond positively to the more considerate child, which reinforced the new behavior.

Cognitive-behavioral therapy, when coupled with medication, can also be quite effective in treating a child with *attention-deficit/hyperactivity disorder.* The child may be able to improve academic performance, as cognitive-behavioral techniques can assist in reducing impulsivity and help a child control her motor activity. However, these techniques must be implemented in the home and in the classroom, as well as in the clinician's office. The clinician often works with the school and family to implement or reinforce good behaviors.

Parent Management Training helps parents learn principles and strategies for managing their child's behavior. In the home, parents are taught to use positive reinforcement—praise and rewards—to help their child to play independently and to improve social interactions. Parents learn to use consequences and mild punishments such as time-outs and the loss of privileges. Self-control techniques such as self-monitoring, self-evaluation, and goal-setting are also taught.

Cognitive-behavioral therapy isn't the answer to all problems in childhood. In some instances, cognitive-behavioral therapy may reduce some symptoms only to have new symptoms surface or the therapy may fail to produce lasting therapeutic change. In others, cognitive-behavioral therapies can produce significant, positive results, especially when the symptoms are mild and the child is motivated and the parents actively involved.

Family Therapy

Research has shown that family-oriented therapy, whether used as the primary treatment or in conjunction with other treatments such as individual, group, or medication therapies, has proved remarkably helpful in treating a wide range of emotional, behavioral, and psychiatric disorders in children, including psychotic disorders, depression and bipolar disorder, anxiety disorders, substance abuse, eating disorders, and conduct disorders.

In many cases, family therapy provides support and education as the family tries to manage a child and her problems. In some cases, parents come into therapy to help their child get better but come to understand that other, family-related problems are finding expression through their youngster's troubles. At first, the issues that come to light in therapy may seem tangential and unrelated, but when marital problems, unresolved grief, or a family secret are unmasked and discussed, therapy may move in an unanticipated but productive direction. With the focus shifted to family tensions, the child may well be freed to proceed in a healthier fashion with development. Family therapy can dramatically alter family relationships in very positive and healthy ways.

A clinician may ask that each family member participate, including siblings and even grandparents. At its best, therapy addresses all family members, their private feelings and thoughts, personal and family developmental history, and biological and health-related concerns. An effective family clinician must engage each family member during the session, using age-appropriate talk or play with the children. The clinician must be able to view each individual within the larger context of the family. The clinician will learn from each member's point of view something of the nature, cause, effects, and possible solutions to the problems of the individual and family.

Therapy can help the family deal with the stress generated by living with and caring for a troubled child. A sibling can feel neglected,

overly burdened, or even embarrassed by another sibling's behavior. During treatment, a parent may be found to have a psychiatric disorder (such as depression), which is causing the parent or other family members distress. Such a therapeutic finding will be incorporated into the treatment, either by making an appropriate referral for the individual to receive treatment or by addressing the issues in family therapy.

Family therapy offers parents and children less defensive ways of communicating with one another. It fosters mutual support, positive reinforcement, direct communication, and more effective problem-solving within the family. It may offer instruction on conflict resolution, and can decrease a parent's likelihood of engaging in physically and emotionally abusive behavior. Working to reduce parent-child power struggles, therapy may bring about more satisfying and appropriate parent-child interactions. It can support parents as they negotiate the precarious balance between furthering appropriate independence in their child and maintaining sufficient supervision and accountability.

Family therapy addresses problems that unwittingly perpetuate or promote symptoms in children, among them a lack of generational boundaries (in which parents or caregivers treat children as peers), severe marital conflict, rigid or chaotic rules, projection of parental feelings onto a child, or neglectful or overly involved relationships.

There are numerous schools of thought and theory that influence family therapy practice. Accordingly, the way in which clinicians frame or understand problems will determine their intervention. If, for example, a clinician observes a problem in the way parents discipline and guide their child, she may use techniques to help parents use positive and negative reinforcement more effectively (see *Cognitive-Behavioral Therapy*, page 407). If a child's symptom serves some function within the family (such as distracting parents from dealing with their conflicts with each other), a clinician may then reframe the symptom in terms of its function and offer the family different, less damaging ways of obtaining comparable benefits.

Some family therapists look at the process by which the family maintains the need to protect and preserve itself and the need to adapt in the face of inevitable developmental and environmental change. Still others examine how communication patterns and unspoken rules maintain or cause problems for the family members.

In some cases the clinician may move the focus away from the nuclear family to the extended family and social support networks, and examine the way in which the parents have brought shadows, expectations, and dysfunctions from their own childhoods into their family life.

A popular tool and technique in family therapy is the *genogram,* a pictorial representation or "map" of the family. By working with the family to sketch out a genogram, the clinician can investigate more closely complex family relationships, family history, and multigenerational issues. As they look at their own diagram, individuals, as well as families, can understand their own history and individual context differently.

Family therapy is diverse, both in theory and in practice. However, an eclectic approach to family therapy tends to be more useful than a strict adherence to a particular school of thought. Most family clinicians draw upon different theories for the unique situations different families present. In short, family clinicians aim at understanding a child's problems within the family context; what is working to cause or maintain the problems; and what assets, strengths, and resources within the family can help resolve the problem.

Group Therapy

Group therapy uses the power of group dynamics and peer interaction to further understanding and hope in participants. Group therapy is used for a wide range of emotional, behavioral, and life problems. Groups in therapy may consist of several families or only adults or child peers.

For children, participating in a group with their peers can help them develop social skills for a greater sense of mastery and self-esteem. Some children find it easier to express feelings in a supportive group of their peers. Similarly, parents feel supported, understood, and gain helpful insight and parenting skills in a support group with other parents facing similar challenges. For both the child and the parent, hearing other people talk about similar problems and ways to resolve them can have powerful, supportive effects.

At any one time in a community, a number of groups, in a number of settings, will be able to address different needs. Groups in schools, community centers, churches and synagogues, health or mental health clinics, residential treatment centers, or hospitals may address such problems as poor peer relations, low academic achievement, and delinquency. Groups can help children deal with divorce and abuse, somatic and terminal illness. There may be groups for children of battered women or alcoholics, crisis and trauma groups, educational and prevention groups, parent and family groups. Such groups may meet once or twice a week or even every day in a hospital, intensive outpatient, or long-term treatment center.

The clinician must balance the composition of the therapy group—offsetting, for example, acting out children with quieter, less demanding, more compliant children. The leader must decide on the play, activities, toys, and themes to be used to engage and interest the children. Preschool boys and girls are typically seen in small groups of three, four, or five. When the children are more active or more disturbed, more than one clinician may participate.

With older children, groups may form not only according to disorder and severity of the difficulties, but according to age: early (5–7), middle (8–10), and late (10–12) childhood. However, ages may be mixed but grouped according to intelligence, physical size, and diagnosis. When more boys than girls are in the group, which is often the case, usually a male clinician participates. Older boys and girls may do better in same-sex groups with the same-gender clinician. Consideration for group therapy usually begins with an inter-view with the clinician and the parents and child.

Once in the group, each member will be asked by the group leader what she wants from group therapy. In turn, the leader will explain what is expected of the members. For progress to be made in groups, participants need to be interested in their own thoughts and feelings; to speak within the group as honestly as possible about those thoughts and feelings; to cultivate an awareness of their own behaviors in relation to the others; and to offer suggestions and feedback about issues under discussion.

Initially, members tend to look to the leader for guidance. As the group progresses, members connect with each other. Eventually, each member of the group will assume responsibility for his or her individual growth, improvement, and progress.

When working with children, a group leader offers support, spontaneity, flexibility, and playful creativity while fostering a sense of safety and trust. The leader must establish adequate limits and rules for the group. Children seem to respond best (as, in all likelihood, do adults) when the group leader assumes an attitude of controlled curiosity and sophisticated ignorance, rather than an overly intellectual or authoritarian approach, which is likely to produce silence, fear, withdrawal, and withholding.

Because young children often communicate with one another without words or symbolic reasoning, groups can be helpful in allowing a child broader expression. Many times, group therapy works to move a child toward greater verbal communication.

Within the group, the clinician observes the behavior of children, clarifies diagnoses, and gradually interprets the meaning of their play and interactions.

Since a child's internal troubles gets cast out into her environment, a group can bring light to the way in which a child relates and copes with other children and physical objects. To that end, some clinicians may encourage group play. Rather than providing structured activity, the clinician will set aside a few uncomplicated toys, such as crayons, paper, pencils, playhouse, play telephone, dolls, or action figures. Children can hold, investigate, and use these objects as props, as they move into an exploration of their own difficult internal subjects.

Group therapy for children may involve a group activity, such as creating a mural, playing games, or participating in psychodrama in which children invent characters or the clinician provides themes for them to act out. Such activities can be particularly helpful when the group is dealing with difficult emotional material. Through these activities, the clinician and children begin to understand the meaning of the material or themes shared. It also prepares children to express themselves more directly with others.

Some groups use discussion of a videotape, physical exercise or games, or genograms, in which the children and clinician create "maps" of each child's family. By mapping the emotional and social landscape of the family, a genogram can help a child focus on questions of her parents' marriage(s) or separation, new family alliances, or catastrophic family events. Storytelling, constructing and

using masks, puppets, and playing computer games are all effective ways of putting children at ease, engaging them in a group process, and moving them toward a safe discussion of their pain and problems.

Often groups are structured to allow for a discussion period, perhaps exploring what went on during the play period or between group sessions. Children are encouraged to talk about whatever is on their minds, including their fantasies and dreams. By turns, the children may formulate summary statements of what the group accomplished in that day's session.

The degree of permissiveness, structure, and limit-setting in a group format depends upon the activity level and expressiveness of the group. With children who are overly aggressive and impulsive, greater vigilance and firmer limits may be more necessary than with shy children. In some groups, the clinician allows each child the freedom to work with one another, intervening only when a child is in danger, hurt, or is threatening another child. Clinicians impart meaning, insight, and interpretations when appropriate. As the child feels accepted into the group and connected to her peers and clinician, she will begin to express her feelings and gain confidence in herself and her role in the group.

Medications

The use of medications in treating psychiatric disorders—*psychopharmacological treatments*—is a most helpful form of individual therapy when there is a clear target symptom or disorder for a particular medication. Some medications are prescribed to facilitate attention and learning; others may be used during particularly stressful times, perhaps in the initial stage of treatment or at a time of crisis. Antipsychotic medications can benefit children with thought disorders, delusions, or hallucinatory experiences.

Parents need complete information about any medication prescribed for their child. They need to understand when and how the medication is to be taken; the goals for medication use; and the possible side effects. The more parents are involved in the decision to use medications, the more supportive they can be. Sometimes, when parents, teachers, or qualified professional clinicians become frustrated and desperate in their efforts to manage especially difficult behavior, they request medication for the child. Such proposals must be carefully evaluated by the child and adolescent psychiatrist because the requests themselves can be impulsive rather than constructive or may serve the classroom or family rather than the individual child.

A child should be given age-appropriate information to help her understand the medication's effects and the reasons for taking it. Young children usually do not have special fears about taking *psychotropic* medications (drugs that affect psychic function, behavior, or experience), though youngsters may overhear or misunderstand her parents, peers, or other family members when they talk about medications, their effects, risks, and expectations.

■ **ISSUING THE PRESCRIPTION**

The procedure for prescribing medications for children begins with a consultation between the child and adolescent psychiatrist, the child, and parents. The child and adolescent psychiatrist needs a clear understanding of the child's medical history and current state of health, any allergies observed in the child or family, and the child's previous experience with any psychiatric medications.

The child and adolescent psychiatrist will define target symptoms and discuss the goals and anticipated effects of the medication. This discussion will also include possible side effects and any precautions parents should take during treatment. The psychiatrist will discuss the anticipated length of treatment; when and what follow-up will be given; and at what point or under what conditions medication will be adjusted or discontinued. A plan will be formulated, on the basis of a baseline mental health status examination, for measuring the child's progress. Medication will be prescribed only after parents have given consent. After the child has begun her course of medication, the psychiatrist will review the youngster's response to and progress on the medication on a regular basis. Dosage adjustments or even changes in medication are made when needed. Discuss with the physician any doubts or concerns you may have about the medication.

Many different medications are prescribed to treat psychiatric disorders in children. The categories of medications include: stimulants, antidepressants, mood stabilizers, anxiolytics, hypnotics, and antipsychotic drugs. See Appendix A: Psychiatric Medications, which contains detailed information about each of these families of medications, including common side effects, generic and brand names, and other important pharmaceutical information.

Community Resources and Prevention Services

Most communities offer resources providing support to children, especially those whose biological vulnerabilities, family lives, and socioeconomic circumstances put them at risk.

These community resources address the temperamental, neurological, cognitive, or physical vulnerabilities of children early in their development. By reducing the risk factors and lessening stress on the children, their parents, and families, some community programs attempt to prevent or limit the later development of behavioral and emotional disorders.

Although the nature and number of programs vary in each community, here are some that may be available in your community.

Prenatal/Infant Development Programs

These programs serve families who are considered to be *at risk* from the prenatal period to the time the child is about four years old. They may be based in a clinic or hospital. Quite often, nurses or professional practitioners bring services into the home during home visits.

During pregnancy, education focuses on such risk factors as inadequate diet, smoking, and alcohol and drug use and abuse. After the baby is born, the nurse or counselor may discuss family planning as well as appropriate parenting practices. In order to improve their parenting skills and interactions with their children, parents may be given instruction in the normal child's physical and psychological development. The program attempts to combat the feelings of isolation that some mothers feel after the birth of a baby. Other programs may offer employment training.

These programs have a range of positive results, including fewer low-birth weight babies, better physical health for mother and child, improved nutrition, fewer accidents and emergency room visits, and reduced incidence of child abuse. Parents benefit from such guidance and a stronger social support network, which can improve their parenting skills and enrich parent-child interactions. In addition, these services improve stability in marital relationships, extend the time between pregnancies, and encourage more frequent and appropriate use of other medical, educational, and social services.

Preschool Programs

These include such programs as Head Start, which was developed in 1960 for disadvantaged children. In Head Start programs, children are given basic preparation for kindergarten and elementary school by introducing them to school materials and subject matter, as well as assistance in developing cognitive and motor skills that children from advantaged homes have more routinely developed. Children involved in high-quality preschools are less likely, later on, to be held back in school, to need special education, and to drop out of high school. In general, social and emotional development is enhanced, which means increased social competence and more positive attitudes and motivation in school. Long-term results also point to lower rates of juvenile crime and arrest, higher rates of employment and earnings, increased self-sufficiency in adulthood, and fewer teen pregnancies.

Attending preschool helps children develop language skills and better prepares them to read and write. Such programs also help children to develop impulse control. Some programs offer home visits and family support and educational services such as parent training and education to teach skills in caregiving and effective child behavior management.

Primary School Intervention Programs

These programs target middle to late childhood, when children are undergoing a period of rapid cognitive and social development. Usually by the fourth or fifth grade, it is apparent which children are at heightened risk for developing conduct disorders and substance abuse problems. These are the children who have trouble performing the expected academic tasks and show poor social competence, poor impulse control, and aggressive behavior. In addition, conditions at home can also increase the risk of these emotional and behavioral problems, including home situations where there are poor parenting practices, high levels of conflict in the family, and poor relationships between children and their parents.

Schools provide excellent settings to address such risk factors and problems at many levels. Children can be seen individually by counselors (social workers, psychologists, or psychiatrists) or in groups. Behaviorally based classroom interventions promote feelings of competence and mastery and prevent problem behaviors. Interventions that foster social and academic competence by increasing awareness of feelings, attitudes, and values can be used in the classroom with significant success.

Community Intervention Programs

These include programs to address specific stresses in a child's life. Some hospitals offer programs which aim to alleviate some of the anxiety children experience when they must spend time in a hospital. Some hospitals or agencies also offer programs for children with chronic physical illnesses.

Children whose parents suffer from serious emotional or psychiatric illnesses or substance abuse are themselves at higher risk for developing emotional and behavioral difficulties. Programs offered through mental health agencies and hospitals can improve family stability and parenting skills, decrease marital discord, and increase the availability of family supports in these difficult situations.

Children of divorce are recognized as being at an increased risk for emotional and behavioral problems. The immediate and long-term effects of parent separation and divorce, as well as the burden of adapting to new family configurations are better known. Some programs offer children and parents who are involved with divorce a chance to participate in preventive interventions that aim to reduce much of the stress of the events. In some states, for example, it is mandated that children have access to special Children of Divorce Intervention Programs before a divorce can be finalized. These programs seem to reduce the risk and promote healthier adaptation for children of divorce.

Big Brother/Big Sister Programs Offer children from single-parent families the opportunity to develop a relationship with an adult, usually of the same gender as the child. The adult offers the child regular assistance, understanding, and acceptance as they share activities and time together.

Foster Homes Offer a homelike environment for children who experience significant turmoil in their lives and must be removed from their own homes in order to assure their safety or adequate care. Foster homes provide the child temporary care and nurture as well as shelter. (See also *Foster Families,* page 210.)

In order to become foster parents, adults must be licensed, but they rarely have any specific training, other than their own life experience. In recent years, there has been an increase in therapeutic foster homes and "special" foster homes, such as those designed for HIV-infected children or abused children. Usually, a child ends up in foster care only after protective services has become involved with a family in which abuse or neglect has occurred. Some parents, when overwhelmed and fragmented, will request temporary placement for their children in a foster-care home.

Intensive Outpatient, Partial Hospitalization, and Day Treatment

Intensive outpatient, partial hospitalization, and day treatment represent important options for providing psychiatric care to children in settings less restrictive than a hospital. Day hospitals and day treatment offer more intensive care for children for whom one or two office visits per week is insufficient. These programs can be located in hospitals, schools, in other mental health settings, or be freestanding. In these programs, the child lives and sleeps at home.

With the advent of managed care and other recent health-care reforms, the demand for partial hospital and outpatient or day-treatment programs has increased, since they provide an alternative to more costly inpatient hospital stays. In many cases, access to these programs makes hospitalization unnecessary. These programs provide short-term crisis intervention, which can be either an alternative to hospitalization or a transitional setting to shorten hospital stays.

Providing intense, highly structured outpatient treatment, day hospitals, and day treatment programs utilize a variety of therapeutic modalities: individual, group, and family therapy (see pages 404, 411, and 409, respectively), educational and/or vocational therapy, recreation and activity therapy, medical and nursing services, and in some cases medications. Such an array of services requires the involvement of an interdisciplinary staff typically drawn from psychiatry, psychology, social work, educational or vocational therapy, occupational or recreational therapy, and nursing.

Day treatment is useful for moderately to severely disturbed children who can be safely managed in less restrictive settings than hospital or residential care. Some communities have specialized day-treatment programs for children with eating disorders, alcohol and drug abusers, and children with nonpsychiatric conditions such as epilepsy, head trauma, asthma, and sickle-cell disease. Preschoolers with developmental delays, victims of physical and sexual abuse, and children with severe emotional and/or behavioral disturbances often do well in these treatment settings.

The goal of these nonresidential programs is to provide treatment for children requiring intensive therapeutic intervention with the least amount of disruption in their normal daily functioning. However, the evaluation process determines whether the child can be treated safely in a community setting or needs a more restrictive setting such as a hospital or residential treatment center. Children who do well in such open treatment systems usually show a greater ability to control their impulses and comply with program rules.

These open systems rely on family supports and strengths as well as community agencies and programs. Because the child remains in the home, nonresidential treatment encourages the child and family to maintain higher levels of interaction and normal functioning than settings that remove the child from the home. Parents, however, must be able to provide adequate control and support at home during evenings and weekends. Techniques that are used in treatment must be used at home. Parents must be receptive to and involved in most treatment strategies and techniques. Parents might also engage in their own therapy and usually must be able to provide transportation for the child to the day-treatment program.

Treatment is based on a plan developed by a treatment team. A child's progress in treatment is continuously monitored, with changes made to the plan as needed. The length of treatment varies according to diagnosis, severity, the needs of the child and family, and on insurance coverage and the managed care company reviewing the treatment, but discharge planning is an integral part of each child's treatment plan. Before the child leaves the treatment milieu for the community, there must be a comprehensive plan for aftercare, including plans for continuation of her therapy, schooling, and follow-up.

Hospitalization

Occasionally because of severe symptoms or a concern for safety of the child or of other children, the youngster will require psychiatric treatment in a hospital. Depending on what's available in the community, a child may be admitted to a special unit in a general hospital or to a psychiatric hospital. The goal of inpatient psychiatric treatment is to provide comprehensive evaluation and treatment, involving a number of different disciplines and treatments.

Today psychiatric hospitals tend to provide

evaluation, crisis-intervention, and crisis stabilization rather than long-term treatment. Specialized multidisciplinary treatment teams with child and adolescent psychiatrists, pediatricians, psychologists, social workers, nurses, and teachers may also have access to high technology diagnostic testing, including brain imaging, electroencephalography, and chromosomal analysis. Treatment typically includes an individualized mix of group, family, and individual psychotherapies, along with medication.

By its very nature, hospital treatment is the most restrictive, taking place in an out-of-home institutional setting. The level of structure varies among psychiatric hospitals and depends largely on whether the admission is voluntary or involuntary; whether the unit is locked or unlocked; on policies regarding parent participation (it may be encouraged or discouraged); and whether visits to the home community are facilitated or prevented.

The average length of stay varies from setting to setting. In many cases, the stay is dictated by diagnostic considerations, the progress of medication therapies, and by funding availability or insurance coverage. In some areas, managed care has reduced the availability and utilization of hospital treatment even though the hospital benefit may be provided by insurance coverage. At present, the stays are typically defined as up to three days for emergencies (see page 400); up to fourteen days for acute conditions; up to thirty days for short-term treatment; between one and three months for intermediate treatment; and more than three months for long-term treatment. Managed care has had a pro-

found impact on the use of inpatient care. Fewer children and adolescents are being admitted to hospitals, lengths of stay have been decreased, and fewer patients gain access to longer-term treatment.

Children may be hospitalized with a broad group of disorders including adjustment disorders, thought disorders and childhood onset psychosis, behavioral disorders, emotional disorders, eating disorders, substance abuse, and pervasive developmental disorders.

Usually hospitals separate patients according to the developmental age of child, much the same way as do schools. For example, there may be programs for children six to twelve (elementary school) and for teenagers (middle school and high school). Inclusion of children and adolescents in psychiatric units for adults is not ordinarily recommended.

Inpatient treatment includes many different modalities and many different clinicians. Special education programs are also an important aspect of inpatient treatment. A majority of children hospitalized on psychiatric inpatient units have significant cognitive and/or academic difficulties. Identification of these disorders and the development of remedial teaching strategies can play an important part in a child's progress.

When appropriately and effectively utilized, hospitalization results in safety, stabilization, and a comprehensive understanding of the child's problems, context, and treatment needs. Often the treatment team can then provide linkages with an array of services in the community, such as school system, day treatment, in-home services, therapeutic foster care, protective services, medical providers, traditional outpatient services, housing resources, and recreation programs. The goal is to enable the child to return to his home and community and continue with healthy development.

Residential Treatment

Some children need stable, long-term treatment, especially when their emotional and therapeutic needs are great, and their family and environmental resources are overwhelmed, inadequate, or uncertain. Residential treatment provides stability, and intensive therapeutic and remedial interventions in a setting away from the child's home.

Residential treatment typically takes place in a campuslike setting that is not a hospital. It provides individually planned programs of mental health treatment services in conjunction with residential care. The professional staff at a residential treatment center may include child-care workers, teachers, social workers, child and adolescent psychiatrists, pediatricians, nurses, and psychologists.

Residential centers offer a setting in which there is space for therapy programs, school, and evening and weekend activity programs. Children live in small groups. Depending on the individual center, children have private or shared bedrooms, separate showers and bath facilities for boys and girls, and communal living and dining rooms. Recreational facilities, classrooms, medical services, and various community resources are usually located nearby.

Each residential center has an admission process. Most are relatively targeted in terms of the type of disorders and age of children they serve.

Residential treatment often suits children who are out of control. These children lack age-appropriate internal controls and therefore require external controls. Children who have moderately severe antisocial (delinquent) and aggressive behaviors, or psychotic symptoms (see *Psychotic Disorders*, page 372) may do particularly well in residential treatment centers. Many children admitted to residential treatment also have severe learning problems.

Children with clinical diagnoses of pervasive or specific developmental disorders, attention-deficit/hyperactivity disorder, conduct disorders, depression, manic-depressive disorder, or severe anxiety disorders may be referred for residential placement. Problems such as organic brain damage; severely disturbed or chaotic families; and impoverished socioeconomic backgrounds may lead a child to residential treatment. A background that includes parental deprivation, loss, and sexual or physical abuse may also lead to residential placement.

Most children admitted to residential treatment have been through the community mental health system with little success. They have often been seen by one or more clinicians and been to a child guidance clinic, juvenile court, or state welfare agency. Typically, previous attempts at outpatient treatment and foster home or other custodial placement have not been able to help the child.

■ ADMITTING THE CHILD

Admission to a residential treatment center usually begins with an intensive evaluation process. Information is gathered from previous clinicians and treatment centers; family and individual interviews, psychological testing, and neurological examinations are conducted when indicated. The needs of the child, the skills and training of the staff, the balance of the child's strengths and problems, and the chance that the child will be helped are some of the variables weighed during the admissions process. Parents may or may not be directly involved in their child's treatment.

The child's evaluation is usually a collaborative effort of the staff. A treatment program is tailored to meet the child's needs and then progress is monitored.

The largest amount of time in the child's life—and therefore, the bulk of the therapeutic work—is spent in group living. Behavioral therapy and psychoeducational principles are applied to address such problematic behaviors as temper tantrums, fighting, withdrawal, bed-wetting, poor feeding habits, and inadequate peer relations. Children are involved in intensive individual and group therapy. Some take medication for specific symptoms or disorders. School problems that are rooted in severe learning disabilities and disruptive behavior are routinely assessed and addressed in the school, either on campus or in the community.

The goal is improvement in the ability to relate to others and to function in and out of school. Many have the opportunity to work through certain types of past trauma during this residential phase of treatment. When children leave residential treatment, they may react with feelings of loss and a temporary regression may occur, with heightened acting out and aggressive behavior.

Follow-up after discharge varies. Many residential treatment centers have their own step-down programs, so that a child moves from residential treatment into a day-treatment program or off-grounds school program. Most children eventually return to their families but continue with community and outpatient treatments in order to further consolidate and enhance progress. Others go into group or foster homes, boarding school, further residential treatment, or custodial care.

APPENDICES

APPENDIX A

Psychiatric Medications

Prescription medications have become an important part of treatment for a number of psychiatric disorders in children and adolescents. However, medications are seldom used in isolation but as one element of an overall approach. A psychiatric medication should be prescribed for your youngster only after a through psychiatric evaluation has been completed (see *The Psychiatric Evaluation*, page 394). These medications cannot cure all problems but can be effective treatments for specific troubling symptoms, problem behaviors, or certain psychiatric disorders.

The medication must be part of a comprehensive treatment plan, which usually includes individual or other psychotherapeutic approaches (see *Individual Psychotherapy,* page 404; *Psychodynamic Psychotherapy,* page 406; *Cognitive-Behavioral Therapy,* page 407; *Family Therapy,* page 409, or *Group Therapy*, page 411). Like other prescription medications, psychiatric medications can only be pre-

scribed by a licensed physician. Psychiatrists, however, are physicians who are specifically trained in using psychiatric medications and, more specifically, child and adolescent psychiatrists are trained to use these medications in young people.

When a child psychiatrist prescribes a medication, both parent and youngster may have concerns and questions. Full explanations should be given for why the medication is being prescribed, what benefits may result, the potential side effects, and other treatment alternatives, if any. (See also *Your Child's Medication: Questions to Ask the Doctor,* page 426).

Most medications have some side effects. These can range from minor (for example, dry mouth, constipation, or stomach upset) to serious (such as liver inflammation, kidney dysfunction, or changes in heart rhythm). Fortunately, the most common side effects are minor and the serious ones rare. Your child's psychiatrist should discuss these risks with you.

YOUR CHILD'S MEDICATION:
QUESTIONS TO ASK THE DOCTOR

When a medication is prescribed for your child or adolescent, you have a responsibility as a parent to learn as much as you can about the medication. The prescribing child psychiatrist will explain to you the expected role the medication is to play in the comprehensive treatment plan, and will monitor and evaluate the effectiveness of the drug. The following issues should also be discussed with you and your child.

◾ **The name of the medication.**
What is the generic name of the medication? The brand name? Are there other brand names by which it is known?

◾ **Action of the medication.**
How does the medication work? How does it affect your child's brain or body to produce the desired emotional, behavioral, or cognitive changes? What is known about its efficacy in other children with similar conditions?

◾ **Instructions.**
How is the medication to be taken—before, after, or with meals? With water? How many times per day? Are certain foods or other medications to be avoided while using the prescribed medication? Are there activities that should be avoided while taking it?

◾ **Side effects.**
What are the potential side effects? Are some of them permanent or life-threatening? What should be done if side effects occur? Is the medication potentially addictive?

◾ **Laboratory tests.**
Are any laboratory tests (for example, electrocardiogram or blood tests) required prior to the youngster's taking the medication? Are lab tests necessary to monitor the effects of the medication during use?

◾ **Indications.**
Why is this medication necessary? Medications are tested in a variety of trials before being marketed. The Food and Drug Administration reviews the data and

deems them sufficient before permitting drugs to be sold. FDA approval will specify that a given medication has efficacy in treating a given disorder—that is the disorder for which the drug is *indicated*. However, it is common that a medication is valuable in treating other disorders for which there are not FDA *indications* and, as a result, the medications may be prescribed in such cases. Be aware that most trials are conducted on adults, most often men. Before your child begins taking a medication, discuss its indications with the prescribing physician.

■ **Drug interactions.**

If your youngster is taking another medication, prescribed for example by his pediatrician for a common disorder like acne or asthma, is there a potential problem? Discuss this, too, with your child's psychiatrist.

■ **Follow-up.**

How often will the child need to see the doctor to determine how the youngster is responding to the medication and whether the dosage should be changed? How long will this medication be necessary?

■ **Cost.**

How much does it cost? Are there less expensive generic brands of the same medication on the market?

Ask these questions *before* your child or adolescent starts taking the medication. If you are not satisfied with all the answers, seek a second opinion.

The Medication Directory

In the pages that follow are individual entries for medications that are commonly prescribed by child and adolescent psychiatrists. The organization is alphabetical; for ease of reference, both brand and generic names are included. Because new products continually arrive on the market, this list cannot be all inclusive. Nor is the inclusion of a medication in these pages an endorsement.

When a medication is first developed, it is given a **generic** name, approved by government agencies, which identifies it as being different from all others. In this appendix, generic names are listed in **boldface** type.

When a medication is marketed, the maker gives it a proprietary name, its *brand* name. Brand names are listed in *italic* type. Brand names are the exclusive property of the original manufacturer who, for a fixed period, has the sole right to sell that medication under its own brand name. When the patent expires, other drug companies may produce and sell the medication under its generic name or their own brand names. That's why some drugs are available under a variety of names.

When taking any medication, your youngster needs to follow carefully the child psychiatrist's instructions regarding administration, dosage, and proper storage. If any side effects occur, consult your pediatrician, psychiatrist, or pharmacist immediately. Always tell your physician about other prescriptions, over-the-counter drugs, and health supplements that your child may be taking. Beneath the entry for each generic name, you will find the medication family to which the medication belongs; the brand names under which it is sold; the common uses and indications; and some of the potential side effects. If you don't see the reason cited that your child is taking a specific medication, ask your doctor. There are occasionally extenuating circumstances for the use of certain medications beyond the typical ones.

■   ■   ■

ADDERALL
> Brand name of the psychostimulant medicationdextroamphetamine/amphetamine.

ALPRAZOLAM
> *Medication Family:*
> A benzodiazepine antianxiety medication
> *Brand Name:*
> Xanax
> *Common Uses and Indications:*
> Separation anxiety disorder, panic disorder, generalized anxiety
> *Potential Side Effects:*
> Drowsiness, lethargy, dependence, loss of inhibition

AMITRIPTYLINE
> *Medication Family:*
> Tricyclic antidepressant medication
> *Brand Names:*
> Elavil, Endep
> *Common Uses and Indications:*
> Depressive disorders

> *Potential Side Effects:*
> Dry mouth, constipation, cardiovascular changes, dizziness

ANAFRANIL
> Brand name of the tricyclic antidepressant medication clomipramine.

ATENOLOL
> *Medication Family:*
> Beta blocker antihypertensive medication
> *Brand Names:*
> Tenormin
> *Common Uses and Indications:*
> Anxiety, performance anxiety, impulse-control disorders
> *Potential Side Effects:*
> Lethargy, numbness in fingers, decreased heart rate and blood pressure

ATIVAN
> Brand name for the antianxiety medication lorazepam.

BENADRYL
> Brand name for the antihistamine medication diphenhydramine hydrochloride.

BENZTROPINE
> *Medication Family:*
> Anticholingeric
> *Brand Names:*
> Cogentin
> *Common Uses and Indications:*
> Control of muscular spasms and other side effects of certain antipsychotic medications
> *Potential Side Effects:*
> Increased heart rate, constipation, dry mouth, confusion, blurred vision

BUPROPION
> *Medication Family:*
> Antidepressant medication
> *Brand Names:*
> Wellbutrin, Zyban
> *Common Uses and Indications:*
> Major depression, attention-deficit/hyperactivity disorder, smoking cessation
> *Potential Side Effects:*
> Appetite reduction, nausea, sleeplessness, dry mouth, constipation; rarely, seizures, dizziness

BUSPAR
> Brand name of the antianxiety medication buspirone.

BUSPIRONE
> *Medication Family:*
> Antianxiety medication
> *Brand Names:*
> BuSpar
> *Common Uses and Indications:*
> Anxiety, extreme anger

> *Potential Side Effects:*
> Nausea, headache

CALAN
> Brand name for the calcium-channel-blocker antihypertensive medication verapamil hydrochloride.

CARBAMAZEPINE
> *Medication Family:*
> Anticonvulsant medication
> *Brand Names:*
> Tegretol
> *Common Uses and Indications:*
> Major depression, bipolar disorder, impulse-control disorder
> *Potential Side Effects:*
> Double vision, nausea, drowsiness, poor coordination, reduced white blood cell count

CAFTAPRES
> Brand name for the antihypertensive medication clonidine.

CHLORPROMAZINE
> *Medication Family:*
> Antipsychotic medication
> *Brand Names:*
> Thorazine
> *Common Uses and Indications:*
> Schizophrenia, psychotic symptoms, agitation
> *Potential Side Effects:*
> Drowsiness, dry mouth, constipation, weight gain, blurred vision, muscle spasms, restlessness, involuntary movements, tremors, blood pressure changes

CLOMIPRAMINE
> *Medication Family:*
> Tricyclic antidepressant medication

Brand Names:
   Anafranil
Common Uses and Indications:
   Obsessive-compulsive disorder
Potential Side Effects:
   Drowsiness, headache, dry mouth, constipation, stomach upset, excess sweating, tremor, cardiovascular and blood pressure effects, weight gain

CLONAZEPAM

Medication Family:
   Antianxiety medication, anticonvulsant
Brand Names:
   Klonopin
Common Uses and Indications:
   Anxiety, panic disorder, separation anxiety, seizures
Potential Side Effects:
   Drowsiness, irritability, dependence, lethargy, diminished inhibitions

CLONIDINE

Medication Family:
   Antihypertensive medication
Brand Names:
   Catapres
Common Uses and Indications:
   Attention-deficit/hyperactivity disorder, Tourette's disorder
Potential Side Effects:
   Drowsiness, cardiovascular and blood pressure changes, stomach upset, depression

CLOZAPINE

Medication Family:
   Antipsychotic medication
Brand Names:
   Clozaril
Common Uses and Indications:
   Schizophrenia and bipolar disorder

Potential Side Effects:
   Drowsiness, exaggerated salivation, constipation, weight gain, nausea, dizziness, decreased white blood cell count, seizures

CLOZARIL

Brand name of the antipsychotic medication clozapine.

COGENTIN

Brand name of the anticholingeric medication benztropine.

CYLERT

Brand name of the psychostimulant medication pemoline.

DALMANE

Brand name of the sedative/hypnotic flurazepam.

DDAVP

Brand name of the analogue of antidiuretic hormone, desmopressin.

DEPAKENE

Brand name of the anticonvulsant medication valproic acid.

DEPAKOTE

Brand name of the anticonvulsant medication valproic acid.

DESIPRAMINE

Medication Family:
   Tricyclic antidepressant medication
Brand Names:
   Norpramin
Common Uses and Indications:
   Depression, attention-deficit/hyperactivity disorder
Potential Side Effects:
   Drowsiness, dry mouth, blood pressure

and cardiovascular effects, weight gain, constipation, blurred vision

DESMOPRESSIN

Medication Family:
Synthetic antidiuretic hormone
Brand Names:
DDAVP
Common Uses and Indications:
Enuresis (bed-wetting)
Potential Side Effects:
Nasal dryness, headaches

DESYREL

Brand name of the antidepressant medication trazodone.

DEXEDRINE

Brand name of the psychostimulant dextroamphetamine.

DEXTROAMPHETAMINE

Medication Family:
Psychostimulant medication
Brand Names:
Dexedrine
Common Uses and Indications:
Attention-deficit/hyperactivity disorder
Potential Side Effects:
Appetite reduction, sleeplessness, irritability, weepiness, increased heart rate, decreased growth rate

DEXTROAMPHETAMINE/AMPHETAMINE

Medication Family:
Psychostimulant medication
Brand Names:
Adderall
Common Uses and Indications:
Attention-deficit/hyperactivity disorder
Potential Side Effects:
Appetite reduction, sleeplessness,

irritability, weepiness, increased heart rate, decreased growth rate

DIAZEPAM

Medication Family:
A benzodiazepine antianxiety medication
Brand Names:
Valium
Common Uses and Indications:
Anxiety, night terrors
Potential Side Effects:
Drowsiness, reduced inhibitions, dependence, lethargy

DILANTIN

Brand name of the anticonvulsant medication phenytoin.

DIPHENHYDRAMINE HYDROCHLORIDE

Medication Family:
Antihistamine
Brand Names:
Benadryl
Common Uses and Indications:
Sedation; control of side effects of antipsychotic medications
Potential Side Effects:
Drowsiness, rash, decreased blood pressure, unsteadiness, gastrointestinal disturbances

DOXEPIN

Medication Family:
Tricyclic antidepressant medication
Brand Names:
Sinequan
Common Uses and Indications:
Major depression
Potential Side Effects:
Dry mouth, constipation, dizziness, cardiovascular changes

EFFEXOR
Brand name of the antidepressant medication venlafaxine.

ELAVIL
Brand name of the tricyclic antidepressant medication amitriptyline.

ENDEP
Brand name of the tricyclic antidepressant medication amitriptyline

ESKALITH
Brand name of the mood stabilizer lithium.

FLUPHENAZINE
Medication Family:
An antipsychotic medication
Brand Names:
Prolixen
Common Uses and Indications:
Psychotic symptoms, schizophrenia, Tourette's and similar conditions
Potential Side Effects:
Drowsiness, restlessness, muscular rigidity, tremor, blurred vision, constipation, dry mouth, involuntary movements, blood pressure changes, weight gain

FLURAZEPAM
Medication Family:
Sedative/hypnotic
Brand Names:
Dalmane
Common Uses and Indications:
Insomnia
Potential Side Effects:
Drowsiness, dizziness, dependence

FLUVOXAMINE
Medication Family:
A selective serotonin-reuptake-inhibitor antidepressant medication

Brand Names:
Luvox
Common Uses and Indications:
Depression, obsessive-compulsive disorder
Potential Side Effects:
Nausea, diarrhea, sleeplessness, jitteriness, stomach upset, excess sweating

FLUOXETINE
Medication Family:
A selective serotonin-reuptake-inhibitor antidepressant medication
Brand Names:
Prozac
Common Uses and Indications:
Obsessive-compulsive disorder, major depression, eating disorders
Potential Side Effects:
Nausea, diarrhea, upset stomach, appetite change, sleeplessness, drowsiness, jitteriness, excess sweating

GUANFACINE
Medication Family:
An antihypertensive medication
Brand Names:
Tenex
Common Uses and Indications:
Attention-deficit/hyperactivity disorder
Potential Side Effects:
Drowsiness, headache, dry mouth, constipation, nausea, cardiovascular and blood-pressure changes

HALDOL
Brand name of the antipsychotic drug haloperidol.

HALOPERIDOL
Medication Family:
Antipsychotic medication

Brand Names:
Haldol
Common Uses and Indications:
Schizophrenia, psychotic symptoms, Tourette's disorder
Potential Side Effects:
Drowsiness, muscle rigidity or tremor, restlessness, dry mouth, blurred vision, constipation, involuntary movements, weight gain

IMIPRAMINE
Medication Family:
Tricyclic antidepressant medication
Brand Names:
Tofranil
Common Uses and Indications:
Attention-deficit/hyperactivity disorder, major depression, panic disorder, separation anxiety disorder, enuresis (bed-wetting)
Potential Side Effects:
Dry mouth, drowsiness, blood pressure and cardiovascular effects, constipation, blurred vision

INDERAL
Brand name of the beta blocker propranolol.

KLONOPIN
Brand name of the benzodiazepine medication clonazepam.

LITHOBID
Brand name of the mood stabilizer medication lithium.

LITHIUM
Medication Family:
Mood stabilizer medication
Brand Names:
Eskalith, Lithobid
Common Uses and Indications:
Bipolar disorder, extreme anger, major depression
Potential Side Effects:
Nausea, vomiting, sedation, diarrhea, weight gain, tremor, acne, increased urination, thirst, decreased concentration, kidney dysfunction, hypothyroidism

LORAZEPAM
Medication Family:
Antianxiety medication
Brand Names:
Ativan
Common Uses and Indications:
Anxiety, agitation, insomnia
Potential Side Effects:
Drowsiness, dizziness, unsteadiness, diminished inhibition, dependence, diminished concentration

LUVOX
Brand name of the selective serotonin-reuptake-inhibitor medication fluvoxamine.

MELLARIL
Brand name of the antipsychotic medication thioridazine.

METHYLPHENIDATE
Medication Family:
Psychostimulant medication
Brand Names:
Ritalin
Common Uses and Indications:
Attention-deficit/hyperactivity disorder, impulsivity
Potential Side Effects:
Appetite reduction, nausea, sleeplessness, headaches, weepiness, increased heart rate, decrease in growth rate

MOBAN

Brand name of the antipsychotic medication molindone.

MOLINDONE

Medication Family:

Antipsychotic medication

Brand Names:

Moban

Common Uses and Indications:

Schizophrenia, psychotic symptoms

Potential Side Effects:

Drowsiness, muscle rigidity or tremor, restlessness, dry mouth, blurred vision, constipation, involuntary movements, blood pressure changes, weight gain

NARDIL

Brand name of the monoamine-oxidase-inhibitor antidepressant medication phenelzine.

NAVANE

Brand name of the antipsychotic medication thiothixene.

NORPRAMIN

Brand name of the tricyclic antidepressant medication desipramine.

NEFAZODONE HYDROCHLORIDE

Medication Family:

Antidepressant

Brand Names:

Serzone

Common Uses and Indications:

Major depression

Potential Side Effects:

Decreased blood pressure, headache, dry mouth, nausea, drowsiness

NORTRIPTYLINE

Medication Family:

Tricyclic antedepressant medication

Brand Names:

Pamelor, Aventyl

Common Uses and Indications:

Attention-deficit/hyperactivity disorder, major depression, panic disorder

Potential Side Effects:

Drowsiness, dry mouth, blood pressure and cardiac effects

OLANZAPINE

Medication Family:

Antipsychotic mediction

Brand Names:

Zyprexa

Common Uses and Indications:

Schizophrenia, psychotic symptoms

Potential Side Effects:

Drowsiness, weight gain, cardiovascular and blood pressure changes, dry mouth, blurred vision, constipation, muscle spasms or rigidity, tremor

ORAP

Brand name for the antipsychotic medication pimozide.

PAMELOR

Brand name of the tricyclic antidepressant medication nortriptyline.

PARNATE

Brand name of the monoamine-oxidase-inhibitor antidepressant tranylcypromine.

PAXIL

Brand name of the selective serotonin-reuptake-inhibitor paroxetine.

PAROXETINE

Medication Family:
A selective serotonin-reuptake-inhibitor antidepressant medication

Brand Names:
Paxil

Common Uses and Indications:
Major depression, obsessive-compulsive disorder

Potential Side Effects:
Nausea, diarrhea, appetite changes, stomach upset, sleeplessness, jitteriness, excess sweating, dry mouth

PEMOLINE

Medication Family:
Psychostimulant medication

Brand Names:
Cylert

Common Uses and Indications:
Attention-deficit/hyperactivity disorder

Potential Side Effects:
Appetite reduction, nausea, sleeplessness, decreased growth rate, irritability, increased heart rate, headaches, liver inflammation

PERPHENAZINE

Medication Family:
Antipsychotic medication

Brand Names:
Trilafon

Common Uses and Indications:
Schizophrenia, psychotic symptoms

Potential Side Effects:
Drowsiness, tremor, muscle rigidity, restlessness, dry mouth, blurred vision, constipation, blood-pressure changes

PHENELZINE

Medication Family:
Monoamine-oxidase-inhibitor antidepressant medication

Brand Names:
Nardil

Common Uses and Indications:
Depression

Potential Side Effects:
Lowered blood pressure, weight gain, dizziness, high-blood pressure after eating foods containing tyramine

PHENYTOIN

Medication Family:
Anticonvulsant

Brand Names:
Dilantin

Common Uses and Indications:
Seizure disorders

Potential Side Effects:
Balance and coordination problems, confusion, slurred speech, nausea, gingival (gum) problems

PIMOZIDE

Medication Family:
Antipsychotic medication

Brand Names:
Orap

Common Uses and Indications:
Tourette's disorder

Potential Side Effects:
Drowsiness, muscle rigidity, tremor, restlessness, dry mouth, blurred vision, constipation, cardiovascular and blood-pressure changes, involuntary movements

PROLIXEN
    Brand name of the antipsychotic
    fluphenazine.

PROPRANOLOL
    Medication Family:
        Beta-blocker antianxiety and
        antihypertensive medication
    Brand Names:
        Inderal
    Common Uses and Indications:
        Anxiety, performance anxiety, impulse-
        control disorders, migraine
    Potential Side Effects:
        Lethargy, depression, decreased heart
        rate, decreased blood pressure, wheezing

PROZAC
    Brand name of the selective serotonin-
    reuptake-inhibitor fluoxetine.

RISPERDAL
    Brand name for the antipsychotic
    risperidone.

RISPERIDONE
    Medication Family:
        Antipsychotic medication
    Brand Names:
        Risperdal
    Common Uses and Indications:
        Schizophrenia, psychotic symptoms,
        impulse-control disorders
    Potential Side Effects:
        Drowsiness, restlessness, weight gain,
        muscle rigidity, decreased blood pressure,
        diminished concentration, dry mouth,
        constipation, blurred vision, involuntary
        movements

RITALIN
    Brand name for the psychostimulant
    methylphenidate.

SERTRALINE
    Medication Family:
        A selective serotonin-reuptake-inhibitor
        antidepressant medication
    Brand Names:
        Zoloft
    Common Uses and Indications:
        Major depression, obsessive-compulsive
        disorder, panic disorder
    Potential Side Effects:
        Nausea, diarrhea, stomach upset, sleep-
        lessness, jitteriness, excess sweating,
        drowsiness

SERZONE
    Brand name of the antidepressant
    medication nefazodone hydrochloride

SINEQUAN
    Brand name of the tricyclic
    antidepressant medication doxepin.

STELAZINE
    Brand name of the antipsychotic
    medication trifluoperazine.

TEGRETOL
    Brand name of the anticonvulsant
    medication carbamazepine.

TENEX
    Brand name for the antihypertensive
    guanfacine.

TENORMIN
    Brand name for the beta blocker atenolol.

THIOTHIXENE
    Medication Family:
        Antipsychotic medication
    Brand Names:
        Navane
    Common Uses and Indications:
        Schizophrenia, psychotic symptoms

Potential Side Effects:
Drowsiness, dry mouth, blurred vision, constipation, muscle rigidity, restlessness, blood pressure changes, weight gain, involuntary movements

THIORIDAZINE
Medication Family:
Antipsychotic medication
Brand Names:
Mellaril
Common Uses and Indications:
Schizophrenia, psychotic symptoms, impulse-control disorders
Potential Side Effects:
Drowsiness, dry mouth, constipation, weight gain, blurred vision, muscle rigidity, restlessness, blood pressure changes, weight gain, involuntary movements

THORAZINE
Brand name of the antipsychotic chlorpromazine.

TOFRANIL
Brand name of the tricyclic antidepressant medication imipramine.

TRANYLCYPROMINE
Medication Family:
Monoamine-oxidase-inhibitor antidepressant medication
Brand Names:
Parnate
Common Uses and Indications:
Major depression
Potential Side Effects:
Decreased blood pressure, dizziness, elevated blood pressure after eating foods containing tyramine, restlessness, jitteriness

TRAZODONE
Medication Family:
Antidepressant medication
Brand Names:
Desyrel
Common Uses and Indications:
Depression, insomnia
Potential Side Effects:
Drowsiness, persistent penile erections, blood pressure changes

TRIFLUOPERAZINE
Medication Family:
Antipsychotic medication
Brand Names:
Stelazine
Common Uses and Indications:
Schizophrenia, psychotic symptoms
Potential Side Effects:
Drowsiness, dry mouth, blurred vision, constipation, muscle rigidity, restlessness, blood pressure change, weight gain, involuntary movements

TRILAFON
Brand name of the antipsychotic perphenazine.

VALIUM
Brand name of the benzodiazepine diazepam.

VALPROIC ACID
Medication Family:
Anticonvulsant medication
Brand Names:
Depakene, Depakote
Common Uses and Indications:
Bipolar disorder, major depression
Potential Side Effects:
Stomach upset, vomiting, nausea, weight gain, drowsiness, tremor, liver toxicity

Venlafaxine

Medication Family:

Antidepressant medication

Brand Names:

Effexor

Common Uses and Indications:

Major depression, obsessive-compulsive disorder

Potential Side Effects:

Drowsiness, dry mouth, nausea, excess sweating, constipation, blurred vision, elevated blood pressure, decreased appetite, tremor

Verapamil Hydrochloride

Medication Family:

Calcium-channel-blocker antihypertensive

Brand Names:

Calan

Common Uses and Indications:

Bipolar disorder, hypertension

Potential Side Effects:

Constipation, low blood pressure, headache, dizziness, fatigue

Wellbutrin

Brand name of the antidepressant medication bupropion.

Xanax

Brand name of the benzodiazepine alprazolam.

Zoloft

Brand name of the selective serotonin-reuptake-inhibitor sertraline.

Zyprexa

Brand name of the antipsychotic medication olanzapine.

Medical, Psychological, Educational, and Developmental Tests

In arriving at a diagnosis, your child's physician, child and adolescent psychiatrist, or other clinician may require specialized information about your youngster. In addition to talking to you, examining your child, and obtaining a range of information about your youngster's symptoms, behavior, and development, the clinician may order one or more diagnostic tests.

The nature of testing will vary according to specific symptoms. If a physician suspects lead poisoning, a blood test may be conducted to determine the serum level of lead. Specialized tests like the Continuous Performance Test may be done to evaluate a youngster's ability to concentrate on specific tasks, which can be useful in diagnosing attention-deficit/hyperactivity disorder. Intelligence and developmental tests may be conducted to evaluate a child's intellectual, speech, motor, and other areas of development.

In the pages that follow, the diagnostic tests most commonly used in evaluating cognitive, behavioral, and developmental problems in children are discussed.

Medical Tests

A wide range of medical tests is routinely used by medical professionals to help diagnose—and often to rule out—many disorders, both psychiatric and physiological. This appendix does not attempt, however, to cover the whole catalogue of medical tests, but only those that are most commonly used by the child and adolescent psychiatrist seeking to diagnose psychiatric disorders.

Blood Tests Blood tests are conducted to identify the presence of certain conditions. A blood sample can be examined in multiple ways. Some tests measure the levels of the different types of blood cells; other seek to identify enzymes, toxins, or certain chemicals in the blood. The volume of blood required for some blood tests is as small as a few drops, in which case a small prick of a fingertip will produce the required amount. For other studies, a larger amount of blood is required, in which case a thin needle inserted into an arm vein will allow the blood to be withdrawn into a syringe. While this is a bit painful, a skilled technician can help the patient relax and make the procedure as easy as possible.

COMPLETE BLOOD COUNT The CBC is the most commonly conducted blood test. Most often done as part of a complete checkup, the CBC measures the amount of hemoglobin in the blood, as well as the red blood cells (*hematocrit*), the number and types of white blood cells, and the platelets (which help in clotting the blood) in a given sample. The CBC can be used to monitor the side effects of certain medications.

BLOOD SERUM CHEMISTRY Blood chemistry tests measure the amounts of sodium, potassium, chloride, and phosphorus (the electrolytes) in the blood; blood sugar (glucose); and a variety of enzymes and chemical by-products produced by the body. Some blood serum chemistry examinations may also be done to monitor the possible side effects of some medications on kidney and liver function.

THYROID FUNCTION Blood may be drawn to measure serum levels of hormones such as thyroxine and thyroid-stimulating hormone. These tests can be used in evaluating certain mood disorders and the possible side effects of some medications.

CHROMOSOMAL ANALYSIS May be done to evaluate for genetic disorders such as Down's syndrome and Fragile-X syndrome.

SCREENING TESTS May be conducted to identify antistreptococcal antibodies, mononucleosis, or Human Immunodeficiency Virus (HIV), each of which can be a factor in certain emotional or behavioral problems. A screening test may also be done to identify elevated levels of lead in the blood, which may be linked to attention-deficit/hyperactivity disorder.

MEDICATION LEVELS Can be measured in monitoring correct dosages of medications such as lithium, carbamazepine, depakote, and certain antidepressants.

SERUM TOXICOLOGY STUDIES May be ordered to identify the presence of unknown drugs, alcohol, or other chemicals in the body which can help explain sudden behavior changes, toxic delirium, or to confirm substance abuse.

Urine Tests Urine tests are a routine part of a comprehensive health examination. Your child's physician will usually order a urinalysis at your youngster's periodic checkups, typically testing for protein and sugar (glucose) as well as a microscopic examination of the sediment in the urine. All your youngster needs to do is provide a small amount of urine in a cup, which is then sealed in a special container, labeled, and sent to a laboratory for testing.

When treating certain psychiatric disorders, there are two other circumstances when urine tests may be appropriate. Some medications, including certain mood stabilizers and antidepressants, may on rare occasions damage the kidneys, so the child and adolescent psychiatrist or other physician may conduct a *routine urinalysis* to monitor kidney function. If substance abuse is suspected, a *urine drug screen* may be ordered to test for the use of drugs. Some substances, like marijuana, may appear in the urine for several days or weeks after use, depending on the amount of substance ingested.

Imaging Tests   For decades, doctors have been employing X-ray examination to view the internal structures of the body. The technology has proven its worth countless times in diagnosing injuries and disorders of the skeleton, the teeth, and a variety of internal organs. Recently, new types of procedures like *computerized tomography* (CT scanning) and *magnetic resonance imaging* (MRI) have added to the range of choices your physician has in seeking to understand the anatomy within the body. For the child and adolescent psychiatrist, too, each of these imaging techniques has a number of uses.

X rays, CT scans, and MRIs each involve immobilizing the patient on a specially designed table, while the X rays or electromagnetic energy are used to create an image. The X ray takes only a few seconds to complete, while the MRI and CT scan may require an hour or more. Other than the discomfort of being still for a period of time, which can sometimes be frustrating for youngsters, none of these examinations result in pain for the child.

THE SKULL X RAY   The skull X ray can be an invaluable tool for evaluating certain conditions that may affect your emotions or behavior. The film image produced can be examined ("read") for evidence of abnormalities or to investigate for skull fractures. The skull X ray can be particularly useful in cases of trauma and physical abuse.

CT SCANS AND MAGNETIC RESONANCE IMAGING.   Like the traditional X ray, the CT scan employs an X-ray beam that passes through the body. In the case of computerized tomography, the beam is then processed by a computer to produce an image. The CT scan is many times more detailed than an X ray.

The MRI is also used to generate a picture of the body's internal structure but, unlike the X ray, the MRI employs electromagnetic energy to provide image information. No ionizing radiation is required, as with conventional X rays and CT scans.

The greater sensitivity of both the MRI and the CT scans mean they are valuable in providing images of soft tissues, the heart, and the blood vessels, as well as the brain. For the child and adolescent psychiatrist, these scanning technologies can be useful in examining for structural changes in the brain that can produce certain emotional and behavioral changes.

Electrical Tests   The human body has its own complex circuitry, and devices have been developed that record electrical activity in the heart and brain. When these recordings are examined, they may reveal a wide variety of symptoms or abnormalities, some of which may prove to be valuable diagnostic clues.

ELECTROCARDIOGRAPH   The EKG or ECG records electrical currents in the heart. The pattern of electrical impulses that is produced can then be examined in detail. For the child and adolescent psychiatrist, an EKG may be used to monitor the side effects of medications that can affect cardiac function. The EKG procedure involves the attachment of electrodes to the chest, wrist, and ankles that record the electrical activity in the heart. Typically about fifteen minutes are required for an EKG, which is painless.

ELECTROENCEPHALOGRAPH The EEG measures and records the patterns of electrical activity that are produced by the brain and is used typically to identify possible seizure disorders. Electrodes will be attached to the child's scalp using a special glue. The electrodes will then detect the electrical activity of the brain, which can be recorded as a "brainwave" on a moving sheet of paper. Typically the test requires only about half an hour. Often the child is given a mild sedative to evaluate patterns of brain activity during sleep. If an unusual seizure disorder or sleep disorder is suspected, the electrodes may be left in place overnight.

Psychological, Educational, and Developmental Tests Many psychological, educational, and developmental tests are in general use. Some are regularly employed in educational settings, so virtually every child of school age will at one time or another take an achievement test in a school setting. Other tests are used either to identify disorders or to explain abnormalities in behavior or development. Thus, when a psychiatric disorder is suspected, one or more developmental tests, adaptive functioning assessments, personality, or neuropsychological tests may be done.

Standardized psychological testing constitutes an important complement to more informal clinical interview techniques. Because most psychological tests were developed using large samples of children, and because the same procedures are used for all youngsters being tested, these psychological tests allow for quantitative comparisons between the performances of specific children and their peers. Specialized tests are recommended for children from whom English is a second language. Only very low or very high scores are interpreted as indicating significant delays or giftednenss.

Psychological testing usually proceeds from a comprehensive examination of such major areas as verbal and visual-spatial skills to more specialized testing of specific problem areas (such as memory or receptive and expressive language). This process ensures that no deficits are missed and that specific problems are examined closely. Each child's unique strengths are identified and specific recommendations for intervention made.

INTELLIGENCE TESTS Intelligence tests are designed to measure children's capacity to learn. These tests can help identify strengths and weaknesses in such areas as comprehension, attention span, math ability, and spatial reasoning. If specific deficits are identified, additional tests of language, memory, spatial perception, or motor functioning may be conducted. In conjunction with achievement tests (see page 442), intelligence tests are used to identify learning disabilities. When mental retardation is suspected, intelligence tests and measures of adaptive functioning (see page 443) are employed.

While there are a number of widely used intelligence tests, the most common are the *Wechsler Intelligence Scale for Children—Third Edition* (WISC-III), which is designed for children six to sixteen years of age; the *Wechsler Pre-School Primary Scale—Revised* (WPPSI-R), an adaptation of WISC-III for children three to seven years of age; and the *Stanford-Binet Intelligence Scale—Fourth Edition,* which can be used for children as young as two years of age. For children aged one to forty-two months, the *Bayley Scales of Infant Development—Second Edition* (BSID—II) are used to assess progress in developing speech, fine and gross motor skills, and socialization.

ACADEMIC ACHIEVEMENT TESTS These tests are used to assess the student's learning potential and the degree to which a child has acquired knowledge compared to other children in the same grade and of the same age. Academic achievement tests are standardized, so they measure school achievement without the potential subjectivity of the teachers. They can be useful in identifying specific learning disorders and academic problems.

Common achievement tests include the *Wide Range Achievement Test—Third Edition* (WRAT-3), which evaluates a child's ability to read, spell, and do arithmetic. The *Woodcock-Johnson Psycho-Educational Battery* measures a child's progress with reading, writing, and arithmetic. The *Wechsler Individual Achievement Test* (WIAT) is a recently developed achievement counterpart to the *Wechsler Intelligence Scale for Children—Third Edition* (WISC-III).

ADAPTIVE FUNCTIONING ASSESSMENTS In assessing a young child, these instruments can be helpful in attempting to quantify various self-help and social skills. Two instruments are commonly used to assess adaptive skills. The *Vineland Adaptive Behavior Scales (VABS)* assess an individual's personal and social functioning. Information is provided by a parent or other respondent familiar with the child, who is interviewed by a trained examiner. The *Scales of Independent Behavior (SIB)* assess skills needed to function independently at home as well as in social and community settings. When used in conjunction with an intelligence test, assessment of adaptive functioning is used to profile mental retardation.

PERSONALITY TESTS Personality is the collection of qualities and characteristics that make a person a distinct individual. Personality testing may be useful in some situations, such as in diagnosing psychosis, evaluating the potential

risk of suicide, or assessing a shy child or one who communicates poorly.

Personality tests seek to discover important psychological themes or issues that may not be apparent from other tests or from observing the child. In a projective test, the child is presented with an ambiguous picture or an incomplete sentence and asked to respond to it. The expectation is that the child's way of perceiving and interpreting the ambiguous stimulus will reveal his or her way of coping with reality. In other words, the child's personality *projects* his own way of thinking onto the picture or sentence. When administered skillfully, personality tests may offer insights into a child's psychological needs, self-image, relationships, coping skills, and defense mechanisms.

Among the many personality tests in use are the *Children's Apperception Test* (CAT), typically used for children three to seven years of age; the *Roberts Apperception Test for Children,* employed with children over seven; and the *Rorschach's Test,* in which children five or older are asked to respond to inkblots.

NEUROPSYCHOLOGICAL TESTING These sophisticated tests are used to identify the presence of brain damage in children, and to determine the extent and even the location of the brain damage. The tests can be used both to diagnose the nature of the brain damage and to direct rehabilitation strategies. The two neuropsychological tests in common use are the *Halstead-Reitan Battery* and the *Luria-Nebraska Neuropsychological Battery (Children's Revision).*

OTHER TESTS There are a number of other instruments that are used in evaluating a child. For children who appear to have attention difficulties, as in diagnoses of attention-deficit/hyperactivity disorder, the tests include the

Continuous Performance Test (CPT) and the *Test of Variable of Attention* (TOVA). When hearing problems are suspected, as may be the case with certain behavioral or learning problems, an *audiological evaluation* or hearing test may be done, either in the pediatrician's office or by an audiologist. Speech and language problems may be evaluated and appropriate therapies designed using such tests as the *Peabody Picture Vocabulary Test* (PPVT), the *Expressive One Word Picture Vocabulary Test* (EOWPVT), and the *Test of Language Competence* (TLC). These tests are usually performed by a speech pathologist.

RATING FORMS AND QUESTIONNAIRES Various surveys may be used to assist with making diagnoses and/or following progress during treatment. These surveys may be completed by the child, the parents, or others involved with the child such as teachers. Many rating scales are available, some of them very specific for what they evaluate (for example, the *Beck Depression Index*). Others are more general.

One commonly used test is the *Child Behavior Checklist* (CBCL), in which parents or teachers are asked to rate a very wide variety of specific behaviors for a particular child. The pattern of responses may then be compared to the standards for the questionnaire to help determine the types and seriousness of the problems. Other rating forms document the seriousness of certain disorders, such as depression or ADHD.

Glossary

Medicine in general and psychiatry in particular make use of technical terms that enable the clinician to identify the symptoms, progress, and other aspects of a patient's health or disorder.

In this book, we have attempted to keep such terms to a minimum, introducing psychiatric and medical terminology only for reasons of specificity or because you, as a parent, will encounter them in discussing your youngster's status with his child and adolescent psychiatrist or other clinicians. The definitions in the following pages are brief and intended to be immediately useful rather than all-inclusive. Particularly when your concern is specific disorders, refer to the main text of the book for comprehensive discussions.

■   ■   ■

Acute. Of short duration or rapid onset.

ADHD. See *Attention-deficit/hyperactivity disorder.*

Affect. Feelings; observable aspects of an emotional state, such as sadness, anger, or euphoria.

Aggression. Forceful action against another person which may be physical, verbal, or symbolic, and is meant to cause pain. Such behavior may be hostile or destructive or it may be for self-protection.

Allergen. Agents, such as pollen particles, dust mites, certain foods, inhalants, and drugs, which may cause an allergic reaction.

Antidepressant. Medication used to treat depression.

Anxiety. Feeling of nervousness, apprehensiveness, fear, or dread.

Anxiolytic. Medication used to treat anxiety.

Articulation disorder. Inability or delay in producing speech appropriate to age and dialect, such as when sounds are omitted, distorted, or substituted, as in saying *w* for *r* and *f* for *th.*

Asperger's disorder. Pervasive disorder of development characterized by seriously impaired social interactions and repetitive behaviors, interests, and activities. Asperger's disorder resembles autism, but language development is less affected in children with Asperger's disorder.

Asthma. Disease of the respiratory system characterized by increased responsiveness to stimuli, including pollens, air pollutants, and *allergens,* in which the smaller bronchial airways constrict causing wheezing and shortness of breath.

Attention-deficit/hyperactivity disorder (ADHD). Disorder characterized by impulsivity, distractibility, inattention, and sometimes excessive activity.

Autism. Pervasive disorder of development that affects socialization, speech, and thinking.

Autonomy. Independent control over one's actions. This term is used to describe the emerging behaviors of children around age two, who have just learned to walk and talk.

Avoidant disorders. Social anxiety, characterized by a child's avoidance of or failure to seek contact with others.

Behavioral. Relating to how a person acts.

Behavioral therapy. See *Cognitive therapy.*

Behavior modification. Method of treatment used to help children change behaviors by rewarding desired behaviors and establishing consequences for undesirable ones.

Bipolar mood disorder. Mood disorder characterized by cycles of depression and mania (excitement).

Birth order. Sequence in which siblings are born within a family.

Body image. Perception an individual has of his or her own body which may include size, shape, and attractiveness.

Bonding. Sense of connection (attachment) between parents and babies that forms the foundation of the parent-child relationship.

Brief reactive psychosis. Short episode of severely disturbed thinking, with loss of contact with reality, in response to a stressful event.

Bruxism. Grinding or clenching of teeth during sleep.

Catatonia. Condition in which a person is unresponsive, immobile, sometimes with rigid muscles, and unable to talk. Catatonia may be seen in schizophrenia or mood disorders.

Cerebral palsy. Disorder resulting from damage to the central nervous system before, during, or shortly after birth. *Spastic* cerebral palsy is characterized by constant muscle spasms. *Nonspastic* cerebral palsy involves involuntary movements of the muscles.

Child Abuse. Pattern of behavior in which an adult beats, batters, sexually molests, exploits, or neglects a child.

Child and Adolescent Psychiatrist. Physician whose education after medical school includes at least three years of speciality training in psychiatry plus two additional years of advanced training with children, adolescents, and families.

Childhood trauma. Horrible, often life-threatening events experienced during childhood, frequently causing stress reactions.

Chronic disease. Disease of long duration, often of slow progression, which may wax or wane over time.

Closed head injury. Injury in which brain tissue remains within the skull but that may lead to brain bruising, swelling, and irreversible damage.

Cognition. Process of thinking characterized by awareness with perception, reasoning, judgment, intuition, and memory.

Cognitive therapy. Method of psychotherapy used to decrease symptoms of depression and anxiety by examining negative thoughts and ideas associated with these feelings.

Colic. Distressing but harmless disorder of infants, usually between two and five months of age, characterized by repeated episodes of uncontrollable crying.

Conduct disorders. Disorder in which behavior exceeds normal range and is socially destructive, such as fighting, stealing, lying, arson, truancy, running away from home, or exploitative actions.

Conflict. Psychic tension that occurs as a result of opposing forces, desires, or needs.

Corporal punishment. Physical punishment such as spanking.

Date rape. Sexual relations between partners known to each other but to which both parties have not consented.

Delinquency. Antisocial, immoral, and illegal actions committed by minors.

Delusion. False and perhaps bizarre belief that cannot be changed by logical arguments or evidence.

Depression. Emotional state or mood characterized by sadness, despair, and loss of interest in usual activities.

Diabetes mellitus. Disorder of carbohydrate metabolism due to a decrease in insulin production that results in increased sugar in the blood and urine.

Diagnosis. The name of a disease or syndrome.

Disorder of written expression. Specific learning disability involving written language and fine motor coordination, problems with visual memory, slowness in finding the correct word, spatial disorganization, and inability to arrange thoughts.

Disorder of attachment. Disorder of parent-infant interaction characterized by the baby's failure to thrive, gain weight, eat well, and to engage in interactions expected for the age.

Dissociation. Involuntary mental and emotional distance or separation from events resembling a self-hypnotic state.

Down's syndrome. Congenital disorder usually caused by an extra chromosome in the twenty-first pair, and characterized by mental retardation and a distinct physical appearance.

Dysfunction. Inadequate, impaired, or abnormal function.

Dyslexia. Specific learning disability involving reading, which may include reversing letters and words and word-blindness.

Dysthymic disorder. Disorder characterized by mild to moderate chronic depression.

Ego. Theoretical concept describing the internal mental function that enables a person to perceive needs and to adapt to the demands of reality.

Empathy. Understanding how others feel.

Encopresis. Repeated elimination of feces by a child who is at least four years old in inappropriate places either involuntarily or intentionally.

Enuresis. Urination in inappropriate places at night (bed-wetting) or during the day (in clothing) in a child past the usual age of toilet training.

Expressive language. Phase of communication involving the process of putting ideas and thoughts into words and then into speech.

Fetal alcohol syndrome. Congenital syndrome caused by exposure to alcohol in utero, characterized by mental retardation and specific physical characteristics.

Fragile-X syndrome. Congenital syndrome caused by an abnormality of the X-chromosome, characterized by mental retardation, specific maladaptive behaviors, and abnormal physical features.

Gender identity. Perception of one's self as male or female, developing in toddlerhood or early childhood, and reinforced by social experience and the changes of puberty.

Genetic. Relating to heredity.

Genogram. Diagram or "map" of a family including notation of medical or psychiatric conditions in family members. A genogram may be useful in investigating complex relationships, family history, and multigenerational issues.

Gestural speech. Physical gestures of a young child that indicate comprehension of speech before the child's expressive language develops, such as pointing at a wanted object or waving good-bye.

Glucose monitoring. Testing to monitor sugars in the urine or blood, usually in a person with diabetes.

Hallucination. Visual, auditory (sound), olfactory (smell), or kinetic (touch) perceptions without external stimulation, such as hearing voices when no one is present.

Handedness. Preference for using the dominant hand, often indicated by learning to write with the right or left hand.

Heredity. Characteristics passed from parent to child through genes.

Human Immunodeficiency Virus (HIV). Virus which causes acquired immune deficiency syndrome (AIDS).

Hyperkinesis. Outdated term for attention-deficit/hyperactivity disorder referring to excessive motor activity.

Hypnotic. Medication used to induce sleep.

Hypoxia. Inadequate oxygen supply to the tissues of the body.

Identification. Unconscious patterning of one's behavior after that of another person. Important in the development of personality and the superego.

Infant. Person between age two weeks until the age (typically eighteen to twenty-four months) at which he or she is expected to be able to walk and use language.

Inhibition of choice. Understanding and ability to act, based on knowing that it is often better to pass on a short-term reward for an ultimately better result.

Insulin. Hormone secreted by the pancreas, essential to the metabolism of glucose.

Language and speech disorders. Abnormal or delayed development of language and speech in children. Typically these include problems with development of expressive language, receptive language, and/or speech and articulation.

Latchkey children. Children who arrive home from school to an empty household because parents work outside the home.

Learning disorders. Disorders characterized by difficulty in processing, learning, or expressing concepts and information, resulting in academic achievement below expected performance for age, schooling, and intellectual abilities.

Major depression. Disorder characterized by persistently depressed mood for at least two weeks accompanied by other related symptoms, including suicidal thinking in severe cases.

Managed care. Medical or mental health care organized under an administrative system that monitors the need, type, and use of medical services, in order to control costs and/or make a profit.

Mania. Mood characterized by extreme excitation, euphoria, grandiosity, irritability, hypersexuality, decreased need for sleep, and rapid speech. Psychotic symptoms may also be associated with mania.

Manic-depressive disorder. See *Bipolar mood disorder.*

Mathematics disorder. Specific learning disorder involving mathematics skills.

Mental retardation. Disorder characterized by subnormal intelligence and delayed self-help skills.

Migraine headache. Headache, often on one side of the head, usually associated with visual symptoms, intolerance of light, nausea, or vomiting, and lasting four to six hours.

Mutism. Lack of speech.

Nebulizer. Machine for making a fine spray or mist, to which medication may be added, usually for treatment of asthma when inhalers do not suffice.

Negativism. Refusal to follow requests or commands with oppositional disagreement.

Neonate. Newborn person up to a few weeks old.

Neurobiological. Regarding the biology of the nervous system.

Neurology. Medical specialty concerned with the function and malfunction of the nervous system.

Nightmare. A "bad dream," the contents of which arouse fear or anxiety.

Night terrors. Harmless sleep disorder that causes the child to scream out and behave uncontrollably; usually of short duration with no memory of the event the next day.

Nonverbal. Without words.

Obsessive-compulsive disorder (OCD). Disorder characterized by intrusive thoughts (obsessions) and repeated, ritualized actions (compulsions).

Object permanence. Mental capacity, obtained by most children at around seven months, to comprehend that an object still exists even when it is out of sight.

OCD. See *Obsessive-compulsive disorder.*

ODD. See *Oppositional defiant disorder.*

Open head injury. Brain damage as the result of a severe skull fracture and open wound to the head.

Oppositional behavior. Behavior that is defined as negative or hostile.

Oppositional defiant disorder (ODD). Disorder characterized by a pattern of uncooperative, defiant, and hostile behavior toward authority figures that seriously interferes with a child's day-to-day functioning.

Parallel play. Pattern of play in which small children play alongside each other with minimum interaction.

Paranoid ideation. Thoughts involving suspiciousness, exaggerated feelings of unfair treatment, or harassment.

Parasomnias. Disturbances which occur during sleep or in the transition between wake and sleep, including night terrors, sleepwalking, and sleep talking.

Parent management training (PMT). Therapy in which parents are taught principles and strategies for managing their child's behavior, including positive reinforcement (praise and tokens) and consequences and mild punishments (time-outs and the loss of privileges).

Personality. Mental traits, characteristics, and styles of behavior which are stable over time.

Person permanence. Mental concept obtained around seven months of age which allows a child to understand that a person exists, even though he or she is out of sight.

Pervasive developmental disorders (PDD). Disorders, including autism, characterized by qualitative impairments in the development of social interaction, communication skills, and in imaginative activity.

Phenylketonuria (PKU). Hereditary disease in which the amino acid phenylalanine is not metabolized. Without strict dietary control, mental retardation develops.

Phobia. Persistent and irrational fear of particular objects, people, animals, or situations.

Pica. Persistent or recurring ingestion of nonfood substances such as clay, dirt, chalk, dried animal feces, paint chips, tiny rocks, or cardboard.

Play therapy. Form of psychotherapy in which a child enacts experiences or emotions through play with dolls, drawings, clay, or other toys.

Postpartum depression. Maternal depression occurring after the birth of a child, often at the time of weaning, with its accompanying hormonal shifts.

Post-traumatic stress disorder (PTSD). Anxiety disorder following exposure to trauma, characterized by recall of the event, and avoidance of stimuli associated with the trauma. See also *Childhood trauma.*

Precocious puberty. Signs of sexual maturation prior to age eight years.

Preferred provider. Physicians, social workers, nurses, or psychologists enrolled by a particular insurer or managed care plan.

Prognosis. Prediction of course, duration, and outcome.

Psychiatric social worker. Person with a master's degree in social work (M.S.W.) or state certification as a licensed clinical social worker (L.C.S.W.).

Psychiatrist. Physician whose education after medical school includes at least four years of speciality training in psychiatry.

Psychoanalyst. Person, usually a physician, trained in the theory of psychoanalysis, a technique employing free association, careful analysis of the relationship between the psychoanalyst and the patient, and interpretation of unconscious thoughts and feelings.

Psychoanalytically oriented psychotherapy. See *Psychodynamic therapy.*

Psychodrama. Therapeutic technique of dramatically enacting, as if in a play, personal or emotional problems.

Psychodynamic therapy. Therapy based on the assumption that a person can develop better control over his or her own behavior, choices, and actions by understanding unconscious thoughts and feelings and interpersonal relationships. Such therapy often combines discussion, explanation, relaxation, and psychological exploration and support.

Psychologist. Person who has a master's, Ed.D., Psy.D., or Ph.D. degree in clinical, school, counseling, experimental, or educational psychology.

Psychopharmacology. Medical speciality concerned with the use of psychoactive medications to alleviate symptoms of emotional, behavioral, or mental disorders.

Psychosis. Severely disturbed mental state characterized by loss of contact with reality that may include disorganized speech or behavior, delusions, and/or hallucinations.

Psychotherapist. Person who uses various psychological principles to help a patient improve behavior, feelings, thinking, or social interactions.

Psychotherapy. Treatment for various emotional, behavioral, or mental problems that uses communication between a trained person and the patient to bring about change and to relieve distress.

PTSD. See *Post-traumatic stress disorder.*

Puberty. Stage of physical development when changes of sexual maturation occur and sexual reproduction first becomes possible.

Rapid eye movement (REM). Description of activity of closed eyes during a particular stage of sleep during which dreams occur. This stage of sleep is also called REM sleep.

Reactive attachment disorder (RAD). Disorder of infancy resulting from severely deficient or abusive parenting, signaled by a child's failure to thrive, to gain weight, and to engage in social interaction expected at his or her age.

Reading disorder. Specific learning disorder characterized by difficulties in visually tracking words, visually discriminating between similar letters (mistaking *d* for *b,* for example), or problems with associating sounds with their symbols and interpreting the meaning of words.

Receptive language. Decoding spoken words and sentences requiring discrimination among sounds (auditory discrimination), interpretation of what is heard, and assignment of meaning to words and sentences.

Reflex. Involuntary neurological response to stimulus.

Regression. Return to an earlier pattern of thinking or acting.

REM. See *Rapid eye movement.*

Role modeling. Method of teaching behavior based on patterning by example.

Schizophrenia. Severe psychiatric disorder characterized by psychosis (inability to think logically and rationally) including catatonia, delusions, hallucinations, paranoia, disorganized language and behavior.

Seizure. Neurological disorder characterized by convulsions or other episodic behavior caused by abnormal electrical discharges in the brain. Epilepsy is one form of seizure disorder.

Selective mutism. Childhood refusal to speak in a specific social circumstance, such as where a child will speak at home but refuse to talk at school.

Self-regulation. Regular pattern of sleep, alertness, and feeding that most newborns develop for themselves, unless prevented by environmental shifts and changes.

Separation anxiety. Emotional response of infants after six or seven months of age when they become capable of understanding they are separate from their parents, evidenced by distress and protest if a parent leaves.

Serotonin. Neurotransmitter (chemical messenger) involved in regulation of sleep, mood, appetite, and sexual function.

Sexual abuse. Behavior in which an adult commits a sexual act with a child or adolescent for gratification of the adult's sexual needs and desires.

Sexually transmitted diseases (STDs). Infections transmitted by sexual activity, including gonorrhea, chlamydia, genital herpes, human papilloma virus (genital warts), HIV, and syphilis.

Sibling. Brother or sister.

Sibling rivalry. Competition between siblings for the affection and attention of parents.

Sleep terror disorder. See *Night terror.*

Social-emotional learning disorder. Diagnosis given to children who are unable to make friends and behave in a socially acceptable way. They fail to interpret appropriately the emotional responses of others and make incorrect inferences about others' intentions and behaviors.

Social referencing. Psychological process in which a child looks to others, such as a parent, for cues on how to respond when confronted with something new or perplexing.

Somatoform disorder. A psychiatric disorder characterized by the development of physical symptoms that suggest a medical condition but are not fully explained by any medical condition.

Spelling disorder. Specific learning disability characterized by difficulty spelling words.

Startle response. Rapid, reflexive reaction to a sudden stimulus.

Stranger anxiety. Normal emotional response of infants occurring around seven months upon hearing, seeing, or being picked up by an unfamiliar person.

STDs. See *Sexually transmitted diseases.*

Stuttering. Involuntary breaks in the rhythm or fluency of speech such as repetition of syllables, prolongation of sounds, and pauses in which the person seems to be struggling to make any sound at all.

Superego. Theoretical concept describing a person's internal mental functions that are expressed in moral attitudes, conscience, and sense of guilt.

Systematic desensitization. Behavioral therapy technique in which the patient is presented with a graduated hierarchy of anxiety-provoking stimuli; a treatment for phobias.

Talk therapy. See *Psychotherapy.*

Tantrum. Fit of uncontrolled anger, rage, and distress.

Temperament. Predisposing characteristics of a person, including the manner of displaying moods and emotions first noted in infancy.

Thought disorders. Disorders characterized by an impairment of thinking including disorganized, incoherent, or vague speech, delusions, hallucinations, or paranoia.

Tics. Involuntary, repetitive muscle contractions, involving any muscle group but most commonly the face, eyes, or neck.

Time-out. Technique used to isolate briefly a disruptive child in order to interrupt and avoid reinforcement of negative behavior.

Toddler. Child from about twelve to thirty-six months; the name refers to the unsteady gait of children this age.

Tourette's disorder. Disorder characterized by multiple motor tics along with vocal tics such as grunting, humming, and tongue-clicking.

Toxic delirium. Disorder in which psychotic symptoms are caused by an ingested chemical or accumulation of the body's toxic by-products.

Tranquilizer. Medication that reduces anxiety, agitation, or emotional tension.

Transitional object. Object such as a blanket, teddy bear, or toy selected by a toddler or preschool child for comfort against anxiety or distress.

Trauma. Injury, physical or psychic, caused by shock, violence, or abuse.

Utilization review. Monitoring of care and services in medical or mental-health setting, for the purposes of improving quality of care and/or containing cost of care.

Verbal. Related to words.

Withdrawing. Retreating or avoiding contact with people and experiences.

Withholding. Keeping information or feelings inside or away from interactions with people.

Index

▪   ▪   ▪

FACTS *for* FAMILIES

Facts for Families© is developed and distributed by the American Academy of Child and Adolescent Psychiatry. These single page fact sheets are designed to provide concise, timely information on child and adolescent development and issues concerning the behavioral, mental, or developmental disorders that may affect them.

Titles Available

#01 Children and Divorce	#34 Children's Sleep Problems
#02 Teenagers with Eating Disorders	#35 Tic Disorders
#03 Teens: Alcohol and Other Drugs	#36 Helping Children After a Disaster
#05 Child Abuse - The Hidden Bruises	#37 Children and Firearms
#06 Children Who Can't Pay Attention	#38 Manic-Depressive Illness in Teens
#07 Children Who Won't Go to School	#39 Children of Parents with Mental Illness
#08 Children and Grief	#40 The Influence of Music and Rock Videos
#09 Child Sexual Abuse	#41 Making Decisions about Substance Abuse Treatment
#10 Teen Suicide	
#11 The Autistic Child	#42 The Continuum of Care
#12 Children Who Steal	#43 Discipline
#13 Children & TV Violence	#44 Children and Lying
#14 Children and Family Moves	#45 Lead Exposure
#15 The Adopted Child	#46 Home Alone Children
#16 Learning Disabilities	#47 The Anxious Child
#17 Children of Alcoholics	#48 Problems with Soiling and Bowel Control
#18 Bedwetting	#49 Schizophrenia in Children
#19 The Child with a Long Term Illness	#50 Panic Disorder in Children and Adolescents
#20 Making Day Care a Good Experience	#51 Questions to Ask about Psychiatric Medications for Children & Adolescents
#21 Psychiatric Medication for Children	
#22 Normality	
#23 Mental Retardation	#52 Comprehensive Psychiatric Evaluation
#24 Know When to Seek Help for Your Child	#53 What is Psychotherapy for Children and Adolescents?
#25 Know Where to Seek Help for Your Child	
#26 Know Your Health Insurance Benefits	#54 Children and Watching TV
#27 Stepfamily Problems	#55 Understanding Violent Behavior in Children
#28 Responding to Child Sexual Abuse	
#29 Children's Major Psychiatric Disorders	#56 Normal Adolescence: the Early Years
#30 Children and AIDS	#57 Normal Adolescence: the Later Years
#31 When Children Have Children	#59 Children Online
#32 11 Questions to Ask Before Psychiatric Hospitalization of Children & Adolescents	#60 Obsessive Compulsive Disorder in Children and Adolescents
	#62 Talking to Your Kids about Sex
#33 Conduct Disorders	#63 Gay and Lesbian Adolescents

Facts for Families are available in English and Spanish on the AACAP Homepage at http://www.aacap.org. Contact Public Information, P.O. Box 96106, Washington, D.C. 20090-6106 for information on ordering full sets suitable for reproduction.

AMERICAN ACADEMY OF CHILD & ADOLESCENT PSYCHIATRY

3615 Wisconsin Avenue, NW ■ Washington, DC 20016-3007 ■ 202.966.7300 FAX 202.966.2891
http://www.aacap.org